Fundamentals of the Irish Legal System

Law, Policy and Politics

Fundamentals of the Irish Legal System

Law, Policy and Politics

SECOND EDITION

Tanya Ní Mhuirthile

BCL (N.U.I.); M.DRA (R.S.A.M.D.); LLB (N.U.I.); PH.D. (N.U.I.); PGDIPTE (Q.Q.I.)

Catherine O'Sullivan

BCL, LLM (N.U.I.); PH.D. (OSGOODE HALL, YORK UNIVERSITY)

Liam Thornton

BCL (INT.) (N.U.I.); PG.CHEP (ULST.); PH.D. (N.U.I.); F.H.E.A. (UK)

ROUND HALL

Thomson Reuters™

Published in 2025 by
Thomson Reuters (Professional) Ireland Limited
(Registered in Ireland, Company No. 80867.
Registered Office and address for service:
Spaces, Office 313, 77 Sir John Rogerson's Quay,
Block C, Dublin 2, D02 VK60)
trading as Round Hall.

Typeset by Carrigboy Typesetting Services
Printed by CPI Group (UK) Ltd, Croydon, CR0 4YY

ISBN (Print): 978-0-41411-523-1
ISBN (ProView): 978-0-41411-525-5
ISBN (Print & ProView): 978-0-41411-524-8
ISBN (eBook): 978-0-41412-3731

A catalogue record for this book is available from the British Library

Preface

It is almost nine years since the first edition of *Fundamentals of the Irish Legal System: Law, Policy and Politics* was published in 2016. We had not meant for so much time to pass before completing a second edition, but life had to be lived, and work responsibilities had to be met. One of the benefits of a second edition is the ability to improve upon the first edition. Some chapters have been significantly restructured to make the issues we discuss easier to understand. In places we provide better, and often more recent, case studies to illuminate legal principles, legal application, and the impact of law on people. Some chapters needed a total rewrite due to significant reforms. *Fundamentals* continues to offer socio-legal insights into law, legal structures, and the role of politics and policy in the Irish legal system. As academics responsible for the teaching and management of introduction to the Irish legal system modules within our respective universities, we wanted a core text that provided a doctrinal description of the Irish legal system, but which also sought to contextualise and situate the Irish legal system in its broader political and societal framework.

As with the first edition, the second edition examines the Irish legal system in a clear and accessible manner, while also requiring students to think about deeper issues relating to how law and legal systems interact with the political system and society. Chapter 1 contains a full explanation of the structure of this book and our conceptual approach to the Irish legal system. *Fundamentals* is divided into three parts, focusing on the rule of law and sources of law, the Irish legal system in action, and legal skills and research. We hope that readers of this text gain a critical appreciation of the structures, processes and actors that make up the Irish legal system.

As with all book projects, colleagues, friends, partners and families have offered guidance and support. A particular thanks to our families who had to endure many months of disruption to family life.

Tanya: While writing this book many people have offered support (and on occasion consolation!). Thank you to you all. I would like to thank my colleagues in DCU, particularly those in the School of Law and Government. My part of this book would never have happened without the cheerful critiques and solid support, particularly during The Big Read, of my co-authors Catherine and Liam—Go Team! My girls Claire, Lorna, Sheelah and Shelley deserve a special mention. Finally, I would like to thank my family: my husband, Mark, and our children, Neasa and Donal, who stoically support me while I pursue those things that are important to me; none are more so than they.

Catherine: The first edition of this book was the product of teaching introduction to law modules over a number of years and in that teaching I was supported by various colleagues at University College Cork, specifically Maria Cahill, Louise Crowley, Fiona Donson, Conor O'Mahony and Fidelma White. I would also like to thank my co-authors, Tanya and Liam, whose thoughtful feedback improved my chapters, and whose good humour throughout the writing and editing process made what can be a tedious process a relatively enjoyable one. Finally, I would like to thank Declan, my partner, my sister and Mum who have provided me with support both during the writing of this book and beyond it.

Liam: Thanks to my husband, Tony, and our dog-child Lobo. Your understanding of me having to work late nights and weekends while completing this book was really appreciated. Thanks are due to my partners in crime, Catherine and Tanya, whose good humour, critical legal insights and proofreading (!) made this a wonderful project to work with them on again. Thanks to all my family members, in particular my Mam, Catherine and my mother-in-law, Sheila. I was fortunate to have one semester research leave that ensured I was able to dedicate focus to updating the book, so a particular word of thanks to the current Dean of UCD School of Law, Professor Laurent Pech. Thanks to my UCD colleagues, both inside and outside the law school. Thanks to John O'Dowd and Tony Kerr SC who alerted me to several journal articles and relevant case law that I have relied on in parts of Chapters 10, 11 and 13.

We would like to express our gratitude to Round Hall for their assistance and support during the (longer than expected) research and writing process. Donough Cassidy, Senior Publisher at Round Hall, deserves special thanks for his patience and generous good cheer while we completed this second edition. Furthermore, we are indebted to him for his professionalism in undertaking copy-editing duties on this text. Donough's keen eye has ensured the highest levels of accuracy in this text. As with all legal texts, while we have gone to great pains to ensure accuracy, the usual disclaimers apply.

We have endeavoured to state the law as it stood on 30 September 2024. Due to a very understanding publisher, we were able to include some minor updates after this time.

Tanya Ní Mhuirthile, School of Law and Government, DCU
Catherine O'Sullivan, School of Law, UCC
Liam Thornton, School of Law, UCD

11 February 2025

Contents

Part III: Legal Skills

Table of Contents

Part II: The Irish Legal System in Action

Part III: Legal Skills

Table of Cases

Ireland

European Union

Council of Europe

United Kingdom

Australia

Canada

South Africa

United States of America

United Nations

International Court of Justice

United Nations Human Rights Committee

Table of Constitutions

Ireland

France

Germany

Latvia

United States of America

Table of Legislation

Ireland

Acts of the Oireachtas

Pre-1922 Acts

Statutory Instruments

Rules of Court

United Kingdom

Argentina

Australia

United States of America

Table of European Law

European Union

Treaties

Regulations

Directives

Decisions

Council of Europe

Table of International Law

Chapter 1

Introduction

1–01 Invasions, conquests, revolutions and a slow path to independence is the story of Ireland. The Irish legal system has developed over hundreds of years, from a colonised country to an independent nation. The legal system continues to develop today. Legal systems do not emerge from thin air. While law and legal systems may have a "relative autonomy",[1] law and legal systems are moulded by citizens' engagement with the political system, coupled with the values and practices of legislators, judges and the legal profession. As Raz, a legal and political scholar, notes, legal systems contain a number of core elements.[2] First, there are institutions whose role it is to create law. Second, courts interpret and assist in the application of law. Third, legal systems, and the rules emerging from legal systems, help individuals understand what they can or cannot do. This book explores the Irish legal system. In Part I, we examine the rule of law and sources of law in the Irish legal system. In Part II, we contextualise and analyse the Irish legal system, examining its institutions and actors. In Part III, we include a dedicated description and reflection of the legal skills processes that you will use, either for one module, or throughout your degree. Given the diversity of those who may have to study law or an introductory module on Irish law and legal systems, we felt it important to include such a section on legal research, reading and writing in this book.

1–02 As will become clear from your engagement with this book, a number of common threads emerge from many of our discussions throughout the chapters. First, the Irish legal system must be placed within its societal and political context. This means that the Irish legal system should be viewed as having a number of functions. While the

---

1 For differing perspectives and critiques as to whether law enjoys a "relative autonomy", see I.D. Balbus, "Commodity Form and Legal Form: An Essay on the 'Relative Autonomy' of Law" (1977) 11(3) *Law & Society Review* 571; J. Raz, *The Concept of a Legal System* (Oxford: Clarendon, 1967); and L.M. Friedman, *The Legal System: A Social Science Perspective* (New York: Russell Sage, 1975).

2 J. Raz, "The Identity of Legal Systems" (1971) 59(3) *California Law Review* 795.

passage of law and its interpretation are of exceptional importance, it is also essential that you critically reflect on the interaction of law with individuals, with political systems (both formal and informal), and with society. Second, the actors within the Irish legal system—politicians, judges, administrative decision-makers and the legal profession—engage with their functions within a societal context. We are all a product of our upbringing, our educational attainment, our social class and our socialisation within the structures of society. Actors in legal systems are no different and it is important to reflect on how all the issues just outlined can impact on the creation, contestation, interpretation and application of legal rules and norms. Third, a core theme that will be evident throughout this book is the impact that legal systems have on individuals. Who is a legal system supposed to serve? Is it some elusive and undefinable "public interest", is it individuals, or is it the legal system in and of itself? Before you can engage in a reflection on all these questions, it is fundamental that you can describe the Irish legal system in its current form and function. At various stages throughout this book, we provide you with legal insights to allow you to understand a particularly important case or issue. At times, we provide a comparative legal focus on how foreign legal systems have dealt with a particular issue. We also consider the roles that societal change and societal agitation play in law reform. To enable you to engage in deep and critical thinking, we also ask you at various stages to reflect on legal questions. The text also uses skills insights to familiarise you with the craft of legal research, reading and writing. With these introductory points made, we now provide a brief outline of the structure of this book.

A. Part I: The Rule of Law and Sources of Law in the Irish Legal System (Chapters 2–6)

1–03 Part I of this book provides a comprehensive overview of the sources of law within the Irish legal system. The concept of the "rule of law" is central to this study. Chapter 2 considers the rule of law. It first defines the concept, then turns to a detailed discussion on how the rule of law applies in an Irish context. Our focus is on four key principles when discussing the rule of law: the principles of legality, equality before the law, the need for an independent judiciary, and the importance of law being public, precise and accessible. Yet, the concept of the rule of law is not without its critiques, and we will sketch some of these concerns towards the end of Ch.2. This chapter also explores how the legal system, at times, does not appear to conform with the principles of the rule of law. We engage with two case studies on law-making and Covid-19, and the rights of children with a disability, to illustrate this point. The primary and secondary sources of law, and the hierarchy of legal sources in the Irish legal system, are also introduced in this chapter. The Constitution, legislation, common law, European Union law and public international law are then considered in detail in Chs 3–6 inclusive.

1–04 The Irish Constitution is the *grundnorm* or basic norm of the Irish legal system. This means that all other sources of law gain their legitimacy from the Irish Constitution. Inferior laws that fail to comply with the Irish Constitution can be declared unconstitutional by the superior courts. As is discussed in Ch.3, the Irish Constitution, as well as providing for the legal organisation of the State, also provides a symbolic function to allow the people to declare what they envisage the purposes of the State to encompass. The Constitution provides the broad contours of how the Irish legal system should operate, and the relationship between the Oireachtas (Parliament and President), the executive (government) and the judiciary. The ability to amend the Constitution and the protection of fundamental rights are also significant matters dealt with in the Constitution and explored in Ch.3. Given that judges are tasked with the role of interpreting the Constitution, Ch.3 also analyses the interpretive tools developed by judges to reveal the meaning of constitutional provisions. In light of the impending 90th anniversary of the Constitution in 2027, and given the enormous social changes over that time, it is unsurprising that the Constitution has been amended on a number of occasions. Two amendments to the Constitution did not require a referendum between 1937 and 1941. These two amendments were introduced during a brief three-year period that permitted the Oireachtas to make changes to the Constitution by way of legislation. All subsequent amendments had to be passed by referendum. These amendments can be categorised as centred on international relations, on the domestic political process, on court-related matters, and on moral/social issues.

1–05 With the Constitution providing the basic law of organisation of the State and the Irish legal system, the heavy lifting as regards law-making is undertaken by the Oireachtas. Chapter 4 explains the difference between primary and secondary legislation, and the limits placed on secondary legislation, which gains its legitimacy and powers from its primary statute. In Ch.7, we will explore the creation of legislation, but in Ch.4 we focus on the role of judges in interpreting legislation created by our elected representatives. As with constitutional interpretation, judges use interpretive techniques, including the literal or purposive approach and a number of other internal and external statutory aids, in order to determine the legislative intent of the Oireachtas. In interpreting legislation, there are a number of presumptions that can be rebutted, as regards the object and purpose of legislation. These too are explored in Ch.4, as is the issue of the complexity of legislative language and how it may offend against the rule of law.

1–06 Chapter 5 introduces the common law as a source of law in the Irish legal system. Unlike the Constitution and legislation, common law emerges from the principles developed by courts in resolving legal disputes. Chapter 5 defines the concept of common law, as well as the all-important principle of precedent and considers how it facilitates and constrains judges as law-makers. The refinement of legal principles employed by judges in coming to a decision, and such principles taking hold and being applied by other judges, is what will establish a judge-made precedent, giving it the status of common law. As we explore in Ch.5, the operation of the doctrine of precedent within the Irish legal system is an issue that you will explore throughout the duration of your legal studies. Judges typically apply or distinguish precedents, and Ch.5 provides you with some analysis as regards the legitimacy of the doctrine of precedent in a modern liberal democratic state like Ireland.

1–07 The Irish legal system does not exist in a vacuum but is shaped and changed by external laws and norms. As indicated in Ch.2, and outlined in more detail in Ch.6, Ireland's membership of the European Union (EU) has a profound impact on the hierarchy of sources of law in the Irish legal system. EU law, within its competences, has primacy over Irish law, because the Constitution provides for this. Chapter 6 introduces the core constitutional principles developed by the Court of Justice of the European Union and how these are received within the Irish legal system through the Irish Constitution and legislation. We briefly consider the institutional structure of the EU. We introduce the forms of law-making. Then the obligation on Ireland to comply with EU law is explored, along with case studies on what occurs when Ireland is in breach of EU law. Chapter 6 also discusses the system of public international law, sometimes known as the law of nations. Unlike EU law, public international law is not automatically binding within the Irish legal system. We identify the sources of public international law and the provisions of the Irish Constitution that engage with international law. As you will discover in Ch.6, individuals cannot challenge the Irish State's alleged failure to comply with its international obligations unless these have been given domestic force of law through legislation. We will also identify where Irish courts have relied upon international treaties, and certain "soft law" international instruments, to assist them in interpreting domestic law. Finally, Ch.6 introduces the Council of Europe, with a particular focus on the European Convention on Human Rights. The Convention, once only applicable to Ireland at the international level, can now be indirectly applied by Irish courts via the European Convention on Human Rights Act 2003.

B. Part II: The Irish Legal System in Action (Chapters 7–13)

1–08 Having considered the rule of law as an underlying feature of the Irish legal system and the hierarchy of sources of law in Ireland, Part II of this book turns to an analysis of the Irish legal system in action. In Ch.7, we describe the process by which legislation, as a source of law, is enacted. We identify the different types of legislation based on the function of each category of legislation. We discuss in detail the various stages that legislation must undergo in both Houses of the Oireachtas. We also pause to consider Bills sponsored by backbench TDs and Senators, known as Private Members' Bills. These are not to be confused with the extremely rare Private Bills, which have a different progression path and which we consider briefly. The Dáil and the Seanad do not enjoy parity of power when it comes to passing legislation, and the differences in powers between the Houses are also discussed. Chapter 7 interrogates the role of the President, as a member of the

Oireachtas, in the enactment of legislation. Finally, the impact that legislation has on the lives of individuals, and society more generally, is explored in the detailed case study on the Gender Recognition Act 2015.

1–09 Leading on from our discussion of how legislation is proposed, enacted and promulgated within the Irish legal system, we turn our attention to processes of law reform in Ch.8. While law can remain relatively static over many decades, the advent of participatory democracy has permitted much wider engagement in processes to bring about law reform. These processes, both formal and informal, as you will discover in Ch.8, can have profound impacts on Irish society. The "insiders" within law reform, politicians, government, the Law Reform Commission and the impact of the judiciary are all analysed. Within the formal law reform mechanisms, we also consider the role and impact of processes such as Constitutional Conventions and Citizens' Assemblies that have emerged in more recent times. It is also important to engage with the "outsiders", who protest, agitate, strategically litigate or engage with the law reform process, in order to reshape society. Chapter 8 provides a dedicated case study on the abortion issue in Ireland, exploring the interaction of "insiders" and "outsiders" in seeking change or in maintaining the law as it already is in this area.

1–10 Throughout the text, you will see constant mention of various courts. It is essential that you have some appreciation of the structure and jurisdiction of the various courts established by law in Ireland, as well as having some insights into alternative dispute resolution. In Ch.9, we explore the constitutional and legislative parameters of the Irish courts system. We describe the first instance and appellate jurisdictions of the Irish courts, reflect on the public administration of justice (other than in exceptional circumstances), and consider how Irish courts engage with non-domestic courts, in particular the Court of Justice of the European Union and the European Court of Human Rights. The final part of Ch.9 examines alternative dispute resolution, with an introduction to some of the formalised alternative non-court mechanisms for resolving disputes: negotiation, conciliation, mediation and arbitration.

1–11 Leading on from our discussions of courts and alternative dispute resolution mechanisms, Ch.10 examines the Irish administrative state and administrative law. The field of administrative law in Ireland is extensive, so Ch.10 offers a substantive overview of law and administration in Ireland. We begin by defining what is meant by the administrative state, before turning our attention to administrative decision-making. We offer just a flavour of the reach of administrative law, with a brief case study on social welfare law. We then introduce you to the superior courts' judicial review jurisdiction, examining this through the lens of one legal area, housing law. Yet administrative law is not just about state administration and the courts. Thus, Ch.10 considers how administrative bodies, such as the various ombudsman offices, can be used to hold the State to account for maladministration. Finally, the chapter considers the nature of parliamentary inquiries, tribunals of inquiry and commissions of investigation. We will tease out the distinctions between these public inquiry mechanisms, including an overview of the reasons why such public inquiries may need to be established.

1–12 Judges and legal practitioners can help to shape both the legal system and society at large. In Ch.11, we examine the role of judges both within the courthouse and in society more generally. The chapter identifies the "traditional" functions and role of judges in interpreting and applying law, but also other areas where judges engage with legal and political systems in Ireland. The independence of the judiciary is a core component of the rule of law, as well as a core constitutional principle. The chapter considers the politics of judicial appointments, given the constitutional role of government to appoint judges. We consider the significant changes made to judicial appointments in Ireland since 1 January 2025, brought about by the full commencement of the Judicial Appointments Commission Act 2023. We focus on the concept of "merit" and on the legislative restrictions on government choice as to who they will appoint to the bench. Given that the 2023 Act has just been commenced at the time of writing, we still do not know how the Judicial Appointments Commission will operate in practice. The question of judicial diversity and whether a judge's class background, gender, race, ethnicity or other intersecting characteristics might impact on their decision will be explored. We provide an introduction to the *Northern/Irish Feminist Judgments* project in Ch.11. Judicial conduct and misconduct will be examined, and the ability to sanction judges under the Judicial Council Act 2019 will be evaluated. Finally, Ch.11 considers the constitutional removal of judges by the Oireachtas for "stated misbehaviour". While the Oireachtas to date has never removed a judge under the Constitution, we survey the times where the possibility that the Oireachtas would remove a judge for stated misbehaviour was live.

1–13 Having considered the part played by judges in the Irish legal system, in Ch.12 we turn to an analysis of the other significant actors on the legal stage: legal practitioners, namely solicitors and barristers. We discuss the historical context that saw these two professions emerge. The role of legal practitioners in upholding the rule of law cannot be underestimated. When the first edition of *Fundamentals of the Irish Legal System* was published in 2016, the Legal Services Regulation Act 2015 still had not been substantially commenced. Therefore, Ch.12 of this second edition explores the operation and impact of the Legal Services Regulatory Authority and its proposals for further reform to legal services. The chapter examines each profession in turn as regards the education and training legal practitioners must complete in order to qualify, as well as proposals for reform on entry routes to qualifying as a legal practitioner. It also explains and evaluates the complaints, investigation and sanction powers of the Legal Services Regulatory Authority against legal practitioners. Finally, we conclude the chapter with a very brief overview of the functions and responsibilities of specific legal officers within the Irish legal system: the Attorney General, the Chief State Solicitor and the Director of Public Prosecutions.

1–14 In Ch.13, we examine access to justice in Ireland. Given that access to justice is a core component of the rule of law, we reflect on a core question in this chapter: whether the Irish legal system facilitates or inhibits access to justice. First, we turn our attention to the question of legal aid in the criminal context, at all stages that people may come into contact with the criminal justice system. We examine the different schemes underpinning criminal legal aid in the contexts of legal advice and solicitor representation at Garda stations; the trial; proceedings for bail, extradition, European arrest warrant and habeas corpus; and whether criminal legal aid can be accessed by those in proceedings involving the Criminal Assets Bureau. Proposed reforms of the criminal legal aid scheme are then outlined. The chapter then considers the development of legal aid in the context of civil law. We introduce civil legal aid, from its tentative beginnings up to its existing legislative basis, the Civil Legal Aid Act 1995. We provide a detailed exploration of entitlement to civil legal aid under the 1995 Act. In particular, we identify and discuss the conditions for entitlement to and exclusions from civil legal aid. The role of the Legal Aid Board in determining entitlement is also considered throughout. As you will see, the system of civil legal aid is very limited, and reform of the system seems unlikely to occur, even where there are strong recommendations for fundamental change.

C. Part III: Legal Skills (Chapters 14–16)

1–15 Part III of this book explores legal research, reading, writing and advocacy. Whether you are studying just a small number of law modules as part of your studies, or are undertaking a law degree, legal communication is essential. By legal communication, we mean the skills you must build in order to properly put across your views. Undertaking any sort of assessment in higher education can be daunting, at least initially. Practice does make perfect. The more you research, the more you read, the more you engage in oral legal argument, and the more you write, the better you will become at legal communication. However, our experience indicates that many students believe that they must learn some sort of new, hidden, legal language. You do not. You need to write clearly. You need to write simply, but not simplistically.

1–16 Within higher education, lectures, seminars and tutorials will only ever introduce you to a topic. There is an expectation that you will read widely beyond the core issues discussed within the formal teaching environment. As we outline in Ch.14, the vast majority of your time studying legal subjects will be spent undertaking independent research. The law library and online legal databases are your apprentice tools for starting your legal research. Chapter 14 provides you with an overview of the library catalogue and a discussion of online legal databases (both open access and subscription) to enable you to excel in your legal research. It is important to emphasise that when conducting "online legal research", you restrict your research to reputable sources. Going on "fishing expeditions" via web search engines (such as Google) is to be avoided at all costs. Web search results do not give any indication of the quality of material that may emerge from a Google search. In addition, and our experience has emphasised the need to highlight this, we wish to note that you should not base any legal analysis on information that you find on Wikipedia. Wikipedia is a wonderful resource; we all browse Wikipedia. However, for the purposes of legal research, Wikipedia should be avoided. It might provide you with an accessible overview of a particular legal concept or idea, or a summary of a case. However, you are in higher education, and summaries of materials for general, non-legal specific audiences do not count as legal research. Reference to Wikipedia in essays and other assignments usually results in a grade penalty being applied. Additionally, we discuss the benefits and risks of using generative artificial intelligence when undertaking research. While conducting your legal research, it is important that you develop a system to effectively record your research. This becomes exceptionally important when coming to finalising an essay or other assignment, as we outline in Ch.14.

1–17 The modalities of research mean that you will, from a very early stage of your studies, have to read law. Reading law can be daunting, but it should not be. In Ch.15, we guide you through the core legal materials that you will have to consult, read and critique throughout your legal studies. The language of legislation and case law can, admittedly, be dense. Over time, as you develop your legal research and legal writing skills, reading law will become less intimidating. Chapter 15 provides an overview of the structure of an Act of the Oireachtas to provide you with some appreciation of the core features that are present within all legislation. As will become familiar to you during your first weeks of study, you will spend a significant amount of time reading cases. As with legislation, at first the structure of case reports will probably be unfamiliar to you. Yet there is a consistency to all case reports in that, generally, you will be provided with the factual reasons that a dispute is before a court, the arguments of the parties to a case, a judge's or judges' evaluation of these arguments, and ultimately a decision or a dissent. Identifying the legal principles that have been applied, or indeed developed, in a particular case takes time and practice. In addition, Ch.15 briefly highlights the importance of also engaging with academic and other commentary on matters of legal and judicial interpretation.

1–18 Chapter 16 provides an introduction to legal writing and advocacy. Ensuring that you engage in excellent written communication is a core responsibility for students. In Ch.16, we reflect on good prose style, meaning, in essence, how to write and, importantly, how to write well. Law is no different from many other arts, humanities and social science subjects. A significant proportion of your time in higher education will involve writing. That may be writing for yourself so as to understand a topic, or writing for assessment in the form of essays, case notes or problem questions. A terminal end-of-semester or end-of-year exam is another key form of assessment. Within all assessments, it is your responsibility to communicate your knowledge, understanding and reflections of a particular issue or issues. Chapter 16 begins with some style points on good prose, reminding readers of the importance of proper sentence formation, grammar and syntax. Chapter 16 also provides you with some advice on how to become a more engaging legal writer. Remember, however, the core of legal writing is communicating your response in an understandable manner. In building a persuasive legal argument, as mentioned above, you must engage in legal research. It is also standard and expected academic practice for you to cite the research you have consulted in essays. We take you through the steps of how to use referencing and citation tools in Microsoft Word, as well as standard legal citation and referencing practices that you are expected to adopt throughout your legal studies. In Ch.16, we introduce you to one specific citation and referencing method, the Oxford Standard for Citation of Legal Authorities (OSCOLA), a form of citation used in many law schools in Ireland.

D. Conclusion

1–19 The aim of this book is to provide you with a detailed description, analysis and critique of the Irish legal system. We have sought to practise what we preach by presenting complex ideas in as accessible a language and style as possible, and by highlighting recent high-profile areas of controversy to ground the material in recent events. The purpose of this is to demonstrate to you that the law is not just to be found in books, but that it surrounds our everyday interactions. For those of you who are interested in becoming a legal practitioner, or using your legal expertise to advocate for law and policy change, it is necessary for you to understand how the law operates in the Irish legal system. This book will provide you with the knowledge and skills to embark on this process.

Part I

The Rule of Law and Sources of Law in the Irish Legal System

Chapter 2

The Rule of Law and Sources of Law in the Irish Legal System

> "The Rule of Law is a dynamic concept for the expansion and fulfilment of which jurists [legal practitioners, judges and other experts in law] are primarily responsible and which should be employed not only to safeguard and advance the civil and political rights of the individual in a free society, but also to establish social, economic, educational and cultural conditions under which his legitimate aspirations and dignity may be realized."
>
> International Congress of Jurists, *The Declaration of Delhi*, 10 January 1959.

In this chapter we:

- introduce the concept of "the rule of law" in the Irish legal system, and many of the areas that are touched upon will be explored throughout this book;
- examine definitions of the rule of law from judges and leading thinkers;
- analyse four key principles of the rule of law that underpin the Irish legal system: legality, equality before the law, judicial independence, and public and precise law;
- link the discussion on the rule of law with the primary and secondary sources of law along with the hierarchy of these sources in the Irish legal system; and
- briefly explore arguments of those who critique the concept of the rule of law.

A. Introduction

2–01 At its most formalistic level, the rule of law means that everything done by the state or an individual must be done in accordance with law.[1] The rule of law should protect against arbitrary power of the state. Nowhere in the Irish Constitution, in Irish legislation or within court decisions can we identify a precise, clearly agreed definition of what is meant by "the rule of law". Bingham's core definition of the rule of law is as follows:

> "[A]ll persons and authorities within the state, whether public or private, should be bound by and entitled to the benefit of laws publicly and prospectively promulgated and publicly administered in the courts."[2]

The rule of law is regarded as being "inherent in the text and structure of our Constitution".[3] The Irish Supreme Court has asserted that "[t]he values of certainty of law and the duty of compliance with the law are fundamentals in any legal system based on the rule of law."[4] Donnelly J. further states that democracy and protection of fundamental and human rights "necessarily encompasses the rule of law."[5]

2–02 Only on very rare occasions has the phrase "the rule of law" appeared in Irish legislation in the sense we are exploring it in this chapter. The preamble to the now repealed Public Safety (Emergency Powers) Act 1923[6] referred to the need to re-establish "the rule of law throughout the country" during the Irish Civil War.[7] This provides us with a sense that the rule of law requires compliance by all with the law.[8] Within a number of legislative enactments where the phrase "the rule of law" is used, it is where the Oireachtas has given permission for public funds to be expended in the international sphere. For example, the Finance (State Guarantees, International Financial Institution Funds and Miscellaneous Provisions) Act 2024 permits Ireland to financially

1 W. Wade and C. Forsyth, *Administrative Law*, 10th edn (Oxford: OUP, 2009), p.17.
2 T. Bingham, "The Rule of Law" (2007) 66(1) *Cambridge Law Journal* 67 at 69, and T. Bingham, *The Rule of Law* (London: Penguin, 2011), p.8.
3 *Conway v An Bord Pleanála* [2024] IESC 34 at para.14 of Collins J.'s judgment.
4 *Gearty v DPP* [2024] IESC 45 at para.16.
5 *Conway v An Bord Pleanála* [2024] IESC 34 at para.6.
6 Statute Law Revision Act 2016 s.1 and Sch.1.
7 See generally, S. Ó Longaigh, *Emergency Law in Independent Ireland 1922–1948* (Dublin: Four Courts Press, 2006).
8 See generally, the Public Safety (Emergency Powers) Act 1923. In relation to this and other legislative "innovations" throughout the Irish civil war, see G. Foster, *The Irish Civil War and Society: Politics, Class and Conflict* (Dublin: Palgrave, 2015), in particular pp.146 and 169.

support Ukraine through a European Union (EU) Bank for Reconstruction and Development. Within this agreement, contained in Sch.1 of this Act, reference is made to the EU member states' commitment to democracy, the rule of law and "market economics".[9] The other manner in which the phrase "the rule of law" appears in Irish legislation is in the sense that legal and/or common law rules might apply or disapply to a given situation. For example, s.24 of the Non-Fatal Offences against the Person Act 1997 provides: "[t]he rule of law under which teachers are immune from criminal liability in respect of physical chastisement of pupils is hereby abolished." The reference to "the rule of law" in this provision does not (necessarily) engage in the debate about what is meant by the concept of "the rule of law". It simply means any past legislation or common law rule no longer applies to a particular circumstance.[10]

2–03 To criticise the action of government or the activities of individuals as being contrary to the rule of law is to suggest that they are acting in an unlawful manner.[11] To fully appreciate the differing definitions, limits and values supposedly imbued within the phrase "the rule of law", you would have to go significantly beyond what is covered in this text.[12] In this chapter, we will first explore differing definitions provided to the concept of the rule of law. We do so, in Section B of this chapter, by introducing you to how judges and legal scholars understand the phrase "the rule of law". In Section C, we explore the rule of law in the Irish legal system, exploring the principles of legality, equality before the law, independence of the judiciary, and the requirement for law to be public, precise and accessible. We also engage with a case study on law and the Covid-19 pandemic. Our attention in Section D briefly turns to critiques of the rule of law. These critiques argue that law can only be understood with reference to political and economic power so that the rule of law cannot simply be understood as a purely legal, non-ideological concept. Given the centrality of the rule of law to legal systems, each chapter of

9 For further examples akin to this where international agreements are contained in a Schedule to an Act and highlight the importance of the rule of law, see Criminal Justice (Mutual Recognition of Probation Judgments and Decisions) Act 2019 Sch.1 and Criminal Justice (Terrorist Offences) Act 2005 Sch.1A.

10 See, e.g. Land and Conveyancing Law Reform Act 2009 s.53, which provides that a past legal rule that emanated from a decision of the courts is abolished prospectively.

11 P. Craig, "Formal and Substantive Conceptions of the Rule of Law" [1997] *Public Law* 467 at 487.

12 You should consult some of the core monographs, textbooks and journal articles referred to throughout this chapter if you wish to further explore this fascinating area.

this text develops further your knowledge and understanding of "the rule of law" in the Irish legal system.[13]

B. Definitions and Concepts: What Is Meant by "the Rule of Law"?

1. Defining the Rule of Law

2–04 As Vaughan and Kilcommins note, "[t]he rule of law has to mean a protection from arbitrary action from both the state and the general populace".[14] Bedner argues that there are three core elements to the rule of law—procedural, substantive and controlling mechanisms—which, taken together, are designed to protect against arbitrary use of state power so as to protect all those within the state.[15] The procedural aspects of the rule of law hold that law is applicable to all, legal rules are clear and determinable, and there is consent (by democracy) to be governed by legal rules.[16] The substantive aspects to the rule of law encompass the protection of fundamental and human rights.[17] The controlling mechanisms embrace the role of an independent courts system and judiciary, coupled with functioning administrative systems, in adjudicating between disputes that may arise between the state and a private individual, or between two or more private individuals.[18]

2–05 Steyn, a former senior British judge and respected author, advances two core meanings of the rule of law.[19] First, the rule of law can be understood as a term of philosophical or institutional morality, with law being an essential force within modern liberal democratic

[13] For a historical overview of the concept of the rule of law within the European legal tradition, see M. Burnay, *Chinese Perspectives on the International Rule of Law* (Cheltenham: Edward Elgar, 2018), Ch.1.

[14] B. Vaughan and S. Kilcommins, *Terrorism, Rights and the Rule of Law: Negotiating Justice in Ireland* (Devon: Willan, 2008), p.9.

[15] A. Bedner, "An Elementary Approach to the Rule of Law" (2010) 2(1) *Hague Journal on the Rule of Law* 48 at 50–51.

[16] A. Bedner, "An Elementary Approach to the Rule of Law" (2010) 2(1) *Hague Journal on the Rule of Law* 48 at 56–63.

[17] A. Bedner, "An Elementary Approach to the Rule of Law" (2010) 2(1) *Hague Journal on the Rule of Law* 48 at 63–67.

[18] A. Bedner, "An Elementary Approach to the Rule of Law" (2010) 2(1) *Hague Journal on the Rule of Law* 48 at 67–69.

[19] J. Steyn, *The Constitutionalisation of Public Law* (London: Constitution Unit, 1999), p.4.

society. Steyn's second core meaning is that the rule of law constrains abuse of power by the state, protecting legal certainty, access to justice, and procedural fairness within administrative and judicial systems. Therefore, the rule of law connotes a system of restricted legal power upon the state that benefits those living in the state, who must know whether their actions are within the limits of legality. Similarly to Bedner, Steyn understands the rule of law as operating to protect citizens from the arbitrary use of state power. Bedner and Steyn's understanding of the rule of law underpin Hogan, Morgan and Daly's and Bingham's definitions of the rule of law.

2–06 Hogan, Morgan and Daly argue that there are four core aspects to the rule of law in the Irish context (we will return to these in more detail in Section C):[20]

1. the principle of legality, where all actions and decisions made by the Government, Oireachtas and public bodies will "be clothed with the necessary legislative powers";[21]
2. all persons, including Government and public officials, are subject to law;[22]
3. the legality of state action is to be determined by an independent judiciary;[23] and
4. law must be "public and precise",[24] so that all those affected by the law must know what they can or cannot do.[25]

2–07 Bingham, another former senior UK judge, provides a substantive elaboration on his meaning of the rule of law. Bingham's core definition, as outlined above, is that all persons are entitled to benefit from law,

[20] G. Hogan, D.G. Morgan and P. Daly, *Administrative Law in Ireland*, 5th edn (Dublin: Round Hall, 2019), paras 2–01 to 2–10.

[21] G. Hogan, D.G. Morgan and P. Daly, *Administrative Law in Ireland*, 5th edn (Dublin: Round Hall, 2019), para 2–02 to 2–05, citing *Albatros Feeds v Minister for Agriculture and Food* [2007] 1 I.R. 221 at 223 per Fennelly J. For a discussion on legislative (statutory) interpretation, see Ch.4. For an outline of the legislative process, see Ch.7.

[22] G. Hogan, D.G. Morgan and P. Daly, *Administrative Law in Ireland*, 5th edn (Dublin: Round Hall, 2019), paras 2–06 to 2–07.

[23] G. Hogan, D.G. Morgan and P. Daly, *Administrative Law in Ireland*, 5th edn (Dublin: Round Hall, 2019), para 2–08. For more on the judiciary, see Ch.11.

[24] See also *Maguire v Ardagh* [2002] 1 I.R. 385 at 567 per Denham J. See Chs 3–5.

[25] G. Hogan, D.G. Morgan and P. Daly, *Administrative Law in Ireland*, 5th edn (Dublin: Round Hall, 2019), paras 2–09 to 2–10.

clearly know what legal rights and obligations they have, and for any disputes to be resolved by an independent judiciary. Bingham argues that in achieving this aim, there are eight interrelated sub-rules.[26] These are:

1. the law must be accessible, predictable and clear;
2. law is preferable to discretion in resolving legal disputes;
3. law should apply equally, unless there are objective reasons to justify distinctions;
4. law must ensure adequate protection of fundamental human rights;
5. access to justice must be obtained without prohibitive cost or inordinate delay;
6. government ministers and public officials must exercise their powers reasonably, in good faith, for the purpose intended and without exceeding limits;
7. adjudicative procedures should be fair; and
8. the state must adhere to its international legal obligations.

2. Principles of the Rule of Law

(a) Legality

2–08 In order to meet Hogan, Morgan and Daly's (HMD) first principle, then, and drawing upon Bingham's analysis, the principle of legality requires a limiting of the role of discretion in the operation of the law (HMD 1 and Bingham 2). This does not mean that there is no place for discretion in the operation of the law. Rather, because modern society is complex, it is recognised that discretion can be useful once it is not exercised arbitrarily or in an unfettered manner.[27] As Donson and O'Donovan note, summarising the views of regulatory scholars, "the rule of law's goal of consistency and certainty is merely one aspect ... to pursue it as an absolute value is not realistic".[28] This explains why administrators may lawfully use their discretion to make decisions as regards priority for social/local authority housing, the grant of planning permission or whether a person should be granted a discretionary social

[26] T. Bingham, *The Rule of Law* (London: Penguin, 2011), Chs 3–10.
[27] T. Bingham, *The Rule of Law* (London: Penguin, 2011), pp.48–54.
[28] F. Donson and D. O'Donovan, *Law and Public Administration in Ireland* (Dublin: Clarus Press, 2015), para.1.18.

welfare payment. It also explains why judges may have discretion as to the sentence an individual convicted of a crime should receive to do justice in individual cases.[29] The principle of legality requires that those who exercise power must do so reasonably, in good faith, for the purpose intended (HMD 1 and Bingham 6), and in accordance with the constraints imposed on us by our membership within a wider international legal community (Bingham 8). This may be implicit in the principle as framed by Hogan, Morgan and Daly, specifically the reference to "clothed with the necessary legislative powers" (HMD 1), i.e. that laws need to derive from a recognised source of law, such as legislation, in order to meet the legality principle. This point will be returned to below when we explore the rule of law and the Covid-19 pandemic in Ireland,[30] as well as state compliance with law, with a consideration of the rights of children with a disability.[31]

(b) Equality

2–09 Equality of all before the law is Hogan, Morgan and Daly's second fundamental principle (HMD 2). Yet, as Bingham's elaboration notes, there can be legitimate and objective reasons to justify distinctions in the applicability of law (Bingham 3). Treating everyone equally can sometimes result in the compounding of disadvantage. This point will also be returned to in Section C of this chapter.[32] Equality before the law also means that proper balance is achieved through the protection of fundamental human rights (Bingham 4). You will note that Hogan, Morgan and Daly do not include this within their definition of the rule of law.

(c) Judicial independence

2–10 An independent judiciary is Hogan, Morgan and Daly's third essential principle (HMD 3) for the operation of the rule of law. Yet an independent judiciary, discussed in detail in Ch.11, is meaningless without fair adjudicative procedures (Bingham 7) and without realistic access to justice (Bingham 5). The latter two points will be returned to in Ch.10 and Ch.13 respectively.

---

29 For discussion on discretion, law and the welfare state, see R. Titmuss, "Welfare 'Rights', Law and Discretion" (1971) 42(2) *The Political Quarterly* 113.

30 See Box 2.2.

31 See Box 2.3.

32 See paras 2–37 to 2–40.

(d) Law as public and precise

2–11 The fourth requirement that the law be public and precise carries with it the obligation that it be accessible (HMD 4 and Bingham 1). There are, however, several problematic elements to this final requirement in practice. As will be discussed in Ch.4, legislative language can be complex and abstract, leading to interpretive difficulties. Moreover, as Bingham noted in the UK context, the legislature engages in "legislative hyperactivity",[33] whereby the law changes so often it is near impossible for anybody to know, even with legal advice, what precisely the law is at any one time.[34] This point is equally true in Ireland.[35] Bingham also accepts that judges have played a role in adding to the confusion as regards what precisely constitutes law, where the short and long-term impact of a decision can be difficult to decipher.[36] This point will be returned to in Ch.5.

3. International and European Indicators of "the Rule of Law"

2–12 While this chapter is focused on the rule of law within the Irish legal system, it is also important to recognise that discussion of the rule of law occurs internationally. The United Nations (UN) offers the following definition of the rule of law (and note how close it is to Bingham's understanding of the rule of law):

> "[The rule of law] refers to a principle of governance in which all persons, institutions and entities, public and private, including the State itself, are accountable to laws that are publicly promulgated, equally enforced and independently adjudicated, and which are consistent with international human rights norms and standards. It requires, as well, measures to ensure adherence to the principles of supremacy of law, equality before the law, accountability to the law, fairness in the application of the law, separation of powers, participation in decision-making, legal certainty, avoidance of arbitrariness and procedural and legal transparency."[37]

---

[33] T. Bingham, *The Rule of Law* (London: Penguin, 2011), p.40.

[34] T. Bingham, *The Rule of Law* (London: Penguin, 2011), pp.40–43.

[35] See Ch.14, Section D (Online Databases) and Ch.15, Section B (Reading Legislation).

[36] T. Bingham, *The Rule of Law* (London: Penguin, 2011), pp.44–47.

[37] United Nations, *Report of the Secretary-General on the rule of law and transitional justice in conflict and post-conflict societies*, UN Doc. S/2004/616, para.6. See also the UN's attempt to provide implementation criteria and indicators to test the robustness

2–13 The Council of Europe's Venice Commission identifies the following five core principles inherent within the rule of law:[38] (i) legality; (ii) legal certainty; (iii) prevention of abuse and misuse of power; (iv) equality before the law and non-discrimination; and (v) access to justice.[39] Yet, neither the UN's nor the Council of Europe's indicators of the rule of law are binding in the Irish legal system.[40]

2–14 EU law has a special status in Irish law, outlined in detail in Ch.6. For now, it is enough to say that Ireland is obliged to comply with EU law. The concept of the rule of law is referenced within the Treaty on European Union (TEU).[41] Article 2 TEU states that the EU is founded "on the values of respect for human dignity, freedom, democracy, equality, the rule of law and respect for human rights".[42] The rule of law was subsequently defined in Article 2 of Regulation (EU, Euratom) 2020/2092 of the European Parliament and of the Council of 16 December 2020:

> "'the rule of law' refers to the Union value enshrined in Article 2 TEU. It includes the principles of legality implying a transparent, accountable, democratic and pluralistic law-making process; legal certainty; prohibition of arbitrariness of the executive powers; effective judicial protection, including access to justice, by independent and impartial courts, also as regards fundamental rights; separation of powers; and non-discrimination and equality before the law. The rule of law shall be understood having regard to the other Union values and principles enshrined in Article 2 TEU …".

2–15 This Regulation establishes a general regime of conditionality for the protection of the Union budget.[43] This Regulation allows the EU to

of the rule of law in a given state: United Nations Department of Peacekeeping Operations (DPKO) and the Office of the United Nations High Commissioner for Human Rights (OHCHR), *The United Nations Rule of Law Indicators: Implementation Guide and Project Tools*, 1st edn (UN: Geneva, 2011).

38 The Council of Europe is a separate body to the European Union; see further Ch.6, Section E.

39 European Commission for Democracy through Law (Venice Commission), *Report on the Rule of Law*, COE Doc. CDL-AD(2011)003rev (4 April 2011).

40 See Ch.6, Section D (public international law) and Ch.6, Section E (Council of Europe).

41 Consolidated Versions of the Treaty on European Union and the Treaty on the Functioning of the European Union [2016] OJ C202/1.

42 See also Article 21 TEU which commits the EU, within the international sphere, to consolidate and support democracy, the rule of law and human rights.

43 See further, L. Pech, "The Rule of Law as a Well-Established and Well-Defined Principle of EU Law" (2022) 14 *The Hague Journal on the Rule of Law* 107.

withhold EU monies from Member States who do not respect the rule of law. This was put in place to inhibit rule of law backsliding that was occurring in two EU Member States. In Poland, the backsliding was regarding threats to judicial independence. In Hungary, this Regulation sought to put pressure on the government to end gross violations of the human rights of asylum seekers and refugees, end legal attacks on opposition politicians and the press, as well as repeal laws and practices designed to hinder academic freedom in universities and law reform campaigns of civil society organisations. Challenges to the consequent withholding of funding from both countries were unsuccessful before the Court of Justice, with the court stating in both cases:

> "The values contained in Article 2 TEU have been identified and are shared by the Member States. They define the very identity of the European Union as a common legal order. Thus, the European Union must be able to defend those values, within the limits of its powers as laid down by the Treaties."[44]

Nonetheless, as Pech and Lobina highlight, the EU's commitment to prevent rule of law backsliding is less than robust, with funding released to Hungary in return for them permitting the EU to assist Ukraine in its war against Russia.[45]

C. The Rule of Law in the Irish Legal System

2–16 In this section we will consider how the rule of law is given effect in the Irish legal system, with reference to judicial pronouncements on its importance. Hogan, Morgan and Daly's four principles outlined in the previous section will provide the framework for this discussion. While we are focusing on the four principles, it is essential to note that these principles are underpinned by: (i) the democratic nature of the State; (ii) the separation of powers;[46] and (iii) the protection of fundamental and

[44] *Hungary v European Parliament and Council of the European Union* (C-156/21) EU:C:2022:97 at para.127; *Poland v European Parliament and Council of the European Union* (C-157/21) EU:C:2022:98 at para.145.

[45] L. Pech, "The Future of the Rule of Law in the EU", *VerfBlog*, 14 December 2023, available at: *https://verfassungsblog.de/the-future-of-the-rule-of-law-in-the-eu*. See further, L. Pech and B. Lobina, *A Guide to Protecting the Rule of Law in European Courts amid Democratic Backsliding* (Prague: CEELI Institute, 2024).

[46] See below Section C.1 and Ch.3, paras 3–04 and 3–19 to 3–23.

human rights. In *Maguire v Ardagh*, Denham J. regarded the rule of law as "a principle fundamental to constitutional justice".[47] The separation of powers has been viewed as an "inherent part of the modern liberal democracy founded on the rule of law".[48] The embedding of the rule of law in the Constitution is important, as the Constitution is the foundation of our legal system and the most important domestic source of law. Accordingly, in this section we will also include an introduction to the various sources of law and the hierarchy of these legal sources in the Irish legal system.

2–17 Denham J. in *TD v Minister for Education* noted that no one branch of the State is solely responsible for upholding the rule of law, but rather:

> "The Constitution of 1937 and the judicial review element is in keeping with a modern democratic state where there are important elements to protect, being of the democratic majority, fundamental rights, and the rule of law. The function of the courts in protecting fundamental rights and the rule of law is part of the balance within a modern constitution. By including such a balance, the democratic values, fundamental rights and the rule of law are protected. The ultimate decision maker is neither a majority of representatives elected (in the executive or the legislature) nor the judges but the people in a referendum. By such a system the fundamental rights and the rule of law are protected."[49]

2–18 The Constitution, as the highest form of law in the State, and in particular Articles 5, 15, 34, 38 and 40–44, "presupposes the existence of a civilised and humane society, committed to democracy and the rule of law and the safeguarding of fundamental rights".[50] As the

---

47 [2002] 1 I.R. 385 at 568.

48 As quoted in *TD v Minister for Education* [2001] 4 I.R. 259 at 329 per Murray C.J. This has been extensively supported in subsequent court decisions: see, e.g. *Irish Human Rights and Equality Commission v Minister for Children, Equality, Disability, Integration and Youth* [2024] IEHC 493 at paras 36 and 59 per O'Donnell J. and *Delaney v Personal Injuries Assessment Board* [2024] IESC 10 at para.60 of Charleton J.'s judgment.

49 [2001] 4 I.R. 259 at 312. See also the decision of Barr J. in the High Court in *Sinnott v Minister for Education* [2001] 2 I.R. 545 at 571.

50 *Connolly v Governor of Wheatfield Prison* [2013] IEHC 334 at para.18 per Hogan J. See also *Lynch and Whelan v Minister for Justice* [2012] 1 I.R. 1 at 18, where Murray C.J., delivering judgment for the Supreme Court, stated: "[t]he sanctity of human life and its protection is fundamental to the rule of law in any society."

Supreme Court observed in *Re Article 26 and the Judicial Appointments Commission Bill 2022*:

> "The entire structure of the Constitution presupposes the existence of a state and a legal system governed by the rule of law. Article 5 describes the State as a democracy, yet without the appropriate rule of law guarantees, the essential democratic character of the State could not be assured ... [T]he Constitution has created a society governed by the rule of law, because it is principally through the enactment of legislation duly passed by a majority in a democratically elected Oireachtas that law is made for the State in accordance with Article 15.2.1°.This in turn means that citizens are entitled to regulate their affairs by reference to legislation enacted by the Oireachtas and, where applicable, by the corpus of common law and pre-1937 legislation carried over by Article 50."[51]

With this in mind, we now turn to consider the principles of legality, equality before the law, judicial independence, and public, precise and accessible law.

1. The Principle of Legality

2–19 The division of power between the legislative, executive and judicial branches of state is known as the separation of powers. This doctrine, enshrined in Article 6 of our Constitution, is an essential element in the rule of law because it sets limits on the nature and exercise of the power given to each branch. Under the classic understanding of the separation of powers, the legislative and executive branches of the State are intended to hold each other accountable to this rule of law standard. In turn, both these branches are intended to be held to account by the courts.

2–20 In reality, this classic conception of the separation of powers where each branch co-equally holds the other to account does not operate in Ireland. That Ireland does not have as "complete [a] separation between those powers" as other jurisdictions was recognised by the Supreme Court in *Barlow v Minister for Agriculture, Food and the Marine*.[52] The

[51] [2023] IESC 34 at para.11.
[52] [2016] IESC 62.

Supreme Court in *Barlow* highlighted that the "distinction [between executive and legislative functions] is often blurred in the Irish context because the executive sits in the legislature and more often than not effectively controls it and in particular the process of legislation."[53] In the European Commission's 2023 Rule of Law Report, concern was expressed about the increasing use of "guillotine motions". Guillotine motions have the effect of reducing the time that parliament can consider draft legislation prior to it becoming law.[54] As the executive has effective control over the legislature, then a majority of the legislature would likely vote to pass legislation in a hurried manner. While the decrease in the use of guillotine motions was acknowledged in the 2024 Report,[55] nonetheless it is evidence of the imbalance in power between the executive and legislative political branches. With this in mind, it is unsurprising that judicial independence has been described by the Irish Supreme Court as the "lynchpin of the constitutional order",[56] as "the most critically important aspect of the separation of powers",[57] and that it is "[a]n independent judiciary [that] guarantees that the organs of state conduct themselves in accordance with the rule of law".[58]

2–21 The judiciary have repeatedly noted that good (in the sense of legal) exercise of executive, legislative and administrative powers is a core component of the rule of law. For example, in *Callely v Moylan* it was stated that the legislature and executive are under a duty to "conduct themselves in accordance with the rule of law".[59] The courts therefore prohibit decision-makers, including government ministers, from exercising discretionary powers in an "autocratic or arbitrary fashion",[60] or for purposes not intended,[61] as this would be contrary to the rule of law and the democratic nature of the State under Article 5 of the

53 [2016] IESC 62 at para.36. See further Ch.6.

54 European Commission, *2023 Rule of Law Report: Country Chapter on the Rule of Law Situation in Ireland* (5 July 2023), p.22.

55 European Commission, *2024 Rule of Law Report: Country Chapter on the Rule of Law Situation in Ireland* (24 July 2024), p.28.

56 *Zalewski v Workplace Relations Commission* [2022] 1 I.R. 421 at para.37.

57 *Re Judicial Appointments Commission Bill 2022* [2023] IESC 34 at para.207.

58 *Curtin v Dáil Éireann* [2006] 2 I.R. 556 at 617.

59 [2014] IESC 26 at para.11 per O'Donnell and Clarke JJ. See also *Curtin v Dáil Éireann* [2006] 2 I.R. 556.

60 *Hussain v Minister for Justice, Equality and Law Reform* [2011] IEHC 171 at para.17 per Hogan J.

61 *Giles J. Kennedy and Co v Law Society of Ireland* [2004] 1 I.L.R.M. 178 at 185 per Kearns J., approving *Three Rivers District Council v Bank of England* [2000] 3 All E.R. 1.

Constitution. This is because, as Clarke J. noted in *Rawson v Minister for Defence*, "if decisions materially affecting the rights and obligations of individuals could be made in an unlawful fashion the rule of law would not be upheld".[62] Indeed, even in cases where a Minister has apparently been granted absolute discretion by legislation, the courts retain a supervisory capacity. As Edwards J. explained in *Damache v DPP*:

> "It was axiomatic that the rule of law requires all decision-makers to act fairly and rationally, meaning that they must not make decisions without reasons. The fact that a power is to be exercised in the Minister's absolute discretion may be relevant to the extent of the courts' power to review the decision, which might perhaps be limited to the question of examining the reasonableness of the decision, but that did not mean that a decision-maker was dispensed from observance of such requirements as the rules of natural and constitutional justice."[63]

2–22 In acting in this manner, the judges are applying and upholding the Constitution, which is the highest-ranking domestic source of law in Ireland. The Constitution, as interpreted by the judiciary, controls and sets the conditions according to which the rule of law operates in Ireland. The Constitution also identifies and ranks the other primary sources of law in Ireland. The identification of the sources is important as, for the legality principle to be met, we need to know which rules are law and need to be obeyed and which rules do not. The establishment of a hierarchy between the sources is essential as it enables disputes between sources of law to be resolved. It is therefore worthwhile at this juncture to consider what the sources of law in Ireland are.

(a) Primary sources of law

2–23 The Constitution is one of four primary sources of law in Ireland. Three of these sources are domestic in origin, and one is external. The three domestic sources are the Constitution, legislation and case law. The fourth primary source is EU law. You will be introduced to each of

[62] [2012] IESC 26 at para.6.1. For a discussion of superior court supervision of Oireachtas Committees to protect natural justice, see Ch.10, paras 10–29 to 10–32.

[63] [2014] IEHC 114 at para.88. See also *Efe v Minister for Justice, Equality and Law Reform* [2011] 2 I.R. 798 at 813 per Hogan J. See discussion of the court's judicial review function in Ch.10, paras 10–17 to 10–19 and Box 10.2.

these sources in detail in Chs 3–6 but, for the purposes of this chapter, we will confine our discussion to a number of key points.

2–24 First, "sources of law" has a specific meaning in law. It refers to those sources that are recognised as containing the rules and principles that comprise the law. Therefore, if a rule does not originate in one of these four sources, it is not a legal rule. The importance of correctly identifying the sources of law cannot be overstated because when you wish to make legal argument in an assignment, in an exam, before a court or to instigate legal reform, the primary basis of this argument must rest on what the law currently provides. As you will discover in other chapters, these sources are informed by and reflect extra-legal political and social considerations, but these extra-legal influences do not have force of law. Force of law is what differentiates legal rules from other categories of rules. Simply put, force of law means that legal rules are enforceable in ways that other social rules are not. For example, if you talk during a movie in the cinema, you might face social reproof, but the consequences of this punishment are unlikely to be felt very deeply or for a long time. By way of contrast, if you fail to abide by a legal rule, then you may be required to pay damages (e.g. for causing injury), you may be required to act against your will (e.g. specific performance of a contractual term), you may not get a benefit that you otherwise would have (e.g. if a will is not made in the prescribed way), or you may suffer a penalty (e.g. be fined or sentenced to prison for committing a criminal offence).

2–25 Second, for the rule of law to operate, it must be possible to resolve conflicts between the primary sources if, and when, this may arise. If this were not possible, then the law would be in a perpetual state of stalemate. This is why the sources of law are not equal in ranking. In Ireland, the highest-ranking domestic source of law is the Constitution, and this is clear from the translation of the Irish. Bunreacht means "basic law". This means that as the basic law of the State, it takes precedence over all other inferior sources of law. Legislation (including statutory instruments), common law, government department circulars and administrative actions of the State that violate the Constitution have no legal effect.[64] A summary of the core provisions of the Constitution is set out below.

[64] However, in the context of the status of law prior to being deemed unconstitutional, see *State (Byrne) v Frawley* [1978] I.R. 326 at 349, where Henchy J. states: "it does

Box 2.1: Legal Insight

Core Provisions of the Irish Constitution

Articles 1–3: The Nation

Articles 4–11: Definition of the State

Articles 12–14: The role and functions of the President

Articles 15–27: The powers (and limits) of the National Parliament (or Oireachtas)

Article 28: The duties of the Government

Article 28A: Local Government

Article 29: International Relations

Article 30: The Attorney General

Articles 31–32: The Council of State

Article 33: The Comptroller and Auditor General

Articles 34–37: The Courts

Articles 38–39: Trial of offences

Articles 40–44: Fundamental rights protections

Article 45: Directive Principles of Social Policy which are "not ... cognisable by any Court under any of the provisions of this Constitution"

Articles 46–47: The power of the people to amend the Constitution in a referendum

Articles 49–50: Repeal of the 1922 Constitution and the continuance of pre-1937 laws that conform with the 1937 Constitution

2–26 The Constitution establishes legislation[65] as the next highest ranking domestic source of law. Article 15.2.1° provides: "[t]he sole and exclusive power of making laws for the State is hereby vested in the Oireachtas: no other legislative authority has power to make laws for the State." Legislation can create, alter or revoke law in Ireland, once the

not necessarily follow that Court Orders lack binding force because they were made in proceedings based on an unconstitutional statute". See also, *Murphy v Attorney General* [1982] I.R. 241 and *A v Governor of Arbour Hill Prison* [2006] 4 I.R. 88. For a discussion on suspended declarations of unconstitutionality, see Ch.3, Section D.5.

65 The different types of legislation, its creation, and the passage of legislation through the Oireachtas are discussed in more detail in Chs 4 and 7.

Act of the Oireachtas complies with the Constitution[66] and with Ireland's obligations under EU law.[67] This Article also clearly limits who has the authority to legislate, i.e. the Oireachtas. The Oireachtas consists of Dáil Éireann (the lower house), Seanad Éireann (the upper house), and the President of Ireland.[68]

2–27 The third primary source of law is the common law,[69] or case law. Common law consists of all previous decisions made by courts over hundreds of years that have legal effect. Such law is known as "judge-made law". Although case law is not expressly mentioned in the Constitution as a source of law, Articles 50 and 15.2.1° implicitly recognise it as a primary source of law and rank it. Article 50 provides that all laws that were in force prior to the enactment of the Constitution will retain force of law so long as they conform to the terms of the Constitution. This means that common law principles that predated the Constitution continue to have force and effect in Ireland, subject both to the terms of the Constitution itself and to the ability of the legislature to overwrite them, as provided for in Article 15.2.1°.

2–28 A hierarchy also operates within the case law system for the same reasons as one operates between the sources of law. Where there is a conflict between two judgments, the ranking of the court that issued the judgment resolves the conflict and enables the smooth operation of the law. Therefore, a judge must generally follow decisions of courts higher up the hierarchy than the court they sit on. While facts can significantly differ in cases, in theory the application of legal principle is to be the same. This will be discussed further in Ch.5. On occasion, higher courts may depart from a long-standing precedent where there have been societal developments. Throughout the duration of your legal studies, you may engage in questions on the political nature of common law and judicial decisions.[70]

2–29 EU law is the fourth and final primary source of law. EU law has a special status in the Irish legal system. Within the EU's legal competence,

---

66 Article 15.4.1°.

67 Article 29.4.3° et seq. The status of EU law within the Irish legal system is discussed in detail in Ch.6, Section C.

68 Article 15.1.2°.

69 For a more detailed consideration of common law, see Ch.5.

70 See further Section D of this chapter and Chs 5 and 11.

EU law is the highest-ranking source of law in Ireland. What this means is that if Irish law, be it the Constitution, legislation, administrative practices or past decisions of Irish courts, conflicts with EU law, then EU law prevails. This is not due to some overarching political monolith usurping Irish sovereignty. This is due to the Irish people deciding that this be so. Article 29.4.6° states:

> "No provision of this Constitution invalidates laws enacted, acts done or measures adopted by the State, before, on or after the entry into force of the Treaty of Lisbon, that are necessitated by the obligations of membership of the European Union ...".

2–30 Therefore, it is only because the Irish people inserted this Article into the Constitution[71] that EU law has primacy over Irish law. While the issue is somewhat more complex than this, for now it can be stated as a general principle. Under the TEU and the Treaty on the Functioning of the European Union (TFEU),[72] the European Council and the European Parliament can legislate[73] in any of the following areas:

- free movement of EU citizens;[74]
- free movement of goods;[75]
- free movement of capital;[76]
- free movement of services;[77]
- fisheries and agricultural policy;[78]
- immigration and asylum (although Ireland must agree to be bound by these measures);[79]
- criminal co-operation, e.g. arrest warrants and extradition.[80]

---

71 It should be noted that the primacy of EU law over domestic law was established prior to Ireland entering the (then) European Economic Community (EEC) in 1973, and prior to the express recognition of the principle of primacy in the Lisbon Treaty. See further, Ch.6, Section C.

72 Consolidated Version of the Treaty on European Union and the Treaty on the Functioning of the European Union [2016] OJ C202/1.

73 The different forms of legislation in the EU are briefly outlined in Ch.6, paras 6–11 to 6–16.

74 Part Three, Title IV, Ch.1 TFEU [2016] OJ C202/47.

75 Part Three, Title II TFEU.

76 Part Three, Title IV, Ch.4 TFEU.

77 Part Three, Title IV, Ch.3 TFEU.

78 Part Three, Title III TFEU.

79 Part Three, Title V, Ch.2 TFEU.

80 Part Three, Title V, Chs 4 and 5 TFEU.

(b) Secondary sources of law

2–31 In addition to the primary sources of law, we have what are known as secondary sources of law. In some instances, these secondary sources are recognised law either in another jurisdiction or at supranational level. In others, the label "source of law" is something of a misnomer but it is nonetheless applied.

2–32 International law (excluding EU law), as traditionally understood, governs legal relations between different states. International law consists of several different sources, including custom, treaties and decisions of international courts and tribunals.[81] Article 29.3 of the Irish Constitution provides: "Ireland accepts the generally recognised principles of international law as its rule of conduct in its relations with other States." Article 29.6 of the Constitution requires an Act of the Oireachtas to incorporate into Irish law treaties that Ireland has signed. In other words, just because Ireland signs an international treaty does not mean that it has legal effect in Ireland. For example, Ireland ratified the European Convention on Human Rights in 1950 but it did not acquire the force of law domestically, and only to the extent provided for, until the Oireachtas passed the European Convention on Human Rights Act 2003.[82] It is only when the Oireachtas incorporates an international treaty into Irish law through legislation that it becomes a primary source of law. However, even if this step of domestic incorporation has not been done, the State still has a responsibility to abide by its international obligations—obligations that may be enforced through international enforcement mechanisms (assuming these exist), rather than through national courts.

2–33 Case law from other common law jurisdictions can also be argued before an Irish court. This case law does not have binding force of law before Irish courts. This is why it is a secondary source of law rather than a primary one. An Irish court can decide to accept or reject the principles articulated in a foreign precedent; it is only if they are accepted that they become incorporated into the body of Irish law, and the source of the principle will be the Irish case that adopted it.[83]

81 See Ch.6, paras 6–63 to 6–67.

82 See further, Ch.6, Section E.

83 For more on precedent, and judicial engagement with case law from foreign jurisdictions, see Ch.5.

2–34 The secondary source of law whose inclusion as a source of law is disputed is scholarly writing. This is textbooks and articles written by academics which analyse and critique the primary sources of law. Traditionally, neither lawyers nor judges cited the works of living authors, partly out of fear that living authors could change their minds and that could lead to inconsistency, and partly because dead authors did not talk back. While arguments from textbooks were gradually accepted before the courts, it was not until 1980 that articles from legal periodicals were given the official stamp of approval. In *Hynes v Independent Newspapers*, Kenny J. noted that the admission of books but the exclusion of articles would create the arbitrary situation whereby an author's views expressed in a textbook could be brought to the court's attention but those expressed in a reputable legal periodical could not.[84] Accordingly, academic work is now cited by judges in their judgments and relied upon by them in coming to decisions, and it is in this limited sense that they can be regarded as a source of law.

2–35 The level of merit accorded to a particular author varies depending on how respected they are within their field. However, the opinion of an author, no matter how respected, is regarded solely as an opinion. A judge is always free to disregard it. For example, in *Re Article 26 and the Judicial Appointments Commission Bill 2022*,[85] the Supreme Court considered the work of Professor David Kenny. While acknowledging the richness of the arguments proffered, the Supreme Court determined that they were not helpful to them in answering the specific question before them, namely whether the use of the term "merit" was unconstitutionality vague. That being said, academic support for a position taken can be reassuring, as McKechnie J. noted:

> "'Whether an interpretation is shared by academics' is not a canon of interpretation, and for good reason: the role of academia in critiquing and developing the law, though of undoubted importance, is markedly distinct from the judicial function. On balance, however, it is at least reassuring at some level that the view which I have reached is shared by so many academic experts in this field of the law."[86]

84 [1980] 1 I.R. 201 at 221.
85 [2023] IESC 34 at para.216. Discussed further in Ch.11, Section D.
86 *DPP v Brown* [2018] IESC 67 at para.139.

2–36 As students, you will spend a lot of time reading chapters from textbooks and articles from law journals. This is because secondary literary sources often offer insightful exploration and analysis of an area of law which can help you to understand the primary sources and can and should be cited by you to support your analysis in exams and assignments. However, it is important to emphasise that a secondary source is not a substitute for reading cases or statutes in their original form. Remember that an opinion of an author is only that—an opinion—and you are free to disagree with them, if you can justify your position with appropriate legal argument.

2. Equality before the Law

2–37 The applicability of the law to the State[87] and to everybody in the State, including to judges themselves, subject to certain exceptions discussed below, is an essential component of the rule of law.[88] As Smyth J. noted in *Flood v Lawlor*, "there are no Untouchables".[89] However, that does not mean that it is impermissible to discriminate as there can be legitimate, objective reasons to treat different categories of person differently. This is known as Aristotelian equality and it recognises the difference between formal equality (treating everyone the same) and substantive equality (generally treating everyone the same, but allowing for differential treatment where appropriate in order to equalise their positions and thereby ensure true equality).[90] Affirmative action policies in respect of groups previously excluded from positions of advancement or power by virtue of their race, class or gender would be the example

87 *Byrne v Ireland* [1972] 1 I.R. 241 at 307 per Budd J.

88 See *Curtin v Dáil Éireann* [2005] IEHC 163.

89 [2001] 1 JIC 1501 (no page or paragraph numbers to which point reference can be made). See also *Howard v Commissioner of Public Works* [1994] 1 I.R. 101 at 159, where Denham J. stated that "the archaic rule based on prerogative had no relevance to a democratic republic, being inconsistent with the rule of law based on the doctrine of equality".

90 See, in particular, Walsh J. in *de Burca v Attorney General* [1976] I.R. 38 at 68, where he stated: "Article 40 does not require identical treatment of all persons without recognition of differences in relevant circumstances but it forbids invidious or arbitrary discrimination. It imports the Aristotelian concept that justice demands that we treat equals equally and the unequals unequally." This dictum has been approved by the Irish courts on a significant number of occasions subsequently. See, for example, *Minister for Justice v Devine* [2012] 1 I.R. 326 at 366 (per O'Donnell J.). In the High Court decision of *Norris v Attorney General* [1984] 1 I.R. 36 at 49, McWilliam J. utilised, in part, the concept of Aristotelian equality, protected under Article 40, in dismissing the plaintiff's challenge to legislation that criminalised male homosexual acts.

par excellence of substantive equality. An Irish example of such a policy is the requirement for political parties to introduce gender quotas to increase female participation in politics.[91] Aristotelian equality is expressly recognised by Article 40.1 of the Constitution:

> "All citizens shall, as human persons, be held equal before the law. This shall not be held to mean that the State shall not in its enactments have due regard to differences of capacity, physical and moral, and of social function."

2–38 The Oireachtas is entitled to have due regard to differences between people or groups in society. An example of this can be seen in the Supreme Court decision of *Emma Y.*[92] "Emma" was an Irish citizen child. Her mother, who was not an Irish citizen, was seeking international protection in Ireland. Ms Y challenged the refusal of the Department of Social Protection to provide Emma with child benefit. The Supreme Court explained the legislative structuring on entitlement to child benefit. Child benefit is not an entitlement of the child, but rather an entitlement of an habitually resident parent.[93] A parent must be living with their child, who is under 16, or under 19 if in full-time education.[94] Persons seeking international protection are never deemed to be habitually resident for the purposes of social welfare law. As Ms Y was seeking international protection, she was not habitually resident so could not meet the legislative conditions for entitlement to child benefit.[95] (It is worth noting that people recognised as being entitled to protection are deemed to be habitually resident.) The Supreme Court held that the Oireachtas

---

91 Part 6 of the Electoral (Amendment) (Political Funding) Act 2012. This will be discussed again further in Ch.3, Box 3.3. For more on this, see I. Bacik, "Electoral (Amendment) (Political Funding) Act 2012" in E. Rackley and R. Auchmuty (eds), *Women's Legal Landmarks* (Oxford: Hart, 2019) and F. Buckley and Y. Galligan, "The 2020 General Election: A Gender Analysis" (2020) 35(4) *Irish Political Studies* 602.

92 *Michael X and Emma Y and others v Minister for Social Protection and others* [2019] IESC 82. A full analysis of this decision can be found in L. Thornton, "*Michael X and Emma Y and others v Minister for Social Protection and others* – Welfare, Immigration and Citizenship" (2021) 3 *Irish Supreme Court Review* 161.

93 Social Welfare Consolidation Act 2005 ss.220(3) and 246. The legislation also provides child benefit to persons who are not a biological parent but who are caring for the child once they meet all relevant legislative conditions. *Michael X and Emma Y and others v Minister for Social Protection and others* [2019] IESC 82 at para.65 per Dunne J. for the court.

94 Social Welfare Consolidation Act 2005 Act s.221(1A).

95 Explained in the decision, *Michael X and Emma Y and others v Minister for Social Protection and others* [2019] IESC 82 at paras 50–63 per Dunne J.

was entitled to impose an immigration restriction on child benefit entitlement. This, the Supreme Court determined, did not offend against the constitutional equality principle.[96] The Oireachtas was entitled to provide for a legislative scheme that excluded international protection applicants, even if the "ripple effect" of this was that Emma's mother did not qualify for child benefit.[97] This was not invidious discrimination against Emma, as according to the Supreme Court, the Oireachtas had a legitimate and rational basis for restricting access to child benefit: to "deter opportunistic [asylum] claims" and "welfare tourism".[98] The decision is concerning as regards its focus on alleged "welfare tourism", with the court in no way finding that Ms Y had engaged in this.[99] However, it does assist us in understanding that legal equality does not mean treating everybody equally; the legislature is permitted to identify a rational distinction for why law applies to one person but not another.[100]

2–39 A further exception to the general principle of equality before the law is where certain categories of person are excluded from the operation of the law to fulfil specific political or policy purposes. For example, foreign diplomats will have immunity for any criminal or civil wrongs that they commit while in Ireland, just as Irish diplomats in foreign countries enjoy similar immunity. This is provided for in international law,[101] as well as in Irish domestic law.[102] The rationale for this, as espoused by the European Court of Human Rights, is as follows: "the grant of immunity to a State in civil proceedings pursues the legitimate aim of complying

[96] See *Michael X and Emma Y and others v Minister for Social Protection and others* [2019] IESC 82, separate concurring decision of O'Donnell C.J., at paras, 21, 22 and 25.

[97] *Michael X and Emma Y and others v Minister for Social Protection and others* [2019] IESC 82 at para.19 per O'Donnell J.

[98] [2019] IESC 82 at para.16 per O'Donnell J.

[99] For more criticism of this aspect of the decision, see L. Thornton, "*Michael X and Emma Y and others v Minister for Social Protection and others* – Welfare, Immigration and Citizenship" (2021) 3 *Irish Supreme Court Review* 161 at 181–184.

[100] See *O'Meara v Minister for Social Protection* [2024] IESC 1 for an example of where the appellant had been excluded from accessing a Widower's Contributory Pension on the basis that he was not married to his deceased partner, with whom he had children. The Supreme Court declared provisions of the Social Welfare Consolidation Act 2005 unconstitutional as there was no reasonable or rational basis for limiting this payment just to those who were married.

[101] Vienna Convention on Diplomatic Relations 1961 (500 U.N.T.S. 95). See further, D. Fennelly, *International Law in the Irish Legal System* (Dublin: Round Hall, 2014), paras 7–111 to 7–115.

[102] Diplomatic Relations and Immunities Act 1967 s.5.

with international law to promote comity and good relations between States through the respect of another State's sovereignty."[103] However, even this has its limits. Traditionally, where an ambassador breached Irish employment law, there was no recourse to law for those at the receiving end of egregious violations of employment rights.[104] This has now significantly changed so that employees of persons with diplomatic immunity or of foreign embassies must now benefit from employment rights legislation.[105]

2–40 In a domestic context, judges have immunity from civil actions (torts) when they carry out their judicial functions. In *Kemmy v Ireland*, the plaintiff had been convicted of rape and sexual assault in December 2000 and sentenced to three years' imprisonment, with two years of the sentence suspended.[106] This conviction was subsequently overturned by the Court of Criminal Appeal after the plaintiff had served his sentence.[107] In overturning the conviction, the Court of Criminal Appeal was highly critical of the trial judge's summing up to the jury, where only the complainant's evidence was read out.[108] The plaintiff was not able to claim damages for time wrongly spent in prison.[109] The plaintiff argued that common law rules granting judges personal immunity from suit were unconstitutional. In rejecting this argument, McMahon J. stated that immunity of judges from being sued was for the benefit of the community as a whole, and not a personal privilege of a judge.[110] This is because a judge who feared that their decisions could render them

[103] *Cudak v Lithuania* [2010] ECHR 370 at para.60. However, see *Calderon v Nasser Rashed Lootah* (UD1219/2013, UD1220/2013, UD1221/2013). This determination is available at: *https://www.workplacerelations.ie.*

[104] For an example of this occurring, see Labour Court Determination No. EDA0417, *Italian Embassy v Damery* (December 2004), discussed in S. Kingston and L. Thornton, *A Report on the Application of the European Convention on Human Rights Act 2003 and the European Charter of Fundamental Rights: Evaluation and Review* (Dublin: Law Society, 2015), p.92.

[105] See, e.g. *Mahamdia v People's Democratic Republic of Algeria* (C-154/11) EU:C:2012: 491 at paras 27 and 57. For application of this in Ireland, see *A Housekeeper v An Embassy* (ADJ-00010792), decision of the Workplace Relations Commission, 10 January 2019.

[106] [2009] 4 I.R. 74 at 77.

[107] [2009] 4 I.R. 74 at 77.

[108] [2009] 4 I.R. 74 at 78.

[109] As to the reasons why this was the case, see s.9 of the Criminal Procedure Act 1993 and [2009] 4 I.R. 74 at 78–79.

[110] See, in particular, [2009] 4 I.R. 74 at 84–95.

personally liable would not exercise those powers impartially. The State had provided a "fair legal system" in which the plaintiff's trial was heard, and where he could appeal his conviction.

3. Independent Judiciary

2–41 Judicial immunity from civil suit in respect of judicial duties derives from the principle of judicial independence. Judges need to be independent from the other branches of state to ensure that they can adjudicate without fear or favour.[111] The importance of judicial independence in protecting the rule of law means that it is also recognised as a constitutional principle. Article 35.2 expressly states: "[a]ll judges shall be independent in the exercise of their judicial functions and subject only to the Constitution and the law."

2–42 Access to the courts for all persons in Ireland has also been viewed as a fundamental component of the rule of law.[112] In *O'Sullivan v Irish Prison Service*, McKechnie J. stated: "it is fundamental to governance based on the rule of law that access to the courts be both meaningful and purposeful. For such right to have any substance this must of course include the potential for an effective remedy."[113]

2–43 As discussed above, the existence of an independent judiciary has been emphasised as essential in Ireland given the imbalance in power between the executive and the legislature.[114] According to the most recent EU Justice Scoreboard, 72 per cent of the general population and 78 per cent of companies perceive the level of judicial independence in Ireland to be "fairly or very good".[115] This placed Ireland seventh of 27 EU Member States in the overall ranking for this criterion. In its 2024 Rule of Law Report, the European Commission also commented favourably on

[111] The function, appointment and removal of judges is considered in Ch.11.

[112] Access to justice is considered in more detail in Ch.13. See also, *Re Article 26 and the Illegal Immigrants (Trafficking) Bill, 1999* [2000] 2 I.R. 360 at 385, *Murphy v Greene* [1990] 2 I.R. 566 at 578 and *White v Dublin City Council* [2004] 2 I.L.R.M. 509 at 533, where the courts emphasised the importance of access to courts to ensure protection of the rule of law.

[113] [2010] 4 I.R. 562 at 603.

[114] See para.2–20.

[115] European Commission, *2024 EU Justice Scoreboard* (June 2024), p.45 (Figure 51) and p.45 (Figure 53).

progress made on a new judicial appointments process that will reduce political influence on appointments.[116]

4. Public, Precise and Accessible Law

2–44 The first element of this principle—that the law must generally be administered in public—is set out in Article 34.1 of the Constitution.[117] It is a long-standing principle, captured by the adage that "justice must not only be done, it must also be seen to be done", and is intended to increase public confidence in the legal system. That the law must be clearly stated and precise is also a well-established principle of Irish law. It helps those subject to the law to understand what they can and cannot do and legitimates their punishment if they chose to breach that law.

2–45 This requirement that the ambit of the law should be clear has been considered particularly in the context of the criminal law because of the potential for abuse of state power that overly broad or imprecise criminal offences could permit. In *King v Attorney General*,[118] the Supreme Court struck down s.4 of the Vagrancy Act 1824, a provision that allowed a person to be imprisoned for up to three months for loitering with intent to commit a criminal offence, on the basis that it offended against a number of constitutional provisions. Henchy J. held:

> "In my opinion, the ingredients of the offence and the mode by which its commission may be proved are so arbitrary, so vague, so difficult to rebut, so related to rumour or ill-repute or past conduct, so ambiguous in failing to distinguish between apparent and real behaviour of a criminal nature, so prone to make a man's lawful occasions become unlawful and criminal by the breadth and arbitrariness of the discretion that is vested in both the prosecutor and the judge, so indiscriminately contrived to mark as criminal conduct committed by one person in certain circumstances when the same conduct, when engaged in by another person in similar

[116] European Commission, *2024 Rule of Law Report: Country Chapter on the Rule of Law Situation in Ireland* (24 July 2024), pp.3–4. The new system for judicial appointments in Ireland is outlined in Ch.11, Table 11.1.

[117] Article 34.1, and some of the exceptions to the principle that it permits, will be discussed further in Ch.9, Section B.4.

[118] [1981] I.R. 233.

circumstances, would be free of the taint of criminality, so out of keeping with the basic concept inherent in our legal system that a man may walk abroad in the secure knowledge that he will not be singled out from his fellow-citizens and branded and punished as a criminal unless it has been established beyond reasonable doubt that he has deviated from a clearly prescribed standard of conduct, and generally so singularly at variance with both the explicit and implicit characteristics and limitations of the criminal law as to the onus of proof and mode of proof, that it is not so much a question of ruling unconstitutional the type of offence we are now considering as identifying the particular constitutional provisions with which such an offence is at variance."[119]

In other words, the offence of loitering with intent was declared unconstitutional because the language was ambiguous and uncertain. It was feared that it could be used in a discriminatory fashion, particularly against those who had prior criminal histories.

2–46 The principle that laws be clearly stated and precise also requires the activity in question to be unlawful when it was committed. A lawful activity cannot be made unlawful retrospectively. This is for the simple reason that the laws to which citizens are subject are required to be known in advance so that citizens can comply with them. The prohibition on retroactivity of law has constitutional status with Article 15.5.1°: "[t]he Oireachtas shall not declare acts to be infringements of the law which were not so at the date of their commission." While no-one disputes the importance of the law being precise, there are some shortcomings in meeting this standard in Ireland. Not only is statutory language complex, and therefore difficult for those without legal training to comprehend,[120] but sometimes those difficulties can also be (in)advertently exacerbated. People must be able to know, even if they require legal advice, what is a legal obligation, and what may be a mere recommendation. This issue came to the fore regarding Irish law and the Covid-19 pandemic.

119 [1981] I.R. 233 at 257.

120 As mentioned at para.2–11. The interpretive difficulties caused by the complexity of statutory language will be considered further in Ch.4, Section H.

Box 2.2: Legal Insight
Legal Clarity? Legal Responses to the Covid-19 Pandemic

The first person to die in Ireland from Covid-19 was on 11 March 2020, the same day the World Health Organization declared that the outbreak constituted a global pandemic. The danger Covid posed to the life, health and socio-economic wellbeing of all who lived in Ireland led to the introduction of two far-reaching statutes: the Health (Preservation and Protection and other Emergency Provisions in the Public Interest) Act 2020 and the Emergency Measures in the Public Interest (Covid-19) Act 2020. Ministers used the broad powers delegated to them by these statutes to take several extraordinary measures to reduce the spread of Covid, including three lockdowns, an eviction ban, and emergency social welfare supports. This was entirely appropriate given the need for Ministers to act quickly in response to a rapidly evolving situation.[121] The legality of these regulations is not at issue. Instead, our focus is on two connected concerns that were raised about them. The first is that government statements—either in speeches or in official websites—did not always accurately reflect the content of those regulations; the second is that there was a lack of precision in their wording, meaning it was not always clear what was proscribed. The rule of law principle that connects these concerns is the requirement that the law should be sufficiently precise to enable all those affected by it to know what they can or cannot do.[122]

The first concern stemmed from instances where public health advice was presented as if it was law. For example, there was never a legal obligation on those aged 70 years and older to "cocoon". This was to stay at home and avoid contact with any person. However, the language used on the website of the Health Service Executive initially suggested otherwise: "you need to cocoon", "you cannot have visitors in your home".[123] While this (in)advertent[124] misrepresentation of public health advice as law may have had good intentions, the effects of such misrepresentations were not benign. Not only were negative

[121] C. Casey and D. Kenny, "The Risk and Rewards of Ireland's Leviathan: Rule of Law Values and the Irish Executive's Crisis Response to COVID-19" (2023) 70 *Irish Jurist* 242 at 245.

[122] See further on this at Ch.11, Section F.3(b) (Golfgate).

[123] C. Casey, O. Doyle and D. Kenny, "The Irish State's COVID-19 Response and the Rule of Law: Causes for Concern" (2021) 110(440) *Studies: An Irish Quarterly Review* 446 at 451.

[124] Casey et al acknowledge that it could have been either; C. Casey, O. Doyle, D. Kenny and D. Lyons, *Ireland's Emergency Powers during the COVID-19 Pandemic* (Irish Human Rights and Equality Commission, February 2021), p.66.

psychological consequences experienced by those who cocooned,[125] but misrepresentations such as these could also

> "... create[] the false impression that there is legislation in force which regulates certain activities when, in truth, there is no such legislation. Were this to happen, then the executive branch would be able to achieve a result which is similar in effect to legislation, i.e. members of the public might well be coerced into complying with the Government's guidance in the mistaken belief that it is legally enforceable ... It is unrealistic to expect that a member of the public will wade through reams of statutory instruments in order to determine what the precise legal requirements are at any given moment."[126]

This observation was made by Simons J. in the context of a challenge to different government communications which had similarly incorrectly suggested the existence of a legal obligation.[127]

The concern that the regulations were imprecise is evidenced most clearly by confusion about whether it was permissible to attend religious services in person. In November 2020, the Department of Health advised that the then-applicable regulations did not prohibit such attendance,[128] yet priests who provided such services were fined for breaching the law.[129] Despite the initiation of legal proceedings in November 2020 seeking clarity on what the legal position was (and whether such a restriction, if it existed, was unconstitutional), it was not until March 2021 that the government confirmed that the regulations did restrict the performance of in-person religious services.[130] Legal certainty was also not helped by the regular and unpredictable amendment of the

[125] L. Bailey et al, "Physical and Mental Health of Older People while Cocooning during the COVID-19 pandemic" (2021) 114(9) *QJM: An International Journal of Medicine* 648.

[126] *Ryanair DAC v An Taoiseach* [2020] IEHC 461 at para.38.

[127] The communications in question suggested that international travellers were legally required to restrict their movement for 14-days after entering the State.

[128] For a full discussion of the various regulations that governed this issue, see O. Doyle, "The evolution of legal prohibitions on religious services", COVID-19 Law and Human Rights Observatory (2 April 2021), available at: *https://tcdlaw.blogspot.com/2021/04/the-evolution-of-legal-prohibitions-on.html.*

[129] C. Casey, O. Doyle and D. Kenny, "The Irish State's COVID-19 Response and the Rule of Law: Causes for Concern" (2021) 110(440) *Studies: An Irish Quarterly Review* 446 at 452–453.

[130] The certainty of this assertion was undermined by the introduction of a new regulation prohibiting in-person religious services in April 2021; O. Doyle, "The evolution of legal prohibitions on religious services", COVID-19 Law and Human Rights Observatory (2 April 2021), available at: *https://tcdlaw.blogspot.com/2021/04/the-evolution-of-legal-prohibitions-on.html.*

regulations. Unless people carefully combed through the text of the then-applicable regulations, they could never be certain what was and was not permitted.[131] Simons J.'s observation applies equally here: as few were likely to do this, the effect was that individuals curtailed their legally permissible actions for fear of breaking the law.

Reflecting on these and other concerns, Casey and Kenny write that lack of transparency and certainty on what the rules are can "sow dangerous confusion, and diminish public trust."[132] In this context, and given the extraordinary nature of the various measures taken, it was unsurprising that a case was taken animated by this distrust. The applicants in *O'Doherty and Waters v Minister for Health* applied for judicial review of various Covid measures in March 2020. The applicants argued that the measures were an unconstitutional and disproportionate response to what they characterised as a seasonal influenza virus. Moreover, it was argued that the Covid measures were part of a global conspiracy to deprive citizens of their rights. In rejecting their application in the High Court, Meenan J. determined that they had not produced any evidence to support these arguments, observing "[u]nsubstantiated opinions, speeches, empty rhetoric and a bogus historical parallel [with Nazi Germany] are not a substitute for facts."[133] This decision was upheld by the Court of Appeal.[134] Leave to appeal to the Supreme Court was granted. While the Supreme Court accepted that, generally, expert evidence is not required to challenge the constitutional validity or proportionality of legislation, in a case where the argument is that the State was lying about the objective of the impugned measures, applicants would be required to adduce "some plausible foundation in evidence" to support such a claim.[135] This the applicants had failed to do.

2–47 Accessibility of law is viewed as a key component of the rule of law.[136] As regards accessibility of law, the case of *Minister for Justice, Equality*

131 C. Casey and D. Kenny, "The Risk and Rewards of Ireland's Leviathan: Rule of Law Values and the Irish Executive's Crisis Response to COVID-19" (2023) 70 *Irish Jurist* 242 at 259–260.

132 C. Casey and D. Kenny, "The Risk and Rewards of Ireland's Leviathan: Rule of Law Values and the Irish Executive's Crisis Response to COVID-19" (2023) 70 *Irish Jurist* 242 at 267.

133 [2020] IEHC 209 at para.56.

134 [2021] IECA 59.

135 [2022] IESC 32 at para.88. For analysis of the Supreme Court case, see S. Glennon, "*O'Doherty and Waters v Minister for Health*: A Missed Opportunity for Judicial Scrutiny of the Response to an Extraordinary Crisis" (2023) 70 *Irish Jurist* 268.

136 *Conway v An Bord Pleanála* [2024] IESC 34 at paras 9 and 12 of Collins J.'s judgment and at para.24 of O'Donnell C.J.'s judgment.

and Law Reform v Tobin (No. 2)[137] is interesting. Here the inaccessibility of legislation to the appellant was challenged. The Oireachtas had passed, and the President signed, the Criminal Justice (Miscellaneous Provisions) Act 2009, which amended the European Arrest Warrant Act 2003. The 2009 Act had not been published on the Oireachtas website prior to the endorsement of a European arrest warrant by the High Court against Tobin.[138] In dismissing the argument that there was no "law", in the sense that the provision was not generally accessible at the time of the authorisation of the warrant, O'Donnell J. stated:

> "The importance of accessibility of law as an essential component of a valid or at least respectable, legal system ... has occupied writers from Roman times to St. Thomas Aquinas, Blackstone, Austin and others. The present situation is of course very far removed from the trick ascribed by Blackstone to Caligula, of complying with the formal requirements of promulgation by publishing laws in small letters on tablets attached to the top of high pillars, but the principle itself is of such fundamental importance to a functioning legal system that even the outer limits of the principle must be carefully respected."[139]

2–48 Like the requirement that the law be precise, issues arise regarding its accessibility. While people who do not have legal training may be able to find primary legislation (e.g. by typing in the name of a statute into a search engine), this presupposes that they know the name of the statute. This is not always a given, due to the frequently broad range of amendments contained in statutes with titles disconnected from the provision being looked for. It also ignores the possibility that they may not know that such a thing as secondary legislation exists, never mind where to find it.[140]

137 [2012] 4 I.R. 147.

138 However, as noted in this case, the attempted effect of the warrant occurred post publication of the 2009 Act on the Oireachtas website; see judgment of O'Donnell J.: [2012] 4 I.R. 147 at 316.

139 [2012] 4 I.R. 147 at 324.

140 Both forms of legislation will be considered in Ch.4.

D. Critiquing the Rule of Law

2–49 Professor Judith N. Shklar has stated:

> "It would not be very difficult to show that the phrase 'the Rule of Law' has become meaningless thanks to ideological abuse and general over-use. It may well have become just another one of those self-congratulatory rhetorical devices that grace the public utterances of Anglo-American politicians. No intellectual effort need therefore be wasted on this bit of ruling-class chatter."[141]

Shklar is not as dismissive of the concept of "the rule of law" as this quote suggests, noting the continued relevance of the rule of law as a concept for political and legal theory.[142] Nonetheless, she does illuminate how the rule of law can be misused, in particular within political and government circles. In the United Kingdom, the former Conservative government were frequently accused of breaking the rule of law. Two examples will suffice: the hosting of parties held in Downing Street during Covid-19,[143] and the failed attempt to off-shore asylum seekers to Rwanda.[144] In Europe, Poland and Hungary had EU funding cut on the basis that actions taken by the ruling parties contravened the rule of law.[145]

2–50 The key problem with the concept of the rule of law is its malleability. Although Section B set out criteria by which we can define what is meant by the rule of law, some criteria we highlighted are not universally regarded as essential components of the rule of law. In *O'Sullivan v Chief Executive of the Irish Prison Service*, McKechnie J. acknowledged this uncomfortable truth: "many of the world's legal systems do not uphold the same principles or rule of law or democracy

[141] See further, J. Shklar, "Political Theory and the Rule of Law" in S. Hoffmann (ed.), *Political Thought and Political Thinkers* (Chicago: UCP, 1998), p.21.

[142] J. Shklar, "Political Theory and the Rule of Law" in S. Hoffmann (ed.), *Political Thought and Political Thinkers* (Chicago: UCP, 1998), pp.21–24.

[143] See comments of Sir Keir Starmer, House of Commons Debate, Vol.87, *Hansard*, 31 January 2022.

[144] R. Green, "Migration Crisis: Rule of law under threat as UK government passes controversial Rwanda deportation law", International Bar Association, 24 May 2024. This plan was subsequently stopped once the British Labour Party entered government; see P. William Walsh, "The UK's former policy to send asylum seekers to Rwanda", Migration Observatory at the University of Oxford, 25 July 2024.

[145] See para.2–15.

which we enjoy here".[146] The reality is that the elasticity of the phrase "the rule of law" can justify the most horrendous legal regimes, once formalistic law-making processes are followed.[147] In such systems, the rule of law becomes rule by law. Chinese law professor Li Shuguang distinguishes between these two concepts as follows: "under the rule of law, the law is preeminent and can serve as a check against the abuse of power. Under rule by law, the law can serve as a mere tool for a government that suppresses in a legalistic fashion."[148] Accordingly, Robert Mugabe, the former President of Zimbabwe who was forced to resign in 2017 after decades of dictatorial rule, was able to state without embarrassment and with questionable sincerity, "[o]nly a government that subjects itself to the rule of law has any moral right to demand of its citizens obedience to the rule of law".[149]

2–51 Some legal theorists accept, in principle, the possibility of the rule of law existing in a non-democratic legal system. Raz, for example, stated:

> "A non-democratic legal system, based on the denial of human rights, on extensive poverty, on racial segregation, sexual inequalities and religious persecution may, in principle, conform to the requirements of the rule of law better than any of the legal systems of the more enlightened Western democracies."[150]

Others suggest that legal systems that do not meet the (mainly) Global North ideal of the rule of law might still be worth supporting. Jeremy Waldron writes:

> "[A] system that comes close to satisfying the ideal [of the rule of law] may make a reasonable claim on our support if there is a

[146] [2011] 1 I.L.R.M. 350 at 381.

[147] J. Shklar, "Political Theory and the Rule of Law" in S. Hoffmann (ed.), *Political Thought and Political Thinkers* (Chicago: UCP, 1998), p.30.

[148] S. Mufson, "Chinese Movement Seeks Rule of Law to Keep Government in Check", *Washington Post*, 5 March 1995, A25, quoted in B.Z. Tamanaha, *On the Rule of Law: History, Politics, Theory* (Cambridge: Cambridge University Press, 2004), p.3.

[149] M. Woolf, "Mugabe Told He Has Lost Moral Right to Govern", *Independent*, 1 August 2002, A8, quoted in B.Z. Tamanaha, *On the Rule of Law: History, Politics, Theory* (Cambridge: Cambridge University Press, 2004), p.2.

[150] J. Raz, "The Rule of Law and Its Virtue" in A. Kavanagh and J. Oberdiek (eds), *Arguing About Law* (Oxon: Routledge, 2009), pp.181–182.

real danger that disobedience and protest against its (admitted) injustices and imperfections may precipitate a collapse into a type of regime that has no respect for legality whatsoever."[151]

2–52 While there are many scholars who would fundamentally disagree with both Raz and Waldron on these points, the fact that the matter is debatable confirms the criticism that is levelled at the rule of law: its inherent lack of an agreed-upon definition. These practical problems in defining the rule of law point to significant issues with the rule of law as an ideal. In particular, the formalistic conception of the rule of law[152] can hide deeply held ideological views on what the purpose of the state is, and what the relationship between a state and its citizens should be. The Critical Legal Studies movement highlights the political nature of the rule of law and of laws generally, challenging the construction of the rule of law as a means of ensuring the neutral application of a neutral law. As Adelman and Foster note, "[t]he reality of power is obscured while the existing political order is rationalised in the rhetoric of equality, rights and the rule of law".[153] Socio-legal scholars similarly draw attention to the fact that law does not have any autonomous or semi-autonomous existence. Instead, it is part of society and a political system, which they argue reflects the power structures of the society.[154]

2–53 This conception of the rule of law as a "loaded ideal" was taken up by Mattei and Nader.[155] They argue, contrary to the orthodoxy that the rule of law developed in England as a means to constrain abuse of power by the monarchy, that it emerged to protect the property and power of the aristocracy, and subsequently the bourgeoisie.[156] The

[151] J. Waldron, "The Rule of Law in Contemporary Liberal Theory" (1989) 2 *Ratio Juris* 79 at 94.

[152] Formalistic in the sense that the law is rational and can be determined by politicians and interpreted by judges.

[153] S. Adelman and K. Foster, "Critical Legal Theory: The Power of Law" in I. Grigg Spall and P. Ireland (eds), *Critical Lawyers Handbook* (Vol.1) (London: Pluto Press, 1992), p.31.

[154] See generally, P. Hirst, *On Law and Ideology* (London: MacMillan, 1975).

[155] U. Mattei and L. Nader, *Plunder: When the Rule of Law Is Illegal* (Oxford: Blackwell, 2008).

[156] The rule of law was also an established principle in Classical Greece, and Greek understandings of the concept informed subsequent understandings of the concept from late Medieval times on. B.Z. Tamanaha, *On the Rule of Law: History, Politics, Theory* (Cambridge: Cambridge University Press, 2004), p.7. See Chs 1 and 2 generally.

emergence of the rule of law, they argue, provided a tool for lawyers to claim a special professional status as guardian of a government of laws. However, these lawyers were, they contend, guardians of a highly unequal and non-democratic society.[157] Moving to the present day, Mattei and Nader note that the concept of the rule of law has been used as a justification for "civilising" countries in the Global South, in particular through colonialism and imperialism.[158] Law, as both correctly note, has sanctioned colonial conquests, such as the scramble for Africa.[159] International economic law has privileged libertarian economic policies at the expense of human rights and distributive justice.[160] The rule of law for them is a rule of "imperial ideology" whereby social justice and solidarity are replaced by efficiency and competition.[161] Democracy, the rule of law and international human rights have all been utilised as tools for the legitimisation of control by the powerful over the powerless. Mattei and Nader state:

> "International human rights is ... a problematic notion because it provides a selective justification for intervention in the internal political business of all states that are not culturally aligned with Western or imperial rule of law. In the age of imperial legal order and brutal plunder in which we are living, it would be naïve to expect otherwise from international law."[162]

2–54 E.P. Thompson, a Marxist historian, viewed the law as purposefully "mystifying and pompous".[163] Thompson argued that the rule of law operated to protect the powerful and to disadvantage the powerless. Thompson examined the Black Act 1723, where the death penalty was extended to a range of different offences, including deer-stealing and tree-

---

[157] U. Mattei and L. Nader, *Plunder: When the Rule of Law Is Illegal* (Oxford: Blackwell, 2008), Ch.1, in particular pp.10–11, pp.12–14 and pp.30–34.
[158] U. Mattei and L. Nader, *Plunder: When the Rule of Law Is Illegal* (Oxford: Blackwell, 2008), p.68.
[159] U. Mattei and L. Nader, *Plunder: When the Rule of Law Is Illegal* (Oxford: Blackwell, 2008), pp.5–6.
[160] U. Mattei and L. Nader, *Plunder: When the Rule of Law Is Illegal* (Oxford: Blackwell, 2008), Ch.2.
[161] U. Mattei and L. Nader, *Plunder: When the Rule of Law Is Illegal* (Oxford: Blackwell, 2008), pp.5–6.
[162] U. Mattei and L. Nader, *Plunder: When the Rule of Law Is Illegal* (Oxford: Blackwell, 2008), p.153.
[163] E.P. Thompson, *Whigs and Hunters: The Origin of the Black Act* (New York: Pantheon Books, 1975), p.267.

cutting in enclosures.[164] Enclosures had previously been common land that all persons could use. However, the emergence of proto-capitalism saw property being individualised and privatised. Many individuals who formerly used the land were now regarded in law as trespassers. This, as Cole notes, was a significant redistribution of property rights from the public to the (already) wealthy and powerful landed elite.[165] Thompson regarded the Black Act 1723 as "a bad law, drawn by bad legislators, and enlarged by the interpretations of bad judges".[166] It is important to note that Thompson did not view all laws as inevitable instruments of injustice. While he accepted that law could be ideological, controlling, manipulative and a tool for oppression, he stated:

> "The essential pre-condition for the effectiveness of law, in its function as ideology, is that it shall display an independence from gross manipulation and shall seem to be just. It cannot seem to be so without upholding its own logic and criteria of equity; indeed, on occasion, by actually *being* just."[167]

2–55 Similarly, while maintaining significant suspicion of common/judge-made law, which he regarded as nothing more than the "common sense of the ruling class",[168] Thompson notes that the rule of law imposes inhibitions upon those in positions of power, and this is "an unqualified human good".[169] So, for Thompson, the rule of law, despite its disadvantages, does act as a constraint on those in positions of power and who rule. Even Shklar, with whose (seeming) dismissal of the concept of the rule of law we opened this section, acknowledges that given the continued political and legal importance of the concept, it cannot be so easily disregarded.[170]

---

[164] E.P. Thompson, *Whigs and Hunters: The Origin of the Black Act* (New York: Pantheon Books, 1975), p.267.

[165] D. Cole, "'An Unqualified Human Good': E.P. Thompson and the Rule of Law" (2001) 28(2) *Journal of Law and Society* 177 at 180–181.

[166] E.P. Thompson, *Whigs and Hunters: The Origin of the Black Act* (New York: Pantheon Books, 1975), p.267.

[167] E.P. Thompson, *Whigs and Hunters: The Origin of the Black Act* (New York: Pantheon Books, 1975), p.263 (emphasis in original).

[168] E.P. Thompson, *Whigs and Hunters: The Origin of the Black Act* (New York: Pantheon Books, 1975), p.266.

[169] E.P. Thompson, *Whigs and Hunters: The Origin of the Black Act* (New York: Pantheon Books, 1975), p.266.

[170] J. Shklar, "Political Theory and the Rule of Law" in S. Hoffmann (ed.), *Political Thought and Political Thinkers* (Chicago: UCP, 1998), p.21. See also, D. O'Donnell, "Some

2–56 You do not have to agree with all (or any) of these critiques. In our view, these critiques of the rule of law are essential. They highlight that the rule of law, even if "an unqualified human good", is not politically neutral. Power and politics have shaped the Irish legal system's understanding of what is meant by "the rule of law". Before concluding this chapter, we engage in a case study on what happens in the Irish legal system when the State decides to ignore or be indifferent to its legal obligations. This example illustrates the limits of legal tools in the face of systemic rights violations.[171]

Box 2.3: Legal Insight
The Rule of Law and State Inaction

The Disability Act 2005 is legislation passed by the Oireachtas. Under Pt 2 of the Disability Act 2005, the Health Service Executive (HSE) has obligations to, amongst other things, provide for the educational needs of children under the age of five with a disability.[172] Once a parent or guardian of a child applies to have an assessment of the child's needs, then strict timelines must be adhered to.[173] The HSE must acknowledge the receipt of an application from a parent/guardian to have a child's health and education needs assessed within 14 days.[174] The HSE must then arrange for an assessment of the health and education needs of a child due to their disability as soon as possible, but no later than three months.[175] This assessment of need is to be conducted without regard to the cost or indeed the capacity of the HSE to deliver the services that may be identified in the needs assessment.[176] Within a further three months, an assessment report must be prepared that includes a

Reflections on the Independence of the Judiciary" in E. Carolan (ed.), *Judicial Power in Ireland* (Dublin: IPA, 2018), pp.254–255, who cautions against viewing judicial decisions as "politically inspired". We return to this issue in Ch.11.

171 For an excellent exploration as to why the judiciary are very reluctant to grant mandatory orders when the State violates the law, in areas of supposed "social and economic controversy", see P. Kenna, "Situating Social Rights: Housing and Redistributive Justice – Post TD" (2022) 6(3) *Irish Judicial Studies Journal* 55.

172 Disability Act 2005 (Commencement) Order 2007 (S.I. No. 243 of 2007). The concept of disability for the purposes of the 2005 Act is set out in s.2, s.7 and s.8 of the Act.

173 Disability Act 2005 s.8.

174 Disability (Assessment of Needs, Service Statements and Redress) Regulations 2007 (S.I. No. 263 of 2007), reg.9.

175 Disability (Assessment of Needs, Service Statements and Redress) Regulations 2007 (S.I. No. 263 of 2007), reg.9.

176 Disability Act 2005 s.8(5). See also, *CM (A Minor) v Health Service Executive* [2021] IECA 283 at para.23.

statement of services that should be provided, albeit resource limitations may prevent these services from being provided.[177]

The assessment of needs report is the gateway to gaining access to services to support the education of children under five with a disability. Yet, the HSE has knowingly and continually breached these statutory obligations. The Ombudsman for Children in the *Unmet Need* report paints a stark picture of the impact of the HSE's failure to comply with the Disability Act 2005:

> "[I]t is reasonable for any parent to expect that they will be able to access services, which will enable them to make the right decision about the care, education and health of their child ... children have been on a waiting list for years to access an assessment of need ... once their child is assessed, they struggle to get any or all of the services recommended to help their child talk, move, learn and grow."[178]

Phelan J. in the case of *CTM (A Minor)* held that "there has been widescale non-compliance [by the HSE] with statutory time-limits across many regions of the country."[179] Hundreds of legal actions have been commenced, many successful, but the HSE continues to ignore its legal obligations.[180] As highlighted by Barr J. in *CM (A Minor)*, "[the HSE] cannot unilaterally elect to disregard a statutory duty placed upon it, simply because it is inconvenient or onerous for it to comply with that duty."[181] Barr J. continued stating that if the HSE did not have the resources to meet its obligations, it could "lobby the Minister [for Health] for a change in the legislation".[182]

In *JF v Health Service Executive*,[183] the assessment of the needs of JF's child should have been completed by October 2016. Given the lack of assessment, JF's child did not have access to services for persons on the Autism Spectrum nor appropriate pre-schooling. In addition, JF could not access the Domiciliary Care Allowance due to the lack of an assessment of needs report. By the time of the court hearing and judgment in 2018, JF's child still had not had their assessment of

[177] Disability Act 2005 s.8(7) and s.11; Disability (Assessment of Needs, Service Statements and Redress) Regulations 2007 (S.I. No. 263 of 2007), reg.10.

[178] Ombudsman for Children, *Unmet Need* (Dublin: OCO, 2020), p.5.

[179] *CTM (A Minor) v Assessment Officer* [2022] IEHC 131 at para.3.

[180] For more, see: Assessment of Needs for Children with Special Education Requirements: Motion, *Dáil Debates*, 8 March 2022; Disability and Special Needs Provision: Motion, *Dáil Debates*, 19 September 2024.

[181] *CM (A Minor) v Health Service Executive* [2020] IEHC 406 at para.117.

[182] [2020] IEHC 406 at para.113.

[183] [2018] IEHC 294.

needs. The HSE argued that due to unprecedented levels of demand for assessments and due to a lack of budgetary resources, it could not complete assessments in line with its statutory obligations. Faherty J. noted that "the diagnosis of disability in childhood ... imports a significant degree of urgency in the assessment of children for disability."[184] Faherty J. stated that the HSE had clearly not met its legislative obligations. These were set down by the Oireachtas and could not simply be set aside by the HSE due to pressures. Faherty J. ordered the HSE to complete the assessment of needs report for JF's child within a set timeline.

Phelan J. in *CTM (A Minor)*[185] has summarised the HSE's obligations relating to assessment of educational needs as follows:

i. There must be a determination of the type and extent of a person's disability under s.2 and s.7 of the Disability Act 2005.
ii. Lack of diagnosis affects children, as regards their statement of needs, in that it limits potential supports for their health and educational needs.[186]
iii. The timeliness of assessing a child's needs is crucial, which is why the Oireachtas required a speedy identification of needs, so that supports can be put in place. Not doing so may impact significantly on a child's quality of life into the future.[187]
iv. A full and comprehensive assessment must be provided. The HSE cannot introduce (in an attempt to shorten waiting lists) a lesser or preliminary assessment system.[188]

In 2024, reflecting on the impact of these (and other) decisions, the High Court acknowledged that "the HSE is prioritising the complaints of parents and guardians of children who have issued proceedings over those that have not."[189] Even where a child does manage to get an assessment of need, the delay in then getting access to supports is deeply concerning.[190] In *JN and TM v Health Service Executive*, 18 months after applying for an assessment of needs, in January 2020, TM was found to require occupational therapy, psychology, physiotherapy and speech and language therapy.[191] The HSE estimated that these services could be provided from March 2023. TM's mother, JN, unsuccessfully appealed under the Disability Act 2005 to an appeals officer, seeking

[184] [2018] IEHC 294 at para.56.
[185] [2022] IEHC 131.
[186] [2022] IEHC 131 at para.134.
[187] [2022] IEHC 131 at para.153.
[188] [2022] IEHC 131 at para.156.
[189] *KR v Health Service Executive* [2024] IEHC 225 at para.17.
[190] *JN and TM v Health Service Executive* [2023] IESC 9.
[191] [2023] IESC 9 at para.1.

to challenge the more than three-year wait TM would have in order to access these essential services.[192] The appeals officer concluded that he did not have the jurisdiction to require the HSE to provide services at an earlier date. The Supreme Court, upholding the decision of the Court of Appeal, accepted that the appeals officer had jurisdiction to determine whether the date the services were to commence was appropriate.[193] This decision is, however, somewhat limited. The Supreme Court stated that services cannot be provided where "the resources necessary for the provision of those services are not available". However, this does not prevent an appeals officer from using their "extensive powers" to enquire as to whether the services could be provided sooner, or in a different area.[194]

So what does this brief review of case law in this field tell us about the rule of law?

1) Where the State, or an organ of the State such as the HSE, breaches the law, the courts will intervene. This, however, will be on a case-by-case basis and does not deal with systemic violations of legal obligations.
2) When an organ of the State such as the HSE continues to breach statutory obligations over a prolonged period of time, the only real remedy parents have is to go to the High Court. Where parents do not have the knowledge or means to do so, their child will not access an assessment of needs as quickly as those who do take a successful High Court action.
3) Thinking deeper on our discussion of the rule of law in this chapter, to what degree is the State complying with the rule of law in this arena, given that an organ of the State, the HSE, has continuously and knowingly violated its statutory obligations? It must be emphasised that this is not some sort of wilful ignorance of its obligations, but rather an inability to meet these due to (alleged) funding constraints.
4) Reflecting on critiques of the rule of law discussed above, and the centrality of law and power, would a private individual be permitted to wilfully ignore their legal obligations without any real consequence?

[192] [2023] IESC 9 at paras 3–5.
[193] [2023] IESC 9, see generally paras 68–71.
[194] [2023] IESC 9 at para.75.

E. Conclusion

2–57 In this chapter we have argued that for a legal system to conform to "the rule of law", several indicators of compliance must be present. These include: that legal and political systems are constrained by having to act lawfully; laws and legal rules should be made public, and apply prospectively; independent judicial and administrative systems are necessary to determine rights and responsibilities of the State and all those within the State; and, for the rule of law to really exist, democracy and protection of fundamental human rights are essential. For some, such a definition may be viewed as much too expansive. For others, this definition hides the historical and continued economic, social and political power that has shaped the meaning of the rule of law.

2–58 There will always be contestation as regards what exactly is meant by the rule of law. This contestation should not be regarded as problematic. In fact, it should be seen as healthy that robust debate exists regarding the utility, or otherwise, of the rule of law. In Ireland, the judiciary highlight the Constitution as providing the underpinning for the Irish political and legal systems to operate within the rule of law. Our discussions and reflections on the rule of law in this chapter show that the meaning of, and interpretation towards, law and legal norms can, and should, be contested. Law does not exist in a societal or political vacuum. Even within the Irish legal system, there are concerns about State compliance with the rule of law in various instances. All subsequent chapters in this text, in essence, engage with the rule of law. After all, if the rule of law is shorthand for a legal and political system in "good order", then examining in detail the Irish legal system provides you with tools to reflect on how well the rule of law is respected and protected in Ireland.

Chapter 3

The Irish Constitution

> "Constitutions ... are a phenomenon of the modern world. It was not until the seventeenth century that the word evoked the idea of a document enunciating the fundamental framework of a government and the basic principles by which a country should be governed. They were a direct product of liberalism and the revolt against the concentration of absolute and arbitrary political power that was a feature of the development of the modern, i.e. post-medieval, state. Constitutions became effective political devices when the politically dominant class in some of the rapidly developing countries of Western Europe and North America felt the need to define and delimit government; to accord a special status to particular rules of law regarded as fundamental; to insist that their governments, hitherto absolute rulers, should abide by the law; and to be willing themselves to do likewise."
>
> B. Chubb, *The Politics of the Irish Constitution* (Dublin: Institute of Public Administration, 1991), pp.4–5.

In this chapter we:

- examine the purposes of constitutions;
- consider the historical context of our current Constitution;
- review the content of the Constitution;
- introduce the main constitutional interpretation techniques used by judges;
- consider reform of the Constitution.

A. Introduction

3–01 The first source of law that we will examine in this book is the highest-ranking domestic source, the Constitution. This is made clear from the translation of the Irish word for the Constitution. "Bunreacht" means "basic law". In this context, "basic" means that the Constitution establishes the legal foundation to which the institutional framework of the State is attached and from which all other laws enacted by the State draw support/legitimacy. In practical terms, this means that every other domestically produced source of law, in addition to every action by an organ of the State, must comply with the provisions of the Constitution in order for them to have force of law in Ireland. We have had two Constitutions in Ireland. The first was the Constitution of the Irish Free State of 1922; the second is the 1937 Constitution and it remains in force today.

3–02 In this chapter we will examine various constitutional provisions, having first considered the legal, symbolic and political purposes that constitutions serve and the historical context behind the drafting of the 1937 Constitution. We will also encounter the concept of judicial review, one form of which is where judges are asked to consider the constitutionality of a Bill or a statute,[1] and be introduced to the various interpretation techniques that judges use when performing this task. As will be clear by the conclusion of this chapter, judges play a very important role in developing and circumscribing Irish law through their function as interpreters of the Constitution. As Gallagher writes, "[t]heir power to interpret the Constitution makes them even more powerful than judges in many other countries".[2] Finally, the various amendments that have been made to the Constitution will be identified and there will be a brief discussion of future reforms.

B. The Purpose of Constitutions

1. Legal Functions

3–03 Constitutions perform a number of functions, both legal and symbolic. Legally, constitutions constitute. This is clear from their name. As Murphy explains, "[t]o constitute means to make up, order, or form: thus, a nation's constitution should pattern a legal system".[3] They do

[1] Another aspect of judicial review will be considered in Ch.10, paras 10–17 to 10–20 and Box 10.2.

[2] M. Gallagher, "The Changing Constitution" in J. Coakley and M. Gallagher (eds), *Politics in the Republic of Ireland*, 7th edn (London, New York: Routledge, 2023), p.78.

[3] W.F. Murphy, "Constitutions, Constitutionalism and Democracy" in D. Greenberg, S.H. Katz, M. Oliviero and S.C. Wheatley (eds), *Constitutionalism and Democracy:*

this in two main ways. First, constitutions define the boundaries of the State over which power is asserted. This is necessary because, as was noted in Ch.2, one of the core components of the rule of law is that rules need to be clearly set down so as to enable those subject to them to conduct themselves accordingly.[4] By defining the parameters of the State, a constitution is the first step in this endeavour. In Ireland, the State is declared to consist of the 26 counties.[5]

3–04 Second, constitutions set out how the legal power held by the State is to be distributed and what limits are to be placed on those who have been tasked with running the country. The clear distribution of power and the imposition of limits on the exercise of that power are essential for the rule of law to operate.[6] In order for laws to be valid, it is necessary that proper procedures are followed, and a constitution establishes what those procedures are. Most constitutions adopt a separation of powers paradigm whereby the powers of the State are divided between different branches of the State—the legislative, the executive and the judicial—to ensure that all power is not vested in any one body or individual. The separation of powers is enshrined in Article 6 of the Irish Constitution and the powers are divided out between the different organs of State in other Articles.[7]

3–05 In addition, each organ of State is typically subject to checks and balances by the other branches as a further protection against abuse of power. The reason for this caution is best articulated by Acton: "[a]ll power tends to corrupt; absolute power corrupts absolutely."[8] Indeed, this understanding of human nature explains why constitutions are necessary in a democracy. Laffin writes:

Transitions in the Contemporary World (Oxford: OUP, 1993), quoted in V.C. Jackson and M. Tushnet (eds), *Comparative Constitutional Law* (New York: Foundation Press, 1999), p.196.

4 Chapter 2, paras 2–05 to 2–06 and paras 2–45 to 2–46.

5 Article 3.1°.

6 See Ch.2, in particular the discussion on the principle of legality at paras 2–19 to 2–21.

7 See paras 3–19 to 3–23. Article 6 of the Constitution states:

"1 All powers of government, legislative, executive and judicial, derive, under God, from the people, whose right it is to designate the rulers of the State and, in final appeal, to decide all questions of national policy, according to the requirements of the common good.

2 These powers of government are exercisable only by or on the authority of the organs of State established by this Constitution."

8 Letter to Bishop Mandell Creighton, 5 April 1887, published in J.N. Figgis and R.V. Laurence (eds), *Historical Essays and Studies* (London: MacMillan, 1907).

> "Constitutions make public policy possible by creating a structured arena within which policy can be formulated. Constitutions give the executive the mandate to govern, yet at the same time they must contain protections against possible abuses of power by those controlling it."[9]

The practical importance of the separation of powers in protecting citizens and non-citizens[10] from the excesses of the State has been recognised in the Irish courts. Barrington J. noted: "the purpose of the theory of separation of powers is to protect the rights of the citizen. Absolute power may not be delegated to any executive agency because to do so would be inconsistent with the rights of the citizen."[11]

3–06 In Ireland, rights provisions can be found throughout the Constitution, but the most well-known rights are to be found in Articles 40–44, in the part of the Constitution titled "Fundamental Rights", and in Article 38 which governs the trial of offences. The protection of specified rights in the Constitution and, as will be seen, unspecified or derived rights, is important because it places such rights "beyond the reach of ordinary politics".[12] Sunstein writes:

> "Constitutional protection of ... rights is not at odds with the commitment to self-government but instead a logical part of it ... Majority rule should not be identified with democracy itself. If a political majority restricts dissenters, or disenfranchises people, [or fails to protect minority groups], it is behaving inconsistently with democracy ... ."[13]

3–07 The fact that constitutions typically cannot be amended easily adds a further layer of protection for the citizens of the State.[14] Different

9 M. Laffin, "Constitutional Design: A Framework for Analysis" (2000) 53 *Parliamentary Affairs* 532 at 533.

10 Some rights in the Constitution are confined to citizens only, e.g. the rights specified in Article 40.1. However, the rights under Articles 41–44 are mostly available to citizens and non-citizens, as is the right to freedom from unlawful detention (Article 40.4.1°). For more, see J.P. Casey, *Constitutional Law in Ireland*, 3rd edn (Dublin: Round Hall Sweet & Maxwell, 2000), pp.444–449.

11 *Laurentiu v Minister for Justice* [1999] 4 I.R. 26 at 70.

12 C.R. Sunstein, *Designing Democracy: What Constitutions Do* (Oxford: OUP, 2001), p.97.

13 C.R. Sunstein, *Designing Democracy: What Constitutions Do* (Oxford: OUP, 2001), p.97.

14 Indeed, some constitutions include unamendable provisions, such as Article V in the US Constitution (equal representation of every state in the Senate), or Article 79(3) of

countries have different mechanisms for the amendment of their constitutions but they are usually more onerous than the ways in which ordinary legislation can be amended. In France, amendments can be made by means of referendum or with the support of three-fifths of the Parliament.[15] In Germany, two-thirds of both Houses of Federal Parliament must support the amendment.[16] In both of these constitutions, certain provisions can never be amended, such as the basic rights provisions in Germany[17] and the republican form of government in France.[18] In Ireland, no provision is exempt from amendment,[19] but any amendment must be with the consent of the people[20] after a referendum campaign is conducted.

2. Symbolic Functions

3–08 The protection of rights, even when it may be politically unpopular to do so—the protection of the rights of the accused or of prisoners' rights being good cases in point—illustrates that, in addition to legal purposes, constitutions also perform symbolic or aspirational ones. Constitutions are texts that set out the "goals, ideals and moral standards by which [the framers and subjects] want others, including their own posterity to judge the community".[21] Sometimes these ideals are honoured more in the breach than in the observance, but their textual existence provides the basis for citizens to argue for change when circumstances allow it. For example, it could have been argued by some of the women who were detained in Magdalene Laundries that they were unlawfully deprived of their liberty (Article 40.4.1°) and were denied their due process right to a fair hearing before a punishment was imposed (Article 38). However,

the German Constitution, which forbids, among others, any amendment that would lessen human dignity.

15 French Constitution, Article 89.

16 German Constitution, Article 79.

17 German Constitution, Article 79(3).

18 French Constitution, Article 89.

19 This was not always the case. Article 51, which was deleted from the 1937 Constitution following the transition period, permitted constitutional amendment by means of ordinary legislation. However, it also provided that neither it nor Article 46, which established the referendum process, could be amended during this three-year period.

20 Only citizens can vote to amend the Constitution: Article 47.3.

21 W.F. Murphy, "Constitutions, Constitutionalism and Democracy" in D. Greenberg, S.H. Katz, M. Oliviero and S.C. Wheatley (eds), *Constitutionalism and Democracy: Transitions in the Contemporary World* (Oxford: OUP, 1993), quoted in V.C. Jackson and M. Tushnet (eds), *Comparative Constitutional Law* (New York: Foundation Press, 1999), pp.198–199.

it is extremely unlikely that any of the women would have thought to argue such points at the time or that any lawyer would have agreed to represent them.[22] Ongoing problems with accessing the redress scheme established in 2013 and revised in 2018 are further evidence of the downplaying of the harm perpetrated against this cohort of women and girls.[23]

3–09 The aspirational nature of particular provisions in a constitution may sometimes be contentious. For example, prior to 1999, Articles 2 and 3 of the Constitution as originally enacted asserted a legal claim over the whole island of Ireland.[24] These provisions reflected nationalist thinking at the time—as Ó Tuathaigh notes, they caused no controversy in either the Dáil or amongst the public prior to enactment[25]—but Unionists regarded them as inflammatory. Part of the Good Friday peace process, which sought to provide a political solution to the Northern Ireland conflict, was a recommendation that this claim of legal right be removed from the Constitution. It was removed by means of a referendum,[26] but an aspiration to a united Ireland is still included in our Constitution. Article 3.1 expresses "the firm will of the Irish Nation ... to unite all the people who share the territory of the island of Ireland ...". However, the fulfilment of this aspiration is stated to be dependent on the consent of the majority of those in Northern Ireland; it is therefore no longer couched as a legal claim of right.

3–10 The introduction of a new constitution is also a symbolic act. Both for new States and for States reconstituting themselves, it represents a rejection of the earlier legal order, either in whole or in part, and it offers the promise of a new beginning. This is so even if the majority of the architecture of the State remains the same, as was the case in Ireland

[22] For a consideration of the role that the Magdalene Laundries played in the Irish carceral context, see S. Kilcommins, I. O'Donnell, E. O'Sullivan and B. Vaughan, *Crime, Punishment and the Search for Order in Ireland* (Dublin: IPA, 2004), Ch.2. The point regarding the disjuncture between formal legal rights and their application is one made by Kilcommins in personal communication.

[23] J. O'Connell, "Magdalene laundries survivor recalls a childhood of relentless abuse and neglect", *Irish Times*, 4 March 2023, available at: *https://www.irishtimes.com/ireland/2023/03/04/magdalene-laundries-survivor-recalls-a-childhood-of-relentless-abuse-and-neglect/.*

[24] *Boland v An Taoiseach* [1974] I.R. 338.

[25] G. Ó Tuathaigh, "Irish Nation-State in the Constitution" in B. Farrell (ed.), *De Valera's Constitution and Ours* (Dublin: Gill & Macmillan, 1988), p.51.

[26] Nineteenth Amendment of the Constitution Act 1998.

when the 1922 Constitution was replaced with the 1937 Constitution. In order to explain what is meant by this, it is necessary to look at why the 1937 Constitution was introduced and how the performance of legal and symbolic functions can be enmeshed.

3. Symbolic and Legal Impetus behind the 1937 Constitution

3–11 When Ireland gained independence in 1922, the terms of that independence were hotly contested, ultimately leading to a civil war between 1922 and 1923. There were five main sources of contention, all of which were incorporated into the Free State Constitution as it was enacted with reference to the 1921 Treaty. The first was the partitioning of Ireland into two discrete legal entities: the 26-county Free State and the six-county Northern Ireland. The second was the continued obligation to pay land annuities to the British Government. This was money provided under the Land Acts of 1891 and 1909 to allow tenant farmers buy their farms. It amounted to £3 million a year, a very significant sum of money at the time.[27] The next three matters of dispute all represented continued Irish subservience to England despite independence. The highest appellate court in Irish law would not be an Irish court, but the British Privy Council. The Governor-General, an office created by the Treaty, would represent the Crown in the Free State and had, in theory, the power to veto legislation passed by the Oireachtas.[28] Finally, the Free State was not a republic but a dominion of the Commonwealth. This meant that the Crown would remain the Head of State and all members of the Oireachtas had to swear an oath of allegiance to the King or Queen.

3–12 Those who supported the Treaty, represented by Cumann na nGaedheal, held power from 1922–1932. However, in 1932, the party opposed to the Treaty won the general election. Fianna Fáil, led by Éamon de Valera, were clear that their stated aim was to dismantle the Treaty. Two legal measures facilitated this process: first, the passing of the Statute of Westminster 1931, which granted dominions constitutional

[27] De Valera still intended to collect the money, but the money would be retained by the Free State. For further discussion of this, see J.C.W. Wylie, *Irish Land Law*, 5th edn (Dublin: Bloomsbury Professional, 2014), pp.28–59.

[28] In practice, the Governor-General never exercised this power, signing all Bills that were forwarded to him. D. Keogh and A. McCarthy, *The Making of the Irish Constitution 1937* (Cork: Mercier Press, 2007), p.40.

independence, i.e. the ability to amend treaties; and second, the 1922 Constitution could be amended by ordinary legislation, leaving it open to relatively easy modification by those who held power.[29]

3–13 Several significant amendments followed. The first of these removed the oath of allegiance in May 1933.[30] The removal of the right of petition to the Privy Council and the reduction of the powers of the Governor-General followed in November 1933.[31] The abdication of Edward VIII provided the opportunity to pass two further amendments.[32] One removed all references to the King and the Governor-General from the Constitution.[33] The other recognised the King but only in regard to external relations with other countries and only when authorised to do so by the Government; Ireland was domestically sovereign, but the King would remain in principle the representative of Ireland in international affairs.[34]

3–14 Accordingly, the majority of the provisions in the 1922 Constitution that were problematic from de Valera's perspective had been deleted. Moreover, de Valera's refusal to pay part of the land annuities owed in 1932, which led to an economic war with Britain, was ultimately resolved in Ireland's favour in the Anglo-Irish Agreements of 1938.[35] In

29 The main difficulty for de Valera was the Seanad, so he abolished it in 1936 by means of another constitutional amendment. By the time it was replaced, 41 of the 83 Articles in the 1922 Constitution has been amended. B. Farrell, "From First Dáil through Irish Free State" in B. Farrell (ed.), *De Valera's Constitution and Ours* (Dublin: Gill & Macmillan, 1988), p.30.

30 Constitution (Removal of Oath) Act 1933. The Seanad's refusal to accept this change, delaying the passage of the Bill, angered de Valera and was one of the factors in his decision to abolish the House. D. Keogh and A. McCarthy, *The Making of the Irish Constitution 1937* (Cork: Mercier Press, 2007), p.46.

31 Constitution (Amendment No. 20) Act 1933, Constitution (Amendment No. 21) Act 1933, and the Constitution (Amendment No. 22) Act 1933. A Bill to remove the oath had been initiated by the Cumann na nGaedheal Government, but it lapsed when the Government fell.

32 Edward VIII abdicated in order to marry Wallis Simpson, a twice-divorced American socialite, following social, moral, political, religious and legal opposition to the match. See further, His Majesty's Declaration of Abdication Act 1936 (1 Edw. 8 & 1 Geo. 6 c. 3) (UK).

33 Constitution (Amendment No. 27) Act 1936.

34 Executive Authority (External Relations) Act 1936. This was done in the hopes that when partition ended, there would still be a connection to the Crown for Unionists. R. Fanning, "Mr de Valera drafts a Constitution" in B. Farrell (ed.), *De Valera's Constitution and Ours* (Dublin: Gill & Macmillan, 1988), p.41.

35 The British Government initially demanded £104 million in settlement but in the end £10 million was agreed upon and trade was opened up again between the two

some senses, therefore, the enactment of the 1937 Constitution was unnecessary. Yet the origins of the 1922 Constitution as one imposed on Ireland under the threat of violence were troubling to de Valera on a symbolic level. He noted: "[n]o matter how republican the Free State Constitution was made by amendment, it could never escape its basis in British law."[36] In advocating for the adoption of the 1937 Constitution, he described it as "a renewed declaration of national independence".[37] He also refused to allow the British dominions secretary to see a draft of the Constitution in April 1937, stating: "the new Constitution should be framed by the representatives of the Irish people solely ... without any consultation with any member of the British Commonwealth."[38] Accordingly, the 1937 Constitution was drafted between 1935 and 1937, was put to a referendum in July 1937, and came into force on 29 December 1937.

3–15 Somewhat unexpectedly then, not only were many of the Articles in the 1937 Constitution worded identically to those in the 1922 Constitution, but the 1937 Constitution also rolled back on some changes previously implemented by de Valera, specifically the reintroduction of the Seanad[39] and the creation of the office of President which in essence fulfilled the functions of the Governor-General.[40] De Valera was clear that "we should not have change simply for change's sake".[41] It would therefore be tempting to regard the 1937 Constitution merely as a symbolic assertion of Ireland's status as an independent, sovereign

countries, a process that had been begun by the Coal-Cattle Pact of 1935. In addition, three ports that had been held by Britain were returned to Ireland. J.A. Murphy, *Ireland in the Twentieth Century* (Dublin: Gill & Macmillan, 1975), p.94.

36 D. Keogh and A. McCarthy, *The Making of the Irish Constitution 1937* (Cork: Mercier Press, 2007), p.62. It is also noteworthy that the word "Republic" does not appear anywhere in the Constitution. This was because de Valera believed that Ireland could not properly be called a republic until the island was united. J.A. Murphy, *Ireland in the Twentieth Century* (Dublin: Gill & Macmillan, 1975), p.89.

37 D. Keogh and A. McCarthy, *The Making of the Irish Constitution 1937* (Cork: Mercier Press, 2007), p.176.

38 D. Keogh and A. McCarthy, *The Making of the Irish Constitution 1937* (Cork: Mercier Press, 2007), p.177.

39 See para.3–12, fn.29.

40 Indeed, Áras an Uachtaráin was the former vice-regal lodge of the Governor-General. However, unlike the Governor-General, the President was directly elected by the people, which was a symbolic difference. See J.P. Casey, *Constitutional Law in Ireland*, 3rd edn (Dublin: Round Hall Sweet & Maxwell, 2000), p.22.

41 67 *Dáil Debates* 40 (11 May 1937), quoted in J. Casey, "Changing the Constitution: Amendment and Judicial Review" in B. Farrell (ed.), *De Valera's Constitution and Ours* (Dublin: Gill & Macmillan, 1988), p.152.

nation. However, it would be wrong to do so. There were important inclusions in the 1937 Constitution which meant that the underlying legal context—the foundations—on which the apparently unaltered apparatus of the State operated was changed. For example, the strengthening of judicial review powers and the requirement that the Constitution could only be amended by the people[42] curtailed the powers of the executive and the legislature. The inclusion of quite lengthy fundamental rights provisions was also a significant change, particularly in the context of the rise of fascism in Europe.

3–16 Any discussion of the drafting of the 1937 Constitution would be incomplete without mentioning a criticism that has frequently been levelled at it, namely that the Catholic Church had undue influence in its drafting.[43] It is undeniable that the rights provisions were influenced by Catholic teaching,[44] as were other provisions in the Constitution such as the wording of the Preamble, the inclusion of five vocational panels in the election of 43 seats to the Seanad (reflecting the then popular Catholic interest in vocationalism),[45] repeated references to the Christian nature of the State, the constitutional recognition of an offence of blasphemy,[46] and the recognition given to the "special position" of the Roman Catholic Church in Article 44 as originally enacted. However, Article 44 shows that while the Church was influential, its influence was not determinative. The failure of Article 44 to recognise the Catholic faith as the established religion of the State was criticised by some.[47] Indeed, it was remarkable

[42] Indeed, the Constitution itself was adopted by means of a referendum, and it was the first ever Constitution to undergo this process. G. Hogan, "Foreword" in D. Keogh and A. McCarthy, *The Making of the Irish Constitution 1937* (Cork: Mercier Press, 2007), p.37.

[43] For further reading, see R.F. Foster, *Modern Ireland 1600–1972* (London: Allen Lane, 1998); T.P. Coogan, *De Valera: Long Fellow, Long Shadow* (London: Hutchinson, 1993); C. Cruise O'Brien, *States of Ireland* (London: Hutchinson, 1972); J.H. Whyte, *Church and State in Modern Ireland* (Dublin: Gill & Macmillan, 1971); D. Fitzpatrick, *The Two Irelands: 1912–1939* (Oxford: OUP, 1998).

[44] Hogan argues that Article 40 owes more to liberal than Catholic ideology. G. Hogan, "Foreword" in D. Keogh and A. McCarthy, *The Making of the Irish Constitution 1937* (Cork: Mercier Press, 2007), pp.21–22. See D. Keogh and A. McCarthy, *The Making of the Irish Constitution 1937* (Cork: Mercier Press, 2007), Ch.4, for an analysis of the influence of Catholic teaching on Articles 40–45.

[45] Article 18.7.1°.

[46] Article 40.6.1°.

[47] This criticism tended to come from religious extremists. J.A. Murphy, *Ireland in the Twentieth Century* (Dublin: Gill & Macmillan, 1975), p.91. See the religious media's generally positive reaction, considered in D. Keogh and A. McCarthy, *The Making of the Irish Constitution 1937* (Cork: Mercier Press, 2007), pp.195–197.

that the Catholic faith was not so endowed given that the majority of European constitutions at that time endowed one faith or another.[48] Lee has also observed that the explicit recognition given to the Jewish faith in the original version of Article 44 was "a gesture not without dignity in the Europe of 1937".[49] Unfortunately, this gesture did not translate into action when Jewish refugees fleeing Nazi Germany sought protection in Ireland in the 1940s.[50]

Box 3.1: Time to Reflect

Constitutional Design—Motivated by Public or Self-Interest?

A question of academic interest has been whether constitutional drafters seek to promote the public interest over their own self-interest. The traditional view has been the former. However, more recently it has been suggested that constitutions reflect and support the interests and concerns of those in power. This point that constitutions are not neutral documents can be supported with reference to both of our constitutions. The 1922 Constitution was designed by those who supported the Treaty and therefore it incorporated that worldview, albeit one formed under threat of the resumption of war.[51] Conversely, the drafters of the 1937 Constitution rejected the Treaty and that informed its design and content. Yet even if constitutions seek to construct the State in a way that suits the ideals of the framers, the idealistic rhetoric often present in constitutions "also pushes a people to renew their better selves".[52] Moreover, the widespread recognition that constitutions are

48 See G. Hogan, "Foreword" in D. Keogh and A. McCarthy, *The Making of the Irish Constitution 1937* (Cork: Mercier Press, 2007), pp.17–19.

49 J.J. Lee, *Ireland 1912–1985: Politics and Society* (Cambridge: CUP, 1989), p.203, quoted in M. Gallagher, "The Changing Constitution" in J. Coakley and M. Gallagher (eds), *Politics in the Republic of Ireland*, 5th edn (London, New York: Routledge, 2010), p.78. See too, D. Keogh, "Church, State and Society" in B. Farrell (ed.), *De Valera's Constitution and Ours* (Dublin: Gill & Macmillan, 1988), p.113. Article 44.1.3° recognised the Church of Ireland, the Presbyterian Church in Ireland, the Methodist Church in Ireland, the Quakers, Jewish congregations "and the other religious denominations existing in Ireland at the date of the coming into operation of this Constitution".

50 D. Keogh, *Jews in Twentieth-Century Ireland: Refugees, anti-Semitism and the Holocaust* (Cork: Cork University Press, 1998), Ch.5.

51 An earlier draft of the 1922 Constitution, which had excluded references to the Crown, was rejected in this manner by the British government; see L. Cahillane, *Drafting the Irish Free State Constitution* (Manchester: Manchester University Press, 2016), Ch.4.

52 W.F. Murphy, "Constitutions, Constitutionalism and Democracy" in D. Greenberg, S.H. Katz, M. Oliviero and S.C. Wheatley (eds), *Constitutionalism and Democracy: Transitions in the Contemporary World* (Oxford: OUP, 1993), quoted in V.C. Jackson and M. Tushnet (eds), *Comparative Constitutional Law* (New York: Foundation Press, 1999), p.197.

living documents, whose provisions have to be interpreted in light of current values and understandings, means that decisions can be based on the text of the constitution that would have been anathema to those who framed it. In Ireland, examples would include *McGee v Attorney General*,[53] a decision that overturned as unconstitutional a ban on the importation of contraceptives, and the case of *Attorney General v X*,[54] which legitimated abortion where there was a threat to the life of the mother. Both of these cases will be considered later in this chapter.

- Do you think that it is appropriate for constitutions to perform symbolic functions?
- If you were asked to design a new constitution for Ireland, what key principles would you include and why?
- What rights would you include/exclude and why?

Reconsider your constitutional design at the end of the chapter.

C. The Irish Constitution

3–17 The Constitution is made up of 50 provisions, called Articles, and these Articles establish the institutions of the State and set out the principles that govern them (Articles 1–37, 45); protect the fundamental rights of the individual (Articles 38, 40–44); set out the process by which the Constitution can be amended (Articles 46–47); and repeal the 1922 Constitution (Articles 48–50).[55] In this section, we will briefly consider each of these aspects of the Constitution.

3–18 As the aim of a constitution is to establish the means by which laws can be enacted and the principles by which the State will be governed, it is obvious that these aims will be stated broadly. This is another reason why "Bunreacht" is a particularly apt word to describe our Constitution. It is bun/basic in the sense of providing the skeleton of the body politic. The flesh is added by the Oireachtas, which drafts legislation to give effect to provisions in the Constitution, and by the judges who interpret what words and phrases in the Constitution mean. For example, Article 36 allows the terms of judicial appointment to be "regulated in

53 [1974] I.R. 284.

54 [1992] 1 I.R. 1.

55 Article 39 defines the offence of treason and while grouped with Article 38 under the trial of offences, it does not otherwise fit into the broad categories outlined above.

accordance with law". The legislature has recently enacted the Judicial Appointments Commission Act 2023 which specifies the particulars of the appointments process.[56] Similarly, the right to a criminal trial in "due course of law" in Article 38.1 has been interpreted by judges as including a wide range of procedural requirements and substantive protections for accused persons, including the right to silence,[57] the presumption of innocence,[58] the right to a reasonably expeditious trial,[59] and rules around the exclusion of unconstitutionally obtained evidence.[60]

1. Institutions of State

3–19 In addition to defining the boundaries of the State, the Constitution sets out the basic governance structure of the State. It asserts that Ireland is "a sovereign, independent, democratic state" (Article 5), and it recognises and establishes the separation of powers (Article 6) by dividing the State's powers between the executive (Articles 28–29), the legislature (Articles 15–27) and the judiciary (Articles 34–37).

3–20 Executive power in domestic (Article 28.2) and international (Article 29.4.1°) affairs is given to the Government, which is comprised of a cabinet of 7 to 15 members (Article 28.1), one of whom is the Taoiseach (Article 28.5) and another the Tánaiste (Article 28.6). Article 28.7 requires that the Taoiseach, the Tánaiste and the Minister for Finance must be members of Dáil Éireann, and that no more than two Ministers can be Senators. Article 28.4.3° provides that the Government acts with collective responsibility, while Article 28.4.1° states that the Government is responsible to the Dáil. It does not explain how the Dáil is to exercise this responsibility, but in practice it is through questions in the Oireachtas and in the various Committees that have been established in line with the Westminster model of Parliament.[61]

56 See Ch.11 for detailed discussion of the judicial appointments process.
57 *Heaney v Ireland* [1994] 1 I.R. 593.
58 *O'Leary v Attorney General* [1993] 1 I.R. 102.
59 *State (O'Connell) v Fawsitt* [1986] I.R. 362.
60 *DPP v JC* [2015] IESC 31.
61 Although the Oireachtas also has elements of the consensus model. See C. Lynch and M. MacCarthaigh, "Parliament" in J. Coakley and M. Gallagher (eds), *Politics in the Republic of Ireland*, 7th edn (London, New York: Routledge, 2023), p.221 and p.239 et seq for further details on the accountability structures within the Oireachtas.

3–21 The Dáil is one of the three elements of the legislature. Article 15.1.2° provides that the Oireachtas comprises the Dáil, the Seanad and the President. The legislative process will be considered in Ch.7, but for present purposes it is sufficient to note that the Oireachtas has been granted "sole and exclusive power" for making domestic law (Article 15.2.1°). This is subject to two important limitations and one directive. First, the Oireachtas cannot enact legislation that is unconstitutional by virtue of Article 15.4. This is where the fundamental rights provisions in particular place limits on the power of the legislature to legislate. Second, as constitutional provisions are often drafted broadly, the judiciary play an important and constitutionally legitimate law-making role both directly in their interpretation of the Constitution, which will be considered in Section D of this chapter, and indirectly via the application of the doctrine of precedent.[62] Finally, the Oireachtas is encouraged in Article 45 to enact laws that will secure equality, protect the interests of workers, facilitate private industry, and safeguard the interests of the most vulnerable in the community, among other aims. However, as Article 45 is directive only, the failure of the Oireachtas to give effect to these social policy guidelines cannot be challenged before the courts.

3–22 The President is the third-named element in the Oireachtas. The President has functions other than legislative which are set out in Articles 12–14. In contradistinction to the mostly ceremonial function the President has in the exercise of these other functions,[63] the President's role in respect of legislation can be important. In the majority of cases, the President simply signs a Bill into law once it has been passed by both Houses. However, pursuant to Article 26, if the President has any doubts about the constitutionality of any Bill (bar Money Bills) or any part thereof, they can refer it to the Supreme Court for its constitutionality to be determined. There have been 16 Article 26 referrals to date.[64] The President is also empowered under Article 27 to refer a Bill that has been deemed to be passed by both Houses pursuant to the Article 23 procedure to the people for a referendum on the Bill or by means

[62] *IRM v Minister for Justice* [2018] IESC 14 at paras 10.24–10.25; *Re JJ* [2021] IESC 1 at para.140. See Ch.5, paras 5–03 to 5–06.

[63] Apart from Article 13.2.2° which concerns the dissolution of the Dáil, which is required to bring about a general election.

[64] The most recent example of such a referral was *Re Article 26 of the Constitution and the Judicial Appointments Commission Bill 2022* [2023] IESC 34.

of dissolving the Dáil.[65] The President has never been called upon to exercise the second of these powers, but it is nonetheless an important check on the abuse of parliamentary majority by the Government. The President also has power to refuse to dissolve the Dáil where the Taoiseach makes a request.[66]

3–23 With regard to the judicial branch of power, the Constitution requires that justice be administered in public (Article 34.1) by independent judges (Article 35) appointed by law (Article 36) in courts of first instance and courts of appeal (Article 34.2). The superior courts are specifically named in the Constitution: the Supreme Court (Articles 34.3.3° and 34.5), the Court of Appeal (Articles 34.2 and 34.4), and the High Court (Article 34.3). The Court of Appeal is a relatively recent addition to our courts system. It was formally established on 28 October 2014 following a referendum on 4 October 2013. The inferior courts are not mentioned by name, but it was envisaged when the 1937 Constitution was drafted that the existing system of other courts—the District and Circuit Courts—would continue. Article 34.3.4° simply notes that they will have local and limited jurisdiction. The courts system will be considered in more detail in Ch.9 and judicial independence in Ch.11.

2. Connected Institutions and Offices

3–24 In addition to these three main powers, the Constitution recognises the democratic value that the direct election of local government provides (Article 28A). It also creates offices and bodies whose function it is to assist the three powers. For example, the Council of State is established by Articles 31–32 to "aid and counsel" the President in the exercise of any of their functions, such as whether to refer a Bill to the Supreme Court under Article 26 or to the people under Article 27. The Comptroller and Auditor General's function is to monitor State spending and to audit the accounts (Article 33). The Attorney General is established by Article 30, and they are the chief legal advisor to the Government.

3–25 Neither the Comptroller and Auditor General nor the Attorney General[67] can be members of the Government. By way of contrast, a

[65] See Ch.7, Section D.

[66] See Ch.7, Section D, paras 7–17 to 7–22.

[67] The Office of the Attorney General is considered further in Ch.12, paras 12–47 to 12–50.

number of members of the Council of State must be members of the Government. Article 31.2 specifies that the Taoiseach and the Tánaiste are part of the Council of State. In addition, the Chairs (Ceann Comhairle in the Dáil and Cathaoirleach in the Seanad) of both the Dáil and the Seanad are also members. Traditionally, the Ceann Comhairle has been a member of the political party in power, but following the inconclusive results of the 2016 General Election, with no one party with sufficient support to form a majority government, it was determined to allow a secret ballot vote for the election of the Ceann Comhairle. Accordingly, it is now possible for persons not connected to the main political party or coalition in power to be elected to the position of Ceann Comhairle.[68] This governmental influence on the Council of State could be regarded as problematic as the President only seeks their advice on decisions that could impact negatively on the Government's position. This potential bias, though, is countered by the fact that former Taoisigh and Presidents, whose political allegiance may lie elsewhere, are also members of the Council of the State and by the fact that the President can appoint up to seven members of their choosing.

3. Fundamental Rights

3–26 The fundamental rights provisions are located in Articles 40–44. These rights are both express and derived. Express rights are those named in the Constitution and these are the right to equality before the law, the right to life, liberty, good name, freedom of expression, assembly and association (Article 40), familial rights (Article 41), the right to education (Article 42), children's rights (Article 42A), the right to private property (Article 43), and the right to free practice of religion (Article 44). Derived rights have been read into the Constitution by the judiciary and are legitimated on the basis that they flow from an existing express right,[69] from the "Christian and democratic nature of the State",[70] from

[68] The results of the 2016 election were inconclusive, with Fine Gael winning marginally more seats than Fianna Fáil. However, the Dáil elected Fianna Fáil TD Seán Ó Fearghaíl to the post. He was re-elected to the post following the 2020 election.

[69] For example, the right to refuse to join a union was found to derive from the right to freedom of association protected in Article 40.6.1°iii in *Educational Co Ltd v Fitzpatrick (No. 2)* [1961] I.R. 345.

[70] *Ryan v Attorney General* [1965] I.R. 294 at 312.

natural law,[71] or as a natural corollary of another derived right.[72] Derived rights were originally known as unenumerated rights but were renamed in *Friends of the Irish Environment CLG v Government of Ireland*.[73] The reason for this renaming will be considered later but it is important for now to be aware that older cases use the terminology of enumerated and unenumerated rights rather than express and derived.

3–27 The first case where a derived right was recognised within the 1937 Constitution was the case of *Ryan v Attorney General*.[74] In this case, the plaintiff challenged the fluoridation of the public water supply, claiming that it would be injurious to her health and the health of her children. This, she argued, would be in breach of her and their right to bodily integrity. There was no such right enumerated in the Constitution but it was argued that it was one of her "personal rights" guaranteed under Article 40.3.1°. In the High Court, Kenny J. rejected previous case law which had determined that the personal rights mentioned in subs.1 were limited to those specified in subs.2. Instead, he found that citizens should have personal rights appropriate to a State defined as "Christian" in the Preamble and "democratic" in Article 5. The Supreme Court agreed, noting that "the 'personal rights' mentioned in section 3, 1° are not exhausted by the enumeration of 'life, person, good name, and property rights' in section 3, 2° as is shown by the use of the words 'in particular' …".[75]

3–28 Unfortunately for the plaintiff, although she successfully established the existence of a derived right to bodily integrity, she did not succeed in proving that the fluoridation of water was injurious to either her health or her children's. Consequently, there was no bodily integrity violation in this particular case. However, Ó Dálaigh C.J. was clear that there were additional unspecified rights within Article 40.3.1°[76] and it was unsurprising that the doctrine of derived rights was a fertile

[71] *McGee v Attorney General* [1974] I.R. 284 at 310. Recourse to natural law was resiled from in *Re Article 26 of the Constitution and the Abortion Information Bill 1995* [1995] 1 I.R. 1.

[72] The right to marry was noted in *Ryan v Attorney General* [1965] I.R. 294. In *McGee*, Griffin J. noted that the right to determine how many children a married couple would have was inherent in that right: *McGee v Attorney General* [1974] I.R. 284 at 333.

[73] [2020] IESC 49 at paras 8.4–8.9.

[74] [1965] I.R. 294.

[75] [1965] I.R. 294 at 344–345.

[76] [1965] I.R. 294 at 344–345.

ground of jurisprudence for a short period of time. Rights unearthed include the rights to free movement within the State and to marry,[77] the right to travel,[78] the right to refuse invasive medical treatment,[79] the right of access to the courts,[80] and the right to privacy.[81] The right to privacy offers a very good illustration of how derived rights are developed, and of some of the strengths and weaknesses of the doctrine.

3–29 The first case to establish that there was a derived right to privacy was *McGee v Attorney General*.[82] This case concerned the constitutionality of s.17 of the Criminal Law Amendment Act 1935 which made it a crime to sell or import contraceptives. McGee had attempted to import spermicidal jelly from England as she had received medical advice that having a fifth child carried a very high risk of death or, if she survived, paralysis. In her previous pregnancies she suffered from toxaemia, hypertension and cerebral thrombosis. She challenged her prosecution on the basis that she had an unenumerated right to marital privacy, which included the right to decide whether and when to have children. The majority of the Supreme Court agreed with her, with three judges locating the right primarily in Article 40.3.1° and one also finding it in Article 41.

3–30 This decision, and the development of the doctrine of derived rights, requires judges who are willing to engage in judicial activism. Judicial activism, in constitutional cases, is where a judge "makes the positive choice of departing from the path adopted by the legislature or the executive" and "call[s] on some element of policy choice or preference" in order to do so.[83] Reaction to the doctrine varies depending on how such activism is regarded. Morgan, for instance, praised the judiciary in the *McGee* case for taking a courageous step in the context of a time where previous attempts to liberalise the law on the availability of contraceptives had failed. In 1969, for example, then Senator Mary Robinson tried to introduce a Private Member's Bill to do just that. It was

77 *Ryan v Attorney General* [1965] I.R. 294.
78 *State (M) v Attorney General* [1979] I.R. 73.
79 *Re a Ward of Court (Withdrawal of Medical Treatment)* [1996] 2 I.R. 79.
80 *McCauley v Minister for Posts and Telegraphs* [1966] I.R. 345.
81 *McGee v Attorney General* [1974] I.R. 284.
82 [1974] I.R. 284.
83 D.G. Morgan, *A Judgment Too Far? Judicial Activism and the Constitution* (Cork: Cork University Press, 2001), pp.7, 8. For further on the origins of this term, see K.D. Kmiec, "The origin and current meanings of judicial activism" (2004) 92 *California Law Review* 1441.

so controversial that the Seanad refused to print and circulate the Bill to enable proper debate.[84] Morgan writes:

> "Thus it might well be said that, in taking this decisive action, the Courts were courageously fulfilling one of their duties, namely to use open-textured areas of the Constitution to keep the laws up to date and in line with the changing needs and values of society, in a situation in which the principal guarantor – the legislature – appeared reluctant to act. The judges were thereby upholding a significant and legitimate personal right."[85]

More recently, and echoing Morgan, de Londras described judicial activism in constitutional interpretation as compensatory: it "compensate[s] for the failure of other organs of the state to advance constitutional evolution in line with the *telos* of the constitution."[86]

3–31 Yet we must be careful not to overstate the effects of judicial activism. Legislative action is still required to give effect to this activism. Following the *McGee* decision, where the executive and legislature were now under a constitutional obligation to enact legislation to regulate the sale of contraceptives, the first attempt failed when both the Taoiseach (Liam Cosgrave) and Minister for Education (Richard Burke) voted against their own Bill. It was not until 1979 that access to contraceptives was finally made legal, for married couples only, in the Health (Family Planning) Act 1979. We see this same legislative inertia around matters of moral concern repeated following *Attorney General v X*,[87] where the Supreme Court held in 1992 that abortion was legally permissible in cases where there was a risk to the life of the mother, including by means of suicide. It was not until 2014 that the legislative framework to give effect to this decision was commenced.[88]

[84] D.G. Morgan, *A Judgment Too Far? Judicial Activism and the Constitution* (Cork: Cork University Press, 2001), p.24. However, it should be noted that Morgan was generally critical of judges for overstepping their constitutionally prescribed role.

[85] D.G. Morgan, *A Judgment Too Far? Judicial Activism and the Constitution* (Cork: Cork University Press, 2001), p.24.

[86] F. de Londras, "In Defence of Judicial Innovation and Constitutional Evolution" in L. Cahillane, J. Gallen and T. Hickey (eds), *Judges, Politics and the Irish Constitution* (Manchester: Manchester University Press, 2017), p.9 at p.19.

[87] [1992] 1 I.R. 1.

[88] Protection of Life During Pregnancy Act 2013, commenced on 1 January 2014.

3–32 Those critical of judicial activism have cited concerns that it was unnecessary, placed the law in a state of uncertainty, and possibly breached the separation of powers. Hogan J., writing extrajudicially, argued that recourse to derived rights in the first tranche of cases post-*Ryan* meant that express rights that could have been relied upon were ignored and have consequently been left under-developed.[89] For example, the protection of the person in Article 40.3.2° and the protection of the inviolability of the dwelling in Article 40.5 could have been invoked in McGee's case instead of the derived right of marital privacy.[90]

3–33 Regarding the uncertainty concern, Kelly writes that the doctrine has

> "... been marked – unfortunately from the point of view of one attempting a systematic exposition of an organic law – by a certain blurring of definition, a certain bursting of conceptual banks, rather as though legal rivers finding their confluence in the estuary of liberty and justice, had had their courses confused by flooding further upstream, leaving a somewhat trackless delta for the constitutional geographer".[91]

This uncertainty is felt particularly by the Oireachtas who, while endeavouring under Article 15.4 to ensure that they do not enact laws that infringe the rights of citizens, are put in the impossible position of not knowing what those rights are.[92] This was articulated most clearly by former Taoiseach Jack Lynch as follows: "it would be a brave man who would predict, these days, what was or was not contrary to the Constitution."[93]

[89] G. Hogan, "Unenumerated Personal Rights: the Legacy of *Ryan v. Attorney General*" in L. Cahillane, J. Gallen and T. Hickey (eds), *Judges, Politics and the Irish Constitution* (Manchester: Manchester University Press, 2017), p.49 at pp.50–51.

[90] Three judges also referred to other express rights in their judgments. G. Hogan, "Unenumerated Personal Rights: the Legacy of *Ryan v. Attorney General*" in L. Cahillane, J. Gallen and T. Hickey (eds), *Judges, Politics and the Irish Constitution* (Manchester: Manchester University Press, 2017), p.49 at p.56.

[91] G. Hogan, G. Whyte, D. Kenny and R. Walsh, *Kelly: The Irish Constitution*, 5th edn (Dublin: Bloomsbury Professional, 2018), para.7.3.76. See also, J.M. Kelly, *Fundamental Rights in the Irish Law and Constitution*, 2nd edn (Dublin: Allen Figgis & Co, 1967), p.42, and G. Hogan, "Unenumerated Personal Rights: Ryan's Case Re-evaluated" (1990–92) 25–27 *Irish Jurist* 95.

[92] J.M. Kelly, *Fundamental Rights in the Irish Law and Constitution*, 2nd edn (Dublin: Allen Figgis & Co, 1967), pp.42–43.

[93] J.M. Kelly, "Preface to the First Edition" in *Kelly: The Irish Constitution*, 4th edn (Dublin:

3–34 Uncertainty also faced litigants whose success or failure seemed to depend not on law but on the beliefs of judges. The prime illustration of this is another privacy case, that of *Norris v Attorney General*.[94] Norris argued that ss.61 and 62 of the Offences against the Person Act 1861, which criminalised homosexual acts between consenting adults, were unconstitutional. Building on *McGee*, he submitted that Article 40.3.1° protected a general right to privacy, of which marital privacy was only one aspect, with which the State could not interfere unless the common good or the protection of public order or morality necessitated it. The Supreme Court accepted that there was a more general right to privacy but the majority did not agree that this included a right to sexual privacy between adult homosexuals. O'Higgins C.J. held that it amounted to "unnatural sexual conduct which Christian teaching held to be gravely sinful" and hence could not be protected by the constitution of a "Christian" state.[95] He also said that male homosexuality increased sexually transmitted infections and was injurious to the institution of marriage which is protected by Article 41.3.1°.[96] This judgment is regarded as one of the worst judgments ever written by the Supreme Court.[97] However, the case is also the source of one of the best, Henchy J.'s dissenting judgment.[98] Henchy J. criticised the High Court judge, and by necessary implication O'Higgins C.J., for placing too much emphasis on religious teachings and ignoring the lack of evidence proffered by the State to support their contention that the ban on homosexual sexual activity was necessary to protect the common good.[99] Norris subsequently took his

Butterworths, 2003), p.xii. The Preface to the first edition is not included in the fifth edition of this text.

94 [1984] I.R. 36.

95 [1984] I.R. 36 at 64.

96 [1984] I.R. 36 at 65.

97 R. Mac Cormaic, *The Supreme Court* (Dublin: Penguin Ireland, 2016), p.207. Hogan J. described it as a "significant wrong turn". G. Hogan, "Re-examining *McGee*, *Norris* and the *X* case" (2021) 65 *Irish Jurist* 25 at 43. Hogan suggests (at 42) that it is important to consider when the decision was made, specifically April 1983 when what would become the Eighth Amendment was working its way through the Oireachtas: "One cannot but sense the unease which *McGee* had caused in certain quarters and certain supporters of the Amendment were also determined ... to ensure that its passage would also serve as a warning to the Supreme Court to leave the delicate and sensitive matters touching on what they saw as the traditional Irish (Catholic) way of life involved in the prohibitions on abortion and homosexuality alone."

98 For praise of the judgment, see, e.g. G. Hogan, "The Judicial Thought and Prose of Mr. Justice Seamus Henchy" (2011) 48 *Irish Jurist* 96 at 116; R. Mac Cormaic, *The Supreme Court* (Dublin: Penguin Ireland, 2016), p.207. McCarthy J. also wrote a dissent.

99 [1984] I.R. 36 at 76–78.

case to the European Court of Human Rights where his arguments were successful.[100] The offences were repealed by the Criminal Law (Sexual Offences) Act 1993.

3–35 The third criticism of the doctrine is that it challenges the separation of powers. The basis for this critique is that, through the identification of rights not specified in the Constitution, the judiciary have taken their constitutionally permissible role to interpret the Constitution too far and have strayed into law-making, a terrain constitutionally reserved for the Oireachtas.[101] Such an incursion is, arguably, particularly inappropriate in the arena of contentious policy issues that require careful consideration by a democratically elected Oireachtas rather than by unelected judges. The separation of powers concern was the prompt for Clarke J.'s decision to relabel unenumerated rights as derived rights in *Friends of the Irish Environment CLG v Government of Ireland*:[102]

> "[8.5] … [T]here is a danger that the use of the term 'unenumerated' conveys an impression that judges simply identify rights of which they approve and deem them to be part of the Constitution.
>
> [8.6] That does not seem to me to have been the process by which the so-called unenumerated rights have come to be identified, but nonetheless it carries a risk of misimpression. It is for that reason that I would consider the term 'derived rights' as being more appropriate, for it conveys that there must be some root of title in the text or structure of the Constitution from which the right in question can be derived …
>
> [8.9] What needs to be guarded against is allowing for a blurring of the separation of powers by permitting issues which are more

[100] *Norris v Ireland* (1991) 13 E.H.R.R. 186.

[101] J.M. Kelly, *Fundamental Rights in the Irish Law and Constitution*, 2nd edn (Dublin: Allen Figgis & Co, 1967), p.45, warned that the courts were in effect "acting as a 'third House of the legislature'". However, if the government is unhappy with what the courts have decided, then they can always put the question to the people in the form of a proposed constitutional amendment. Hogan J. described such a referendum as a "final appeal" to the people in *Delaney v PIAB* [2024] IESC 10 at para.17. Such attempts were made with various proposals to roll back on the *X* case which were rejected by the people. For other examples, see F. de Londras, "In Defence of Judicial Innovation and Constitutional Evolution" in L. Cahillane, J. Gallen and T. Hickey (eds), *Judges, Politics and the Irish Constitution* (Manchester: Manchester University Press, 2017), p.9 at p.22.

[102] [2020] IESC 49.

properly political and policy matters (for the legislature and the executive) to impermissibly drift into the judicial sphere. Where it is possible properly to derive rights from the Constitution then no such risk arises. Where, however, judges are simply asked to identify rights which they consider might be 'a good thing' then the separation of powers is truly blurred … ."

3–36 It should, however, be noted that whatever the pros and cons of the doctrine, the identification of derived rights requires a judiciary willing to engage in such activism, and there was a period of decline in judicial receptiveness to derived rights from the 1990s until relatively recently. The decline is linked to the comments of Keane C.J. in *TD v Minister for Education*,[103] a case in which the plaintiffs sought the recognition of a new socio-economic derived right, namely that the State be obligated to devote resources to provide costly high-support units for minors with behavioural issues. Keane C.J. cited his own comments in *O'T v B*, where he called for judicial restraint in the identification of new rights.[104] He continued:

> "… I would have the gravest doubts as to whether the courts at any stage should assume the function of declaring what are today frequently described as 'socio-economic rights' to be unenumerated rights guaranteed by Article 40. In my view, however, the resolution of that question must await a case in which it is fully argued."[105]

He also agreed with Murphy J. that it was significant that all of the personal rights provisions in the Constitution, with the exception of the education provisions, were civil and political rights rather than socio-economic. Murphy J. drew attention to the fact that the only reference to any socio-economic rights in the Constitution was in Article 45, an Article that cannot be relied on in court.[106]

3–37 Yet, despite "more than one obituary being written for the doctrine",[107] there has been a recent revival of interest in derived rights,

103 [2001] 4 I.R. 259.
104 [1998] 2 I.R. 321, quoted in *TD v Minister for Education* [2001] 4 I.R. 259 at 281.
105 [2001] 4 I.R. 259 at 282.
106 [2001] 4 I.R. 259 at 317.
107 C. O'Mahony, "Unenumerated Rights: Possible Future Directions after NHV?" (2017) 40(2) *Dublin University Law Journal* 171 at 171.

with a particular focus on derived rights connected to the concept of human dignity. In *NHV v Minister for Justice and Equality*, it was determined that asylum seekers have a right to seek work on this basis.[108] Even in cases where the identification of a derived right has not survived appeal, the courts have not firmly shut the door on the recognition of future derived rights. In *Carter v Minister for Education and Skills*, the High Court identified a new right of access to third-level education.[109] The State's appeal was successful, but one of the reasons for this outcome was that Humphreys J. had unilaterally introduced the idea of a derived right. Indeed, when he had invited Carter's team to make such arguments, they declined to do so. In upholding the State's appeal, the Court of Appeal stated: "this Court should not express any view on whether such a right exists as it was not claimed by the respondent nor were the parties who were necessary to be heard on such an issue before the court."[110]

3–38 In *Friends of the Irish Environment CLG v Government of Ireland*, the right to an environment consistent with human dignity, which had been identified by the High Court in *Friends of the Irish Environment CLG v Fingal County Council,*[111] was rejected by the Supreme Court both because it was superfluous—it added nothing to the already identified rights to life and to bodily integrity—and because it was too vague.[112] However the Supreme Court also noted obiter that if a person, rather than a corporate entity, took a case asserting a right to a healthy environment, the rights to life and bodily integrity as well as other constitutional rights could be engaged.[113] It also acknowledged that future derived rights could stem from the concept of dignity.[114] While the terrain on which the fight for a right to a healthy environment may have shifted following the recent success of such arguments before the European Court of Human

[108] [2017] 2 I.L.R.M. 105. The derived right to work had been established in cases such as *Landers v Attorney General* (1975) 109 I.L.T.R. 1, *Murtagh Properties v Cleary* [1972] I.R. 330, *Murphy v Stewart* [1973] I.R. 97, and *Cafolla v O'Malley* [1985] 1 I.R. 486, but Clarke J. grounded it in the concept of dignity as provided for in the Preamble and in Article 40.1: [2017] 2 I.L.R.M. 105 at paras 15 and 17.

[109] [2018] IEHC 539 at para.42.

[110] [2019] IECA 162 at para.46.

[111] [2017] IEHC 695 at para.264.

[112] [2020] IESC 49 at para.8.11.

[113] [2020] IESC 49 at paras 8.14–8.17.

[114] [2020] IESC 49 at para.8.6.

Rights in *Verein KlimaSeniorinnen Schweiz and Others v Switzerland*,[115] *Carter* and *Friends of the Environment* indicate that there is still life in the doctrine of derived rights in Ireland in appropriate cases.

4. Acceptable Rights Infringements

3–39 No right protected in the Constitution is absolute. Many of the rights provisions include express limitations on the exercise of such rights. For example, the right to equality in Article 40.1 is tempered by the fact that the State is entitled "to have due regard to differences of capacity, physical and moral, and of social function". A variety of rights enshrined in Articles 40.6.1° and 44 are protected "subject to public order and morality". Property rights in Article 43 can be "regulated by the principles of social justice". The rights enumerated in Article 40.3 and those derived from the phrase "in particular" are guaranteed merely "as far as practicable", and the State is simply obliged to protect them "as best it may from unjust attack".

3–40 Accordingly, when legislation is challenged on the basis that it infringes particular rights, that legislation can be justified by the State in one of two ways. In some cases, the State may argue that the infringement vindicates and protects the superior personal rights of other citizens. For example, in the case of *MD v Ireland*, it was held that an exemption of liability section that applied only to girls under the age of 17 was permissible on the basis that the legislature was entitled to have regard to the fact that only girls can become pregnant.[116] In other cases, the State may argue that the rights infringement is justified on the basis that it protects the common good, "that is the good of society as a whole".[117] For example, in *Norris v Attorney General*,[118] it was held that

[115] [2024] ECHR 304, application no. 53600/20. In this case, the European Court of Human Rights found that the Swiss government had failed to meet its duties under the European Convention of Human Rights to take sufficient actions to protect the applicants, who were a group of women aged 64 and older, from the effects of climate change. Note that an applicant cannot take a case to the European Court of Human Rights unless they have exhausted all domestic remedies. See further Ch.6, Section E.3.

[116] [2012] 1 I.R. 697 at 718–719. The impugned section was s.5 of the Criminal Law (Sexual Offences) Act 2006. Section 5 exempts girls under the age of 17, but not boys under the age of 17, from prosecution if they have sexual intercourse with another underage person of the opposite sex.

[117] F. Ryan, *Constitutional Law* (Dublin: Round Hall Ltd, 2001), p.126.

[118] [1984] I.R. 36. See also Ch.6, Section E. Irish law in this area was found to breach the

it was appropriate to criminalise homosexual sexual activity to protect individual and public health and to safeguard the institution of marriage from unjust attack. However, as the subsequent decriminalisation of homosexual activity between adult males in the Criminal Law (Sexual Offences) Act 1993 shows us, what measures are regarded as necessary to protect the common good can and do change.

3–41 In deciding whether a legislative provision is constitutional, the courts typically apply the proportionality principle. This principle was articulated as follows by Costello J. in *Heaney v Ireland*:

> "In considering whether a restriction on the exercise of rights is permitted by the Constitution, the courts in this country and elsewhere have found it helpful to apply the test of proportionality, a test which contains the notions of minimal restraint on the exercise of protected rights, and of the exigencies of the common good in a democratic society ... The means chosen must ... :
> (a) be rationally connected to the objective and not be arbitrary, unfair or based on irrational considerations;
> (b) impair the right as little as possible; and
> (c) be such that their effects on rights are proportional to the objective ... ."[119]

It was further explained in *Rock v Ireland* that "the function of the Court is not to decide whether a perfect balance has been achieved, but merely to decide whether, in restricting individual constitutional rights, the legislature has acted within the range of what is permissible".[120] As such, the legislature is not obliged to have taken the "best" approach to the regulation of an issue, just a legitimate one. More recently, the Supreme Court has noted that the proportionality test is not to be treated "as an almost mathematical formula providing a scientifically measurable and repeatable result wherever and however applied" and that "different articles of the Constitution contain different limiting provisions, and thus the application of a proportionality test in the case of any given right must take account of the particular constitutional text."[121]

right to private life under Article 8 of the European Convention on Human Rights by the European Court of Human Rights.

119 [1994] 3 I.R. 593 at 607.

120 [1997] 3 I.R. 484 at 501.

121 *O'Doherty and Waters v Minister for Health* [2022] IESC 32 at para.57 per O'Donnell C.J.

3–42 On occasion, it has been stated in court that there is a hierarchy of rights, with the right to life at the apex of that hierarchy. In *Re a Ward of Court*, Denham J. described the right to life as "the pre-eminent personal right".[122] On other occasions, the courts have acknowledged that it is not possible to set a fixed hierarchical list of rights. As Egan J. noted in *Attorney General v X*:

> "[T]he right to life might not be the paramount right in every circumstance. If, for instance, it were necessary for a father to kill a man engaged in the rape of his daughter in order to prevent its continuance, I have no doubt but that the right of the girl to bodily integrity would rank higher than the right to life of the rapist."[123]

Accordingly, when rights come into conflict with one another, it is for the judiciary to decide which right takes precedence through a balancing exercise.

Box 3.2: Case Focus
***Fleming v Ireland* [2013] IEHC 2; [2013] IESC 19**
Is the Right to Die a Corollary of the Right to Life?

In *Fleming v Ireland*,[124] the appellant argued that there was a derived right to die as a corollary of the express right to life provided for in Article 40.3.2°. She then argued that s.2(2) of the Criminal Law (Suicide) Act 1993, which prohibited assisted suicide, was contrary to Article 40.3 of the Constitution because it discriminated against disabled persons who were not able to die by suicide without another's assistance. The appellant was unable to end her own life because her multiple sclerosis had deteriorated to the point where she was confined to a wheelchair and unable to use her upper or lower limbs.

The appellant drew from the prior Supreme Court decision of *Re a Ward of Court*[125] to support her claim that there was a constitutional right to die. In that decision, permission was given to withdraw medical treatment from a woman who had been in a persistent vegetative state for a prolonged period of time which would lead to her inevitable death on the following basis:

---

122 [1996] 2 I.R. 79 at 160.
123 [1991] 1 I.R. 1 at 92.
124 [2013] IEHC 2; [2013] IESC 19.
125 [1996] 2 I.R. 79.

> "As the process of dying is part, and an ultimate inevitable consequence, of life, the right to life necessarily implies the right to have nature take its course and to die a natural death and, unless the individual concerned so wishes, not to have life artificially maintained by the provision of nourishment by abnormal artificial means, which have no curative effect and which is intended merely to prolong life."[126]

The State focused on the next paragraph in the *Re a Ward of Court* judgment, where Hamilton C.J. stated emphatically, obiter:

> "This right, as so defined, does not include the right to have life terminated or death accelerated and is confined to the natural process of dying. No person has the right to terminate or to have terminated his or her life or to accelerate or have accelerated his or her life."[127]

Although the Supreme Court in *Fleming* ultimately rejected the appellant's argument that s.2(2) was unconstitutional, it did so not on the basis that the right to die was incompatible with the constitutional protection of the right to life, but on the basis that any relaxation on the absolute prohibition on assisted suicide required careful consideration of policy issues that were best left to the executive. The court stated:

> "Nothing in this judgment should be taken as necessarily implying that it would not be open to the State, in the event that the Oireachtas were satisfied that measures with appropriate safeguards could be introduced, to legislate to deal with a case such as that of the appellant. If such legislation was introduced it would be for the courts to determine whether the balancing by the Oireachtas of any legitimate concerns was within the boundaries of what was constitutionally permissible. Any such consideration would, necessarily, have to pay appropriate regard to the assessment made by the Oireachtas both of any competing interests and the practicability of any measures thus introduced."[128]

As such, while there is no constitutional right to suicide,[129] the Constitution does not necessarily prohibit the enactment of legislation to allow for assisted suicide in limited circumstances. The *Fleming* case

126 [1996] 2 I.R. 79 at 124.
127 [1996] 2 I.R. 79 at 124.
128 [2013] IESC 19 at para.108.
129 [2013] IESC 19 at para.137.

therefore is an example of judicial restraint, where the judiciary defer to democratically elected representatives on policy issues.

The problem, however, is that the executive has been notoriously slow to legislate on morally contentious matters. It took over 20 years for any government to pass legislation to give effect to a legal right to abortion in the very limited circumstances established by *Attorney General v X*,[130] despite various contemporary polls suggesting that the majority of Irish people supported access to abortion,[131] a support confirmed by the passage of the constitutional amendment to remove Article 40.3.3° from the Constitution in 2018. Moreover, the intense controversy that had surrounded the enactment of the Protection of Life During Pregnancy Act 2013 meant that the then-government was reluctant to get involved in legislating in another life/death moral issue. The then-Taoiseach Enda Kenny was clear about this in response to questions from John Halligan TD on 29 May 2013, a month after the Supreme Court judgment in the *Fleming* case was issued. Halligan asked the Taoiseach if the Government would commit, or consider committing, to the introduction of measures to allow for assisted suicide. The Taoiseach said he would not.[132]

Marie Fleming died in December 2013 but her advocacy continued to inform calls to legalise assisted suicide. In 2018, the Joint Committee on Justice and Equality published the *Report on the Right to Die with Dignity*.[133] They were unable to reach a consensus on the introduction of legislative change. In 2021, the Justice Committee reviewed the Dying with Dignity Bill 2020, a Private Member's Bill that sought to introduce assisted dying, and recommended that it not proceed but that a special Committee be established to consider ways forward.[134] The resultant Joint Committee on Assisted Dying published a report in March 2024. The Report recommends the introduction of legislation to permit and regulate assisted dying. They recommend that only those who have been

---

130 [1992] 1 I.R. 1.

131 See "Poll finds 64 per cent support at least legislating for X Case", *TheJournal.ie*, 10 January 2013, available at: *http://www.thejournal.ie/abortion-support-poll-red-c-paddy-power-748560-Jan2013/* and J. Corcoran and J. Drennan, "Support for suicide down: poll", *Sunday Independent*, 19 May 2013. Support for abortion in a case where the risk to the mother's life was due to suicide was down from 58% to 53%.

132 Dáil Debates (29 May 2013).

133 Joint Committee on Justice and Equality, *Report on the Right to Die with Dignity* (32/JAE/18, June 2018), available at: *https://data.oireachtas.ie/ie/oireachtas/committee/dail/32/joint_committee_on_justice_and_equality/reports/2018/2018-06-25_report-on-the-right-to-die-with-dignity_en.pdf.*

134 Joint Committee on Justice, *Report on Scrutiny of the Dying with Dignity Bill 2020 [PMB]* (33/JC/11, July 2021), available at: *https://opac.oireachtas.ie/Data/Library3/Documents%20Laid/2021/pdf/Report20on20Scrutiny20of20the20Dying20with20Dignity20Bill202020 _210721_153302.pdf.*

diagnosed with an incurable and irreversible disease/illness/medical condition that is advanced, progressive and will cause death within six months (or within 12 months if the condition is neurodegenerative) and causes suffering that cannot be relieved in a manner that they find tolerable, should be allowed to access assisted dying.[135] The matter now rests with the executive and legislature.

5. Additional Rights

3–43 Rights can be found in provisions other than the fundamental rights provisions. The most obvious location of additional rights is in Article 38 which governs the right of an accused to a fair trial. As with Article 40.3, derived rights have been found to be implicit in the Article 38.1 right that "[n]o person shall be tried on any criminal charge save in due course of law." In *Heaney v Ireland*, Costello J. stated that the phrase "due course of law"

> "... implies a great deal more than a simple requirement that trials are to be held in accordance with laws enacted by parliament. It is an Article couched in peremptory language and has been construed as a constitutional guarantee that criminal trials will be conducted in accordance with the basic concepts of justice."[136]

Accordingly, a wide range of procedural requirements and substantive protections have been read into Article 38.1. These include the right to silence,[137] the presumption of innocence,[138] the right to a reasonably expeditious trial,[139] and rules around the exclusion of unconstitutionally obtained evidence.[140]

3–44 The right to trial by jury is established by Article 38.5. Although the Constitution provides exceptions to this general right, where the trial

[135] Recommendation 27, Joint Committee on Assisted Dying, *Final Report of the Joint Committee on Assisted Dying* (33/JCAD/01, March 2024), available at: *https://data.oireachtas.ie/ie/oireachtas/committee/dail/33/joint_committee_on_assisted_dying/reports/2024/2024-03-20_final-report-of-the-joint-committee-on-assisted-dying_en.pdf.*

[136] [1994] 3 I.R. 593 at 605.

[137] *Heaney v Ireland* [1994] 1 I.R. 593.

[138] *O'Leary v Attorney General* [1993] 1 I.R. 102.

[139] *State (O'Connell) v Fawsitt* [1986] I.R. 362.

[140] *DPP v JC* [2015] IESC 31.

of an offence does not fit into one of these exceptions, it is obligatory. Ó Dálaigh C.J. noted in *Re Haughey* that "[t]rial by jury of non-minor offences is mandatory, it is not simply a right to be adopted or waived at the option of the accused".[141]

3–45 Rights provisions that are not so obvious include the right to judicial independence. Erroneously, this right is often thought of as being a personal right of judges, but this assumption was corrected by Murray C.J. in *Curtin v Clerk of Dáil Éireann*:

> "The principle of judicial independence does not exist for the personal or individual benefit of the judges, even if it may have that incidental effect. It is a principle designed to guarantee the right of the people themselves from whom, as Article 6 proclaims, all powers of government are derived, to have justice administered in total independence, free from all suspicion of interference, pressure or contamination of any kind. An independent judiciary guarantees that the organs of the State conduct themselves in accordance with the rule of law."[142]

3–46 The Constitution also contains various civil rights. These include the right to vote in Dáil (Article 16.2) and presidential (Article 12.2) elections, and the right of any citizen to run for Dáil or Seanad election once they attain the age of 21 (Articles 16.1 and 18.2). It is odd that these rights do not come instantly to mind when we think of our rights, considering how hard fought the right to vote and to hold public office has been in Ireland as elsewhere. Moreover, citizens have the right to vote to amend (or not) the Constitution and seven referendums have focused on changes to voting.[143] The referendum process will be considered briefly in the next section.

Box 3.3: Legal Insight
Representation and Voting Milestones in Ireland

Ireland is a representative democracy, i.e. an individual or individuals is/are elected to represent the interests of their constituents and their

[141] [1971] I.R. 217 at 252.
[142] [2006] 2 I.R. 556 at 617. This case will be discussed further in Ch.11, paras 11–70 to 11–71.
[143] See para.3–83.

country. While this system causes many problems, not least of which is that our elected representatives tend to focus on local rather than on national matters, to the possible detriment of the latter,[144] it nonetheless recognises the principle that politicians should reflect the interests of those they serve. It has not always been thus. It was not until 1829 that a Catholic could hold public office without taking the Oath of Supremacy.[145] This meant that very few Catholics held public office in Ireland, despite the majority of the population being Catholic. Thomas Wyse calculated in 1828 that merely 39 of 2,062 offices connected with the administration of justice in Ireland were held by Catholics.[146] Daniel O'Connell and Richard Lalor Shiel founded the Catholic Association in 1823 with the purpose of putting pressure on the Crown to repeal the Oath by electing Catholics to office who would not take the Oath. Once repealed, O'Connell became the first Catholic to take a seat at Westminster.

A current matter of debate on the issue of representativeness is whether Irish political life is deficient because so few women hold public office.[147] In the 2011 General Election, 25 female TDs were elected to Dáil Éireann. This meant that women accounted for 15 per cent of our national representatives. A similarly low percentage—16 per cent—was elected at local level in the 2009 city and county council elections.[148] Steps were taken to redress this imbalance. Part 6 of the Electoral Amendment (Political Funding) Act 2012 sets gender quotas in respect of electoral candidates designed to increase female participation in politics. Parties who fail to nominate sufficient women to reach these quotas will have funding cut. This measure has had some success. Following the 2016 General Election, women accounted for 22 per cent of our TDs, even after the number of available seats was reduced from 2011, representing an increase of 40 per cent. Women won 22.5 per cent of Dáil seats in the 2020 General Election and 25 per cent in the 2024 General Election. From data compiled on 183 countries on 1 December 2024, Ireland ranked 97th in terms of the percentage of

[144] M. Gallagher and L. Komito, "The Constituency Role of Dáil Deputies" in J. Coakley and M. Gallagher (eds), *Politics in the Republic of Ireland*, 6th edn (London, New York: Routledge, 2018), p.190 at pp.208–210.

[145] This oath required the oath-taker to recognise the Crown as head of the Church and renounce any other such claimants, in particular the Pope.

[146] D.J. Hickey and J.E. Doherty, *A Dictionary of Irish History 1800–1980* (Dublin: Gill & Macmillan, 1987); cf. Catholic emancipation.

[147] For detailed discussion of this issue, see Y. Galligan and F. Buckley, "Women in Politics" in J. Coakley and M. Gallagher (eds), *Politics in the Republic of Ireland*, 5th edn (London, New York: Routledge, 2018), p.254 at p.258 et seq.

[148] Presentation by Prof. Gail McElroy, *Second Report of the Convention on the Constitution* (May 2013), section 5.2, available at: *https://citizensassembly.ie/wp-content/uploads/Role-of-Women-Woemn-in-Politics.pdf.*

female parliamentarians.[149] The Convention on the Constitution voted narrowly to reject a proposal that the Constitution should be amended to place a duty on the State to take positive action to enhance women's participation in politics and public life,[150] but 97 per cent were in favour of a proposal that the Government should take action to encourage such greater participation. In 2021, the Citizens' Assembly recommended that the quota system be extended to local and European elections.[151]

In terms of the eligibility to vote, the right of men to vote was traditionally connected to property ownership, which effectively disenfranchised the majority of the Irish male population. However, a series of reforms in the 1800s gradually increased the proportion of the adult male population eligible to vote by reducing the amount of property they had to hold.[152] The right to vote for women was only provided for in 1918, and then only to women aged 30 and older.[153] This 1918 Act also extended the right of men to vote by again reducing the property eligibility criteria. In 1923, the property eligibility criteria were abolished by the Electoral Act 1923, with age now being the only criterion of importance. Section 1 of the 1923 Act set 21 as the relevant age, and for the first time men and women were on an equal footing. In 1973, a referendum was passed reducing the voting age to 18.[154]

The importance of voting in connecting citizens to the political process has been emphasised in more recent calls to further extend the right of suffrage to those under the age of 18. In January 2013, the Convention on the Constitution heard submissions on whether the right to vote should be extended to those aged 17. A slim majority of

[149] *https://data.ipu.org/women-ranking/?date_month=12&date_year=2024.* This data is updated monthly.

[150] 50% voted no, 49% voted yes, and 1% had no opinion. See *Second Report of the Convention on the Constitution* (May 2013), section 2.2.

[151] Citizens' Assembly, *Report of the Citizens' Assembly on Gender Equality* (June 2021), p.69, available at: *https://citizensassembly.ie/wp-content/uploads/2023/02/report-of-the-citizens-assembly-on-gender-equality.pdf.* Even though the quota system does not currently apply to local elections, Galligan and Buckley have described a "quota diffusion effect", as local elections provide a main route to the Dáil. They report that there was a 78% increase in women candidates at local level between 2009 and 2019. Y. Galligan and F. Buckley, "Women in Politics" in J. Coakley and M. Gallagher (eds), *Politics in the Republic of Ireland*, 5th edn (London, New York: Routledge, 2010), p.254 at p.262.

[152] Representation of the People (Ireland) Act 1832, Reform Act 1850, Representation of the People Act 1884.

[153] Representation of the People Act 1918.

[154] Fourth Amendment of the Constitution Act 1972, passed by the people on 5 January 1973.

the Convention members recommended that it should be.[155] Of those who were in favour of reducing the age, there was greater support for it to be reduced to 16.[156] The Fine Gael/Labour Government did not hold a referendum on this issue during its tenure in office. The Electoral Commission was asked by the Minister for Housing, Local Government and Heritage, Darragh O'Brien, to consider the issue in July 2023[157] and it is included in the draft research programme for 2024–2026 produced by the Electoral Commission in November 2023.[158]

Finally, the courts have insisted that constitutional rights regarding suffrage are respected. As enacted in 1937, Article 18.4 of the Constitution provided that three Senators would be elected by graduates of Trinity College Dublin and three by graduates of the National University of Ireland. This provision was amended in 1979 to allow the Oireachtas to extend suffrage to graduates from other higher education institutions. No legislation was enacted to give effect to this amendment. Following the judgment in *Heneghan v Minister for Housing, Planning and Local Government*,[159] the Oireachtas is now obliged to extend the right to vote to other third-level institutions to give effect to the intention of the people when they voted for this amendment. The Oireachtas has until 25 May 2025 to put in place legislation to modify the system by which these six seats are elected.[160]

6. Amendment of the Constitution and the Continuance of Pre-Constitution Laws

3–47 The amendment of the Constitution is governed by Articles 46 and 47. In order for the Constitution to be amended, the Dáil and the Seanad must pass a Bill, which is then put to the people for their approval or rejection (Article 46.2). If the change is accepted by the majority of voters (Article 47.1), the President must sign the Bill into law (Article 46.5), assuming that proper procedures have been followed.[161]

155 52% were in favour, 47% opposed, and 1% had no opinion. See *Second Report of the Convention on the Constitution* (May 2013), section 2.1.

156 48% recommended the age of 16, 39% the age of 17, and 14% had no opinion.

157 C. McQuinn, "Scrapping byelections and lowering voting age could be studied by Electoral Commission", *Irish Times*, 9 August 2023, available at: *https://www.irishtimes.com/politics/2023/08/09/scrapping-byelections-and-lowering-voting-age-to-be-studied-by-electoral-commission/*.

158 At the time of writing in April 2024, the research programme had not been finalised.

159 [2023] IESC 7.

160 [2023] IESC 18. This case will be discussed further in Section D.5.

161 If proper procedures have not been followed, then the referendum result can be challenged before the High Court pursuant to ss.42–58 of the Referendum Act 1994.

3–48 Referendums seek to ensure that any changes to the Constitution are the result of considered reflection rather than a knee-jerk reaction by a particular government in power. Indeed, as Gallagher observes, "[o]n only one occasion (the referendum to approve the Constitution in 1937) have the people approved a proposal not backed by the major opposition party".[162] However, this is not to say that the people are immune from knee-jerk reactions. It is well-recognised that voters often do not vote on the substance of a proposed amendment; instead, their vote is utilised to support or punish the ruling political parties.[163] Referendums will be discussed further in Section E of this chapter.

3–49 The final three Articles in the Constitution repeal the Free State Constitution (Article 48), transfer powers, functions, rights and prerogatives from the State to the people (Article 49), and allow laws that were in existence prior to the enactment of the 1937 Constitution to continue to have legal force only if they are consistent with the provisions of the 1937 Constitution (Article 50). There were an additional 13 Articles in the Constitution (Articles 51–63) that existed primarily to allow for the transition between the two Constitutions. For example, Article 58 allowed the courts established and judges appointed under the 1922 Constitution to continue to operate. Provision was made for the deletion of Article 51 after a three-year transition period[164] and the remaining Articles were deleted "after the date on which the first President shall have entered upon his office".[165] In 2013, a new Article was temporarily added to the Constitution by the Thirty-third Amendment of the Constitution. Article 64 enabled the Chief Justice to transfer cases from the abolished Court of Criminal Appeal to the newly established Court of Appeal.[166]

162 M. Gallagher, "The Changing Constitution" in J. Coakley and M. Gallagher (eds), *Politics in the Republic of Ireland*, 6th edn (London, New York: Routledge, 2018), p.57 at p.66.

163 Such an impulse is lessened when voters are informed about the substantive issue. See M. Marsh, "Voting Behaviour" in J. Coakley and M. Gallagher (eds), *Politics in the Republic of Ireland*, 5th edn (London, New York: Routledge, 2010), pp.187–188.

164 Article 51.4.

165 Article 52.1. However, Article 52.2 provided that, despite their deletion from the official text of the Constitution, they would "continue to have force of law".

166 Article 64.7 provided that the text of Article 64 would be omitted from the Constitution a year after the establishment date of the Court of Appeal.

D. Constitutional Interpretation

3–50 Constitutions require interpretation because "[g]overnance is an activity ... that must constantly address new and emerging issues."[167] The Constitution is routinely interpreted by the legislature and the executive in how they practise their respective roles. This is made most evident in pronouncements from the Government that they have obtained advice from the Attorney General that a particular piece of legislative reform is not permissible because such legislation would be unconstitutional. However, in this section we will focus on how the third branch of power, the judiciary, approaches the question of constitutional interpretation. This is because judges have been allocated power under the Constitution to strike down legislation that they determine to be unconstitutional.

3–51 Judges are asked to engage in this form of judicial review in two circumstances.[168] The first is where someone argues that a constitutional right has been infringed; such a challenge would either be based on Article 34.3.2° (for a statute enacted after the adoption of the 1937 Constitution) or on Article 50 (for pre-1937 Constitution statutes). In such cases, an individual argues that a section (or sections) of a statute is contrary to an identified provision of the Constitution. We have encountered numerous examples of such challenges in this chapter, including the *McGee* case.[169] The Supreme Court, the Court of Appeal and the High Court have jurisdiction to review the constitutionality of any statute under Article 34 or Article 50, as appropriate.

3–52 The second is by means of the Article 26 procedure. As noted previously, Article 26 is invoked when the President is uncertain about the constitutionality of a Bill or part thereof passed by both Houses. The Bill is forwarded to the Supreme Court for its assessment of the Bill's constitutionality. The Supreme Court is not interested in the "mere hypothesis or possibility" that the Bill might, if enacted, infringe an Article of the Constitution; it will only declare a Bill to be unconstitutional that

---

[167] F. de Londras, "In Defence of Judicial Innovation and Constitutional Evolution" in L. Cahillane, J. Gallen and T. Hickey (eds), *Judges, Politics and the Irish Constitution* (Manchester: Manchester University Press, 2017), p.9 at p.10.

[168] See also, Ch.10, paras 10–17 to 10–19 and Box 10.2.

[169] See para.3–29.

would, if enacted, result in a "concrete and foreseeable" infringement.[170] If the Supreme Court finds that any part of the Bill is unconstitutional, then that Bill cannot be signed into law. If, however, the Bill is found to be constitutional, it must be signed into law by the President "as soon as may be",[171] and the entire Act is immune from any constitutional challenge in the future.

3–53 In exercising their judicial review function, judges have recourse to a number of constitutional interpretation principles. Some of these principles contradict one another, which means that this can be a confusing area of law. Indeed, it has been observed that given the lack of consistency in the methods chosen, a suspicion can arise that a judge, having decided what outcome they want, picks the approach that helps them reach that result.[172]

3–54 One means of allaying this concern would be to have a hierarchy of principles, such as set out in *Bacik v An Taoiseach* where the High Court summarised the key constitutional interpretive principles identified from various precedents.[173] However in *Heneghan v Minister for Housing, Planning and Local Government*, the Supreme Court urged caution regarding the adoption of such a mechanical approach. Murray J. stated:

> "[I]n undertaking the exercise of constitutional interpretation the courts must incline more to flexibility in subordinating the strictly literal interpretation of the text in order to attain a construction that is both internally harmonious, and that achieves a clearly ascertainable purpose, than might be the case when conducting the exercise of interpreting ordinary legislation."[174]

This view aligns with that of Casey, who wrote:

> "Constitutional interpretation is not, and cannot be, a mechanical process leading to a preordained conclusion. No matter how

[170] *Re Article 26 of the Constitution and the Judicial Appointments Commission Bill 2022* [2023] IESC 34 at para.238.

[171] Article 26.3.3°.

[172] G. Hogan, G. Whyte, D. Kenny and R. Walsh, *Kelly: The Irish Constitution*, 5th edn (Dublin: Bloomsbury Professional, 2018), para.1.1.12.

[173] [2020] IEHC 313 at para.80.

[174] [2023] IESC 7 at para.85.

> inevitable a given judgment makes a particular conclusion seem, that conclusion results from a creative choice, and there will inevitably be room for differences of view as to its 'correctness'."[175]

Accordingly, inconsistency in approach is unavoidable. With this in mind, we turn now to consider these key interpretive principles.

1. Presumption of Constitutionality

3–55 Whether a statute is being considered under Article 26 or Article 34, it is presumed that the impugned statute, like all statutes enacted after the 1937 Constitution was adopted, is constitutional and the burden of proving that it is not rests on the person alleging unconstitutionality. The presumption of constitutionality derives from the separation of powers, whereby the Oireachtas has been given the power to enact legislation, and from Article 15.4, which requires the Oireachtas to pass constitutional legislation. The presumption therefore expects that the legislature intends to enact constitutional legislation and that the judiciary should demonstrate the "respect which one great organ of the State owes to another".[176]

3–56 The presumption of constitutionality carries with it an obligation on the judiciary to interpret impugned section(s) as constitutional if such an interpretation is reasonably possible. This is known as the double construction rule. This rule was defined as follows in *McDonald v Bord na gCon*:

> "[O]ne practical effect of this presumption is that if in respect of any provision or provisions of the Act two or more constructions are reasonably open, one of which is constitutional and the other or others are unconstitutional, it must be presumed that the Oireachtas intended only the constitutional construction and a Court called upon to adjudicate upon the constitutionality of the statutory provision should uphold the constitutional construction. It

[175] J.P. Casey, *Constitutional Law in Ireland*, 3rd edn (Dublin: Round Hall Sweet & Maxwell, 2000), p.383. See also, O. Doyle and T. Hickey, *Constitutional Law: Text, Cases and Materials*, 2nd edn (Dublin: Clarus Press, 2019), paras 4.30–4.32. For an excellent analysis of this in the context of a single judgment, see O. Doyle, "The Duration of Primary Education: Judicial Constraint in Constitutional Interpretation" (2002) 10 *Irish Student Law Review* 222.

[176] *Buckley v Attorney General* [1950] I.R. 67 at 80.

is only when there is no construction reasonably open which is not repugnant to the Constitution that the provision should be held to be repugnant."[177]

3–57 There are limits on the use of the double construction rule. It was emphasised in *East Donegal Co-operative Livestock Mart Ltd v Attorney General* that "[i]n seeking to reach an interpretation or construction in accordance with the Constitution, a statutory provision which is clear and unambiguous cannot be given an opposite meaning".[178] This is because if the courts did so, they would be "replac[ing] one form of unconstitutionality with another form of unconstitutionality (judicial legislating)".[179] Another limit is illustrated by the case of *A, B, C v Minister for Foreign Affairs and Trade* where Murray J. held that "[t]he double construction rule allows the adjustment of a single statutory provision so as to align it with constitutional requirements, it does not thereby permit the imposition of an entirely new legislative regime."[180] This case concerned s.7(1) of the Irish Nationality and Citizenship Act 1956 which provides that a child attains Irish citizenship if one of their parents was an Irish citizen at the time of their birth. A and B were a same-sex married couple. C's genetic parent was B, an English citizen, and his legal parent was A, an Irish citizen.[181] An application for citizenship for C was refused because A was not C's parent, understood to mean either a mother or a father. The family argued that "parent" should be construed to include a person who became a legal parent after the birth of the child. The Supreme Court did not agree, determining that the meaning of "parent" within the legislation was clear and that the proposed interpretation would fundamentally alter how citizenship by descent was regulated by the 1956 Act.[182]

3–58 Another corollary of the presumption of constitutionality is the principle of self-restraint.[183] According to this principle, if it is possible to

[177] [1965] I.R. 217 at 239.
[178] [1970] I.R. 317 at 341.
[179] D. Dodd, *Statutory Interpretation in Ireland* (Dublin: Tottel Publishing, 2008), para.11.48.
[180] [2023] IESC 10 at para.92.
[181] Under English legislation, it is possible for a non-genetic parent to be identified as a child's legal parent on their birth certificate.
[182] [2023] IESC 10 at paras 91–92 per Murray J.
[183] *McDaid v Sheehy* [1991] 1 I.R. 1 at 17. This principle, however, is subject "to the overriding consideration of doing justice between the parties": *Murphy v Roche* [1987] I.R. 106 at 111.

resolve the legal dispute by means of an alternative legal route, without recourse to the Constitution, then the courts will do this. This is another means by which the judiciary respects the constitutional allocation of the power to legislate to the Oireachtas.

3–59 Finally, the presumption of constitutionality only applies to statutes that have been passed after the enactment of the Constitution. As Ryan explains, "[l]ogically, one cannot assume that a piece of legislation passed before the 1937 Constitution was created with the Constitution's terms in mind".[184] Accordingly, the presumption of constitutionality does not apply to a statute whose constitutionality is being challenged under Article 50.

2. Literal or Harmonious Approach?

3–60 The literal approach is when a word or phrase in a constitutional provision is given its ordinary/most obvious meaning. Some constitutional provisions can only be given such a meaning. For example, Article 21 requires Money Bills to be initiated in the Dáil. This could hardly be interpreted as allowing the Seanad to initiate such a Bill. However, in interpreting constitutional provisions, a harmonious approach is generally favoured over a literal one. This is because, as noted above, the Constitution is not just a legal document but it is also a political one with various aspirations included in it. As such, the traditional canons of interpretation, one of which is the literal rule, are not always appropriate.[185] The harmonious approach requires a court to look beyond the plain meaning of the words in a particular Article and to interpret that Article with reference to other Articles so as to ensure that the various provisions work in harmony with one another.

3–61 A controversial example of this approach is the case of *O'B v S*.[186] In this case, the defendant's father had died intestate and the question before the court was whether she, as a daughter born outside marriage, was his "issue" pursuant to s.67(3) of the Succession Act 1965. If it was found that she was not, she further argued that such treatment was discriminatory and contrary to Article 40.1. Having found that she was

[184] F. Ryan, *Constitutional Law*, 3rd edn (Dublin: Round Hall, 2018), p.14.
[185] *Attorney General v Paperlink Ltd* [1984] I.L.R.M. 373 at 385. For further discussion of the canons of interpretation, see Ch.4, Sections D and E.
[186] [1984] I.R. 316.

not his "issue", the Supreme Court determined that the discrimination was not prima facie permissible under the terms of the proviso to Article 40.1, as being born outside marriage was not a difference of capacity or social function. However, because Article 41 permitted discrimination in favour of the marital family, a legislative provision that gave effect to that constitutional preference could not be contrary to Article 40.1:

> "Legislation which differentiates citizens or which discriminates between them does not need to be justified under the proviso if justification for it can be found in other provisions of the Constitution. Legislation which is unjust, unreasonable or arbitrary cannot be justified under any provision of the Constitution. Conversely, if legislation can be justified under one or more Articles of the Constitution, when read with all the others, it cannot be held to be unjust within the meaning of any Article ... ."[187]

Three years later, the distinction between children born inside and outside marriage was abolished by the Status of Children Act 1987, which provided that all children are equal before the law.

3. The Purposive Approach

3–62 The purposive approach seeks to construe constitutional provisions in line with the purpose the Article was intended to fulfil, which allows for a slightly broader interpretation of words than a strict literal approach would allow. In *Sullivan v Robinson*, O'Byrne J. held that "[a] Constitution is to be liberally construed so as to carry into effect the intentions of the people as embodied therein".[188] This is because the Constitution is generally concerned with setting out the broad principles according to which the State is to be run rather than specifying the detail. An example of a case in which the purposive approach was used is the previously encountered case of *Ryan*.[189] In the High Court, Kenny J. interpreted the phrase "personal rights" in Article 40.3.2° to include rights not specifically enumerated in the Constitution but which would accord with "the Christian and democratic" State that the Constitution was intended to create and regulate.[190]

[187] [1984] I.R. 316 at 335 per Walsh J.
[188] [1954] I.R. 151 at 174.
[189] *Ryan v Attorney General* [1965] I.R. 294 at 312. See para.3–27.
[190] D.G. Morgan, *A Judgment Too Far? Judicial Activism and the Constitution* (Cork: Cork University Press, 2001), pp.98–99.

4. The Historical or Living Document Approach?

3–63 The historical approach seeks to interpret the Constitution with reference to what the intention of the drafters and the people was when they adopted the Constitution or the referendum. This is gleaned either from an understanding of the attitudes that existed in 1937 or at the time the relevant referendum was held.[191] Conversely, the living document approach considers that the meaning of words in the Constitution can and should change as society changes. Which approach is preferred "reflects ... deep but competing commitments over the extent to which constitutional law is a matter of social fact or moral aspiration."[192]

3–64 An example of a case where both approaches were used is *McGee*, where the criminalisation of the importation of contraceptives was challenged.[193] In the High Court, the closeness in time between the passage of the Criminal Law Amendment Act 1935 and the enactment of the 1937 Constitution was determinative in upholding its constitutionality. O'Keeffe P. wrote:

> "The section impugned was barely two years on the statute book when the Constitution was adopted. If the submission of the plaintiff is correct, then public opinion as to what were fundamental rights must have been such as to require that the rights guaranteed to individuals by the Constitution were inconsistent with the continued legality of the section. I consider that the best test of the position is to be found in the views expressed when the section was being passed into law since, in point of time, this was so close to the enactment of the Constitution by the people. I find that the section was adopted without a division ... I cannot think that this reflects a public opinion in favour of the existence of such a right of privacy as is alleged by the plaintiff to be guaranteed under the Constitution."[194]

Walsh J. rejected this historical approach in the Supreme Court and preferred the living document approach. He wrote:

---

[191] See further para.3–66.

[192] C. Casey and O. Doyle, "Foreword: The Constitution under the New Supreme Court" (2024) 44(1) *Dublin University Law Journal* 5 at 50.

[193] *McGee v Attorney General* [1974] I.R. 284. See para.3–29.

[194] [1974] I.R. 284 at 292–293.

> "It is but natural that from time to time the prevailing ideas of [prudence, justice and charity] may be conditioned by the passage of time; no interpretation of the Constitution is intended to be final for all time. It is given in the light of prevailing ideas and concepts."[195]

3–65 There appears to be a general judicial preference for the living document approach. O'Donnell C.J. explained why, beautifully, in *Jordan v Minister for Children and Youth Affairs*:[196]

> "[215] ... [A] constitution is to some extent an ongoing conversation across the generations. While Bunreacht na hÉireann is emphatically the people's Constitution, it must be remembered that the youngest living person who can be said to have adopted the Constitution in 1937 will be 100 years old next year. When we speak therefore of the people adopting and giving to themselves this Constitution, that necessarily comprehends also the acceptance of the Constitution by subsequent generations, and the accretions to it by the process of constitutional interpretation.
>
> [216] The force and value of the Constitution comes in part from its age, and the respect which is paid to our predecessors who attempted to express an enduring statement of those core truths that they held to be fundamental and applicable in whatever circumstances. Of course the Constitution speaks in the present tense and would be of little value if it was not capable of addressing important contemporary issues. ... Part of the value of the Constitution is that it is at one and the same time both old and ageless, and it gets some of its strength from the fact that it has been tried and tested through different generations in different circumstances. The process of constitutional interpretation is part of that historical continuum and an important exercise in the intergenerational conversation and solidarity. ..."

3–66 However, a general preference for the living document approach does not mean that the historical approach is never used. In *Zappone and Gilligan v Revenue Commissioners*,[197] Dunne J. upheld as constitutional the Revenue Commissioners' decision to limit the definition of

[195] [1974] I.R. 284 at 319.
[196] [2015] 4 I.R. 232.
[197] [2006] 2 I.R. 417.

marriage for taxation purposes to a heterosexual couple on the basis that this would have been the understanding of marriage at the time the Constitution was adopted and was the understanding adopted in various judgments since 1937.[198] Moreover, both approaches are in fact codependent. Expressing a preference for the living document approach in *Sinnott v Minister for Education*, Murray J. observed: "this does not mean ... that it can be divorced from its historical context. Indeed, by definition, that which is contemporary is determined by reference to its historical context."[199] Both approaches also share a common problem, namely, how a judge is supposed to decipher what historical or current attitudes were/are.[200] As Kelly observes, "[t]o read public opinion out of the fact of enactment of the very statute which is under challenge seems a dubious method of interpretation".[201] The one situation where this problem is eased is when the text at issue was inserted into the Constitution by means of a referendum. In *Heneghan v Minister for Housing, Planning and Local Government*, it was determined that the explanatory statement that is included on polling cards and displayed in the polling station could be relied upon to assist in interpreting such a provision. This is because such statements are "as reliable an account of what the People might reasonably have believed they were voting for" and because they are drafted by the Houses of the Oireachtas for this purpose which gives an indication of what they, as an institution, believed was being proposed.[202]

5. Effect of Finding of Unconstitutionality

3–67 Whether a statutory provision was passed pre- or post-1937, once it has been found to be unconstitutional it has no further legal effect. The finding of unconstitutionality is, however, confined to the (sub) section(s) challenged. Indeed, where possible, the courts will seek to

---

198 [2006] 2 I.R. 417 at paras 238–239. This understanding of marriage was changed with the passage of the Thirty-fourth Amendment in 2015 which allowed for the recognition of same-sex marriage.

199 [2001] 2 I.R. 545 at 680.

200 J.P. Casey, *Constitutional Law in Ireland*, 3rd edn (Dublin: Round Hall Sweet & Maxwell, 2000), p.382.

201 G. Hogan, G. Whyte, D. Kenny and R. Walsh, *Kelly: The Irish Constitution*, 5th edn (Dublin: Bloomsbury Professional, 2018), para.1.1.73.

202 [2023] IESC 7 at paras 107–109 per Murray J. It is inappropriate to refer to the views of individual parliamentarians though. See para.87 per Murray J. and para.35 per Hogan J., citing *Crilly v T & J Farrington Ltd* [2001] 3 I.R. 251. See further Ch.4, Section F.2(c).

sever the offending word or words from a (sub)section in order to save the remainder of the section.[203] If the unconstitutional provision or part thereof was passed after 1937, it is said to be void ab initio, i.e. it never had legal effect and nothing done in accordance with it was valid.

3–68 The effect is the same for any provision or part thereof declared unconstitutional that was passed prior to 1937; it is said never to have survived the adoption of the 1937 Constitution because it was not consistent with it, as required by Article 50. A declaration of unconstitutionality in such instances has rather dramatically been described as a "judicial death certificate, with the date of death stated as the date when the Constitution came into operation".[204]

3–69 However, this principle that the provision never had legal effect either from the date of its adoption or from the enactment of the Constitution is not absolute. This was noted in *Murphy v Attorney General* where a married couple who had successfully argued that provisions in the Income Tax Act 1967 that penalised married couples were unconstitutional could only recoup the unconstitutionally deducted tax from the year they began their proceedings. The Supreme Court reasoned as follows:

> "Up to that year the State was entitled, in the absence of any claim of unconstitutionality, to act on the assumption that the taxes were validly imposed ... Equally, every taxpayer whose income tax was deducted ... could not avoid having imputed to him the knowledge that the tax he was paying was liable to be immediately spent by the State. As time went by, his right to complain of the State's unjust enrichment ran the risk of being extinguished by *laches* on his part."[205]

3–70 The reason why limits need to be placed on the operation of this principle of absolute retroactivity is made most apparent in cases where criminal offences have been declared to be unconstitutional. In *A v Governor of Arbour Hill Prison*,[206] the applicant issued habeas

[203] As required by the wording of Article 15.4.2° ("to the extent only of such repugnancy") and Article 50 ("to the extent to which they are not inconsistent therewith").
[204] *Murphy v Attorney General* [1982] I.R. 241 at 307.
[205] [1982] I.R. 241 at 318.
[206] [2006] 4 I.R. 88.

corpus proceedings challenging the legality of his continued detention for sex with an underage girl after that offence was declared to be unconstitutional in *CC v Ireland*[207] because it did not allow for the defence of honest mistake. The Supreme Court rejected his challenge and declared that it was possible to be imprisoned for an offence that never existed because unlimited retroactivity would be contrary to the public interest, the common good and social order. Murray C.J. held:

> "Absolute retroactivity based solely on the notion of an Act being void *ab initio* so as to render any previous final judicial decisions null would lead the Constitution to have dysfunctional effects in the administration of justice ... The application of a principle of absolute retroactivity ... would render null and of no effect final verdicts or decisions affected by an Act which at the time had been presumed or acknowledged to be constitutional and otherwise had been fairly tried. Such unqualified retroactivity would be a denial of justice to the victims of crime and offend against fundamental and just interests of society."[208]

3–71 This point was elaborated upon by Geoghegan J.:

> "It cannot have been the intention of the draftsmen of the Constitution and more properly of the Oireachtas and perhaps more properly still of the people that if a statutory provision creating an offence was found to be unconstitutional, every past conviction and sentence, perhaps going back a large number of years were *ipso facto* nullities. ... If such was the devastating effect of a declaration of unconstitutionality in all cases, it would fly in the face of common sense, would be manifestly unjust and would be contrary to any good order in a civilised society."[209]

3–72 Hardiman J. noted that the applicant was debarred from relying on *CC* to obtain his release for two further reasons: first, he had not challenged the constitutionality of the law when he was tried; second, he would not have been able to do so, as he could not on the facts of his case have raised the defence of honest mistake as he knew the age of the girl with whom he had sex. The effect of this decision was that although a

[207] [2006] 4 I.R. 1.
[208] [2006] 4 I.R. 88 at 130.
[209] [2006] 4 I.R. 88 at 197.

section (or part thereof) is technically void, that unconstitutionality does not begin to crystallise until a challenge is or could be brought against that statute on that basis.

3–73 The *A* case is also significant because Denham J. noted obiter that it might be appropriate to follow the Canadian example and suspend the effect of a declaration of invalidity in certain circumstances to give the legislature time to carefully consider how best to remedy the defect and adopt the appropriate measures. This approach would accord with the courts' jurisdiction to administer justice.[210] The Irish Supreme Court duly adopted a variation of this practice in *NHV v Minister for Justice and Equality*. Instead of declaring that s.9(4) of the Refugee Act 1996, which absolutely and indefinitely prevented asylum seekers from working, was contrary to the Constitution and suspending the effect of that declaration (as would be the case in Canada), the Supreme Court held that the provision was "in principle" contrary to the Constitution. It then adjourned the matter for six months to give the State time to prepare submissions to the court to assist it in deciding when the declaration of unconstitutionality would be made.[211] When the case appeared before the Supreme Court again, the court emphasised that the approach taken in *NHV* was reserved for exceptional cases.[212] The court also stated that it would not engage in detailed oversight of the legislature's choices.[213]

3–74 The procedure adopted in *NHV* when a provision is "in principle" unconstitutional—proceedings are adjourned to give the parties time to prepare submissions about how long the declaration of unconstitutionality should be suspended, after hearing which the court sets a date on which the declaration will be issued—was subsequently followed in *PC v Minister for Social Welfare*.[214] It was confirmed in *Heneghan v Minister for Housing, Planning and Local Government (No. 1)* that this was the correct approach.[215]

[210] [2006] 4 I.R. 88 at 153–154.
[211] [2017] 2 I.L.R.M. 105 at para.21.
[212] [2017] IESC 82 at paras 2–3.
[213] The court said that it would issue a declaration of invalidity in February 2018. By this stage, a temporary employment permits system had been put in place, operated by the Department of Business, Enterprise and Innovation. This system was replaced in July 2018 when Ireland opted in to the EU (recast) Reception Conditions Directive (2013/33/EU).
[214] [2018] IESC 57.
[215] [2023] IESC 7 at para.160 per Murray J.

3–75 In *Heneghan (No. 1)*, it was determined that the declaration of invalidity could only be prospective, i.e. from the date on which the declaration is issued, in that case due to the nature of the constitutional deficiency.[216] Heneghan successfully argued that ss.6 and 7 of the Seanad Electoral (Universities Members) Act 1937 were in breach of Article 18.4.2° of the Constitution. This Article, which was inserted into the Constitution in 1979, enabled the Oireachtas to extend the franchise of the six university seats beyond its current constituency of Trinity College Dublin and the National University of Ireland graduates, but no such legislation was passed. Heneghan was a graduate of the University of Limerick and thus excluded from this aspect of the Seanad franchise.[217] The reason the declaration of invalidity could not be retrospective in any way was because it would result in "a constitutional impasse".[218] As O'Donnell C.J. explained in *Heneghan (No. 2)*:

> "[Absolute retroactivity] would have the effect of invalidating all past elections, and therefore, any legislation enacted by the legislature so elected, and also and at the same time, preventing the problem from ever being cured, since on this view there would be no validly elected legislature that could enact the curative legislation."[219]

Accordingly, the date on which the declaration of unconstitutionality will be issued is 31 May 2025—one year and nine months after *Heneghan (No. 2)*—in recognition of the possibility that a general election could be called before the corrective legislation is passed.[220] It was also theoretically accepted that an initial period of suspension could be extended but only in exceptional cases.[221]

3–76 The main benefit of suspended declarations of unconstitutionality is that they give the legislature time to carefully consider how to fill the lacuna that will follow the issuing of a declaration of unconstitutionality rather than enacting rushed and possibly flawed legislation. It also has

[216] [2023] IESC 7 at para.159 per Murray J.

[217] There are 60 Senators. Six are elected by the university franchise, 43 by members of the incoming Dáil, members of the outgoing Seanad, and members of city/county councils, and 11 are nominated by the Taoiseach.

[218] [2023] IESC 7 at para.68 per Hogan J.

[219] [2023] IESC 18 at para.15.

[220] [2023] IESC 18 at para.37. The Seanad Electoral (University Members) (Amendment) Act 2024 was signed into law in October 2024.

[221] [2023] IESC 18 at para.35.

the benefit of improving judicial review because it "liberat[es] judges from the more stark (and in many respects unnecessarily broad) consequences of invalidating a law."[222] As Hogan J. explained in *AB v Director of St Loman's Hospital*:

> "The lesson of *NHV* is that the judiciary should not have to watch helplessly as a finding of unconstitutionality leads on with remorseless logic to invalidate and unravel a large variety of administrative decisions, often in a chaotic and disruptive fashion and with possibly unforeseen consequences for third parties ... ."[223]

In that case, the relevant provision was s.15(3) of the Mental Health Act 2001 which allowed for involuntary detention in the Central Mental Hospital to be extended but did not allow for a review of the mental health status of the detainee outside of the two stated periods. The Court of Appeal agreed that this provision would be unconstitutional because it allowed for the involuntary detention of a person who was no longer suffering from a mental disorder, but it deferred issuing the declaration because doing so immediately would mean that there would be no legal basis for the continued detention of many vulnerable patients whose release could endanger themselves or others.[224]

3–77 There are two main negatives to suspended declarations. The first is conceptual. How can this approach co-exist with the concept of void ab initio? If a provision is void ab initio then there is nothing to delay suspending because it was never law at all.[225] The second is more practical, and because of that, more meaningful. Delaying the declaration of unconstitutionality means that those affected by that "in principle" unconstitutional provision continue to have their rights infringed. As Carolan writes:

> "[T]here are *prima facie* rule of law issues about the enforcement of a legal situation that is unconstitutional. There is a discomforting dissonance about the position in which courts may find themselves

[222] G. Hogan, G. Whyte, D. Kenny and R. Walsh, *Kelly: The Irish Constitution*, 5th edn (Dublin: Bloomsbury Professional, 2018), para.6.2.399.
[223] [2018] IECA 123 at para.111.
[224] [2018] IECA 123 at para.110.
[225] G. Hogan, G. Whyte, D. Kenny and R. Walsh, *Kelly: The Irish Constitution*, 5th edn (Dublin: Bloomsbury Professional, 2018), para.6.2.403.

> following such a ruling: declaring something to be unconstitutional while obliged to uphold and enforce it, even against litigants in whose favour the declaration was made. This has led some courts in Canada to grant personal exemptions to individual litigants under which the invalid-but-in-force law cannot be applied to them. The difficulty is that this arguably replaces a concern about legality with one about equality before the law."[226]

3–78 While this was a moot point for NHV because he had been granted refugee status, others who were still in the asylum system continued to be prohibited from working. In *PC v Minister for Social Protection*, O'Donnell J. acknowledged the effect on individual litigants of a delayed declaration but affirmed that it was still appropriate to delay in exceptional cases because "the striking down of an unconstitutional provision must be balanced against, and sometimes outweighed by, other countervailing factors".[227]

3–79 Whatever the validity of these concerns, the practice is now part of Irish law. However, we can also learn from the Canadian experience. After a period where the procedure was used liberally, the Canadian Supreme Court in *Ontario (AG) v G* decided that the issuing of a suspended declaration should be rare and should be limited to cases where the harms caused by an immediate declaration would endanger a compelling public interest.[228] The majority did not identify categories of cases where a compelling public interest would arise but the dissenting judgments sought to be narrower and more prescriptive. Three dissenters wanted to limit the use of the procedure to cases where rule-of-law concerns were engaged and where public safety was endangered. One of the three would also permit it in cases where under-inclusive legislation conferred a benefit. In *Heneghan (No. 2)*, the Supreme Court observed that

> "... both the theory and practice in this jurisdiction, has come closest to the views of the dissenters in *G*, but what is significant

---

[226] E. Carolan, "A Dialogue-Orientated Departure in Constitutional Remedies? The Implications of NHV v Minister for Justice for Inter-Branch Roles and Relationships" (2017) 40(1) *Dublin University Law Journal* 191 at 195.

[227] [2018] IESC 57 at para.21.

[228] [2020] SCC 38. For more on this case, see D. Lalor, "*Ontario (Attorney General) v G* and 'Principled' Remedial Discretion: Lessons for Ireland" (2021) 5(2) *Irish Judicial Studies Journal* 55.

... is that ... even [judges and academics] most opposed to the use of suspended declarations, accept[] that there is a core of cases in which the remedy is properly applied, and most obviously, in cases which give rise to rule of law concerns, particularly in the field of electoral law."[229]

E. Reform of the Constitution

3–80 In order for the Constitution to be reformed, the referendum process must be administered. However, the decision to bring a constitutional amendment before the people is a political one: the running of a referendum campaign is expensive, and the Government is clearly reluctant to spend money on one unless it is actually necessary or is perceived to be so. In this section, we will review the amendments accepted and rejected. In total, 45 amendments have been put before the people[230] and they have voted to amend the Constitution 30 times. We will also consider various reports that have recommended the reform of other Articles. The issue of reform is particularly pertinent in light of the increasing pace at which amendments have been proposed, suggesting that the 1937 Constitution might no longer be fit for purpose. For the first 46 years of its life, the Constitution was amended only eight times, but from 1984 onwards, 34 amendments have been proposed (of which 31 have been put before the people).[231]

[229] [2018] IESC 18 at para.23.

[230] This figure includes a double-counting of the Twenty-eighth Amendment, as it was put to the people twice, and excludes the first two amendments, as these were made not by the people but by the Oireachtas by means of ordinary legislation, as permitted by Article 51 during the first three years of the life of the Constitution.

[231] The Twenty-second Amendment was withdrawn before being put to the people. See para.3–84 for further information, and Ch.11, para.11–74. The first version of the Children's Rights Amendment (Thirty-first Amendment) included text to allow for the imposition of strict and absolute liability offences "committed against or in connection with children under the age of 18". However, following consultation, this version of the proposed text was replaced by the text that was adopted by the people in 2015. It was intended to hold the Forty-first Amendment, to ratify an agreement regarding a Unified Patent Court, in June 2024 to coincide with the local and EU elections, but it has been decided to suspend this until a later date: Press Release, "Government defers date for referendum on a Unified Patent Court" (16 April 2024), available at: *https://enterprise.gov.ie/en/news-and-events/department-news/2024/april/20240416.html*. For a full list of all referendums that have been held, see *https://www.electoralcommission.ie/referendums-info/previous-referendums/*.

1. Categories of Amendments of the 1937 Constitution

3–81 The reasons that prompt the amendment of the Constitution are varied. Sometimes an amendment is necessary for international relations reasons, such as the various referendums that ratify European Union (EU) Treaties. Such referendums are required for legislation from the EU to be recognised in Irish law because Article 15.2.1° preserves legislative autonomy for the Oireachtas. Accordingly, in 1972 the Third Amendment inserted Article 29.4.3° into the Constitution to allow Ireland join the European Economic Community (as it then was). Each successive EU Treaty has similarly required ratification by the people, and the continued proliferation of subsections of Article 29. In total, including the 1972 amendment, there have been 10 referendums on EU Treaties.[232] All bar two were accepted by the people. The Nice Treaty was rejected by the people when proposed as the Twenty-fourth Amendment in 2001, but accepted in 2002 as the Twenty-sixth Amendment. The Twenty-eighth Amendment on the Lisbon Treaty was held twice, first rejected by the people in 2008 but accepted in 2009.

3–82 A referendum was also necessary to ratify the 1998 British-Irish Agreement, known as the Good Friday Agreement. Part of this Agreement required the modification of Articles 2 and 3 of the Constitution, the amendment of which was accepted by the people in 1998.[233] A consequence of this Nineteenth Amendment was that anyone born on the island of Ireland could claim citizenship. Concerned about the prospect of citizenship tourism,[234] the Government tabled the Twenty-seventh Amendment which limited the right of citizenship to persons who had a citizen parent. This amendment was accepted by the people in 2004.

3–83 The remaining amendments can be grouped into four main categories: referendums on the domestic political process, on court-related matters, on moral/social issues, and two amendments that did not require a referendum. Of the 10 referendums concerning the domestic

[232] The Third, Tenth, Eleventh, Eighteenth, Twenty-third, Twenty-fourth, Twenty-sixth, Twenty-eighth (held twice), and the Thirtieth. For further exploration of this, see Ch.6, para.6–37.

[233] See para.3–09.

[234] M. Gallagher, "The Changing Constitution" in J. Coakley and M. Gallagher (eds), *Politics in the Republic of Ireland*, 5th edn (London, New York: Routledge, 2010), p.82.

political process, the issue that has been put to the people the most has been voting. There have been seven referendums on voting, four of which were accepted by the people. These lowered the voting age to 18 (Fourth Amendment), extended voting rights in the Seanad (Seventh Amendment), granted the right to vote in Dáil elections to certain non-citizens (Ninth Amendment), and recognised local government and required elections to be held every five years (Twentieth Amendment). Two proposals put to the people in 1959 and 1968 to change our voting system from proportional representation to "first past the post"[235] were rejected by the people. The 1968 referendum also proposed that rural voters could be over-represented, which was also rejected. Additional referendums on the political process are the Seventeenth Amendment on the confidentiality of government meetings (accepted by the people) and the Thirty-second Amendment which sought to abolish the Seanad (rejected). In May 2015, a referendum on reducing the minimum age a presidential candidate must attain before being eligible (Thirty-fifth Amendment) was rejected.

3–84 All four referendums on court-related matters that have been put before the people have been accepted by them. These legitimated adoption orders that were not made by a court (Sixth Amendment), allowed a court to refuse bail to an accused person on the grounds that they might commit a further crime while on bail (Sixteenth Amendment), allowed for a reduction in judicial pay (Twenty-ninth Amendment), and established the Court of Appeal (Thirty-third Amendment). A fifth court-related proposal, the Twenty-second Amendment which proposed to set up an impeachment process for judges, was never put to the people as a dispute arose in the Dáil about the percentage of votes that would be required.[236]

3–85 There have been 16 referendums on moral/social issues, the most divisive of which have been the six referendums on abortion. The first inserted the Eighth Amendment which protected the right to life of the

[235] Proportional representation allows voters to select a number of candidates in order of preference, i.e. first choice, second choice, etc. The candidate(s) that win do so on the basis of the first preference votes received and/or through the allocation of votes transferred to them. First past the post is a system where a voter is only permitted to select one candidate and the candidate with the simple majority of votes is elected.

[236] The 2001 Bill proposed a two-thirds vote as compared to the simple majority that is currently required under Article 35.4.1.° See further, Ch.11, para.11–74.

unborn; the next four were attempts to expand or limit that protection with reference to the *X* case, where the Supreme Court established that the mother's right to life trumps that of the unborn where there is a risk to her life, including due to the risk of suicide.[237] The two that sought to limit the ambit of this case were rejected by the people; the two that gave effect to it were accepted.[238] The Eighth Amendment was repealed by the Thirty-sixth Amendment in 2018.

3–86 The most common subject of amendment under the moral/social category focuses on families: their form, the rights and duties within them, and their dissolution. Two referendums sought to expand the definition of the family. The first, the Thirty-fourth Amendment which proposed allowing same-sex marriage, was passed by a majority in May 2015. The second, the Thirty-ninth Amendment which proposed including non-marital families within the definition of family, was rejected in March 2024. The relationship between the rights of children and parents in the family was recalibrated by the Thirty-first Amendment in 2012.[239] The Fortieth Amendment proposed removing reference to women's duties in the home and inserting a new provision about the care provided by family members. It was rejected in March 2024.[240] Finally, the issue of divorce was put to the people on three occasions. In 1986, the people rejected removing the prohibition on divorce that was in the Constitution. The 1996 referendum that introduced divorce was also contentious but was accepted by the people by a very slim majority. The Thirty-eighth Amendment in 2019 subsequently widened access to divorce.

3–87 Two of the three remaining moral/social category amendments relate to offences. The death penalty was abolished in 2002 (Twenty-first Amendment) and the offence of blasphemy was removed from the Constitution in 2018 (Thirty-seventh Amendment). Finally, the special position of the Catholic Church was removed from Article 44 of the Constitution in 1972.

---

[237] *Attorney General v X* [1992] 1 I.R. 1.

[238] For further discussion on the Eighth Amendment, see Ch.8, Box 8.3.

[239] The legitimacy of the result was queried before the courts, delaying its insertion into the Constitution, but the challenge was unsuccessful: *Jordan v Minister for Children and Youth Affairs* [2015] IESC 33.

[240] See para.3–91 et seq.

3–88 Amendments that do not fit into any of the above categories are the first two amendments, which were passed without a referendum, as was permitted during the first three years of the life of the Constitution.[241] The First Amendment extended the scope of Article 28.3.3° to allow for the suspension of provisions of the Constitution during times of emergency, whether the State was a party to the conflict or not;[242] the Second Amendment contained miscellaneous amendments designed to tidy up the Constitution, some of which were significant changes.[243]

2. Recommendations on Further Reform

3–89 There is no shortage of reports on how the Constitution can be reformed. The first Constitution reform report was issued in 1967 but though the majority of its recommendations were unanimous, only one was implemented.[244] This was the removal of the "special position" of the Catholic Church from Article 44 in 1973. The next report was issued by the Constitution Review Group in 1996,[245] which was referred to an All-Party Oireachtas Committee on the Constitution. This Committee published 10 reports between 1997 and 2006.[246] A number of amendments to the Constitution derived from this process, specifically the amendments on cabinet confidentiality (Seventeenth Amendment), local government (Twentieth Amendment) and the abolition of the death penalty (Twenty-first Amendment). A proposed amendment on the establishment of a judicial impeachment procedure (Twenty-second Amendment) was withdrawn during the legislative process over concerns regarding the voting process.

3–90 The All-Party Oireachtas Committee on the Constitution was replaced by a Joint Committee on the Constitution in 2007 which issued two reports, one on freedom of expression in 2008, the other on the

---

241 Article 51, which was deleted from the Constitution following the transition period.

242 This amendment was adopted in September 1939 at the outbreak of World War II.

243 See J.P. Casey, *Constitutional Law in Ireland*, 3rd edn (Dublin: Round Hall Sweet & Maxwell, 2000), pp.24–25 for a discussion of these amendments and their scope.

244 *Report of the Committee on the Constitution*, Pr. 9817 (Dublin: Stationery Office, 1967).

245 *Report of the Constitution Review Group*, Pr. 2632 (Dublin: Stationery Office, 1996). This report can be accessed at: *https://citizensassembly.ie/wp-content/uploads/Report-of-the-Constitution-Review-Group-1996.pdf.*

246 These reports can also be accessed at: *https://citizensassembly.ie/previous-assemblies/2013-2014-convention-on-the-constitution/our-constitution/.*

referendum process in 2009. In 2012, a Convention on the Constitution was established, comprising 100 members, 66 of whom were ordinary citizens randomly selected from the electoral register. It published nine reports.[247] Two referendums were held in May 2015 arising out of the Convention on the Constitution. The Thirty-fourth Amendment proposed expanding the definition of marriage to include same-sex couples. The Thirty-fifth Amendment sought to lower the minimum age a candidate for the presidency must attain before they can be eligible for election, from 35 to 21. The former was accepted by the people, the latter rejected.

3–91 Citizens' Assemblies have also played an important role in proposing constitutional reform.[248] The Citizens' Assembly on the Eighth Amendment recommended repeal of that Amendment and its replacement with text that permitted the Oireachtas to legislate for abortion.[249] This proposal was put to the people in 2018 and was passed. The Citizens' Assembly on Gender Equality recommended, among other reforms, that Article 41 be amended to include non-marital families within the constitutional definition of family and that reference to women's duties in the home be removed.[250] Variations on the recommendations made by this Citizens' Assembly were put to the people in March 2024. Both amendments were rejected. In 2018, the Citizens' Assembly also considered how referendums should be run and while the majority of these recommendations do not involve constitutional change, their recommendations are nonetheless significant. They recommended that a permanent Electoral Commission be established to inform the public about referendums, rather than ad hoc Referendum Commissions.[251] This came to pass with the enactment of the Electoral Reform Act 2022

247 All nine reports are available at: *https://citizensassembly.ie/previous-assemblies/2013-2014-convention-on-the-constitution/reports-recommendations/.*

248 Discussed in greater detail in Ch.8, Section B.5, paras 8–22 to 8–27.

249 Citizens' Assembly, *First Report and Recommendations of the Citizens' Assembly: The Eighth Amendment of the Constitution* (29 June 2017), p.3, available at: *https://citizensassembly.ie/wp-content/uploads/2023/02/FirstReport_EIGHTAMENDMENT.pdf.*

250 Citizens' Assembly, *Report of the Citizens' Assembly on Gender Equality* (June 2021), pp.50–58, available at: *https://citizensassembly.ie/wp-content/uploads/2023/02/report-of-the-citizens-assembly-on-gender-equality.pdf.*

251 Citizens' Assembly, *Report and Recommendations of the Citizens' Assembly on the Fourth and Fifth Topics: The Manner in which Referenda Are Held & Fixed Term Parliaments* (21 June 2018), p.10, available at: *https://citizensassembly.ie/wp-content/uploads/2023/02/Final-Report-on-Manner-in-which-Referenda-are-Held-Fixed-Term-Parliaments.pdf.*

and the Electoral Commission was active during the campaigns for the Thirty-ninth and Fortieth Amendments. Sixty-nine per cent of the Citizens' Assembly recommended the facilitation of citizens' initiatives to propose amendments to the Constitution.[252] This proposal would require a constitutional amendment. It remains to be seen whether this proposal will gain political traction.

3–92 The referendum on marriage equality is an example of the blending of the symbolic and legal effects of constitutional provisions. Some argued that there was no need to open up the definition of marriage to same-sex couples as many (but not all) of the rights and obligations of marriage were conferred on such couples by means of the Civil Partnership and Certain Rights and Obligations of Cohabitants Act 2010. Others argued that through the symbolic and legal prioritisation of heterosexual marriage in Article 41, the Constitution props up homophobic aspects of our culture which impacts negatively on society generally and on homosexual people in particular. It is notable that since the passing of the marriage equality referendum, the Government has amended s.37 of the Employment Equality Act 1998 to offer homosexual and lesbian teachers some protection within religious-run institutions.[253] Prior to this amendment, gay and lesbian teachers and medical staff felt unable to disclose their sexual orientation for fear of being dismissed. Religious-run institutions were previously exempted from the obligation not to discriminate on the basis of sexual orientation, as priority was given to the religious ethos of the institution.

3–93 Finally, Article 45 of the Constitution directs the Oireachtas to take account of various principles when enacting laws. These principles are in the arena of socio-economic rights but, unlike the civil and political rights we have looked at up to this point, the Constitution provides that they are non-cognisable in court. The sole cognisable socio-economic right that is explicit in the Constitution is located outside Article 45: the

[252] Citizens' Assembly, *Report and Recommendations of the Citizens' Assembly on the Fourth and Fifth Topics: The Manner in which Referenda Are Held & Fixed Term Parliaments* (21 June 2018), p.11, available at: *https://citizensassembly.ie/wp-content/uploads/2023/02/Final-Report-on-Manner-in-which-Referenda-are-Held-Fixed-Term-Parliaments.pdf*.

[253] Equality (Miscellaneous Provisions) Act 2015, passed on 10 December 2015. This Act was commenced on 1 January 2016. See the Equality (Miscellaneous Provisions) Act 2015 (Commencement) Order 2015 (S.I. No. 610 of 2015).

provision of education under Article 42. The courts have also reaffirmed the existence of the derived socio-economic right to seek work in *NHV v Minister for Justice and Equality*.[254] In the panel discussion in the Convention on the Constitution on whether economic, social and cultural rights should be better protected in our Constitution, it was postulated that if such rights had been cognisable at the time of the financial crisis, then it and the subsequent budgetary responses would have been handled differently by the Government.[255] In the end, when asked to consider if the Constitution should be amended to provide stronger protection for economic, social and cultural rights, 85 per cent of the Convention on the Constitution members said "yes".[256] They also recommended the specific enumeration of some economic, social and cultural rights. These included housing, social security, rights for persons with disabilities, healthcare, and language and cultural rights. To date, despite attempts by opposition members of the Oireachtas, there has been no referendum on adding socio-economic rights to the Constitution.

3–94 This raises the question as to whether courts should recognise more socio-economic rights as derived rights. The general tenor of jurisprudence in this arena is that protection (or not) of socio-economic rights is best left to the executive. In the seminal case of *O'Reilly v Limerick Corporation*, this argument was accepted by the High Court, where Costello J. determined that decisions on the distribution of public resources (in this case, on the provision of resources for halting sites) must be done fairly and with reference to the common good, such a decision being properly for the executive rather than the judiciary.[257] Accordingly, the courts were precluded by the separation of powers from adjudicating on the claim.[258] Costello J. suggested instead that

[254] [2018] 1 I.R. 246, in particular see 313–318.

[255] It was noted that the Latvian Government was helped in its negotiations with international lenders because it could refer to specific socio-economic rights in the Latvian Constitution that had to be protected. *Eighth Report of the Convention on the Constitution: Economic, Social and Cultural (ESC) Rights* (March 2014), p.25, available at: *https://citizensassembly.ie/wp-content/uploads/ESC-Rights.pdf.*

[256] *Eighth Report of the Convention on the Constitution: Economic, Social and Cultural (ESC) Rights* (March 2014), p.6.

[257] [1989] I.L.R.M. 181. It is worth noting that Costello J. subsequently resiled from this position: L. Thornton, "Declan Costello (1926-2011) & Irish Socio-Economic Rights Jurisprudence", available at: *https://liamthornton.ie/2011/06/08/declan-costello-1926-2011-irish-socio-economic-rights-jurisprudence/.*

[258] [1989] I.L.R.M. 181 at 195.

Travellers should argue their case "in Leinster House rather than in the Four Courts".[259] Yet, as Whyte noted, the problem with such an approach is that minority needs are not prioritised or protected because of the limited political influence of minority constituents.[260] Similarly, in *TD v Minister for Education*, Keane C.J. spoke of his "gravest doubts" that judges should recognise any form of socio-economic right as being derived from Article 40.[261]

3–95 There does seem to be some movement from this position, evidenced by the *NHV* case and other judgments. In *Re Health (Amendment) (No. 2) Bill 2004*, the Supreme Court stated that "in a discrete case ... the normal discretion of the Oireachtas in the distribution or spending of public monies could be constrained by a constitutional obligation to provide shelter and maintenance for those with exceptional needs."[262] Similarly, Mac Eochaidh J. held in *CA and TA v Minister for Justice and Equality* that in an appropriate case where the State breached a socio-economic right, a court can require the State to "spend money" in order to remedy this rights breach.[263] However, it appears that the correct case has not yet been put before the courts. For a brief moment, it was hoped that *BM and JM v Minister for Social Protection*[264] would be the one. In this case, Hyland J. in the High Court had rejected the argument that Article 41.2 of the Constitution could be utilised to require the State to further financially support a mother who was providing round-the-clock care to her son who had a disability. In granting a "leap-frog" appeal, the Supreme Court noted that this was an issue of systemic importance and they would consider whether, if at all, Article 41.2 requires support for carers at a particular financial level.[265]

3–96 However, the Supreme Court's decision in *BM and JM v Minister for Social Protection* did not provide the hoped-for outcome and aligns with other cases where judges are asked to vindicate socio-economic

[259] [1989] I.L.R.M. 181 at 195.

[260] G. Whyte, "Welfare Law – Travellers and the Law" (1988) 10 D.U.L.J. 189 at 195–196.

[261] [2001] 4 I.R. 259 at 282. See also the comments of Murphy J. in *TD v Minister for Education* [2001] 4 I.R. 259 at 316.

[262] [2005] 1 I.R. 105 at 166.

[263] [2014] IEHC 532 at para.12.6. See further, *Fundamentals of the Irish Legal System*, 1st edn (Dublin: Round Hall, 2016), pp.42–45.

[264] [2023] IEHC 359.

[265] [2023] IESCDET 131 at paras 9 and 14.

rights.[266] The appellant mother was entitled to carer's allowance, a means-tested social welfare benefit.[267] The entire family income is considered when determining what weekly rate a carer may be entitled to. The appellant argued that taking her partner's income into account breached the State's obligations under Article 41.2. The net effect of this was to reduce BM's carer's allowance payment by half. The Supreme Court determined that Article 41.2 of the Constitution "is not readily capable of legal assessment or application in the same way as other, differently expressed, constitutional rights."[268] The Oireachtas was (and is) entitled to legislate to grant differentiated rates of entitlement to carer's allowance based on entire household income.[269] Article 41.2 was interpreted as having "no bearing" on this case.[270] Collins J. held that Article 41.2 "does not commit the State to the provision of any particular form or level of support or giving individual mothers any legally enforceable right to support from the State."[271]

Box 3.4: Time to Reflect

At the beginning of the chapter you were asked to draft your own Constitution. Return to that draft now and ask yourself the following questions:

- Is there anything in your original draft that you would amend?
- Are there additional points that you think should be included that did not occur to you when you first drafted it?
- Have you included rights in your Constitution that are not included in the 1937 one? Why (not)?

F. Conclusion

3–97 In this chapter we have considered the legal and symbolic functions that constitutions perform and we have examined the provisions of the Irish Constitution, paying particular attention to the rights provisions. As

[266] [2024] IESC 51.
[267] See Collins J.'s succinct summary of legislative entitlement to carer's allowance: [2024] IESC 51 at paras 6–17 of his decision.
[268] [2024] IESC 51 at para.105 per Collins J.
[269] [2024] IESC 51 at paras 120–122 per Collins J.
[270] [2024] IESC 51 at para.123 per Collins J.
[271] [2024] IESC 51 at para.120 per Collins J.

should be clear from this discussion, the Constitution is an enormously important legal document in the regulation of the State and in protecting us from abuses by the State. This importance is emphasised by the fact that, unlike other legal rule forms, amendment of the Constitution is not possible merely on the whim of the executive or legislature. Equally, however, because the Constitution performs such important legal and symbolic functions, its provisions need to be continually under review to ensure that it reflects the interests of an evolving society. The recognition that the Constitution is a living document by judges in their interpretation of constitutional provisions goes some way towards ensuring that this is done, but we too have a role to play in the process of updating. If we believe that the Constitution needs to be reformed, then it is incumbent on us to make these wishes known to our elected representatives. While constitutions do derive from a particular historical and philosophical perspective, as noted in the opening quote to this chapter, unlike that quote, it is not just the interests of the "politically dominant class" that the 1937 Constitution represents. As the Preamble to the Constitution provides, "[w]e the people of Éire ... [d]o hereby adopt, enact and give to ourselves this Constitution".

Chapter 4

Legislation

> "To reach a conclusion on this matter involved the court in wading through a monstrous legislative morass, staggering from stone to stone and ignoring the marsh gas exhaling from the forest of schedules lining the way on each side. I regarded it at one time, I must confess, as a slough of despond through which the court would never drag its feet, but I have, by leaping from tussock to tussock as best I might, eventually, pale and exhausted, reached the other side … ."
>
> *Davy v Leeds Corporation* [1964] 1 W.L.R. 1218 at 1224–1225 per Harman L.J.

In this chapter we:

- define primary and secondary legislation;
- evaluate the status of secondary legislation in Ireland;
- explore the role of the judge in interpreting legislation;
- introduce the main statutory interpretation techniques used by judges;
- consider why statutory interpretation questions arise.

A. Introduction

4–01 Legislation is written law that has gone through the various stages of the legislative process, a process that will be considered in Ch.7. Legislation is the second highest ranking domestically produced source of law in Ireland and this positioning is set and protected by the Constitution. Legislation is clearly stated to be of lesser authority than the Constitution in Article 15.4.2° where it is provided that any piece of legislation that is contrary to the Constitution is invalid. Those to whom the Constitution gives power to enact domestic legislation are directed in Article 15.4.1° to do so with the Constitution's supremacy in mind.

4–02 Exclusive law-making power is given to the Oireachtas, which comprises both Houses of Parliament and the President, by Article 15.2.1°. This means that, as is to be expected in a constitutional democracy, valid legislation can only be enacted by representatives who have been elected by the people either directly (as in the case for TDs, the President, and for some Senators) or indirectly (remaining Senators).[1] The vesting of the law-making function in the legislature has consequences for the third-ranked domestically produced source of law: the common law. Common law will be considered in the next chapter, but for present purposes it is sufficient to note that common law principles derive from the judgments of judges handed down in courts over the centuries. Article 15.2.1° means that the Oireachtas is entitled to abolish or modify any common law principle and once the legislature has intervened, judges must apply the new law as written.

4–03 In this chapter, our focus is on legislation. We will first consider the differing types of legislation that are enacted in Ireland. We will then explain why problems arise in interpreting legislation, and will encounter the various techniques that the courts have developed to resolve these problems. As will be clear by the end of the chapter, although legislation outranks case law as a source of law, judges still perform an important function in determining the meaning to be given to a particular word or phrase in a contested legislative provision. Therefore, as with Ch.3, we will spend a lot of time considering case law in this chapter.

B. Primary and Secondary Legislation

4–04 Legislation is divided into two categories: primary and secondary. Primary legislation is any statute that has gone through the legislative process and it consists of sections and subsections that set out legal rules, procedures and penalties, and establishes governance mechanisms. This is what most people think of when they think of legislation. However, when we speak of legislation as a primary source of law, we are referring not only to primary legislation but also to secondary legislation, as the latter derives from and gives effect to the former.

---

[1] Senators are indirectly elected by the people in the sense that Senators are selected from vocational panels by outgoing Senators and incoming Dáil deputies and county councillors. For further on the composition of the Oireachtas, see Ch.7, para.7–14.

4–05 Most pieces of primary legislation contain a provision or provisions allowing a designated person or body to enact secondary or delegated legislation. This is for two main reasons. First, as you will discover in Ch.7, the legislative process is very time-consuming and in order to use legislative time more efficiently, the Oireachtas tries to simplify the process by leaving a lot of the detail out of the primary Act and delegating the detail to some person or body. This allows the Oireachtas to focus on the principles and policies sought to be implemented by the Bill in question. Second, the detail in delegated legislation is often very technical and complicated, and it is a more efficient use of time and resources to delegate the detail to those with expertise in the area rather than leaving it to the Oireachtas. Given the amount of secondary legislation enacted each year, this seems like a sensible division of labour.[2]

4–06 It is important to emphasise that secondary legislation can only exist if the primary Act has a section or sections identifying a person or body to whom power is delegated and specifying what powers they have. If a statute does not contain such a provision or provisions, then there can be no delegated legislation attached to that particular statute. This is why the primary piece of legislation is often called the parent Act. There can be no child (secondary legislation) without a parent (primary legislation). The subordinate status of secondary legislation also explains why the powers of the delegate are limited to, for example, giving effect to the principles and policies of the parent Act. How a court determines whether a delegate has strayed too far into the legislative domain will be considered in more detail in Section B.2(b)(i) below.

1. Primary Legislation

4–07 Primary legislation can be subdivided into three main categories:

(a) Acts to amend the Constitution;
(b) Public General Acts; and
(c) Private Acts.

[2] In 2022, 52 statutes were enacted as compared to 747 statutory instruments. In 2023, the respective numbers were 41 and 711. It has been noted that figures such as these are in fact a dramatic under-estimate of the amount of delegated legislation enacted, as there are other categories of secondary legislation not included in this tally. R. Byrne, P. McCutcheon, L. Cahillane and E. Roche-Cagney, *Byrne and McCutcheon on the Irish Legal System*, 7th edn (Dublin: Bloomsbury Professional, 2020), para.13.124.

(a) Acts to amend the Constitution

4–08 As noted in Ch.3, the Constitution can only be amended by the people by means of a referendum. Accordingly, unlike ordinary legislation, the passing of a statute to amend the Constitution by the Oireachtas does not bring about the desired change. The legislative process is different to that of ordinary legislation, in that the proposed addition (for example, the insertion of Article 40.3.3° into the Constitution in 1983), deletion (for example, the removal of Article 40.3.3° from the Constitution in 2018) or amendment (for example, the removal of the "special position" of the Catholic Church and the recognition given to other named religious denominations from Article 44 in 1973) of existing constitutional wording is put to the people for us to vote on whether we accept or reject it prior to the legislation being sent to the President for signature.

(b) Public General Acts

4–09 The majority of legislation passed by the Oireachtas falls into this category. Public General Acts are statutes that are directed at the community at large. This means that everyone is or could be subject to their provisions. For example, the majority of us do not commit serious criminal offences. However, if we were to commit a serious offence, then we would be subject to the penalties set in a statute for that offence. If you committed a theft, the maximum penalty you would face is set at 10 years' imprisonment in s.4 of the Criminal Justice (Theft and Fraud Offences) Act 2001. Similarly, the majority of us do not care full-time for persons with medical needs, but if such a necessity arose, then we could be eligible for the carer's allowance, the basis for which is set out in ss.179–186 of the Social Welfare Consolidation Act 2005, as amended.[3] These two examples illustrate that public general legislation does not always impact on us directly, but that it could, depending on our personal circumstances and context.

(c) Private Acts

4–10 The final category of primary legislation is Private Acts. These statutes are directed at an individual body/bodies or person/people. For example, the MacSwiney (Pension) Act 1950 was enacted to provide

[3] Further details are fleshed out by the Social Welfare (Consolidated Claims, Payments and Control) Regulations 2007 (S.I. No. 142 of 2007).

an annual pension for Muriel MacSwiney who was widowed when her husband, Terence MacSwiney, died in 1920 during a hunger strike when he was imprisoned for sedition during the War of Independence.[4] This form of statute is very rare. Only four Private Acts were enacted between 1992 and 2012.[5] Between then and December 2024, only one further such statute has been enacted: the Royal Hibernian Academy (Amendment) Act 2023. Because a Private Act is directed at an individual or at a body, it can affect an individual's rights and duties and, for this reason, the legislative process for Private Bills differs from that of other legislation. This will be discussed further in Ch.7.[6]

Box 4.1: Key Provisions to Look for in Legislation[7]

A statute is divided into sections and subsections. Larger statutes have Parts and sometimes Schedules. Parts group relevant sections together for ease of reference. For example, the Digital Services Act 2024 has four Parts and all of the sections relating to the amendment of the Broadcasting Act 2009 are to be found in Pt 2. Parts can be further subdivided into chapters, again for organisation purposes, e.g. Pt 3 of the Digital Services Act 2024 consists of 39 sections divided between 10 chapters. Schedules are appendices to the statute and contain material that would clutter the Act if included in the sections, e.g. the Misuse of Drugs (Amendment) Act 2015 has two schedules, the first of which inserts a list of 51 drugs into the Schedule of controlled drugs in the Misuse of Drugs Act 1977.

When reading a statute for the first time, there are two key sections that you should always look for. These are the interpretation/definition section and the commencement section. The interpretation/definition section, typically s.1 or s.2, provides definitions of various words or phrases that will be used in the statute. It is an important section for statutory interpretation purposes and will be discussed further in Section F of this chapter. In statutes up until late 2005, the word "interpretation" was used

4 At the time of his death, MacSwiney was the serving Lord Mayor of Cork. For more on his life and death, see D. Hannigan, *Terence MacSwiney: The Hunger Strike that Rocked an Empire* (Dublin: O'Brien Press, 2010).

5 Houses of the Oireachtas Joint Committee on Standing Orders (Private Business), *Report on the Revision of Standing Orders Relative to Private Business 1939* (Dublin: Houses of the Oireachtas, 2012), p.1. These were the Limerick Markets Act 1992, the Altamont (Amendment of Deed of Trust) Act 1993, the Trinity College, Dublin (Charters and Letters Patent Amendment) Act 2000, and the Royal College of Surgeons in Ireland (Charters Amendment) Act 2003.

6 See Ch.7, Box 7.3.

7 For further on this, see Ch.15, Section B.

to describe this section. The word "definition" was used for the first time in the Adoptive Leave Act 2005 and is the word currently used.

The commencement section, typically the first or last section of a statute,[8] gives power to a designated person or body to commence the statute either in whole or in part. This means that one or more sections of the statute did not come into force on the day the President signed the statute. For example, the Public Health (Sunbeds) Act 2014 was signed into law on 24 June 2014. However, s.25(2) provides that the Act, either in whole or in part, does not come into force until the Minister for Health issues commencement orders. This provision allows the Minister to commence different sections on different days, and even to commence different subsections of a section on different days. For example, s.17(1)(a)–(k), (m) and (2)–(5) were commenced on 17 July 2014 by the Public Health (Sunbeds) Act 2014 (Commencement) Order 2014.[9] However, s.17(1)(l) was not commenced until 2 March 2015 by the Public Health (Sunbeds) Act 2014 (Commencement) Order 2015.[10] The entire Act, bar s.14, has been commenced at the time of writing.[11]

If the section you think may be applicable to a legal question you have been asked to answer has not been commenced, then it is legally irrelevant as it is not yet law. In order to see if the statute/section has been commenced, you should use the Irish Statute Book website (*www.irishstatutebook.ie*). This resource will be discussed in detail in Ch.14.[12] If a statute does not have a commencement section, then the entire Act comes into force on the date it is signed into law by the President.[13]

You can easily determine if an Act has either of these sections by looking at the arrangement of sections/table of contents at the beginning of the statute or by looking at the marginal notes (words in the margin of the statute summarising the content of the section) or section headings (marginal notes moved to the top of each section). The arrangement of sections/marginal notes combination was used in statutes prior to the enactment of the Protection of Life During Pregnancy Act 2013, which was signed into law in July 2013. Every statute passed since July 2013, including this Act, uses the table of contents/definitions combination.

8 Sometimes the commencement section may be exclusive to one Part of a statute. For example, the entirety of the State Airports (Shannon Group) Act 2014 commenced on the date of enactment, bar Pt 6 which required commencement orders pursuant to s.43.

9 S.I. No. 299 of 2014.

10 S.I. No. 37 of 2015.

11 The failure to commence s.14 was one of several examples given by Sheehy Skeffington in an article where she questions whether a delegate's failure to commence provisions without valid articulated reasons contravenes the separation of powers and amounts to an unconstitutional repeal or amendment of primary legislation; P. Sheehy Skeffington, "Commencement Orders: A Creeping Incursion into the Legislature's Law-Making Domain?" (2018) 59 *Irish Jurist* 93 at 116.

12 See Ch.14, Section C.1(a).

13 Article 25.4.1°.

2. Secondary Legislation

4–11 Secondary legislation can only exist if a primary parent Act explicitly identifies a person or body to whom power is delegated and specifies the terms of that delegated power. Sometimes the delegate is given quite limited technical powers, such as issuing commencement orders or changing fines payable. In other cases, the delegate may be able to play a significant part in how the law in question operates.[14] For example, s.2(2) of the Misuse of Drugs Act 1977 empowers the delegate to designate a substance, product or preparation as a controlled drug, the unlawful possession of which becomes a criminal offence. Section 78(1) of the Health Act 2004 gives the delegate very wide discretion to give effect to the principles and policies contained in it:

> "The Minister may make regulations—
> (a) for any purpose in relation to which regulations are provided for in this Act,
> (b) for prescribing any matter or thing referred to in this Act as prescribed or to be prescribed, and
> (c) generally for the purpose of giving effect to this Act."

It would be wrong to assume that these powers can be exercised without limit. We will consider these limits in Section B.2(b) below.

4–12 Frequently, the designated delegate is the Minister with responsibility for the area in question. The Minister for Health and Children is the relevant delegate in the Health Act 2004.[15] While you might query a Minister's knowledge of their portfolio, particularly if they have just been assigned new responsibility, it is worth remembering that they are supported by experts in their Department and they also engage in consultation with interested groups in the exercise of their powers. In other cases, the Oireachtas has delegated power to other persons/bodies, including local authorities, various boards and QUANGOs (Quasi-Autonomous Non-Governmental Organisations). The reason for

[14] L. Cherkassky et al, *Legal Skills* (Hampshire: Palgrave Macmillan, 2011), p.9; E. Finch and S. Fafinski, *Legal Skills*, 8th edn (Oxford: OUP, 2021), p.27.

[15] Although s.78 does not state which Minister, if you look up the interpretation section of the Health Act 2004, you will find that the Minister for Health and Children is identified as the relevant Minister. In 2011, the portfolios of health and children were divided into separate ministries and the relevant Minister today is the Minister for Health.

this is simple: the Oireachtas wishes to delegate the detail to those who have expertise in the area in question. It makes sense that the Medical Council would be better placed to organise its own functioning, including the running of the Fitness to Practise Committee, than a Minister; hence, s.11 of the Medical Practitioners Act 2007 empowers the Medical Council to do this.

4–13 The Oireachtas has a limited role to play in the passing of some delegated legislation. Secondary legislation takes the form of statutory instruments, or SIs, and a parent Act generally provides that SIs drafted by a delegate should be laid before one or both Houses of the Oireachtas for a specified period of time. In other words, the draft SI is made available for viewing by members of the relevant House(s). At the expiry of this period of time, the relevant House(s) can pass the SI either by

- positive resolution (Oireachtas must approve of the SI in its entirety[16]), or
- negative resolution (Oireachtas must not vote against the SI).

The parent Act will usually state which of the above is required. For example, s.80 of the Health Act 2004 requires a negative resolution within 21 sitting days of the regulation or order being laid before it. In practice, however, it is unlikely that any piece of delegated legislation would be rejected, as they are typically enacted by Ministers and the party whip system can be used to ensure their passage.[17] It has also been found that SIs that require review do not seem to attract any more attention than those that do not, with Hunt unable to find a single SI that had been annulled.[18] This is an issue because, as will be discussed in Section B.2(b)(i) below, this "dormant force for ensuring democratic accountability"[19] has assumed

[16] Unlike primary legislation, TDs or Senators are not able to table amendments to the SI, so it is either passed in its entirety or annulled in its entirety. It is very unlikely that a statutory instrument will be annulled, as they generally are produced by Ministers and the Government controls both Houses of the Oireachtas.

[17] R. Byrne, P. McCutcheon, L. Cahillane and E. Roche-Cagney, *Byrne and McCutcheon on the Irish Legal System*, 7th edn (Dublin: Bloomsbury Professional, 2020), para.13.166. The party whip is a member of the political party who has been appointed to ensure that all other members adhere to the party line when votes are cast. If they refuse to do so, then the errant TDs/Senators will be disciplined by the party.

[18] B. Hunt, *The Role of the Houses of the Oireachtas in the Scrutiny of Legislation* (Dublin: Houses of the Oireachtas, 2010), p.83.

[19] C. O'Brien, "The Principles and Policies Test and the Constitutional Requirement for Certainty" (2018) 41 *Dublin University Law Journal* 79 at 96. O'Brien proposes

greater (but not determinative) importance in assessing whether a delegated power is constitutional or not following the Supreme Court decision in *Bederev v Ireland*.[20]

(a) Categories of secondary legislation

4–14 Section 1(1) of the Statutory Instruments Act 1947 defines a statutory instrument as an "order, regulation, rule, scheme or bye-law made in exercise of a power conferred by statute". An order is an instrument that has a "once-off" effect. The orders that you will most commonly encounter in the course of your legal studies will be commencement orders, discussed previously. To repeat, if a delegate has been given power to commence various section(s) or Part(s) of a statute, then those section(s) or Part(s) do not have force of law until they are commenced.

4–15 Regulations flesh out and give effect to the aims and objectives established in the parent Act. An example would be the Organisation of Working Time (Determination of Pay for Holidays) Regulations 1997,[21] which was enacted to give effect to provisions in the Organisation of Working Time Act 1997. That Act regulates the number of hours that can be worked, the minimum number of holiday days one is entitled to, holiday pay, and rest breaks. The Regulations set out in more detail how holiday pay is to be calculated. Rules generally refer to provisions that concern the operation of the courts, for example the Rules of the Superior Courts 1986.[22] Schemes usually set a scale of fees and charges. Byrne et al give the example of s.15(5)(a) of the Central Bank Act 1989, which enables the Central Bank of Ireland to make "schemes for granting pensions, allowances and gratuities on retirement or death" to its employees.[23]

4–16 A bye-law was defined in the English case of *Kruse v Johnson* as "an ordinance affecting the public or some portion of the public, imposed by

a more vigorous review process where a delegate is tasked with bringing criminal offences into law because of the specific constitutional considerations raised by the criminalisation of behaviour.

20 [2016] IESC 34. See also *Delaney v Personal Injuries Assessment Board* [2024] IESC 10. These cases are discussed in further detail in Section B.2(b)(i).

21 S.I. No. 475 of 1997.

22 S.I. No. 15 of 1986.

23 R. Byrne, P. McCutcheon, L. Cahillane and E. Roche-Cagney, *Byrne and McCutcheon on the Irish Legal System*, 7th edn (Dublin: Bloomsbury Professional, 2020), para.13.127.

some authority clothed with statutory powers ordering something to be done or not to be done, and accompanied by some sanction or penalty for non-observance".[24] This definition was affirmed as being applicable in Ireland by the Supreme Court in *State (Harrington) v Wallace*.[25] Bye-laws are frequently enacted by bodies such as city and county councils to regulate issues such as littering and parking. However, they are not confined to minor matters and can attract significant penalties. For example, then-TDs Clare Daly and Mick Wallace were each convicted of two charges of breaching airport bye-laws at Shannon Airport when they entered a restricted area on 22 July 2014 to inspect US military airplanes that were refuelling there.[26] They were fined €1,000 for each charge, amounting to €4,000 between them. Their refusal to pay the fines resulted in their brief imprisonment in December 2015.[27]

4–17 Section 2(1)(b) of the Statutory Instruments Act 1947 requires that certain SIs must be publicised in *Iris Oifigiúil*, specifically those enacted by the President, the Government or a member of Government, a Minister of State or a body that exercises a governmental or administrative function. The reason for this is that these bodies could implement SIs with far-reaching implications for the public at large, and by requiring them to publish in *Iris Oifigiúil*, it is hoped that the general public becomes aware of any obligations that might arise.

(b) Limits on secondary legislation

4–18 Although provisions that delegate the power to enact secondary legislation can seem very broad—for example, see the terms of s.78(1) of the Health Act 2004 above—the scope of the power to delegate is subject to four important limitations, and if any are breached, then the lawfulness of either the section in the statute that grants the delegate power or the delegated legislation enacted by such a delegate can be challenged. The first three limitations are constitutional, with two focusing on the section of the parent Act that authorises the creation of delegated legislation, and the third on the delegate. First, the parent

[24] [1898] 2 Q.B. 91 at 96.
[25] [1988] I.R. 290 at 294.
[26] Article 4(1) of the Airport Bye-Laws 1994 (S.I. No. 425 of 1994). They were convicted on 22 April 2015.
[27] F. Kelly and K. Hayes, "Wallace and Daly spend brief spell in Limerick Prison", *Irish Times*, 10 December 2015.

Act must not give unlimited powers to the delegate that permit them to assume legislative power, as such a function is the exclusive purview of the Oireachtas. Second, the Oireachtas cannot empower a delegate to breach the Constitution. Third, the functions given to the delegate must not offend against the separation of powers. If the parent Act allows for any of these things, then that section is unconstitutional. However, in deciding these issues, the courts apply the presumption of constitutionality previously considered in Ch.3, Section D.1.

4–19 The fourth limitation focuses not on the parent Act but on the delegated legislation enacted. The delegate must exercise their powers only to give effect to the parent Act. If the delegate goes beyond the powers granted to them by the parent Act in enacting secondary legislation, then they are acting ultra vires (beyond their powers). In such cases, the secondary legislation is declared to be unlawful; the section in the parent Act that authorises the delegate to enact secondary legislation is not affected. Let us turn now to consider the application of these limitations.

(i) Constitutional considerations

4–20 The original test for establishing whether a statutory section that empowers a delegate to enact delegated legislation is permissible under Article 15.2.1° was set in *Cityview Press Ltd v An Chomhairle Oiliúna*, where the Supreme Court held:

> "[T]he test is whether that which is challenged ... is more than the mere giving effect to principles and policies which are contained in the statute itself. If it be, then it is not authorised; for such would constitute a purported exercise of legislative power by an authority ... not permitted to do so under the Constitution. On the other hand ... if the law is laid down in the statute and details only are filled in or completed by the designated Minister or subordinate body ... there is no unauthorised delegation of legislative power."[28]

This test became known as the "principles and policies" test. A policy is "an objective of some sort which parliament wishes to achieve by

[28] [1980] I.R. 381 at 399.

effecting an alteration of the law".[29] A principle sets boundaries on how the delegate can attain those objectives.[30]

4–21 Originally having "almost canonical status" regarding the appropriate limits to be placed on the exercise of delegated powers,[31] more recently the courts have begun to depart from the principles and policies test as articulated in *Cityview*. For example, in *DPP v McGrath*, the *Cityview* test was described as helpful but "cannot be considered an infallible guide".[32] Instead of requiring the parent Act to set out all the principles and policies that will guide the delegate's choices, the question has instead become whether the delegated power is limited or unlimited. That limitation can be in the form of principles and policies, but delegated powers can also be bounded by other means. In *Bederev v Ireland*, parliamentary supervision of the delegate's actions through the power to review and annul proposed secondary legislation prior to its taking effect was recognised as one such limit, although not necessarily a decisive one.[33] Similarly, in *Delaney v Personal Injuries Assessment Board*, legislative oversight was highlighted but it was also stated that it was not determinative of whether the delegation of power in question was constitutional or not.[34]

4–22 In *O'Sullivan v Sea Fisheries Protection Authority*, O'Donnell J. reframed the question from whether the primary legislation had set all

[29] *Laurentiu v Minister for Justice* [1999] 4 I.R. 26 at 90.

[30] C. O'Brien, "The Principles and Policies Test and the Constitutional Requirement for Certainty" (2018) 41 *Dublin University Law Journal* 79 at 83, citing N. Maddox, "Legislation by Delegation – The Principles and Policies Test in Irish Law" (2004) 22 *Irish Law Times* 293.

[31] *Collins v Minister for Finance* [2013] IEHC 530 at para.99.

[32] [2021] IESC 66 at para.68.

[33] [2016] IESC 34 at para.24. This was in addition to the principles and polices that could be identified within the statute. For criticism of *Bederev*, see M. Cahill and S. Ó Conaill, "Judicial Restraint Can Also Undermine Constitutional Principles: An Irish Caution" (2017) 36(2) *University of Queensland Law Journal* 259 at 267–268; L. Cahillane, "Principles, Policies and Fair Procedures after *O'Sullivan v Sea Fisheries Protection Authority* and *Crayden Fishing Company Ltd v Sea Fisheries Protection Authority*" (2019) 1 *Irish Supreme Court Review* 51 at 58, citing G. Hogan, G. Whyte, D. Kenny and R. Walsh, *Kelly: The Irish Constitution* (Dublin: Bloomsbury Professional, 2018), p.304.

[34] See [2024] IESC 10 at para.173 (per Collins J), and at para.46 (per Charleton J). While Collins and Charleton JJ. were in the minority in finding that the delegated legislation at issue was constitutional, Collins J.'s discussion of the delegation of legislative power issue was concurred with by other judges. See, e.g. Faherty J. at para.27 and Haughton J. at para.88.

principles and policies (the *Cityview* approach) to: "[i]s the area of rule-making delegated, so broad as to constitute a trespass by the delegate or subordinate on an area reserved to the Oireachtas by Article 15.2.1?"[35] He continued that while it may be necessary to look for principles and policies to limit the scope of what would otherwise be an impermissibly wide delegation power, it would not be necessary to look for them where a power is narrowly defined and constrained within the statute. This broadening of approach was confirmed in *Náisiúnta Leictreach Contraitheoir Éireann Cuideachta Faoi Theorainn Ráthaíochta (NECI) v Labour Court* where the Supreme Court held that principles and policies in a piece of legislation are "a series of indicators or pointers to the ultimate issue: whether or not the Oireachtas has acted as sole *legislator*, or has impermissibly delegated legislative power."[36] MacMenamin J. explained:

> "[R]ather than seeking all principles and policies, a court should ask the question as to whether the absence of such principles and policies actually trespasses on the power of the Oireachtas? For this purpose, a focus on the breadth or narrowness of the delegation may be a useful heuristic. This may involve an approach whereby, within a narrow area of delegation, a court should consider whether the legislature has considered the possible choices, and found them all to be acceptable. This must, surely, be the correct approach, again based on the text of the Constitution itself."[37]

4–23 MacMenamin J. in *NECI* also helpfully summarised and endorsed Charleton J.'s discussion in *Bederev* of what the appropriate approach of a court should be when faced with a question of whether there has been an unconstitutional abrogation of legislative power:

> "First, an assessment of the Act in order to determine whether or not it contains sufficient principles and policies, should be based on a reasonable, but not far-reaching, examination of the provisions. Second, the purpose of the various principles and policies criteria is to ask whether the legislation sets boundaries, in the sense of defining rules of conduct, or guidelines. Third, does the legislation have defined subject matter, and contain basic conditions of fact and

35 [2017] IESC 75 at para.40.
36 [2021] IESC 36 at para.55 (emphasis in original).
37 [2021] IESC 36 at para.67.

law? Fourth, is the legislative purpose of the provisions discernible by identification of objectives or outcomes, as well as principles? Fifth, is the power delegated sufficiently delimited? Sixth, does the exercise of the subordinate power contain sufficient safeguards? Seventh, the primary question, is there an abdication by the Oireachtas of its constitutional role? These are the key questions."[38]

4–24 It has been argued by academics that *Cityview* has been de facto overruled,[39] with Casey asserting that efforts in *NECI* to suggest doctrinal continuity with *Cityview* were "artificial".[40] However, judges in subsequent cases have continued to insist that there is doctrinal continuity.[41] Whether *Cityview* has been de facto overruled or not, Cahillane has observed that even when it was the governing precedent, the principles and policies test it articulated "may not have been as helpful to judges as first thought", with very few cases ever found to breach it.[42] Cahillane (considering *O'Sullivan*) and Casey (considering *NECI*) both agree that the revised test is a more accurate reflection of how the courts have, in practice, assessed whether a delegation of powers was unconstitutional.[43]

4–25 In assessing the constitutionality or not of a provision, the presumption of constitutionality is also relevant. This presumption was

[38] [2021] IESC 36 at para.63.

[39] M. Cahill and S. Ó Conaill, "Judicial Restraint Can Also Undermine Constitutional Principles: An Irish Caution" (2017) 36(2) *University of Queensland Law Journal* 259 at 268, discussing *Bederev v Ireland* [2016] IESC 34. They argue that this has negative implications for the separation of powers.

[40] C. Casey, "The Supreme Court and the Reformation of the Non-Delegation Doctrine: *Náisiúnta Leictreach Contraitheoir Éireann v The Labour Court*" (2022) 4 *Irish Supreme Court Review* 39 at 52.

[41] For example, Haughton J. writes in *Delaney v Personal Injuries Assessment Board* [2024] IESC 10 at para.88 that the *Cityview* "principles and policies" test was "amplified" in *Bederev v Ireland* [2016] IESC 34. Hogan J. does acknowledge that the test "has moved on somewhat", referring to *NECI* and *McGrath*; *Delaney v Personal Injuries Assessment Board* [2024] IESC 10 at para.63.

[42] L. Cahillane, "Principles, Policies and Fair Procedures after *O'Sullivan v Sea Fisheries Protection Authority* and *Crayden Fishing Company Ltd v Sea Fisheries Protection Authority*" (2019) 1 *Irish Supreme Court Review* 51 at 56.

[43] L. Cahillane, "Principles, Policies and Fair Procedures after *O'Sullivan v Sea Fisheries Protection Authority* and *Crayden Fishing Company Ltd v Sea Fisheries Protection Authority*" (2019) 1 *Irish Supreme Court Review* 51 at 58; C. Casey, "The Supreme Court and the Reformation of the Non-Delegation Doctrine: *Náisiúnta Leictreach Contraitheoir Éireann v The Labour Court*" (2022) 4 *Irish Supreme Court Review* 39 at 49. But see M. Cahill, "From *Cityview* to *NECI* and Judicial Virtues in Action: Afterword to the Foreword by Conor Casey and Oran Doyle" (2024) 44(2) *Dublin University Law Journal* 3 at 9.

discussed in Ch.3, Section D.1, but in brief it provides that if there are two or more possible plausible interpretations to be given to a provision, one of which renders the provision constitutional and the other(s) not, then the provision should be given its constitutional interpretation. In the context of delegated legislation, the courts will construe the powers given to the delegate by the parent Act as narrowly as possible in order to ensure that the section at issue accords with the Constitution. This is both to respect the separation of powers and to give effect to legislative intent.[44] Although the Oireachtas does not draft delegated legislation, it has made a decision to delegate power to someone to do so and that clearly expressed intention is to be respected by the courts.

4–26 The second constitutional limitation placed on the Oireachtas when granting a delegate legislative powers is that the delegate cannot be empowered to breach the Constitution. This is because, pursuant to Article 15.4, the Oireachtas cannot enact unconstitutional legislation. The third constitutional limitation is an application of the separation of powers. In *Delaney v Personal Injuries Assessment Board*,[45] it was found that the Personal Injuries Guidelines, developed under the auspices of the Judicial Council Act 2019 and adopted by the judiciary following a vote, were unconstitutional because they compromised judicial independence. Explaining why he concurred with Faherty and Haughton JJ., Hogan J. was concise:

> "The essential neutrality of judicial adjudication and the disinterested application of the law is irrevocably compromised if judges are seen to have been involved in the making of laws affecting the substantive law which they are then called upon to apply."[46]

However, this does not mean that judges cannot be given delegated powers. Haughton J. gave examples of judges performing constitutionally valid non-judicial functions such as sitting on Committees that set the rules of various courts and on the Judicial Appointments Commission.[47]

---

44 For a contrary view of this use of the presumption of constitutionality, see M. Cahill and S. Ó Conaill, "Judicial Restraint Can Also Undermine Constitutional Principles: An Irish Caution" (2017) 36(2) *University of Queensland Law Journal* 259 at 265.

45 [2024] IESC 10.

46 [2024] IESC 10 at para.65.

47 [2024] IESC 10 at paras 114–117.

If powers are to be delegated to the judiciary, the nature of these powers must be assessed to ensure that judicial independence is not breached or at risk of being perceived so. For the conferral of delegated powers on a judge to be constitutional, two questions must be answered in the affirmative:

1. Does the judge consent to the assumption of the non-judicial function?
2. Is the non-judicial function compatible with the judge's judicial functions?[48]

(ii) Statutory purpose

4–27 The fourth way the lawfulness of a piece of secondary legislation can be challenged is on the basis that it is ultra vires. Here the focus is not on the parent Act but on the SI itself. Because the delegate's powers come from a parent Act, it makes sense that they can only enact delegated legislation that implements the aims and objectives of the parent Act. If a delegate tries to go beyond the powers given to them in the statute, then they are acting ultra vires and the delegated legislation is invalid.

4–28 In order to be intra vires (within the powers), delegated powers must be exercised in good faith and the means by which the aims and objectives are achieved must be reasonable. These requirements are not usually expressly enumerated in the parent Act but have been read into statutes by the courts. In *Cassidy v Minister for Industry and Commerce*,[49] it was determined that good faith did not preclude the existence of multiple motives behind the passing of a ministerial order. The question to be asked was stated by Henchy J. as follows:

> "Where a power to legislate for a particular purpose is delegated and the power is exercised *bona fide* and primarily for that purpose, I consider that the exercise of that power is not vitiated if it is aimed also at the attainment of a subsidiary or consequential purpose which is not inconsistent with the permitted purpose. If the law

[48] [2024] IESC 10 at paras 130–131 per Haughton J., and at paras 68–72 per Faherty J., endorsing *Grollo v Commissioner of Australian Federal Police* (1995) 131 A.L.R. 225.
[49] [1978] I.R. 297.

were otherwise, many delegated powers would be unexercisable, for the permitted purpose frequently encompasses of necessity the attainment of other purposes … ."[50]

4–29 The Supreme Court considered how the existence of bad faith might be established in *Listowel UDC v McDonagh*.[51] The court determined that it would be permissible to consider matters such as what happened in the council meeting where the bye-law was passed, the views of the council members and officials on the bye-law, and the veracity of the opinions they expressed.[52]

4–30 With regard to the reasonableness criterion, *Cassidy* is also pertinent. It was determined that in order for a piece of secondary legislation to be unreasonable, it must effect "such manifest arbitrariness, injustice or partiality that a court would say: 'Parliament never intended to give authority to make such rules; they are unreasonable and *ultra vires*'."[53] This position was reaffirmed in *Island Ferries Teoranta v Minister for Communications, Marine and Natural Resources*.[54]

C. The Judge's Role in Interpreting Legislation

4–31 Courts are frequently called upon to resolve disputes concerning the meaning to be given to a contested word or phrase in a domestically produced piece of legislation, primary or secondary. Indeed, it has been noted by a former Chief Justice, Murray C.J., that questions of statutory interpretation constitute "a high proportion of the decisions on law which the Courts routinely make".[55] When the dispute concerning meaning is resolved, the interpretation of the word or phrase given by the court becomes part of the body of law governing that particular area. In other words, the legislation is now no longer to be read in isolation but has

50 [1978] I.R. 297 at 309.
51 [1968] I.R. 312.
52 R. Byrne, P. McCutcheon, L. Cahillane and E. Roche-Cagney, *Byrne and McCutcheon on the Irish Legal System*, 7th edn (Dublin: Bloomsbury Professional, 2020), para.13.163.
53 [1978] I.R. 297 at 311, quoting Diplock L.J. in *Mixnam's Properties Ltd v Chertsey UDC* [1964] 1 Q.B. 214 at 237.
54 [2015] IESC 95 at para.21.
55 Murray C.J., "Foreword" in D. Dodd, *Statutory Interpretation in Ireland* (Dublin: Tottel Publishing, 2008).

taken on the meaning ascribed to it by the judge or judges who heard the case. Accordingly, the judicial role in interpreting legislation is an important one.

4–32 Judges use various interpretive techniques to deduce the meaning of statutory provisions. However, their use of these techniques is constrained by Article 15.2 of the Constitution, whereby sole legislative power is vested with the Oireachtas. In practical terms, this means that the court is not permitted to interpret legislation in a way that changes the meaning of that legislation; it must interpret the contested word or phrase in a way that best gives effect to what the legislature intended when they enacted the legislation in question. This is known as seeking to give effect to legislative intent. The problem with the concept of "legislative intent" is that it is, in reality, a legal fiction.[56] As you will discover when we look at the legislative process in Ch.7, the enactment of legislation is a very cumbersome process, and while different political parties or individual TDs and Senators might agree to pass a particular piece of legislation, they may have different reasons for supporting it. Alternatively, the opposition parties may be fundamentally opposed to the passage of a particular piece of legislation but they lack the numbers to cause it to founder. In such cases, it would be impossible to speak of a single legislative intent behind the passing of these pieces of legislation. Moreover, as will be discussed later, the subjective intent of individual legislators is irrelevant to the interpretation of legislation.[57] In recognition of these realities, more recently the Supreme Court has described the judges' role in interpreting legislation as being "to ascertain the legal effect attributed to the legislation by a set of rules and presumptions the common law (and latterly statute) has developed for that purpose."[58] Nonetheless, the phrase "legislative intent" continues to be used, not least because it has a statutory basis in s.5 of the Interpretation Act 2005.[59]

[56] A legal fiction is a "fact" created by the court and treated as though it were true even when it is not/cannot be. An example that you might be familiar with is the idea of a corporation as a legal person. We know that a corporation is a business entity, not a person, but the law has granted it personhood in order to affix liability to it rather than to the individuals who operate it.

[57] See Section F.2(c).

[58] *Heather Hill Management Co CLG v An Bord Pleanála* [2022] IESC 43 at para.114.

[59] See further para.4–34.

4–33 In *Heather Hill Management Co CLG v An Bord Pleanála*, the Supreme Court brought together recent decisions and set out four general principles:

(1) Words in a statute should be given their ordinary and natural meaning;
(2) These words, where necessary, should be looked at in the context of the section and the statute as a whole and, if necessary, any past legislation on the same issue;
(3) A court should utilise the canons, maxims, principles and rules of interpretation; and
(4) If this still results in ambiguity, then the court will "seek to discern the intended object of the Act and the reasons the statute was enacted".[60]

The next three sections of this chapter will consider the main statutory interpretation methods used by judges in applying these principles.

4–34 Before we look at these methods, though, a note of caution. As with constitutional interpretation,[61] you will find considerable variety in the approaches individual judges take to statutory interpretation. This "judicial à-la-carteism" is possible because of the variety of interpretive methods available to judges.[62] This is why, for example, you will find that some judges tend to prefer the purposive approach, even though the literal approach is supposed to be the primary approach in Irish law[63] and is indirectly codified as such in s.5 of the Interpretation Act 2005 (the "2005 Act");[64] why the same judge can use different statutory interpretation techniques in respect of two different sections in the same statute;[65] and why two judges in the same case will use different approaches to construe the same provision.[66] Indeed, it was contended in 2010 that

[60] [2022] IESC 43 at para.106.
[61] Considered in Ch.3, Section D.
[62] Law Reform Commission, *Report on Statutory Drafting and Interpretation: Plain Language and the Law* (LRC 61-2000), para.1.10.
[63] Law Reform Commission, *Report on Statutory Drafting and Interpretation: Plain Language and the Law* (LRC 61-2000), para.1.09.
[64] It is indirect because the focus of s.5 is when the literal approach can be departed from.
[65] See *Gooden v St Otteran's Hospital* [2005] 3 I.R. 617, where Hardiman J. applied the purposive approach to one provision in the Mental Treatment Act 1945 and the literal approach to another.
[66] *Lawlor v Flood* [1999] 3 I.R. 107. This case will be discussed further at para.4–37.

legislative attempts to rein in judicial departure from the literal rule with s.5 of the 2005 Act have had "negligible impact on judicial practice".[67] Ten years later, McKechnie J. noted in *AWK (Pakistan) v Minister for Justice and Equality* that despite s.5 of the 2005 Act having been in existence for 15 years at that point, "its full effect and implications have yet to work their way through the case law."[68]

4–35 It is therefore useful to think of these various statutory interpretation techniques as tools rather than as rules, despite the use of the latter term in *Heather Hill Management Co.*[69] As Holland and Webb put it, using the word "rule" "gives the impression that if you follow a particular pattern you will not go wrong. [The word 'rule' also conveys a false] aura of scientific authenticity ... when the reality is ... that interpreting any document is more of an art than a science."[70] This view arguably has more force in Ireland because legislation is subservient to the Constitution. As Curran and Daly write:

> "[There is] a remarkable disparity between the courts' description of statutory interpretation as a mechanical, uncreative process centred around the retrieval of legislative intent, and the far-reaching judicial power inherent in the use of constitutional principles (as well as other public values) as supplementary sources of statutory meaning."[71]

D. The Literal Approach

4–36 Originally there were three canons of interpretation: the literal rule, the golden rule, and the mischief rule. These have been replaced by the literal approach (which is based on the literal rule) and the purposive approach (which is an amalgamation of the golden and mischief rules).

[67] P. Brady, "Constitutional Interpretation and the Irish Supreme Court: some reflections on a neighbouring common law court's approaches to interpretation", Statute Law Society Conference 2010 (Supreme Court, London, 9 October 2010), p.2. Section 5 of the 2005 Act will be considered in more detail in Section F.2(a).

[68] [2020] IESC 10 at para.46.

[69] *Heather Hill Management Co CLG v An Bord Pleanála* [2022] IESC 43 at para.114, quoted at para.4–33.

[70] J. Holland and J. Webb, *Learning Legal Rules*, 11th edn (Oxford: OUP, 2022), p.247. See also, E. Finch and S. Fafinski, *Legal Skills*, 8th edn (Oxford: OUP, 2021), p.76.

[71] C. Curran and E. Daly, "Reappraising the Constitutional Justification for Intentionalism and Literalism in Statutory Interpretation" (2013) 36 *Dublin University Law Journal* 155 at 181.

In this section, we will focus on the literal approach. The literal approach requires the judge to give the word or words in a statute their literal, ordinary and natural meaning. It works from the presumption that the legislature chose the word or words at issue for a reason and, in making that choice, the legislature understood them to have their ordinary meaning. If the legislature had wanted an ordinary word to have a special meaning, then they could have said so by defining it, typically but not exclusively, in the interpretation/definition section of the statute. An example of this is *Bookfinders Ltd v Revenue Commissioners*,[72] where it was held that the bread used to make sandwiches in Subway could not be classified as "bread" for taxation purposes because its sugar content was too high. For bread to be "bread" under the definition set out in paragraph (xii)(d)(II) of the Second Schedule to the Value Added Tax Act 1972, it could not have more than 2 per cent sugar content; the bread used by Subway had 10 per cent.[73]

4–37 The literal approach is promoted as the primary principle of statutory construction in Ireland[74] and has been put on a statutory footing by s.5 of the 2005 Act. It holds this position because it is thought to be the best means of deciphering legislative intent. The prioritising of legislative intent by the courts has its basis in Article 15.2.1°, whereby the Constitution has vested the legislative function in the Oireachtas, and in Article 6 which enshrines the separation of powers. See, for example, the following comments of Denham J. in *Lawlor v Flood*:

> "In applying the ordinary meaning of the words, the Court is enforcing the clear intention of the legislature. This aspect of statutory construction is an essential part of the separation of powers. Further, it is an illustration of appropriate respect by one organ of government to another."[75]

It is, however, interesting that while Denham J. found the literal approach determinative in this case, Hamilton C.J. did not find it similarly useful and he turned to another approach,[76] showing that what is obvious to one judge is not necessarily so to another.

72 [2020] IESC 60.
73 [2020] IESC 60 at paras 92 and 95.
74 *AWK (Pakistan) v Minister for Justice and Equality* [2020] IESC 10 at para.34.
75 [1999] 3 I.R. 107 at 136.
76 Hamilton C.J. used the *in pari materia* technique to divine the purpose of the provision: [1999] 3 I.R. 107 at 119–120. This technique will be considered in Section F.2(b).

4–38 A much-cited example of the application of the literal rule/approach is *Inspector of Taxes v Kiernan*.[77] The question in this case was whether the respondent taxpayer was a "dealer in cattle" for the purposes of s.78 of the Income Tax Act 1967 (the "1967 Act"). He was a pig farmer. He based his case on the fact that in older statutes, the word "cattle" was defined in the interpretation section as including pigs. However, the fact that the interpretation section in the 1967 Act did not include such a clause was determinative:

> "When the legislature used the word 'cattle' ... without ... giving it a definition, was it intended that the word should comprehend pigs? That the word has, or has been held to have, that breadth of meaning in other statutes is not to the point. A word or expression in a given statute must be given meaning and scope according to its immediate context, in line with the scheme and purpose of the particular statutory pattern as a whole, and to an extent that will truly effectuate the particular legislation or a particular definition therein."[78]

Therefore, a dealer in cattle did not include pigs in the specific context of the 1967 Act because an ordinary person would not consider that the word "pigs" included cattle.

4–39 The *Kiernan* case is also important because it emphasises that the literal meaning of a word is what the hypothetical person on the street would understand by the word. As such, recourse should only be made to a dictionary when "alternative meanings, regional uses or other obliquities are shown to cast doubt on the singularity of its ordinary meaning".[79] However, in practice, reference to dictionaries is frequent to confirm the ordinary meaning of a word.[80] In *Delaney v Personal Injuries Assessment Board*, where the meaning of "guidelines" was relevant to one of the issues, Charleton J. observed that, as "every permutation of argued meaning has been contended for to the point of an equation with solid law", recourse to the dictionary was necessary to find that "singularity of ... ordinary meaning".[81]

77 [1981] I.R. 117.
78 [1981] I.R. 117 at 121.
79 [1981] I.R. 117 at 122.
80 R. Byrne, P. McCutcheon, L. Cahillane and E. Roche-Cagney, *Byrne and McCutcheon on the Irish Legal System*, 7th edn (Dublin: Bloomsbury Professional, 2020), para.14.206.
81 [2024] IESC 10 at para.15.

4–40 The literal approach, when strictly invoked, can sometimes lead to a result that could not have been the legislature's intention. However, the courts justify giving a word/phrase such an interpretation on the basis that they cannot amend the clearly written text of a piece of legislation because it would amount to a usurpation of the legislative function. This is so even if the judicial amendment would lead to a more equitable result or to a result that better gives effect to the known or presumed legislative purpose. In *Heather Hill Management Co*, Murray J. acknowledged that the application of well-established statutory interpretation techniques might lead to a result never intended by the Oireachtas, but observed:

> "That is the price of an approach which prefers the application of transparent, coherent and objectively ascertainable principles to the interpretation of legislation, to a situation in which judges construe an Act of the Oireachtas by reference to their individual assessments of what they think parliament ought sensibly to have wished to achieve by the legislation … ."[82]

Consequently, the courts cannot fill in loopholes in legislation or fix obvious errors.

4–41 In *McGrath v McDermott*,[83] the appellants offset capital gains against losses they engineered to reduce their tax bill using a loophole in the Capital Gains Tax Act 1975. The Inspector of Taxes asked the Supreme Court to close this loophole so as to condemn tax-avoidance schemes that were not technically prohibited by statute law. The Supreme Court refused, stating:

> "The courts have not got a function to add to or delete from express statutory provisions so as to achieve objectives which to the courts appear desirable. In rare and limited circumstances words or phrases may be implied into statutory provisions solely for the purpose of making them effective to achieve their expressly avowed objective."[84]

---

82 [2022] IESC 43 at para.114.

83 [1988] I.R. 258.

84 [1988] I.R. 258 at 276. Following this decision, the Oireachtas filled the loophole with legislation: s.86 of the Finance Act 1989.

An example of "rare and limited circumstances" where it is appropriate to imply words or phrases into a statutory provision is the previously encountered situation in Section B.2(b)(ii) where courts read in the good faith and reasonableness requirements for the intra vires exercise of delegated powers. Reading in these requirements does not change the content of the section; it simply ensures that the powers are implemented in accordance with the requirements of constitutional and natural justice.

4–42 In *State (Murphy) v Johnston*,[85] the Supreme Court similarly refused to fix an obvious error in a statute on the basis of the separation of powers. The accused was charged with drink driving pursuant to s.49 of the Road Traffic Act 1961. Section 22 of the Road Traffic (Amendment) Act 1978 allowed a certificate issued by the Medical Bureau of Road Safety to be entered as evidence of the concentration of alcohol in the accused's body. Section 23 of the 1978 Act provided that this certificate was also evidence that the Bureau had complied with the requirements imposed on it "under Part III of the Act of 1968" to ensure that the samples were properly tested. Unfortunately, s.23 should have read "under Part V of the Act of 1968". The certificate was therefore found to be defective.[86]

E. The Purposive Approach and Other Exceptions to the Literal Approach

4–43 The literal approach has never been the sole statutory interpretation technique utilised by judges when resolving statutory interpretation issues. There are three well-established exceptions to its operation. The first is the purposive approach and it is invoked where the literal approach would result in an absurdity. In such cases, an alternative construction can be given to the word or phrase in question. Section 5 of the Interpretation Act 2005 (the "2005 Act") codifies this common law exception to the literal approach. The second and third focus on situations where the application of the literal approach would be inappropriate either because technical or legal language is used, in which case that

85 [1983] I.R. 235.

86 The "Act of 1968" refers to the Road Traffic Act 1968. However, this was not ultimately fatal to the accused's conviction, as other provisions in the 1978 Act meant that proof of compliance with the provisions of Pt V of the 1968 Act was no longer necessary for a successful prosecution under s.49 of the 1961 Act.

is the meaning that should be given to the contested word(s), or where the legislative provision in question is directed at a particular class of people rather than directed at the general population. Well-established common law statutory interpretation techniques, which would include these exceptions, continue to co-exist with s.5 of the 2005 Act.[87] Each of these exceptions will now be considered in turn.

1. The Purposive Approach

4–44 The purposive approach derives from two of the three original canons of construction: the golden and mischief rules. The golden rule was invoked in cases where the use of the ordinary meaning of the word would lead to an absurd, unjust or inconsistent result. In such a case, the golden rule operated to allow judges to look for an alternative meaning, generally a secondary or less common meaning of the word, which avoided the contrary or absurd result and so protected the reputation of the law. In looking for this secondary meaning, the judge looked only within the four corners of the statute in order to ensure the consistent and smooth running of the legislation in question, i.e. they looked at other elements within the statute, such as the long title and other sections to get a better sense of what the legislature intended.

4–45 The mischief rule also asked judges to look for the purpose of the legislation but allowed them to look beyond the four corners of the statute. The rule developed in the sixteenth century and was outlined in *Heydon's Case*:

> "And it was resolved that … four things are to be discerned and considered:
> 1st What was the common law before the making of the Act,
> 2nd What was the mischief and defect for which the common law did not provide,
> 3rd What remedy the Parliament hath resolved and appointed to cure the disease of the Commonwealth, and
> 4th The true reason of the remedy … ."[88]

---

[87] Although these two exceptions were not discussed, see generally *Heather Hill Management Co CLG v An Bord Pleanála* [2022] IESC 43 at paras 123–128.

[88] (1584) 3 Co. Rep. 7a at 7b.

In other words, when judges applied this rule, they asked themselves what mischief the legislation in question was enacted to prevent and then interpreted the contested term(s) to best give effect to that purpose.

4–46 These rules have been brought together in the purposive approach. In *DPP (Ivers) v Murphy*, Denham J. stated that the mischief rule was now known as the purposive approach.[89] Section 5 of the 2005 Act further subsumes the golden rule into it. Section 5 provides that where a word/phrase in a primary or secondary piece of legislation is obscure or ambiguous, or where a literal interpretation would result in an absurdity, the word/phrase is to be given a construction "that reflects the plain intention of the Oireachtas or parliament concerned[90] ... where that intention can be ascertained from the Act as a whole".[91] While the phrase "from the Act as a whole" might be thought to preclude reference to material outside of the four corners of the statute, this is not the case. Murray J. held in *Heather Hill Management Co* that this phrase needs to be read in conjunction with "plain intention", with the result that judges are permitted to consider external statutory interpretation aids[92] as long as the meaning thereby ascertained is reconcilable with the "Act as a whole".[93]

4–47 A pre-2005 Act example that illustrates the purposive approach well is *Nestor v Murphy*.[94] Here, the husband and wife defendants agreed to sell their house to the plaintiff and signed a contract to that effect. However, they subsequently changed their mind and sought to withdraw from the contract. The plaintiff applied to the court for specific performance of the contract, i.e. he sought to enforce the contract and force the defendants to sell the house as originally agreed. The defendants argued that the contract was rendered void by s.3(1) of the Family Home Protection Act 1976 because the wife had not given her written consent to the making of the contract of sale prior to the

[89] [1999] 1 I.L.R.M. 46 at 59.

[90] Any statute passed pre-1922 or under the 1922 Constitution that does not offend the terms of the 1937 Constitution. It can also encompass regulations and directives from the European Parliament.

[91] This wording follows very closely the wording suggested by the Law Reform Commission in its *Report on Statutory Drafting and Interpretation: Plain Language and the Law* (LRC 61-2000), para.2.44.

[92] See further Section F.2.

[93] [2022] IESC 43 at para.127.

[94] [1979] I.R. 326.

signing of it. Henchy J. determined that the purpose of the statute was to protect both spouses' interests in the family home and it existed to prevent one spouse from unilaterally disposing of the family home without the consent of the other. Accordingly, he determined that the section in question should be read to protect a spouse who has not participated in the sale of the family home and not to allow spouses who have changed their mind about a sale to withdraw from it.

4–48 However, the courts will only embrace the purposive approach when it is necessary to avoid an absurdity, and not in cases where the literal approach would lead to an unfair or unreasonable result. In *Rafferty v Crowley*,[95] Murphy J. did not apply the purposive approach to s.80 of the Building Societies Act 1976, which prevented a building society from issuing a loan where the security for that loan was property that was subject to a prior loan/charge. In this case, the prior charge in question was miniscule and it was argued that its existence would not be contrary to the purpose of the statute, which was to ensure that, in cases of default, the building society would be able to recoup the money lent through the sale of the property in question. While Murphy J. agreed with the plaintiff that the construction she suggested was a sensible one, it was not permissible as, unlike *Nestor v Murphy*, the literal approach did not lead to a "pointless absurdity".[96] The legislature had exempted charges on land of a minor nature from other statutes and it could have chosen to do so in the Building Societies Act 1976.[97]

4–49 A pointless absurdity would be an interpretation that would negate the intent of the section. For example, in *DPP (Ivers) v Murphy*, Denham J. declined to interpret s.6 of the Criminal Justice (Miscellaneous Provisions) Act 1997 in the way argued for by the accused, on the basis that it would lead to "the absurd result that the garda is required to be in court to prove that his presence is not required!"[98] Section 6 was designed to remove the need for a garda to testify about the circumstances of an arrest where that arrest was conducted without a warrant; it allowed for a certificate detailing the circumstances of the arrest to be entered

[95] [1984] I.L.R.M. 350.
[96] [1984] I.L.R.M. 350 at 353.
[97] The Building Societies (Amendment) Act 1988 was passed in the aftermath of this decision.
[98] [1999] 1 I.R. 98 at 111.

into evidence instead. The accused's preferred interpretation would have required the garda to come into court to testify that the arrest was otherwise than under a warrant before the certificate could be entered into evidence.

4–50 Of course, whether the purposive approach is considered to be necessary or not will depend on the judge(s) hearing the case. This is because there is no legislative definition of what constitutes an absurdity and what is absurd to one judge might not be to another.[99] That being said, the adoption of different approaches can lead to the same conclusion. The previously mentioned case of *Lawlor v Flood* provides such an example.[100] In that case, Hamilton C.J. applied the purposive approach to interpret s.4 of the Tribunals of Inquiry (Evidence) (Amendment) Act 1979, while Denham J. applied the literal approach.[101] Both approaches led to the same result: a finding that tribunals of inquiry had lesser powers than the High Court. That both approaches could yield the same result should not be surprising. As Dodd notes, "[t]he legal meaning derived from the literal and purposive interpretation in the majority of cases coincide ... The literal interpretation of the text chosen by the Oireachtas usually carries out the intended purpose."[102]

4–51 Yet, just because both approaches can yield the same result, this does not mean that the interpretations derived are the same. As the case of *Jones v Minister for Justice and Equality* illustrates, which approach is adopted (or prevails on appeal) can determine how broadly or narrowly a statutory regime applies in the future to others such as you, your family, your friends or your clients. In *Jones*, s.15(1)(c) of the Irish Nationality and Citizenship Act 1956 (the "1956 Act"), as amended, was considered.

[99] The Court of Appeal looked up the dictionary definition of "absurd" in *McDonagh v Chief Appeals Officer* [2020] IECA 5 at para.61. However, synonyms for "absurd" are as open to judicial subjectivity as "absurd"; R. Byrne, P. McCutcheon, L. Cahillane and E. Roche-Cagney, *Byrne and McCutcheon on the Irish Legal System*, 7th edn (Dublin: Bloomsbury Professional, 2020), para.14.53. It was also pointed out by McKechnie J. that the word "absurd" (and indeed the words "obscure" and "ambiguous") was not "clear of uncertainty"; *AWK (Pakistan) v Minister for Justice and Equality* [2020] IESC 10 at para.46.

[100] [1999] 3 I.R. 107, considered at para.4–37.

[101] Section 4 provides: "A tribunal may make such orders as it considers necessary for the purposes of its functions, and it shall have, in relation to their making, all such powers, rights and privileges as are vested in the High Court or a judge of that Court in respect of the making of orders."

[102] D. Dodd, *Statutory Interpretation in Ireland* (Dublin: Tottel Publishing, 2008), para.6.32.

This subsection sets out one of the criteria that applicants for citizenship must meet, namely "continuous residence" in the State for the year prior to application. Jones had been outside the State for 100 days, 97 of which were for holidays and three for work. Although the Minister for Justice exercised a discretionary policy permitting applicants to leave Ireland for short periods (generally up to six weeks, but this could be extended where exceptional and unavoidable circumstances applied), Jones had exceeded this leeway. Accordingly, Jones's application was rejected. Barrett J. in the High Court interpreted "continuous residence" literally, i.e. unbroken or uninterrupted residence, and thus upheld the Minister's decision to reject Jones's application.[103] However, he also determined that the discretionary policy was ultra vires because the 1956 Act did not confer any authority on the Minister to introduce one.[104] The Court of Appeal also upheld the Minister's refusal but rejected Barrett J.'s "overly" literal interpretation of "continuous" as it gave rise to an absurdity, i.e. it would mean that citizenship applicants would be tethered to Ireland for the year prior to their application, unable to leave the country even for a few hours for valid reasons (e.g. travelling to London for work purposes or taking a day trip to Newry), and it would operate to exclude most applicants for citizenship.[105]

4–52 Finally, the purposive approach is generally not applied to specific categories of statute, namely criminal, taxation and conveyancing statutes. This common law rule was given partial statutory footing when the use of the purposive approach to statutes that impose "a penal or other sanction" was exempted from s.5 of the 2005 Act. The phrase "or other sanction" was held to include taxation statutes, unless the legislature declared otherwise, in *Bookfinders Ltd v Revenue Commissioners*.[106] The reason for generally requiring such statutes to be interpreted literally is because of the possible negative implications of those statutes for individuals. A strict literal meaning limits the range of words or phrases in a statute and allows people to regulate their affairs

103 [2019] IEHC 519 at para.3.
104 [2019] IEHC 519 at para.2.
105 [2019] IECA 285 at paras 47–51, 63.
106 [2020] IESC 60 at paras 46, 54. However O'Donnell J. (at para.47) also held that understanding the purpose of the statute can assist with the interpretation of a word or phrase in a taxation statute.

with more certainty[107]—an important facet of the rule of law.[108] However, this is not to say that the purposive approach can never be used, and where a strict literal reading would disadvantage an accused person or a person being asked to pay more taxes, the purposive approach has been invoked. For example, in *DPP v Tivoli Cinema Ltd*, the word "seat" in s.20 of the Intoxicating Liquor Act 1927 was interpreted to include "a place for standing", on the basis that the section in question was a penal one and that "before a criminal sanction can be applied the defendant is entitled to know by clear and unambiguous language that such sanction will be applied in specific circumstances".[109]

2. Technical or "Legal" Language

4–53 The technical or legal language exception states that where the words in the statute are legal terms of art, they will bear their special legal meaning as opposed to their ordinary literal one. The case that best illustrates this exception is *Minister for Industry and Commerce v Pim Brothers Ltd*.[110] In this case, the question before the High Court was whether a notice on a coat in a window display stating how much the coat cost and what the weekly payment would be, without specifying the credit terms, was an offer for sale (in which case the defendant had breached the law which governed credit-sales schemes) or an advertisement that the coat was available for sale (in which case the defendant had not broken the law). The court determined that it was the latter because displaying an item for sale is not the same as offering it for sale within contract law terms. This is because in order for a legal offer to be made, the purchaser would have to be told what the credit terms are.

3. Where Directed at a Particular Class

4–54 The third exception to the literal approach is where the statute is directed at a particular class of persons. In such cases, the words of the statute are interpreted according to how members of that class would understand them. In *Minister for Industry and Commerce v Hammond*

[107] D. Dodd, *Statutory Interpretation in Ireland* (Dublin: Tottel Publishing, 2008), para.6.51.
[108] See Ch.2, paras 2–06 to 2–07.
[109] [1999] 2 I.R. 260 at 268.
[110] [1966] I.R. 154.

Lane Metal Co Ltd,[111] it was held that the scrap metal industry distinction between "scrap lead" and "battery lead" was relevant in interpreting the phrase "scrap lead" in the Emergency Powers (Scrap Lead) (Mixed Prices) Order 1945, as that Order was directed at the scrap metal industry rather than at the public at large.

F. Statutory Aids to Finding Legislative Intent

4–55 In addition to the primary aids to interpretation—the literal and purposive approaches which both have a statutory basis in the Interpretation Act 2005 (the "2005 Act")—judges can also have recourse to secondary aids to construction. These aids, which assist judges in determining what the literal or purposive meaning of a word or phrase is, can be found within the four corners of the statute itself or extrinsic to it. In this section we will briefly consider some of the main internal and external statutory construction tools.

1. Internal Statutory Aids

4–56 There are three main categories of internal statutory aid that we will look at in this section. The first is other parts of the statute, such as other sections and the long title. The second and third focus on the context of the word or phrase in question. The courts will either interpret the word/phrase with reference to the ordinary rules of grammar or with reference to well-established legal maxims.

4–57 The section of most interest to judges when looking for the meaning to be given to a contested word or phrase is the interpretation/definition section. Most statutes have a section that defines various terms used in a statute. To return to an earlier example, s.78(1) of the Health Act 2004 provides as follows:

> "The Minister may make regulations—
> (a) for any purpose in relation to which regulations are provided for in this Act,
> (b) for prescribing any matter or thing referred to in this Act as prescribed or to be prescribed, and
> (c) generally for the purpose of giving effect to this Act."

[111] [1947] Ir. Jur. Rep. 59.

Section 79, however, does not state which Minister may make such regulations. Instead it is necessary to go to s.2 which provides that "[i]n this Act", the Minister is the Minister for Health and Children.[112]

4–58 The reason why courts look at the interpretation/definition section was explained concisely by Murnaghan J. in the case of *Mason v Leavy*: "[w]here a statute ... defines its own terms and makes what has been called its own dictionary, a court should not depart from the definitions given the statute and the meanings assigned to the words used in the statute."[113] Some sections in a statute will also include definitions for a particular word or words used in that section only. For example, s.7(6) of the Non-Fatal Offences against the Person Act 1997, which criminalises the unlawful possession of a syringe, states that "[i]n this section 'blood' includes any fluid or substance resembling blood".[114] Murnaghan J.'s reasoning is equally applicable in such instances.

4–59 In addition to referring to other sections of a statute, courts have also sometimes had recourse to the long title of a statute. The long title is situated on the first page of the statute on which sections appear. An example is the long title of the Court of Appeal Act 2014:

> "An Act to provide, in pursuance of Article 34 of the Constitution, for the establishment of the Court of Appeal referred to in paragraph ii of Article 34.2 of the Constitution; to specify the jurisdiction of the court; to provide, in relation to the said court, for matters supplementary to the court and the judges and officers of that court; to provide that the Supreme Court may, in certain circumstances, hear certain applications made to it in respect of decisions of the Court of Appeal or the High Court otherwise than with an oral hearing; to provide that the Chief Justice or the President of the Court of Appeal may issue directions in relation to the conduct of appeals or applications made to the Supreme Court or the Court of Appeal; to make provision in relation to the conduct of proceedings before those courts; for those purposes, to amend the Courts (Establishment and Constitution) Act 1961, the Courts

[112] See para.4–12, fn.15.

[113] [1952] I.R. 40 at 47.

[114] Other examples in that statute, as amended, are ss.9(2), 12(2), 14(2), 15(2), 18(3), 23(2) and 25(3).

(Supplemental Provisions) Act 1961 and certain other enactments; to provide for the repeal of certain enactments; and to provide for related matters."

In *DPP v Quilligan*, McCarthy J. opined that the long title "is the plainest of all guides to the general objectives of a statute".[115]

4–60 A second technique is to apply the ordinary rules of grammar to the wording of the section in question. For example, in *Dunnes Stores Ireland Co v Ryan*, the use of the present tense in s.19(2)(f) of the Companies Act 1990[116] was determinative:

> "The language used in s 19(2)(f), using as it does the present tense in contrast to the past tense employed in the other subparagraphs, makes it clear that the examination of books or documents authorised under that subparagraph is related to continuing or future illegal acts or omissions of the company and not to acts or omissions which have occurred in the past."[117]

Section 19(2)(f) pertained to the power of the Minister to require the production of certain documents to establish if the company in question was governed by the Companies Acts.

4–61 The third and related technique is to focus on the specific context of the contested word or phrase and interpret it with reference to that context. The reason for this is simple. As Dodd explains, "[j]ust as with ordinary language, words in a statute can normally only be understood in the sentence in which they appear ... The linguistic context may make plain the intended meaning of the words or expression."[118] In seeking to provide such context, judges typically invoke one of three maxims:

(a) *Expressio unius est exclusio alterius*;
(b) *Ejusdem generis*; or
(c) *Noscitur a sociis*.

---

[115] [1987] I.L.R.M. 606 at 635.
[116] Since repealed and replaced by the Companies Act 2014.
[117] [2002] 2 I.R. 60 at 80.
[118] D. Dodd, *Statutory Interpretation in Ireland* (Dublin: Tottel Publishing, 2008), para.5.62.

(a) *Expressio unius est exclusio alterius*

4–62 *Expressio unius est exclusio alterius* means that to express one thing is to exclude another. The easiest way to illustrate this maxim is with reference to a relatively straightforward statutory example. Section 1(1) of the Punishment of Incest Act 1908, as amended, provides as follows:

> "Any male person who has carnal knowledge of a female person, who is to his knowledge his grand-daughter, daughter, sister, or mother, shall be guilty of an offence and shall be liable on conviction on indictment to imprisonment for a term not exceeding 10 years."[119]

Re-read the section with the following question in mind: is a man who has sex with his grandmother guilty of incest? Do not proceed to the next paragraph without answering this question.

4–63 The section clearly states that incest is committed when he has sex with "his grand-daughter, daughter, sister, or mother" (*expressio unius*). There is, however, no mention of his grandmother (*est exclusio alterius*). Applying the maxim leads to the inevitable conclusion that he is not guilty of incest for having sex with his grandmother.[120]

4–64 The maxim was relied upon by the Supreme Court in *Kiely v Minister for Social Welfare*.[121] The court determined that because art.11(5) of the Social Welfare (Insurance Appeals) Regulations 1952 only allowed written statements to be admitted as prima facie evidence in appeals against a refusal of benefits, this meant that written statements could not be accepted in any other circumstances.[122]

---

[119] The offence for a female accused is located in s.2 of the Punishment of Incest Act 1908.

[120] This relates to one of the purposes of the prohibition on incest—the fear that children born of incest will have genetic difficulties. As grandmothers are, in theory, less likely to be fertile, they are at low risk of pregnancy. Consequently, they need not be included in the prohibition.

[121] [1977] I.R. 267.

[122] [1977] I.R. 267 at 279.

(b) *Ejusdem generis*

4–65 *Ejusdem generis* means that where a general word follows particular words that establish a *genus* (i.e. type or group), it takes its meaning from them. If a wealthy stud farm-owning relative died and he left you his "dogs, cats and other animals", would you inherit the stud horses? Here the general words are "other animals". If the particular words that precede them, namely "dogs, cats", constitute a *genus*, then the general words will take their meaning from them. As dogs and cats belong to the *genus* of domestic animals, the question becomes whether stud horses are a member of this class. If yes, then you will inherit them; if no, then you do not. Unfortunately for you, stud horses are not domestic animals so you do not inherit them.

4–66 An example of the maxim being applied in practice is the case of *C.W. Shipping Co Ltd v Limerick Harbour Commissioners*.[123] Here the question was whether a tug boat was a "lighter, ferry-boat or other small boat", as set out in s.53(1) of the Harbours Act 1953. O'Hanlon J. found:

> "I consider that the words 'or other small boat' should be construed as being *ejusdem generis* with the specific, descriptive words which immediately precede them, and I do not regard a tug as being of the same *genus* as a lighter or a ferry-boat. It is a very specialised type of craft designed for carrying out towing (or occasionally pushing) of much larger vessels, and not for the carriage for hire of persons or goods."[124]

4–67 The maxim would not apply where only one word is mentioned prior to the general word or where the grouped words do not establish a *genus*. With regard to the former, one word does not establish a category. To return to the will example, if the will said "dogs and other animals" then you would have a claim to the valuable stud horses. Similarly, with regard to the latter, you would also inherit the stud horses if the will said "dogs, shoe boxes, the chandelier in the dining room, and other animals".

---

[123] [1989] I.L.R.M. 416.

[124] [1989] I.L.R.M. 416 at 424.

(c) *Noscitur a sociis*

4–68 *Noscitur a sociis* is a broader statement of the previous maxim and, translated, means a thing is known by its associates. Black J. explained the reason for its existence by way of analogy in *People (AG) v Kennedy*: "[a] small section of a picture, if looked at close-up, may indicate something quite clearly; but when one stands back and examines the whole canvas, the close-up view of the small section is often found to have given a wholly wrong view of what it really represented."[125] Kennedy's appeal against his conviction for a number of offences against various Emergency Powers Orders was successful and he was acquitted. The Attorney General sought to appeal his acquittal. The text of s.29 of the Courts of Justice Act 1924 did not limit the right of appeal to a convicted person; however, looking at the word "appeal" elsewhere in the statute, Black J. found that when it was first used, the word was limited to the convicted party only. Applying *noscitur a sociis*, he determined that the word "appeal" in s.29 should similarly be understood as applying to the convicted party only.

2. External Statutory Aids

4–69 In this section we will look at four external aids, i.e. materials that exist outside the statute whose word/phrase is at issue, that can be referred to by judges when trying to determine what the legislature intended when they included the contested word/phrase. This discussion will also bring external materials that are excluded from judicial consideration to our attention.

(a) *Interpretation Act 2005*

4–70 The 2005 Act sets out specific rules according to which statutes can be interpreted. It replaces a multitude of old interpretation statutes, bar one, the Interpretation (Amendment) Act 1997.[126] The 2005 Act primarily updates and repeats what went before but pulls everything together. For example, s.18 of the 2005 Act is simply a restatement of s.11 of the Interpretation Act 1937. Section 18 provides (and s.11

[125] [1946] I.R. 517 at 536.

[126] This statute provides that common law offences, when abolished or amended by statute, can still be prosecuted in their common law form if they were committed prior to the abolition/amendment.

provided) that singular words can be read as incorporating the plural and vice versa, and that "he" incorporates "she".

4–71 We have already encountered s.5 of the 2005 Act in our discussion of the literal and purposive approaches in Sections D and E above. As noted there, s.5 indirectly affirms the literal approach as the primary approach to statutory interpretation in Ireland by permitting departure from the literal meaning of a provision in certain circumstances. In doing this, it puts the purposive approach on a statutory footing, despite not using the word purposive "or any derivative thereof":[127]

> "In construing a provision of any Act (other than a provision that relates to the imposition of a penal or other sanction)—
> (a) that is obscure or ambiguous, or
> (b) that on a literal interpretation would be absurd or would fail to reflect the plain intention of [the Oireachtas or parliament concerned[128]] ...
>
> the provision shall be given a construction that reflects the plain intention of the Oireachtas or parliament concerned, as the case may be, where that intention can be ascertained from the Act as a whole."

(b) Other statutes

4–72 Other statutes can be relevant to statutory interpretation in three ways. The first two are only relevant when the other statutes are *in pari materia* with the statute whose provision is being queried. In order to be *in pari materia*, the statutes in question must have "a common subject matter or purpose".[129] The third way in which other statutes can be relevant for statutory interpretation purposes is where they are earlier incarnations of the legislative provision at issue.

4–73 First, the courts can look to a group of statutes in order to get a sense of what the legislature intended with regard to the area of law as a whole. In *People (AG) v Boggan*, O'Daly J. stated:

---

[127] *AWK (Pakistan) v Minister for Justice and Equality* [2020] IESC 10 at para.46.
[128] See para.4–46, fn.90.
[129] *Murphy v Dublin Corporation* [1976] I.R. 143 at 149.

> "The problem of the meaning of s 27 of the [Courts of Justice Act 1924] is a question of construction but s 27 cannot be considered in isolation ... [T]he Courts of Justice Acts, 1924 and 1936, are *in pari materia* and they are therefore ... to be taken together as forming one system, and as interpreting and enforcing each other."[130]

4–74 Second, the courts will sometimes refer to the judicial interpretation that was given to a particular word or phrase in a prior statute that is *in pari materia*. As Griffin J. stated in *Cronin v Youghal Carpets (Yarns) Ltd*:

> "It is a well-established principle to be applied in the consideration of an Act that, where a word or expression in an earlier Act has received a clear judicial interpretation, there is a presumption that the subsequent Act which incorporates the same word or expression in a similar context should be construed so that the word or expression is interpreted according to the meaning that has previously been ascribed to it, unless a contrary intention appears."[131]

4–75 Third, a comparison of old and new versions of a statute reveals legislative intent because any amendment is clear evidence that the legislature acted deliberately to change the law governing that area. In *CC v Ireland*, the legislative history of s.1(1) of the Criminal Law Amendment Act 1935 (the "1935 Act"), which criminalised sexual intercourse with a girl who was under the age of 15, was considered by the Supreme Court.[132] CC was charged under this provision and one of his grounds of appeal was that the defence of mistake should be read into the 1935 Act. The Supreme Court rejected this ground of appeal on the basis that the equivalent section in the prior incarnation of the 1935 Act—the Criminal Law Amendment Act 1885—had included a defence of honest mistake. The 1935 Act removed this defence and the clear inference of this removal was that the legislature intended the offence with which CC was charged to be a strict liability one.[133]

[130] [1958] I.R. 67 at 87.
[131] [1985] I.R. 312 at 321.
[132] [2005] IESC 48.
[133] The provision in question was subsequently found to be unconstitutional because it did not allow for the defence of honest mistake: *CC v Ireland* [2006] IESC 33.

(c) Pre-parliamentary materials

4–76 The courts allow pre-parliamentary materials to be opened in evidence before them as a means of discerning legislative intent. Pre-parliamentary materials would include Law Reform Commission Consultation Papers, Issues Papers and Reports; and Green and White Papers.[134] All of these pre-parliamentary materials come from official sources. Materials that come from unofficial sources, such as a letter from the Department of Industry and Commerce,[135] are excluded.

4–77 An example of a case where a Law Reform Commission Report was found to help resolve an interpretation question is *Whitely v Minister for Defence*.[136] This case concerned a claim for damages for hearing loss incurred by the plaintiff when he underwent training in the armed forces 30 years prior. The question before the court was whether this claim was statute barred, as s.3 of the Statute of Limitations (Amendment) Act 1991 (the "1991 Act") requires an individual to bring a claim within three years of the date at which they had knowledge of the injury and how significant it was. The point of contention was the meaning to be given to the word "significant". The plaintiff, relying on English precedent, argued that while he had knowledge that he had been injured in 1979 or 1980, he only became aware that the injury was "significant" in 1993. Therefore, his "date of knowledge" was 1993 and he was not statute barred, as he initiated the claim in 1995. However, the defendant drew the court's attention to the Law Reform Commission Report that informed the content of the 1991 Act. The Law Reform Commission had recommended that the English approach should not be followed, in particular recommending that a definition not be given to the word "significant", as had been done in England. Quirke J. held that the obvious implication of the Oireachtas's decision not to define the word "significant" in the 1991 Act was that the Oireachtas had accepted the Law Reform Commission's recommendation. Accordingly, the plaintiff lost his case.

---

[134] A "Green Paper" is a discussion document setting out ideas and inviting comment and views from individuals and relevant organisations. A "White Paper" is not as discursive but sets out the Government's perspective on the issue. R. Byrne, P. McCutcheon, L. Cahillane and E. Roche-Cagney, *Byrne and McCutcheon on the Irish Legal System*, 7th edn (Dublin: Bloomsbury Professional, 2020), para.13.59. For further discussion of these resources, see Ch.8, Sections B.1 and B.2. The interpretive status of explanatory memoranda that accompany Bills is uncertain. See *Iurescu v Minister for Justice and Equality* [2019] IEHC 535 at para.48; Byrne et al, para.14.204.

[135] *Minister for Industry and Commerce v Hales* [1967] I.R. 50.

[136] [1997] 2 I.L.R.M. 416.

4–78 By way of contrast, parliamentary materials are not allowed as interpretive aids. Parliamentary materials include previous drafts of a Bill before it became law, parliamentary debates during the passage of a Bill, and the political background in which a particular Act came into force. Initially, it appeared as though parliamentary debates might be allowed as an interpretive aid. In the High Court decision of *Wavin Pipes v Hepworth Iron Co Ltd*,[137] Costello J. acknowledged the value of referring to parliamentary proceedings, and he stated that the parliamentary history of the statute in question was very helpful to him in determining the meaning of the phrase at issue in that case.

4–79 However, the Supreme Court unanimously ruled in *Crilly v Farrington*[138] that parliamentary materials should be excluded from consideration. This decision was prompted by three main concerns: first, that inclusion of parliamentary materials would undermine traditional canons of interpretation, which were regarded as "more sophisticated and neutral aids";[139] second, that it would add to legal costs, as solicitors would be obliged to carefully read all parliamentary debates before advising a client, which would take a lot of extra time and be quite an onerous task;[140] and, third, that their inclusion could inhibit legislative debate. Murray J. noted:

> "A minister or promoter of a bill may feel constrained when intervening in the cut and thrust of parliamentary debate to choose her or his words carefully for fear of giving rise to any misunderstanding as to her or his intent on a subsequent parsing of those words in a court of law ... Statements, calculated or otherwise, promoting a bill passing through a politically contentious process would not necessarily constitute a neutral aid to construction. If the courts were to [adopt this process] ... it would place an onus on other members of the Oireachtas to examine his or her spoken words for its implications as to the ultimate effect of a bill when it becomes law. They would have to do so from a perspective which they have never had to do and which does not currently arise."[141]

137 (1982) 8 F.S.R. 32.
138 [2001] 3 I.R. 251.
139 [2001] 3 I.R. 251 at 299.
140 [2001] 3 I.R. 251 at 298.
141 [2001] 3 I.R. 251 at 297–298.

4–80 There was also concern expressed that focusing on the statements of one or a few speakers would be problematic from a constitutional perspective. Murray J. noted:

> "Any proposal that the courts should go behind the constitutionally expressed will of the Oireachtas so as to rely on the statement of one member of one house, whatever his or her status, must be approached with circumspection and constitutional prudence. To go behind a will so expressed so as to look at such statement and impute an intent expressed by one member to the Oireachtas as a whole may, and I use that word guardedly, risk compromising the legislative process and the role of other members of the Oireachtas."[142]

4–81 While the Supreme Court made some compelling points in *Crilly*, it is worth noting that, in some instances, reference to parliamentary debates could resolve the dispute very easily. An Irish case that very clearly illustrates this is *Minister for Justice, Equality and Law Reform v Dolny*.[143] Here the issue was what meaning should be given to the word "assault" in s.3 of the Non-Fatal Offences against the Person Act 1997, specifically whether it should carry the meaning given to that word in s.2. Had it been permissible to refer to the Dáil Debates, it would have been obvious that the answer was "yes". When the then-Minister for Justice, Nora Owen, introduced ss.2 and 3 of the Non-Fatal Offences against the Person Bill 1997 to the Dáil in April 1997, she stated:

> "The first substantive section of the Bill before the House is section 2. This section replaces the common law offences of assault and battery usually referred to as 'common assault' with the new offence of assault ...
>
> Section 3 deals with the more serious offence of assault causing harm ... Under the present law, consent cannot be a defence to a charge of causing actual bodily harm. The Law Reform Commission recommended that such a rule is no longer appropriate and I have accepted that view. Since section 3 is framed by reference to an assault and consent is a defence to simple assault, it will also be a defence where actual bodily harm is caused. We are not talking here of cases of serious harm which are covered by the next section."[144]

142 [2001] 3 I.R. 251 at 296. See too McGuinness J. at 302.
143 [2008] IEHC 326; [2009] IESC 48.
144 477 *Dáil Debates* 976–977 (15 April 1997).

Precluded from accessing this information, the opposite conclusion was reached by Peart J. in the High Court, where he determined that the s.2 and s.3 offences were entirely separate and that the definition provided in s.2 was irrelevant to s.3.[145] This interpretation, which was upheld on appeal before the Supreme Court,[146] was subsequently overturned in *People (DPP) v Brown*.[147] Again however, the Minister's remarks were excluded with reference to *Crilly*.[148] More recently, the *Crilly* approach was stated to be as applicable to constitutional interpretation as it is to the interpretation of ordinary legislation.[149]

4–82 What is particularly interesting in relation to the *Dolny* case in light of concerns raised in *Crilly* was that the text of ss.2 and 3 went through the legislative process unaltered and without any critical comment. As such, it would not have been inappropriate to impute Minister Owen's intent to the legislature as a whole. If the legislature had disagreed with her, then someone would have said something. The use of parliamentary debates in this case would have met the second and third criteria in the *Pepper v Hart*[150] test that is used in England.

Box 4.2: International Perspective—*Pepper v Hart*

For centuries, the UK courts were precluded from referring to parliamentary debates, known as Hansard.[151] Article 9 of the Bill of Rights 1689 prevented it on the basis that their inclusion would impinge on the freedom of parliamentary speech. The exclusionary rule was put on a judicial footing in the case of *Millar v Taylor*,[152] yet as Beaulac notes, "the very founding case on the exclusionary rule seems to be of somewhat dubious origin", as Willes J. referred to parliamentary material in coming to his conclusion.[153] A limited opening up of parliamentary debates as

[145] For a critique of this decision, see C. O'Sullivan, "The Importance of Correct Statutory Interpretation Technique—The Case of *Minister for Justice, Equality and Law Reform v Dolny*" (2010) 46 *Irish Jurist* 146.

[146] [2009] IESC 48.

[147] [2018] IESC 67.

[148] [2018] IESC 67 at para.194 per McKechnie J.

[149] *Heneghan v Minister for Housing, Planning and Local Government* [2023] IESC 7 at para.87 (per Murray J.) and para.35 (per Hogan J.).

[150] [1992] 3 W.L.R. 1032.

[151] After the Hansard family of printers who began publishing the parliamentary debates in 1774.

[152] (1769) 98 E.R. 201 at 217.

[153] S. Beaulac, "Parliamentary Debates in Statutory Interpretation: A Question of Admissibility or of Weight?" (1998) 43 *McGill Law Journal* 287 at 292.

recorded in Hansard was permitted with the passing of a resolution by the Parliament in 1818, but this option was never availed of.[154] Change came in 1992 with the House of Lords' decision in *Pepper v Hart*.[155]

This change was prompted by two factors. First, it was revealed that judges frequently took "a surreptitious peek" at Hansard without informing the parties.[156] This was clearly problematic, as it is a basic requirement of the adversarial system that judges should only decide cases with reference to arguments put before them in order to ensure that both sides are able to address all arguments that may affect their case. Second, as it was standard practice within EU case law for reference to be made to EU parliamentary debates, when interpreting English laws drafted in response to EU legislation, judges began to refer to Hansard when interpreting that legislation.[157] It accordingly made sense to open up that practice to legislation with domestic origins.

Pepper v Hart established three criteria that must be met before parliamentary debates can be admissible in argument:

(a) legislation is ambiguous or obscure, or leads to an absurdity;
(b) the material relied upon consists of one or more statements by a minister or other promoter of the Bill, together if necessary with such other parliamentary material as is necessary to understand such statements and their effect; and
(c) the statements relied upon are clear.[158]

The general rule of exclusion remains; Lord Browne-Wilkinson was adamant that it would only be in rare cases that such materials would be admissible. This has proven to be the case. Although judges have on occasion relied on Hansard, very few cases have been found to meet the criteria above and so justify the admission of the material.[159] Indeed, it seemed for a period in the mid to late-1990s that judges in the House of Lords were more reluctant to allow in parliamentary debates than were judges in the Court of Appeal.[160]

---

154 Law Reform Commission, *Report on Statutory Drafting and Interpretation: Plain Language and the Law* (LRC 61-2000), para.5.53.

155 [1993] 1 All E.R. 42.

156 A. Lester, "Pepper v. Hart Revisited" (1994) 15 *Statute Law Review* 10 at 17. See too the admission of Denning L.J. in his Court of Appeal judgment in *Davis v Johnson* [1978] 2 W.L.R. 182 at 192–193. He was reprimanded by the House of Lords on appeal: [1979] A.C. 264 at 337.

157 J. Holland and J. Webb, *Learning Legal Rules*, 11th edn (Oxford: OUP, 2022), pp.272–273.

158 [1993] 1 All E.R. 42 at 69 per Lord Browne-Wilkinson.

159 J. Holland and J. Webb, *Learning Legal Rules*, 11th edn (Oxford: OUP, 2022), pp.275, 282.

160 S. Vogenauer, "A Retreat from *Pepper v Hart*? A Reply to Lord Steyn" (2005) 25(4) *Oxford Journal of Legal Studies* 629.

Pepper v Hart was subject to significant critique and, for a period, various predictions as to its demise were made. These prophecies have proven unfounded. Even its most influential critic, Lord Steyn—somewhat surprisingly one of the six judges who established the rule in *Pepper v Hart*[161]—sees a limited role for its continued existence, specifically in the context of preventing the executive from stating that the legislation was intended to mean one thing in the legislative process and then arguing that it meant something else in court.[162] Calls for its repeal are also likely to fall on deaf ears. Lord Steyn has suggested that the executive is unlikely to pass legislation to abolish it, as the decision is primarily to its advantage.[163]

It is, however, important to note that many of the same concerns that the Supreme Court raised in *Crilly* have been raised in the context of *Pepper v Hart*. Like the Irish Supreme Court, the separation of powers implications of reading legislative intent from the speech of a member of the executive have been highlighted as problematic:

> "To give to the executive, which promotes a Bill, the right to put a gloss on the Bill, is a substantial inroad on a constitutional principle, shifting legislative power from Parliament to the executive ... *Pepper v Hart* treats ... ministerial policy as canonical. It treats them as a source of law. It is in constitutional terms a retrograde step: it enables the executive to make law."[164]

Yet in the 1930s, it was argued in the US that reference to parliamentary debates was a way of protecting the separation of powers by curbing undemocratic judicial law-making. Landis differentiated the fictitious legislative intent that judges appealed to in their decision-making with the reality of that intent that could be discerned easily when the "records of legislative assemblies [were] opened and read".[165] Relatively liberal use was historically made of parliamentary materials in the US, so common in fact that it was wryly suggested that "only when legislative history is doubtful do you go to the statute".[166]

[161] Seven judges heard the case; five judgments were written.

[162] J. Steyn, "Pepper v Hart; A Re-examination" (2001) 21(1) *Oxford Journal of Legal Studies* 59 at 67.

[163] J. Steyn, "Pepper v Hart; A Re-examination" (2001) 21(1) *Oxford Journal of Legal Studies* 59 at 70.

[164] J. Steyn, "Pepper v Hart; A Re-examination" (2001) 21(1) *Oxford Journal of Legal Studies* 59 at 68.

[165] J. Landis, "A Note on 'Statutory Interpretation'" (1930) 43 *Harvard Law Review* 886 at 888. Parliamentary materials were relied on in the US for the first time in 1860 in *Dubuque & Pacific Railroad Co v Litchfield* 64 U.S. (23 How) 66.

[166] F. Frankenfurter, "Some Reflections on the Reading of Statutes" (1947) 47 *Columbia Law Review* 527 at 543. There has been a shift in the opposite direction under the

Concern about increased research costs was the primary reason Lord Mackay dissented in *Pepper v Hart*.[167] However, referring to practice in Australia and New Zealand where parliamentary materials were admissible, Lord Browne-Wilkinson noted that there had not been a significant increase in the cost of litigation in either jurisdiction.[168] To address costs concerns, though, Lord Browne-Wilkinson suggested that if irrelevant parliamentary materials were introduced, then the party who introduced them would be liable for costs.[169] Lord Griffiths also noted that modern technology "greatly facilitates" the location of relevant passages from Hansard, thus reducing the anticipated costs.[170] A Practice Direction issued after *Pepper v Hart* requires any party seeking to introduce Hansard to provide copies to the court and to all other parties in advance of the court hearing.[171]

A final argument in favour of excluding parliamentary materials, not referenced in *Crilly*, is the rule of law concern that the law must be public and precise. Citizens should not need to refer to such materials in order to divine whether a statutory provision applies to them. However, Magyar dismisses this argument on the basis that, "[w]ith or without recourse [to legislative history], people are regularly cautioned to consult a legal professional when they have a legal problem ... Case law poses at least as much challenge to a lay person as legislative history."[172]

As is clear from the foregoing discussion, parliamentary debates are admissible in other major common law jurisdictions. In this regard, Dodd observes that Ireland "has the distinction of refusing to follow the modern trend".[173] In the UK, the US, New Zealand and Canada, the move away from the strict exclusionary rule was judicial in origin.[174] The sole

influence of Scalia J. and Thomas J., who were critical of the use of parliamentary materials. Gorsuch J. and Kavanaugh J., appointed since Scalia J.'s death, also favour Scalia J.'s approach to legislative history. While parliamentary materials are still legally admissible, lawyers are less inclined to include them because the bench as a whole is less receptive to them. J.J. Magyar, "The slow death of dogma? The prohibition of legislative history in the 20th century" (2021) 50(2–3) *Common Law World Review* 120 at 144.

167 [1993] 1 All E.R. 42 at 48.

168 [1993] 1 All E.R. 42 at 66.

169 [1993] 1 All E.R. 42 at 67.

170 [1993] 1 All E.R. 42 at 50.

171 Supreme Court Practice Direction (Hansard: Citation) [1995] 1 W.L.R. 192. For the citation of subsequent consolidating directions, see J. Holland and J. Webb, *Learning Legal Rules*, 11th edn (Oxford: OUP, 2022), p.278.

172 J.J. Magyar, "The slow death of dogma? The prohibition of legislative history in the 20th century" (2021) 50(2–3) *Common Law World Review* 120 at 150.

173 D. Dodd, *Statutory Interpretation in Ireland* (Dublin: Tottel Publishing, 2008), para.9.04. See too, J.J. Magyar, "The slow death of dogma? The prohibition of legislative history in the 20th century" (2021) 50(2–3) *Common Law World Review* 120.

174 For specifics as to the admissibility of parliamentary materials in these jurisdictions,

jurisdiction in which parliament took the initiative was at federal level in Australia. There, s.15AB was inserted into the Acts Interpretation Act 1901 by s.7 of the Acts Interpretation Amendment Act 1984. It provides:

> "(1) Subject to subsection (3), in the interpretation of a provision of an Act, if any material not forming part of the Act is capable of assisting in the ascertainment of the meaning of the provision, consideration may be given to that material:
> (a) to confirm that the meaning of the provision is the ordinary meaning conveyed by the text of the provision taking into account its context in the Act and the purpose or object underlying the Act; or
> (b) to determine the meaning of the provision when:
> (i) the provision is ambiguous or obscure; or
> (ii) the ordinary meaning conveyed by the text of the provision taking into account its context in the Act and the purpose or object underlying the Act leads to a result that is manifestly absurd or is unreasonable."

This provision goes further than *Pepper v Hart* as it allows for reference to be made to parliamentary materials even in cases where the text appears unambiguous, in order to ensure that the apparent literal meaning is the meaning that was intended. However, s.15AB(3) acknowledges the value of "persons being able to rely on the ordinary meaning", so it is for the court to determine the weight to be given to the parliamentary material in question.

4–83 *Pepper v Hart* may impact on the development of Irish law in a rather unexpected way. In their practice of statutory interpretation, judges are frequently directed to jurisprudence from England. If the case in question is an instance where *Pepper v Hart* was applied, this would result in the undesirable outcome that the stated intentions of elected representatives in Westminster would hold more weight in Irish law than what our own TDs and Senators say.

Beaulac's article is a comprehensive introduction: S. Beaulac, "Parliamentary Debates in Statutory Interpretation: A Question of Admissibility or of Weight?" (1998) 43 *McGill Law Journal* 287. For the US, see J.J. Magyar, "The slow death of dogma? The prohibition of legislative history in the 20th century" (2021) 50(2–3) *Common Law World Review* 120.

(d) EU materials and international treaties

4–84 Where domestic legislation is enacted in response to our obligations under an international treaty or EU law,[175] it makes sense that our interpretation of that legislation should conform to the objectives of its source. This necessitates reading not only the relevant EU legislation (Directive, Regulation or Treaty), but also the preparatory materials. This means that different rules apply to parliamentary debates at EU and international level (which are admissible in Irish courts) than apply to Oireachtas debates. The Supreme Court in *Crilly* acknowledged this lack of uniformity in approaching the parliamentary materials produced by different entities—one domestic, the other not—but determined that it did not matter: "[i]nternational treaties are a different and specific matter."[176] The reason why a different approach was permissible was to ensure inter-jurisdictional consistency in the interpretation of the treaty in question.

G. Presumptions

4–85 The final interpretive tool that we will consider in this chapter is presumptions. Presumptions are assumptions judges make when construing legislation. However, these presumptions are not determinative and can be rebutted by evidence to the contrary. There are numerous presumptions, but we will only focus on a number of key ones, namely:

(1) presumption of constitutionality;
(2) presumption that all words bear a meaning;
(3) presumption that statutes should be given an updated meaning;
(4) presumption against retrospective effect;
(5) presumption of compatibility with EU law;
(6) presumption of compatibility with international law; and
(7) presumption that penal and revenue statutes be construed strictly.

[175] EU and international law will be discussed in Ch.6.
[176] [2001] 3 I.R. 251 at 282.

1. Presumption of Constitutionality

4–86 We have previously encountered the presumption of constitutionality in Ch.3 and a summary of the presumption was provided in this chapter.[177] Where the presumption is invoked, one of three outcomes is possible:

(1) the legislative provision is found not to offend the Constitution;
(2) the legislative provision has one or more possible meanings, one of which is constitutional and the others not. In such a case, using the double construction rule, judges are required to select the constitutional meaning; or
(3) the legislative provision in question cannot be saved by the double construction rule and it is declared to be unconstitutional.

In the second and third cases, you can see the primacy of the Constitution as a source of law over law enacted by the legislature as, in both, what the legislature intended is either irrelevant (situation 3) or modified perhaps in ways that the legislature could never have intended because "it assumes that constitutional restrictions are determinate and foreseeable in advance of constitutional litigation"[178] (situation 2).

2. Presumption that All Words Bear a Meaning

4–87 This presumption is based on the idea that each word inserted into a piece of legislation is carefully chosen by the legislature and, accordingly, each is intended to bear a meaning. This point was made by Egan J. in *Cork County Council v Whillock*:

> "There is abundant authority for the presumption that words are not used in a statute without a meaning and are not tautologous or superfluous, and so effect must be given, if possible, to all the words used, for the legislature must be deemed not to waste its words or say anything in vain."[179]

---

[177] See para.4–25 and Ch.3, Section D.1.

[178] C. Curran and E. Daly, "Reappraising the Constitutional Justification for Intentionalism and Literalism in Statutory Interpretation" (2013) 36 *Dublin University Law Journal* 155 at 174. See too at 169–170.

[179] [1993] 1 I.R. 231 at 239.

3. Presumption that a Statute Should Be Given an Updated Meaning

4–88 The presumption that words in statutes should be given an updated meaning exists to extend the life of statutes, as it recognises that circumstances change, and so reduces the need for constant revision of legislative provisions. It presumes that the legislature did not intend to enact a piece of legislation just for the time in which it was enacted but intended that it would govern future similar circumstances. The presumption has been given legislative effect by s.6 of the Interpretation Act 2005 which provides:

> "In construing a provision of any Act or statutory instrument, a court may make allowances for any changes in the law, social conditions, technology, the meaning of words used in that Act or statutory instrument and other relevant matters, which have occurred since the date of the passing of that Act or the making of that statutory instrument, but only in so far as its text, purpose and context permit."

The limits imposed by s.6 are similar to those that were previously imposed by the common law presumption. In *Keane v An Bord Pleanála*, it was clearly stated: "a distinction must be made between giving an updated construction to the general scheme of the legislation and altering the meaning of particular words used therein."[180]

4. Presumption against Retrospective Effect

4–89 Retrospective effect is where a statute "takes away or impairs any vested right acquired under existing laws, or creates a new obligation, or imposes a new duty, or attaches a new disability in respect to transactions or considerations already past."[181] This definition, provided in *Craies on Statute Law*, has been cited with approval in all of the cases that will be considered under this heading. The presumption against retrospective effect is a long-standing common law presumption and the policy rationale underlying it is that it would be "unjust to declare acts

[180] [1997] 1 I.R. 84 at 193.
[181] W.F. Craies, *Craies on Statute Law*, 7th edn (London: Sweet & Maxwell, 1971), p.387.

to be unlawful which were lawful at the time of their commission".[182] It is therefore unsurprising that the presumption has been given constitutional footing in Article 15.5 which provides that "[t]he Oireachtas shall not declare acts to be infringements of the law which were not so at the date of their commission."

4–90 However, as with all of the presumptions, it is not absolute and it can be rebutted. In *Hamilton v Hamilton*,[183] a distinction was drawn between legislation that governed procedural rather than substantive law. The latter category, as it impacted on vested rights, could not have retrospective effect. *Hamilton* concerned the Family Home Protection Act 1976 and the plaintiff wife sought to rely on this statute to retrospectively invalidate the sale of her family home which occurred before the 1976 Act came into effect. O'Higgins C.J. determined that she could not avail of the statute because it concerned substantive law: "this Act sets out to alter the law. It is not an Act dealing merely with form or procedure. It is an Act which declares to be unenforceable and void certain transactions which were previously regarded in law as binding and valid."[184] It was, however, also held that it was permissible for the legislature to state in legislation that it was intended to have retrospective effect or it could be read in by necessary implication.

4–91 An example of retrospective effect being read in by necessary implication is *Chestvale Properties Ltd v Glackin*.[185] In this case, it was held that the only way an inspector could carry out his duties under the Companies Act 1990 was to demand access to documents created prior to the enactment of the statute. Accordingly, his powers operated retrospectively despite the Act's silence on that point.

4–92 It was firmly established in *Re Hefferon Kearns Ltd (No. 1)*[186] that the phrase "infringements of the law" in Article 15.5 of the Constitution was not confined to criminal offences but also encompassed civil liability. Murphy J. held:

[182] R. Byrne, P. McCutcheon, L. Cahillane and E. Roche-Cagney, *Byrne and McCutcheon on the Irish Legal System*, 7th edn (Dublin: Bloomsbury Professional, 2020), para.14.119.
[183] [1982] I.R. 466.
[184] [1982] I.R. 466 at 473.
[185] [1993] 3 I.R. 35.
[186] [1993] 3 I.R. 177.

> "[T]here seems to be no reason why a tort would not be described as 'an infringement of the law.' ... [I]n practical terms a citizen might have as much and more reason to be aggrieved if his actions which at the time of their performance were wholly innocent were to attract substantial civil liability than he would be if the same actions were to be transmuted into a criminal activity punishable by a nominal fine."[187]

5. Presumption of Compatibility with EU Law

4–93 Any domestic Act or statutory instrument enacted in response to our EU obligations is presumed to be compatible with EU law. Accordingly, it should be interpreted in a manner that ensures this compatibility, in a manner similar to the presumption of constitutionality.[188] This can have the effect of overriding the literal approach. For example, in *Murphy v Bord Telecom Éireann*, the literal reading that would normally be given to ss.2 and 3 of the Anti-Discrimination (Pay) Act 1974 was superseded by an interpretation that rendered the section compatible with the EU treaties from which it derived its origin.[189]

6. Presumption of Compatibility with International Law

4–94 There is also a presumption that the Oireachtas intends to abide by obligations imposed by international law. This presumption arises out of Article 29.3 of the Constitution which provides that "Ireland accepts the generally recognised principles of international law as its rule of conduct in its relations with other States." In *O'Domhnaill v Merrick*, Henchy J. considered, obiter, the relevance of the European Convention on Human Rights when asked to determine if a claim for damages was statute barred by the Statute of Limitations 1957. He stated: "one must presume that the statute was enacted (there being no indication in it of a contrary intention) subject to the postulate that it would be construed and applied in accordance with the State's obligations under international law, including any relevant treaty obligations."[190] Since this judgment was issued, the European Convention on Human Rights Act

[187] [1993] 3 I.R. 177 at 187.
[188] *Dowling v Ireland* [1991] 2 I.R. 379 at 386.
[189] [1989] I.L.R.M. 53 at 60.
[190] [1984] I.R. 151 at 159. This comment was obiter as the point was not argued before him.

2003 was passed and, pursuant to s.2, Irish courts are obliged to interpret domestically produced legislation in a Convention-compliant manner. This will be considered further in Ch.6.[191] Finally, as international law is subordinate to the Constitution, if the particular piece of international law is incompatible with any of our domestically produced pieces of law (namely the Constitution, legislation or common law), then this presumption cannot apply. For examples, see the discussion in Ch.6.[192]

7. Presumption that Penal and Revenue Statutes Be Construed Strictly

4–95 We have encountered the consequence of this presumption previously when we noted that, in general, penal and revenue statutes are interpreted literally rather than purposively in order to limit the penalty or financial liability imposed on those subject to them.[193] Where the language in a penal or taxation statute is ambiguous and open to a broad or narrow reading, then the narrow one is taken. Henchy J. stated the general principle in *Inspector of Taxes v Kiernan*:

> "[I]f a word or expression is used in a statute creating penal or taxation liability, and there is a looseness or ambiguity attaching to it, the word should be construed strictly so as to prevent a fresh imposition of liability from being created unlawfully by the use of oblique or slack language ... ."[194]

In this case, which concerned taxation and the meaning to be given to the phrase "dealer in cattle", Henchy J. found that there was no ambiguity.

4–96 However, it has been emphasised in more recent case law that the presumption of strict construction only applies where ambiguity remains after the other interpretive approaches have been used. In *People (DPP) v TN*, where s.9 of the Waste Management Act 1996, which imposed criminal liability, was considered, the Supreme Court held:

> "The principle does not mean that whenever two potentially plausible readings ... are available, the court must automatically adopt the

[191] See Ch.6, paras 6–92 to 6–97.
[192] See Ch.6, paras 6–70 to 6–84.
[193] See para.4–52.
[194] [1981] I.R. 117 at 122.

> interpretation which favours the accused: it does not mean that where the defendant can point to any conceivable uncertainty or doubt regarding meaning ... he is entitled to a construction which benefits him. Rather, it means that where ambiguity should remain following the utilisation of the other approaches and principles of interpretation at the Court's disposal, the accused will then be entitled to the benefit of that ambiguity. The task for the Court ... remains the ascertainment of the intention of the legislature through, in the first instance, the application of the literal approach to statutory interpretation."[195]

This judgment was quoted from extensively in *Bookfinders Ltd v Revenue Commissioners* where it was held to be "clearly applicable" to a case where a taxation statute was the subject of litigation.[196]

H. Reasons Why Legislative Interpretation Questions Arise

4–97 New or amending legislation is typically prompted by a particular legal problem or set of problems that need(s) to be regulated or prevented. For example, the penalty points system was introduced in October 2002 by the Road Traffic Act 2002 to respond to high rates of fatalities on our roads.[197] In other instances, it performs a codification function whereby existing common law rules and principles are placed on a statutory footing. For example, s.28 of the Non-Fatal Offences against the Person Act 1997 abolished the common law offences of assault, battery, assault occasioning actual bodily harm, kidnapping and false imprisonment, and replaced them with statutory offences, based on modified and updated forms of the prior common law offences. In either case, legislation is enacted for a particular purpose; it is "deliberate law-making".[198] In addition, legislation generally takes quite some time to go through the legislative process. As such, one would expect legislation to be carefully considered and drafted, with the result that legislation is

[195] [2020] IESC 26 para.119.

[196] [2020] IESC 60 at para.54. The excerpts from *People (DPP) v TN* [2020] IESC 26 were quoted at paras 53 (quoting paras 62–67) and 55 (quoting para.119).

[197] See *https://www.rsa.ie/services/licensed-drivers/penalty-points/how-it-works*.

[198] R. Byrne, P. McCutcheon, L. Cahillane and E. Roche-Cagney, *Byrne and McCutcheon on the Irish Legal System*, 7th edn (Dublin: Bloomsbury Professional, 2020), para.13.05.

easy to read and understand. Unfortunately, this is not usually the case. Legislative provisions are notoriously difficult to read. This is for a number of reasons—historical, cultural, pragmatic, political and linguistic. Each of these reasons will be considered in turn in this section.

1. Historical

4–98 The verbose quality of legislation originated from a time where legislative drafters were paid by the word.[199] Unfortunately, over time this archaic, convoluted, and entirely mercenarily-motivated way of legal writing acquired the status of orthodoxy and this form of legislative language (and legal language generally) persists today, even though drafters are no longer paid by the word. Even relatively short sections can be rendered difficult to understand because of poor drafting practices. Take, as an example, s.4(1) of the Criminal Justice Act 1964 which defines the offence of murder:

> "Where a person kills another unlawfully the killing shall not be murder unless the accused person intended to kill, or cause serious injury, to some person, whether the person actually killed or not."

In contrast to good writing practice, we are not told directly what murder is but have to pick through a confusingly written sentence that starts by telling us what it is not. The doctrine of transferred malice is tacked on at the end of the sentence, further complicating the definition provided. This reflects a long-standing legal convention that sections in statutes should be a single sentence, which can lead to unwieldy, multi-clause sentences that are very difficult to read. If, however, the above section was broken down into two sentences, and the important information placed first, then the definition of murder would be much more comprehensible: "[m]urder is the unlawful killing of another where the accused intended to kill or cause serious injury. The deceased need not be the intended victim." In addition, this simplified definition is eight words shorter than the current statutory one.

4–99 Poorly drafted and unnecessarily complicated legislation has been criticised by judges. One of the strongest examples of this is Hardiman

[199] F. Woleslagel, "The 'KISS' Principle of Jury Communication" (1975) 14 *Washburn Law Journal* 252 at 253.

J.'s damning appraisal of s.1 of the Interpretation (Amendment) Act 1997 in *DPP v Devins*, where he stated:

> "This, frankly, is the sort of legislative provision which exposes the law to ridicule ...
>
> This section is of a complexity and, more important, of a degree of uncertainty, which would baffle even the most enthusiastic or concerned of readers ...
>
> It appears to me that this is a state of the law which makes absolute nonsense of the presumption that every citizen is presumed to know the law ... ."[200]

2. Cultural

4–100 It has been suggested that the complexity of legal language is a deliberate strategy employed by lawyers to justify their continued existence and high legal fees. If the law was easy to understand, it is posited, then ordinary people would not need to hire lawyers to explain the law to them and to wield it in their interests. Mellinkoff writes: "[w]hat better way of preserving a professional monopoly than by locking up your trade secrets in the safe of an unknown tongue?"[201]

4–101 That being said, it is worth noting that sometimes legal ideas are expressed in complex ways not to obfuscate but because they are complex. It is also the case that legal knowledge will often be required to understand the law, no matter how simply it is expressed. This is because words that might mean one thing in ordinary language can mean something entirely different in a legal context. This is a point we have come across when we looked at one of the exceptions to the literal approach, e.g. *Minister for Industry and Commerce v Pim Brothers Ltd*[202] and the offer to sell. In other words, legal knowledge will often be required to fully understand the scope of a provision. As Coshott writes, "[t]o use a metaphor, it is like arguing that if science were expressed as plainly as possible, we would no longer need scientists."[203]

[200] [2012] 4 I.R. 491 at 532.

[201] D. Mellinkoff, *The Language of Law* (Boston: Little Brown and Co, 1963), p.iv, quoted in G. Carey, "Practice and Procedure: Towards Simpler Language" (2000)18 *Irish Law Times* 177 at 177.

[202] [1966] I.R. 154. See para.4–53.

[203] D. Coshett, "Living in the Past: The Critics of Plain Language" (2014) 16 *European Journal of Law Reform* 541 at 546.

3. Pragmatic

4–102 Enacting legislation is but one aspect of a TD's or Senator's job and they do not wish to revisit the same problems repeatedly. For this reason, they, through the Office of the Parliamentary Counsel to the Government, try pragmatically to future-proof legislation by attempting to cover all possible contingencies, and this sometimes leads to overly lengthy and complex sections. In the 1975 Renton Report on statutory drafting, Lord Denning wrote:

> "It is because the judges have not felt it right to fill in the gaps and have been giving a literal interpretation ... that the draftsman has felt that he has had to try and think of every conceivable thing and put it in as far as he can so that even the person unwilling to understand will follow it. I think the rules of interpretation which the judges have applied have been one of the primary causes why draughtsmen have felt that they must have a system of over-detail, over-long sentences, and obscurity."[204]

4–103 In addition, legislators and parliamentary drafters, like lawyers and judges who reason by analogy when engaging with precedent,[205] do not wish to reinvent the wheel every single time a new piece of legislation is enacted. Accordingly, they follow the style, structure and language of previous statutes. This has the benefit of ease, but it also has the advantage of legal certainty because the language used may have been considered by judges in prior cases and moving to simpler language risks reopening previously settled matters to litigation.[206]

4. Political

4–104 As you will discover in Ch.7, the legislative process does not always focus on producing the best legislation possible to resolve the problems that have been identified. Instead, the party or coalition in power will often use the party whip system to block tabled amendments by opponents and/or block Private Members' Bills. In addition, Bills can be pushed through the legislative process for political reasons, with the result that the legislation in question is deficient in some ways.

---

[204] D. Renton, *The Preparation of Legislation: Report of a Committee Appointed by the Lord President of the Council*, Cmnd. 6053 (London: H.M.S.O., 1975), para.19.1.

[205] See Ch.5, Section C.3.

[206] G. Carey, "Practice and Procedure: Towards Simpler Language" (2000)18 *Irish Law Times* 177 at 178.

4–105 The phenomenon of rushed legislation is not new, and a well-established legal adage is "rushed legislation is bad legislation". An example of such legislation is the Credit Institutions (Financial Support) Act 2008, legislation that put in place the bank guarantee on 30 September 2008. This legislation issued a blanket €440 billion guarantee of all liabilities in the Irish banking system without the legislators knowing the full extent of the liabilities of the banks in question. The lack of careful consideration that went into the drafting of this legislation was revealed by the Oireachtas Banking Inquiry, where Brendan McDonagh stated that members of the National Treasury Management Agency who were present in Government Buildings on the night when the legislation was being drafted were not consulted by the Government for their input into the extent and nature of the guarantee.[207] Both Irish Nationwide and Anglo Irish Bank subsequently were put into liquidation, while Allied Irish Banks and Bank of Ireland required significant recapitalisation by the State. As a consequence, the bank guarantee has cost taxpayers approximately €64 billion. It has been described by the former Central Bank Governor, Patrick Honohan, as "one of the most expensive banking crises in world history".[208]

5. Linguistic

4–106 It should be acknowledged that even in cases where the legislation on point can seem clear, disputes as to meaning can still arise. This is both because parties in conflict will find interpretations that support their claims and because language is not fixed. Not only can words have multiple meanings but those meanings can shift over time. The word "gay" is a good example. Initially, in and around the twelfth century, it meant happy, colourful or carefree. By the mid-seventeenth century, these meanings still attached to the word, but the sense of "carefree" was expanded to include someone who was self-indulgent and/or immoral. The immorality aspect of the word was further developed, and by the nineteenth century, a gay man was someone who slept with female sex workers. From the 1920s on, probably in reaction to the rather clinical-sounding descriptor "homosexual", men who were

[207] C. Hancock, "Nama chief was 'surprised by scale' of bank guarantee", *Irish Times*, 22 April 2015; Joint Committee of Inquiry into the Banking Crisis, *Report of the Joint Committee of Inquiry into the Banking Crisis*, vol.1 (January 2016), p.245.

[208] V. Browne, "Let's own up to our part in the burst bubble", *Irish Times*, 6 April 2011.

attracted to men began to use the word "gay" to describe their sexual orientation. This meaning of the word went mainstream in the 1960s. From the 1980s on, "gay" acquired the meaning of something stupid or of poor quality. Originally, this meaning was tied to the meaning of "gay" as homosexual, and in the context of a homophobic society, it is not surprising that it was meant in a derisive way.

Box 4.3: Legal Insight
Plain English Movement

The plain English movement began in the US in the 1960s with the publication of David Mellinkoff's *The Language of the Law*,[209] moving to the UK in 1979 with the foundation of the Plain English Campaign.[210] The core aim of the movement was to remove legalese as much as possible from legal writing. Legalese is the unnecessarily complicated, archaic and specialised language that is often used to express legal ideas and principles. This would include words such as "herein", "heretofore", "aforesaid" and "aforementioned", a resistance to describing things in ordinary language,[211] and the unnecessary use of synonyms.[212]

Legalese can make it difficult for laypersons to know what the law is. Indeed, in extreme cases, it can make it difficult for lawyers and judges. This is problematic because "[a] society whose regulations are incomprehensible lives with the Rule of Lottery, not of Law".[213] Such comments, made by Lord Simon in the UK, take on added significance in Ireland where it is a constitutional principle that not only must justice be done, it must be seen to be done.[214] Carey writes that "providing for comprehensible legal language fits squarely within such a principle which is an essential element of our constitutional democracy".[215]

[209] Boston: Little, Brown, 1963.

[210] For more information about this organisation, please visit *www.plainenglish.co.uk.*

[211] The Law Reform Commission notes, for example, that e-mail is referred to as "electronic communication" in s.12 of the Electronic Commerce Act 2000. *Report on Statutory Drafting and Interpretation: Plain Language and the Law* (LRC 61-2000), para.6.08.

[212] This would include phrases such as "give and bequeath" and "null and void". Law Reform Commission, *Report on Statutory Drafting and Interpretation: Plain Language and the Law* (LRC 61-2000), para.6.11.

[213] Lord Simon, "The Renton Report—Ten Years On" (1985) 6(1) *Statute Law Review* 133, quoted in G. Carey, "Practice and Procedure: Towards Simpler Language" (2000) 18 *Irish Law Times* 177 at 180. As noted in Ch.2, Section B.1, people need to know what the rules are so that they can comport themselves to abide by them.

[214] Article 34 of the Constitution requires that justice must be administered in public for this very reason. See also, *O'Reilly v Cassidy* [1995] 1 I.L.R.M. 306 at 310.

[215] G. Carey, "Practice and Procedure: Towards Simpler Language" (2000)18 *Irish Law Times* 177 at 180.

The plain English movement advocates that legal documents should be free of jargon and easily understood by a layperson. The movement has had some success in terms of requiring or encouraging the publication of materials in plain English where directed at particular sectors of society.[216] There has, however, been some debate about its applicability in the context of legislative drafting. This debate has focused on who the intended audience of legislation is. If the intended audience of legislation is laypeople, then clearly it is desirable to adopt plain English principles in legislative drafting. However, if the intended audience of legislation is not laypeople, then plain English principles are not as necessary.

In its 2000 *Report on Statutory Drafting and Interpretation: Plain Language and the Law*, the Law Reform Commission gave qualified approval to the use of plain English in statutes on the basis that it would reduce the number of situations where judges would be required to interpret legislation. While it acknowledged that slightly more complex language may be required sometimes to ensure legal certainty, it stated that in many situations, plain English would be preferable.[217] The comments of Hardiman J. in *DPP v Devins*, quoted above, are also relevant here.[218]

Byrne et al, however, suggest that the focus of the plain English movement on legislation is somewhat misplaced. They suggest that statutes are not really addressed at laypeople but at regulators, lawyers and other professionals and that the aims of legislation in terms of precision and comprehensiveness can and must sometimes militate against simplicity and comprehensibility.[219] This does not mean that legislation is poorly written; it just means that it is doing its job. Hunt notes that laypeople rarely read statutes and asks: "is it reasonable to ask drafters to play to an audience who are not even in the auditorium?"[220]

However, both points can be challenged. First, it is assumed that legislation is easily comprehended by the professionals who regularly

[216] For example, in 1977, New York passed legislation requiring plain English in consumer contracts and leases. The Plain Writing Act 2010 requires federal agencies to use plain English in any document they produce. The EU, in its Unfair Consumer Contract Terms Directive (Directive 93/13/EEC), requires simplified contracts where they are directed at consumers. Ireland has implemented this with the European Communities (Unfair Terms in Consumer Contracts) Regulations 1995 (S.I. No. 27 of 1995), as amended. The National Adult Literacy Agency is also a major proponent of the use of plain English in Ireland. See *https://www.nala.ie/plain-english/*.

[217] Law Reform Commission, *Report on Statutory Drafting and Interpretation: Plain Language and the Law* (LRC 61-2000), para.6.22.

[218] See para.4–99.

[219] R. Byrne, P. McCutcheon, L. Cahillane and E. Roche-Cagney, *Byrne and McCutcheon on the Irish Legal System*, 7th edn (Dublin: Bloomsbury Professional, 2020), para.13.104.

[220] B. Hunt, "Plain Language in Legislative Drafting: Is It Really the Answer?" (2002) 23 *Statute Law Review* 24 at 29.

use it, and this is not always the case. Referring to the UK Tax Rewrite Project, the Law Reform Commission notes that simplifying language through the use of mathematical formulae instead of cumbersome multi-clause sentences would be of benefit to tax practitioners—the intended audience of such legislation.[221] Second, while it might be true that laypeople rarely read statutes, when statutes are so difficult to read, this is hardly surprising. It is, however, undeniable that those opposed to the use of plain English in statutes are correct when they state that complex language is sometimes necessary to convey complex ideas, and that simplicity can sometimes militate against accuracy, which can lead to uncertainty and litigation.

A middle road might therefore be appropriate. It is indisputable that legislation, no matter how clearly written, will never be comprehensible to all. As Hunt memorably puts it, "[t]he language of our legislation cannot be reduced to baby talk for consumption by the masses".[222] However, the current situation, though improving,[223] causes difficulties not just for laypersons but for those whose job it is to engage with legislation on a regular basis. Therefore, simplifying the language in statutes, where it is possible to do so, would benefit the professionals who engage with them on a regular basis, with the consequential side effect of making them more readable for laypeople.[224]

In cases where complexity is inevitable, the publication of leaflets and guides in plain English could address the deficit in information for laypeople. This indeed is a solution that has been proposed by Byrne et al.[225] Hunt also advocates the dissemination of information about the content of law in leaflets and guides, and is implicitly critical of the fact that, in Ireland, this role is currently performed by a number of different entities rather than coming from a centralised body.[226]

[221] Law Reform Commission, *Report on Statutory Drafting and Interpretation: Plain Language and the Law* (LRC 61-2000), para.6.28.

[222] B. Hunt, "Plain Language in Legislative Drafting: Is It Really the Answer?" (2002) 23 *Statute Law Review* 24 at 44.

[223] Hunt notes that the Office of Parliamentary Counsel to the Government incorporated many of the Law Reform Commission's proposals into its drafting manual. B. Hunt, "Plain Language in Legislative Drafting: Is It Really the Answer?" (2002) 23 *Statute Law Review* 24 at 40–41. We see too the use of the word "contents" instead of "arrangement of sections" and "definitions" instead of "interpretation" since July 2013. The former word in both pairings is an example of the "familiar vocabulary" advocated by the Law Reform Commission, i.e. standard words used in various forms of documentation.

[224] D. Coshett, "Living in the Past: The Critics of Plain Language" (2014) 16 *European Journal of Law Reform* 541 at 550.

[225] R. Byrne, P. McCutcheon, L. Cahillane and E. Roche-Cagney, *Byrne and McCutcheon on the Irish Legal System*, 7th edn (Dublin: Bloomsbury Professional, 2020), paras 13.104–13.106.

[226] B. Hunt, "Plain Language in Legislative Drafting: Is It Really the Answer?" (2002) 23 *Statute Law Review* 24 at 43.

I. Conclusion

4–107 The opening quote to this chapter captures wonderfully the difficulty that can be experienced when trying to make sense of legislative provisions. In evocative prose, the process of understanding poorly drafted legislative language is compared by Harman L.J. to an arduous journey.[227] It is undeniable that you too will face similar quests in your encounters with legislative language. The hope is that with perseverance and with the statutory interpretation techniques that you have been introduced to in this chapter, you too will succeed. For Harman L.J., the techniques that assisted him were the legislative history of the statute in question and a careful reading of a particularly convoluted section about which he observed, "I do not wonder at anybody getting tired reading this section".[228] The consolation to be taken from this is that judges struggle with legislative language too, and the problem lies not with you but with the language itself, a point made forcefully by Hardiman J. in *DPP v Devins*.[229] As with every other aspect of the law, the more you familiarise yourself with the language used, the better you will become at understanding it and proposing solutions to the question of what the legislature intended when the provision or provisions were phrased that way. Bon voyage.

[227] *Davy v Leeds Corporation* [1964] 1 W.L.R. 1218 at 1224–1225.
[228] *Davy v Leeds Corporation* [1964] 1 W.L.R. 1218 at 1226.
[229] [2010] 4 I.R. 491 at 532. See para.4–99.

Chapter 5

The Common Law Doctrine of Precedent

> "The doctrine of judicial precedent is ... really the lawyer's term for legal experience. We all tend to repeat the same things we have done before if they proved successful: law is essentially no different ... The US judge, Oliver Wendall Holmes Jr., once said that: 'The life of the Law has not been logic; it has been experience.' Miles Kingston put it rather more cynically in *Punch*: judicial precedent means; 'A trick which has been tried before, successfully.'"
>
> J. Holland and J. Webb, *Learning Legal Rules*, 11th edn (Oxford: OUP, 2022), p.135.

In this chapter we:

- introduce you to the concept of "judge-made" common law;
- define the doctrine of precedent;
- learn how to work with precedent;
- examine how the doctrine operates in Irish courts;
- consider the advantages and disadvantages of precedent.

A. Introduction

5–01 The phrase "common law" has two different meanings in Irish law. The first is when it is used to describe the system of law that was developed in England following the Norman invasion in 1066 and imported here by Henry II around 1172.[1] When Ireland is described as a common law jurisdiction, this is the sense that is meant. The second

[1] R. Byrne, P. McCutcheon, L. Cahillane and E. Roche-Cagney, *Byrne and McCutcheon on the Irish Legal System*, 7th edn (Dublin: Bloomsbury Professional, 2020), para.1.11. For a comprehensive discussion of pre-Norman Irish law, in the realms of law of the person, law of property and offences, see F. Kelly, *A Guide to Early Irish Law* (Dublin: Dublin Institute for Advanced Studies, 2003 reprint).

sense is more limited and it refers to law developed by the courts over the centuries through cases. This is to distinguish case law from law created by the Oireachtas.[2] When we refer to case law as a primary source of law, we are applying this second meaning of the phrase "common law".

5–02 Historically, the majority of law was judge-made. This changed in common law jurisdictions in the eighteenth and nineteenth centuries when Parliament in the UK began to assert its primacy. In part, this shift was necessitated by the Industrial Revolution which wrought massive changes socially, culturally, politically and economically—changes that a system based on appellate court judgments utilising archaic procedures could not respond to rapidly enough. Manchester writes: "[u]p to a point ... delay and expense was tolerable in a society which was relatively static. It was less likely that a more dynamic commercial and industrial world would be content with such a system."[3] Change also came about as a result of the Enlightenment era, where judge-made law was criticised for being the product of unelected judges rather than democratically elected representatives.[4]

5–03 This prioritisation of legislation enacted by democratically elected representatives over laws created by unelected judges has constitutional status in Ireland by virtue of Article 15.2.1° of the Constitution. As noted in Ch.4, Article 15.2.1° provides that "[t]he sole and exclusive power of making laws for the State is hereby vested in the Oireachtas: no other legislative authority has power to make laws for the State." However, judges are still lawmakers, even though they might sometimes baulk at describing themselves as such for fear of being accused of breaching the separation of powers. We have previously encountered judicial law-making in Ch.3 and Ch.4. In Ch.3, we noted that the Constitution provides the framework for our legal and political system. It does not, however, provide a lot of detail. That detail is fleshed out by the courts when constitutional issues are raised before them. As such, judicial decisions put flesh on the skeleton of the Constitution and establish the meaning and ambit of constitutional provisions. Something similar

2 See Ch.7.

3 A.H. Manchester, *A Modern Legal History of England and Wales 1750–1950* (London: Butterworths, 1980), p.2.

4 The Enlightenment era was a period of intellectual advancement in Europe between the Glorious Revolution (1688) and the French Revolution (1789). The critique of precedent developed in this period will be considered further in Section E of this chapter.

occurs when there is disagreement over the meaning of a word/phrase/section in a piece of legislation. As we learned in Ch.4, the interpretation that results from the resolution of the dispute becomes part of the body of law governing that particular area. In other words, the legislative provision is now no longer to be read in isolation, but it takes on the meaning ascribed to it by the judge or judges who heard the case.

5–04 However, while judges make law when they interpret constitutional and legislative provisions, they do not and cannot act as legislators. Unlike legislation which, as discussed in Ch.4, is "deliberate law-making",[5] judicial law-making can best be described as consequential law-making. Clarke C.J. put it thus in *IRM v Minister for Justice and Equality*:

> "Law may in some sense be made by judicial decision, but even in the most important cases raising issues of obvious national consequence ... law made by courts is always made indirectly, and only because it is a necessary and indeed essential consequence of the performance of the judicial function of resolving the particular dispute."[6]

There are, accordingly, limits on what judges can do in making consequential law, one of the most important of which for the purposes of this chapter is the obligation to abide by the doctrine of precedent. Precedent is a method of working with case law that is integral to the common law tradition and part of our constitutional order.[7]

5–05 Judges are accorded more law-making leeway in the development of common law principles, as the legislature has not yet asserted its authority over them. In *Iarnród Éireann v Ireland*, Keane J. confirmed that Article 50 of the Constitution provided for the continuation of the power of judges to develop common law principles "in light of changing social conditions in Ireland and decisions in other common law jurisdictions."[8]

[5] R. Byrne, P. McCutcheon, L. Cahillane and E. Roche-Cagney, *Byrne and McCutcheon on the Irish Legal System*, 7th edn (Dublin: Bloomsbury Professional, 2020), para.13.05. See Ch.4, para.4–97.

[6] [2018] IESC 14 at para.10.25.

[7] *Jordan v Minister for Children and Youth Affairs* [2015] IESC 33 at para.64 per O'Donnell J.; *O'Meara v Minister for Social Protection* [2024] IESC 1 at paras 51–53 per O'Donnell C.J.

[8] [1996] 3 I.R. 321 at 366–367.

However, in recognition of the primacy of the legislature,[9] judges prefer to develop the common law interstitially or incrementally.[10] This does not mean that bigger steps are not sometimes taken. In his judgment in *People (DPP) v McNamara*,[11] Charleton J. changed the much-criticised test for provocation from an entirely subjective one to one that is objective with subjective elements.[12] In doing so, he explicitly relied on the fact that the defence was governed by the common law rather than by legislation, and also referenced Article 50.[13]

5–06 As common law principles have force of law in Ireland only if they are consistent with the terms of the Constitution (Article 50), and as they can be overruled by legislation (Article 15.2.1°), the law as articulated by judges places third in the hierarchy of domestic sources.[14] However, despite being the lowest-ranked domestically-produced source of law, in practical terms you will spend more time reading cases than either legislative or constitutional provisions. This is for two main reasons, the first of which has been considered in the previous chapters and summarised above—namely, they are essential reading to understand what constitutional or legislative provisions mean. The second reason is that a significant number of legal principles have their origins in case law, and many of these have simply been transplanted from the common law into statute law. Consequently, judicial elaboration on these concepts remains relevant to assist in understanding their application.

5–07 In this chapter, our focus is on the cases that are the product of our common law system. Specifically, we will examine what is meant by precedent, how you can work with precedent in order to support legal argument and how the doctrine operates in the Irish courts, and we will consider the extent to which precedent is an apparent rather than an actual constraint on judicial decision-making. This will entail a

9 This primacy is subject to the requirement that the legislature act within the terms of the Constitution; Article 15.4.1°.

10 *Delaney v Personal Injuries Assessment Board* [2024] IESC 10 at para.18 per Hogan J., quoting Holmes J.'s dissent in *Southern Pacific v Jenson* 244 U.S. 205 (1917) at 221.

11 [2020] IESC 34.

12 For a discussion of the criticisms, see L. Campbell, S. Kilcommins, C. O'Sullivan and A. Cusack, *Criminal Law in Ireland: Cases and Commentary*, 2nd edn (Dublin: Clarus Press, 2021), Ch.27, Section 2.B.

13 [2020] IESC 34 at paras 30–31.

14 These sources are considered in Ch.2, paras 2–23 to 2–36, and Chs 3 and 4 respectively.

consideration of the advantages and disadvantages of the doctrine of precedent.

B. The Doctrine of Precedent

5–08 Precedent, like common law, has more than one meaning and in this chapter we are focused on two, both of which are essential to understanding the doctrine of precedent. First, in its most common iteration, the word "precedent" is used as synonymous with the word "case". In this sense, you will often hear of a particular case being cited as the precedent for a particular legal principle, e.g. *Ryan v Attorney General*[15] established the doctrine of derived (previously unenumerated) rights in Irish law. However, to be more precise, it is not the case that is the precedent, rather the case contains the precedent, i.e. the statement of law/legal principle that is binding on future courts where a similar issue is raised. To continue with the example of *Ryan*: the principle of derived rights that was established in that case (and applied to recognise the existence of the right to bodily integrity) was also applied in subsequent cases to identify other derived rights, such as the right to marital privacy[16] and the right to refuse invasive medical treatment.[17] Second, the word "precedent" also describes the method by which we determine whether a case is binding on a particular issue and/or binds a particular court. We will consider both meanings in this section.

1. Precedent within a Case

5–09 As noted above, it is not the case that is the precedent, rather the case contains the precedent, i.e. the statement of law/legal principle that is binding on future courts where a similar issue is raised. The binding part of a judgment is the ratio decidendi, or rationes decidendi if there is more than one binding part. As each issue raised in a case requires a ratio to resolve it, there is typically more than one ratio in a case, as most appellate cases involve multiple issues.[18] However, in your research or in answering a particular legal query, you might be interested in only

---

15 [1965] I.R. 294. For more on this, see Ch.3, Section C.3.

16 *McGee v Attorney General* [1974] I.R. 284.

17 *Re a Ward of Court (Withdrawal of Medical Treatment)* [1996] 2 I.R. 79.

18 As will be discussed further in Section C.1, oftentimes the ratio of a case will only become clear through its interpretation and application in subsequent cases.

one of those issues, so your focus will be on the ratio that correlates to it. Costello J. in the High Court case of *Considine v Shannon Regional Fisheries Board* gave a very good definition of the ratio, where he said that it could be "discovered by determining what proposition of law justified the decision in the light of the material facts which the court decided".[19]

5–10 By way of contrast, obiter dictum—or its plural, obiter dicta—is only persuasive for future courts. "Obiter dictum" means "a thing said by the way". As such, an obiter is a peripheral statement of a legal principle that is not directly relevant to the case in question. An obiter most frequently arises when a judge, discussing the principle in the case before them, notes in passing that the same principle would be equally applicable to different facts, or notes that a related principle might be relevant also. A good example is the decision of McCarthy J. in the case of *Rooney v Connolly*.[20] This case concerned the duty of care an occupier owes to protect those who enter their property from concealed dangers that were known to the occupier. McCarthy J. clearly signaled the obiter in his judgment:

> "The plaintiff's legal advisors chose to advance the case as being that of a licensee; I consider that these status distinctions are wholly artificial and do not properly form part of our law, but I must await a decision of the Court as a whole before I can know if my view will prevail. I recognise that the point has not been argued in the course of this appeal but, subject to whatever inference may properly be drawn from that factor, I think it right to express my view in what I hope are clear terms. In my view, the liability, if any, of the occupier of premises to any person injured thereon should be tested in the same manner as any other action laid in negligence - whether or not there was a failure to take reasonable care, with such guidance as to the application of that principle as may be necessary in the circumstances of a particular case."[21]

5–11 In some instances, a case might be more notable for an obiter statement made by the judge rather than how and why the court came

[19] [1994] 1 I.L.R.M. 499 at 501.
[20] [1987] I.L.R.M. 768.
[21] [1987] I.L.R.M. 768 at 788.

to the conclusion that resolved the case. A good example of this is the case of *DPP v Bartley.*[22] In this case, the accused pleaded guilty to various counts of sexual offences against his stepsister. In line with precedents on point, the trial judge sentenced him, taking account of a number of factors such as his confession, his guilty plea, and the effects of his abuse on the victim. However, in addition to setting the relevant sentence, Carney J. took the opportunity to criticise the gardaí for their failure to investigate the complainant's report of the abuse when she initially raised it when she was 12-and-a-half years old. As a result of the failure to take her complaint seriously, the complainant was abused for a further 25 years. Carney J. endorsed, obiter, a case in England that held that members of the police are required by their office to act in certain instances.[23] This obiter is regarded as putting the gardaí on notice that failure to investigate a credible complaint of a crime could render them liable for a common law criminal offence.[24]

5–12 Although an obiter is not binding, it can be highly persuasive and what was an obiter in one judgment can become the ratio of another. An example of this is *State (Raftis) v Leonard*,[25] in which Murnaghan J. in the High Court reluctantly followed two pre-independence decisions because the Supreme Court in a post-1922 judgment had approved them obiter. He concluded that the views of the Supreme Court should be "given the weight of an opinion of the Court and, as such, an acceptance that the law was as stated therein".[26]

5–13 These examples show why an obiter should not be disregarded, but caution is urged before defaulting to them. As the Supreme Court observed in *IRM v Minister for Justice and Equality*, an obiter is uttered in a different context from the ratio, the latter being formed in response to the "intense focus of adversarial argument".[27] Accordingly, when assessing whether an obiter in one case could form the ratio in another:

---

22 Unreported, High Court, Carney J., 13 June 1997.

23 *R. v Dytham* [1979] Q.B. 722.

24 This case is discussed further in para.5–61. For the relevant text of the judgment, see L. Campbell, S. Kilcommins, C. O'Sullivan and A. Cusack, *Criminal Law in Ireland: Cases and Commentary, 2nd edn* (Dublin: Clarus Press, 2021), para.3.25. See also, *X, Y and Z v United Kingdom* (1997) 24 E.H.R.R. 143.

25 [1960] I.R. 381.

26 [1960] I.R. 381 at 419.

27 [2018] 1 I.R. 417 at para.163.

> "The court's task … becomes … a consideration as to whether the [obiter] observations, detached as they are from the core focus of the case in which they are made, are nevertheless correct and can properly be applied when an issue is properly raised which it is necessary to decide in order to resolve the dispute between the parties."[28]

5–14 Dissenting judgments are also only persuasive on future courts but, like obiter statements, they can be very influential and should not be ignored. Dissents are issued by a judge when they disagree in whole or in part with the reasoning or conclusions of the majority. The "in whole or in part" is important. Cases are often complex, raising more than one issue, and a judge could be with the majority for some issues—their judgment may in fact contain important statements of principle that form part of the ratio on those issues—and not for others. For example, Collins J.'s reasoning in *Delaney v Personal Injuries Assessment Board* on whether the delegation of power to the judiciary by the Judicial Council Act 2019 to draft personal injury guidelines unconstitutionally usurped the legislative role was concurred with by the majority.[29] He determined that it did not, as the delegation of power was appropriately circumscribed by the text of the statute.[30] However, he was in the minority on the subsequent question of whether the delegation was nonetheless unconstitutional because it constituted a breach of judicial independence. He held that the delegation respected the separation of powers as the judiciary, collectively, were the most qualified group to whom power to set personal injury guidelines could be delegated, as the awarding of damages was closely connected to the judicial function.[31] The majority disagreed. For them, "[t]he essential neutrality of judicial adjudication and the disinterested application of the law is irrevocably compromised if judges are seen to have been involved in the making of laws affecting the substantive law which they are then called upon to apply."[32]

---

28 [2018] 1 I.R. 417 at para.164.

29 See, e.g. Faherty J., [2024] IESC 10 at para.27, and Haughton J., [2024] IESC 10 at para.88.

30 [2024] IESC 10 at paras 176–187. For discussion of the constitutional limits placed on the delegation of legislation, see Ch.4, Section B.2(b)(i).

31 [2024] IESC 10 at para.267, 275 per Collins J.

32 [2024] IESC 10 at para.65 per Hogan J. See further para.4–26 and Ch.11, paras 11–06 to 11–09.

5–15 While some are critical of what they regard as the egotism of dissents,[33] this view is not widely shared. Dissenting judgments have value both before and after they are delivered in court. As part of the collegiate judgment drafting process, judges share their views on the case and the existence of a dissenting voice encourages the majority to justify and refine their reasoning.[34] After the finalised judgments are released, dissents can result in legal change over time. Sometimes, a dissent may "soar with passion and ring with rhetoric", seeking "to sow seeds for future harvest".[35] Such dissents promote a vision of justice that has applicability beyond the specifics of the case before the court and the judge speaks not just to their peers, but also to society and subsequent generations.[36] They show us that even when the majority held views that are offensive to modern eyes and ears, there were judges who recognised "the truly horrendous mistake"[37] that was being made and sought to hold the majority to account. The most famous example of such a dissenting judgment in Irish law is that of Henchy J. in *Norris v Attorney General*.[38] *Norris* concerned a constitutional challenge to ss.61

[33] See, e.g. M. Kirby, "Judicial Dissent – Common Law and Civil Law Traditions" (2007) 123 *Law Quarterly Review* 369 at 423.

[34] Justice R.B. Ginsburg, "The Role of Dissenting Opinions" (2010) 95 *Minnesota Law Review* 1 at 3. As Byrne et al note, there is little information about the practice of collegiate drafting of judgments in Irish courts, but it is clear that Supreme Court judges share their draft judgments with one another as they frequently refer to each other's judgments and why they (dis)agree with them; R. Byrne, P. McCutcheon, L. Cahillane and E. Roche-Cagney, *Byrne and McCutcheon on the Irish Legal System*, 7th edn (Dublin: Bloomsbury Professional, 2020), para.4.66. This practice of sharing draft judgments is not confined to the Supreme Court. In an interview with the *Irish Times*, recently retired Supreme Court Judge Marie Baker revealed that in the High Court case of *PP v Health Service Executive* [2014] IEHC 622, she and the two other colleagues who had been empanelled to hear the case worked together to draft the judgment; M. Carolan, "'I cried all the way home': retired judge recalls 'heartbreaking' case of brain-dead pregnant woman", *Irish Times Weekend*, 27 July 2024, p.8. The *PP* case concerned a woman, NP, who was brain-dead but was being kept alive artificially as she was pregnant at the time in order to preserve the life of the foetus. The case was taken in the context of a time when Article 40.3.3° had not been removed from the Constitution. The High Court permitted the withdrawal of life support because the medical evidence was clear that the chance of the child surviving to viability was "virtually non-existent" due to the deterioration of NP's body.

[35] Justice W.J. Brennan, "In Defense of Dissents" (1985) 37 *Hastings Law Journal* 427 at 431.

[36] Justice W.J. Brennan, "In Defense of Dissents" (1985) 37 *Hastings Law Journal* 427 at 432.

[37] Justice R.G. Ginsburg, "The Role of Dissenting Opinions" (2010) 95 *Minnesota Law Review* 1 at 5, quoting Justice A. Scalia, "Dissents" (1988) 12(1) *Organization of American History Magazine* 18.

[38] [1984] I.R. 36.

and 62 of the Offences against the Person Act 1861, which criminalised homosexual acts between consenting adults. The majority, regarding homosexual sex as unnatural and sinful, determined that the provisions were constitutional.[39] Henchy J.'s dissent was eloquent and humane, and is recognised as being one of the best judgments ever written by the Supreme Court.[40] It continues to exert an influence today.[41]

5–16 Other times, what was a dissent in one case becomes the ratio in another when the exact same issue is argued before the courts. Keane J.'s dissent in *Shannon Regional Fisheries Board v Cavan County Council*[42] provides an example of this instance. Keane J. advocated for the recognition of a distinction between strict and absolute liability offences in Irish criminal law, with a due diligence defence available to those accused of strict liability offences. In coming to this conclusion, he applied the Canadian case of *R. v City of Saulte Ste. Marie*.[43] His position did not find the support of the majority in 1997 but it found favour with judges in later cases. In 2006, the Canadian case and Keane J.'s dissent were approved of obiter by Hardiman J. in *CC v Ireland*.[44] In 2008, Keane J.'s dissent was adopted by McCarthy J. in *Reilly v Patwell*.[45]

5–17 Accordingly, judges are generally encouraged to write a dissent if they do not agree with the majority on an issue or issues, because they create opportunities for the law to be honed and evolve. There are, however, two exceptions to this statement. The first is to be found in Article 26.2.2°. This Article provides that, in a case where a Bill is sent to the Supreme Court to have its constitutionality assessed prior to being signed into law, the Supreme Court is required to speak with one voice. No dissenting opinion, if one exists, may be published. When the Constitution was enacted in 1937, the single-judgment rule did not form

39 [1984] I.R. 36 at 64.

40 For praise of the judgment, see, e.g. G. Hogan, "The Judicial Thought and Prose of Mr. Justice Seamus Henchy" (2011) 48 *Irish Jurist* 96 at 116; R. Mac Cormaic, *The Supreme Court* (Dublin: Penguin Ireland, 2016), p.207. This case is also discussed in Ch.3, Section C.3.

41 In *Simpson v Ireland* [2019] IESC 81, MacMenamin J. held (at para.88) that Henchy J.'s dissent correctly identified the main features of the right to privacy. See too, N. Ní Loinsigh, "Judicial Dissent in Ireland: Theory, Practice and the Constraints of the Single Opinion Rules" (2014) 51(1) *Irish Jurist* 123 at 142.

42 [1997] 3 I.R. 267.

43 [1978] 2 S.C.R. 1299.

44 [2006] IESC 33, [2006] 4 I.R. 1 at 78.

45 [2008] IEHC 446.

part of Article 26.2.2°. It was added to it in 1941 by the legislature during the three-year period when the Constitution could be amended without a referendum.[46] In Dáil debates around this amendment, de Valera declared that he wanted the certainty and finality of a single judgment.[47] He was also probably influenced by his disquiet following the first Article 26 referral to the Supreme Court.[48] In Sullivan C.J.'s judgment for the court in that case, where the constitutionality of a Bill that sought to increase the security of the State during the Emergency was reviewed, it was noted that the decision was not unanimous.[49]

5–18 The second exception is s.40(2) of the Offences against the State Act 1939. This section prohibits reference to dissent, if any exists, in judgments released by the Special Criminal Court. No reasons were given for the inclusion of the single-judgment rule in the debates around the 1939 Act, and the section passed without discussion or amendment, but given the political sensitivities of a non-jury court in the context of concern about the existential threat posed to the fledgling State by links between the IRA and Nazi agents,[50] it was presumably determined that the existence of dissent could undermine the legitimacy of the court's decision to convict or acquit.

2. Precedent as Method

5–19 The second way in which the word "precedent" is used is as a method by which:

(i) we identify and extract rules and principles from an earlier judgment; and
(ii) we determine whether the principles extracted must be followed or whether they can be departed from.

[46] Second Amendment of the Constitution Act 1941. The Second Amendment also inserted a single-judgment rule into Article 34.4.5° but this was subsequently removed by the Thirty-third Amendment which created the Court of Appeal: Thirty-third Amendment of the Constitution (Court of Appeal) Act 2013.

[47] N. Ní Loinsigh, "Judicial Dissent in Ireland: Theory, Practice and the Constraints of the Single Opinion Rules" (2014) 51(1) *Irish Jurist* 123 at 136–137.

[48] See further, N. Ní Loinsigh, "Judicial Dissent in Ireland: Theory, Practice and the Constraints of the Single Opinion Rules" (2014) 51(1) *Irish Jurist* 123 at 133–137.

[49] *Re Article 26 of the Constitution and the Offences against the State (Amendment) Bill 1940* [1940] I.R. 470 at 475.

[50] A. Harrison, *The Special Criminal Court: Practice and Procedure* (Dublin: Bloomsbury Professional, 2019), paras 1.09–1.10.

When we talk about precedent in this sense, we are referring to the doctrine of precedent, also known as stare decisis ("let the decision stand"). Point (i) requires us to be familiar with the distinction between ratio and obiter, namely that the former is the binding part of the judgment and the latter merely persuasive, and to tailor our analysis accordingly. Embedded within point (ii) are two steps: first, it is necessary to identify which court produced the ratio and which court it will be argued before; second, it must be determined whether the ratio is relevant to the question asked.

5–20 The first step is important because all rationes are not created equal. The doctrine of precedent requires a hierarchy of courts for it to function effectively; without a hierarchy of courts, it would be difficult to assess the relative authority of competing precedents. In Ireland, as in other common law jurisdictions, inferior courts must follow the relevant prior rationes of superior courts. The latter are binding on the former. By way of contrast, the rationes of inferior courts are merely persuasive for superior courts. The latter can choose to follow or depart from the former. It is worth noting here that the superior courts have adopted some flexibility with respect to following their own prior decisions. In general, superior courts will follow their own prior decisions. However, in exceptional circumstances they will depart from them. We will return to this point in Section D of this chapter.

5–21 The hierarchy of courts is established by the Constitution of Ireland. Article 34 names the superior courts. These are the High Court (Article 34.3), the Court of Appeal (Article 34.2 and 34.4) and the Supreme Court (Article 34.3.3° and 34.5). The Court of Criminal Appeal was a legislatively created superior court,[51] but it was abolished and replaced by the Court of Appeal, which was established on 28 October 2014.[52] However, the decisions of the Court of Criminal Appeal continue to form part of criminal law precedent unless the Court of Appeal or the Supreme Court overrules them.[53]

51 Section 3(1) of the Courts (Establishment and Constitution) Act 1961.

52 Section 6 of the Court of Appeal Act 2014; Court of Appeal Act 2014 (Commencement) (No. 2) Order 2014 (S.I. No. 479 of 2014).

53 For example, in the first judgment posted on the *courts.ie* website heard by the Court of Appeal—*DPP v Walsh* [2014] IECA 10—the prior Court of Criminal Appeal judgment of Keane J. in *People (DPP) v TB* [1996] 3 I.R. 294 was cited approvingly. The precedents of the Court of Criminal Appeal have been repeatedly applied by the Court of Appeal in subsequent judgments.

5–22 Two Articles provide for our inferior courts. Article 34.3.4° does not name the District Court and Circuit Court, simply noting that "Courts of First Instance shall … include Courts of local and limited jurisdiction" and permits their establishment by legislation. It is very rare that either of these courts sets precedents.[54] This is because these courts tend not to issue written judgments due to the volume of cases they hear[55] and because, typically, the cases heard before these courts, while of significance for the individuals involved, may not involve broader issues of legal import. If such questions do arise, they are forwarded to the superior courts by way of a case stated procedure or by means of an appeal on a point of law.[56] The doctrine of precedent requires written judgments in order to function, as they provide a record of the legal reasoning used by the judge(s) to come to their decision. This legal reasoning forms the basis for the precedent.

5–23 Article 38.3.1° allows for the establishment of special courts when it is determined that "the ordinary courts are inadequate to secure the effective administration of justice, and the preservation of peace and order." Part V of the Offences against the State Act 1939 provides for the establishment of the Special Criminal Court.[57] Unlike the District Court and Circuit Court, the practice of the Special Criminal Court is to issue written judgments[58] which means it is possible to extract precedents. However, given the fact-focused nature of the judgments that emanate from the Special Criminal Court, where the court explains how existing legal principles were applied to the facts of the case before it, precedents are rarely created.[59]

---

[54] One such example is *Minister for Industry and Commerce v Hammond Land Metal Co Ltd* [1947] Ir. Jur. Rep. 59, where a Circuit Court decision on the literal rule not applying in cases where a statute is directed at a particular class of persons, was reported; discussed in Ch.4, para.4–54.

[55] In 2022, the District Court resolved 367,592 matters and the Circuit Court 61,406. This is in comparison to 2,234 appeals that were resolved by the Court of Appeal and 241 by the Supreme Court in the same year. Courts Service, *Annual Report 2022* (Dublin: Courts Service, 2023), p.45. This is only the tally of resolved matters; it does not include cases that were not completed within the reporting period.

[56] This will be considered in Ch.9, para.9–70.

[57] See generally Ch.9, but in particular Section C.5.

[58] A. Harrison, *The Special Criminal Court: Practice and Procedure* (Dublin: Bloomsbury Professional, 2019), para.3.130. Three judges hear individual cases before the Special Criminal Court and a single judgment is issued. As noted in para.5–18, it is not permitted to disclose the existence of a dissenting opinion.

[59] An example is *DPP v Kelso* [1984] I.L.R.M. 329.

5–24 The second step embedded in point (ii) is to determine if the ratio is relevant to the question under consideration. Just because a ratio derives from a superior court does not mean that it is automatically binding on an inferior court. A precedent is only applicable to a new case if the precedent raises the same types of questions or points of law as the original case did. If it does not, then the precedent is not useful in resolving the questions that arise in the new case and can be disregarded. This practice is expressed by the well-known legal adage: treat like cases alike and different cases differently.

5–25 The logic of the adage is irreproachable. If a prior case has decided a point of law, then it makes sense that it would be helpful in a future case raising the same or similar points of law.[60] As Byrne et al note, "the seeking of guidance for current practice from past events [is] common in many walks of life. Children pleading with their parents frequently claim parity with their perceived equals ('every other child in my class was allowed to stay up to watch the football match')".[61] In other words, there is no need to reinvent the wheel. The second part of the adage is also important, as recognising differences allows for some flexibility in the doctrine of precedent, but it also creates room for arbitrariness. We will come back to these points in Sections C and E below.

C. Working with Precedent

1. A Chain Novel

5–26 In addition to providing a helpful definition of the ratio in *Considine v Shannon Regional Fisheries Board*, Costello J. observed that it is not always easy to identify what the ratio is in a particular case.[62] This is because a court rarely expressly states "the ratio decidendi of this case is X". This is not to make it difficult for you to locate the ratio, but it is to allow later courts to extrapolate it from the reasoning employed in the decision, which gives the law room to evolve. It is not the role of a judge to set a precedent. It is their function to answer the legal issue(s) arising before them by applying the relevant law. Law is made

[60] J. Holland and J. Webb, *Learning Legal Rules*, 11th edn (Oxford: OUP, 2022), p.135.
[61] R. Byrne, P. McCutcheon, L. Cahillane and E. Roche-Cagney, *Byrne and McCutcheon on the Irish Legal System*, 7th edn (Dublin: Bloomsbury Professional, 2020), para.12.01.
[62] [1994] 1 I.L.R.M. 499 at 501.

as a consequence of this function. Indeed, a judge may not realise the wider significance of the judgment they are writing or which part of the judgment will be designated as the ratio in future cases. In some ways, then, it is erroneous to speak of there being a single ratio waiting to be found for each issue in a case. In reality, what the ratio of a case is often only becomes apparent following interpretation and application by a subsequent court or courts. A very good example of this is a case that originated in Scotland, *Donoghue v Stevenson*,[63] which has been followed in Irish law.

5–27 *Donoghue v Stevenson* involved a woman who ordered ginger beer and ice-cream to make an ice-cream float. She added some ginger beer to her ice-cream, consumed part of the mix, and then added more ginger beer, at which point a decomposed snail fell out of the bottle. The bottle was made of dark opaque glass so the snail was not visible prior to being dislodged from it. Donoghue sued the manufacturer of the ginger beer for negligently causing her to suffer shock and gastroenteritis. The question before the court was whether the manufacturer was liable for its defective product. The House of Lords, in a 3:2 decision, said "yes".

5–28 There are two key passages in the lead judgment given by Lord Atkin, one of which is stated in quite broad terms, the other more narrowly. The first statement is:

> "The rule that you are to love your neighbour becomes in law: You must not injure your neighbour and the lawyer's question: Who is my neighbour? receives a restricted reply. You must take reasonable care to avoid acts or omissions which you can reasonably foresee would be likely to injure your neighbour. Who then, in law, is my neighbour? The answer seems to be – persons who are so closely and directly affected by my act that I ought reasonably to have them in contemplation as being so affected when I am directing my mind to the acts or omissions which are called into question."[64]

The second statement appears later in the judgment:

> "A manufacturer of products, which he sells in such a form as to show that he intends them to reach the ultimate consumer in the form

[63] [1932] A.C. 562.
[64] [1932] A.C. 562 at 580.

> in which they left him with no reasonable possibility of immediate examination [on the consumer's part], and with the knowledge that the absence of reasonable care in the preparation or putting up of the products will result in an injury to the consumer's life or property, owes a duty to the consumer to take that reasonable care."[65]

Box 5.1: Time to Reflect

- If you were a lawyer when the case was first published in 1932, which statement would you have thought was the ratio?
- Refer back to the definitions of ratio and obiter. Which statement is directly relevant to the case in question and which statement do you think goes beyond it?

5–29 It is likely that the majority of people who read the case in 1932 would have assumed that the second statement was the ratio, as it responded more directly to the issue of the case: whether the manufacturer was liable for its defective product. By contrast, they would have dismissed the first statement as obiter, as it seemed more abstract and went beyond the specific legal question asked. For example, a leading textbook published in 1934 wrote: "[w]e cannot do more than take Lord Atkin's general principle as a useful guide and it cannot be regarded as an authoritative proposition of law."[66] However, in subsequent cases, courts focused on the first quote—the neighbour principle—and have applied it to develop the tort of negligence in ways that would never have been envisaged by the parties, lawyers or judges involved in the seminal case. As such, what was originally thought to be an obiter statement in the case is now regarded as the ratio.[67] This outcome was by no means guaranteed. If subsequent lawyers had focused on the second statement, then the ratio from *Donoghue v Stephenson* would have been relevant to a much narrower range of situations. It may even have sunk into obscurity. However, they did not, and today the neighbour principle has been applied in Irish law to negligence claims involving occupiers'

65 [1932] A.C. 562 at 599.

66 A. Goodhart, *Salmond on Torts*, 8th edn (London: Wildy & Sons, 1934), quoted in J. Holland and J. Webb, *Learning Legal Rules*, 11th edn (Oxford: OUP, 2022), p.206.

67 E. Finch and S. Fafinski, *Legal Skills*, 8th edn (Oxford: OUP, 2021), p.156.

liability[68] and professional liability[69] and has been adopted throughout the common law world.[70]

5–30 This case demonstrates that the identification of the ratio is an interpretive choice. It also shows how framing the ratio in a case in narrow or broad terms can determine its subsequent usefulness as a precedent. The more broadly stated a ratio is, the greater the range of possible fact scenarios it can be applicable to, as it can be expanded to accommodate new circumstances. This accounts for the success of the generic "neighbour principle". By way of contrast, the narrower the ratio is stated, the smaller its reach and relevance.

5–31 The easiest way of conceptualising how the ratio of a case can come into focus through an accumulation of interpretive choices made by judges in subsequent cases is to think of the doctrine of precedent as operating like a chain novel. The first decision in the chain, Case A, is the introductory chapter and it sets the scene for everything that follows. It determines what the key principles are for that area of law. The court hearing the next case, Case B, refers to the reasoning in Case A and decides how broadly or narrowly it wishes to apply the reasoning in Case A to its case—whether, for example, to apply the manufacturer owes a duty of care statement or the neighbour principle statement in *Donoghue v Stevenson*. The choice of the court in Case B sets the parameters of the choice for the court in Case C and so on and so on. The more cases in the chain, the more certain the ratio in Case A becomes. O'Donnell J. put it thus in *Gillen v Commissioner of An Garda Síochána*:

> "[T]he *ratio* of any case, and its binding effect, is determined not by what the court itself decides, or indeed any independent analysis of the decision, but rather the manner in which subsequent courts treat the decision. It is accordingly necessary to consider the subsequent case law."[71]

---

68 *McNamara v Electricity Supply Board* [1975] I.R. 1; *Rooney v Connolly* [1987] I.L.R.M. 768. These judicial developments were reformed by the legislature in the Occupiers' Liability Act 1995.

69 *Securities Trust Ltd v Hugh Moore & Alexander Ltd* [1964] I.R. 417.

70 See B. McMahon and W. Binchy, *Law of Torts*, 4th edn (Dublin: Bloomsbury Professional, 2013), paras 6.07–6.36.

71 [2012] 1 I.R. 574 at 600.

2. Selecting the Ratio

5–32 In light of the centrality of identifying and applying the ratio to legal method, this uncertainty about what the ratio is or might be in a given case is understandably disconcerting for the student encountering case law for the first time. However, it is worth remembering that uncertainty is part and parcel of everyday life. Even the apparent certainties of science are subject to change. For example, Newton's laws of gravity were unaltered for centuries but they were upended by Einstein's Theory of Relativity.[72] We cope with uncertainty in our daily lives (will it rain today or not?) because we have developed mechanisms to help us do so (bring an umbrella just in case). This is because experience has taught us how best to accommodate uncertainty. It is also possible to acquire experience with regard to locating and framing the ratio. This is through the practice of reading cases regularly. You might not be able to say with confidence that the ratio of the case is X, but with practice you will be able to say with confidence where that ratio is likely to be located. With more practice, and depending on what use you wish to make of it, you will be able to say what you think the ratio might be in broad or narrow terms.[73]

5–33 The first step in this process is to become familiar with the typical structure of cases so you will know where to focus your attention. Judgments typically follow a set structure and most have four parts:

(a) facts that raise particular legal issues;
(b) a summary of the law that the opposing parties argue governs those issues;
(c) application of the relevant law to material facts of the case; and
(d) a decision.[74]

Part (a) is self-explanatory. A case would not be before the courts unless there was a legal dispute. The recitation of the facts that precipitated the dispute, the legal issues raised by the dispute, and the procedural history of the case are laid out first. In part (b), the judge sets out the

[72] J. Holland and J. Webb, *Learning Legal Rules*, 11th edn (Oxford: OUP, 2022), p.180.
[73] For more on reading cases see Ch.15, Section C.
[74] If there is only one judgment issued by the court, then this is the structure that the judgment will follow. If there are multiple judgments, the lead judgment will follow this structure. The remaining judgments will omit (a) and may omit (b). Their focus will be on where they agree or disagree with the lead judgment, i.e. (c) and (d).

constitutional provisions and/or domestic or EU legislation, if any, relevant to those issues and summarises all of the precedents that were raised by opposing legal counsel in their arguments for their respective clients. The judge typically does this neutrally, preferring to evaluate the competing claims in part (c) of the judgment. Note that it is very rare for a case to involve all four primary sources of law. This is because parties to a case will only raise the law that they think is relevant to the legal issues raised. Some cases raise questions pertaining to EU law, others raise constitutional and/or legislative matters which may be assisted with reference to relevant interpretive case law, while others might be entirely based on the common law where there is no higher primary source of law governing that particular legal area.

5–34 As noted above, in part (c) the judge evaluates the arguments put forth by opposing counsel. It is in this evaluation process, where the judge reasons out which side's arguments are more convincing, that the ratio is to be found. To repeat Costello J.'s words from *Considine v Shannon Regional Fisheries Board*: "[t]he *ratio* of a case is discovered by determining what proposition of law justified the decision in the light of the material facts which the court decided."[75] Accordingly, when reading this portion of the judgment, you should focus on those passages where the judge identifies the "rule" or "principle" that governs the issue(s) and on why that rule/principle was applied in the way that it was to the facts of the case. This will help you to decide if a particular case is binding or not in a similar or slightly different factual scenario.

5–35 This focus on the judge's or judges' legal reasoning process is important. Many students are distracted by the facts of cases and focus on the result obtained, part (d), rather than on the reasoning process that led to that result. This means that when you read a case, you are not concerned about *who* won or lost the case but *why* they won or lost the case, i.e. the legal basis for the decision. How to read cases and to present the results of your research in the appropriate manner will be discussed in more detail in Chs 15–16.

5–36 Finally, it should be noted that it is rare for a student to read a case without some sense of its context or relevance. Typically, you read a case

[75] [1994] 1 I.L.R.M. 499 at 501.

because it has been included in a reading list or has been emphasised as being particularly important by the lecturer. Frequently, the case is one that has been considered in subsequent cases and, as such, its ratio is well established. Accordingly, the difficulty most commonly experienced by students is not with identifying the ratio, but with deciding whether or not it applies to a new fact situation and whether or not you wish it to.

3. Analogising and Distinguishing

5–37 The processes of analogising and distinguishing are the tools that lawyers, judges and you will use when faced with a precedent that, at first glance, appears binding on them/you. An analogy is made when a court/lawyer/you determine(s) that the reasoning and principle applied in the precedent should be applied to the new case either because of the similarity of the facts raised in both cases or because the issues are similar. A decision is distinguished when a court/lawyer/you decide(s) that the facts/issues raised in the prior case are not relevant to the new case. This justifies the court/the lawyer/you taking a different approach to that taken in the precedent.

5–38 Professor Goodhart explains one basis on which a court (and, by necessary implication, you) can analogise with or distinguish from a previous case: focus on the material facts of the case. He writes:

> "If [the material facts in both cases] are identical, then the first case is a binding precedent for the second, and the court must reach the same conclusion as it did in the first one. If the first case lacks any material fact or contains any additional ones not found in the second, then it is not a direct precedent."[76]

This observation ties in with Costello J.'s focus on the material facts in his definition of the ratio in *Considine v Shannon Regional Fisheries Board*.[77] Professor Goodhart also supplies welcome advice for how you can discern which facts are (im)material when the judge does not specifically state their status:

[76] A.L. Goodhart, "Determining the *Ratio Decidendi* of a Case" (1930) 40 *Yale Law Journal* 161 at 180.

[77] [1994] 1 I.L.R.M. 499 at 501.

> "The difficulty in these cases is to determine whether a court has or has not considered the fact immaterial. Evidence of this implication is found when the court, after having stated the facts generally, then proceeds to choose a smaller number of facts on which it bases its conclusion. The omitted facts are presumably held to be immaterial."[78]

Another basis on which you can analogise with or distinguish from a prior decision is to focus on the legal issues raised. If they are not sufficiently similar to justify utilising the same principle to resolve them, then you will distinguish the new case from the prior one; if they are sufficiently similar, then you will analogise.

5–39 Whether you analogise with or distinguish from a prior case will depend on the degree of similarity or difference between it and the new case and whether the prior case helps or hinders the position that you wish to advance. If the principle articulated in precedent X is one that you think will be or should be applied to new situation Y, then, by means of reasoning by analogy, you would draw attention to the similarities between both cases and show how the principle articulated in X would resolve the legal issue in Y. If, however, you think that the principle is not relevant or should not be, then you would frame the ratio in X in narrow terms and emphasise the differences between both cases, showing that X is not the best means of resolving the legal problems raised in Y.

5–40 These processes of analogising and distinguishing are not unique to law. You draw analogies and make distinctions every day.[79] For example, you and your friend both like medical drama series and she asks your advice about whether she should start *The Good Doctor*, as she knows that you watched it. You know that she likes *Grey's Anatomy* but dislikes *New Amsterdam*. If you analogise *The Good Doctor* with *Grey's Anatomy*, then she is more likely to want to watch it. If you analogise it with *New Amsterdam*, then she is unlikely to wish to view it. Holland and Webb give a good example of everyday distinguishing:

> "At its simplest level, you distinguish physical objects – a television from a [Personal Video] recorder for example … At a more complicated

[78] A.L. Goodhart, "Determining the *Ratio Decidendi* of a Case" (1930) 40 *Yale Law Journal* 161 at 175. See generally at 173 et seq.

[79] J. Holland and J. Webb, *Learning Legal Rules*, 11th edn (Oxford: OUP, 2022), p.195.

level ... we all distinguish the faces of billions of people, despite the fact that they are built of the same, limited number of component parts. We would submit that, saying *exactly* why Deb and Jane are not the same person might, in the end, be more difficult than distinguishing between [case X and case Y] ... ."[80]

D. Precedent in the Irish Courts

1. The Vertical Operation of the Doctrine of Precedent

5–41 As noted in Section B, one of the preconditions for the doctrine of precedent to operate effectively is that there must be a clear hierarchy of courts. This chain of command must exist so that each court knows whether another court's decision is binding on it or whether it is merely persuasive. Generally, a court must follow the relevant decisions of courts superior to it in the judicial hierarchy. In Ireland, Article 34.2 of the Constitution establishes that there are three layers to our courts system: first-instance courts, a court of appeal and a court of final appeal. In ascending order of ranking, these courts are the District and Circuit Courts (Article 34.3.4°), the High Court (Article 34.3.1°), the Court of Appeal (Article 34.4) and the Supreme Court (Article 34.5). The Special Criminal Court (Article 38.3.1°) is a first-instance court that sits outside the "ordinary" court structure[81] but is not entirely disconnected from it. Cases can be directed to it from other first-instance courts[82] and appeals lie to the Court of Appeal[83] and Supreme Court.[84]

80 J. Holland and J. Webb, *Learning Legal Rules*, 11th edn (Oxford: OUP, 2022), p.195 (emphasis in original).

81 Article 38.3.1° provides for the establishment of first-instance special courts in circumstances where "the ordinary courts are inadequate to secure the effective administration of justice, and the preservation of peace and order."

82 It is more common for cases to be sent from the District Court than from the Circuit Court or Central Criminal Court; A. Harrison, *The Special Criminal Court: Practice and Procedure* (Dublin: Bloomsbury Professional, 2019), paras 3.37–3.44.

83 Section 44(1) of the Offences against the State Act 1939, as substituted by s.32 of the Criminal Procedure Act 2010, provides for an appeal from conviction or sentence for the accused. The DPP has three routes to appeal. First, they may seek clarification on a point of law on a without prejudice basis following an acquittal pursuant to s.34 of the Criminal Procedure Act 1967, as amended. Second, they may seek the quashing of an acquittal via s.23 of the Criminal Procedure Act 2010, as amended. Finally, they may wish to appeal a sentence for being unduly lenient, relying on s.2(1) of the Criminal Justice Act 1993.

84 Only where a case meets the criteria in Article 34.5.3°; Courts of Justice Act 1924 s.29(3), as substituted by s.22 of the Criminal Justice Act 2006.

5–42 As this ranking of the courts is prescribed by the Constitution, it is the constitutional duty of all inferior courts to abide by and apply relevant precedents issued by courts superior to them. Moreover, as the ultimate guardian of the Constitution, it is the duty of the Supreme Court to ensure that this vertical hierarchy is respected. The Supreme Court has rarely had to admonish lower courts for disregarding its precedents. Indeed, as we noted when we encountered the case of *State (Raftis) v Leonard*, such is the respect that the lower courts have for the judgments of the Supreme Court that a judge followed an obiter statement from that court despite disagreeing with it.[85] On the atypical occasion that a lower court has not complied with an applicable Supreme Court precedent, the Supreme Court has emphatically asserted its position at the top of the curial hierarchy. In the High Court case of *McDonnell v Byrne Engineers*, Murnaghan J. refused to follow the formula for the assessment of damages that had been set by the Supreme Court in *Carroll v Clare County Council*[86] and stated that he had no intention of doing so in any future cases.[87] On appeal to the Supreme Court, O'Higgins C.J. reprimanded Murnaghan J. for his refusal to respect this constitutionally mandated hierarchy:

> "[U]nder the Constitution, the Supreme Court was the final court of appeal. As such, it had the duty, when necessary to declare what legal principles should apply to cases that were reviewed by the court. Where necessary, it had the duty to lay down guidelines for all courts and all judges as to the manner in which such cases were to be tried.
>
> It was equally the duty of all other courts and judges to follow directions as to law and procedures as given by the Supreme Court."[88]

He continued: "[i]t is with real concern that this court notes that ... the trial judge [has refused to follow the *Carroll* guidelines]. ... This court will not permit this situation to continue and shall insist that its directions be respected and obeyed."[89]

85 [1960] I.R. 381 at 419 per Murnaghan J. See para.5–12.
86 [1975] I.R. 221.
87 *Irish Times*, 4 October 1978, p.13.
88 *Irish Times*, 4 October 1978, p.13.
89 *Irish Times*, 4 October 1978, p.13.

5–43 The Supreme Court's zealousness in protecting its position at the top of the hierarchy has led to some questionable decisions. For example, in *State (Harkin) v O'Malley*,[90] O'Higgins C.J. held that the High Court was bound to follow an erroneous earlier Supreme Court decision. He held that only the Supreme Court has the power to overrule a previous Supreme Court decision, be it wrongly decided or not. While this decision accords with the letter of Article 34, it is certainly arguable that it was unnecessary to give effect to that Article. To recognise that a prior Supreme Court decision was made *per incuriam* (in ignorance of a relevant law or precedent), as was the case in *State (Harkin)*, is not to disrespect the Supreme Court's position at the top of the hierarchy. In order to come to such a decision, the lower court must give careful attention to the Supreme Court precedent and the error must be clearly evident. It is therefore not a matter of the lower court manipulating or disregarding a higher court precedent in order to avoid being bound by it. Instead, it respects precedent by requiring precedents to be correct in law. In practical terms, too, this decision is problematic. Requiring an individual to appeal a case all the way to the Supreme Court in order for an obvious error to be rectified seems to be an unnecessary waste of that individual's time and money.

5–44 This criticism also applies to cases where the Supreme Court exercises its position at the top of the hierarchy of courts to protect the position of other courts in the hierarchy. In *O'B v Patwell*,[91] the Supreme Court held that a lower court is required to follow a decision of a higher court (in this case, two prior Court of Criminal Appeal decisions) even when it is believed to be erroneous and it is correctly anticipated that it would be overruled by the Supreme Court.

2. The Horizontal Operation of the Doctrine of Precedent in the Supreme Court

5–45 The position historically was that precedent operated just as rigidly horizontally as it did vertically. In other words, courts of co-ordinate jurisdiction were as bound by their own prior judgments as inferior courts were by the judgments of superior courts. The precedent for this

90 [1978] I.R. 269.
91 [1994] 2 I.L.R.M. 465.

position was *London Tramways Co v London County Council*.[92] In this case, Halsbury L.J. set a strict rule requiring the House of Lords to abide by its own prior decisions:

> "Of course I do not deny that cases of individual hardship may arise and there may be a current of opinion in the profession that such and such a judgment was erroneous; but what is that occasional interference with what is perhaps abstract justice, as compared with the inconvenience—the disastrous inconvenience—of having each question subject to being re-argued and the dealings of mankind rendered doubtful by reason of different decisions, so that in truth and in fact there would be no real final Court of Appeal?"[93]

However, this ruling no longer represents the legal position either in the UK or in Ireland. Ireland departed from the precedent first in 1964 with the case of *State (Quinn) v Ryan*.[94] The UK followed suit in 1966.[95]

5–46 Quinn was an Irish national who, when he lived in England, had allegedly committed larceny. On his release from Mountjoy Prison, he was handed over to the English authorities by the gardaí and was transported to Northern Ireland where he could be processed for trial. This was done without any judicial oversight of the Irish courts, as would normally be required where an Irish citizen was extradited to face criminal charges in another country. The reason for not bringing Quinn before an Irish court was s.29 of the Petty Sessions (Ireland) Act 1851. Under this statute, passed when Ireland was part of the UK, a person could be removed from Ireland to England without appearing before the national courts. Two prior Supreme Court decisions had upheld the constitutionality of the statute.[96]

---

[92] [1898] A.C. 375.

[93] [1898] A.C. 375 at 380.

[94] [1965] I.R. 70.

[95] *Practice Note* [1966] 1 W.L.R. 1234.

[96] *State (Dowling) v Kingston (No. 2)* [1937] I.R. 699, when the provision had been challenged under the 1922 Constitution, and *State (Duggan) v Tapley* [1962] I.R. 62, when it was challenged under the 1937 Constitution. It should, however, be noted that Walsh J. rejected arguments that these cases had decided the issue, as they had focused on whether s.29 was unconstitutional with regard to specific Articles of both Constitutions rather than considering a question of general repugnancy: *State (Quinn) v Ryan* [1965] I.R. 70 at 128–129. Ó Dálaigh C.J. and Kingsmill Moore J. agreed that the two cases did not decide the issue before the court: [1965] I.R. 70 at 119–121, 123.

5–47 Walsh J. found that s.29 was unconstitutional and he did so on the basis that the Supreme Court was not "the successor" of the House of Lords but was an independent Irish creation, established under the provisions of the 1937 Constitution by the Courts (Supplemental Provisions) Act 1961.[97] Therefore, just because *London Tramways* bound the House of Lords to follow its own prior decisions, this foreign decision did not similarly bind the Supreme Court in respect of its practice. However, Walsh J. emphasised that he was not abandoning the doctrine of stare decisis:

> "This is not to say, however, that the Court would depart from an earlier decision for any but the most compelling reasons. The advantages of *stare decisis* are many and obvious so long as it is remembered that it is a policy and not a binding rule."[98]

5–48 *State (Quinn)* was considered and applied in *Attorney General v Ryan's Car Hire Ltd.*[99] The issue in this case was whether an Air Corps pilot, who had been involved in an off-duty car crash involving another (hired) car, was a servant of the Minister for Defence. If he was, the State would be entitled to damages from the car rental company which they could use to offset the cost of the wages and medical treatment they provided to the injured pilot. Like *State (Quinn)*, there were two previous Supreme Court decisions on this point that held that such a person was a servant of the State. However, Kingsmill Moore J. declined to follow these two decisions. Having cited *State (Quinn)* and rejected *London Tramways*, he stated:

> "The law that we have taken over is based on the following of precedents and there can be no question of abandoning the principle of following precedent as the normal, indeed almost universal, procedure. To do so would be to introduce into our law an intolerable uncertainty. But where the Supreme Court is of the opinion that there is a compelling reason why it should not follow an earlier decision of its own, or of the Courts of ultimate jurisdiction which preceded it, where it appears to be clearly wrong, is it bound to perpetuate the error?

97 [1965] I.R. 70 at 126.
98 [1965] I.R. 70 at 127.
99 [1965] I.R. 642.

> ... In my opinion the rigid rule of *stare decisis* must in a Court of ultimate resort give place to a more elastic formula. Where such a Court is clearly of opinion that an earlier decision was erroneous it should be at liberty to refuse to follow it, at all events in exceptional cases."[100]

The language here specifically references Walsh J.'s statement in *State (Quinn)* that one could refuse to follow stare decisis in compelling circumstances,[101] and makes explicit that compelling circumstances are the exception rather than the norm.

5–49 The decision in *Ryan's Car Hire* is important for a number of reasons. First, it showed that the new principle of flexibility regarding prior Supreme Court precedents established in *State (Quinn)* was not confined to questions concerning the constitutionality of legislation, as may have been initially thought, but had more general application.[102] Second, it confirmed Walsh J.'s point that the doctrine of precedent was still important in Irish law. Although Kingsmill Moore J. did not respect *Minister for Finance v O'Brien*[103] and *Attorney General v Córas Iompair Éireann*[104] by overruling them, his rejection of those decisions was based on the precedent set by Walsh J. in *State (Quinn)*. He found that there were exceptional and compelling circumstances, as per *State (Quinn)*, to legitimate the departure. Finally, the focus on the Supreme Court's status as a "court of ultimate resort"[105] is important because it provides additional legitimation for the relaxation of the strict rule of precedent, untainted by the suspicion that political motives underlay the judgment in *State (Quinn)*.[106] It makes sense that the Supreme Court should exercise some flexibility as it is the final domestic court to which parties in conflict can bring disputes. It could bring the administration of justice into disrepute if such a court were unable to depart from its own prior decisions, even when such decisions were no longer appropriate in light of changes in law and/or society.

[100] [1965] I.R. 642 at 653–654.
[101] Having quoted the passage quoted in para.5–47; [1965] I.R. 642 at 653.
[102] R. Byrne, P. McCutcheon, L. Cahillane and E. Roche-Cagney, *Byrne and McCutcheon on the Irish Legal System*, 7th edn (Dublin: Bloomsbury Professional, 2020), para.12.38.
[103] [1949] I.R. 91.
[104] 90 I.L.T.R. 139.
[105] [1965] I.R. 642 at 654.
[106] G. Hogan, "Irish Nationalism as a Legal Ideology" (1986) 75(300) *Studies: An Irish Quarterly Review* 528 at 532.

5–50 This consideration was foregrounded by Henchy J. in his judgment in *McNamara v Electricity Supply Board*.[107] In a case concerning an occupier's liability to trespassers, Henchy J. departed from the old rule which said occupiers only had an obligation not to set a trap for such persons, on the basis that it ran counter to modern decisions, such as *Donoghue v Stevenson*,[108] and because it was "unsuitabl[e] to modern social conditions".[109]

5–51 However, in *Mogul of Ireland Ltd v Tipperary (North Riding) County Council*,[110] Henchy J. was far less willing to depart from precedent and this case has been pointed to as the decision that returned focus to the exceptional and compelling circumstances limitation made in *State (Quinn)* and *Ryan's Car Hire*. According to Henchy J.:

> "A decision of the full Supreme Court ... given in a fully-argued case and on a consideration of all the relevant materials, should not normally be overruled merely because a later Court inclines to a different conclusion. Of course, if possible, error should not be reinforced by repetition or affirmation, and the desirability of achieving certainty, stability, and predictability should yield to the demands of justice. However, a balance has to be struck between rigidity and vacillation, and to achieve that balance the later Court must, at the least, be *clearly* of opinion that the earlier decision was erroneous."[111]

Indeed, Henchy J. extended the rationes of both decisions by adding an additional limitation:

> "Even if the later Court is clearly of the opinion that the earlier decision was wrong, it may decide in the interests of justice not to overrule it if it has become inveterate and if, in a widespread or fundamental way, people have acted on the basis of its correctness to such an extent that greater harm would result from overruling it than from allowing it to stand."[112]

---

107 [1975] I.R. 1.
108 [1932] A.C. 562.
109 [1975] I.R. 1 at 23.
110 [1976] I.R. 260.
111 [1976] I.R. 260 at 272–273 (emphasis in original).
112 [1976] I.R. 260 at 273.

5–52 The *Mogul* approach has been repeated in multiple cases, such as *Hynes-O'Sullivan v O'Driscoll*[113] and *O'Brien v Mirror Group Newspapers Ltd.*[114] However, it was noted by the two dissenting judges in *SPUC v Grogan (No. 5)* that the *Mogul* limitations did not apply in cases concerning citizens' constitutional rights because it would be unconstitutional to deny such rights.[115] Byrne et al note that the majority did not disagree with their general observations on this point.[116] More recent cases have muddied the waters somewhat. In *People (DPP) v JC*,[117] which overturned the exclusionary rule regarding unconstitutionally obtained evidence set by *People (DPP) v Kenny*,[118] the Supreme Court agreed with the dissenting judges in *SPUC*,[119] but the result was to reduce, not improve, the rights of accused persons.[120] O'Donnell C.J. similarly endorsed the *SPUC* judgments in *O'Meara v Minister for Social Protection*,[121] but then seemed to align the approach to constitutional rights more with *Mogul* when he held obiter (as, in his view, it was unnecessary to overrule *State (Nicolaou) v An Bord Uchtála*[122] to resolve the issue raised in the case before him) that "it would ... require a high degree of assurance that a decision was wrong, and that it can and should be corrected, to overrule such a long-established [constitutional precedent]."[123]

5–53 The *JC* case is also interesting as an illustration of the fact that judges hearing the same case can disagree on whether a previous decision was clearly erroneous or not. MacMenamin J., in one of the three majority judgments, observed that "[t]ime, context and attitudes are always relevant [in the application of constitutional rights]. The question, now, is whether there is available a better formulation of the exclusionary rule based on 'better reasoning' or empirical experience?"[124]

---

[113] [1989] I.L.R.M. 349.
[114] [2001] 1 I.R. 1.
[115] [1998] 4 I.R. 343 per Denham J. at 376 and Keane J. at 389.
[116] R. Byrne, P. McCutcheon, L. Cahillane and E. Roche-Cagney, *Byrne and McCutcheon on the Irish Legal System*, 7th edn (Dublin: Bloomsbury Professional, 2020), para.12.48.
[117] [2017] 1 I.R. 417.
[118] [1990] 2 I.R. 110.
[119] [2017] 1 I.R. 417 at para.490 per O'Donnell J.
[120] For further Information, see Y.M. Daly, "Overruling the Protectionist Exclusionary Rule: *DPP v JC*" (2015) 19(4) *International Journal of Evidence and Proof* 270.
[121] [2024] IESC 1 at para.50.
[122] [1966] I.R. 567. This case set the precedent that the family protected by Article 41 of the Constitution is the family based on marriage.
[123] [2024] IESC 1 at para.123.
[124] [2017] 1 I.R. 417 at para.897.

He determined that there was. McKechnie J. disagreed on the basis that no such empirical evidence had been placed before the Supreme Court:

> "[743] It is for me of the utmost concern and of striking significance that the D.P.P. has failed to identify, in any concrete context, the problems which she suggests, at the highest level of generality, exist with *The People (Director of Public Prosecutions) v. Kenny* [1990] 2 I.R. 110. The exclusionary rule as therein announced is said by her 'to frustrate prosecutions' and that it 'regularly does [so] in practice'. Apart from this entirely unsupported assertion, nothing else is offered by way of empirical evidence. ...
>
> [760] So why is that decision wrong, plainly wrong, and what are the compelling reasons advanced by the D.P.P., which would justify the application of the 'overruling jurisdiction' above referred to? When one looks at the principles in *Attorney General and Another v. Ryan's Car Hire Ltd*. [1965] I.R. 642 and *Mogul of Ireland v. Tipperary (N.R.) C.C.* [1976] I.R. 260, it is very difficult to see how it is, if one is to apply those principles in a detached and objective manner ... ."

5–54 The changed reality in which overruling is now a possibility has modified judicial decision-making in arguably unexpected ways. For example, in *Finucane v McMahon*,[125] Griffin J. and Finlay C.J. decided to accede to the majority decision to overrule a prior Supreme Court decision even though they believed it to be correctly decided. They determined that strong dissents on their part could lead to appeals in the future and that, in the interests of consistency, the Supreme Court decision should be a unanimous one. Griffin J. wrote:

> "... I should like to say, having regard to the importance of precedent in our system of jurisprudence as providing a degree of certainty upon which members of the public are entitled to rely in the conduct of their affairs, the principles established in and the conclusions reached by the majority of the Court, are those which should now be applied in all cases in which the [point of law in question] is in issue."[126]

125 [1990] 1 I.R. 165.
126 [1990] 1 I.R. 165 at 218.

Although their restraint has been praised as "commendably statesmanlike",[127] silence in this instance would have been more effective in achieving the façade of unanimity than revealing the existence of dissent within the judicial ranks. Nonetheless, this judgment has provided an example for others to follow where silence would have raised questions. In *ACC Loan Management Ltd v Connolly*,[128] Hogan J. resiled from his dissenting judgment in *de Kretser v Ulster Bank (Ireland) Ltd*.[129] While he still believed that his approach in *de Kretser* was correct, because the majority decision in *de Krester* had been accepted in *Curran v Bank of Ireland*,[130] he chose to "adopt ... as his own" the majority view in *de Krester* in order "that the basic principles underlying it may clearly represent the decision of this Court".[131]

5–55 Finally, it was suggested in *Doyle v Hearne*[132] that the Supreme Court would be less willing to review a previous Supreme Court judgment if it had been issued by a full sitting of the court. At the time, a full sitting would consist of five judges, but cases would also have been heard before a division of three judges. Since that decision, it has been decided to empanel seven judges for exceptional cases.[133] This case also established that the decision to overrule a prior precedent need not be a unanimous one.

3. The Horizontal Operation of the Doctrine of Precedent in the Other Appellate Courts

5–56 The cases considered thus far have focused on the circumstances in which the Supreme Court can overrule its own prior decisions. It was unsurprising when the other courts showed a willingness, in theory at least, to follow suit in respect of their own prior decisions. In *Kearns v*

[127] R. Byrne, P. McCutcheon, L. Cahillane and E. Roche-Cagney, *Byrne and McCutcheon on the Irish Legal System*, 7th edn (Dublin: Bloomsbury Professional, 2020), para.12.56.
[128] [2017] IECA 119.
[129] [2016] IECA 371.
[130] [2016] IECA 399.
[131] [2017] IECA 119 at para.26, quoting Finlay C.J. in *Finucane v McMahon* [1990] 1 I.R. 165 at 207.
[132] [1987] I.R. 601.
[133] The first occasion this occurred was for the case of *Sinnott v Minister for Education* [2001] 2 I.R. 545. Cases involving an assessment of whether the President has become permanently incapacitated or the constitutionality of a Bill must be heard before a Supreme Court of "not less than five judges" pursuant to Articles 12.3.1° and 26.2.1° respectively.

Manresa Estates Ltd,[134] Kenny J. chose to follow two prior High Court judgments, but stated: "[a]lthough I am not bound by decisions of other judges of the High Court, the usual practice is to follow them unless I am satisfied that they were wrongly decided."

5–57 Matters for courts lower in the hierarchy than the Supreme Court are slightly complicated by the fact that they, unlike the Supreme Court, are not the court of "ultimate resort".[135] In *Irish Trust Bank Ltd v Central Bank of Ireland*, Parke J. refused to depart from an earlier High Court decision because it was possible for an appellate court to overrule such a decision.[136] He did, however, accept that in principle it was possible for the High Court to overrule the decision of a co-ordinate court:

> "I fully accept that there are occasions in which the principle of stare decisis may be departed from but I consider that these are extremely rare. A Court may depart from a decision of a Court of equal jurisdiction if it appears that such a decision was given in a case in which either insufficient authority was cited or incorrect submissions advanced or in which the nature and wording of the judgment itself reveals that the judge disregarded or misunderstood an important element in the case or the arguments submitted to him or the authority cited or in some other way departed from the proper standard to be adopted in judicial determination."[137]

Clarke J., in his frequently cited judgment in *Re Worldport Ireland Ltd*, appended the additional consideration that "the judgment sought to be revisited was delivered a sufficiently lengthy period in the past so that the jurisprudence of the court in the relevant area might be said to have advanced in the intervening period".[138] After his elevation to the Supreme Court, he confirmed that the *Re Worldport* approach was correct in *Kadri v Governor of Wheatfield Prison*.[139]

---

[134] Unreported, High Court, Kenny J., 25 July 1975.
[135] *Attorney General v Ryan's Car Hire Ltd* [1965] I.R. 642 at 654.
[136] [1976–1977] I.L.R.M. 50 at 53.
[137] [1976–1977] I.L.R.M. 50 at 53.
[138] [2005] IEHC 189 at para.14.
[139] [2012] IESC 27 at paras 2.1–2.2.

5–58 The High Court's respect for its own prior precedents is "especially evident"[140] in *AG v Residential Institutions Redress Board*,[141] where the judge in question, Hogan J., reluctantly followed the prior co-ordinate precedent. Although there are cases where the High Court has departed from its own decisions, Byrne et al are correct in their observation that "the gravitational pull of precedent is stronger in the High Court than in the Supreme Court".[142]

5–59 The decisions of the Court of Appeal, established in 2014, are intended to be "final and conclusive"[143] but an appeal to the Supreme Court is possible where a case raises an issue of "general public importance" or an appeal is determined to be "in the interests of justice".[144] The Court of Appeal therefore is, apart from exceptional cases, the "court of ultimate resort" in the majority of cases. This status might have supported it in choosing to adopt the same approach to precedent as the Supreme Court. Yet in *ACC Loan Management Ltd v Connolly*,[145] Hogan J. cited Parke J.'s comments in *Irish Trust Bank Ltd v Central Bank of Ireland* and assumed the High Court's approach to its own prior decisions "by analogy".[146] However, it is worth noting that the Court of Appeal's partial predecessor, the Court of Criminal Appeal,[147] was willing to depart from its own prior decisions, even though a similar limited right of appeal to the Supreme Court existed.[148] In *People (Attorney General) v Moore*, Davitt P. stated:

> "There remains the question whether we are bound to accept and apply the principle enunciated in *O'Neill's case* even though we differ from it to the extent we have indicated ... We are not

[140] R. Byrne, P. McCutcheon, L. Cahillane and E. Roche-Cagney, *Byrne and McCutcheon on the Irish Legal System*, 7th edn (Dublin: Bloomsbury Professional, 2020), para.12.66.

[141] [2012] IEHC 492.

[142] R. Byrne, P. McCutcheon, L. Cahillane and E. Roche-Cagney, *Byrne and McCutcheon on the Irish Legal System*, 7th edn (Dublin: Bloomsbury Professional, 2020), para.12.67.

[143] Article 34.4.3°.

[144] Art.34.5.3°.

[145] [2017] IECA 119.

[146] [2017] IECA 119 at para.25.

[147] Partial predecessor both because the new Court of Appeal hears civil and criminal appeals, as compared to the Court of Criminal Appeal which could only hear the latter, and because the Court of Criminal Appeal was a creature of statute whereas the Court of Appeal is named in the Constitution. The Court of Appeal described the Court of Criminal Appeal as its predecessor in *DPP v Cotter* [2014] IECA 40 at para.1.

[148] Section 29 of the Courts of Justice Act 1924, as substituted by s.22 of the Criminal Justice Act 2006.

> unmindful of the principle of *stare decisis* and of the desirability of having uniformity in judicial decisions interpreting the law. We think, however, that the interests of justice will best be served by giving effect to our own opinions, even though they differ from some of those expressed in *O'Neill's* case ... ."[149]

While it is surprising, in light of its constitutional status, that the Court of Appeal took a more restrictive approach to precedent than did the statutory Court of Criminal Appeal,[150] it remains an open question as to whether the interests of justice in criminal cases may result in a more flexible approach to criminal appeals.[151]

4. Pre-1922 Decisions

5–60 The decisions of *State (Quinn)* and *Ryan's Car Hire* effectively resolved another question that had troubled Irish judges for some time. The question was whether pre-1922 House of Lords decisions were binding on them, subject of course to the requirement that they were consistent with the Constitution,[152] because at that time the House of Lords was the final court of appeal in Ireland. The initial position was that the pre-1922 decision would have had to have been accepted in Irish law prior to 1922.[153] In a later decision, it was suggested that all pre-1922 House of Lords decisions were binding, whether they had been adopted into Irish law or not.[154] However, due to *State (Quinn)* and *Ryan's Car Hire*, the focus is no longer on pre-1922 decisions as a group, but on each individual decision if, and when, it is argued before the Supreme Court. Each decision is binding to the same extent that prior Supreme Court decisions are binding, presuming they survived the transition into law following the adoption of the 1937 Constitution.

---

149 [1964] Ir. Jur. Rep. 6 at 12–13, considering *People (Attorney General) v O'Neill* [1964] Ir. Jur. Rep. 1.

150 In the first edition of this textbook, it was postulated that the Court of Appeal would adopt the same approach as the Court of Criminal Appeal. This did not come to pass. See *Fundamentals of the Irish Legal System*, 1st edn (Dublin: Round Hall, 2016), para.5–51.

151 R. Byrne, P. McCutcheon, L. Cahillane and E. Roche-Cagney, Byrne and McCutcheon on the Irish Legal System, 7th edn (Dublin: Bloomsbury Professional, 2020), para.12.76.

152 Article 50 of the 1937 Constitution.

153 *Exham v Beamish* [1939] I.R. 336.

154 *Minister for Finance v O'Brien* [1949] I.R. 91.

5. Foreign Precedents

5–61 The judgments of foreign courts are only persuasive for Irish courts because it would be inappropriate for a sovereign nation to be bound by non-national judgments.[155] This is so irrespective of the calibre of the judge who made the decision or the court from which it emanated. In practical terms, this means that a District Court judge is entirely free to disregard precedent from the supreme court of any other jurisdiction. However, foreign precedents can be particularly persuasive where there is an absence of relevant Irish precedent. This often happens because Ireland is a small jurisdiction and issues frequently arise here many years after they arose and were settled in another jurisdiction. For example, although the decision in *DPP v Bartley*[156] only endorsed *R. v Dytham*[157] obiter,[158] it is likely that Carney J. took the opportunity that the facts of the *Bartley* case presented to promote *Dytham*, because he knew that it was unlikely that a case raising the precise issue that arose in *Dytham* would appear before the Irish courts in the immediate future. He was correct in this surmise. No criminal case has addressed this issue since.

5–62 Foreign judgments are also very persuasive when we have enacted legislation which is based on the legislation from that jurisdiction. For example, we frequently enact legislation that draws very liberally from UK legislation. Indeed, Black J. is said to have noted the "scissors and paste penchant of our Legislature" for UK legislation.[159] If there is a dispute about what a particular word means in the statute, and the UK courts have already considered that word, then it makes sense to look at the arguments raised in those cases, as they might help resolve the dispute in our jurisdiction. It is for the judge hearing legal arguments based on UK case law to decide if they are persuaded by them. An example of a case where they were not is *People (DPP) v TN* where the meaning given to the word "manager" by the UK courts was not accepted, despite the section in question having been copied from that jurisdiction after the UK courts had interpreted it:

[155] The exception, of course, would be where we have legally agreed to be bound by the judgments of non-national courts. This will be discussed further in Ch.6.
[156] Unreported, High Court, Carney J., 13 June 1997.
[157] [1979] Q.B. 722.
[158] Discussed at para.5–11.
[159] *Breathnach v McC* [1984] 1 I.R. 340 at 346 per McWilliam J.

"The Oireachtas, in choosing the words which it did, must have known that they would fall to be construed by the Irish courts in accordance with the usual principles, canons and maxims of interpretation. The Court cannot substitute, for this approach, the assumption urged on behalf of the Appellant [that the Oireachtas must have known how the UK courts had interpreted that word when they copied it and intended to adopt it]. Therefore, I do not accept that the use of this formulation establishes that the legislature intended for the section to be construed in line with the UK authorities."[160]

5–63 In terms of who we cite and how frequently, Byrne et al have gathered data from the headnotes of Irish reported judgments in 1995, 2005, 2011 and 2018.[161] This data complements and updates a study conducted by Boyle and Greer in 1983.[162]

Table 5.1: Citation of Irish and foreign precedents before Irish courts

	1921–1975	1995 (IR and ILRM)	2005 (IR)	2011 (IR)	2018 (ILRM)
Ireland	48%	59.5%	61.88%	61.8%	71.5%
England or Scotland	50%	33%	28.9%	28.3%	13.6%
United States	N/A	2.4%	0.7%	2.3%	2.3%
Canada	N/A	0%	1.24%	0.68%	0.7%
Australia	N/A	1.2%	0.88%	2.1%	0.7%
EU courts	N/A	3.2%	4.96%	3.2%	1.9%
European Court of Human Rights	N/A	N/A	N/A	4.7%	9%

This data only tells us the jurisdiction from which the cited cases derived; it does not tell us whether the cited cases were adopted. That proviso

160 [2020] IESC 26 at para.112 per McKechnie J.

161 Table compiled from data presented in R. Byrne, P. McCutcheon, L. Cahillane and E. Roche-Cagney, *Byrne and McCutcheon on the Irish Legal System*, 7th edn (Dublin: Bloomsbury Professional, 2020), paras 12.86–12.92. Cases reported in both the *Irish Reports* and the *Irish Law Reports Monthly* are not double-counted.

162 C.K. Boyle and D.S. Greer, *The Legal Systems, North and South* (Dublin: Stationery Office, 1983), p.46.

made, it is clear that the most significant external source of precedent is the UK. This would make sense given our historical links with that jurisdiction but our reliance on UK cases has declined, most likely due to the fact that we have built up our own stock of precedents. Byrne et al also highlight the increasing citation of European Court of Human Rights (ECtHR) jurisprudence before Irish courts.[163] This trend is prompted by the enactment of the European Convention of Human Rights Act 2003 which gives principles set in ECtHR case law additional (but not binding) weight before the Irish courts.[164]

5–64 Our historical reliance on judgments from the UK, England and Wales in particular, had led some to suggest they are (and should be) adopted by Irish courts unless they are incompatible with our Constitution or erroneous. In his High Court judgment in *Irish Shell v Elm Motors*, Costello J. made a general observation that could be interpreted in this vein.[165] McCarthy J. was critical of this view in the Supreme Court:

> "Whilst the judgments in cases decided in the English courts at all levels will, on a great many occasions, provide convenient and, indeed, convincing statements of principle and attractive arguments in favour of such principles, they are no more than that and must be examined and questioned in the light of a jurisprudence whose fundamental law is radically different in its denial of a supremacy of parliament and its upholding of three co-equal organs of government in the Legislature, the Executive, and the Judiciary."[166]

In other words, we in Ireland have a written Constitution and England does not. He continued, with clear parallels to the reasoning in *State (Quinn) v Ryan*:

[163] R. Byrne, P. McCutcheon, L. Cahillane and E. Roche-Cagney, *Byrne and McCutcheon on the Irish Legal System*, 7th edn (Dublin: Bloomsbury Professional, 2020), para.12.92.

[164] See *Seredych v Minister for Justice and Equality (No. 2)* [2018] IEHC 307 on the effect of s.4 of the 2003 Act. This case and the 2003 Act are discussed further in Ch.9, Section E.2.

[165] [1984] 1 I.R. 200 at 212. Costello J. stated: "[t]he High Court is not bound to follow the decisions and judgments to which I have referred if there are compelling reasons for rejecting them."

[166] [1984] 1 I.R. 200 at 227.

> "In no sense are our Courts a continuation of, or successors to, the British courts. They derive their powers from a Constitution enacted by the people and would, in my view, find more appropriate guidance in the decisions of courts in other countries based upon a similar constitutional framework than in what, at times, appears to be an uncritical adherence to English precedent which, itself, appears difficult to reconcile from time to time ...."[167]

5–65 Undaunted, Costello J. repeated this position in *Tromso Sparebank v Beirne (No. 2)*[168] and in *M McM v J McC*,[169] although in the latter case he declined to follow the English precedents in question. It would seem from the statistics above that Costello J.'s sense that cases from the UK, especially those from England and Wales, carry additional weight before Irish courts is one shared by Irish lawyers. They would not continue to open so many such cases before Irish courts if they thought that they had little likelihood of success.

E. The Advantages and Disadvantages of Precedent

5–66 The doctrine of precedent evolved in a time when the majority of law-making was done by judges. There was, accordingly, concern that if a judge could decide whatever he (and it could only have been "he" then) wanted in every single case, the law would be applied inconsistently, unfairly, and it would be difficult for people to predict the outcome of a case, which could deter people from taking a case in circumstances when they should. The doctrine was therefore intended to have three main benefits: certainty, stability and predictability.[170] These are laudable aims and they are connected to the rule of law, most clearly the principle of equality as expressed in the maxim "treat like cases alike and different cases differently", but also in the principle that the law should be public and precise so that people can make informed decisions about how to act within or outside of the law.[171] In *O'Meara v Minister for Social Protection*, O'Donnell C.J. emphasised that "the principle of *stare decisis*

---

167 [1984] 1 I.R. 200 at 227, having cited *State (Quinn) v Ryan* [1965] I.R. 70 earlier on the page.
168 [1989] I.L.R.M. 257 at 261.
169 [1994] 1 I.R. 293.
170 *Attorney General v Ryan's Car Hire Ltd* [1965] I.R. 642 at 654.
171 See further Chapter 2, Section B.

is not an historical oddity of the common law; it is ... a fundamental component of the rule of law in any common law system."[172]

5–67 The benefits of certainty, stability and predictability have been referenced in various cases where the role of precedent was considered. For example, in setting the strict approach in *London Tramways*, Halsbury L.J. focused on the unpredictability that would ensue if each legal issue could be reopened in subsequent cases.[173] This was so appalling a vista that he was prepared to tolerate injustice in individual cases. He stated:

> "[W]hat is that occasional interference with what is perhaps abstract justice as compared with the inconvenience—the disastrous inconvenience—of having each question subject to being re-argued and the dealings of mankind rendered doubtful by reason of different decisions, so that in truth and in fact there would be no real final Court of Appeal?"[174]

Even in *State (Quinn)* and *Ryan's Car Hire*, where the strict rule of precedent was first departed from, the benefits of the doctrine were acknowledged. In *State (Quinn)*, it was acknowledged by Walsh J. that "[t]he advantages of *stare decisis* are many and obvious",[175] without specifying what those advantages were. Kingsmill Moore J. in *Ryan's Car Hire* recognised that certainty, stability and predictability were desirable, but not at all costs, and he reiterated that precedent was not being abandoned because "it would introduce into our law an intolerable uncertainty".[176]

5–68 Yet these benefits carry with them negative side-effects, particularly the risk of injustice in individual cases. As noted above, Halsbury L.J. was prepared to tolerate this, citing the inconvenience of having to decide each question afresh. Kingsmill Moore J. was particularly critical of this pragmatic statement, noting:

[172] [2024] IESC 1 at para.51.
[173] [1898] A.C. 375 at 380.
[174] [1898] A.C. 375 at 380. The one exception for Halsbury L.J. would be where a precedent was shown to be founded on an error of law: [1898] A.C. 375 at 380–381.
[175] [1965] I.R. 70 at 127.
[176] [1965] I.R. 642 at 653.

> "This argument from inconvenience would come more suitably from the mouth of an executive official than from that of a judge. The plea that 'it is expedient that one man should die for the multitude' must always be met uncompromisingly by a judge with the words, 'I find no fault in this just man,' and he must not falter in his determination. However desirable certainty, stability, and predictability of law may be, they cannot in my view justify a Court of ultimate resort in giving a judgment which they are convinced, for compelling reasons, is erroneous."[177]

Henchy J., despite retrenching the doctrine of precedent in *Mogul*, agreed that justice was an important consideration and that, in some cases, achieving it was more important than maintaining certainty, stability and predictability.[178]

5–69 Whatever weight one gives to these values, it is arguable that the doctrine of precedent is not and has never been a real constraint on judges because there are a variety of ways by which judges can pay lip service to the doctrine and yet not be bound by it. As noted in the introduction, Enlightenment philosophers were critical of the doctrine, none more so than Jeremy Bentham (1748–1832). Bentham advocated legislative codification of the law to take law-making out of judicial hands. His critique was two-fold. When precedent operated as it was supposed to, so that judgments written in a different time and context continued to exert influence in the changed conditions of the present, he argued that this was problematic because it fossilised the law. He wrote: "the more antique the precedent – that is to say, the more barbarous, inexperienced, and prejudice-led the race of men, by, and among whom the precedent was set – the more unlike that the same *past* state of things ... is the *present* state of things."[179]

5–70 However, precedent did not always operate in this way, and that was equally undesirable because it created the very conditions of uncertainty, instability and unpredictability that it was supposed

[177] *Attorney General v Ryan's Car Hire Ltd* [1965] I.R. 642 at 654.

[178] [1976] I.R. 260 at 272. However, he also stated that sometimes it may be more unjust to depart from precedent than to apply it, even when that precedent was erroneously decided: [1976] I.R. 260 at 273.

[179] J. Bentham, *The Works of Jeremy Bentham*, vol.9 (London: Simpkin, Marshall, 1843), p.323 (emphases in original).

to prevent. This was because, through the use of natural law, legal fictions, and the ability to depart from prior decisions by distinguishing them, judges were effectively unfettered in their application of the law. Bentham wrote that natural law was "private opinion in disguise" and "the mere opinion of men self-constituted into legislatures".[180] He was equally critical of legal reasoning; he wrote that the "most prompt and perhaps the most usual translation of the phrase 'contrary to reason', is 'contrary to what I like'."[181]

5–71 His criticisms regarding the manipulability of precedent remain as valid today as they were when he wrote them. Distinguishing, which as we already know is a way that a judge/lawyer/you can assert that a previous apparently relevant decision should not be applied because of some difference between the two cases, is a much-used tool in legal circles. It is easy to invoke because no two cases are ever exactly the same. There are always factual differences that can be pointed to which legitimate an alternative approach. It is not suggested that distinguishing is always used for the purpose of avoiding precedent—indeed, it is rare that distinguishing a case entirely frees a judge to do what they want; ruling out one line of precedent frequently places the case within and under another line. However, it cannot be denied that distinguishing can be particularly useful where there is a superior court precedent by which an inferior court does not wish to be bound. It can also be used by courts of co-ordinate jurisdiction where they are unable to depart from a prior precedent because it does not fall into the *Mogul* criteria.

5–72 Even in circumstances where superior court judges can overrule the prior decision, sometimes they choose not to out of deference to their colleagues who decided the prior case. Griffin J. was critical of this practice in *McNamara v Electricity Supply Board*, where he stated that it was preferable to overrule a decision than to distinguish it if that decision is no longer an appropriate precedent: "[i]f, by reason of its rigidity or harshness, a rule is found to be unsatisfactory, it is undesirable that efforts to circumvent it should be made rather than that it should be

[180] Quoted in G.J. Postema, *Bentham and the Common Law Tradition* (Oxford: Clarendon Press, 1986), p.629.

[181] Quoted in G.J. Postema, *Bentham and the Common Law Tradition* (Oxford: Clarendon Press, 1986), pp.269–270.

reconsidered."[182] This distinction between overruling and distinguishing is not as clear-cut as it might appear. Byrne et al note that distinguishing a decision can amount to overruling it because the relevance of the previous case becomes limited to cases with almost identical facts which, as noted above, are few and far between.[183] In addition, once a case has been distinguished by one court, it is more likely to be distinguished by other courts, further reducing its value as a precedent.

5–73 The re-labelling of a ratio in a previous case as obiter is another means by which the doctrine can be set aside. A series of cases, commencing in 1982 with *People (DPP) v Shaw*[184] and concluding in 1990 with *People (DPP) v Kenny*,[185] illustrates this method. At issue in these cases was what the legal test should be for excluding/including unconstitutionally obtained evidence. In *Shaw*, Griffin J. stated that the test set in *People (Attorney General) v O'Brien*[186] was in fact obiter. He wrote: "the test in *People (Attorney General) v O'Brien* went beyond the issue presented to the Court in that case; it therefore lacks the authoritativeness that it would possess if it were a necessary element of the *ratio decidendi* of that decision."[187] He then proposed an alternative test that was accepted as correct by the majority of the court.

5–74 However, two months later, a different panel of Supreme Court justices came to a different conclusion in *People (DPP) v Lynch*.[188] They disagreed both with the new test formulated by Griffin J. and with his classifying of the test in *People (Attorney General) v O'Brien* as obiter. Instead, they found that Griffin J.'s own test was obiter on the exact same legal basis that Griffin J. had labelled the *O'Brien* test obiter: "[i]t was not submitted in *Shaw's case*, nor was it the subject of any argument addressed to the Court, that *O'Brien's case* did not apply to statements or admissions made by an accused person."[189]

182 [1975] I.R. 1 at 32.
183 R. Byrne, P. McCutcheon, L. Cahillane and E. Roche-Cagney, *Byrne and McCutcheon on the Irish Legal System*, 7th edn (Dublin: Bloomsbury Professional, 2020), para.12.11.
184 [1982] I.R. 1.
185 [1990] 2 I.R. 110.
186 [1965] I.R. 142.
187 [1982] I.R. 1 at 58.
188 [1982] I.R. 64.
189 [1982] I.R. 64 at 83.

5–75 The *O'Brien* test, as modified by *People (DPP) v Kenny*,[190] continued to set the rule on the admissibility of unconstitutionally obtained evidence until 2015,[191] but in a number of cases post-*Lynch*, Griffin J. continued to unsuccessfully put forward his own test. In *People (DPP) v Healy*, Griffin J. noted:

> "I have had the advantage of reading in advance the judgment which McCarthy J. is about to deliver. In it he expresses the opinion that the examination of *The People (Attorney General) v. O'Brien* in *The People (D.P.P.) v. Shaw* and its reasoning, was not necessary for the decision in *Shaw's case*. I respectfully disagree ... ."[192]

Again, in *People (DPP) v Kenny*, he persevered:

> "[m]y judgment in *The People (D.P.P.) v. Shaw* had the support of Henchy J., Kenny J. and Parke J. Having carefully considered all the arguments advanced in this case I can see no reason why I should resile from what I said in that case."[193]

5–76 With reference to this line of cases, Byrne et al note that "a cynic could be led to the conclusion that the attribution of [the] status of *obiter dictum* to a proposition of law is little more than a device to evade the application of a statement of law which the court dislikes".[194] While this supposition may be concerning, indicating quite clearly that the composition of the court matters in what the ultimate decision is, it is worth noting that if a line of precedent does injustice or is perceived to, then it is always open to the Oireachtas to enact legislation to change that law. The legislature has been given primacy to make law in our jurisdiction under Article 15.2.1° of the Constitution, and once the law is changed by the legislature, then the old line of precedent is no longer valid. Accordingly, while the substance of Bentham's criticisms of precedent remains valid, the operation of the doctrine has been radically

---

190 [1990] 2 I.R. 110.

191 *People (DPP) v Kenny* [1990] 2 I.R. 110 was overruled in a 4:3 split judgment in *People (DPP) v JC* [2015] IESC 31.

192 [1990] I.R. 73 at 85.

193 [1990] 2 I.R. 110 at 137.

194 R. Byrne, P. McCutcheon, L. Cahillane and E. Roche-Cagney, *Byrne and McCutcheon on the Irish Legal System*, 7th edn (Dublin: Bloomsbury Professional, 2020), para.12.143.

transformed in the context of a legal system where it is now the lowest ranking domestically produced source of law.

F. Conclusion

5–77 In this chapter we have examined precedent both as a synonym for case law and as a method by which the authority of an individual case can be determined. As with our discussion of legislative language in Ch.4, we have learned that working with the doctrine of precedent is a skill that will take practice—the experience mentioned in the opening quote.[195] While it is clear that the tensions between the desirability of certainty, stability and predictability versus the benefits of flexibility and individual justice cannot be resolved, your awareness of these tensions should help you realise that the doctrine of precedent is not as unyielding as it is often presented. It will also provide you with a vocabulary to legitimate the approach you take when arguing for or against the application of a particular precedent to a new fact situation.

[195] J. Holland and J. Webb, *Learning Legal Rules*, 11th edn (Oxford: OUP, 2022), p.135.

Chapter 6

European Union Law and Public International Law in the Irish Legal System

> "Strictly speaking, there is no such thing as international law, for there is nobody authorized to pass such laws, no tribunal to interpret them, and no executive authorized to enforce them."
>
> C.E. Gillette, "Mexico: Its People and Its Problem" (1914) 54(1) *The Annals of the American Academy of Political and Social Science* 201 at 201.

In this chapter we:

- explore aspects of international law and the Irish legal system;
- undertake an introductory overview of the institutions and law-making functions of the European Union;
- examine the status of European Union law in the Irish legal system, noting that EU law has primacy in areas of its competence. This will include case studies on Irish compliance and non-compliance with EU law;
- consider the sources of public international law, and reflect on the domestic legal status of international agreements, international custom and "soft" law in the Irish legal system;
- outline the place of the European Convention on Human Rights and its legal status in Irish law.

A. Introduction

6–01 Public international law is known as the law of nations.[1] The essence of international law is that it contains the rules that govern relations between sovereign states only.[2] Nonetheless, depending on

1 E. de Vattel, *The Law of Nations (1797)* (Philadelphia: Nicklin, 1835) (reprint), p. lv.

2 For a concise historical development of international law, see J. Crawford, *Brownlie's*

the form and legal status of aspects of international law, individuals may derive rights under international law. Notwithstanding the absence of any superior authority to enforce international law and ensure state compliance,[3] international law is considered by (most) states as binding upon them.[4] That states consider international law binding upon them does not, in and of itself, stop states violating international law. International law is generally based on state consent. Each state is sovereign. Jebbers defines state sovereignty as follows:

> "States are the main subjects of international law and are generally considered to be sovereign, implying that they need not accept any authority from above or from anyone else unless they choose to."[5]

6–02 Article 29 of the Irish Constitution, titled "International Relations", identifies the status of certain forms of international law in the Irish legal system. Within Article 29, European Union (EU) law has a very special status. EU law has primacy over any conflicting domestic laws, policies and practices. In Section B we sketch the scope of EU law, identifying the primary and secondary sources of EU law. We then turn our consideration to the direct effect and primacy of EU law. A brief sketch of the competences of the core EU institutions is then provided. In Section C we undertake a consideration of the primacy of EU law in the Irish legal system. The core constitutional provisions giving effect to EU law are identified. Some consideration is also provided to the extension of EU competences and referendums in Ireland. Attention then turns to the reception of EU law into the Irish legal system, including a consideration of the European Communities Act 1972 (as amended). The manner in which EU law impacts the usual process by which measures become law

Principles of Public International Law, 9th edn (Oxford: OUP, 2019), pp.5–10. For a sustained critique of international law and its modern-day origins based on imperialism and colonialism, see A. O'Donoghue, *On Tyranny and the Global Legal Order* (Cambridge: CUP, 2021), Ch.5, and E. Tendayi Achiume, "Migration as Decolonization" (2019) 71 *Stanford Law Review* 1509.

3 While we see below that there are international adjudicatory bodies, such as the International Court of Justice, jurisdiction is generally based on consent, and even if consent is provided and a determination is reached, the imposition of sanctions depends (mainly) on the political will of the State; see paras 6–63 to 6–69.

4 However, for broader issues of international law, compliance and the rule of law, see R. Collins, "The Rule of Law and the Quest for Constitutional Substitutes in International Law" (2012) 83(1) *Nordic Journal of International Law* 87.

5 J. Jebbers, *International Law*, 4th edn (Oxford: OUP, 2024), p.74.

in the Irish legal system is explored, as well as the impact of EU law on courts and tribunals in Ireland. We finish our brief exploration of EU law with a case study on Ireland's failure to comply with a key aspect of EU law.

6–03 In Section D of this chapter, we provide an overview of public international law. We identify the sources and scope of public international law, highlighting the at times problematic aspect of state compliance with international law. Our focus then turns to international law within the Irish legal system, the Constitution and how courts engage with aspects of international law. As we will discover, for international law that is not given domestic effect in line with constitutional requirements, Irish law prevails. However, at the level of the law of nations, Ireland is still bound to follow the conflicting public international law, but individuals will often lack the necessary standing or right to challenge Ireland's alleged non-compliance with international law before Irish courts. In Section E, we consider the Council of Europe and its most well-known treaty, the European Convention on Human Rights. People in Ireland can, once satisfying strict admissibility requirements, challenge aspects of Irish law, policy or practice before the European Court of Human Rights. An individual will have to evidence that they are a victim of a Convention rights violation for which Ireland is responsible. Finally, we examine the European Convention on Human Rights Act 2003, which, to a degree, makes Convention rights enforceable within the domestic legal system.

B. Law of the European Union

6–04 The EU has been in constant development since the end of World War II.[6] Initially, a community of just six states in the field of coal and steel,[7] it has evolved over the last few decades to now include 27 Member States. This has reflected sustained attempts to move towards a more integrated Europe.[8] What follows is a substantive, but in no way

[6] R. Schuman, *A New Ideal for Europe: The Schuman Declaration, 1950–2000* (Luxembourg: Office for Official Publications of the European Communities, 1950).

[7] L.F. Duchêne, *Jean Monnet: The First Statesman of Interdependence* (New York: Notron, 1994).

[8] See generally, J. Mayoral, *Democratic Improvements in the European Union under the Lisbon Treaty: Institutional changes regarding democratic government in the EU* (Fiesole: European Union Democracy Observatory, Robert Schuman Centre for

exhaustive, introduction to the EU, EU law and its impact in the Irish legal system.[9]

1. The Primary Sources and Scope of EU Law

6–05 The primary sources of EU law are two treaties: the Treaty on European Union (TEU) and the Treaty on the Functioning of the European Union (TFEU).[10] The TEU and TFEU (collectively, the EU treaties) are binding agreements between EU Member States, and most importantly are based on state consent. That is, if states had not signed and ratified the treaties, they would not have any legal obligations. As witnessed in Britain's exit from the European Union (Brexit), states can decide to leave the EU if they so choose. The TEU and the TFEU establish the aims and objectives of the EU, create the EU institutions and demarcate their roles and powers, and identify the areas in which the EU must or may adopt laws and how legal proposals become law, as well as the relationship between the EU and its Member States. Every action taken by the EU is founded on treaties. The EU cannot act outside these explicit competences. Competences may be exclusive, shared or supporting.

6–06 Exclusive competence means that only the EU can legislate in this area, and EU Member States, as they agreed in the treaties, cannot legislate in these areas. There are five areas of exclusive EU competence, identified in Article 3 TFEU as: the creation and maintenance of a customs union, competition rules for the functioning of the EU's internal market, monetary policy for EU Member States, conservation of marine biological resources under a common fisheries policy, and a common commercial policy.

Advanced Studies, European University Institute, 2011) and J.C. Piris, *The Lisbon Treaty: A Legal and Political Analysis* (Cambridge: Cambridge University Press, 2010).

[9] For a more detailed exploration of EU law, see P. Craig and G. de Búrca (eds), *Evolution of EU Law*, 3rd edn (Oxford: OUP, 2021); D. Chalmers et al, *European Union Law*, 5th edn (Cambridge: CUP, 2024); P. Craig and G. de Búrca, *EU Law: Text, Cases and Materials*, 8th edn (Oxford: OUP, 2024). For a discussion on democratic governance and the European Union, see S. Bredt, "Prospects and Limits of Democratic Governance in the EU" (2011) 17(1) *European Law Journal* 35; C. Shore, "European Governance or Governmentality: The European Commission and the Future of Democratic Government" (2011) 17(3) *European Law Journal* 287; G. de Búrca, "The Quest for Legitimacy in the European Union" (1996) 59 *Modern Law Review* 349.

[10] Consolidated versions of the Treaty on European Union and the Treaty on the Functioning of the European Union [2016] OJ C202/1.

6–07 Shared competences are those that EU Member States may legislate for domestically, but where EU laws are introduced within these areas, EU law must be applied by Member States. Article 4 TFEU identifies shared competences as including (indicative):

- free movement of EU citizens and workers;[11]
- free movement of goods;[12]
- free movement of capital;[13]
- free movement of services;[14]
- fisheries and agricultural policy;[15]
- immigration and asylum (although Ireland has to agree to be bound by these measures);[16] and
- criminal co-operation, e.g. arrest warrants and extradition.[17]

6–08 Supporting competences, identified in Article 6 TFEU, relate to the ability of the EU to support Member States and potentially coordinate actions, but not to legislate or introduce any legal obligations on Member States, in areas such as health, industry, culture and tourism, education, vocational training and youth.

6–09 Only when implementing EU law, Member States are bound by the Charter of Fundamental Rights of the European Union (the "Charter"). The Charter identifies key individual rights all citizens and persons in the EU must enjoy, such as the right to life, freedom of expression, the right of non-EU citizens to seek asylum and so on. The Charter sought to consolidate various rights that had been acknowledged as existing under a wide variety of international and European regional human rights law.[18]

---

[11] Part Three, Title IV, Ch.1 TFEU.
[12] Part Three, Title II TFEU.
[13] Part Three, Title IV, Ch.4 TFEU.
[14] Part Three, Title IV, Ch.3 TFEU.
[15] Part Three, Title III TFEU.
[16] Part Three, Title V, Ch.2 TFEU.
[17] Part Three, Title V, Chs 4 and 5 TFEU.
[18] The Charter confirms all the rights found in the case law of the Court of Justice of the European Union and entrenches within EU law the rights and freedoms enshrined in the European Convention on Human Rights and other rights and principles resulting from the common constitutional traditions of EU countries and other international instruments. It establishes a series of individual rights and freedoms, including third-generation rights such as data protection; contains guarantees on bioethics; and provides for transparent administration. For more, see S. Peers, T. Hervey, J. Kenner,

6–10 The principle of subsidiarity is established in Article 5 TEU. It aims to ensure that interventions and decisions relating to EU law are taken at the most appropriate level, whether this is the European, national or local level. The decision should be taken as locally as possible and only moves up the ranks to be taken by the EU if a decision at the highest level would result in a more effective action than one taken at national or local level. The principle of subsidiarity is also the subject of the Protocol on the Application of the Principles of Subsidiarity and Proportionality.[19] This Protocol identifies three criteria that establish when intervention at EU level is desirable and appropriate: (1) where the action has transnational aspects that cannot be resolved by EU Member States; (2) where action, or lack of action, at the national level could be contrary to the requirements of the TFEU; and (3) where taking the action at EU level has clear advantages.[20] In addition, since the TFEU, there has been a role for national parliaments in Member States to ensure that the EU respects the principle of subsidiarity.[21]

2. Secondary Sources of EU Law

6–11 In the Irish legal system, the Constitution is the primary law of the State. As we have already explored in Chs 3–5, and as will be discussed in Ch.7 when discussing the legislative process, other

and A. Ward (eds), *The EU Charter of Fundamental Rights: A Commentary*, 2nd edn (London: Bloomsbury Publishing, 2021). For a discussion on the impact of the EU Charter of Fundamental Rights on Irish Law, albeit now somewhat dated, see S. Kingston and L. Thornton, *A Report on the Application of the European Convention on Human Rights Act 2003 and the European Charter of Fundamental Rights: Evaluation and Review* (Dublin: Law Society, 2015), Ch.5.

19 Protocol (No 2) TFEU.

20 For more on the principle of subsidiarity, see N.W. Barber, "The Limited Modesty of Subsidiarity" (2005) 11(3) *European Law Journal* 308; P. Kiiver, "The Treaty of Lisbon, the National Parliaments and the Principle of Subsidiarity" (2008) 15 *Maastricht Journal of European and Comparative Law* 77; K. van Kersbergen and B. Verbeek, "The Politics of International Norms: Subsidiarity and the Imperfect Competence Regime of the European Union" (2007) 13(2) *European Journal of International Relations* 217.

21 F. Fabbrini and K. Granat, "'Yellow card, but no foul': The role of the national parliaments under the subsidiarity protocol and the Commission proposal for an EU regulation on the right to strike" (2013) 50(1) *Common Market Law Review* 115. For a specific analysis of the relationship between the Oireachtas and the EU, see G. Barrett, *The Oireachtas and European Union: The Evolving Role of a National Parliament in European Affairs* (Dublin: Houses of the Oireachtas, 2013). For a broader exploration of national parliaments and the European Union, see G. Barrett, *The Evolving Role of National Parliaments in the European Union: Ireland as a Case Study* (Manchester: MUP, 2018).

sources of law also exist. The EU legal system is no different. The TEU and TFEU are in essence the constitutional foundations of the EU. These establish the broad parameters of EU law, allocate powers to respective institutions, and permit secondary forms of law to further ensure the aims and objectives of the EU under the two treaties are met. In the EU legal system, when it legislates in areas of its exclusive or shared competences, secondary law can be adopted. These secondary laws must conform to the EU treaties, otherwise the Court of Justice of the European Union can strike these laws down. The EU legislative process is briefly introduced below, when discussing the institutions of the EU.

6–12 Article 288 TFEU identifies these secondary laws as follows:

> "To exercise the Union's competences, the institutions shall adopt regulations, directives, decisions, recommendations and opinions.
>
> A regulation shall have general application. It shall be binding in its entirety and directly applicable in all Member States.
>
> A directive shall be binding, as to the result to be achieved, upon each Member State to which it is addressed, but shall leave to the national authorities the choice of form and methods.
>
> A decision shall be binding in its entirety. A decision which specifies those to whom it is addressed shall be binding only on them.
>
> Recommendations and opinions shall have no binding force."

6–13 Regulations: A "regulation" is a binding legislative act. It must be applied in its entirety across the EU. Regulations set out legally enforceable rules and, once they come into force, automatically become law in all EU Member States. There is no need for any further domestic legislative act. Consequently, regulations have direct effect.[22] Regulations are ordinarily employed for areas that do not overlap with domestic laws of Member States. For example, when the EU wanted to protect the names of agricultural products coming from certain areas, such as Parma ham, the Council adopted a regulation.[23]

[22] The doctrine of direct effect is explained more fully at paras 6–18 to 6–19. See also *Variola v Amministrazione delle Finanze* [1973] E.C.R. 981.

[23] Council Regulation (EEC) No 2081/92 of 14 July 1992 on the protection of geographical indications and designations of origin for agricultural products and foodstuffs [1992] OJ L208/1. This was updated more recently by Commission Implementing Regulation (EU) No 1208/2013 of 25 November 2013 approving minor amendments to the

6–14 Directives: A "directive" is a form of legislation setting out a goal that all EU Member States must achieve. However, it is up to the individual countries to decide how to go about achieving that goal. Directives often set time limits for a Member State to "transpose" and implement a directive into national law. This often requires either the introduction of new legislation or amendments to existing national legislation to conform with EU legal obligations. Unlike a regulation, a directive is not directly applicable immediately but establishes the rules that must be implemented by all Member States on a particular topic.[24] Whether a directive has direct effect depends on "whether the nature, general scheme and wording of the provisions in question are capable of having direct effects on the relations between Member States and individuals".[25]

6–15 Other sources: Other sources of EU law include decisions, recommendations and opinions. A "decision" usually has limited scope and is binding on those to whom it is addressed (e.g. an EU country or an individual company) and is directly applicable. Between 1991 and 2007, Ireland provided Apple Sales International with unlawful state aid. Ireland did this through making various interpretations to its taxation system that provided Apple with a competitive advantage. No other company had benefited from this. In 2016, the European Commission issued a decision directing Apple to pay back (what is now) €14.1 billion that Ireland had in essence waived through purposefully underestimating Apple's tax liability.[26] Apple, supported by Ireland, sought to have this decision annulled. Ultimately, in September 2024, the Court of Justice held that the decision of the Commission was correct.[27] A "recommendation" is not binding and does not have any legal consequences. A recommendation allows the institutions to make their views known and to suggest a line of action without imposing any legal obligation on those to whom it is addressed. An "opinion" is an instrument that allows the institutions to make a statement in a non-binding fashion, without imposing any legal obligation on those to whom it is addressed. It can be issued by

specification for a name entered in the register of protected designations of origin and protected geographical indications (Prosciutto di Parma (PDO)) [2013] OJ L317/8.

24 See further *Inter-Environnement Wallonie v Région Wallone* [1997] E.C.R. I-7411.

25 *Van Duyn v Home Office* [1974] E.C.R. 1337 at para.12.

26 Commission Decision (EU) 2017/1283 of 30 August 2016 on State aid SA.38373 implemented by Ireland to Apple [2017] OJ L187/1.

27 *European Commission v Ireland and Others* (C-465/20 P) EU:C:2024:724.

the main EU institutions: the European Commission, the Council of the European Union, and the European Parliament. Other EU bodies, such as the Committee of the Regions and the European Economic and Social Committee, give opinions from their specific regional or economic and social viewpoints on draft EU legal measures. For example, in 2015 the Committee of the Regions issued an opinion on how best to ensure a fair and efficient corporate tax system in the EU.[28] In 2024, the European Economic and Social Committee issued an opinion on protecting work–life balance and made suggestions for EU legal reform.[29]

6–16 What occurs if national law does not conform with EU law? As we explore below, EU law will prevail over conflicting domestic legal norms. In Ireland, this is because the Irish people have passed constitutional amendments giving explicit recognition to the primacy of EU law.

3. Direct Effect and Primacy of EU Law

6–17 EU law is inherently different to other kinds of international law. The way Member States have agreed to organise the EU is such that the interaction between EU law and national laws is much more defined and tangible than the interaction between national law and non-EU international laws. This is most evident in the direct effect and primacy of EU law. EU law must also abide by the constitutional principle of subsidiarity.[30]

(a) Direct effect

6–18 Direct effect means that a provision of EU law can be enforced by an EU citizen without the need for any intermediate step to make that provision part of the domestic legal order. The first case to establish this right was *Van Gend en Loos*.[31] This case concerned the imposition of a customs tariff which the applicant claimed was contrary to (then) Article

[28] Committee of the Regions, *A Fair and Efficient Corporate Tax System in the European Union: 5 Key Areas for Action*, CDR 3865/2015, 17 June 2015.

[29] European Economic and Social Committee, *Ensuring a needs-based work-life balance for all*, SOC/808, 23 October 2024.

[30] For more on the nature of EU law, see P. Craig and G. de Búrca, *EU Law: Text, Cases and Materials*, 8th edn (Oxford: OUP, 2024), Ch.8.

[31] *NV Algemene Transporten Expeditie Onderneming van Gend en Loos v Nederlandse Administratie der Belastingen* (Case 26/62) [1963] E.C.R. 1.

12 of the EC Treaty.[32] That article prohibited the introduction of customs duties or equivalent measures on imports and exports between Member States. As the article addressed the Member State, the respondent argued that it could not be relied upon by an individual against a Member State. The Court of Justice found in favour of the applicant and held:

> "[T]he Community constitutes a new legal order of international law for the benefit of which the states have limited their sovereign rights, albeit within limited fields, and the subjects of which comprise not only Member States but also their nationals. Independently of the legislation of Member States, Community law therefore not only imposes obligations on individuals but is also intended to confer upon them rights which become part of their legal heritage. These rights arise not only where they are expressly granted by the Treaty, but also by reason of obligations which the Treaty imposes in a clearly defined way upon individuals as well as upon the Member States and upon the institutions of the Community."[33]

6–19 The decision in *Van Gend en Loos* has been described as "ground-breaking".[34] The Court of Justice ruled that once a regulation or directive was: (a) clear and precise, (b) unconditional, (c) did not require implementing measures to be taken by a Member State or the Union, and (d) did not leave discretion to the Member State or Union institutions, it has direct effect.[35] The impact of *Van Gend en Loos* is that the Court of Justice enabled individuals to raise rights arising from EU law before national courts and, in this way, it empowers individuals to enforce compliance with EU law.[36] As national courts must apply those laws emanating from the EU, the result of the concept of direct effect is that these EU laws bind the Irish State. Direct effect can be vertical,

---

32 Now Article 30 TFEU.

33 [1963] E.C.R. 1 at 12.

34 P. Craig and G. de Búrca, *EU Law: Text, Cases and Materials*, 8th edn (Oxford: OUP, 2024), p.218.

35 [1963] E.C.R. 1 at 13.

36 For more on direct effect, see P. Pescatore, "The Doctrine of 'Direct Effect': An Infant Disease of Community Law" (2015) 2 *European Law Review* 135; A. von Bogdandy, "Pluralism, Direct Effect, and the Ultimate Say: On the Relationship between International and Domestic Constitutional Law" (2008) 6(3–4) *International Journal of Constitutional Law* 397; S. Prechal, "Does Direct Effect Still Matter?" (2008) 37(5) *Common Market Law Review* 1047; T.A. Börzel, "Participation through Law Enforcement: The Case of the European Union" (2006) 39(1) *Comparative Political Studies* 128.

in that an individual can invoke a provision of EU law to assert rights against a Member State in the national courts. Direct effect may (and only may) be horizontal, that is, applying between two private parties.

(b) Primacy

6–20 Declaration No. 17 of the TFEU provides:

> "[I]n accordance with well settled case law of the Court of Justice of the European Union, the Treaties and the law adopted by the Union on the basis of the Treaties have primacy over the law of Member States, under the conditions laid down by the said case law."

6–21 Primacy or supremacy of EU law over national laws is inherent within the EU legal system, as we explore in relation to Ireland below.[37] Declaration No. 17, introduced in the Lisbon Treaty in 2009, provides a codified expression of the doctrine of primacy. Note that Declaration No. 17 begins with "in accordance with well settled case law ...", indicating that well before Declaration No. 17 came into effect, EU law already had primacy over conflicting domestic legal norms. In *Van Gend en Loos*, the Court of Justice alluded to this concept when it noted that the (then) European Economic Community (EEC) had created a new legal order of international law which necessitated Member States limiting their sovereignty to benefit from the new structures in place under the treaties. The extent of this limit on sovereignty of Member States was examined directly in the *Costa* case.[38] The plaintiff in the case, Costa, owned shares in an electricity company and opposed the nationalisation of the electricity sector in Italy; as such, he refused to pay his electricity bill. He was sued by ENEL, the national electricity company created following nationalisation, for non-payment of bills, and argued in his defence that the nationalisation of the electricity industry violated (then) Article 37 of the EEC Treaty which concerned state monopolies.[39] The Court of Justice found as follows:

---

[37] For a more detailed discussion of the emergence of the principles of direct effect and primacy of EU law, see B. de Witte, "Direct Effect, Primacy, and the Nature of the Legal Order" in P. Craig and G. de Búrca (eds), *Evolution of EU Law*, 3rd edn (Oxford: OUP, 2021), Ch.7. See also, M. Avbelj, "Supremacy or Primacy of EU Law—(Why) Does It Matter?" (2011) 17(6) *European Law Journal* 744.

[38] *Flaminio Costa v ENEL* (Case 6/64) [1964] E.C.R. 585.

[39] Now Article 37 TFEU.

> "By creating a Community of unlimited duration, having its own institutions, its own personality, its own legal capacity and capacity of representation on the international plane and, more particularly, real powers stemming from a limitation of sovereignty or a transfer of powers from the States to the Community, the Member States have limited their sovereign rights, albeit within limited fields, and have thus created a body of law which binds both their nationals and themselves."[40]

6–22 In reaching this conclusion, the Court of Justice drew on several general aspects of the treaties, including the requirement to ensure the attainment of treaty objectives[41] and the prohibition of discrimination,[42] both of which would be infringed if national legislation could supersede the Union rules. The Court of Justice stressed that the binding nature and direct applicability of regulations[43] would be meaningless if newer national legislation could displace them. Thus, the Court of Justice concluded:

> "[T]he law stemming from the treaty, an independent source of law, could not, because of its special and original nature, be overridden by domestic legal provisions, however framed, without being deprived of its character as Community law and without the legal basis of the Community itself being called into question."[44]

6–23 The doctrine of primacy identified in *Costa* was reinforced in subsequent case law. It was strengthened considerably in *Internationale Handelsgesellschaft*[45] where the Court of Justice ruled that it triumphed even over a fundamental rule of national constitutional law:

> "Recourse to the legal rules or concepts of national law in order to judge the validity of measures adopted by the institutions of the community would have an adverse effect on the uniformity and efficacy of Community law. The validity of such measures can only be judged in the light of community law. In fact, the law stemming

40 [1964] E.C.R. 585 at 593.
41 Article 5 of the EEC Treaty (now Article 4(3) TEU).
42 Article 7 of the EEC Treaty (now Article 18 TFEU).
43 Article 189 of the EEC Treaty (now Article 288 TFEU).
44 [1964] E.C.R. 585 at 594.
45 *Internationale Handelsgesellschaft mbH v Einfuhr- und Vorratsstelle für Getreide und Futtermittel* (Case 11/70) [1970] E.C.R. 1125.

from the Treaty, an independent source of law, cannot because of its very nature be overridden by rules of national law, however framed, without being deprived of its character as Community law and without the legal basis of the Community itself being called into question."[46]

6–24 The question as to whether national laws enacted prior to the relevant Union law continued to be valid was clarified in the *Simmenthal* case.[47] The Court of Justice ruled that the introduction of a Union measure not only prevented the adoption of new conflicting national laws but also rendered inapplicable any conflicting previously existing domestic provisions. The Court of Justice continued:

> "[I]n accordance with the principle of the precedence of Community law, the relationship between provisions of the Treaty and directly applicable measures of the institutions on the one hand and the national law of the Member States on the other is such that those provisions and measures not only by their entry into force render automatically inapplicable any conflicting provision of current national law but—in so far as they are an integral part of, and take precedence in, the legal order applicable in the territory of each of the Member States—also preclude the valid adoption of new national legislative measures to the extent to which they would be incompatible with Community provisions.
>
> Indeed, any recognition that national legislative measures which encroach upon the field within which the Community exercises its legislative power or which are otherwise incompatible with the provisions of Community law had any legal effect would amount to a corresponding denial of the effectiveness of obligations undertaken unconditionally and irrevocably by Member States pursuant to the Treaty and would thus imperil the very foundations of the Community."[48]

[46] [1970] E.C.R. 1125 at 1134.
[47] *Amministrazione delle Finanze dello Stato v Simmenthal SpA* (Case 106/77) [1978] E.C.R. 629.
[48] [1978] E.C.R. 629 at 643.

Box 6.1: Brexit

On 23 June 2016, the United Kingdom (UK) voted to leave the EU in the Brexit referendum. Brexit was formalised and the UK officially left the EU at 23:00 on 30 January 2020. A key reason for the UK leaving the EU was due to the principle of primacy of EU law. A majority of the British public wished to have Britain regain its sovereignty over all areas of exclusive and shared EU competences. El-Enany and Kennan aptly conceive of Brexit as nothing more than "imperial nostalgia" and an expression of post-colonial melancholy by the majority of British people.[49] Negotiating Brexit was a nuanced matter. Many aspects of this negotiation brought the island of Ireland to the fore, among other things, in terms of the Single European Market and the possible need for a hard border to be reinstated on the island, which was ultimately decided against.[50] Nonetheless, the impact of Brexit on how EU law interacts with the Irish legal system is limited. As this is an introductory textbook which in this chapter examines the interaction between international law within our domestic legal system, a detailed consideration of Brexit is outside the scope of this text.

6–25 Before considering the impact of EU law on the Irish legal system, we briefly sketch the institutions of the EU and their respective powers and competences.

4. The Institutions of the EU

6–26 Article 13 TEU identifies the institutions of the EU as: (a) the European Commission; (b) the European Council; (c) the Council of the European Union; (d) the European Parliament; and (e) the Court of Justice of the European Union. In addition, the European Central Bank and the Court of Auditors are identified as EU institutions, but we will not discuss

[49] See N. El-Enany and S. Keenan, "Beware the Ivory Dwellings of the Left: Political Purity in the Face of Fascism", *Critical Legal Thinking*, 2 December 2016, *https://criticallegalthinking.com/2016/12/02/beware-ivory-dwellings-left-political-purity-face-fascism/* and N. El-Enany, "Things Fall Apart: From Empire to Brexit Britain", IPR Blog, 2 May 2017, *https://blogs.bath.ac.uk/iprblog/2017/05/02/things-fall-apart-from-empire-to-brexit-britain/*.

[50] Protocol on Ireland and Northern Ireland (2020), available at: *https://commission.europa.eu/strategy-and-policy/relations-united-kingdom/eu-uk-withdrawal-agreement/windsor-framework_en#protocol-on-ireland-and-northern-ireland*; F. Fabbrini, *The Law and Politics of Brexit* (Oxford: OUP, 2017); F. Fabbrini, *The Withdrawal Agreement* (Oxford: OUP, 2020).

the latter two institutions any further. We are focusing just on how laws are made in the EU, and the role of each of the EU institutions. When engaging with this issue, we can only provide the briefest of overviews.[51]

(a) European Commission

6–27 The European Commission, based in Brussels, is the executive branch of the EU and is the "guardian of the treaties".[52] The Commission is composed of one Commissioner from each of the 27 EU Member States, acting in the interests of the EU, and not in the interests of their national government.[53] The Commission has the exclusive power to initiate EU legislation. The Commission also supervises the implementation of EU law. These powers are subject to some reviews and controls by the European Parliament and the Council of the European Union.[54] The Commission is the external face of the EU and represents the interests of the EU as a whole on the international stage and can represent the EU and negotiate treaties in the area of foreign affairs. The Commission is also responsible for the day-to-day running of the EU. The Commission manages the budget of the EU and is responsible for allocating funding. The process of appointment and election of the President of the Commission is set down by the TEU.[55] The European Council[56] nominates, on the basis of qualified majority vote, the person who this institution seeks to have nominated as the President of the Commission.[57] This nomination must proceed to the European Parliament, where the Parliament is free to elect (or not) the President of the Commission.[58] If the President of the Commission does not obtain a majority of votes in the European Parliament, the European Council must propose a new candidate.[59] Thereafter, the Council adopts a proposed list of Commissioners (this is compiled based on the nominations of each Member State). The European Parliament then votes to approve

[51] For more on the institutions of the EU and law-making powers, see P. Craig and G. de Búrca, *EU Law: Text, Cases and Materials*, 8th edn (Oxford: OUP, 2024), Chs 3, 6 and 7, which discuss legislation, decision-making, and democracy in the EU.
[52] Article 17 TEU.
[53] Article 245 TFEU.
[54] Article 17 TEU.
[55] See generally, Articles 14(1), 15 and 17(7) TEU.
[56] Article 15 TEU.
[57] Article 17(7) TEU.
[58] Article 14(1) TEU.
[59] Article 17(7) TEU.

the entire list of President and Commissioners, following an opportunity for the relevant parliamentary committee to interrogate the proposed Commissioner to determine their suitability to act on that brief.[60] The only exception to this is the appointment of the High Representative for Foreign Affairs and Security Policy, who is one of the Vice-Presidents in the Commission.[61]

(b) European Council

6–28 The European Council consists of Heads of State of EU Member States, the President of the Commission, and the High Representative for Foreign Affairs and Security Policy.[62] The role of the European Council is to define the political direction and priorities of the EU at a high level.

(c) Council of the European Union

6–29 The Council of the European Union is the institution that represents the Member States within the EU in the day-to-day operation of the EU. The Council consists of government representatives at ministerial level. Depending on what will be discussed at the Council level, a different national government minister may attend a Council meeting. An important function of the Council is to consider laws proposed by the Commission and determine, along with the European Parliament, if these laws should be adopted. EU Member States play a fundamental role in determining what should or should not be EU law, subject of course to these being within the competence of the EU. The voting system for the Council is outlined in Article 238 TFEU. Each Member State government minister has one vote in the Council. Voting in certain limited areas is by majority, that is, a minimum of 14 Member States voting in favour. Most decisions of the Council occur under a qualified majority system. A qualified majority means at least 55 per cent of Member States vote

[60] For the 1999 non-approval of appointees to the Commission, see Committee of Independent Experts, *First Report on Allegations Regarding Fraud, Mismanagement and Nepotism in the European Commission* (Brussels: Committee of Independent Experts, 1999). In 2014, the Parliament rejected the proposed Commissioner for Slovenia, and the Slovene Government withdrew its initial candidate and put forward a new candidate, who was accepted by the Parliament; see P. Spiegel and A. Barker, "Parliament rejects Bratusek for European Commission job", *Financial Times*, 8 October 2014, and S. Lynch, "European Parliament backs final Commission nominee", *Irish Times*, 22 October 2014.

[61] The High Representative is appointed by the European Council, with the agreement of the President of the Commission; see Article 18(1) TEU.

[62] Article 15 TEU.

in favour of a legislative proposal. These 55 per cent of Member States must represent at least 65 per cent of the total EU population.[63] In several policy areas, the Council must act unanimously. The treaties identify the type of voting system that must be used. Along with the European Parliament, the Council is central to decisions as to what will become EU law. In this way, the Council is part of the decision-making triangle, together with the Commission and the Parliament, and its powers encompass the common policy domains covered by the treaties establishing the EU.

(d) European Parliament

6–30 The legal status of the European Parliament derives jointly from Article 14 TEU, which defines its main features, and Articles 223–234 TFEU, which lay down the operating rules and contain a series of provisions that refer to it explicitly or implicitly as an institution.[64] Unlike the Irish Parliament, the European Parliament has no power to initiate legislation.[65] Craig and de Búrca note that, over time, the power of the European Parliament has been greatly strengthened from an institution that was intended to assume a consultative and supervisory role to one that exercises substantial powers in relation to legislation, budgets and supervision.[66] The European Parliament is the only democratically-elected EU institution. The Parliament is now a co-legislator along with the Council of the EU, whereby all EU laws proposed by the Commission must be voted upon by both respective bodies. The Parliament votes by majority. There are currently 720 Members of the European Parliament (MEPs), elected by EU citizens across the 27 Member States.[67] Given the significant differences in population across Member States, the size of the population (somewhat) reflects the number of MEPs that each country elects. At present, Ireland is represented by 14 MEPs, whereas Spain

[63] Article 238 TFEU.

[64] Other features of the Parliament's status are to be found in the protocols annexed to the treaties, including Protocol (No 2) on the Application of the Principles of Subsidiarity and Proportionality, and Protocol (No 7) on the Privileges and Immunities of the European Union.

[65] Article 13 TEU.

[66] P. Craig and G. de Búrca, *EU Law: Text, Cases and Materials*, 8th edn (Oxford: OUP, 2024), p.85. See further, B. Rittberger, *Building Europe's Parliament, Democratic Representation Beyond the Nation State* (Oxford: OUP, 2005).

[67] European Council Decision (EU) 2023/2061 of 22 September 2023 establishing the composition of the European Parliament [2023] OJ L238/114.

elects 61 MEPs. MEPs are the representatives of the citizens of Europe. All MEPs are elected for a five-year term of office. As such, their mandate is a representative one and they exercise their mandate independently and may not be bound by any instructions from national authorities, EU institutions, private interest groups, non-governmental organisations, etc.[68]

(e) Court of Justice of the European Union

6–31 The Court of Justice of the European Union (CJEU) consists of three courts: the General Court, the Court of Justice, and "specialised courts".[69] The court at the top of the apex is the Court of Justice, and we will restrict our exploration just to the Court of Justice. The Court of Justice is the judicial arm of the EU.[70] The Court of Justice is responsible for "the interpretation and application of Treaties [to ensure] the law is observed". The Court of Justice is responsible, inter alia, for ensuring Member States, and others, comply with EU law, be this the treaties, a regulation, directive or decision.[71] Like domestic courts, the Court of Justice provides authoritative and binding interpretation of EU law. The Court of Justice is composed of 27 judges and 11 Advocates General.[72] The Court of Justice may sit as a full court, known as a Grand Chamber with 15 judges, or in Chambers of three or five judges.[73] Article 19(3) TEU provides that the Court of Justice must,

> "(a) rule on actions brought by a Member State, an institution or a natural or legal person;
> (b) give preliminary rulings, at the request of courts or tribunals of the Member States, on the interpretation of Union law or the validity of acts adopted by the institutions;
> (c) rule in other cases provided for in the Treaties."

68 Article 2(1) of Decision (2005/684/EC, Euratom) of the European Parliament of 28 September 2005 adopting the Statute for Members of the European Parliament [2005] OJ L262/1; rule 2 of the European Parliament's Rules of Procedure.

69 Article 19(1) TEU. For more, see D. Chalmers et al, *European Union Law*, 5th edn (Cambridge: CUP, 2024), Ch.4.

70 See further, Ch.9, paras 9–75 to 9–78.

71 Protocol (No 3) on the Statute of the Court of Justice of the European Union.

72 For more on the role of Advocates General in the CJEU, see L. Clément-Wilz, "The Advocate General: A Key Actor of the Court of Justice of the European Union" (2012) 14 *Cambridge Yearbook of European Legal Studies* 587.

73 Article 16 of Protocol (No 3) on the Statute of the Court of Justice of the European Union.

6–32 As the supreme judicial authority on the interpretation of EU law, the Court of Justice is charged with interpreting and resolving disputes that arise in relation to EU law. Most legal actions relate to Member States' and/or institutions' obligations under EU law. Given the need for one legal interpretation of EU law in 27 legal systems, it is not surprising that there is a requirement for a definitive ruling on the meaning and impact of EU law. Domestic courts and tribunals, when determining issues of EU law, may, where it is appropriate, request a preliminary reference from the Court of Justice.[74] National courts or tribunals will provide the Court of Justice with (i) the factual background of the case; (ii) the matters of EU law the national court/tribunal has determined to be of relevance to the case; (iii) an explanation of what aspect of EU law requires interpretation; and (iv) the national court/tribunal may (but is not obliged to) provide the Court of Justice with analysis of what the decision-maker(s) think is meant by the EU law they are referring to the Court of Justice. The preliminary reference procedure therefore allows the Court of Justice to provide a definitive interpretation of EU law. Once the Court of Justice provides the national court/tribunal with an answer as to the meaning/application of EU law, it is then for the national court/tribunal to finalise the domestic legal proceedings and apply EU law in the manner prescribed by the Court of Justice. Since September 2024, the General Court of the EU is empowered to determine certain preliminary references for the first time.[75] Where a national court/tribunal requests a preliminary reference and this relates to a number of specified fields of EU law,[76] the General Court will provide a response to the national court/tribunal. The rationale for this significant change is that the areas of law with which the General Court will engage are well-established.

[74] Article 267 TFEU. On whether national courts or tribunals are obliged to refer, or have a discretion to refer, see *Srl CILFIT and Lanificio di Gavardo SpA v Ministry of Health (CILFIT)* [1982] E.C.R. 3415, and I. Maher, "National Courts as Community Courts" (1994) 14(2) *Legal Studies* 226. The role of Irish courts and their power to refer to the CJEU is considered in Ch.9, paras 9–75 to 9–78.

[75] Regulation (EU, Euratom) 2024/2019 of the European Parliament and of the Council of 11 April 2024 amending Protocol No 3 on the Statute of the Court of Justice of the European Union [2024] OJ L 12 August 2024.

[76] Article 1(4) of Regulation (EU, Euratom) 2024/2019 inserts Article 50b into Protocol No 3 on the Statute of the Court of Justice of the European Union. This provides (with some important exceptions) for six legal areas within which the General Court will hear and determine preliminary references. These include: the common system for value added tax; excise duties; the Customs Code; aspects of tariff classification; passenger rights in relation to delayed and/or cancelled transport services; and the system for greenhouse gas emission allowance trading.

Extensive legal interpretation within these fields has already occurred in the Court of Justice. The Regulation effecting this change also noted the significant workload of the Court of Justice responding to preliminary references. This was resulting in significant delays in the Court of Justice providing a response to the preliminary reference.[77]

6–33 Legal action can be commenced by Member States, potentially other institutions of the EU,[78] and those against whom a decision is issued by the Commission. In general, subject to very important exceptions, individuals cannot directly bring a challenge to a measure of EU law to the Court of Justice. It is important to note that the CJEU, generally,[79] does not have jurisdiction to determine issues relating to common foreign and security policy. However, the CJEU has noted that this exclusion from jurisdiction is interpreted "narrowly",[80] in that the CJEU can ensure institutions of the EU are acting within their competences.

6–34 The Court of Justice determines cases in a large number of legal fields. Some key examples include:

- actions for failure to fulfil obligations;[81]
- actions for annulment and for a declaration of failure to act, which is an infringement of the treaties. This action can be brought by Member States, or potentially other institutions of the EU;[82]
- acts of, or failures to act by, the European Parliament or the Council;
- appeals against decisions given by the General Court and review of decisions given by that court in appeal proceedings;[83]
- requests for an opinion on the compatibility of the EU's international agreements with the provisions of the EU treaties;[84]

77 See Recitals (5) to (22) of Regulation (EU, Euratom) 2024/2019. This Regulation further transfers jurisdiction from the Court of Justice to the General Court of decisions from several EU bodies, agencies and offices; see generally, Article 1(6) of Regulation (EU, Euratom) 2024/2019, which substitutes Article 58a of Protocol No 3 on the Statute of the Court of Justice of the European Union.

78 Articles 263 and 265 TFEU.

79 Article 275 TFEU.

80 *European Parliament v Council of the European Union* (C-658/11) EU:C:2014:2025 at para.70.

81 Articles 258–260 TFEU.

82 Articles 263 and 265 TFEU.

83 Article 256(1) and (2) TFEU.

84 Article 218 TFEU.

- the compatibility of certain agreements with the provisions of the European Atomic Energy Community Treaty, which relates to civil use of nuclear power.[85]

C. Primacy of EU Law in the Irish Legal System

1. The Irish Constitution and EU Law

6–35 As briefly mentioned in Ch.2, and discussed above, EU law has primacy over Irish law,[86] including Irish constitutional law. This, as explained in Ch.3, is due to the Irish people passing constitutional amendments that gave, initially implicit, but now explicit, recognition to the primacy of EU law.[87] Article 5 of the Irish Constitution provides: "Ireland is a sovereign, independent and democratic state." Given that membership of the EU entails a transfer of sovereignty, or a pooling of sovereignty, across many legal areas, it is not surprising that the Constitution needed to be changed when Ireland first joined the European Economic Community (EEC), one of the forerunner bodies to the EU. Baker J. in *Costello v Government of Ireland* describes one aspect of the notion of sovereignty in the Irish legal system:

> "The essence of this sovereignty is the ability and willingness to engage as an equal partner in international affairs, and sovereignty is thus not to be seen as either one-dimensional or a blunt refusal to be influenced by external actors. It involves an engagement with and openness to other states which can and does impact on domestic policy and thinking."[88]

6–36 The Constitution is an expression of Ireland's sovereignty. The Oireachtas has the power to make laws, the government to make executive decisions, and the Irish courts to make judicial decisions.[89] The people (i.e. citizens) have the sovereign right to change any aspect of the Constitution, as the sovereignty of the State derives from the people.[90]

---

85 Articles 103–105 EAEC Treaty.
86 See Ch.2, paras 2–29 to 2–30.
87 See Ch.3, para.3–81.
88 [2022] IESC 44, judgment of Baker J. at para.7.
89 [2022] IESC 44, judgment of O'Donnell C.J. at para.11.
90 [2022] IESC 44, judgment of O'Donnell C.J. at para.173.

6–37 The relevant Irish constitutional provisions on Ireland's legal relationship with EU law are as follows:

- Article 29.4.3° permits Ireland to become a member of the European Atomic Energy Community (EAEC).
- Article 29.4.4° affirms Ireland's commitment to the EU "within which the member states of that Union work together to promote peace, shared values and the well-being of their peoples".
- Article 29.4.5° permits Ireland to ratify the Treaty of Lisbon. As outlined above, the Treaty of Lisbon includes the Treaty on the Functioning of the European Union (TFEU) and the Treaty on European Union (TEU). Both treaties together are, in essence, the constitutional underpinnings of the EU.
- Article 29.4.6° states that no provision of the Irish Constitution "invalidates laws enacted, acts done or measures adopted by the State, before, on or after" the coming into force of the various EU treaties.
- Article 29.4.7° provides that Ireland may exercise discretion to implement various aspects of EU law that do not automatically apply in Ireland, such as the Schengen common travel area, aspects of EU immigration and asylum law, and aspects of EU criminal law. Prior to Ireland being bound by the legal measures in these fields, a resolution of both Houses of the Oireachtas must be passed.
- Article 29.4.8° permits Ireland to agree to decisions, regulations or other acts adopted under the EU treaties in certain areas, but this is subject to the agreement of both Houses of the Oireachtas.
- Article 29.4.9° prevents Ireland from entering a common EU security and defence policy with other members of the EU. This relates to peacekeeping, conflict prevention and strengthening international security in accordance with the principles of the United Nations Charter.
- Article 29.4.10° permits Ireland to ratify the Treaty on Stability, Coordination and Governance in the Economic and Monetary Union. This also provides, akin to Article 29.4.6°, that no provision of the Constitution "invalidates laws enacted, acts done or measures adopted by the State that are necessitated by the obligations of the State" under this Treaty.

6–38 The interaction between Irish domestic law and EU law turns on the way EU law was incorporated into the Irish legal system. EU law may be directly applicable in Irish law; in other words, there is no need for any intermediate step to give laws developed in the EU legal force in Ireland. Yet, Article 15.2.1° of the Irish Constitution stipulates that only the Oireachtas may make laws for the Irish State. How then is it possible to reconcile the dissonance between the position of the Oireachtas as sole law-maker for Ireland with legislation that originates from the EU? This is permissible because of the referendum that enabled Ireland to join the EU (EEC as it then was) in 1972. The insertion of Article 29.4.6° means that the normal manner in which primary legislation is adopted in Ireland does not have to occur when Ireland is implementing EU law. Where the State must comply with EU law, even where there is a conflicting primary legislative measure in place, the relevant government minister may amend the law by statutory instrument, rather than by the Oireachtas enacting primary legislation.[91]

2. Extension of EU Competences and Referendums in Ireland

6–39 As can be seen from the discussion on referendums in Ch.3, the issue of ratification of EU treaties by way of referendums has come before the people on a relatively regular basis.[92] The fact that the ratification of both the Nice Treaty and the Lisbon Treaty had to be put to the people twice demonstrates that while EU law is binding on Ireland, it is only permitted to impact on the legislative freedom of the Oireachtas in so far as we consent to this state of affairs. Theoretically, Ireland could withdraw from the EU and, by so doing, be exclusively responsible for its own law-making.

6–40 It was this very question concerning the interaction between the law-making powers of the Oireachtas and the EU that was at issue in *Crotty v An Taoiseach*.[93] Specifically, the plaintiff challenged the decision of the Oireachtas to enact the European Communities (Amendment) Act 1986. The 1986 Act sought to incorporate the Single European Act

[91] European Communities Act 1972. See also *Meagher v Minister for Agriculture and Food* [1994] 1 I.R. 329 and *Sam McCauley Chemists v Pharmaceutical Society of Ireland* [2008] 1 I.R. 16.

[92] See Ch.3, para.3–80.

[93] [1987] I.R. 713.

(SEA) into Irish law. Crotty argued that ratification of the SEA would give the European institutions excessive law-making power and encroach upon the law-making power of the Oireachtas. Thus, he sought an injunction restraining the Irish Government from depositing instruments of ratification of the SEA. The Supreme Court acknowledged that there was an extension to the aims of the European Communities in the SEA. This, however, did not represent an alteration of the essential scope of the founding treaties. The Supreme Court in *Crotty* accepted that the European Communities were a "developing organism".[94] The plaintiff in *Crotty* was successful on one key ground: the Government could not transfer a competence to the EU that was beyond the original treaty that Ireland signed. The Supreme Court held that the provisions of Title III of the SEA (on common foreign and security policy) were unconstitutional (by a majority of 3:2) and contrary to Article 5 of the Constitution on the sovereignty of the State. This necessitated a referendum to amend the Constitution.[95]

6–41 The question of whether every international agreement made by the EU requires ratification by referendum arose before the Supreme Court in the case of *Pringle v Ireland*.[96] The plaintiff, an independent TD, challenged ratification by the State of the European Stability Mechanism (ESM) as part of the EU's response to the financial crisis.[97] He argued that ratification of the ESM would impinge on and diminish Ireland's sovereignty in relation to budgetary, economic and fiscal policy. The purpose of the ESM was to preserve the EU's single currency, the euro, which was then seen to be under existential threat. The Supreme Court rejected the plaintiff's argument that a referendum was required to ratify the ESM. Denham C.J. stated that, in contrast to *Crotty*, there was no abdication of freedom of action in the formulation of foreign policy, no attempt by Government to make a binding commitment to alienate other states in the conduct of foreign relations, nor any attempt at a fundamental transformation of the definition of sovereignty. On that basis, it was found that the decision to ratify was "a policy decision

94 [1987] I.R. 713 at 770.

95 For a discussion of *Crotty* and the impact of the requirement to hold referendums to ratify EU treaties, see G. Barrett, "Building a Swiss Chalet in an Irish Legal Landscape? Referendums on European Union Treaties in Ireland and the Impact of Supreme Court Jurisprudence" (2009) 5 *European Constitutional Law Review* 32.

96 [2012] IESC 47.

97 Treaty establishing the European Stability Mechanism (2012), Doc. No. 42012A0202(01).

within the executive power, pursuant to the Constitution and so did not involve an impermissible transfer of sovereignty".[98]

6–42 According to Rainford, the "boldest assertion of state sovereignty against an international treaty since *Crotty*"[99] is to be found in the decision of *Costello v Government of Ireland*.[100] The appellant, Costello, challenged the ratification of the Comprehensive Economic and Trade Agreement (CETA) between the EU and Canada. The appellant argued that CETA was unconstitutional on two core grounds. The first was that it infringed the powers of the Oireachtas under Article 15.2. This claim failed. The second core ground of challenge was that judicial sovereignty would be infringed if CETA became applicable to and within Ireland. The judgments of the Supreme Court in the main focused on the "investor-state dispute settlement" mechanism established in CETA.[101] In essence, this would establish a permanent investor court system to deal with disputes under CETA. The decisions of the investor court dispute settlement mechanism, pursuant to CETA, would in most circumstances have automatic effect in Irish domestic law. There would not be the possibility of an appeal of a decision to the Irish courts. The applicant in *Costello* argued that this would create a parallel system of justice in Ireland and would breach "judicial sovereignty".[102] The High Court

[98] [2012] IESC 47 at para.17(xiii). The case also considered questions of EU law, which the Supreme Court sent on a reference to the Court of Justice—*Pringle v Government of Ireland* (C-370/12) EU:C:2012:756. The three questions referred by the Supreme Court may be summarised as follows: (1) whether the ESM Treaty was compatible with the EU Treaties; (2) whether the amendment to Article 136 TFEU to facilitate the ESM was lawful (a focus of this question was whether it was permissible for EU Heads of Government to amend the TFEU by use of the simplified amendment procedure); and (3) whether eurozone states were entitled to join the ESM before the Article 136 TFEU amendment came into force. At the time, the earliest date that the amendment could come into effect was 1 January 2013. The Court of Justice rejected Mr Pringle's arguments and found that adherence to the ESM Treaty was compatible with EU law. The Court of Justice also found that the amendment to Article 136 TFEU was not legally necessary as a prerequisite to activation of the ESM. For an analysis of the *Pringle* case, see J. Noonan and M. Linehan, "Thomas Pringle v The Government of Ireland, Ireland and the Attorney General" (2014) 17(1) *Irish Journal of European Law* 129, and C.W. Herrmann, "Pringle v Ireland Case C-370/12" (2013) 107(2) *American Journal of International Law* 410.

[99] S. Rainford, "*Costello v Ireland* and an Irish Constitutional Identity" (2023) 7(1) *Irish Judicial Studies Journal* 70.

[100] [2022] IESC 44.

[101] Article 8.22.1, Consolidated Text of the Comprehensive Economic and Trade Agreement (CETA) (2016).

[102] [2022] IESC 44, judgment of Dunne J. at para.280 and judgment of Hogan J. at para.227.

rejected Costello's argument, and a "leap-frog" appeal was permitted by the Supreme Court.

6–43 In his skilful judgment, Hogan J. reiterated that, owing to our dualist approach to international law, CETA on its own cannot impact the law in Ireland. In coming to this conclusion, Hogan J. referred to s.25 of the Arbitration Act 2010. Section 25 of the 2010 Act would bring CETA into conflict with the Constitution, because the High Court would not be able to refuse enforcement of the investor-state dispute settlement.[103] Hogan J. held:

> "[T]he [2010] Act serves as a sort of make-shift pontoon bridge by which a CETA Tribunal award is enabled to cross that legal Rubicon from the realm of international law into an enforceable judgment recognised as such by our own legal system on a more or less automatic basis."[104]

6–44 Hogan J. then identified a potential solution to this issue that would not necessitate a referendum.[105] The Oireachtas could amend the 2010 Act and make the enforcement of the CETA investor court award subject to three conditions. First, that the award would not "materially compromise" the constitutional identity of the State. Second, the award would not be enforced by the High Court where it violated "fundamental principles" of the Irish constitutional order. Third, the award would not "materially compromise" Ireland's obligations under EU law, including the Charter of Fundamental Rights of the European Union. The majority of the Supreme Court agreed that Hogan J.'s proposal would remove any issue regarding unconstitutionality from CETA. Therefore, it was possible to ratify CETA without requiring a referendum.

3. The Reception of EU Law into the Irish Legal System

(a) EU law, the Executive and the Oireachtas

6–45 As well as the Constitution being relevant, domestic legislation in Ireland fleshes out how EU law will be received into the Irish legal system.

---

[103] [2022] IESC 44 at para.236 per Hogan J.
[104] [2022] IESC 44 at para.84.
[105] [2022] IESC 44 at paras 233–237.

Section 2 of the European Communities Act 1972 (as amended)[106] provides that the EU treaties, as well as EU secondary law, "shall be part of the domestic law" of Ireland. The way EU law has been incorporated into the Irish domestic legal system differs depending on whether the measure of EU law is a regulation or a directive. Regulations have automatic effect in the Irish legal system without the necessity of any other domestic legal measures being brought into force. Where appropriate, Ireland may still need to introduce primary or secondary legislation to identify how EU regulations will be received into the Irish legal system. Directives, since they leave it to Member States to implement, will generally be reflected in Irish law through domestic ministerial regulations. Section 3 of the 1972 Act states that a government minister may repeal, amend or apply EU law through the making of (domestic) regulations (secondary law). So, in this way, domestic secondary regulations can, in effect, modify or disapply Acts of the Oireachtas, where those regulations are giving effect to EU law. The institutions of the EU are indifferent as to how Member States give domestic legal effect to EU legal rule. It is for each Member State to simply give legal effect to EU law.

6–46 In some limited fields, Ireland must introduce criminal offences pursuant to our obligations under EU law. Where the maximum fine is not greater than €500,000 or the maximum period of imprisonment is not greater than three years, a government minister may establish a criminal offence by ministerial regulation.[107] In this field, such regulations creating criminal offences as required by EU law must be laid before the Houses of the Oireachtas within 21 days, and a decision can be made to annul the domestic regulations.[108] This has never happened to date. In *Gearty v DPP*, the issues of law before the Supreme Court related to the protection of bogland, required under EU law, and the protection of habitats of flora and fauna. These protections are established in a variety of EU directives. The appellants had unlawfully cut turf and were prosecuted. The criminal penalty for this was established by means of secondary legislation. In dismissing the appeal, the Supreme Court highlighted that:

[106] European Communities Act 1972 s.2(1), as substituted by European Union Act 2009 s.3.

[107] European Communities Act 1972 s.3, as amended by European Communities Act 2007 s.2 and European Union Act 2009 s.4.

[108] European Communities Act 1972 s.3A, as inserted by European Communities Act 2007 s.3.

> "The normative legitimacy of the power to create indictable offences, effected to implement EU law, derives from EU law obligations."[109]

6–47 So, often when implementing EU law, government ministers will in essence act as the conduit through which EU law is given domestic legal effect. This may introduce new rights, obligations, liabilities or restrictions into Irish law. The legal measure would have gone through the necessary legislative procedure at the EU level. When a minister adopts a (domestic) regulation to give effect to EU law, the 1972 Act (as amended) is the legal basis that permits them to use secondary legislation. This power of the minister is not unrestricted and does have limits. A good illustration of this is in the *Friends of the Irish Environment* decision. The minister introduced secondary legislation purporting to implement aspects of EU law. This secondary legislation permitted turf-cutting at a vast scale. Rather than having to get permission for this, a licence could be granted to permit the cutting of turf. This secondary legislation had the effect of amending an Act of the Oireachtas. However, what the minister sought to do was (knowingly) undermine EU environmental law.[110] Simons J., in striking down the offending ministerial regulation, captures the essence of this (references added):

> "Secondary legislation which is inconsistent with EU legislation cannot be said to give effect to the 'principles and policies'[111] contained in the EU legislation. Nor can it be said to be 'incidental, supplementary and consequential' to the EU legislation or 'necessitated' by the Irish State's membership of the European Union. Rather, it is contrary to EU law."[112]

6–48 Simons J. in *Friends of the Irish Environment* also highlighted a second potential restriction on a minister's power to make regulations to give effect to EU law. With directives in particular, the Minister may

[109] [2024] IESC 45 at para.52.

[110] *Friends of the Irish Environment Ltd v Minister for Communications, Climate Action and Environment* [2019] IEHC 646.

[111] *Maher v Minister for Agriculture* [2001] 2 I.R. 189 at 254, where Fennelly J. stated that this may be the case "where the delegated legislation represents an exercise of a power or discretion arising from Community-law secondary legislation". Note that the principles and policies test is no longer the sole test for interpreting secondary legislation in Ireland. See Ch.4, paras 4–20 to 4–30.

[112] *Friends of the Irish Environment Ltd v Minister for Communications, Climate Action and Environment* [2019] IEHC 646 at para.157.

have a particular policy choice to make. The directive may give a wide discretion for the State to do something or not to do something. Where this occurs, and where the policy choice may impact on the existing primary legislation, then it is possible (and only possible) that the Oireachtas may have to amend the legislation to give effect to EU law.[113] The difficulty here, then, is: when may primary legislation be needed? This is challenging to pinpoint; as O'Donnell J. stated in *O'Sullivan*,[114] measures of EU law may be replete with policy choices, but often the power of Member States to implement the policy is "severely reduced".[115] Once the Minister is acting as a "delegate" implementing EU law, as domestically permitted by the 1972 Act, then it is unlikely that using secondary legislation will fall foul of Article 15.2.1° of the Constitution.

(b) Irish courts and tribunals and EU law

6–49 Maher and Riordan have succinctly summarised how EU law impacts on Irish courts: "Irish courts are not exclusively national courts. They form an integral part of a pan-European Union legal network where domestic courts are increasingly viewed … as European Courts."[116] The volume of litigation involving aspects of EU law has increased significantly in the last number of decades in Ireland.[117] Irish courts and tribunals' use of the preliminary reference procedure has substantially increased. In Rodger et al.'s 2021 study, they argue that the Irish Supreme Court's increased number of preliminary references "shows a robust dialogue with the CJEU and the marked openness of the Supreme Court to make references".[118]

6–50 For an Irish court or tribunal to make a preliminary reference to the CJEU, there must be a genuine dispute between the parties on matters of interpretation or application of EU law.[119] Courts of final appeal,

[113] *Friends of the Irish Environment Ltd v Minister for Communications, Climate Action and Environment* [2019] IEHC 646 at para.170.

[114] *O'Sullivan v Sea Fisheries Protection Authority* [2017] IESC 75.

[115] *O'Sullivan v Sea Fisheries Protection Authority* [2017] IESC 75 at para.43.

[116] I. Maher and R. Riordan, "The Supreme Court and EU Law: Reshuffling Institutional Balance" (2020) 2 *Irish Supreme Court Review* 1 at 1 (reference omitted).

[117] B. Rodger, I. Maher and R. Riordan, "A Decade of EU Law in the Courts of Scotland and Ireland: National Legal Systems Compared" (2021) 41 *Legal Studies* 311 at 322–323.

[118] B. Rodger, I. Maher and R. Riordan, "A Decade of EU law in the Courts of Scotland and Ireland: National Legal Systems Compared" (2021) 41 *Legal Studies* 311 at 332.

[119] *Foglia v Novello* (Case 244/80) [1981] E.C.R. 03045.

such as the Supreme Court, must make a preliminary reference where an interpretation of the EU treaties or secondary law is necessary to deliver a decision, and/or there is a question regarding the validity of an EU law.[120] Lower courts and tribunals may also refer questions to the CJEU. There is no obligation on any court to refer questions to the CJEU where questions of EU law are not relevant to the decision, the CJEU has already provided a materially identical answer of legal interpretation in another decision, and/or application of EU law is so obvious that there is no need to refer matters to the CJEU.[121] The Supreme Court has held that the referral of a preliminary reference by a lower court can be appealed, although this would be the exception rather than the rule.[122]

6–51 It is not only courts that can request preliminary references to the CJEU. Some domestic decision-making tribunals may also request a preliminary ruling. The tribunal should generally be established by law, must be independent and permanent, and its jurisdiction must be compulsory. In Ireland, bodies such as the Workplace Relations Commission and the International Protection Appeals Tribunal may refer questions to the CJEU for determination.

6–52 When applying EU law, even the lowliest tribunal may disapply or ignore conflicting domestic legislative provisions or past judicial decisions of superior courts, if tribunals need to do so to give effect to EU law.[123] In *Workplace Relations Commission*,[124] the Supreme Court argued that domestic legal processes should be followed so that bodies other than the superior courts should not have the power to disapply conflicting domestic law. This argument was rejected by the Court of Justice. The Court of Justice noted that this disapplication did not necessarily mean to "strike down" formally the offending domestic legal provision, as this may be a power the tribunal did not have.[125]

[120] Article 267 TFEU.

[121] For a detailed exploration of this, with reference to Court of Justice decisions, see D. Chalmers et al, *European Union Law*, 5th edn (Cambridge: CUP, 2024), Ch.4 and Ch.5, and P. Craig and G. de Búrca, *EU Law: Text, Cases and Materials*, 8th edn (Oxford: OUP, 2024), Ch.14.

[122] See, e.g. *Data Protection Commissioner v Facebook Ireland Ltd* [2019] IESC 46, in particular para.2.8 and para.6.10.

[123] *Minister for Justice and Equality and Commissioner of An Garda Síochána v Workplace Relations Commission* (C-378/17) EU:C:2018:979, in particular paras 32–52.

[124] *Minister for Justice, Equality and Law Reform and Commissioner of An Garda Síochána v Workplace Relations Commission* [2017] IESC 43.

[125] *Minister for Justice and Equality and Commissioner of An Garda Síochána v Workplace Relations Commission* (C-378/17) EU:C:2018:979 at para.32.

Box 6.2: Legal Insight
Irish Legislation, EU Law, and Clashing Interpretations of EU Law in Irish Courts[126]

International protection applicants, also known as asylum seekers, have a right to have their claims for international protection determined in Ireland.[127] If applicants meet the strict criteria for the recognition of refugee status or the grant of subsidiary protection, then they are recognised as having a protection need. However, deciding on entitlement to international protection takes an extraordinarily long time in Ireland. Ireland is bound by several measures of EU asylum and protection law, including the Reception Conditions Directive Recast 2013 (the "RCDr 2013").[128] This is given domestic legal effect in the Reception Regulations 2018 (the "2018 Regulations").[129] One of the rights recognised in the RCDr 2013 and the 2018 Regulations is the right of international protection applicants to apply to enter the labour market where a first-instance decision has not been made on their international protection claim for a period of six months.[130] When Ireland transposed the RCDr 2013 into domestic law via the 2018 Regulations, it excluded protection applicants where there was a possibility that there would be a removal to another EU Member State to determine their protection claim under the "Dublin system".[131]

The International Protection Appeals Tribunal (IPAT) can determine whether protection applicants are entitled to reception conditions under

[126] For more in-depth discussion of this case study, see L. Thornton, "Clashing Interpretations of EU Law in Domestic Courts" (2021) 26(2) *European Public Law* 243.

[127] For a comprehensive overview of international protection law in Ireland, see C. Hughes and S. Hughes, *International Protection Act 2015: Annotated* (Dublin: Clarus Press, 2020).

[128] Directive 2013/33/EU of the European Parliament and Council of 26 June 2013 laying down standards for the reception of applicants for international protection (recast) [2013] OJ L180/96.

[129] European Communities (Reception Conditions) Regulations 2018 (S.I. No. 230 of 2018). For why this measure became part of Irish law, see L. Thornton, "Clashing Interpretations of EU Law in Domestic Courts" (2021) 26(2) *European Public Law* 243 at 243–245.

[130] RCDr 2013 art.15; 2018 Regulations reg.11. Note that the EU directive requires Member States to permit international protection applicants to enter the labour market within nine months where there has been no first-instance decision on the protection claim. Between 2018 and 2021, Ireland adopted a nine-month limit. Since 2021 in Ireland, an international protection applicant waiting for six months on a first-instance decision on their protection claim may apply to access the labour market; see European Communities (Reception Conditions) (Amendment) Regulations 2021 (S.I. No. 52 of 2021) reg.3.

[131] L. Thornton, "Clashing Interpretations of EU Law in Domestic Courts" (2021) 26(2) *European Public Law* 243 at 246–247.

the 2018 Regulations. A series of IPAT decisions determined that Ireland had failed to properly transpose EU law. EU law, according to IPAT, entitled all protection applicants, including those who may be removed to another EU Member State to have their protection claim assessed, to be able to access the labour market. IPAT therefore ignored the 2018 Regulations and directly applied the RCDr 2013.[132] In a different decision a short time later, *KS (Pakistan)*,[133] Humphreys J. stated that Ireland was entitled to create different types of protection applicants who had different rights. For protection applicants who may be removed from Ireland to another EU Member State, Humphreys J. would have concluded that they were not entitled to enter the labour market. As Ireland may not have been the EU Member State responsible for determining their protection claim, then the applicants could remove themselves to this EU Member State and exercise their right to work there. Humphreys J. did accept that this may not be the correct interpretation of EU law, so he referred a series of questions to the Court of Justice to get a definitive answer on what the correct interpretation of EU law in this field was.

While awaiting a decision of the Court of Justice, Humphreys J. invited IPAT to follow his approach to resolving this question, and refuse labour market access to protection applicants who may be removed from Ireland to another EU Member State.[134] Tribunal Member Carroll of the IPAT, in a subsequent decision, declined to follow the approach of Humphreys J. and provided detailed reasons as to why her interpretation of EU law was correct.[135] Nothing would have prevented Tribunal Member Carroll from simply making a decision and granting the protection applicant access to the labour market. Nonetheless, in a legally astute move, Tribunal Member Carroll made her own preliminary reference to the Court of Justice.

In January 2021, the Court of Justice responded to Humphreys J. and Tribunal Member Carroll's preliminary reference. The Court of Justice determined that Irish law was in breach of EU law by attempting to create two types of protection applicant. Once a protection applicant was in Ireland and met the requisite conditions to access the labour market, then this legal right had to be implemented. This, the Court of

[132] L. Thornton, "Clashing Interpretations of EU Law in Domestic Courts" (2021) 26(2) *European Public Law* 243 at 256–262.

[133] *KS (Pakistan) and MHK (Bangladesh) v International Protection Appeals Tribunal* [2019] IEHC 176.

[134] The rationale for the decision of Humphreys J. is discussed in L. Thornton, "Clashing Interpretations of EU Law in Domestic Courts" (2021) 26(2) *European Public Law* 243 at 252–256. See [2019] IEHC 176 at para.37.

[135] The rationale for the decision of Tribunal Member Carroll is discussed in L. Thornton, "Clashing Interpretations of EU Law in Domestic Courts" (2021) 26(2) *European Public Law* 243 at 261–262.

Justice noted, included protection applicants who may (and only may) be removed from Ireland where a decision on their removal had not been made within the requisite time period. Once a protection applicant had not contributed to delaying the determination of their removal decision, they were entitled to access the labour market.[136] This case was rather unusual in that it was quite clear that Ireland was in significant breach of EU law, with this being expertly set down by Tribunal Member Carroll in the original IPAT decision. Subsequently, secondary legislation brought Irish law into conformity with its legal obligations under the RCDr 2013.[137]

4. Compliance with EU Law: A Case Study on the Right to Shelter for International Protection Applicants

6–53 While EU law has primacy over Irish domestic law, this should not be confused with guaranteeing Irish compliance with EU law. As discussed above, domestic courts will often ensure the State is complying with its EU legal obligations. At times, of course, domestic courts cannot guarantee compliance, which is why the European Commission, as guardian of the treaties, may commence legal action before the Court of Justice to compel a Member State to comply. If a Member State does not comply with deadlines for implementation of EU law, the Commission might initiate "infringement proceedings" against it under Article 258 TFEU. This initially may result in the Court of Justice declaring that an EU Member State is in breach of its obligations under EU law. If a Member State continues to breach EU law after this decision, the Commission may refer the matter again to the Court of Justice, which has the power to impose large fines on Member States. In February 2024, for example, the Court of Justice held that Ireland had failed to transpose the Audiovisual Media Services Directive into Irish law.[138] As Ireland had failed to ensure compliance with EU law, it was fined a lump sum payment of €2.5 million.[139] A daily penalty payment was also imposed on Ireland, so that each day that Ireland continues to fail to give domestic legal effect to this measure of EU law, the State will pay €10,000 per day to the EU.[140]

[136] *K.S and others v International Protection Appeals Tribunal* (C-322/19 and C-385/19) EU:C:2021:11, in particular paras 86–93 for the operative part of the judgment.

[137] European Communities (Reception Conditions) (Amendment) (No. 2) Regulations 2021 (S.I. No. 178 of 2021).

[138] *European Commission v Ireland* (C-679/22) EU:C:2024:178.

[139] *European Commission v Ireland* (C-679/22) EU:C:2024:178 at para.88.

[140] *European Commission v Ireland* (C-679/22) EU:C:2024:178 at para.99.

6–54 Should delayed implementation of EU law result in a person suffering loss, this may be recoverable as damages from the Member State. This is known as the principle of state liability, also referred to as "*Francovich* damages",[141] after the case that established this right. This power was successfully invoked in Ireland in *Tate v Minister for Social Welfare*[142] due to the failure of the Irish Government to implement Directive 79/7/EEC on equal treatment between men and women in social welfare where there was a delay of two years. The Court of Justice found Ireland at fault and ordered the Irish State to pay IR£265 million in arrears to 7,000 women affected. It must be recognised that, in general, Ireland has a good record of compliance with EU law. Nonetheless, this does not mean it is perfect.

6–55 Of the estimated 117.31 million persons who are seeking asylum or otherwise forcibly displaced, about 19.5 million are in Europe.[143] It is estimated that since 2015, over 30,000 migrants have died attempting to cross the Mediterranean.[144] Russia's illegal war on Ukraine has resulted in a significant number of Ukrainian citizens arriving in Europe. Ukrainian citizens fleeing Ukraine are entitled to "temporary protection" status.[145] Persons with the status of temporary protection in Ireland are not international protection applicants (asylum seekers). In this part of the chapter, we are exploring the violation of EU rights of international

---

141 *Francovich v Italy* (C-6 & 9/90) [1991] E.C.R. I-5357. Under the Insolvency Protection Directive (Directive 80/987/EEC, now 2008/94/EC), EU Member States were expected to enact provisions in their national law to give a minimum level of insurance for employees who had wages unpaid if their employers went insolvent. The plaintiff worked for a company that went bankrupt and neither he nor his former colleagues received payment for the wages owed. The Directive was meant to be implemented by 1983, but five years later they had been paid nothing, as the company liquidators had informed them that no money was left. They successfully brought a claim against the Italian State, arguing that it must pay damages to compensate for their losses instead, on account of a failure to implement the Directive.

142 [1995] 1 I.R. 418.

143 United Nations High Commissioner for Refugees, *Global Trends 2023* (Geneva: UN, 2024).

144 UN International Organization for Migration (IOM), *Missing Migrants Project, https://missingmigrants.iom.int/*. For a visual map of the main entry and often perilous routes migrants may have to use, see United Nations High Commissioner for Refugees, *Global Trends 2023* (Geneva: UN, 2024), p.14.

145 International Protection Act 2015 s.50. See also, Immigration Service Delivery, *Information on Temporary Protection for People Fleeing the Conflict in the Ukraine*, available at: *https://www.irishimmigration.ie/*. For updated statistics, see Eurostat, *Temporary Protection for Persons Fleeing Ukraine: Monthly Statistics*, available at: *https://ec.europa.eu/eurostat/statistics-explained/*.

protection applicants in Ireland only. We are not exploring the legal status of persons entitled to temporary protection.

6–56 Since 2022, in particular, thousands of single men seeking international protection have not been offered shelter or accommodation in Ireland.[146] As noted above, Ireland's EU legal obligations are established in the Reception Conditions Directive Recast 2013 (RCDr) and the domestic transposition Reception Regulations 2018. EU law and Irish law require the following:

- A person is seeking international protection and their protection claim has not yet been determined.[147]
- International protection applicants, *without their own means*, are entitled to "material reception conditions". These include housing, food, a daily expenses allowance and a clothing allowance. In Ireland, the Minister for Children, Equality, Disability, Integration and Youth is responsible for providing material reception conditions for persons seeking international protection.[148] The Department of Social Protection provides the daily expenses allowance and clothing allowance.[149] Material reception conditions must ensure an adequate standard of living for international protection applicants. International protection applicants seeking provision of material reception conditions must evidence that they lack the means to support themselves.
- In Ireland, international protection applicants are now accommodated in direct provision accommodation centres, in private hotels, bed and breakfasts, hostels, or in serviced tented accommodation sites.[150]

---

[146] For an overview of current statistics, see Department of Children, Equality, Disability, Integration and Youth, *Statistics on International Protection Applicants Not Offered Accommodation*, available at: *https://www.gov.ie/en/publication/ec5f2-statistics-on-international-protection-applicants-not-offered-accommodation/.*

[147] RCDr 2013 art.2; 2018 Regulations reg.2.

[148] Disability, Equality, Human Rights, Integration and Reception (Transfer of Departmental Administration and Ministerial Functions) Order 2020 (S.I. No. 436 of 2020) transfers the functions of the Department of Justice to the Department of Children.

[149] RCDr 2013 art.17; 2018 Regulations reg.2 et seq. For more on international protection applicants and their very limited social welfare entitlements, see L. Thornton, "Augmenting Social Welfare for Asylum Seekers in Ireland" (2020) 42(4) *Journal of Social Welfare and Family Law* 441.

[150] For critiques of the system of direct provision, its history, continuation and proposals for abolition (that will now not occur), see L. Thornton and A. Ogunsanya, "Ending Direct Provision? February 2021–September 2022: A Review of the Implementation of

6–57 Where accommodation is not provided, then the weekly payment available to these men is €113.80 per week.[151] Those men not offered accommodation are also provided with information on various charities who may be in a position to offer them support (e.g. provision of tents, sleeping bags, hygiene facilities, hot meals, etc). The broader socio-political context in Ireland has shown that where accommodation is sourced within a given village, town or city, there are often protests, particularly so if single men will be present in the accommodation. There have been several cases of suspected arson on premises that were to provide accommodation for international protection applicants.[152]

6–58 In April 2023[153] and August 2024,[154] the High Court granted declarations that Ireland was not only in breach of its legal obligations under the RCDr 2013 and the 2018 Regulations, but also that Ireland was breaching the dignity of people seeking protection by not providing people with even basic shelter, food and hygiene facilities. In the case of *SY (a child)*, the Child and Family Agency initially determined that SY was an adult (over 18), and only subsequently accepted that SY was a child. SY had to sleep rough for a number of weeks, did not have access to showering or other hygiene facilities, had to defecate on the street and had to beg. He had irregular access to food. The State had provided him with a €25 Dunnes Stores (supermarket) voucher and a list of charities he could potentially gain support from. SY was provided with accommodation after he commenced the legal action, but the High Court still proceeded to give a decision as there were many others similarly situated to SY, so the decision in this case would in effect be the

the White Paper on Ending Direct Provision" (Cork: Nasc, 2023), available at: *https://papers.ssrn.com/sol3/papers.cfm?abstract_id=4688677.*

151 This is known as "Homeless Daily Expenses Allowance", see Department of Children, Equality, Disability, Integration and Youth, *Statistics on International Protection Applicants Not Offered Accommodation*, available at: *https://www.gov.ie/en/publication/ec5f2-statistics-on-international-protection-applicants-not-offered-accommodation/.*

152 See generally, B. Cannon and S. Murphy, "'We're not right-wing or racist but …': Far-right myth and distributive conflict in asylum seeker related protest in the Republic of Ireland, November 2022–July 2023" (2024) 32(1–2) *Irish Journal of Sociology* 225, and J. Laurence, F. McGinnity and K. Murphy, *Attitudes towards Immigration and Refugees in Ireland: Understanding Recent Trends and Drivers* (Dublin: ESRI, 2024).

153 *SY (a child) v Minister for Children, Equality, Disability, Integration and Youth* [2023] IEHC 187. See also *IKA v Minister for Children, Equality, Disability, Integration and Youth* [2023] IEHC 283.

154 *Irish Human Rights and Equality Commission v Minister for Children, Equality, Disability, Integration and Youth* [2024] IEHC 493.

decision in all these other cases.[155] The Minister for Children, Equality, Disability, Integration and Youth argued that since it was accepted that the State had breached its EU and domestic legal obligations,[156] there was no need for the court to issue a declaration on this matter. In granting the declaration, Meenan J. in the High Court stated:

> "There is nothing academic or theoretical about the rights which the applicant seeks to enforce. Being denied 'material reception conditions' has a direct impact on the applicant's quality of life to the extent that it deprives him of the most basic standard of living."[157]

6–59 The Department of Children, Equality, Disability, Integration and Youth treated SY in a humiliating and debasing manner, and failed to uphold SY's human dignity as required by the Irish Constitution and Article 1 of the EU Charter of Fundamental Rights.[158] Meenan J. acknowledged that the Department had made extensive efforts, but simply could not find suitable accommodation. Meenan J. held that this was not a defence to breaching the law.[159] In August 2024, the Irish Human Rights and Equality Commission were granted a declaration that the Minister was breaching the RCDr 2013 and the 2018 Regulations.[160] This was due to the violation of unaccommodated international protection applicants' rights to shelter, food and hygiene. While the High Court accepted there had been some (minimal) improvements post the decision in *SY*, these did not have the effect of excusing Ireland's continued breach of EU and Irish law.[161] The High Court declined to grant a mandatory order that would have obliged the Minister to provide shelter to all unaccommodated international protection applicants.[162] The High Court was of the view that the State would respond to the declaration granted adequately.[163] In November 2024, the State appealed this decision.

[155] *SY (a child) v Minister for Children, Equality, Disability, Integration and Youth* [2023] IEHC 187 at paras 32–36.

[156] [2023] IEHC 187 at para.20 and paras 39–40.

[157] [2023] IEHC 187 at para.40.

[158] [2023] IEHC 187 at para.51.

[159] [2023] IEHC 187 at paras 30(ii) and (ii) and para.46.

[160] *Irish Human Rights and Equality Commission v Minister for Children, Equality, Disability, Integration and Youth* [2024] IEHC 493. While this is a detailed decision, the core of the decision in essence follows the findings of law of Meenan J. in *SY*.

[161] [2024] IEHC 493 at para.262.

[162] [2024] IEHC 493 at para.263.

[163] [2024] IEHC 493 at para.262.

6–60 As the EU rights of unaccommodated international protection applicants are being violated, this opens up the possibility of entitlement to *Francovich* damages. This has previously occurred in the High Court decision of *X and Y v Minister for Justice and Equality (No. 1)*.[164] The right to material reception conditions protected under the RCDr 2013 is clear and precise. These were not provided to X and Y for a significant period of time. In *X and Y v Minister for Justice and Equality (No. 2)*, Barrett J. made an order for €1,500 damages against the State for breaching the applicants' rights to material reception conditions.[165] In the more recent decision of *SA and RJ v Minister for Children, Equality, Disability, Integration and Youth*,[166] the applicant, SA, had not been provided with material reception conditions for a period of 71 days.[167] RJ had not been provided with material reception conditions for 64 days.[168] Both argued before the High Court that the breach of their rights to be provided with material reception conditions under the RCDr 2013 meant that the State was liable to pay *Francovich* damages. Ireland argued that the applicants were not entitled to damages due to the extraordinary situation whereby the Department of Children, Equality, Disability, Integration and Youth could not source accommodation for them, and therefore could not provide them with other material reception conditions.[169] The Department in particular referred to the number of people entitled to temporary protection from the Ukraine who needed shelter.[170] This defence is known as *force majeure*.

6–61 The State acknowledged that it was in a financial position to secure accommodation but had simply been unable to do so.[171] Ferriter J. in the High Court noted that EU law was unclear as to whether a *force majeure* defence could nullify an individual's entitlement to *Francovich* damages. Ferriter J. therefore posed a number of questions to the CJEU seeking clarification on whether *force majeure* can prohibit the award of *Francovich* damages.[172] Pending the CJEU's decision,[173] the case will

---

164 [2019] IEHC 133.
165 [2019] IEHC 226 at para.3.
166 [2023] IEHC 717.
167 [2023] IEHC 717 at para.23.
168 [2023] IEHC 717 at para.38.
169 [2023] IEHC 717 at paras 84–88.
170 [2023] IEHC 717 at paras 54–59.
171 [2023] IEHC 717 at para.116.
172 [2023] IEHC 717 at paras 118–119.
173 Case C-97/24, Reference for a preliminary ruling from High Court (Ireland) made on 6

not be finalised and no decision will be taken as to whether the State has liability to pay damages for breaching an international protection applicant's right to material reception conditions.

6–62 Since all of the recent decisions discussed above were delivered, the number of unaccommodated international protection applicants continues to increase (at the time of writing). Given that the State, on its own admission, is breaching their EU and domestic legal obligations, what might that tell us about, or assist us in understanding, not only Ireland's compliance with EU law, but also more broadly about the rule of law?

D. Public International Law and the Irish Legal System

1. The Scope and Sources of Public International Law

6–63 Bingham argues that the rule of law entails a state's compliance with its international legal obligations.[174] The sources of international law are set out in Article 38 of the Statute of the International Court of Justice: (a) international treaties or conventions; (b) international custom; (c) general principles of law "recognized by civilized nations"; and (d) as a subsidiary means for determining rules of law, "judicial decisions and teachings of the most highly qualified publicists of the various nations". Crawford notes that sources (a) and (b) above are "the most important" sources of public international law, but cautions against reading sources (a)–(d) from top to bottom, as a hierarchy of international law.[175] International law is generally based on the principle of consent or state practice; that is, states either consenting to be bound by an international treaty or convention, or adopting a course of conduct in their relations with other states (custom) that the state feels legally obliged to adopt.[176]

February 2024 – *S.A., R.J. v Minister for Children, Equality, Disability, Integration and Youth*, available at: *https://eur-lex.europa.eu/eli/C/2024/3309/oj.*

174 T. Bingham, *The Rule of Law* (London: Penguin, 2011), Ch.10. See Ch.2, para.2–07 and para.2–32. This chapter does not consider private international law; see further, W. Binchy, *Irish Conflicts of Law*, 2nd edn (Dublin: Bloomsbury Professional, 2021); R. Byrne, J.P. McCutcheon, L. Cahillane and E. Roche-Cagney, *Byrne and McCutcheon on the Irish Legal System*, 7th edn (Dublin: Bloomsbury Professional, 2020), paras 17.88–17.95; J. Hill and M. Ní Shúilleabháin, *Clarkson & Hill's Conflict of Laws*, 5th edn (Oxford: OUP, 2016).

175 J. Crawford, *Brownlie's Principles of Public International Law*, 9th edn (Oxford: OUP, 2019), p.22.

176 However, for an alternative argument against this general proposition, but which

6–64 These consent and state practice principles are subject to exceptionally important qualifications. There can be no violation by states of laws pertaining to the commission of genocide, crimes against humanity, or crimes against peace. Certain aspects of the laws of war, prohibition of slavery, the prohibition of torture, and the prohibition of apartheid are further examples of international legal obligations upon states, regardless of whether states have agreed to this. Unfortunately, examples can be provided throughout the globe of states that violate these fundamental norms of international law. Yet, even though we can point to breaches of these fundamental norms, the violators often claim they accept these international legal obligations, and sometimes (rather brazenly) claim they fully comply with their legal obligations in the face of overwhelming evidence that they do not.[177]

6–65 There are a wide variety of international treaties, in areas as diverse as the law of the sea,[178] diplomatic immunities law,[179] criminal law,[180] human rights,[181] aviation law,[182] and taxation law.[183] These are just miniscule examples of legal fields within public international law. The Law Reform Commission in 2018 identified over 1,400 international treaties that Ireland has signed and ratified.[184] So, Ireland has agreed to be

also explores the basis for the consent principle in international law, see A. Guzman, "Against Consent" (2012) 52(4) *Virginia Journal of International Law* 747.

177 For more on this concept known within international law as *jus cogens*, see M.N. Shaw, *International Law*, 9th edn (Cambridge: CUP, 2021), pp.104–109, and J. Klabbers, *International Law*, 4th edn (Cambridge: CUP, 2023), pp.61–64.

178 United Nations Convention on the Law of the Sea 1982 (1833 U.N.T.S. 3).

179 Vienna Convention on Diplomatic Relations 1961 (500 U.N.T.S. 95); Vienna Convention on Consular Relations 1963 (596 U.N.T.S. 261).

180 See, e.g. Rome Statute of the International Criminal Court 1998 (2187 U.N.T.S. 3), and the constitutional provision relating to this international agreement, below at para.6–70.

181 See, e.g. International Covenant on Civil and Political Rights 1966 (999 U.N.T.S. 171); International Covenant on Economic, Social and Cultural Rights 1966 (993 U.N.T.S. 3 and 171); International Convention on the Rights of the Child, UN Doc. A/44/49 (1989). For more on Ireland and its international human rights obligations, see E. Dewhurst, N. Higgins and L. Watkins, *Principles of Irish Human Rights Law* (Dublin: Clarus Press, 2012).

182 See, e.g. Convention on Civil Aviation 1944 ("Chicago Convention"), reproduced at (1994) 15 U.N.T.S. 295.

183 See, e.g. Convention on the Elimination of Double Taxation in Connection with the Adjustment of Profits of Associated Enterprises, done at Brussels on 23 July 1990 (*Irish Treaty Series*, No. 24 of 2009).

184 Law Reform Commission, *Draft Inventory of International Agreements Entered into by the State* (LRC IP 14-2018). See pp.i–ii of this inventory to get a greater understanding of just how many fields of international law there are.

bound by freely accepted international legal obligations in these fields. Ireland has agreed with other states that their actions will conform to the obligations they have agreed to. There is no world parliament, there is no world executive, nor is there a world court or world army. This then raises the issue of compliance. When considering the interaction of Irish law and public international law and assessing the question of compliance, remedies available to individuals, as opposed to remedies that may be available to Ireland against other states, can be somewhat limited.

6–66 As this book explores the Irish legal system, the focus of this chapter will be on the interactions between international law and the domestic legal system. Public international law depends on states abiding by the obligations they have freely accepted. This, it goes without saying, is not always the case. Domestic political expediency can often trump compliance with international legal obligations. It can be tempting to view international law as being merely political agreement. This, at least to an extent, is true. One only must view how international obligations can be set aside for imperialistic ambitions. Russia's illegal war on Ukraine is one such example.[185] Russia has ignored the provisional measures indicated by the International Court of Justice to cease its military operation in Ukraine.[186] In the Middle East, the International Court of Justice requires Israel to refrain from acts that may constitute genocide in Gaza, Palestine.[187] The Court additionally required Israel to provide unhindered aid access, as well as requiring Israel to immediately stop its military actions in Rafah in May 2024. Israel has totally ignored these provisional measures.

6–67 Some states adopt a monist approach to international legal obligations, where "in principle international law has primacy over national

[185] A. Ahmad Haque, "An Unlawful War" (2022) 116 *American Journal of International Law: Unbound* 155.

[186] *Ukraine v Russian Federation*, ICJ GL. No. 182, 16 March 2022 at paras 78–83.

[187] See, generally, the various provisional measures indicated by the International Court of Justice in *Application of the Convention on the Prevention and Punishment of the Crime of Genocide in the Gaza Strip (South Africa v Israel)*, available at: *https://www.icj-cij.org/case/192/provisional-measures.* Discussed in: British Institute of International and Comparative Law, *Reflections on the South Africa v. Israel Case at the International Court of Justice* (9 February 2024); M. Gureghian Hall, "Assessing the Contents of the ICJ's Latest Provisional Measures Order in South Africa v. Israel", *EJIL: Talk!* 6 June 2024; and Tor Krever et al, "On International Law and Gaza: Critical Reflections" (2024) 12(2) *London Review of International Law* 217.

law at national as well as international level".[188] We have already discussed how Irish law interacts and engages with EU law, a form of international law incorporated into the Irish legal system, and issues of compliance. Ireland is not a monist legal system; Ireland has a dualist legal system. This means that international legal obligations are only incorporated into the Irish legal system if the Oireachtas determines that they should be. As Murray C.J. noted in *McD v L*, "[a]ccording to the concept of dualism, at national level national law always takes precedence over international law."[189] While this approach makes sense domestically, it is worth noting, as Murray C.J. did, that the enforcement bodies of international law do not accept reliance "on [domestic] constitutional provisions as an excuse for not fulfilling international obligations which they have undertaken". Within the field of international law, international law takes precedence over any conflicting domestic legal norms.

6–68 One example of the limitations of international law will suffice for our purposes. There are clear international obligations on Ireland[190] to not engage in torture, and to prevent state officials or private persons from having any hand, act or part in torture. There is also a positive obligation on Ireland to investigate allegations of torture, detect torture and punish those who engage in torture.[191] A particularly shameful aspect of Ireland's breach of international law emerges from the Afghan and Iraq wars during the 2000s. Extraordinary rendition is the illegal kidnapping, sometimes torture, sometimes detention without trial, and sometimes execution of prisoners and others who are deemed a threat

---

188 *McD v L* [2010] 2 I.R. 199 at 246 per Murray C.J. Murray C.J. does note that very few states are wholly monist. For an exploration of the monism/dualism distinction, see J.G. Starke, "Monism and Dualism in the Theory of International Law" (1936) 17 *British Yearbook of International Law* 66, and on the approach of the Irish legal system, see D. Fennelly, *International Law in the Irish Legal System* (Dublin: Round Hall, 2014), paras 1–18 to 1–30.

189 *McD v L* [2010] 2 I.R. 199 at 245.

190 Based on Article 3 of the European Convention on Human Rights and obligations under the UN Convention against Torture. However, the Criminal Justice (United Nations Convention against Torture) Act 2000 limits the domestic obligation to the prosecution of torture, or, under s.3 of the 2000 Act, to the prosecution of a person who "does an act with the intent to obstruct or impede the arrest or prosecution of another person, including a person who is a public official, in relation to the offence of torture".

191 The sources and the precise contours of these obligations are considered in Irish Human Rights Commission, *Extraordinary Rendition: A Review of Ireland's International Obligations* (Dublin: IHRC, 2007), Ch.3.

to a state.[192] During the Afghan and Iraq wars, extraordinary rendition was practised by a number of countries, in particular by (but not limited to) the United States. During these conflicts, US aircraft often refueled in Shannon Airport, Co. Clare. Some of these US aircraft were engaged in extraordinary rendition. The Irish Government, publicly at least, stated that it had assurances from the United States that renditions did not take place through Irish airspace, nor did rendition flights take place through Shannon Airport. In any event, the Government stated that members of the public who were concerned about rendition could complain to the Gardaí and provide the Gardaí with evidence that renditions were occurring.[193] These public assurances dissipated in private; the former Minister for Foreign Affairs, Dermot Ahern, told the US Ambassador to Ireland that he was "quite convinced that at least three flights involving renditions had refuelled at Shannon Airport before or after conducting renditions elsewhere".[194]

6–69 The US Ambassador thanked Dermot Ahern for the government's strong rejection of the (then) Irish Human Rights Commission (IHRC) report on extraordinary rendition.[195] The US Ambassador, in a leaked communication to the US Government, noted the concerns of the Minister for Foreign Affairs. The then Minister stated that he "would pay a severe political price if it ever turned out that rendition flights had entered Ireland". The UN Committee against Torture in 2011 expressed concern

> "... at the various reports of [Ireland's] alleged cooperation in a rendition programme, where rendition flights use [Ireland's] airports and airspace. The Committee is also concerned at the inadequate response by [Ireland] with regard to investigating these allegations".[196]

[192] For a legal-political background to these practices, see Amnesty International, *Below the Radar: Flights to Torture* (Dublin: A.I., 2006).

[193] Irish Human Rights Commission, *Extraordinary Rendition: A Review of Ireland's International Obligations* (Dublin: IHRC, 2007), p.19.

[194] See Confidential Brief by Ambassador Thomas C. Foley on meeting with Minister for Foreign Affairs, Dermot Ahern, made public by Wikileaks and accessible at: *https://wikileaks.org/plusd/cables/07DUBLIN916_a.html.*

[195] Irish Human Rights Commission, *Extraordinary Rendition: A Review of Ireland's International Obligations* (Dublin: IHRC, 2007).

[196] Committee against Torture, *Concluding Observations: Ireland*, UN Doc. CAT/C/IRL/CO/1 (17 June 2011), para.9.

The UN Committee against Torture recommended that Ireland adopt "specific measures" to investigate the allegations of extraordinary rendition through Ireland.[197] Ireland has failed to conduct any investigation into the allegations of extraordinary rendition, showing to a degree the limitations of international law. More recently, concerns have been raised regarding the potential use of Irish airspace by airlines moving munitions to Israel as part of the conflict in Palestine.[198] In October 2024, responding to these concerns, the government accepted that there may have been flights that entered into Irish airspace to facilitate the transfer of weapons to Israel.[199] The position of the Irish government remains:

> "We all agree that we do not want to facilitate the carriage of munitions, particularly if they are engaged or used in, or enable, what is an ongoing tragedy and travesty in Gaza, south Lebanon, the West Bank and the Middle East."[200]

2. The Constitution and International Law

6–70 Article 29 of the Constitution is titled "International Relations". The constitutional provision encompasses the approach of Ireland to international law. How the government wishes to conduct its relations with other sovereign states is a matter for the government of the day.[201] If the government wishes to enter an international, bilateral or multilateral treaty, convention agreement, etc., there is no requirement for the government to seek permission from the Oireachtas to do so, unless it results in a charge on public funds. Ireland's compliance with, or violation of, such an international agreement is "resolved" at the level of international law.[202] The relevant constitutional provisions relating to public international law are:

- Article 29.1 declares that Ireland "affirms its devotion to the ideal of peace and friendly co-operation amongst nations founded on international justice and morality".

[197] Committee against Torture, *Concluding Observations: Ireland*, UN Doc. CAT/C/IRL/CO/1 (17 June 2011), para.9.
[198] N. O'Connor and M. O'Cearbhaill, "Taoiseach: 'No consent sought' by Israeli arms shipment flight which crossed Irish airspace", *TheJournal.ie*, 26 August 2024.
[199] Dáil Debates, *Air Navigation Orders*, 17 October 2024.
[200] Minister Eamon Ryan, Dáil Debates, *Air Navigation Orders*, 17 October 2024.
[201] *Barlow v Minister for Agriculture, Food and the Marine* [2016] IESC 62 at para.34.
[202] *Barlow v Minister for Agriculture, Food and the Marine* [2016] IESC 62 at para.34.

- Article 29.2 commits Ireland to "pacific" settlement of disputes with other states through arbitration or judicial determination.
- Article 29.3 states that Ireland "accepts the generally recognised principles of international law as its rule of conduct in its relations with other States".
- Article 29.4 provides that the government is vested with the power to determine Ireland's relations with other states.[203]
- Article 29.5 provides that any international agreement entered into by the government must be placed before Dáil Éireann.[204] Where this international agreement results in any charge on public funds, the Dáil must approve this international agreement.
- Article 29.6 states that an international agreement only becomes applicable within Ireland if it is approved by the Oireachtas.
- Article 29.7 enables Ireland to enter into the British-Irish Agreement, including the establishment of cross-border bodies.[205]
- Article 29.8 permits Ireland to exercise extra-territorial jurisdiction to the degree permitted by "generally recognised principles of international law".
- Article 29.9 permits Ireland to ratify the Rome Statute of the International Criminal Court.[206]

6–71 Ireland is a member of the United Nations (UN), the Council of Europe, the World Health Organization, the World Trade Organization, the International Labour Organization, the World Bank, the International Monetary Fund, the Organisation for Economic Co-operation and Development, and many other bodies too numerous to mention.[207] Ireland's membership of international organisations and relations with other sovereign states are matters for government. Ireland has

---

[203] Article 29.4.

[204] Article 29.5.1°.

[205] Article 29.7.

[206] For an excellent description and evaluation of all of these constitutional provisions, see D. Fennelly, *International Law in the Irish Legal System* (Dublin: Round Hall, 2014), in particular Ch.2, and G. Hogan et al, *Kelly: The Irish Constitution*, 5th edn (Dublin: Bloomsbury Professional, 2018), Ch.5.3.

[207] For an overview of the role and remit of some of these organisations, see C. Archer, *International Organisations*, 4th edn (Oxon: Routledge, 2015), and J. Klabbers, *An Introduction to the Law of International Organisations*, 4th edn (Cambridge: CUP, 2022). For a review of Ireland's engagement with some of these organisations, see B. Tonra and E. Ward (eds), *Ireland in International Affairs: Interests, Institutions and Identities* (Dublin: IPA, 2002).

recognised the jurisdiction of certain international courts and tribunals, including, since 1953, the European Court of Human Rights,[208] since 2002, the Permanent Court of Arbitration,[209] and since its membership of the UN, the International Court of Justice (ICJ). The ICJ generally only has jurisdiction if both states to a dispute consent to the ICJ exercising this jurisdiction. In 2011, Ireland recognised the compulsory jurisdiction[210] of the ICJ to deal with disputes involving other states who have also recognised the compulsory jurisdiction of the ICJ.[211] Ireland also recognises the jurisdiction of the International Criminal Court,[212] and this court, as noted above, has constitutional recognition.[213]

6–72 The powers of the executive in international relations are not unlimited. This is well illustrated in *Barlow v Minister for Agriculture, Food and the Marine*. The plaintiffs sought to challenge the failure of the government to legislate for a fishing agreement that permitted fishing for mussel seed by Northern Irish vessels in Irish waters. This right for Northern Irish fishing vessels was established by means of a Voisinage (neighbourhood) Agreement under the London Fisheries Convention 1964.[214] Rather than this being recognised in legislation, it was agreed to through a series of letters by civil servants in the Irish Department of Agriculture and Fisheries and the British Ministry of Agriculture.[215] The plaintiffs argued that "[t]he Constitution requires that all executive action be governed by the rule of law so that the executive cannot take action without reference to a particular statutory provision or common law rule that justifies their action."[216]

[208] See paras 6–87 to 6–91.
[209] For information on Ireland bringing the United Kingdom before the Permanent Court of Arbitration in relation to the operation of the Sellafield nuclear power plant, see "The Mox Plant Case: *Ireland v United Kingdom*" (2003) 42 *International Legal Materials* 1187.
[210] Department of Foreign Affairs, "Declaration accepting the compulsory jurisdiction of the International Court of Justice", 15 December 2011.
[211] This explicitly excludes any judicial determination before the ICJ on the constitutional status of Northern Ireland.
[212] International Criminal Court Act 2006.
[213] See para.6–70.
[214] European Fisheries Conference, London, *Final act of the European Fisheries Conference, London, December 3, 1963 to March 2, 1964, with fisheries convention, protocol of provisional application and agreements as to transitional rights* (London: H.M.S.O., 1964).
[215] Discussed in detail in the High Court decision in *Barlow v Minister for Agriculture, Food and the Marine* [2014] IEHC 471 at paras 12–15.
[216] [2014] IEHC 471 at para.10.

6–73 In the High Court, Birmingham J. accepted that "the executive now acts pursuant to law and the Constitution".[217] However, he stated that the court must restrain itself from interfering within the realm of foreign affairs, especially when this involved relations with Britain.[218] Ultimately, Birmingham J. stated that the departmental communications did not have to be laid before the Dáil, and dismissed the plaintiffs' action.[219] On appeal, the Supreme Court set aside the High Court decision. O'Donnell J., delivering judgment for the Supreme Court, focused on Article 10 of the Constitution: the State's ownership of all natural resources. The Supreme Court concluded that the government could not divest the natural resources of the State, unless the Oireachtas provided for this in law, through legislation.[220] The Supreme Court granted a declaration that fishing for mussel seeds by Northern Irish vessels in (the Republic of) Ireland's waters is not permitted by law.[221] The Sea-Fisheries (Amendment) Act 2019 restored the rights of Northern Irish fishers to fish in Irish waters.

6–74 The next section will provide a select overview of the interaction of Irish law with international law. This will briefly explore the interaction of Irish law with international treaties (not incorporated into domestic Irish law) and customary international law, and will focus on the status of one international agreement in Irish law: the European Convention on Human Rights.

3. Reliance on International Treaties and Custom in Irish Courts

6–75 An international treaty that has not been incorporated into Irish law does not give rise to actionable rights for individuals in Ireland. Since this issue first arose in the late 1950s, the Irish courts have categorically determined that treaties and conventions that are not brought into the domestic legal order by the Oireachtas in the constitutionally prescribed manner under Article 29.6 do not directly confer rights on individuals. The decision of *Re Ó Laighléis* continues to be relevant to the interaction of Irish law with international law.

[217] [2014] IEHC 471 at para.23.
[218] [2014] IEHC 471 at para.27.
[219] [2014] IEHC 471 at para.29, placing reliance on *State (Gilliland) v Governor of Mountjoy Prison* [1987] I.R. 201.
[220] [2016] IESC 62 at para.66.
[221] [2016] IESC 62 at para.73.

Box 6.3: Case Focus
***Re Ó Laighléis* [1960] I.R. 93**

Ireland signed the European Convention on Human Rights (the "Convention") in 1953. Nonetheless, the Convention was not part of Irish law at that time. In *Re Ó Laighléis*, the applicant had been interned under the Offences against the State (Amendment) Act 1940. As the 1940 Act had been subjected to an Article 26 reference to the Supreme Court before the President signed it into law, it was immune from constitutional challenge before the courts. Undaunted, the applicant sought an inquiry into the legality of his detention under Article 40.4.2° of the Constitution and asserted that the internment power conflicted with the right to liberty in Article 5 of the Convention and the right to a fair trial in Article 6 of the Convention. The Supreme Court, in a judgment delivered by Maguire C.J., rejected the suggestion that the Convention was in any respect relevant to the validity of the 1940 Act:

> "The insuperable obstacle to importing the provisions of the Convention ... into the domestic law of Ireland—if they be at variance with that law—is, however, the terms of the Constitution of Ireland. By Article 15.2.1° of the Constitution it is provided that 'the sole and exclusive power of making laws for the State is hereby vested in the Oireachtas: no other legislative authority has power to make laws for the State.' Moreover, Article 29, the Article dealing with international relations, provides at section 6 that 'no international agreement shall be part of the domestic law of the State save as may be determined by the Oireachtas.' ... [T]he Court ... cannot accept the idea that the primacy of domestic legislation is displaced by the State becoming a party to the Convention ... ."[222]

The Supreme Court found that as the Oireachtas had not made the Convention part of the domestic law of the State, the Supreme Court could not allow the rights contained in the Convention to grant rights or impose obligations beyond those contained in domestic law. No argument can prevail against the express command of Article 29.6 of the Constitution before judges whose declared duty it is to uphold the Constitution and the laws. Thus, the Supreme Court refused to allow Convention rights to displace national legislation. Furthermore, the Convention had been signed over a decade following the enactment of the 1940 Act and could not be retrospectively permitted to influence

[222] [1960] I.R. 93 at 124–125.

the interpretation of legislation that existed prior to the signing of the Convention by the State.

In 2003, Ireland indirectly incorporated the Convention into domestic law by means of the European Convention on Human Rights Act 2003.[223] As a result, parties before the domestic courts can now make legal arguments based on the 2003 Act before the Irish courts.[224] We will explore the Convention and the 2003 Act below.

6–76 The Universal Declaration of Human Rights (UDHR) is a 1948 UN General Assembly Resolution.[225] UN General Assembly resolutions are not one of the sources of international law. The UDHR sought to provide an overview of the key human rights that all people should enjoy. The UDHR acknowledges rights including: right to freedom from torture, criminal due process rights, entitlement to vote, right to marry, right to an adequate standard of living, etc. UN General Assembly Resolutions are just resolutions. They are not international treaties that states sign up to. Yet, what is the legal value of the UDHR in the Irish legal system? A short few years after its adoption by the UN General Assembly (and before Ireland was a member of the UN), Maguire C.J. in the Supreme Court case of *State (Duggan) v Tapley* stated:

> "The Declaration ... though of great importance and significance in many ways, is not a guide to discover the existing principles of international law."[226]

In 2017, the Supreme Court in its determination in *Gibbons v Addington* again emphasised that the UDHR "is not directly applicable in this State".[227] This does not mean the UDHR is totally irrelevant within the Irish legal system. For example, in *Delaney*, it was noted that Article 10

[223] To understand why this phraseology is used, see para.6–93.

[224] For a comprehensive review of the Convention and the European Convention on Human Rights Act 2003, see generally, F. de Londras and C. Kelly, *European Convention on Human Rights Act: Operation, Impact and Analysis* (Dublin: Round Hall, 2010); S. Egan, L. Thornton and J. Walsh (eds), *Ireland and the European Convention on Human Rights: 60 Years and Beyond* (Dublin: Bloomsbury, 2014); S. Kingston and L. Thornton, *A Report on the Application of the European Convention on Human Rights Act 2003 and the European Charter of Fundamental Rights: Evaluation and Review* (Dublin: Law Society, 2015).

[225] Universal Declaration of Human Rights, adopted 10 December 1948, UNGA Res 217 A(III).

[226] [1952] I.R. 62 at 83.

[227] [2017] IESCDET 137 at para.28.

of the UDHR recognises the importance of judicial independence.[228] In *Simpson*, the Supreme Court highlighted that the principle of human dignity is inherent within Article 1 of the UDHR.[229] However, a claim before an Irish court can never be solely based on the UDHR. At most, judges may refer to the UDHR as noting broad principles of rights that are recognised. Courts will then indicate similar domestic or European legal rights that do have the force of law in Ireland.

6–77 Ireland has signed and ratified a whole host of UN human rights treaties. Each of these treaties will recognise/acknowledge the existence of particular human rights. These treaties will usually create a treaty body. The task of the treaty body will be to review state compliance with treaties at regular intervals. Some UN human rights treaties to which Ireland is a state party permit individuals to petition a treaty body by means of an individual communication.[230] United Nations human rights treaty bodies should not be viewed as courts. At best, UN human rights treaty bodies can be viewed as providing authoritative guidance that states are free to accept or reject.[231] The Irish courts have ruled explicitly that individuals may not rely on UN human rights treaties that Ireland has signed and ratified.[232] Again, this does not prevent judges referencing these treaties in thinking broadly about a particular rights claim that is made by an applicant. The Supreme Court in *NHV* recognised that freedom of work is a derived constitutional right. In coming to this decision, the Supreme Court referred to the International Covenant on

[228] *Delaney v Personal Injuries Assessment Board* [2024] IESC 10 at para.106 of Haughton J.'s judgment. See also *Minister for Justice v Adams* [2024] IEHC 435 at para.58 and *Simpson v Governor of Mountjoy Prison* [2019] IESC 81 at para.90.

[229] *Simpson v Governor of Mountjoy Prison* [2019] IESC 81 at para.90.

[230] For a full exploration of the role of UN Treaty Bodies, see S. Egan, *The UN Human Rights Treaty System* (Dublin: Bloomsbury, 2014).

[231] For further exploration of this, see M. O'Flaherty, "The Concluding Observations of the United Nations Human Rights Treaty Bodies" (2006) 6(1) *Human Rights Law Review* 27. In *Grant v South West Trains Ltd* (C-249/96) [1998] E.C.R. I-621 at para.46, the Court of Justice said that the Human Rights Committee is not a judicial body and its findings have no force of law.

[232] Looking just at the UN Convention on the Rights of the Child (CRC), while the courts at times will refer to the rights protected, the CRC cannot be solely pleaded as a basis for seeking relief in an Irish court. See, e.g. *Dos Santos v Minister for Justice and Equality* [2015] IECA 210 at para.17 per Finlay Geoghegan J. Note the decision in *Brophy v DPP* [2024] IEHC 392, where Phelan J., acknowledging that the CRC is not part of domestic law, nonetheless quoted extensively from the CRC and the comments of the UN Committee on the Rights of the Child (at paras 48–50).

Economic, Social and Cultural Rights (ICESCR).[233] The Supreme Court cited the General Comment of the UN Committee on Economic, Social and Cultural Rights on the right to work.[234] The Committee's General Comment states:

> "The right to work is essential for realizing other human rights and forms an inseparable and inherent part of human dignity. Every individual has the right to be able to work, allowing him/her to live in dignity. The right to work contributes at the same time to the survival of the individual and to that of his/her family, and insofar as work is freely chosen or accepted, to his/her development and recognition within the community."[235]

The Supreme Court said that while not fully endorsing the Committee's conception of the right or freedom to work under Article 6 of the ICESCR, the court did state that "the thinking is broadly consistent with that which was the background to the Constitution".[236]

6–78 Irish courts "will strive, if possible, to ensure that Irish implementing legislation is interpreted in a manner consistent with the international law obligations".[237] This, however, has limits. In *Kavanagh v Governor of Mountjoy Prison*,[238] the applicant had been tried before the Special Criminal Court.[239] He brought a complaint to the UN Human Rights Committee,[240] a treaty body established under the International Covenant on Civil and Political Rights (ICCPR). The UN Human Rights Committee determined that the failure in Ireland by the Director of Public Prosecutions to provide reasons and the means for Kavanagh to challenge his denial of a jury trial meant that his rights under Article 26 of the ICCPR (equality before the law) were violated. Kavanagh sought to contest his criminal conviction on the basis that this finding by the

233 *NHV v Minister for Justice and Equality* [2018] 1 I.R. 246.

234 [2018] 1 I.R. 246 at 315–316, citing General Comment No. 18, ICESCR, *The Right to Work* (Article 6), UN Doc. E/C.12/GC/18 (6 February 2006).

235 General Comment No. 18, ICESCR, *The Right to Work* (Article 6), UN Doc. E/C.12/GC/18 (6 February 2006), para.1.

236 [2018] 1 I.R. 246 at 316.

237 *Sweeney v Governor of Loughan House Open Centre* [2014] IESC 42 at para.2.6.

238 [2002] 3 I.R. 97.

239 See Ch.9, paras 9–08, 9–14 and 9–49 to 9–53.

240 *Kavanagh v Ireland*, Communication No. 819/1998, ICCPR, UN Doc. CCPR/C/71/D/819/1998 (2001).

UN Human Rights Committee should bind and be followed by domestic courts. Kavanagh argued that, by making the decision, this was now a general principle of law, as envisaged by Article 29.3 of the Constitution. Rejecting this contention, Fennelly J. held: "[i]t is patent that [Article 29.3] confers no rights on individuals. No single word ... even arguably expresses an intention to confer rights capable of being invoked by individuals."[241] The Supreme Court also rejected Kavanagh's argument that he had a legitimate expectation that Ireland would comply with its freely accepted international obligations under the ICCPR.[242]

6–79 Even where international agreements are reproduced within Irish legislation, this does not necessarily mean that these international agreements are incorporated into Irish law. A case in point is the International Protection Act 2015. Schedules 1 and 2 of the 2015 Act contain the text of the Geneva Convention on the Status of Refugees 1951 and its 1967 Protocol. Section 2 of the 2015 Act indicates that these international agreements are included within the 2015 Act for "convenience of reference". So does this mean that all provisions of the Refugee Convention are now part of domestic law? The answer to this is "no". Article 31 of the Refugee Convention provides that Contracting States shall not impose penalties on account of a refugee's illegal entry or presence within a country. This is subject to two important caveats: that the person comes "directly" from the territory that they face persecution in, and they present themselves to the authorities without delay. Good cause also must be shown for the illegal entry or presence. In *NS*,[243] O'Higgins J. noted that when the Oireachtas sought to give effect to international conventions in Irish law, the wording used in legislation was that the international convention will have "the force of law in the State".[244] As the Refugee Convention does not have the force of law

[241] [2002] 3 I.R. 97 at 126.

[242] See, in particular, [2002] 3 I.R. 97 at 127–129.

[243] *NS v Judge Anderson* [2004] IEHC 440 at paras 16–21. Although this case related to the now repealed Refugee Act 1996, the exact same formulation is used in the International Protection Act 2015. See *KN v Minister for Justice and Equality* [2020] IESC 32 at para.82.

[244] O'Higgins J. referred to a number of Acts of the Oireachtas designed to bring international conventions into force in the State, including the Diplomatic Relations and Immunities Act 1967, the Child Abduction and Enforcement of Custody Orders Act 1991, and the Air Navigation and Transport (International Conventions) Act 2004; [2004] IEHC 440 at para.15.

in Ireland, Ireland may prosecute persons seeking protection in Ireland who do not have a passport when entering Ireland.[245]

6–80 Within international law, various international organisations may provide guidance as to the interpretation of an international treaty. For example, the United Nations High Commissioner for Refugees (UNHCR) has published a handbook and guidelines on determining refugee status.[246] At best, this can be seen as "soft law". Irish courts have cited with approval the UNHCR Handbook on multiple occasions, although noting that it does not have force of law in Ireland. Rather, it is a "useful" and "authoritative" tool to consider when determining the scope and ambit of domestic law pertaining to the refugee definition and procedures for determining protection status.[247] In *Re Article 26 and the Judicial Appointments Commission Bill 2022*, the Supreme Court considered several different guidance and international documents pertaining to best practices in judicial appointments and the principle of merit.[248] While these did not form part of the operative reasoning in finding the Judicial Appointments Commission Bill 2022 to be constitutional, it is nonetheless indicative of a willingness to at least consider authoritative, albeit non-binding, "soft law". Whelan J.'s analysis in *SK v AL* captures well the precise status of "soft law" in the Irish legal system as "representative of international juristic thinking in an area".[249]

6–81 In *Re Ó Laighléis*, Maguire C.J. stated categorically that Article 29.3 of the Constitution "clearly refer[s] only to relations between states and confer[s] no rights on individuals".[250] Subsequent challenges

[245] For many years, Ireland rarely prosecuted protection applicants who arrived in Ireland without their passport. This has changed very significantly; see Immigration Policy, *Dáil Debates*, 26 September 2024, in particular contributions by the then Minister for Justice, Helen McEntee. See further, C. O'Carroll, "Surge in number of people charged with arriving into Ireland without a passport", *TheJournal.ie*, 18 August 2024.

[246] UNHCR, *Handbook and Guidelines on Procedures and Criteria for Determining Refugee Status* (Geneva: UNHCR, 2019).

[247] See, e.g. *VZ v Minister for Justice* [2002] 2 I.R. 135 at 148 and *KN v Minister for Justice and Equality* [2020] IESC 32 at para.26.

[248] [2023] IESC 34 at para.123. This decision is discussed in detail in Ch.11, paras 11–40 to 11–43.

[249] [2019] IECA 177 at para.59. The decision in *SK* related to aspects of private international law, but arguably the principle also applies vis-à-vis public international law.

[250] [1960] I.R. 94 at 124. See also *Murphy v GM* [2001] 4 I.R. 113 at 158, where Keane C.J. stated that Article 29.3 only refers to "relations with other sovereign states at an international level".

by individuals who attempted to argue that Ireland was in breach of customary international law have also failed. In *Horgan v An Taoiseach*,[251] Edward Horgan sought a declaration that Ireland was participating in the illegal war against Iraq and that this was contrary to Ireland's international legal obligations.[252] Ireland permitted US military aircraft to stop over and refuel in Shannon Airport, and also permitted troop movements, munitions of war and war supplies to be transferred in Shannon. This, according to the plaintiff, was contrary to Articles 28.3 and 29.3 of the Constitution and international law. Counsel for Ireland noted that Article 29.3 did not confer any cause of action on persons to challenge the State's approach to its international relations.[253] Kearns J. did not rule on the legality or the illegality of the Iraq war.[254] In accepting the State's proposition that individuals were conferred no rights under either Article 29.1 or 29.3 of the Constitution, Kearns J. stated that these were "aspirational or declaratory provisions which cannot be made the subject matter of binding legal norms".[255] The Dáil had determined that it was not going to participate in the Iraq war, while also maintaining a long-standing position of permitting US aircraft involved in the conflict to move through Shannon Airport.[256] A subsequent case,[257] in which an applicant sought to challenge the government permitting US aircraft to land and refuel, and transport ammunition to Afghanistan, was also unsuccessful for similar reasons to those outlined in *Horgan*. These cases involved litigants inviting the Irish courts to engage in decisions on the occurrence of war, its legality, and the operation of Irish neutrality. The courts did not want to supplant their assessment of international

[251] [2003] 2 I.R. 468.

[252] [2003] 2 I.R. 468 at 472–475. Horgan argued that Ireland was in violation of the Hague Convention (V) Respecting the Rights and Duties of Neutral Powers and Persons in Case of War on Land 1907, and the 1923 Hague Convention Draft Rules of Aerial Warfare, which, it was argued, were reflective of customary international law. For a detailed exploration through a series of articles and reflections on the legality or illegality of the Iraq war, including arguments that counter our assertion that the war was illegal, see (2003) 97 *American Journal of International Law* 553–658.

[253] [2003] 2 I.R. 468 at 493–501.

[254] [2003] 2 I.R. 468 at 503. Kearns J. recognised that while the Iraq war was the "elephant in the room", it would not be appropriate for a domestic court to rule on the legality or illegality of an international conflict.

[255] [2003] 2 I.R. 468 at 513.

[256] Counsel for the Taoiseach noted that landing and over-flight facilities for the US military forces were not withdrawn in any conflicts in which the US participated since 1953, including Vietnam, Lebanon, the first Iraq war, Somalia, Bosnia and Kosovo; [2003] 2 I.R. 468 at 485–487.

[257] *Dubsky v Ireland* [2005] IEHC 442.

customary law for the government's interpretation and operation of its international legal obligations (which, in any event, were far from precise and clear). With key aspects of the relationship between public international law and the Irish legal system considered, we now turn to discuss the European Convention on Human Rights and Irish law.

E. The Council of Europe, the European Convention on Human Rights and Irish Law

1. The Council of Europe

6–82 The Council of Europe was established in 1949 and predates the establishment of the European Union.[258] The Council of Europe is an entirely separate organisation to what we now call the European Union. The purpose of the Council of Europe is established in its 1949 founding Statute.[259] Its primary objectives are "to achieve a greater unity between its members for the purpose of safeguarding and realising the ideals and principles which are their common heritage and facilitating their economic and social progress."[260] This is to be achieved through discussions of matters of common concern amongst the Member States and undertaking common action in "social, cultural, scientific, legal and administrative matters" as well as the "further realisation of human rights and fundamental freedoms".[261] Member States of the Council of Europe must accept the principle of the rule of law, ensure protection of rights and freedoms to all persons within their jurisdiction, and collaborate "sincerely and effectively" with the Council and other Member States.[262]

---

[258] This part of the chapter is focusing only on the Convention, and not the role played by the Council of Europe and its bodies (other than the European Court of Human Rights). For an exhaustive exploration of the totality of the Council of Europe, see Council of Europe, *The Council of Europe: An Overview—Upholding Human Rights, Democracy and the Rule of Law* (Strasbourg: COE Publications, 2023), and B. Rainey et al, *Jacobs, White and Ovey: The European Convention on Human Rights*, 8th edn (Oxford: OUP, 2021), Ch.1.

[259] Council of Europe, *Statute of the Council of Europe* (1949) E.T.S. 1, 5 May 1949.

[260] Council of Europe, *Statute of the Council of Europe* (1949) E.T.S. 1, 5 May 1949, Article 1(a).

[261] Council of Europe, *Statute of the Council of Europe* (1949) E.T.S. 1, 5 May 1949, Article 1(b).

[262] Council of Europe, *Statute of the Council of Europe* (1949) E.T.S. 1, 5 May 1949, Article 3.

6–83 The governance of the Council includes a Consultative Assembly, along with a Committee of Ministers.[263] Since 2004, the Consultative Assembly has been known as the Parliamentary Assembly. The Parliamentary Assembly should not be confused with a parliament; it is an advisory body only. As per Article 22 of the Statute, the role of the Parliamentary Assembly as a "consultative organ" is to "debate matters within its competence under this Statute and present its conclusions, in the form of recommendations, to the Committee of Ministers."[264] Membership of the Parliamentary Assembly is determined by national parliamentarians of Member States. Ireland has four full members of the Parliamentary Assembly, with four substitute members.[265] These members are chosen in relation to political party strength in the Oireachtas.

6–84 The Committee of Ministers is composed of one representative from each Member State. This will usually be (but not always) the Foreign Minister/Secretary of a Member State. The Committee of Ministers is the decision-making body of the Council of Europe. However, the Committee of Ministers' powers are limited.[266] Advice and recommendations on matters within the scope of the Council of Europe's competences can be issued. One of its clearest powers is the ability to expel a Member State from the Council of Europe. On 16 March 2022, the Committee of Ministers expelled Russia from the Council of Europe due to its illegal invasion of Ukraine.[267] This was the only expulsion from the Council of Europe to have occurred since its foundation. The full work of the Committee of Ministers is beyond the scope of this text, except for one important role: the supervision of the execution, or state compliance with, judgments made by the European Court of Human Rights, discussed below.

[263] Council of Europe, *Statute of the Council of Europe* (1949) E.T.S. 1, 5 May 1949, Article 10.

[264] For more on this, see Council of Europe, *The Council of Europe: An Overview* (Strasbourg: COE Publishing, 2024).

[265] For a current list of Irish parliamentarians who are members of the Parliamentary Assembly, see: *https://www.oireachtas.ie/en/inter-parliamentary-work/council-of-europe/*.

[266] Council of Europe, *Statute of the Council of Europe* (1949) E.T.S. 1, 5 May 1949, Articles 15–21.

[267] For more on this, see K.D. Magliveras, "Legal and Procedural Issues Arising from the Expulsion of the Russian Federation from the Council of Europe" (2023) 23(1) *International and Comparative Law Review* 96.

2. The European Convention on Human Rights

6–85 There are 225 treaties, conventions, agreements and charters that Council of Europe Member States can sign and ratify, across fields of education, social rights, nationality, military service, crime, protection of animals, and artificial intelligence.[268] Membership of the Council of Europe does not entail a Member State having to sign or ratify all such treaties. The most well-known treaty of the Council of Europe is the European Convention on Human Rights (the "Convention").[269] The Convention was opened for signature and ratification in Rome on 4 November 1950 and entered into force in 1953. As an instrument, it protects core civil and political rights. Like much of modern international human rights law, the Convention was negotiated by states after the horrors of World War II.[270] The rationale behind the Convention was to create human rights that could be enforced in courts of law, "to act as a bulwark against totalitarian regimes."[271] The Convention was seen as a means to prevent states from hiding behind the shield of state sovereignty in the face of accusations of human rights abuses.[272] The Convention takes "the first steps for the collective enforcement of certain of the rights stated in the Universal Declaration."[273]

6–86 The rights and freedoms protected by the Convention include the right to life,[274] the right to be free from torture, inhuman or degrading

---

[268] For a full list of all Council of Europe treaties, etc., see: *https://www.coe.int/en/web/conventions/full-list.*

[269] Council of Europe, Convention for the Protection of Human Rights and Fundamental Freedoms, 4 November 1950 (E.T.S. No. 5). The Convention has been amended and extended on a significant number of occasions via Protocols. For a full list of these protocols, see: *https://www.coe.int/en/web/conventions/full-list*. For a full overview of the rights protected in the Convention, see, generally, D.J. Harris et al, *Law of the European Convention on Human Rights*, 5th edn (Oxford: OUP, 2023), and B. Rainey et al, *Jacobs, White & Ovey: The European Convention on Human Rights*, 8th edn (Oxford: OUP, 2021). For a brief summary of the relationship between the Convention and Irish law, see S. Kingston and L. Thornton, *A Report on the Application of the European Convention on Human Rights Act 2003 and the European Charter of Fundamental Rights: Evaluation and Review* (Dublin: Law Society, 2015), pp.18–32.

[270] B. Rainey et al, *Jacobs, White and Ovey: The European Convention on Human Rights*, 8th edn (Oxford: OUP, 2021), pp.4–5.

[271] D. Maxwell-Fyfe, *Collected Edition of the Travaux Préparatoires of the European Convention on Human Rights* (The Hague: Martinus Nijhoff Publishers, 1985), p.82.

[272] A. Lester and D. Pannick (eds), *Human Rights Law and Practice*, 2nd edn (London: LexisNexis, 2004), p.5, para.1.14.

[273] Preamble, para.5 of the ECHR.

[274] Article 2 of the ECHR.

treatment or punishment,[275] freedom from slavery and forced labour,[276] the right to liberty and security,[277] the right to a fair trial[278] and the right to respect for family and private life.[279] In addition to these rights, other rights such as freedom of expression[280] and freedom of religious practice are also protected.[281] Article 13 of the Convention guarantees the right to an effective remedy for a breach of Convention rights. Article 14 of the Convention states that there can be no discrimination in the enjoyment of Convention rights "on any ground such as sex, race, colour, language, religion, political or other opinion, national or social origin, association with a national minority, property, birth or other status." In addition to the rights agreed within the Convention, a number of other rights were added by means of Protocols which Contracting States are at liberty to sign and ratify. Some significant rights are protected within these protocols, including the right to property and the right not to be denied an education.[282] Further rights protected by additional protocols include freedom of movement for those lawfully in a country,[283] prohibition of collective expulsions of aliens,[284] procedural protection for aliens in the event of expulsion,[285] and the abolition of the death penalty.[286] Protocol No. 12 is a free-standing prohibition of discrimination on "any ground such as sex, race, colour, language, religion, political or other opinion, national or social origin, association with a national minority, property, birth or other status."[287] While some of the rights outlined above are

[275] Article 3 of the ECHR.
[276] Article 4 of the ECHR.
[277] Article 5 of the ECHR.
[278] Article 6 of the ECHR.
[279] Article 8 of the ECHR.
[280] Article 10 of the ECHR.
[281] Article 9 of the ECHR.
[282] Protocol No. 1 of 20 March 1953.
[283] Article 2 of Protocol 4, 16 September 1963.
[284] Article 4 of Protocol 4.
[285] Article 1 of Protocol 7, 22 November 1984.
[286] Article 1 of Protocol 13, 3 May 2002. But see *Al-Saadoon and Mufdhi v United Kingdom* (App. No. 61498/08), judgment of the ECtHR (Fourth Section), 2 March 2010. The ECtHR determined that Article 2 of the Convention, due to consistent state practice, had in effect been amended to prohibit the death penalty.
[287] Article 1 of Protocol 12, 4 November 2000. Where discrimination is found, then there will be a consideration as to whether there is any objective or reasonable justification, in that the discrimination may pursue a legitimate aim or where there is a "reasonable relationship of proportionality between the means employed and the aims sought to be realised". See Council of Europe, *Explanatory Report on Article 12* (Strasbourg: COE Publishing, 2008), para.18.

absolute,[288] other rights are qualified.[289] Each of these rights have been subject to extensive interpretation by the European Court of Human Rights.

3. The European Court of Human Rights

6–87 Since its foundation in 1959, the European Court of Human Rights (ECtHR)[290] has been the guardian of the Convention. The ECtHR has played a pivotal role in developing the key principles of Convention law. Cases may be brought by individuals and groups[291] or by a Contracting State against another Contracting State.[292] States are only obliged to abide by the judgments of the ECtHR to which it is a party.[293] The ECtHR has emphasised that the rights protected under the Convention are to be "practical and effective" and not merely "illusory".[294] Individuals for the first time within international law exercised rights before an independent human rights court against actions of the state.[295] States parties to the Convention agreed to limit their sovereignty and abide by the judgment of the ECtHR in favour of an applicant. While national human rights protections offer the best guarantee to individuals that the state will protect their human rights, internationalised enforcement mechanisms provide

[288] Such absolute rights include Article 2 (right to life), Article 3 (prohibition of torture, inhuman or degrading treatment), Article 4(1) (prohibition of slavery and servitude), Article 7 (prohibition of retroactive offences), Article 13 (right to an effective remedy), and Article 14 (prohibition of discrimination). In addition, Article 1 of Protocol 13 absolutely prohibits the imposition of the death penalty.

[289] Some of the qualified rights within the Convention include Article 6 (which allows for a trial otherwise than in public where it is the interests of morals, public order or national security, protection of young people, or where publicity would prejudice the interests of the parties); Articles 8–11 may be subject to restrictions prescribed by law and necessary in a democratic society "in the interests of national security, public safety or the economic well-being of the country, for the prevention of disorder or crime, for the protection of health or morals, or for the protection of the rights and freedoms of others." The right to property may be restricted in accordance with the general interest or to secure payment of taxation. Once an interference with Convention rights is shown, it is for the state to bring itself within the limitations prescribed. Central to the ECtHR determination of the issue will be the proportionality of the measures introduced by the Contracting State.

[290] Article 19 of the ECHR.

[291] Article 34 of the ECHR.

[292] Article 33 of the ECHR.

[293] Article 46 of the ECHR.

[294] See *Airey v Ireland* (1979) 2 E.H.R.R. 305 at para.24. This decision is discussed in detail in Ch.13, Box 13.2.

[295] L.A. Lester and D. Pannick (eds), *Human Rights Law and Practice*, 2nd edn (London: LexisNexis, 2004), p.6, para.1.15.

incentives for states to comply with their international obligations.[296] The ECtHR is responsible for determining whether, in admissible cases,[297] a Contracting State has complied with its Convention obligations.[298]

6–88 The ECtHR comprises 46 judges, one from each Contracting Party. Judges are nominated by each Contracting Party (three nominations are made). Judges are elected by the Parliamentary Assembly of the Council of Europe for one non-renewable nine-year term.[299] The ECtHR is based in Strasbourg, and judges work full-time. The ECtHR can sit in four formations: a single judge, a Committee of three judges, a Chamber of seven judges, or a Grand Chamber of 17 judges. Ireland was one of the first states to appear before the ECtHR.[300] Article 35 of the Convention identifies the admissibility requirements that must be met for the ECtHR to hear an application. After exhausting domestic remedies, an applicant must lodge their case before the ECtHR within four months. The Convention rights violation must evidence a "significant disadvantage" to the applicant, unless respect for human rights protected by the Convention requires an examination on the merits of the application. The case must not be manifestly ill-founded nor an abuse of process. Most applications made to the ECtHR are inadmissible on one or more of these grounds.[301]

6–89 Article 46 of the Convention obliges the offending state to abide by the decision of the ECtHR. De Londras and Dzehtsiarou explain this succinctly: "execution of ECtHR judgments is very simply a requirement

---

[296] J.G. Merrills, *The Development of International Law by the European Court of Human Rights*, 2nd edn (Manchester: Manchester University Press, 1993), p.1.

[297] Council of Europe, *Practical Guide on Admissibility Criteria* (Strasbourg: COE Publications, 2023).

[298] For a more detailed review of the administration of the ECtHR, in particular in terms of judicial composition into chambers and the Grand Chamber, see J. Gerards, *General Principles of the European Convention on Human Rights*, 2nd edn (Cambridge: Cambridge University Press, 2023), Ch.9.

[299] On Ireland's system for appointing a judge to the ECtHR, see Ch.11, Table 11.1, p.493.

[300] For an excellent analysis and reflection on Ireland, the Convention and the ECtHR, see S. Egan, "Introduction" in S. Egan, L. Thornton and J. Walsh (eds), *Ireland and the European Convention on Human Rights: 60 Years and Beyond* (Dublin: Bloomsbury, 2014), in particular pp.3–20.

[301] See Council of Europe, *Analysis of Statistics 2023* (Strasbourg: COE Publications, 2024), p.11. This provides a review of a number of inadmissible decisions between 1999 and 2023.

of the Rule of Law; adherence to an existing legal obligation."[302] Where the ECtHR makes a finding that a violation of the Convention has occurred, it may order one or more of the following remedies: just satisfaction, non-pecuniary damages, "individual measures" and/or "general measures". For example, in *Drozdyk and Mikula*,[303] the ECtHR found a violation of the applicant's property rights under Article 1 of Protocol 1. The ECtHR ordered Ukraine to restore the applicants' legal title to the property, along with an award of non-pecuniary damages to one of the applicants.[304] In *Ibrahim*, the ECtHR held that the adoption of the applicant's biological child, for several reasons, violated their right to private and family life under Article 8 of the ECHR. As the applicant had not made a claim for non-pecuniary damages, the ECtHR awarded legal costs only.[305] The ECtHR has on occasion indicated that states may need to change domestic law or practice to prevent a continuing violation of Convention rights.[306] This is known as a "general measure", designed to prevent similar Convention violations in the future. In *JB and others*, the ECtHR ordered Malta to amend its laws to ensure the effective independence of its Immigration Appeals Board, due to concerns around its impartiality and terms of office of its members and pressure that could be placed on the Board by the executive branch of government.[307]

6–90 Once a decision has been delivered by the ECtHR that a state has violated the Convention, the state will have to provide the Committee of Ministers with an update regarding compliance with this decision (or more accurately, the subgroup that supervises execution of judgments).[308] As Rainey and others note:[309]

[302] F. de Londras and K. Dzehtsiarou, *Great Debates on the European Convention on Human Rights* (London: Palgrave, 2018), p.176.

[303] *Drozdyk and Mikula v Ukraine* (App. Nos. 27849/15 and 33358/15), judgment of the ECtHR (Fifth Section), 24 October 2024.

[304] *Drozdyk and Mikula v Ukraine* (App. Nos. 27849/15 and 33358/15), judgment of the ECtHR (Fifth Section), 24 October 2024, at para.68 et seq.

[305] *Ibrahim v Norway* (App. No. 15379/16), judgment of the ECtHR (Grand Chamber), 10 December 2021, at paras 171–176.

[306] See decisions discussed in F. de Londras and K. Dzehtsiarou, *Great Debates on the European Convention on Human Rights* (London: Palgrave, 2018), pp.172–174.

[307] *JB and others v Malta* (App. No. 1766/23), judgment of the ECtHR (Second Section), 22 October 2024, at paras 162–168.

[308] For further detail and analysis on the supervision/execution of judgments by the Committee of Ministers, see F. de Londras and K. Dzehtsiarou, *Great Debates on the European Convention on Human Rights* (London: Palgrave, 2018), Ch.8.

[309] B. Rainey et al, *Jacobs, White and Ovey: The European Convention on Human Rights*, 8th edn (Oxford: OUP, 2021), p.60.

> "[T]he entire Convention system depends on the willingness of the Contracting States to be bound by the Court's judgments. The Committee has few tools at its disposal in the face of persistent refusal to execute a judgment."

At times, it can take many years for a state to comply with a decision of the ECtHR, and sometimes a state simply will not comply with a decision. In 2010 in *McFarlane*,[310] Ireland was found to have breached Article 6 (fair and prompt trial), in conjunction with Article 13 (right to an effective remedy). It took over 10-and-a-half years for criminal charges against the applicant to conclude. The delays were due to significant underinvestment and backlogs in the Irish courts system. In September 2023, the Committee of Ministers determined that the judgment still had not been fully executed by Ireland, some 13 years later.[311] The Committee of Ministers accepted that Ireland had make significant strides in reducing criminal trial backlogs; however, these still remained. By September 2024, the Committee of Ministers noted the significant number of new judicial appointments and the structural changes that were occurring to ensure that a trial would happen in a reasonable timeframe. Ireland has also introduced legislation: the Court Proceedings (Delays) Act 2024.[312] This Act provides the possibility to gain a declaration that court proceedings have been unduly delayed, as well as potentially a right to compensation for people subject to such delays.[313]

6–91 Excluding procedural decisions, there have been 25 judgments where the ECtHR determined that Ireland had violated at least one article of the Convention. In 11 judgments, no violation of the Convention occurred, and there was one friendly settlement.[314] These statistics indicate Ireland has one of the best rights-compliance records relating to Convention rights protection in the Council of Europe. In decisions

[310] *McFarlane v Ireland* (2011) 52 E.H.R.R. 20.

[311] Committee of Ministers, "H46-18 McFarlane v Ireland", CM/Del/Dec(2023)1475/H46-18, 19–21 September 2023.

[312] For a fuller review of the measures Ireland is taking to comply with this 2010 decision, see Committee of Ministers, "H46-14 McFarlane v Ireland", CM/Notes/1507/H46-14.

[313] At the time of writing (October 2024), this Act had not yet commenced.

[314] Council of Europe, *Violations by State and Article* (Strasbourg: COE, 2023), p.1. For statistics from 1959–2021, see *https://www.echr.coe.int/documents/d/echr/Stats_violation_1959_2021_ENG*; for statistics for 2022, see *https://www.echr.coe.int/documents/d/echr/Stats_violation_2022_ENG*; and, for statistics for 2023, see *https://www.echr.coe.int/statistical-reports*.

that found Ireland had violated Convention rights, this has resulted in law being modified. Ireland was required to: put in place a system of civil legal aid;[315] amend the law to stop the criminalisation of gay men and other men who had sex with men; strengthen the rights of natural fathers; provide access to abortion within Ireland's (then) constitutional limitations; and protect the rights of accused to have solicitors present during questioning by Gardaí.[316]

4. The European Convention on Human Rights Act 2003

6–92 As was discussed above in *Re Ó Laighléis*,[317] the Convention did not have domestic effect in Ireland until the coming into force of the European Convention on Human Rights Act 2003 (the "2003 Act").[318] The 2003 Act emerged in part from commitments Ireland made as part of the Belfast/Good Friday Agreement, which secured (relative) peace in Northern Ireland.[319] In *Dublin City Council v Fennell*,[320] Kearns J. highlighted that prior to the 2003 Act, while the Convention was binding on Ireland, it was not binding in Ireland.[321] The Convention did not impose any domestic legal obligations that persons could rely upon in Irish courts. Decisions of the ECtHR had, at best, persuasive authority but these could not displace Irish law. So, the only manner in which people in Ireland could have had their Convention rights vindicated was through taking a case to the ECtHR.

6–93 In *Foy v An tArd-Chláraitheoir (No. 2)*, McKechnie J. described the position of the Convention and the 2003 Act within Irish law as follows:

315 See further, Ch.13, Box 13.3.

316 S. Kingston and L. Thornton, *A Report on the Application of the European Convention on Human Rights Act 2003 and the European Charter of Fundamental Rights: Evaluation and Review* (Dublin: Law Society, 2015), pp.25–28, Table 2.1, outlines the measures taken (or not) by Ireland to ensure compliance with the decisions of the ECtHR up to 2015. See also *Doyle v Ireland* (App. No. 51979/17), judgment of the ECtHR (Fifth Section), 23 May 2019 (right to lawyer present), and see Ch.13, paras 13–10 to 13–11.

317 See Box 6.3.

318 For an excellent analysis of the introduction of the 2003 Act, see F. de Londras and C. Kelly, *The European Convention on Human Rights Act: Operation, Impact and Analysis* (Dublin: Round Hall, 2010).

319 The Belfast Agreement: An Agreement Reached at the Multi-Party Talks on Northern Ireland, 10 April 1998, para.6(9), available at: *https://www.dfa.ie/media/dfa/alldfawebsitemedia/ourrolesandpolicies/northernireland/good-friday-agreement.pdf*.

320 [2005] 1 I.R. 604.

321 [2005] 1 I.R. 604 at 614.

> "It is a misleading metaphor to say that the Convention was incorporated into domestic law. It was not. The rights contained in the Convention are now part of Irish law. They are so by reason of the Act of 2003. That is their source. Not the Convention. So, it is only correct to say, as understood in this way, that the Convention forms part of our law."[322]

As was confirmed by the Supreme Court in *Fennell*, the 2003 Act does not have retrospective effect.[323] Therefore, the Convention is indirectly incorporated into Irish law at a sub-constitutional level. O'Malley J. in *AC v Cork University Hospital* stated that the 2003 Act is "not intended to weaken rights established in national law, and is primarily concerned with ensuring the application of minimum standards rather than with imposing uniformity."[324] Irish courts remain free to go beyond the minimum standards set by the Convention.[325] Clarke C.J. in *Fox v Minister for Justice*[326] explored the relationship between the Constitution and the Convention. Clarke C.J. highlighted that the Irish Constitution is subject to its own interpretive values and is an "autonomous human rights instrument".[327] Nonetheless, he stated that it would be good practice for Irish courts, where appropriate, to use "similar language and structure to that adopted by the ECtHR in analysing rights guaranteed by both the Constitution and the ECHR".[328] In *Middlecamp v Minister for Justice*, Hogan J. held that the protection of the "inalienable and imprescriptible" rights of the family based on marriage contained in Article 41 of the Constitution went further than the mere "respect" for family life under Article 8 of the Convention.[329] In *Clare County Council v McDonagh*, Hogan J. further emphasised that a court should not "engage with a provision of the ECHR in proceedings involving an organ

---

322 [2007] IEHC 470 at para.93. This case is discussed in detail in Ch.7, paras 7–24 to 7–25. See also *Fox v Minister for Justice* [2021] IESC 61 at para.3.2.

323 [2005] 1 I.R. 604 at 627–631.

324 [2019] IESC 73 at para.319. See further, I. O'Malley (writing extrajudicially), "Ireland and the European Convention on Human Rights" (2023) 7(2) *Irish Judicial Studies Journal* 10.

325 S. O'Leary, "Why the European Convention on Human Rights Still Matters" (2023) 7(2) *Irish Judicial Studies Journal* 20 at 30.

326 [2021] IESC 61.

327 [2021] IESC 61 at para.12.14.

328 [2021] IESC 61 at para.12.15.

329 [2023] IESC 2 at para.16.

of State without also engaging at the same time with the corresponding provision of the Constitution."[330]

6–94 Since the coming into force of the 2003 Act, legal practitioners before the Irish courts have sought to use the rights under the Convention across a whole range of fields, including administrative law, employment law, immigration and asylum law, housing law and torts.[331] The 2003 Act imposes several duties: an interpretive duty on courts to interpret Irish law in a Convention-compliant manner; an obligation on "organs of state" to act in a Convention-compliant manner; and where courts cannot interpret Irish law in a Convention-compliant manner, and where no other remedy is available, they can grant a declaration of incompatibility. We now turn to briefly consider each of these issues in turn.

(a) Interpretive obligation

6–95 Section 2 of the 2003 Act requires Irish courts to interpret statutory provisions and rules of law in a Convention-compliant manner.[332] This applies to statutes and rules of law both prior and subsequent to the 2003 Act coming into force.[333] So the courts' "interpretive task" is to engage with the 2003 Act to identify the correct meaning of Irish rules of law.[334] It is the legislature that requires courts to interpret all laws, including statutes, in a way that respects the State's obligations under the Convention.[335] In determining Convention compliance, courts, but not tribunals,[336] must take "judicial notice" of judgments, decisions, declarations and advisory opinions of the ECtHR. Irish courts are also required to take notice of any decision of the European Commission on Human Rights and any decision or opinion of the Committee of Ministers.[337] Humphreys J. in *Seredych v Minister for Justice and Equality*

[330] [2022] IESC 2 at para.54.
[331] See also Ch.8, 8–36 to 8–40.
[332] Section 2 of the 2003 Act. Section 2(2) of the 2003 Act states that this applies to statutory provisions and rules of law in force before and after the coming into operation of the 2003 Act. See further, G. Hogan, "Incorporation of the ECHR: Some Issues of Methodology and Process" in U. Kilkelly (ed.), *ECHR and Irish Law*, 1st edn (Bristol: Jordans, 2004), p.28.
[333] European Convention on Human Rights Act 2003 s.2(2).
[334] *Dowling v An Bord Pleanála* [2024] IEHC 249 at para.51.
[335] *Dowling v An Bord Pleanála* [2024] IEHC 249 at para.46.
[336] See generally, *MOI v Refugee Appeals Tribunal* [2014] IEHC 291.
[337] Section 4 of the 2003 Act. Protocol No. 11 of the Convention abolished the European Commission on Human Rights (1953–1998) and enlarged the ECtHR.

(No. 2) stated that the obligation to take "judicial notice" of ECtHR decisions meant examining the "principles as set out in well-established case law that a court must follow, not any and every individual case however outlying."[338] To take "judicial notice" does not mean that the decisions of the ECtHR are binding precedents on Irish courts.[339] This obligation to interpret existing law in a Convention-compliant manner is not a power of the Irish courts to rewrite legislation so as to bring law in line with the Convention. The Supreme Court has emphasised that where courts are called upon to interpret a statutory provision in a Convention-compliant manner, the courts should not engage in a "redrafting exercise" to read legislation in such a manner.[340]

(b) Obligation to act in a Convention-compliant manner and damages

6–96 Section 3 of the 2003 Act requires an "organ of the State"[341] to undertake its functions in a Convention-compliant manner.[342] An "organ of the State" includes a tribunal or any other body that is established by law, or a body that exercises legislative, executive or judicial power. This definition does not include the President, the courts, either House of the Oireachtas or any committees therein. All state bodies must act in a manner compatible with the State's Convention obligations.[343] This includes bodies such as the Gardaí, city and county councils,[344] the Health Service Executive,[345] An Bord Pleanála,[346] the Workplace Relations Commission, and all other bodies exercising a decision-making function,[347] including government departments.[348] Where it is proved that an organ of State had not acted in a Convention-compliant manner, a person may commence proceedings in the Circuit Court or the High Court for damages.[349] An award of damages is the only remedy

---

338 [2018] IEHC 307 at para.7.
339 *Mahon v Keena* [2010] 1 I.R. 336 at 355 per Fennelly J.
340 *Ryan v Clare County Council* [2014] IESC 67 at para.54.
341 European Convention on Human Rights Act 2003 s.1.
342 European Convention on Human Rights Act 2003 s.3(1).
343 *Corcoran v Commissioner of An Garda Síochána* [2023] IESC 15 at para.102 of Hogan J.'s decision.
344 See, e.g. *O'Donnell v South Dublin County Council* [2015] IESC 28.
345 See, e.g. *Health Service Executive v HH* [2024] IEHC 564.
346 See, e.g. *Weston v An Bord Pleanála* [2008] IEHC 71.
347 See, e.g. *Zalewski v Workplace Relations Commission* [2022] 1 I.R. 421.
348 See, e.g. *MK (Albania) v Minister for Justice and Equality* [2022] IESC 48.
349 European Convention on Human Rights Act 2003 s.3(2). An award of damages is limited to that available within each court as if it were exercising its tort jurisdiction.

available.[350] The courts have determined that the 2003 Act does not permit them to grant an injunction to prevent a potential breach of Convention rights, no matter how likely it is that Convention rights will be breached.[351] There may of course in such a situation be other legal avenues to obtain an injunction.

(c) Declaration of incompatibility

6–97 Where it is not possible to interpret existing Irish law in a Convention-compliant manner, and if no other remedy exists, the superior courts may grant a declaration of incompatibility.[352] The declaration of incompatibility is a "purely domestic invention", and only arises where there is no possibility of interpreting a rule of law in a Convention-compliant manner.[353] The Taoiseach is obliged to bring the offending rule or statute to the attention of the Oireachtas within 21 days. Whether or not the Oireachtas will remedy this non-compliance with the Convention is solely for the Oireachtas to determine.[354] As noted by Hogan J. in his judgment in *O'Meara v Minister for Social Protection*, a declaration of incompatibility is a "less effective remedy" than a declaration of unconstitutionality. A declaration of incompatibility does not affect the validity, continuing operation or enforcement of the statutory provision in question.[355] If a person is granted a declaration of incompatibility, the individual is entitled to apply for an ex gratia payment to the Attorney General.[356] The government, in its sole discretion, will then consider whether any payment will be made.[357] Since the coming into force of the 2003 Act, there have been two declarations of incompatibility granted by the courts, in the areas of housing law and gender identity

[350] *Coyne v An Bord Pleanála* [2023] IEHC 412 at para.251. See also, European Convention on Human Rights Act 2003 s.3A, as inserted by Irish Human Rights and Equality Commission Act 2014 s.54. Section 3A of the 2003 Act establishes the right of a person deprived of their liberty to seek damages.

[351] *Pullen v Dublin City Council (No. 2)* [2009] I.L.R.M. 484.

[352] European Convention on Human Rights Act 2003 s.5(1).

[353] *II (Nigeria) v Minister for Justice and Equality* [2019] IEHC 729 at para.29.

[354] European Convention on Human Rights Act 2003 s.5(3).

[355] [2024] IESC 1 at para.46.

[356] To date, one such ex gratia payment of "about €50,000" has been made; R. Mac Cormaic, "Compensation paid to Lydia Foy over gender recognition failures", *Irish Times*, 3 November 2014.

[357] European Convention on Human Rights Act 2003 s.5(2)(c). The government may appoint an adviser who will examine the level of payment that may be made. In doing so, the adviser is to have regard to the level of damages that the ECtHR awards.

law.[358] It took the legislature eight years to respond to the declaration of incompatibility on gender identity law, and two years to respond to the declaration of incompatibility on housing law.[359] In *AB v Clinical Director of St Loman's Hospital*,[360] the High Court had granted a declaration of incompatibility finding that provisions of the Mental Health Act 2001 breached Convention rights. However, the Court of Appeal overturned the declaration of incompatibility and instead declared provisions of the Mental Health Act 2001 to be unconstitutional.[361]

F. Conclusion

6–98 In the opening quote of this chapter, written in 1914, there is a fairly stark statement as regards what the author considered the irrelevance of international law. The juncture of law and politics becomes more visible when we discuss international law and state compliance. Over 100 years later, this assessment clearly has to be reconsidered. Ireland's membership of the EU has transformed the Irish legal system. The constitutional foundations of the EU, as established in the treaties, create a supranational legal order. The institutions of the EU all have clearly demarcated roles, in terms of creating and implementing EU law, with the Court of Justice the interpreter of EU law. The Court of Justice was responsible for shaping the underlying EU constitutional principles of primacy and direct effect. The impact of the Court of Justice on providing the foundational bedrock to the EU should not be underestimated. It is exclusively because of the Irish people amending their Constitution that EU law is enabled, in its areas of competence, to have primacy over conflicting domestic laws. The Irish courts have ensured that fundamental changes to the EU's competences must be approved by the Irish people.

358 S. Kingston and L. Thornton, *A Report on the Application of the European Convention on Human Rights Act 2003 and the European Charter of Fundamental Rights: Evaluation and Review* (Dublin: Law Society, 2015), pp.39–42 and 51–52.

359 See further, T. Ní Mhuirthile, "Article 8 and the Realisation of the Right to Legal Gender Recognition" in S. Egan, L. Thornton and J. Walsh (eds), *Ireland and the European Convention on Human Rights: 60 Years and Beyond* (Dublin: Bloomsbury, 2014). See now the Housing (Miscellaneous Provisions) Act 2014 and the Gender Recognition Act 2015.

360 [2017] IEHC 360.

361 [2018] 2 I.L.R.M. 242.

6–99 The reception of EU law into the Irish legal system has been nothing short of revolutionary (in a constitutional sense). The government may, in most cases, bring Irish law into conformity with EU law by means of secondary legislation. This does significantly diminish the legislative role of the Oireachtas. It is important to highlight that this was the effect of the Irish people voting to join the EU. Irish courts and tribunals when interpreting and implementing EU law become, in essence, branches of the Court of Justice. The Court of Justice, in matters of EU law, is therefore at the apex of the Irish courts system. Even the lowliest Irish tribunal may apply EU law, and ignore conflicting domestic laws, without this issue ever going near the superior courts. Ireland has a generally good compliance record with EU law. Nonetheless, as outlined in the case study on international protection applicants, when EU legal compliance relates to people who are made vulnerable by the state and society, even EU law may at times not be implemented.

6–100 The place of public international law in the Irish legal system differs significantly from the status of EU law in Ireland. The sources of public international law, while generally clear, lack any one judicial body to provide authoritative interpretations, although there are a plethora of international courts and tribunals within various fields that do command respect for decisions by many states, albeit certainly not all. State consent to international law is, in most instances, required. Holding states to account for breaches of their international legal obligations can be difficult. This is due to the sovereign nature of states. The sovereign nature of a state requires non-interference by other countries in the domestic affairs of any other state. Again, this does not prevent imperialistic reach and ambition of the most powerful countries in the globe interfering with or extinguishing sovereignty of countries. Within the Irish legal system, the government (of the day) determines the extent that the Irish State is bound by international law. Where the government signs and ratifies international agreements, only where the Oireachtas legislates to give domestic effect would people/bodies be able to rely on these in domestic courts. Irish courts may still seek to engage with international law, even with treaties that do not have domestic effect.

6–101 The European Convention on Human Rights and its place in the Irish legal system is rather unique. The Convention, indirectly, forms part of Irish law. Decisions of the European Court of Human Rights are now cited liberally by Irish courts in areas of Convention relevance. The Irish courts have proved to be willing to engage with the jurisprudence of the ECtHR, and to use the 2003 Act as a means of interpreting Irish law in a manner that corresponds to the Convention meaning. This does not mean Ireland is always in compliance with the Convention; however, Ireland does have an exceptional compliance record given the small number of judgments against Ireland at the ECtHR. It often, unfortunately, can take some time for Ireland to comply with decisions of the ECtHR. This is even an issue domestically, as witnessed with the significant period of time the Oireachtas has taken to remedy declarations of incompatibility. The interrelationship between the rights protected in the Convention and the Constitution has resulted, in particular throughout the early 2020s, in a rich judicial discourse. This discourse has explored the cross-pollination of rights interpretation, the extent that constitutional and Convention rights are similar, and how they differ.

Part II

The Irish Legal System in Action

Chapter 7

The Legislative Process in Ireland

"[T]o retain respect for laws and sausages, one must not watch them in the making."

> Often attributed to Otto Von Bismark, the poet and lawyer John Godfrey Saxe is much more likely to be the source of the aphorism. See F.R. Shapiro (ed.), *The Yale Book of Quotations* (New Haven: Yale University Press, 2006), p.86.

In this chapter we:

- consider the purpose of the legislative process;
- examine the manner in which draft legislation passes through the Oireachtas;
- discuss the balance of power between the Dáil and the Seanad as regards legislation;
- analyse the role of the President in the enactment of legislation;
- provide a case study on the legislative process.

A. Introduction

7–01 Legislation is one of the primary sources of law in Ireland. It is written law that has been enacted by the legislature, or the Oireachtas as it is known in Ireland. In Ch.4, we considered the different types of legislation, both primary[1] and secondary,[2] and we also analysed in detail the rules of legislative interpretation.[3] This chapter will focus on the process of how legislation is made. Enacting legislation is governed both by the Constitution[4] and the rules of parliamentary procedure.[5]

1 See further, Ch.4, Section B.1.
2 See further, Ch.4, Section B.2.
3 See further, Ch.4, Sections C–H.
4 Articles 20–27 of the Constitution.
5 Consolidated Dáil Standing Orders 2020 (with updates up to 2023), available at: *https://data.oireachtas.ie/ie/oireachtas/parliamentaryBusiness/standingOrders/dail/2023/2023-09-28_consolidated-d-il-ireann-standing-orders-september-2023_*

While the title of Articles 20–27 of the Constitution is "Legislation", it does not set down the process for passing legislation, except in limited circumstances discussed below. Many different actors play a role in the development of legislation. Not all of these are part of the formal law-making process. Thus, contributors to legislation include: the relevant Minister; Oireachtas members, i.e. TDs and Senators; parliamentary drafters who produce the text of legislation; activists and advocates who lobby public representatives regarding legislation; and academic and other experts and civic society groups who may advise the Oireachtas. In this chapter, we will discuss how the formal rules and official actors mould the making of our law. In Ch.8, we will examine law reform more generally and consider the contributions that those not connected with the Oireachtas can make to the process of law reform.[6]

7–02 Legislation can have many purposes: to regulate, to authorise, to prohibit, to fund, to sanction, to grant, to declare, and/or to restrict any manner of activities and/or rights. Morse identifies "timely responsiveness" as the principal purpose of legislation.[7] By this he means that legislation "should be responsive to the needs of the people—it should be protective of their interests—and it should be enacted when the need arises, before wrong is wrought".[8] Linde contends that to be lawful, legislation must have an identifiable purpose: it is a rational means towards legitimate ends.[9] He asks the question: "would anyone defend the validity of a law that does not reasonably serve some purpose?"[10] Therefore, all legislation should be functional.

en.pdf. Seanad Standing Orders consolidated to 2023, available at: *https://data.oireachtas.ie/ie/oireachtas/parliamentaryBusiness/standingOrders/seanad/2023/2023-03-08_modifications-to-seanad-eireann-standing-orders-relative-to-public-business-2020_en.pdf*. It is worth bearing in mind that standing orders change from time to time, therefore it is important to ensure that you remain up-to-date by checking the most recent versions available at: *https://www.oireachtas.ie/en/how-parliament-is-run/*.

6 Chapter 8, Section C.

7 H.N. Morse, "Theories of Legislation" (1965) 14 *DePaul Law Review* 51 at 51.

8 H.N. Morse, "Theories of Legislation" (1965) 14 *DePaul Law Review* 51 at 51.

9 H.A. Linde, "Due Process of Lawmaking" (1975–76) 55 *Nebraska Law Review* 197 at 205.

10 H.A. Linde, "Due Process of Lawmaking" (1975–76) 55 *Nebraska Law Review* 197 at 205.

Box 7.1: Legal Insight
Functional Categorisation of Legislation[11]

Legislation can be categorised based on its underlying purpose in a number of different ways.

Public General Acts: These are pieces of legislation that address the public at large in a very broad range of areas. Examples include the Policing, Security and Community Safety Act 2024, the Road Traffic Act 2024 and the Employment (Collective Redundancies and Miscellaneous Provisions) and Companies (Amendment) Act 2024.

Private Acts: These are legislative enactments addressed at a particular (and limited) section of the community such as local authorities or private bodies. Examples include the Royal College of Surgeons in Ireland (Charters Amendment) Act 2003, the Trinity College, Dublin (Charters and Letters Patent Amendment) Act 2000 and the Limerick Markets Act 1992.

Money/Taxation Acts: This type of legislation concerns public spending and taxation. Examples include the Finance (No. 2) Act 2023 and the Finance (State Guarantees, International Financial Institution Funds and Miscellaneous Provisions) Act 2024.

Acts to Amend the Constitution: This kind of legislation enables the text of the Constitution to be altered in a particular way. Examples include the Thirty-eighth Amendment of the Constitution (Dissolution of Marriage) Act 2019 and the Thirty-seventh Amendment of the Constitution (Repeal of offence of publication or utterance of blasphemous matter) Act 2018.

Private Members' Bills: These are draft pieces of legislation that are introduced before the Houses of the Oireachtas by an Oireachtas member who is not a Government Minister. An example of such legislation is the Intoxicating Liquor (Amendment) Bill 2017, introduced in the Seanad by Senators Billy Lawless, Michael McDowell, Gerard P. Craughwell and Victor Boyhan, which became the Intoxicating Liquor (Amendment) Act 2018. It amended various Licensing Acts to enable pubs and other licensed premises to trade on Good Friday.

Consolidation Acts: These Acts streamline or "consolidate" the law in a particular area. Examples include the Companies Act 2014 and the Civil Registration Act 2004.

7–03 The Constitution provides in Article 28.4.1° that the Government is responsible to Dáil Éireann. In reality, the Government is in the driving seat of legislative initiation in Ireland. The political parties making up

[11] For a review of the structure of legislation, see Ch.4, Box 4.1. For an insight into how to read legislation, see Ch.15, Section B.

the Government will (almost always) vote for legislation that has been introduced by the Government. Where the Government loses a vote in the Dáil, unless it can subsequently get a motion of confidence passed, an election usually follows. Outside this exceptional circumstance, at the beginning of each parliamentary term the Government publishes its legislative programme. This document identifies the legislation that the Government intends to introduce during the current term. For example, on 16 January 2024, the Chief Whip—the Government Minister responsible for progression of legislation through the Oireachtas—published the legislative programme for the spring session of 2024.[12] This programme identified six categories of legislation:

A. Legislation for Priority Publication Spring Session 2024.
B. Legislation for Priority Drafting Spring Session 2024.
C. All Other Legislation Spring Session 2024.
D. Bills currently on the Dáil and Seanad Order Paper, as of 16 January 2024.
E. Bills published since Government came to office on 27 June 2020.
F. Bills enacted since Government came to office on 27 June 2020.

Each of these lists is organised by Department so, at a glance, you can ascertain what the legislative priorities for any particular ministry is in a given Dáil term. In the spring session of 2024, the Department of Justice had most Bills on the "A" list, with five Bills for publication, while the Departments of Agriculture, Food and the Marine; Children, Equality, Disability, Integration and Youth; Defence; Education; and Public Expenditure, National Development Plan Delivery and Reform all listed only one Bill for publication during that time.[13] Examples of such priorities include: updating defamation law, following a statutory review of the Defamation Act 2009; introducing mandatory drug testing following serious road collisions; enhancing enforcement and regulatory provisions in the Companies Act 2014; and prohibiting conversion therapy/practices. In this chapter, we analyse the process through which these Bills are transformed into Acts of the Oireachtas, or statutes.

[12] H. Naughton, *Government Legislation Programme Spring 2024* (Dublin: Department of An Taoiseach, 2024).

[13] H. Naughton, *Government Legislation Programme Spring 2024* (Dublin: Department of An Taoiseach, 2024).

B. Legislation in the Houses of the Oireachtas

7–04 As mentioned above, the formal process by which a Bill progresses through the Houses of the Oireachtas is outlined in the Standing Orders of both the Dáil[14] and Seanad.[15] The Standing Orders regulate how the business of the Oireachtas is conducted and this includes delineating how legislation is introduced and progressed through the Houses of the Oireachtas. Bills can begin their legislative journey in either the Dáil or the Seanad. Thus, under Article 28.2 of the Constitution, Government Ministers, who are ordinarily members of the Dáil, can attend and be heard in both Houses. There are five stages to the legislative process in the initiating House, and when the Bill progresses to the second House, it undergoes the process afresh, although there is no need to repeat Stage 1. For ease of discussion, as we outline the process, we will assume that the legislation has begun its journey in the Dáil.

1. Pre-Legislative Consideration

7–05 One of the primary commitments contained in the Programme for Government 2011–2016 was the promise to introduce Dáil reform.[16] The *Irish Times* reported in 2008 that only one Private Member's Bill of the 87 proposed by opposition TDs between January 2002 and June 2007 was enacted.[17] Acknowledging that the then system ensured that the Government had a monopoly on legislation and a "stranglehold" on the business of the Dáil, the incoming Government proposed to

> "... enhance the democratic process by involving public representatives at an earlier stage of the legislative process, particularly before Bills are published. We will amend cabinet procedure instructions so as to allow government to publish the general scheme of a Bill so that Oireachtas Committees can debate and hold hearings at an early stage."[18]

[14] Dáil Éireann, Standing Orders of Dáil Éireann relative to Public Business (2020).

[15] Seanad Éireann, Standing Orders of Seanad Éireann relative to Public Business (2025).

[16] Government of Ireland, *Programme for Government 2011–2016* (Dublin: Department of An Taoiseach, 2011), pp.18–26.

[17] Coroners (Amendment) Bill 2005 proposed by Pat Rabbitte TD. For further discussion of Private Members' Bills, see Box 7.2.

[18] Government of Ireland, *Programme for Government 2011–2016* (Dublin: Department of An Taoiseach, 2011), p.21.

As a consequence of this commitment in 2011, the pre-legislative consideration process was introduced to the Houses of the Oireachtas and formalised in parliamentary procedure in November 2013.[19] Standing Order 174A of the Standing Orders of Dáil Éireann states that prior to its presentation or introduction under Stage 1, the proposing Minister must give a draft Heads of Bill or General Scheme to the relevant Joint Oireachtas Committee. Under Standing Order 30(1), the Business Committee of the Dáil may consider a request for a waiver on the requirement to send the legislation for pre-legislative consideration. Any decision on such a request must, under Standing Order 30(2), be notified in writing to (a) the relevant member of Government or Minister of State, (b) the relevant Select Committee, and (c) in the case of a Private Member's Bill, the member in charge of the Bill. Where the Business Committee decides to issue a waiver, under Standing Order 30(3), the Clerk of the Business Committee must send a message in writing to this effect to the Clerk of the Dáil, and the Ceann Comhairle must communicate this to the Dáil at the first convenient opportunity.

7–06 Once the legislation has been referred by the proposing Minister, Joint Oireachtas Committees are empowered (but not obliged) under Standing Orders to consider the General Scheme. On receipt of a General Scheme (a draft of the Bill), a Committee will decide whether and how to conduct pre-legislative scrutiny. During the 31st Dáil (2011–2016), 52 legislative proposals underwent pre-legislative scrutiny. The majority of these processes, 46 in total, produced Committee Reports, while on six occasions the process concluded with a letter from the Committee to the Minister.[20] The shape and focus of these reports has evolved over time. In general, they seek to highlight the main provisions of the proposed legislation and to identify the policy issues underpinning each head. As the Committees can, and do, seek input from a variety of stakeholders, experts and interested parties, reflections on these submissions and the recommendations they contain also form part of the Committee's report.[21]

[19] Dáil Éireann, Standing Orders of Dáil Éireann relative to Public Business (2011), Standing Order 123A. Now replaced by Dáil Éireann, Standing Orders of Dáil Éireann relative to Public Business (2020), Standing Order 174A.

[20] Oireachtas Library and Research Service, *Pre-Legislative Scrutiny (PLS) by Parliament* (Dublin: Houses of the Oireachtas, 2016), p.3.

[21] Oireachtas Library and Research Service, *Pre-Legislative Scrutiny (PLS) by Parliament* (Dublin: Houses of the Oireachtas, 2016), p.3.

7–07 As discussed above, the purpose behind the introduction of the pre-legislative consideration process was to increase the involvement of Oireachtas members in the legislative drafting process.[22] Furthermore, by involving interested parties and experts at an early stage in a formal way, the quality of the legislation produced can be informed by their expertise.[23] Additionally, as North notes, it can promote democracy by enabling the community to "feel involved" in the law-making process.[24] It also enables the Oireachtas to examine the policy underpinning the legislation before a Bill's text is firmly "entrenched".[25] This reflects the reality that the legislative process does not start with the formal publication and introduction of a Bill into Parliament.[26] The published Bill is the outcome of a long process involving a Minister and their Department, on the one hand, and the drafters in the Office of the Attorney General, on the other.[27] As discussed in Ch.8, the process of law reform can involve both formal[28] and informal mechanisms.[29] Thus, many actors, other than legislators, can have an input in shaping the overall policy underpinning proposed legislation. A beneficial feature of pre-legislative consideration is that it enables Oireachtas members "to engage with Departmental officials before the process has too far gone".[30] Furthermore, it facilitates Oireachtas members to engage with the public, civic society groups, advocacy groups, stakeholders and experts to develop legislation before the Bills are fully drafted.[31]

7–08 Pre-legislative consideration has been welcomed as a means of achieving a better balance of power between the executive and the

---

22 Government of Ireland, *Programme for Government 2011–2016* (Dublin: Department of An Taoiseach, 2011), p.21.

23 G. Power, *Parliamentary Scrutiny of Draft Legislation 1997–1999* (London: UCL Constitution Unit, 2001), p.43.

24 P. North, "Law Reform: Problems and Pitfalls" (1999–2000) 33(1) *University of British Columbia Law Review* 37 at 40.

25 M. Korris, "Standing Up for Scrutiny: How and Why Parliament Should Make Better Law" (2011) 63(3) *Parliamentary Affairs* 564 at 565.

26 M. Korris, "Standing Up for Scrutiny: How and Why Parliament Should Make Better Law" (2011) 63(3) *Parliamentary Affairs* 564.

27 J. Smooker, "Making a Difference: The Effectiveness of Pre-Legislative Scrutiny" (2006) 59(3) *Parliamentary Affairs* 522 at 523.

28 See Ch.8, Section B.

29 See Ch.8, Section C.

30 G. Power, *Parliamentary Scrutiny of Draft Legislation 1997–1999* (London: UCL Constitution Unit, 2001), p.43.

31 G. Power, *Parliamentary Scrutiny of Draft Legislation 1997–1999* (London: UCL Constitution Unit, 2001), pp.33–34.

legislature.[32] Martin noted that of the Bills he analysed in his report for the Oireachtas Library and Research Service on the impact of pre-legislative scrutiny on legislative and policy outcomes, 41.7 per cent of committee recommendations were accepted by Ministers and included in the final draft of the Bill as initiated.[33] His research also revealed that a comparison of the Bills that had, and had not, undergone pre-legislative consideration demonstrated that the pre-legislative scrutiny did not simply pre-empt the Stage 3 Committee Stage of the legislative process, as in both scenarios Bills continued to be amended at the formal Committee Stage.[34] In other words, he found that pre-legislative consideration has had a distinct impact on legislative outcomes in the 31st Dáil, and this impact was separate from that of the formal legislative process.[35] Reflecting on the efficacy of pre-legislative consideration before the 31st Dáil, Lynch and Martin found that pre-legislative consideration can have a significant impact on legislative outcomes, such as with the Gender Recognition Bill 2014,[36] but that it does not always lead to significant changes in legislation.[37] They found that one of the most interesting features of pre-legislative consideration was how it continued to exert an influence once a Bill had progressed through the formal legislative stages, as issues identified in submissions and hearings before the Committee at the pre-legislative stage and/or the recommendations of the Committee could frame subsequent debate on the legislation.[38] Thus, they conclude that pre-legislative consideration impacts both the drafting and subsequent legislative progress of Bills presented to the Oireachtas.[39] Once the pre-legislative consideration of a Bill has been completed by the Joint Oireachtas Committee, the

32 D. Farrell, E. O'Malley, T. Reidy and J. Suiter, "Proposals for Dáil Reform Just Don't Cut It: No Incentive to Be Aggressive in Holding Executive to Account", *Irish Times*, 16 September 2013; M. MacCarthaigh, "Executive Accountability to Dáil Still the Elephant in the Room", *Irish Independent*, 22 July 2013.

33 S. Martin, The Impact of Pre-Legislative Scrutiny on Legislative and Policy Outcomes (Dublin: Oireachtas Library and Research Service, 2017), p.6.

34 S. Martin, The Impact of Pre-Legislative Scrutiny on Legislative and Policy Outcomes (Dublin: Oireachtas Library and Research Service, 2017), p.31.

35 S. Martin, The Impact of Pre-Legislative Scrutiny on Legislative and Policy Outcomes (Dublin: Oireachtas Library and Research Service, 2017), p.31.

36 See case study at Section E below.

37 C. Lynch and S. Martin, "Can Parliaments Be Strengthened? A Case Study of Pre-Legislative Scrutiny" (2020) 35(1) *Irish Political Studies* 138 at 154.

38 C. Lynch and S. Martin, "Can Parliaments Be Strengthened? A Case Study of Pre-Legislative Scrutiny" (2020) 35(1) *Irish Political Studies* 138 at 154.

39 C. Lynch and S. Martin, "Can Parliaments Be Strengthened? A Case Study of Pre-Legislative Scrutiny" (2020) 35(1) *Irish Political Studies* 138 at 154.

draft of the Bill is complete and it continues to the formal parliamentary legislative process.

2. Stage 1: Introduction

7–09 The first stage of the formal legislative process in the Oireachtas is the introduction of the Bill. This stage consists of the proposer of the legislation receiving permission from the House to circulate the Bill.[40] Generally, there is little opposition to this proposal. This is a relatively informal process. Legislation can also be introduced before the House by way of formal presentation and there is no need for the House to consent. Any member of the Government, Minister of State or a private member, nominated for the purpose,[41] may present a Bill without the need for permission from the Dáil.[42] A similar provision exists in the Seanad for the leader of the Seanad, and appropriately nominated Senators.[43]

3. Stage 2: Debate on General Provisions

7–10 The second stage of the legislative process does not focus on the details of the Bill but is concerned with the general principles and policies underpinning it.[44] In a case where the proposer is a Minister, they speak first, outline the main provisions of the Bill and explain the Government's policy reasons for its enactment.[45] Each opposition spokesperson in the relevant area is then given an opportunity to respond either supporting or opposing the Bill.[46] Where the Bill has been subjected to pre-legislative consultation, the Chairperson or Vice-Chairperson of the relevant Joint Oireachtas Committee, or their nominee, may speak to the work of the Committee during this process.[47] At this point, the floor is opened to other TDs who may wish to contribute to the debate.[48] The order and duration of these contributions is agreed by the party whips—those TDs who have been given the responsibility of organising the business of the

40 Standing Order 174(2) of Dáil Éireann. For Bills initiated in the Seanad, the relevant provision is Standing Order 144 of the Standing Orders of Seanad Éireann.
41 Such nominations are governed by Standing Order 169(1) of Dáil Éireann.
42 Standing Order 174(3) of Dáil Éireann.
43 Standing Order 145 of Seanad Éireann.
44 Standing Order 176(1) of Dáil Éireann; Standing Order 149(1) of Seanad Éireann.
45 Standing Order 176(2)(i) of Dáil Éireann; Standing Order 149(1) of Seanad Éireann.
46 Standing Order 176(2)(ii) of Dáil Éireann; Standing Order 149 of Seanad Éireann.
47 Standing Order 176(2)(iii) of Dáil Éireann; Standing Order 149(2)(ii) of Seanad Éireann.
48 Standing Order 176 of Dáil Éireann.

Dáil on behalf of their parties. At the end of the second stage, a vote is taken on the motion that begins the stage, i.e. "that the Bill be now read a second time".[49] Technically, a Bill proposed by a Minister could be rejected at this point, yet given the controlling numbers of Government TDs, such a defeat rarely occurs.[50] It is at this stage that the majority of Private Members' Bills fail. If a Bill successfully passes this stage, it then proceeds to the third stage, also known as committee stage.

4. Stage 3: Consideration by Committee of the Details

7–11 The detailed analysis of the Bill happens at the third stage.[51] The task of conducting this comprehensive consideration is usually delegated to a subcommittee of Dáil members,[52] although the entire Dáil retains the right to conduct this examination.[53] At this point, the general purpose of the Bill can no longer be considered. The work of the committee is restricted to a section-by-section analysis[54] and a consideration of any potential amendments to the provisions in the Bill.[55] The chief advantages of delegation to a committee are that it is those Dáil members who are interested in the area who will examine the Bill and, as a result, this frees up Dáil time to attend to other business.[56] At committee stage, the committee has the power to amend the Bill as it sees fit, providing that amendments do not conflict with the general principles of the Bill debated in Stage 2.[57] Once the committee has completed its analysis, it can order the Bill to be printed and place its report before the Dáil.[58] At this point, the Bill progresses to the fourth stage.

49 Standing Order 176(1) of Dáil Éireann; Standing Order 149(1) of Seanad Éireann.
50 R. Byrne, P. McCutcheon, L. Cahillane and E. Roche-Cagney, *Byrne and McCutcheon on the Irish Legal System*, 7th edn (Dublin: Bloomsbury Professional, 2021), para.13.37.
51 Standing Order 181(1) of Dáil Éireann; Standing Order 150(1) of Seanad Éireann.
52 This could be either a Special Committee or a Select Committee. Membership of these committees for each House is determined based on party representation in that House. The principal distinction between the Special and the Select Committee is that the latter has the power to send for persons, papers and records.
53 Standing Order 181(2) of Dáil Éireann; Standing Order 150(2) of Seanad Éireann.
54 Standing Order 184 of Dáil Éireann; Standing Order 152 of Seanad Éireann.
55 Standing Order 185 of Dáil Éireann; Standing Order 153 of Seanad Éireann.
56 R. Byrne, P. McCutcheon, L. Cahillane and E. Roche-Cagney, *Byrne and McCutcheon on the Irish Legal System*, 7th edn (Dublin: Bloomsbury Professional, 2021), para.13.38.
57 Standing Order 187(1) of Dáil Éireann; Standing Order 154 of Seanad Éireann.
58 Standing Order 188 of Dáil Éireann; Standing Order 155 of Seanad Éireann.

5. Stage 4: Report Stage

7–12 The fourth stage enables the Dáil to consider the work done by the committee in the third stage. Where the committee did not make any amendments to the Bill, it can proceed directly to the fifth stage.[59] Any amendments made by the committee are considered by the Dáil at this fourth stage.[60] Further amendments may be made at this stage, but where these have previously been rejected by the committee at the third stage, they shall not be permitted.[61] This power is regularly employed by the proposing Minister in circumstances where they have given an undertaking to consider certain amendments with their officials at the third stage. These are usually tabled during this fourth stage.[62] The Bill then progresses to the fifth stage.

6. Stage 5: Final Stage

7–13 The fifth and final stage of the passage through either House consists of a vote on the motion "[t]hat the Bill do now pass".[63] At this point, no further amendments, bar verbal ones, are permitted.[64] Any errors of typography can be corrected by order of the Clerk of the relevant House.[65] Where this fifth stage is the final stage of the progress of the Bill through the first House, it will now pass to the second House for consideration. When the second House has completed its deliberations on the Bill, it will be sent to the President for their signature. When a Bill fails to pass through both Houses of the Oireachtas before a general election is called, it lapses, although there is provision in the Standing Orders for lapsed Bills to be restored.[66]

59 Standing Order 189(1) of Dáil Éireann; Standing Order 160 of Seanad Éireann.
60 Standing Order 189(2) of Dáil Éireann; Standing Order 159 of Seanad Éireann.
61 Standing Order 191 of Dáil Éireann; Standing Order 159 of Seanad Éireann.
62 R. Byrne, P. McCutcheon, L. Cahillane and E. Roche-Cagney, *Byrne and McCutcheon on the Irish Legal System*, 7th edn (Dublin: Bloomsbury Professional, 2021), para.13.41.
63 Standing Order 194 of Dáil Éireann; Standing Order 163(1) of Seanad Éireann.
64 Standing Order 194 of Dáil Éireann; Standing Order 163(2) of Seanad Éireann.
65 Standing Order 196 of Dáil Éireann; Standing Order 166 of Seanad Éireann.
66 Standing Order 198 of Dáil Éireann; Standing Order 169 of Seanad Éireann.

Box 7.2: Legal Insight
Private Members' Bills

A Bill that has not been introduced by a Minister, Minister of State or the Leader of the Seanad is known as a Private Member's Bill. In other words, this is a Bill proposed by an ordinary backbench TD or Senator.

Such Bills undergo a similar process as Government legislation, although there are some slight variations. Any private member may propose a Bill for consideration on the Thursday fortnightly sessions of the Dáil, which are set aside for this purpose.[67] Where more than one TD indicates an intention to propose legislation on any given Thursday, the Business Committee determines which Bills will be considered on that date.[68]

From a practical perspective, Private Members' Bills do not make a quantifiably significant contribution to legislation because the vast majority of them are either opposed by the Government and fail at the second stage of the legislative process, or are taken over by the relevant Minister and become Government-sponsored legislation.[69] Former Minister Ruairí Quinn noted, with dismay, "[t]he convention ... of not accepting legislative initiatives from the other side, irrespective of their merits or demerits".[70] Often Private Members' Bills can be used strategically to highlight an issue or attempt to force the Government to legislate on a particular topic. We will return to this point in our consideration of the passage of the Gender Recognition Act 2015 below.

Despite the difficulties for Private Members' Bills making the statute book, some notable Private Members' Bills have become law. Significant examples of legislation that have been introduced on foot of Private Members' Bills include the Judicial Separation and Family Law Reform Act 1989, the Electoral (Amendment) Act 1996 and the Coroners (Amendment) Act 2005.

---

67 Standing Order 160 of Dáil Éireann.

68 Standing Order 160(1)(2) of Dáil Éireann.

69 R. Byrne, P. McCutcheon, L. Cahillane and E. Roche-Cagney, *Byrne and McCutcheon on the Irish Legal System*, 7th edn (Dublin: Bloomsbury Professional, 2021), para.13.42.

70 R. Quinn, 394 *Dail Debates* Col.1452 (13 December 1989).

C. Difference in Power between the Dáil and Seanad as Regards the Legislative Process

7–14 The Constitution grants to the Oireachtas the sole and exclusive power to make law.[71] However, power is not distributed equally between both Houses of the Oireachtas. The Dáil is a house of representatives who are elected from amongst the people by a general election.[72] The membership of the Dáil, called Teachtaí Dála (TDs for short), varies from time to time but can be no less than one member for each 30,000 of the population, and no more than one member for each 20,000 of the population.[73] By contrast, membership of the Seanad is confined to 60 members.[74] The electorate is also much more limited. Eleven members are appointed by the Taoiseach,[75] three are elected by graduates of the National University of Ireland,[76] a further three are elected by graduates of the University of Dublin,[77] and the remaining 43 are elected from panels of candidates,[78] in the fields of national language and culture, agriculture, labour, industry and commerce and public administration and social service.[79] Only those who are members of the incoming Dáil, members of the outgoing Seanad or members of county councils or city councils may vote to select those remaining 43 senators.[80] The Dáil, being the house elected by popular vote, has more power than the Seanad. As outlined above,[81] Bills can be initiated in either House of the Oireachtas. Where a Bill that has been passed by the Dáil is rejected or amended by the Seanad, under Article 23.1.1° the Dáil can pass a resolution within 180 days which deems the Bill to have been passed by both Houses. Effectively, this provision permits the Dáil to overrule the Seanad. Furthermore, where a Bill was initiated in the Seanad and amended during its passage through the Dáil, it is treated as if it were initiated in the Dáil and the Seanad is required to consider it afresh.[82]

---

71 Article 15.2.1° of the Constitution.
72 Article 15.1.2° of the Constitution.
73 Article 16.2.2° of the Constitution.
74 Article 18.1 of the Constitution.
75 Article 15.1.2° of the Constitution.
76 Article 18.4.1°(i) of the Constitution.
77 Article 18.4.1°(ii) of the Constitution.
78 Article 18.4.1°(iii) of the Constitution.
79 Article 18.7.1° of the Constitution.
80 *https://www.citizensinformation.ie/en/government-in-ireland/houses-of-the-oireachtas/the-seanad/#l9d8b9.*
81 Paragraph 7–04.
82 Article 23.2 of the Constitution.

7–15 While Bills can be initiated in either House, Money Bills can only originate from the Dáil.[83] A Money Bill is one that will result in public expenditure.[84] Additionally, the Seanad is prevented from amending a Money Bill and can merely posit recommendations.[85] Such recommendations must be made within 21 days.[86] Where the Bill is not returned to the Dáil within the 21-day period, or where the Seanad makes recommendations that the Dáil does not accept, the Bill is deemed to have passed both Houses at the end of the 21 days.[87]

7–16 The second constitutionally enshrined distinction in the powers of the Seanad is contained in Article 24. This Article facilitates an abridgement of the time available to the Seanad within which to consider a Bill. It is a somewhat complicated procedure. The Taoiseach can certify in writing that any Bill, except one containing a proposed amendment to the Constitution, is considered by the Government to be "urgent and immediately necessary for the preservation of the public peace and security, or by reason of the existence of a public emergency, whether domestic or international".[88] Notification of this certification must be communicated to the President and to the Chairperson of each House of the Oireachtas. Quite what emergency would justify such a certification is not clarified, and Morgan has suggested that it ranges from "either a nuclear attack or, at the other extreme, an outbreak of small pox in one town".[89] Yet, this power is not unrestrained. The continued legitimacy of legislation introduced under these emergency conditions is dependent upon subsequent ratification by both Houses of the Oireachtas. If resolutions from both Houses confirming the continued force of the legislation for an extended period of time have not been passed within 90 days of its entry into force, the legislation ceases to be law.[90] To date, Article 24 has not been invoked. As Byrne et al note, the Seanad has in any event tended to facilitate the speedy passage of urgent legislation.[91]

[83] Article 21 of the Constitution.
[84] Article 22.1.1° of the Constitution.
[85] Article 21.1.1° of the Constitution.
[86] Article 21.2.1° of the Constitution.
[87] Article 21.2.2° of the Constitution. See further *Collins v Minister for Finance* [2013] IEHC 530 at para.86.
[88] Article 24.1 of the Constitution.
[89] D.G. Morgan, *Constitutional Law of Ireland*, 2nd edn (Dublin: Round Hall Press, 1990), p.95.
[90] Article 24.3 of the Constitution.
[91] R. Byrne, P. McCutcheon, L. Cahillane and E. Roche-Cagney, *Byrne and McCutcheon on the Irish Legal System*, 7th edn (Dublin: Bloomsbury Professional, 2020), para.13.23.

Box 7.3: Legal Insight
Private Acts of the Oireachtas

A Private Bill specifically promotes the interests of chartered corporations, statutory bodies established by Private Acts of Parliament, and private individuals by providing them with the opportunity to petition Parliament for specific relief of a nature limited to a particular location or interest.[92] Private Bills are very rare. The Houses of the Oireachtas Joint Committee on Standing Orders (the "Committee"), in its report published in 2012, noted that only four such Acts had been enacted in the previous 20 years.[93] The Directory of Private Acts on *www.irishstatutebook.ie* provides a comprehensive list of all Private Acts passed since 1925.[94] Given the relative rarity of Private Bills, the Committee considered whether the Private Bill procedure should be "dispensed with in its entirety".[95] Ultimately, it accepted the legal advice tendered that chartered corporations have a common law right to petition the Oireachtas to enact legislation amending the Charter or Private Act that governs them.[96] Thus, the Committee turned its attention to the question of how best to reform the Private Bills procedure. The reforms it suggested were appended to its report and, on 27 November 2012, these were adopted without amendment and came into effect.[97]

The process by which Private Bills are enacted is as follows:

92 Houses of the Oireachtas Joint Committee on Standing Orders (Private Business), *Report on the Revision of Standing Orders Relative to Private Business 1939* (Dublin: Houses of the Oireachtas, 2012), p.1, available at: *https://opac.oireachtas.ie/AWData/Library3/Report_of_the_Joint_Committee_on_Standing_OrdersFinal_115007.pdf.*

93 Houses of the Oireachtas Joint Committee on Standing Orders (Private Business), *Report on the Revision of Standing Orders Relative to Private Business 1939* (Dublin: Houses of the Oireachtas, 2012), p.1.

94 See Chronological Table of Private Acts, available at: *www.irishstatutebook.ie/eli/isbc/patoc.html.*

95 Houses of the Oireachtas Joint Committee on Standing Orders (Private Business), *Report on the Revision of Standing Orders Relative to Private Business 1939* (Dublin: Houses of the Oireachtas, 2012), p.1.

96 Houses of the Oireachtas Joint Committee on Standing Orders (Private Business), *Report on the Revision of Standing Orders Relative to Private Business 1939* (Dublin: Houses of the Oireachtas, 2012), p.1.

97 Appendix 2, "Draft Standing Orders of the Dáil and Seanad relative to Private Business" in Houses of the Oireachtas Joint Committee on Standing Orders (Private Business), *Report on the Revision of Standing Orders Relative to Private Business 1939* (Dublin: Houses of the Oireachtas, 2012). As the Standing Orders were accepted without amendment, Appendix 2 remains their sole location ("Private Business Standing Orders 2012").

- **Notices by advertisement**: Prior to formal introduction before the Houses of the Oireachtas, notice of intended Private Bills must be published in a newspaper published or circulated in the locality, *Iris Oifigiúil*, and the Houses of the Oireachtas website.[98] This notice shall contain a clear and concise summary of the Bill.[99]
- **Application for Private Bill**: An application to introduce Private Bills must include the short title of the Bill[100] and a copy of the Bill.[101] This should be drafted in the usual manner for private legislation[102] and be accompanied by an explanatory memorandum.[103] The application, including the required documentation, should be deposited in the Private Bills Office[104] and copies should be lodged with each Department of Government and at the Office of the Attorney General.[105] Where the Bill relates to a charitable foundation, a copy must also be lodged with the Charities Regulatory Authority.[106]
- **Consent of chartered corporation**: Where the Bill relates to a chartered corporation, evidence of the consent of the corporation must also be furnished to the Joint Committee on Private Bills ("Private Bill Committee").[107]
- **Petition against an application for a Private Bill**: Those who wish to oppose a Private Bill have one month from the date of the deposit of the Bill to petition against its enactment.[108]
- **Consideration by Private Bill Committee**: Once the Private Bill Committee is satisfied that the technicalities are in order,[109] it formally considers the application for the Bill.[110] The promoter of the Bill, any petitioner against it and their counsel or agents are entitled to be heard during this consideration process.[111] The Private Bill Committee also considers any reports from the offices notified under Standing Order 5(1) of Private Business Standing Orders 2012.[112]
- **Decision of the Private Bill Committee**: Where the Private Bill Committee is satisfied that the proposed Bill complies with the

[98] Standing Order 8(1) of Private Business Standing Orders 2022.
[99] Standing Order 8(4)(b) of Private Business Standing Orders 2022.
[100] Standing Order 4(2)(a) of Private Business Standing Orders 2022.
[101] Standing Order 4(2)(b)(ii) of Private Business Standing Orders 2022.
[102] Standing Order 4(2)(a) of Private Business Standing Orders 2022.
[103] Standing Order 4(2)(b)(iii) of Private Business Standing Orders 2022.
[104] Standing Order 4(1) of Private Business Standing Orders 2022.
[105] Standing Order 5(1) of Private Business Standing Orders 2022.
[106] Standing Order 5(1)(c) of Private Business Standing Orders 2022.
[107] Standing Order 7 of Private Business Standing Orders 2022.
[108] Standing Order 9(3) of Private Business Standing Orders 2022.
[109] Standing Order 13(1) of Private Business Standing Orders 2022.
[110] Standing Order 14 of Private Business Standing Orders 2022.
[111] Standing Orders 15(5) of Private Business Standing Orders 2022.
[112] Standing Orders 15(3)(c) of Private Business Standing Orders 2022.

standing orders, it publishes its report forthwith.[113] Where the Private Bill Committee is not satisfied that the Bill complies with the standing orders, it may recommend amendments,[114] and the proposer may re-present the Bill.[115] If, following re-presentation, the Private Bill Committee finds that the Bill does not comply with the standing orders, it shall proceed and report accordingly.[116]

- **Report of the Private Bill Committee**: A report noting that the proposed Bill is a true Private Bill may recommend amendment in order to ensure compliance with the requirement of the offices notified under Standing Order 15(4). The report shall be furnished to the Ceann Comhairle of the Dáil and the Cathaoirleach of the Seanad who shall cause a copy of the report to be laid before each House for its consideration. The Bill and explanatory memorandum shall thereafter be printed at the cost of the promoter.[117]
- **Introduction to the Seanad:** The Bill then proceeds to first stage in the Seanad and from this time it progresses as any Public Bill through the Oireachtas.[118]

D. The Role of the President in the Legislative Process

7–17 The Oireachtas is the law-making organ of the State. Yet, it does not consist exclusively of the Dáil and the Seanad. The third actor in the Oireachtas is the President, and this chapter now turns to an examination of the role of the President in the legislative process. Once a Bill has passed both Houses of the Oireachtas, it is presented to the President to be signed, which must be done between five and seven days of receipt.[119] Under Article 25.2.2°, the President may sign a Bill before the fifth day, should the Seanad agree. This provision makes no mention of the Dáil having a role to play in this regard, so this is one area where the Seanad can exercise a legislative power denied the Dáil.[120] A Bill that has been subject to an Article 24 abridgement process

113 Standing Order 16(1) of Private Business Standing Orders 2022.
114 Standing Order 17 of Private Business Standing Orders 2022.
115 Standing Order 17(2) of Private Business Standing Orders 2022.
116 Standing Order 17 of Private Business Standing Orders 2022.
117 Standing Order 19(5) of Private Business Standing Orders 2022.
118 Standing Order 19(1)(b) of Private Business Standing Orders 2022.
119 Article 25.2.1° of the Constitution.
120 Examples of legislation signed before the fifth day include the Offences against the State (Amendment) Act 1985 and the Anglo Irish Bank Corporation Act 2009.

must be signed by the President on the day it is presented to them.[121] By signing the Bill, it is transformed into an Act of the Oireachtas and becomes law. The final stage of the process is the promulgation of the Act. This is done by publishing a notice in *Iris Oifigiúil*.[122] Where the Bill is one that contains a proposed amendment to the Constitution, then the President may not sign it until it has been voted upon by referendum of the people.[123] Once the referendum has passed, the Bill must be signed "forthwith"[124] by the President and promulgated in the usual fashion.[125] Promulgation is a fundamental aspect of the legislative process, as it ensures that the law is public and knowable—essential elements of the rule of law.[126] Once the Act has been signed by the President, Article 25.4.5° requires that a copy of it is enrolled in the record of the office of the Registrar of the Supreme Court. It is this enrolled copy that becomes the definitive version of the text of the Act should a dispute arise. Under the Constitution, there are two circumstances where the President may refuse to sign a Bill, and we will now consider these in turn.

1. Article 26

7–18 Article 26 permits the President to refuse to sign a Bill where they have concerns regarding its constitutionality. However, it does not enable an outright refusal to sign. Rather, the President may, on the advice of the Council of State, refer the Bill to the Supreme Court to have its constitutionality tested. The Supreme Court is then required to pronounce whether the Bill, or any provision of the Bill, is repugnant to the Constitution. There are three categories of Bill that are excluded from the Article 26 reference procedure. These are Money Bills, Bills signed following an Article 24 abridged process, and a Bill that contains a proposal to amend the Constitution.[127]

---

[121] Article 25.3 of the Constitution.

[122] Article 25.4.2° of the Constitution.

[123] Article 46.2 of the Constitution.

[124] Article 46.5 of the Constitution.

[125] However, as was seen with the passage of the Thirty-first Amendment of the Constitution (Children) Act 2012, while it was passed by a majority in a referendum on 10 October 2012, it was not signed by the President until 28 April 2015. This was due to a legal challenge to the result. The challenge was rejected; see *Jordan v Minister for Children and Youth Affairs* [2014] IEHC 327 and *Jordan v Minister for Children and Youth Affairs* [2015] IESC 33. For more on the referendum process, see Ch.3, Section E.1.

[126] Discussed in Ch.2, Section C.4.

[127] Article 26 of the Constitution.

7–19 When adjudicating on Article 26 cases, the Supreme Court must consist of at least five judges.[128] This judicial panel must consider every question that the President has referred to it. Generally, however, the President poses one simple question, namely, whether the Bill is repugnant to the Constitution. The procedure for such hearings is set down in Article 26.2.1° and requires that the Attorney General present arguments in favour of the constitutionality of the Bill while the court appoints counsel to argue the contrary. The court must issue its verdict in open court as soon as possible and no later than 60 days following the reference by the President. Article 26.2.2° declares that the decision of the majority shall be the decision of the court and no dissenting opinion may be issued. Thus, Article 26.2.2° preserves the one-judgment rule that was otherwise removed by the Thirty-third Amendment of the Constitution.[129] Where the Supreme Court finds that a Bill is constitutional, the President must sign it into law "as soon as may be"[130] once the court's decision has been pronounced. Where the Supreme Court pronounces a Bill constitutionally repugnant, the President must refuse to sign the Bill.[131]

7–20 Referring a Bill to the Supreme Court under Article 26 has advantages and disadvantages. First, where a Bill is found to be constitutional, once enacted it can never again be challenged in any court. In its report, the Constitution Review Group noted that awareness of the potential immunity of legislation considered under an Article 26 reference can cause inflexibility in the procedure which may not always be appropriate and, consequently, the Review Group recommended removing the immunity.[132] Second, the Supreme Court reaches its decision on the constitutionality or otherwise of the Bill in abstract circumstances. There are no parties to ground the arguments and thus no factual context to inform the judgment. Finally, it is interesting that the "one judgment" rule persists in relation to Article 26. It was explicitly removed from Article 34.4.5° by the Thirty-third Amendment, which also established the Court of Appeal. However, the wording of

[128] Article 26.2.1° of the Constitution.
[129] See further, Ch.15, para.15–20, fn.14.
[130] Article 26.3.3° of the Constitution.
[131] Article 26.3.1° of the Constitution.
[132] *Report of the Constitution Review Group* (Pn 2632) (Dublin: Stationery Office, 1996), para.15.196.

that amendment did not address the existence of the one-judgment rule in Article 26 and, consequently, it continues to apply in that context.[133]

2. Article 27

7–21 Article 27 also enables the President to refuse to sign a Bill where it contains a proposal of "national importance".[134] However, the President may only take such a step on receipt of a petition signed by a majority of the Seanad and not less than one-third of members of the Dáil.[135] The President may then consult with the Council of State prior to making their decision regarding refusal.[136] The purpose of the refusal is to facilitate a referendum so that the people may have the opportunity to vote on the Bill.[137] The President will then sign the Bill should the people approve it.[138] Alternatively, the President can require that the Dáil be dissolved and a new Dáil assembled following a general election. Should this reassembled Dáil approve the Bill, then the President will sign it into law.[139] Whichever strategy is chosen will ensure that there is popular support for this legislation. Article 27 has never been invoked.

3. Article 25

7–22 Article 25.2.2° of the Constitution permits the President to sign legislation before the fifth day should the Seanad agree, and the Seanad has been accommodating in cases where legislation was (perceived to be) urgently required. Examples include the Irish Bank Resolution Corporation Act 2013 and the Misuse of Drugs (Amendment) Act 2015. Some commentators suggest that the existence of Article 25 is intended to redress the power imbalance between the Houses of the Oireachtas, particularly in circumstances where the Dáil has overruled the Seanad.[140]

[133] See further, N. Ní Loinsigh, "Judicial Dissent in Ireland: Theory, Practice and the Constraints of the Single Opinion Rule" (2014) 51 *Irish Jurist* 123 at 133–134.
[134] Article 27.1 of the Constitution.
[135] Article 27.1 of the Constitution.
[136] Article 27.4 of the Constitution.
[137] Article 27.5.1° i of the Constitution.
[138] Article 27.5.1° i of the Constitution.
[139] Article 27.5.1° ii of the Constitution.
[140] R. Byrne, P. McCutcheon, L. Cahillane and E. Roche-Cagney, *Byrne and McCutcheon on the Irish Legal System*, 7th edn (Dublin: Bloomsbury Professional, 2021), para.13.27.

E. Case Study: the Gender Recognition Act 2015

7–23 This chapter now turns to consider a case study charting the introduction of one piece of legislation: the Gender Recognition Act 2015. We have chosen to examine this particular legislative journey as it encompasses all aspects of the law-making and law reform processes. Thus, it was the subject of strategic litigation, advocacy and activism.[141] Furthermore, introducing legislation on this issue was considered by a special interdepartmental group. It was among the first pieces of legislation to undergo pre-legislative consideration and both the shape of the legislation and the policy position underpinning it changed considerably as it progressed through the Oireachtas. As such, a close study of the passage of the Gender Recognition Act 2015 demonstrates the impact that all the stages of the legislative process can have on legislation.

7–24 The impetus for the introduction of legislation on gender recognition was the judgment of McKechnie J. in *Foy v An tArd Chláraitheoir (No. 2)*.[142] Lydia Foy was a male-to-female transgender woman who petitioned the Registrar General for a change in the gender marker on her birth certificate from male to female so that she could be recognised by the law as a woman. In the first case on this point, *Foy v An tArd Chláraitheoir (No. 1)*,[143] the court ruled that legal gender in Ireland is determined by the congruence of the chromosomes, gonads and genitals at the moment of birth.[144] On the basis of this common law test, Foy could not be legally recognised as a woman as her body was congruent with the male sex at birth. Foy appealed the decision to the Supreme Court on the basis of the decision of the European Court of Human Rights in *Goodwin v UK*,[145]

[141] See Ch.8, Section C for a more detailed analysis of the informal processes of law reform.

[142] [2007] IEHC 470. For a more detailed analysis of the *Foy* cases, see T. Ní Mhuirthile, "Legal Recognition of Preferred Gender Identity in Ireland: An Analysis of Proposed Legislation" in E. Kiely and M. Leane (eds), *Sexualities in Irish Society: A Reader* (Dublin: Orpen Press, 2014), p.127.

[143] [2002] IEHC 116.

[144] [2002] IEHC 116 at para.121.

[145] (2002) 35 E.H.R.R. 18, where the Strasbourg Court upheld the right to recognition as part of one's right to respect for private and family life under Article 8 of the European Convention on Human Rights. For more on the evolution of case law before the Strasbourg Court on the right to recognition, see T. Ní Mhuirthile, "Article 8 and the Realisation of the Right to Legal Gender Recognition" in S. Egan, L. Thornton and J. Walsh (eds), *Ireland and the European Convention on Human Rights: 60 Years and*

the introduction of the European Convention on Human Rights Act 2003 (the "2003 Act") and the Civil Registration Act 2004 (the "2004 Act"), which established a new system of civil registration and repealed all previous legislation on the issue. As these developments had not been considered as part of the original hearing, the Supreme Court remitted the case back to the High Court. Unusually, by agreement of the parties, the remitted action was again heard by McKechnie J., on the basis that he was familiar with the medical evidence and understood the issues involved. Given the absence of any new evidence, the court found that the principle of res judicata (it is already decided) applied.[146]

7–25 Independently, Foy made a fresh application for a change in the gender marker on her birth certificate under the 2004 Act.[147] The Registrar General refused the request and Foy began judicial review proceedings which were heard together with the hearing in the remitted case. In essence, the core of the argument in *Foy (No. 2)* was that if the new system of registration introduced under the 2004 Act did not permit an amendment of the birth certificate to reflect her preferred gender identity, then this amounted to a breach of her rights under Article 8 of the European Convention on Human Rights (ECHR). In considering this argument, McKechnie J. found that it did not.[148] However, he did find that the failure of the Irish State to provide some mechanism by which the preferred gender identity of Foy could be recognised amounted to a breach of her right to recognition under Article 8 of the ECHR.[149] Consequently, he issued a declaration of incompatibility under s.5 of the 2003 Act.[150]

7–26 The State appealed the decision, but shortly after, the then-Minister for Social Protection, Éamon Ó Cuiv, announced the establishment of a Gender Recognition Advisory Group (GRAG) to examine how best to

Beyond (Dublin: Bloomsbury Professional, 2014), p.201.

146 [2007] IEHC 470 at para.12.

147 Section 62(2)(b) of the Civil Registration Act 2004.

148 [2007] IEHC 470 at para.64.8. McKechnie J. found that the birth register is a record of historical fact: "[i]t is not intended to and does not record any other major event in a person's existence or even in death. In particular, it is not intended to be a document of current identity although in practice this has not always been the case."

149 [2007] IEHC 470 at para.100.

150 For more on the declaration of incompatibility, see Ch.6, Section E.4(c) and Ch.8, Section B.6(b).

introduce legislation on the issue in Ireland.[151] The State withdrew the appeal and settled the case.[152] The GRAG published its report on 15 June 2011 and the legislative scheme it outlined was a close copy of the scheme in the UK Gender Recognition Act 2004. Under the proposed scheme, a person whose birth was registered in Ireland, was at least 18 years of age, had a clear and settled intention to live in the preferred gender permanently, and had lived in that gender for at least two years, could apply to be legally recognised. In addition to these criteria, the applicant had to supply evidence of a diagnosis of gender identity disorder (GID), or evidence of having undergone gender reassignment surgery, or evidence of legal recognition of preferred gender identity by another jurisdiction. Furthermore, persons in an existing valid marriage or civil partnership were excluded from the scheme.[153]

7–27 Three criticisms emerged with this proposed scheme. First, the requirement to have a diagnosis of GID pathologised access to the legal rights contained in the scheme. By the time of publication of the GRAG report, discourse in international human rights had begun to stress that medical diagnosis should not serve a gate-keeping function in terms of access to legal rights.[154] Furthermore, defining access in relation to a specific diagnostic label such as GID would exclude other potential applicants, including intersex people,[155] who may need to exercise the rights contained in the scheme. Second, the requirement for applicants to be single mandated dissolution of marriages and civil partnerships that had survived the transition of gender in one spouse/partner, which it was argued would be an undue interference with the special constitutional position of the family based on marriage, as contained

[151] See Gender Recognition Advisory Group, *Report of the Gender Recognition Advisory Group* (Dublin: Department of Social Protection, 2011), p.6.

[152] T. Ní Mhuirthile, "Legal Recognition of Preferred Gender Identity in Ireland: An Analysis of Proposed Legislation" in E. Kiely and M. Leane (eds), *Sexualities in Irish Society: A Reader* (Dublin: Orpen Press, 2014), p.144.

[153] Gender Recognition Advisory Group, *Report of the Gender Recognition Advisory Group* (Dublin: Department of Social Protection, 2011), pp.3–4.

[154] Council of Europe Commissioner for Human Rights, *Discrimination on Grounds of Sexual Orientation and Gender Identity in Europe* (Strasbourg: Council of Europe Publishing, 2011); *Yogyakarta Principles on Sexual Orientation and Gender Identity* (2007), available at: *http://yogyakartaprinciples.org/principles-en/yp10/*.

[155] "Intersex" is an umbrella term for a variety of conditions where a person's body combines both male and female biological traits, or where the body does not develop along typical male or female lines.

in Article 41.3.1° of the Constitution.[156] Finally, the scheme made no provision for applicants under 18 years of age. This was of particular concern in relation to intersex children and registering for school in the context of the provision of single-sex education, where the gender marker on official documentation did not match the social gender in which the child lived.[157]

7–28 Following publication of the GRAG report, there was a delay in Government-sponsored legislation on the issue. However, in early 2013, two different Private Members' Bills were introduced to the Oireachtas on the issue: Aonghus Ó Snodaigh's Gender Recognition Bill 2013 ("Ó Snodaigh's Bill"), introduced in the Dáil on 22 May 2013, and Katherine Zappone's Legal Recognition of Gender Bill 2013 ("Zappone's Bill"), introduced in the Seanad on 27 June 2013. Both drew inspiration from the Gender Identity Act 2012 in Argentina which adopted a self-declaration model of recognition and did not require diagnosis.[158] Nor did they require that applicants be single. While Ó Snodaigh's Bill contained a provision in s.6 for under-18s to make an application to the District Court for recognition, Zappone's Bill enabled parents and guardians to make an application on behalf of their child in s.2(4), and enabled a child between the ages of 16 and 18 to make an application on their own initiative without the need for parental consent in s.2(5).

7–29 In July 2013, the Minister for Social Protection published the General Scheme of the Gender Recognition Bill 2013 (the "2013 General Scheme"). This draft legislation proposed a scheme similar to that outlined in the GRAG report. The 2013 General Scheme underwent

---

[156] T. Ní Mhuirthile, "Legal Recognition of Preferred Gender Identity in Ireland: An Analysis of Proposed Legislation" in E. Kiely and M. Leane (eds), *Sexualities in Irish Society: A Reader* (Dublin: Orpen Press, 2014), pp.150–152. At this stage in the progress of the legislation, Irish law only recognised opposite-sex marriages. The marriage equality referendum had not yet been held. See para.7–32.

[157] See *S v An Bord Uchtála*, unreported, High Court, Sheehan J., 9 December 2009. This case was a judicial review of the refusal of the Adoption Board to amend the gender marker of the intersex child on the Register of Intercountry Adoptions. The court granted the amendment in an ex tempore judgment. For analysis, see T. Ní Mhuirthile, "Building Bodies: A Legal History of Intersex in Ireland" in S. Tiernan, S. McAvoy, J. Redmond and M. McAuliffe (eds), *Sexual Politics in Ireland* (Dublin: Irish Academic Press, 2014), p.154.

[158] An English translation of Argentina's gender identity law, as approved by the Senate of Argentina on 8 May 2012, is available at: *https://gate.ngo/wp-content/uploads/2012/05/GATE_English-Translation-of-Argentinas-Gender-Identity-Law_2012.pdf.*

pre-legislative consideration by the Joint Oireachtas Committee on Education and Social Protection (the "Joint Committee") in October 2013. During two days of public hearings, the Joint Committee heard from trans people[159] and parents of trans children, the civil servants leading the drafting process, medical professionals, academic lawyers, NGOs and civic society groups. The Joint Committee published its report on the 2013 General Scheme in January 2014.[160] In its report, the Joint Committee recommended that the minimum age for applicants be reduced to 16 years for the grant of a Gender Recognition Certificate and that measures should be put in place to address the day-to-day concerns of under-16s.[161] On the criterion that the applicant be single, the Joint Committee stated its belief "that the fact that a person is in an existing marriage or a civil partnership should not prevent him or her from qualifying for a Gender Recognition Certificate, and urges the Minister to revisit this issue".[162] On the diagnosis issue, the Joint Committee recommended a reconsideration of the current wording in the Bill and a sensitivity to avoid stigmatisation of applicants.[163]

7–30 In June 2014, the Minister published a Revised General Scheme of Gender Recognition Bill 2014 (the "2014 Revised Scheme"). Although Head 5 of the 2014 Revised Scheme maintained the requirement that potential applicants be single, there were some significant shifts of

---

[159] Terminology in relation to gender identity is highly contested and each term has a specific meaning. "Transgender" refers to a person whose gender identity and/or gender expression differs from the sex assigned to them at birth. This term can include diverse gender identities. "Transsexual" refers to a person whose gender identity is "opposite" to the sex assigned to them at birth. The term connotes a binary view of gender, moving from one polar identity to the other. Transsexual people may or may not take hormones or have surgery. Finally, "trans" is a commonly used shorthand that can encompass both these different terms. For more on gender identity terminology, see TENI, "Helpful Terms and Definitions", available at: *https://teni.ie/resources/trans-terms/*.

[160] Joint Oireachtas Committee on Education and Social Protection, *Report on the General Scheme of a Gender Recognition Bill 2013* (Dublin: Houses of the Oireachtas, 2014).

[161] Joint Oireachtas Committee on Education and Social Protection, *Report on the General Scheme of a Gender Recognition Bill 2013* (Dublin: Houses of the Oireachtas, 2014), p.37.

[162] Joint Oireachtas Committee on Education and Social Protection, *Report on the General Scheme of a Gender Recognition Bill 2013* (Dublin: Houses of the Oireachtas, 2014), p.37.

[163] Joint Oireachtas Committee on Education and Social Protection, *Report on the General Scheme of a Gender Recognition Bill 2013* (Dublin: Houses of the Oireachtas, 2014), p.37.

position on the part of the Department evident in the 2014 Revised Scheme. On the diagnosis point, Head 6 no longer required medical certification of a particular diagnosis but instead sought supporting statements from two medical professionals that the applicant has transitioned or is transitioning. In response to the recommendation by the Joint Committee on the age limit, Head 7 proposed an exemption from the minimum age requirement of 18 years for those between the ages of 16 and 18 following a successful application to the Circuit Court, which was supported by the consent of the parent or guardian of the applicant child and supporting statements from medical professionals. The 2014 Revised Scheme was the subject of a detailed analysis by the Irish Human Rights and Equality Commission (the "Commission").[164] The Commission welcomed the shift in relation to trans youth as considerably enhancing their options.[165] Yet the Commission also reiterated the shortcomings of the scheme as revised from the perspective of divorce, diagnosis and children under 16 years of age.[166]

7–31 In December 2014, the full text of the Gender Recognition Bill 2014 (the "2014 Bill") was finally published, and on 17 January 2014, it was initiated in the Seanad. This draft had again changed from the 2014 Revised Scheme. Most notably, s.9 of the 2014 Bill changed the evidential requirement from a "supporting statement" in Head 6 of the 2014 Revised Scheme to a requirement for "medical certification" by two medical professionals following "medical evaluation" of the applicant. It was posited in debate on the floor of the Seanad that this was in essence diagnosis in disguise. The requirement for "medical evaluation" was removed from the text of the 2014 Bill at the report stage in the Seanad and the new s.10(1)(g) merely required medical certification.

7–32 There was one final change to the Bill prior to its enactment into law. The diagnosis requirement was removed entirely from the text of the draft legislation by 17 June 2015 and a self-declaration model was adopted. Section 10 of the 2014 Bill as passed by the Dáil no longer required any form of medical certification. Surprisingly, despite the

[164] *Observations on the Revised General Scheme of the Gender Recognition Bill 2014* (Dublin: Irish Human Rights and Equality Commission, 2014).

[165] *Observations on the Revised General Scheme of the Gender Recognition Bill 2014* (Dublin: Irish Human Rights and Equality Commission, 2014), pp.2–3.

[166] *Observations on the Revised General Scheme of the Gender Recognition Bill 2014* (Dublin: Irish Human Rights and Equality Commission, 2014).

passing of the marriage equality referendum on 23 May 2015 while the Bill was working its way through the Dáil, the Gender Recognition Act 2015 was still enacted with the requirement of being single intact. This requirement was only subsequently removed by amendment via s.24 of the Marriage Act 2015.

F. Conclusion

7–33 This chapter has examined the formal process by which a Bill becomes an Act. We have considered briefly the purposes of legislation. We have examined how the introduction of pre-legislative consideration has recalibrated the influence between the Oireachtas and the executive so that the legislature and other non-government actors have more substantial input. The legislative process itself was outlined in detail and we considered each step a Bill must undergo to become law. The difference in power that each House of the Oireachtas wields in the process was considered, as was the role of the President. The case study on the Gender Recognition Act 2015 reveals that there is room within the formal process for accommodating amendments and changes in policy.

Chapter 8

Law Reform

> "Changing the law can be a tricky business. Seen from the perspective of non-governmental organisations, law reform can mean years of lobbying governments and politicians for change; seen from inside government, law reform may signify months or years of consultation, drafting bills, and holding one's breath for Parliament; seen from Parliament, law reform may mean a relatively simple examination and passage of a Bill or months of political haggling; from the perspective of the public, law reform may appear variously political, idealistic, long and drawn out or hasty. Law reform is all of these things."
>
> L. Barnett, "The Process of Law Reform: Conditions for Success" (2011) 39 *Federal Law Review* 161 at 161.

In this chapter we:

- identify formal mechanisms of law reform;
- consider informal ways to reform the law;
- examine how reform of the law reflects the aspirations of how society views itself, or wishes to view itself;
- discuss the impact of reform of the law in response to a moment of crisis.

A. Introduction

8–01 Law reform is the process by which the law is amended and changed. As a term, it suggests that these changes will improve the law. Law reform can be prompted by both formal and informal processes. Formal processes can include government department initiatives such as Green and White Papers, consultation papers, issues papers, seminar papers, discussion papers and reports from the Law Reform Commission, reports from tribunals, formal court statements, reports from citizens' assemblies or constitutional referendums. Informal processes are less readily identifiable and include strategic litigation, advocacy and activism. These formal and informal processes will be considered in this chapter. Unusually, Irish formal law reform projects engage regularly with Irish citizens through both direct democratic mechanisms (e.g. referendums to change the Constitution) and deliberative democratic mechanisms (e.g. citizens' assemblies). Thus, it is not surprising that Ireland has a reputation as both "one of the most frequent users of constitutional referendums in Europe"[1] and "at the vanguard of deliberative innovations, particularly for citizens' assemblies."[2] Informal law reform processes such as activism and strategic litigation are inherently led by citizens. Consequently, the Irish people, in whom sovereignty has always been identified as a core component of the Irish Constitution,[3] are regularly intimately involved in the process of law reform in Ireland.

8–02 Reform of the law is a constant process, mainly progressed through legislation, but also on occasion through constitutional referendum. Article 15.2.1° of the Constitution provides that "[t]he sole and exclusive power of making laws for the State is hereby vested in the Oireachtas". Practically speaking, the main mechanism to effect legal change and reform of the law is through the introduction of legislation. Each Act of the Oireachtas changes the law as it is enacted. Thus, law is ever-changing. In Ch.7, we examined the legislative process by which Acts of the Oireachtas are introduced. In this chapter, we consider the tools that can be used to prompt the introduction of legislation before the Houses of the Oireachtas to bring about legal change.

B. Formal Mechanisms of Law Reform

8–03 As outlined above, there are a number of different formal ways by which the law can be reformed. These include exploratory policy documents that invite public comment, such as Green and White Papers,

1 T. Reidy and J. Suiter, "Direct and Deliberative Democracy" in J. Coakley, M. Gallagher, E. O'Malley and T. Reidy (eds), *Politics in the Republic of Ireland*, 7th edn (Abingdon: Routledge, 2024), p.193.

2 T. Reidy and J. Suiter, "Direct and Deliberative Democracy" in J. Coakley, M. Gallagher, E. O'Malley and T. Reidy (eds), *Politics in the Republic of Ireland*, 7th edn (Abingdon: Routledge, 2024), p.193.

3 E. Daly and T. Hickey, *The Political Theory of the Irish Constitution: Republicanism and the Basic Law* (Manchester: Manchester University Press, 2015), p.1.

reports and consultation papers from the Law Reform Commission, court decisions and referendums.

1. Green Papers

8–04 Green Papers are tentative policy documents published by the Government, or the European Union, to stimulate discussion in a particular policy area. They operate as a very preliminary step towards law reform without committing the Government to a particular policy. In essence, the Green Paper outlines current thinking on the policies that underline the operation of the law in particular areas. Green Papers invite discussion, feedback and critique from interested parties, both inside Government and in the wider civic society. Interested individuals or organisations may put forward proposals on how that policy ought to be developed. Green Papers enable government departments to test and refine a policy, to identify potential weaknesses at an early stage, and to involve the community at large in the development of policy. As the Department of Defence *Green Paper on Defence* noted in its opening sentence, "[t]he goal of this Green Paper is to initiate and inform a broad consultative process, which will in turn inform the development of a new White Paper on Defence".[4] Green Papers are intended to be conversation starters at a moment when a department is considering a complete revision of policy, as in the example from the *Green Paper on Defence* where there had been no policy review in 13 years.[5] Green Papers may also be a precursor to the introduction of policy in an entirely new area. Once submissions are received from interested parties, these are read by the Department and may form part of the considerations refining the policy that may be published as a White Paper. For example, the *Green Paper on Energy Policy in Ireland*, published in March 2014, produced over 1,240 submissions to the Department of Communications, Energy and Natural Resources.[6] Resulting from these submissions, the Department held a series of seminars on the priority areas both in Dublin and around the country. The final White Paper, entitled *Ireland's Transition to a Low Carbon Energy Future 2015–2030*, was published on 16 December 2015.[7]

[4] Department of Defence, *Green Paper on Defence* (Dublin: Stationery Office, 2013), p.3.

[5] Department of Defence, *Green Paper on Defence* (Dublin: Stationery Office, 2013).

[6] Department of Communications, Energy and Natural Resources, *Green Paper on Energy Policy in Ireland* (Dublin: Stationery Office, 2014).

[7] *Ireland's Transition to a Low Carbon Energy Future 2015–2030* (Dublin: Department of Communications, Energy and Natural Resources, 2015).

2. White Papers

8–05 If the Green Paper is intended to promote discussion on an issue, the White Paper is a firm policy proposal. Where it is intended that the policy outlined in the White Paper will result in the introduction of legislation, the position adopted in the White Paper is not intended to be absolute. Rather, it invites feedback on these proposals. As Doerr notes, a White Paper is a "tool of participatory democracy".[8] The White Paper then enables scrutiny of the proposed change by the relevant Oireachtas Committee, members of the Oireachtas and other interested parties.

8–06 Alternatively, where there is no legislative underpinning, but rather the outline of a new policy for a department, the White Paper marks a formal statement of that policy. For example, the *Green Paper on Defence* discussed above prompted written submissions, follow-on meetings with selected authors of those submissions, and the establishment of an interdepartmental group and two further groups comprising civil and military personnel from the Defence Organisation and an External Advisory Group to advise the Minister on the development of the new policy in the area of defence.[9] Prior to final publication of the White Paper, the Minister held a symposium for a final round of debate on key policy principles, which facilitated a final opportunity for input from stakeholders and international experts.[10] Consequently, the final *White Paper on Defence* is the result of an extensive research and consultation process and is the policy of the State for the next 10 years in the area of defence.

3. Law Reform Commission Consultation Papers and Reports

8–07 While both Green and White Papers originate within Government, many formal mechanisms prompting reform of the law are initiated outside the corridors of power. First and foremost among these are Law Reform Commission consultation papers and reports. The Law Reform Commission Act 1975 (the "1975 Act") established the Law Reform

[8] A.D. Doerr, "The Role of White Papers" in G.B. Doern and P. Aucoin (eds), *The Structures of Policy-making in Canada* (Toronto: MacMillan, 1971), p.185.
[9] Department of Defence, *White Paper on Defence* (Dublin: Stationery Office, 2015), p.6.
[10] Department of Defence, *White Paper on Defence* (Dublin: Stationery Office, 2015), pp.6–7.

Commission. The function of the Commission is set out in s.4 of the 1975 Act as "keep[ing] the law under review and ... [the Commission] shall undertake examinations and conduct research with a view to reforming the law and formulate proposals for law reform". There are three aspects to this task: developing law, codifying law and consolidating law.

8–08 The intention behind the establishment of the Commission was that there would be a statutory body, independent of the Oireachtas, capable of addressing specific reform proposals, while also having the capacity to undertake a general analysis of the state of the law and put forward an agenda for reform. As Baroness Hale, the first woman appointed to the Law Commission in the United Kingdom, has noted, many of the areas on which these kinds of commissions focus are those in which "[g]overnments were simply not sufficiently interested to waste valuable time and resources putting them right. They were far too busy running the country to concern themselves with 'lawyers' law'".[11] The job that the Commission performs in terms of keeping the Statute Book under review and up-to-date is an important one, which the Attorney General at the time of the Commission's establishment stated, "in light of many years of neglect ... must be considered an arduous one".[12]

8–09 The Commission consists of five people: a President and four other members appointed by the Government.[13] Commissioners serve a five-year renewable term of office.[14] By custom, at least one Commissioner occupies a full-time position. To be eligible for appointment as a Commissioner, a potential candidate must be a judge, a barrister or solicitor, or a teacher of law.[15] Additionally, and unusually, the 1975 Act recognises that non-lawyers may make a valuable contribution to the process of law reform, and if a candidate possesses other special experience, qualification or training which the Government considers

[11] The Rt Hon. Baroness Hale of Richmond, *Law Maker or Law Reformer: What is a Law Lady for?*, 11th Annual John Maurice Kelly Memorial Lecture, delivered at the Faculty of Law UCD on 21 January 2005 (Dublin: University College Dublin Faculty of Law, 2005), p.10.

[12] D. Costello, "Law Reform: A New Departure" (1976–1977) 1 *Dublin University Law Journal* 6 at 7.

[13] Law Reform Commission Act 1975 s.3(1). For the profiles of the current membership, see: *http://www.lawreform.ie/law-reform/who-we-are.329.html*.

[14] Law Reform Commission Act 1975 s.3(8).

[15] Law Reform Commission Act 1975 s.3(7).

appropriate, then that person can be appointed as a Commissioner.[16] Indeed, one of the very first Commissioners was a social scientist.[17] The independence of the Commission is provided for in s.3 of the 1975 Act, which requires any Commissioner who is nominated to stand for election to either House of the Oireachtas, or who is entitled under the standing orders of either House to sit in the Oireachtas, to resign their position as Commissioner.[18]

8–10 The Commission is supported in its task by a staff of full and part-time researchers and other support staff.[19] Lawyers, whether practising or academic, with a proven track record in research, form the research staff. They are involved in all aspects of the work of the Commission.

8–11 Aside from its regular work updating and maintaining the Legislation Directory and producing Revised Acts,[20] the Commission identifies its work priorities in two ways: (1) as a result of public consultation, and (2) as a result of specific requests from the Attorney General. To date, the Commission has engaged in five programmes of law reform. The first lasted from 1977–2000 and covered a very wide range of areas. Since then, the programme has been revised more regularly. The second programme ran from 2000–2008, the third from 2008–2014, the fourth from 2013–2019, and the current (fifth) programme was adopted by the Government in March 2019.

8–12 When devising a new programme of law reform, the Commission engages in a wide-ranging public consultation, holding a variety of public meetings around the country, inviting members of the public to identify those areas of the law where they feel that reform is required. In addition, the Commission invites submissions of reform suggestions via email or post. Such submissions need not take any special format: interested people can communicate with the Commission in their preferred manner to let it know what reforms they think are necessary.[21] The feedback from

---

[16] Law Reform Commission Act 1975 s.3(7).
[17] D. Costello, "Law Reform: A New Departure" (1976–1977) 1 *Dublin University Law Journal* 6 at 7.
[18] Law Reform Commission Act 1975 s.3(12) and (13).
[19] Law Reform Commission Act 1975 s.10.
[20] For more information on both the Legislation Directory and Revised Acts, see Ch.14, para.14–25.
[21] *https://www.lawreform.ie/contact-us.50.html.*

all this public consultation is considered and a list of priority issues is identified which then forms the next programme of law reform.

8–13 In addition to the issues identified through public consultation, the Attorney General may request that the Commission examine the law in relation to specific issues.[22] Between its establishment in 1975 and 2019, the Attorney General requested that the Commission examine the law in 24 areas. These covered a variety of issues, from the domicile of married women[23] to mandatory sentencing.[24] In response to these requests, the Commission has produced 47 reports which examined in detail the law in relation to these issues and made various reform proposals.[25]

8–14 The Commission invites consultation at various points in its research process. Since 2013, the Commission has published Issues Papers, Seminar Papers and Discussion Papers in a few select areas. These publications provide a summary or outline of a particular project on which the Commission is working or about to commence work. The aim of publishing the Papers is to inspire feedback, comment and suggestions from the public and from issue experts, which will assist the Commission in relation to the very specific questions identified in the Paper. These Papers are circulated to the legal professions, to other professional groups who may have an interest in or specialist knowledge on the issue, and are published directly on the Commission's website. Members of the public are also invited to comment. Crucially, these Papers are intended as discussion documents. They are not the final perspective of the Commission on the topic but are intended to provoke debate and assist the Commission to tease out the law and any potential reform. Any submissions received on foot of these Papers are treated confidentially by the Commission.[26]

---

[22] Law Reform Commission Act 1975 s.4(2)(c).

[23] Law Reform Commission, *Report on Domicile and Habitual Residence as Connecting Factors in the Conflict of Laws* (LRC 7-1983), p.1.

[24] Law Reform Commission, *Report on Mandatory Sentences* (LRC 108-2013), paras 1–2.

[25] For details of all Attorney General requests and the reports that have resulted from the investigations, see further: *http://www.lawreform.ie/Attorney_General_References/Default.246.html*.

[26] For further details on current projects and the current calls for consultation, see: *https://www.lawreform.ie/press-room.7.html*.

8–15 The next stage at which the Commission solicits feedback is when the Consultation Paper is published. A Consultation Paper usually contains a detailed summary of the Irish law on the area. It also examines the relevant law from other jurisdictions to assess how the practice there compares to the law in Ireland. This can include an analysis of any reform, or proposed reform, of the law in those jurisdictions. Finally, the Consultation Paper includes provisional proposals for reform of Irish law. Once the Consultation Paper is published, comments and feedback are welcomed and the Commission issues a call for public consultation, inviting written submissions on all aspects of the Paper. These submissions are then considered by the Commission and the results of the consultation process inform the development of the final Report. The final stage is the publication of the Law Reform Commission Report. This Report contains the Commission's final conclusions at the end of this extensive period of research, consultation and reflection. It contains the summary of recommended reforms the Commission has to offer in the area and often will contain draft legislation.

8–16 It is clear that public consultation is central to the work of the Law Reform Commission and it engages the public at a variety of stages in its processes. Such consultation is neither an example of direct democracy nor deliberate democracy but it does aim to capture public sentiment on the issues that the Law Reform Commission considers. North identifies five advantages to the inclusion of extensive public consultation in the process of developing suggestions for law reform.[27] These are: (1) the gathering of factual evidence; (2) the provision of technical advice and critiques of current and proposed reforms from both experts and lay people directly affected by the area of law; (3) the promotion of democracy by enabling the community to "feel involved" in the law reform process; (4) the reformer is enabled to gauge the weight of public opinion on social issues raised by particular projects; and (5) it "flushes out" the identity and opinions of potential opponents to the reform so that opposition can be "neutralized".[28]

---

[27] P. North, "Law Reform: Problems and Pitfalls" (1999–2000) 33(1) *University of British Columbia Law Review* 37.

[28] P. North, "Law Reform: Problems and Pitfalls" (1999–2000) 33(1) *University of British Columbia Law Review* 37 at 39–40.

8–17 North recognises that not all these advantages are wholly "respectable", particularly in the context of the "neutralization" of opposition.[29] Yet, for any reform suggestion to become law, it will have to endure the legislative process. If all potential opponents have become partners in ensuring the law is successfully passed, this process will be considerably easier.

8–18 Biribonwoha considers the role that legislative drafters have to play in the law reform process.[30] He notes that, ordinarily, the drafter of proposed legislation only receives instructions after the policy underpinning the law has been agreed. By the time the drafter gets involved, those who have prepared the policy have moved on to new projects and are no longer immersed in this issue. Consequently, he cautions that certain aspects of the proposed reform might not be realised, either because the drafter does not fully understand exactly what the reformer wishes to achieve, or because the proposed reform might not be possible in that exact way due to some other technical hindrance the reformer had not considered. While it is not the job of legislative drafters to determine the policy-making aspects of law reform, Biribonwoha suggests that their particular skillset would be most useful in helping law reformers achieve their vision. Thus, he recommends that those with expertise in legislative drafting should be included at an earlier stage in the law reform process so that the draft legislation that law reform commissions produce is accepted, unchanged, by governments.

8–19 The final aspect of interest in relation to the Law Reform Commission is its Implementation Table.[31] Here it tracks the impact of the proposed reforms. In a simple table, it notes the name of the report, the summary of recommendations, whether any draft legislation was included in the report and any information on implementation. This table details exactly which aspects of the recommendations have been implemented (and the relevant statutory provisions that contain the reform) or are being considered (and notes the body that has the recommendation under

[29] P. North, "Law Reform: Problems and Pitfalls" (1999–2000) 33(1) *University of British Columbia Law Review* 37 at 40.

[30] P.P. Biribonwoha, "The Role of Legislative Drafting in the Law Reform Process" (2006) 32(4) *Commonwealth Law Bulletin* 601.

[31] Available at: *http://www.lawreform.ie/publications/table-of-implementation-of-law-reform-commission-recommendations.171.html*.

consideration). So it is easy to trace how successful the Commission has been in bringing about reform of the law. In this regard, many proposals were eventually adopted, albeit, on occasion, some time after the recommendations of the Commission were made. For example, in 2006 the Commission published its *Report on Vulnerable Adults and the Law*.[32] It took nine years for some of these recommendations to be implemented into legislation, with the passage in December 2015 of the Assisted Decision-Making (Capacity) Act 2015. An even longer delay in implementing some of the Commission's recommendations was evident in the field of property and conveyancing law. The Commission had issued several reports on various aspects of land and conveyancing law from 1991 onwards.[33] Some of these recommendations were not implemented, while those that were came into effect with the Land and Conveyancing Law Reform Act 2009.

4. Reports of Tribunals of Inquiry

8–20 Tribunals of inquiry are established on a statutory basis to investigate matters of public concern. As discussed in Ch.10,[34] these public inquiries are formed under the terms of the Tribunals of Inquiry (Evidence) Acts 1921–2011. Such public inquiries are established on an ad hoc basis, as the need arises for some instance to be investigated. As Hardiman and Scott note, these tribunals are "investigatory bodies set up to examine policy failures, shortcomings in executive functioning, or suspicion of political malpractice".[35]

8–21 As discussed in Ch.10, there have been tribunals of inquiry established to investigate all manner of events in Ireland. At the

[32] LRC 83-2006.

[33] See generally, *Report on Land Law and Conveyancing Law: (3) The Passing of Risk from Vendor to Purchaser* (LRC 39-1991); *Report on Land Law and Conveyancing Law: (4) Service of Completion Notices* (LRC 40-1991); *Report on Interests of Vendor and Purchaser in Land during the Period between Contract and Completion* (LRC 49-1995); *Report on the Rule against Perpetuities and Cognate Rules* (LRC 62-2000); *Report on the Variation of Trusts* (LRC 63-2000); *Report on the Acquisition of Easements by Prescription and Profits à Prendre* (LRC 66-2002); *Report on Land Law and Conveyancing Law: (7) Positive Covenants over Freehold Land and Other Proposals* (LRC 70-2003); *Report on Reform and Modernisation of Land Law and Conveyancing Law* (LRC 74-2005).

[34] Chapter 10, paras 10–29 to 10–39.

[35] N. Hardiman and C. Scott, "Governance as Polity: An Institutional Approach to the Evolution of State Functions in Ireland" (2010) 88(1) *Public Administration* 170 at 183.

conclusion of each tribunal, a report is published that details the findings of the tribunal and makes recommendations for legal change. Hogan and Morgan note that these recommendations are not binding on the Minister to whom the report is addressed, nor to any other responsible decision-making authority.[36] Nonetheless, the reports of tribunals of inquiry may, but are not guaranteed to, prompt reform of the law.

Box 8.1: Case Focus

The Tribunal of Inquiry into Certain Planning Matters and Payments (Mahon Tribunal)

This Tribunal has the distinction of being the longest running and most expensive public inquiry held in Ireland.[37] It was established in November 1997 to investigate allegations of corrupt payments to politicians in relation to issues surrounding planning permissions and land rezoning in Dublin County Council in the 1990s.[38] Its final report was published in March 2012.[39]

Originally chaired by Judge Fergus Flood (and known as the Flood Tribunal), when he retired, he was replaced by Judge Alan Mahon as chair. Judges Mary Faherty and Gerald Keys were added to the Tribunal to support its work. The Tribunal organised its activities into 11 modules to facilitate investigation.

The Final Report contained 64 different recommendations, which were broadly divided into seven different areas: planning; conflicts of interest; political finance; lobbying; bribery, corruption in office, money laundering and the misuse of confidential information; asset recovery; and miscellaneous matters.[40] In response to these recommendations, the Department of the Environment, Community and Local Government published a detailed document outlining how it would respond to each of the suggestions made.[41] Some of these responses were already

[36] G. Hogan, D.G. Morgan and P. Daly, *Administrative Law in Ireland*, 5th edn (Dublin: Round Hall, 2019), para.8–02.

[37] It was reported in the *Irish Times* in August 2014 that the Tribunal cost €159 million (€100 million less than had been previously reported). See O. Kelly, "6,000 social housing units to be provided this year", *Irish Times*, 14 August 2014.

[38] Resolution of Dáil Éireann, passed on 7 October 1997; 481 *Dáil Debates* (7 October 1997).

[39] *Final Report of the Tribunal of Inquiry into Certain Planning Matters and Payments* (Dublin: Stationery Office, 2012), available at: *https://www.planningtribunal.ie/reports/*.

[40] See above.

[41] Department of the Environment, Communications and Local Government, *Tribunal of Inquiry into Certain Planning Matters and Payments (Mahon Tribunal): Response to*

underway by the time of the publication of the Final Report, given the lengthy duration of the Tribunal.

Examples of some of the legislation that has been enacted containing reforms based on the recommendations of the Mahon Tribunal include the Electoral (Amendment) Act 2012, the Electoral (Amendment) (Political Funding) Act 2012, the Protected Disclosures Act 2014 and the Regulation of Lobbying Act 2015.

5. Constitutional Conventions and Citizens' Assemblies

8–22 In recent years a new type of formal law reform project has emerged. The Constitutional Convention and Citizens' Assemblies reflect Elster's observation that "[t]he idea of deliberative democracy, or decision making by discussion among free and equal citizens, is having a revival."[42] In many ways, the existence of these mechanisms is a reaction to the increased mistrust in politics and politicians and the rise in populism.[43] The OECD reports that between 2021 and 2023, 156 representative deliberative processes were initiated or completed in OECD and EU member states.[44]

8–23 The Constitutional Convention was established in 2012.[45] Members of the Convention included an independent chairperson, 33 publicly elected representatives (29 members of the Oireachtas and four members of the elected officials from Northern Ireland), and 66 members of the public, chosen at random by a polling company to ensure balanced representation of the electorate as regards age, gender and geographical location.[46] The Resolution establishing the Convention delegated to it a series of issues regarding potential constitutional reform to be explored

Final Report Recommendations, available at: *https://assets.gov.ie/132530/56376a00-4d49-41f6-8295-62aef46b9de1.pdf*.

42 J. Elster, "Introduction" in J. Elster (ed), *Deliberative Democracy* (Cambridge: Cambridge University Press, 1998), p.1.

43 E. Bertsou and D. Caramanai, "People Haven't Had Enough of Experts: Technocratic Attitudes Among Citizens in Nine European Democracies" (2022) 66(1) *American Journal of Political Science* 5.

44 OECD Deliberative Democracy Database (2023), available at: *https://airtable.com/appP4czQIAU1My2M3/shrX048tmQLI8yzdc*.

45 *https://citizensassembly.ie/previous-assemblies/2013-2014-convention-on-the-constitution/*.

46 Behaviours & Attitudes, "Constitutional Convention: Members of the Public Recruitment Process", available at: *https://citizensassembly.ie/wp-content/uploads/BehaviourAndAttitudes.pdf*.

in-depth.[47] These issues referred to the Convention covered a broad range of aspects of life and legal reform, specifically:

- the reduction of the Presidential term from 7 to 5 years and aligning elections with the local and European elections;
- the reduction of the voting age to 17 years;
- the review of the Dáil electoral system;
- enabling Irish citizens living abroad to vote in Presidential elections at local embassies;
- the introduction of same-sex marriage;
- amending the clause relating to women in the home and encouraging greater participation of women in public life;
- increasing the participation of women in politics;
- removing the offence of blasphemy from the Constitution;
- the Convention considered other amendments that had not been specifically referred to it, including:
  - Dáil reform, and
  - economic, social and cultural rights.

8–24 Over 18 months, the Convention considered these 10 issues in depth. Its deliberations resulted in some changes to the Constitution, including the introduction of marriage equality following the referendum on 22 May 2015.[48]

8–25 Despite being initially dismissed by some as a "charade",[49] focusing mostly on "inconsequential issues",[50] by the completion of its programme of work, the Convention was largely considered positively.[51]

[47] The resolution is available at: *https://citizensassembly.ie/wp-content/uploads/Terms_of_Reference.pdf.*

[48] Thirty-fourth Amendment of the Constitution (Marriage Equality) Act 2015.

[49] C. O'Mahony, "This So-called Constitutional Convention is a Charade", *Irish Times* (7 June 2012), available at: *https://www.irishtimes.com/opinion/this-so-called-constitutional-convention-is-a-charade-1.1064539.*

[50] C. O'Mahony, "This So-called Constitutional Convention is a Charade", *Irish Times* (7 June 2012).

[51] M. Wall, "Change we can believe in? Ireland's Constitutional Convention has delivered", *The Journal* (23 July 2013), available at: *http://www.thejournal.ie/readme/column-change-we-can-believe-in-ireland%E2%80%99s-constitutional-convention-has-delivered-1003278-Jul2013/*; D. Farrell, "The Irish Constitutional Convention offers a potential route-map for renewing UK democracy", *Democratic Audit UK* (10 October 2014), available at: *http://www.democraticaudit.com/?p=8625*; J. Suiter, D. Farrell, C. Harris and E. O'Malley, "People with Politicians: Innovations in Deliberative Democracy", Paper presented at ECPR General Conference, 3–6 September 2014; I.

8–26 The perceived success of the Convention is reflected in the establishment of various Citizens' Assemblies in the years since examining in detail the issues that have been referred to them for consideration.[52] Citizens' Assemblies differ from the Constitutional Convention in that they are made up of an independent chairperson and 99 members of the public chosen at random.[53] Thus, the public representatives who formed one-third of the membership of the Constitutional Convention no longer play a part. Like the Convention, Citizens' Assemblies are established on foot of a resolution of the Houses of the Oireachtas. Assemblies have considered matters as diverse as the Eighth Amendment of the Constitution,[54] fixed-term parliaments,[55] biodiversity,[56] gender equality[57] and whether there should be a directly elected mayor for Dublin.[58]

8–27 Walsh and Elkink report that 78 per cent of respondents in the 2020 Irish Election Study agreed or strongly agreed with the statement that "politics in Ireland would benefit from more Citizens' Assemblies".[59]

Bacik, "Can a Constitutional Convention Offer Real and Radical Change?", LSE Blog (15 December 2014), available at: *https://eprints.lse.ac.uk/83163/*.

52 See *https://citizensassembly.ie* for details of the work of each of the Citizens' Assemblies.

53 See Citizens' Assembly, "FAQ: What is a Citizens' Assembly?", available at: *https://citizensassembly.ie/faq/*.

54 Terms of Reference for the 2016–2018 Citizens' Assembly, available at: *https://citizensassembly.ie/overview-previous-assemblies/2016-2018-citizens-assembly/terms-of-reference/*. Ultimately this led to the Thirty-sixth Amendment of the Constitution Act 2018, which repealed and replaced the language in Article 40.3.3°. See discussion in Box 8.3 for more information. *https://www.referendum.ie/archive/referendum-on-the-regulation-of-termination-of-pregnancy-thirty-sixth-amendment-of-the-constitution-bill-2018/*.

55 Terms of Reference for the 2016–2018 Citizens' Assembly, available at: *https://citizensassembly.ie/overview-previous-assemblies/2016-2018-citizens-assembly/terms-of-reference/*.

56 Terms of Reference for the Citizens' Assembly on Biodiversity Loss, available at: *https://citizensassembly.ie/citizens-assembly-on-biodiversity-loss/terms-of-reference/*.

57 Terms of Reference for the Citizens' Assembly on Gender Equality, available at: *https://citizensassembly.ie/overview-previous-assemblies/assembly-on-gender-equality/terms-of-reference/*. The proposed Thirty-ninth and Fortieth Constitutional Referendums regarding the language of Article 41, which resulted from this report, were put to a public vote on 8 March 2024 and were defeated comprehensively. See further: *https://www.referendum.ie*.

58 Terms of Reference for the Dublin Citizens' Assembly, available at: *https://citizensassembly.ie/dublin-citizens-assembly/terms-of-reference/*. In 2024, the Local Government (Mayor of Limerick) and Miscellaneous Provisions Act 2024 was enacted. Following an election in June 2024, John Moran became Limerick's first directly-elected mayor.

59 C.D. Walsh and J.A. Elkink, "The Dissatisfied and the Engaged: Citizen Support for Citizens' Assemblies and Their Willingness to Participate" (2021) 36(4) *Irish Political Studies* 647 at 660.

Thus, it seems that this type of law reform mechanism will continue to feature in the Irish legal landscape.[60]

6. Court Mechanisms

8–28 One of the courts' functions is to interpret the law.[61] In carrying out this task, courts may also be asked to test the legality of the law. This can happen in two instances: (1) where a party before the courts argues that a particular legislative provision is contrary to the Constitution, and thus asks that it be declared unconstitutional, as was examined in Ch.3; or (2) where a party before the courts argues that a particular legal provision is incompatible with Ireland's obligations under the European Convention on Human Rights Act 2003, as was examined in Ch.6. In either case, should the court declare a law unconstitutional or incompatible, this may prompt reform of the law. That said, as will be discussed below, the response of the Oireachtas to such a declaration may depend on which declaration is handed down by the court and the importance of the issue at stake.

(a) Declaration of unconstitutionality

8–29 As the fundamental source of law in Ireland, all laws passed by the Oireachtas must be in accordance with the provisions of the Constitution. As discussed in Ch.3, there is a presumption that all laws passed by the Oireachtas are constitutional.[62] Furthermore, there is an obligation on the courts to interpret impugned sections of legislation as constitutional where this is reasonably possible.[63] However, where it is not reasonable to interpret a section of legislation as constitutional, the courts retain the authority to strike it down as unconstitutional.[64] This is a necessary aspect of the courts performing the checks-and-balances aspects of their duties under the separation of powers. Where a section of legislation has been declared unconstitutional by the courts, the effect of this is that it immediately gives rise to a lacuna (or gap) in the

---

[60] See further, T. Reidy and J. Suiter, "Direct and Deliberate Democracy" in J. Coakley, M. Gallagher, E. O'Malley and T. Reidy, *Politics in the Republic of Ireland*, 7th edn (Abingdon: Routledge, 2024), pp.204–210.

[61] See further discussion on the role of the courts in Ch.9, Sections A and B. See also Ch.4, Sections C–G inclusive, where the various statutory interpretation techniques that judges use to enable them to perform this function are described.

[62] See further, Ch.3, Section D.1.

[63] *McDonald v Bord na gCon* [1965] I.R. 217 at 239.

[64] Article 15.4 of the Constitution.

law.[65] This gap occurs as the law that is found to be unconstitutional is considered instantly invalid and, furthermore, it is acknowledged never to have been valid.[66] Therefore, this gap will need to be filled, which is where the prompt for law reform emerges. Most regularly, this will require the introduction of new legislation that directly addresses the troublesome issue identified by the courts.

Box 8.2: Case Focus

***NHV v Minister for Justice and Equality* [2017] IESC 35**

The appellant in this case was a Burmese Rohingya asylum seeker who had been living in Direct Provision in Ireland for eight years by the time the judgment was handed down. He argued that the ban on asylum seekers in Ireland working until their application for asylum had been assessed (contained in s.9(4) of the Refugee Act 1996) was unconstitutional as it contravened the right to work, an unenumerated right under Article 40.3.

In his judgment, O'Donnell J. notes the comments by Hogan J. in the Court of Appeal that the existence of a right to work had long been established in Irish law.[67] In explaining the applicability of this right, O'Donnell J. determined that this was not an enforceable obligation, but rather a freedom to seek work, which could not be infringed without "substantial justification".[68]

In assessing whether s.9(4) of the Refugee Act 1996 amounted to such a substantial justification, the court held that "work is connected to the dignity and freedom of the individual which the Preamble tells us the Constitution seeks to promote".[69] Therefore, the court concluded that freedom to work, or seek work, is an inherent part of human personality which under Article 40.1 must be extended equally to both citizens and non-citizens.[70]

Nonetheless, the court recognised that there may be instances where it would be legitimate to distinguish between citizens and non-citizens and to limit the exercise of the right for non-citizens.[71] Considering s.9(4) in this light, O'Donnell J. found that it "does not merely limit the right

65 G. Hogan, G. Whyte, D. Kenny and R. Walsh, *Kelly: The Irish Constitution*, 5th edn (Dublin: Bloomsbury Professional, 2018), paras 4.5.28–4.5.29.

66 *Murphy v Attorney General* [1982] I.R. 241. However, on important qualifications to this principle, see Ch.3, Section D.5.

67 [2017] IESC 35 at para.12.

68 [2017] IESC 35 at para.12.

69 [2017] IESC 35 at para.15.

70 [2017] IESC 35 at para.17.

71 [2017] IESC 35 at para.18.

severely: it removes it altogether."[72] The absence of a time limit after which an asylum seeker would be permitted to seek work, notwithstanding the fact that a determination of their application had not yet been made, was the central point grounding this finding.[73] Thus, the court found that "in principle"[74] s.9(4) of the Refugee Act 1996 was unconstitutional.

From a practical perspective, the court delayed activation of the declaration to enable the State to consider its decision, and to put in place a framework for protection applicants to enter employment.[75] Subsequently, the Supreme Court provided a short additional period of time for the State to put in place necessary measures to give effect to the declaration of unconstitutionality.[76] On 9 February 2018, the legislative measures prohibiting protection applicants from entering employment in Ireland were formally declared unconstitutional.

The State responded by opting into and implementing the Recast EU Reception Directive in July 2018.[77] Thus, asylum seekers, including those under the age of 18,[78] may now be provided with labour market access if they have not received a first-instance decision on their claim after nine months,[79] through no fault of their own.[80]

(b) Declaration of incompatibility

8–30 The possibility of issuing a declaration of incompatibility is to be found in s.5 of the European Convention on Human Rights Act 2003 (the

---

72 [2017] IESC 35 at para.19.

73 [2017] IESC 35 at para.19.

74 [2017] IESC 35 at para.11.

75 On the issue of suspended declarations of unconstitutionality, see E. Carolan, "A 'Dialogue-Oriented Departure' in Constitutional Remedies? The Implications of NHV v Minister for Justice for Inter-Branch Roles and Relationships" (2017) 40(1) *Dublin University Law Journal* 191.

76 See *NHV v Minister for Justice and Equality* [2017] IESC 82. The Supreme Court stated, at para.7 of this judgment, that "the Court feels that the balance of justice would be met by affording a relatively brief period to the State to, as it were, take whatever measures it considers necessary prior to a declaration of inconsistency with the Constitution being made. But the Court would wish strongly to emphasise that what is envisaged is not that there will be any further hearing, sitting, consideration of submissions, receipt of letters or the like. What follows is simply an indication of what the Court will do."

77 European Communities (Reception Conditions) Regulations 2018 (S.I. No. 230 of 2018).

78 European Communities (Reception Conditions) Regulations 2018 (S.I. No. 230 of 2018), reg.16.

79 European Communities (Reception Conditions) Regulations 2018 (S.I. No. 230 of 2018), reg.11(4)(a).

80 European Communities (Reception Conditions) Regulations 2018 (S.I. No. 230 of 2018), reg.11(4)(b).

"2003 Act").[81] Unlike the declaration of unconstitutionality, a declaration of incompatibility does not render a legislative provision void. Rather, it identifies to the Oireachtas that there is a piece of legislation that needs revision, or an area of law on which the Oireachtas needs to legislate for the first time. The manner in which the 2003 Act incorporates the European Convention on Human Rights (the "Convention") into Irish law ensures that the declaration of incompatibility will be the remedy of "last resort".[82] First, the 2003 Act requires that the courts interpret legislation in a manner compatible with the State's obligations under the Convention.[83] Second, the 2003 Act requires all organs of the State to carry out their duties in a Convention-compliant manner.[84] Finally, it is only when a human rights violation has been identified that is impossible to remedy using any other legal mechanism that a court can issue a declaration of incompatibility under s.5 of the 2003 Act.

8–31 The first declaration of incompatibility issued arose out of the *Foy v An tArd Chláraitheoir*[85] cases that we considered in Ch.7.[86] However, as de Londras notes, the declaration of incompatibility is intended to prompt a political and not a legal resolution to the difficulty identified.[87] Accordingly, there is no urgency surrounding a declaration of incompatibility, which means that the incompatibility is resolved at the leisure of the legislature. For example, the declaration of incompatibility that was handed down on 14 February 2008 following *Foy v An tArd Chláraitheoir (No. 2)*[88] took over seven years to be resolved with the enactment and commencement of the Gender Recognition Act 2015 on 8 September 2015.[89] Accordingly, de Londras is critical of the declaration

---

81 Previously discussed in Ch.6, para.6–97. For a full review of the 2003 Act and a discussion of its utilisation in Irish courts, including discussion on the limits of the 2003 Act, see S. Kingston and L. Thornton, *A Report on the European Convention on Human Rights Act 2003 and the European Charter of Fundamental Rights: Evaluation and Review* (Dublin: Law Society of Ireland, 2015).

82 F. de Londras, "Declarations of Incompatibility under the ECHR Act 2003: A Workable Transplant?" (2014) 35(1) *Statute Law Review* 50 at 61.

83 European Convention on Human Rights Act 2003 s.2.

84 European Convention on Human Rights Act 2003 s.3.

85 *Foy v An tArd Chláraitheoir (No. 1)* [2002] IEHC 116; *Foy v An tArd Chláraitheoir (No. 2)* [2007] IEHC 470.

86 Chapter 7, Section E.

87 F. de Londras, "Declarations of Incompatibility under the ECHR Act 2003: A Workable Transplant?" (2014) 35(1) *Statute Law Review* 50 at 53–54.

88 [2007] IEHC 470.

89 See also, Ch.6, para.6–94.

of incompatibility, yet such a declaration can nonetheless provide the impetus for change. Again, the *Foy* series of litigation is illustrative. Where there is a delay by the State in responding to a declaration, the instigation of further proceedings querying the persistence of the delayed response to the declaration can prompt political action.[90] Thus, while it may take some time, the declaration of incompatibility can ultimately prompt law reform.

(c) Decisions from non-domestic courts

8–32 Decisions of both the Court of Justice of the European Union (CJEU)[91] and the European Court of Human Rights (ECtHR)[92] can also prompt reform of the law in Ireland. As already discussed in previous chapters,[93] the law of the European Union (EU) ranks above that of the domestic legal framework in specified areas of competence. For example, on 16 July 2009 in *Commission of the European Communities v Ireland*,[94] the Court of Justice held that Ireland had failed to implement EU VAT legislation contained in Directive 2006/112/EC in relation to State and local authorities. The case came to the attention of the Commission following a complaint from the operator of a private car park adjacent to a local authority car park. The local authority car park did not have to impose a VAT levy of 21.5 per cent, which had to be imposed on customers by the private car park operator. This permitted the local authority to gain a clear competitive advantage. In April 2010, the law was reformed to ensure that the State would be considered a "taxable person" where failure to do so "would likely create a significant distortion of competition".[95] By contrast, the impetus to implement a ruling from the ECtHR is less pressing. For example, in 1988, prior to the introduction of the European Convention on Human Rights Act in 2003, in the *Norris* case[96] the ECtHR ruled that the continued criminalisation of homosexual activity between consenting male adults amounted to a violation of Article 8 of the Convention, which concerns respect for

[90] I. Bacik, "Commentary on *Foy v An tArd Chláraitheoir*" in M. Enright, J. McCandless and A. O'Donoghue (eds), *Northern/Irish Feminist Judgments: Judges' Troubles and the Gendered Politics of Identity* (Oxford: Hart, 2017), Ch.29.

[91] Chapter 6, Section B.4.

[92] Chapter 6, paras 6–86 and 6–91.

[93] See Ch.2, paras 2–29 to 2–30; Ch.3, para.3–81; and Ch.6, Section C.

[94] (C-554/07) [2009] E.C.R. I-00128.

[95] Finance Act 2010 s.117(1)(b).

[96] *Norris v Ireland* (1991) 13 E.H.R.R. 186.

privacy. It was not until 1993 that the law was finally reformed when the Criminal Law (Sexual Offences) Act 1993 was introduced some five years after the decision was handed down.[97] Comparing the responses of the Government to each court ruling, it is clear that decisions of the CJEU have a much more profound and immediate impact on reform of the law than those from the ECtHR.

7. Referendums

8–33 As the primary source of law in the State, any amendment to the Constitution necessarily reforms the law. Referendums have been considered at length in Ch.3 on the Constitution.[98] Once the text of the Constitution has been altered, then the law has also changed. This may require the introduction of legislation to ensure that any new incompatibilities between the Constitution as amended and the existing law are erased. For example, prior to 2015, the institution of civil marriage was confined to those in heterosexual relationships. The successful passage of the Thirty-fourth Amendment of the Constitution on Marriage Equality required the introduction of legislation—the Marriage Act 2015. Consequently, civil marriage is now available to all couples regardless of their sexual orientation.

C. Informal Mechanisms

8–34 Having considered the formal mechanisms by which the law is reformed, this chapter now turns to an examination of the less clearly defined ways by which the Oireachtas becomes seized with the importance of introducing legislative change. This is sometimes described, at least by lawyers and the lawyerly-minded, as public interest law. Public interest law originated in the United States in the 1960s.[99] Public interest law is not a subset of law—such as social welfare law, company law, banking law—but rather is a way to describe utilising law

[97] S. Kingston and L. Thornton, *A Report on the Application of the European Convention on Human Rights Act 2003 and the European Charter of Fundamental Rights: Evaluation and Review* (Dublin: Law Society, 2015), pp.25–28, Table 2.1., outlines the measures taken (or not) by Ireland to ensure compliance with decisions of the ECtHR.

[98] See further, Ch.3, Section E.1.

[99] For a discussion of public interest law in the United States, see C.R. Halpern, "Public Interest Law: Its Past and Future" (1974) 58(3) *Judicature* 118, and A. Southworth, "Conservative Lawyers and the Contest Over the Meaning of 'Public Interest Law'" (2005) 52 *UCLA Law Review* 1123.

as one of many tools to advance the civil, political, economic, social and cultural rights of those who are, in some way, excluded from society.[100] Litigation is but one strategy that may be used within public interest law. Political lobbying and building mass movements for social change are an inherent part of lawyering in the public interest.[101] Whyte notes that, ideally, pressing social issues for minority groups in Irish society should be progressed through the political system rather than the courts.[102] But political realities mean that advocating on behalf of marginalised (and oft-maligned) groups within Irish society may win little public support at the ballot box. However, many lawyers may be wary of viewing law as a political means of changing society. Often, it is activists and societal advocates who push issues onto the legal and/or political agenda. As Gordon, although focusing on the United States, notes:

> "Until very recent times, elite lawyers (with a few exceptions like the antislavery lawyers) left the defense of pariahs, dissenters, and subordinate groups to lawyers at the fringes of the profession—Jews, Communists, blacks, women. It has only been after those activists succeeded in promoting a rights revolution, supported by the highest precincts of the judiciary, that the respectable bar embraced their causes."[103]

With these issues in mind, we now consider informal mechanisms for prompting law reform, including advocacy, activism and strategic litigation.

1. Advocacy/Activism

8–35 The most common way by which people attempt to engage in law reform is through advocacy and/or activism. This can take many forms, including signing petitions, attending public meetings, letter writing, protest and formal lobbying of politicians in an attempt to change the law. Often people will coalesce around a particular issue—the introduction

[100] See C. Harlow, "Public Law and Popular Justice" (2002) 65(1) *Modern Law Review* 1.
[101] H.J. McCammon and A.R. McGrath, "Litigating Change? Social Movements and the Court System" (2015) 9(2) *Sociology Compass* 128.
[102] G. Whyte, *Social Inclusion and the Law: Public Interest Law in Ireland*, 2nd edn (Dublin: IPA, 2015), p.1.
[103] R.W. Gordon, "The Role of Lawyers in Producing the Rule of Law: Some Critical Reflections" (2010) 11 *Theoretical Inquiries in Law* 441 at 456.

of water charges being a good example—and mobilise in a number of different ways to try to encourage politicians to change the law in the way that a particular group wishes. Engaging in advocacy and activism can be a long and thankless process, with no guarantee of legal change at its conclusion. Furthermore, where the law does change, it may cause other unexpected issues to be raised such that the campaign continues and/or counter campaigns are launched. The most infamous example of the (un)intended consequences that followed a legal reform in Ireland was the inclusion of the Eighth Amendment in the Constitution in 1983.

Box 8.3: Issue Focus
The Abortion Issue in Ireland

Abortion was outlawed in Ireland under the Offences against the Person Act 1861 (the "1861 Act"). Sections 58 and 59 of the 1861 Act criminalised those who procured a miscarriage or those who assisted with procuring a miscarriage. This pre-independence legislation was carried over by Article 50 to become part of Irish law by the 1937 Constitution.

When introduced, ss.58 and 59 were also the law in England and Wales. This changed in 1967 when the Abortion Act 1967 was introduced. While the enactment of the English law did not change the law in Ireland, the effect of its introduction was felt here. Irish women could now travel to England to avail of safe and lawful abortions.[104] This growing trend towards the liberalisation of abortion laws caused people in Ireland to fear that Ireland might also follow suit.[105]

A case, *McGee v Attorney General*,[106] on a seemingly unrelated issue of the availability of contraception for use by married people, caused disquiet in relation to abortion in Ireland. In this case, the Supreme Court found that the right to privacy included a right to marital privacy, which enabled married couples to control the number and spacing of their children through the use of contraception. The unease surrounding *McGee* was amplified as the US Supreme Court ruled in *Roe v Wade*[107] that the right to privacy under the Due Process Clause of the 14th Amendment to the US Constitution extended to a woman's decision to have an abortion. Thus, there was a concern that abortion might

[104] J.A. Quinlan, "The Right to Life of the Unborn—An Assessment of the Eighth Amendment to the Irish Constitution" (1984) *Brigham Young University Law Journal* 371 at 377.

[105] See above.

[106] [1974] I.R. 284.

[107] 410 U.S. 113 (1973). Since overturned in *Dobbs v Jackson Women's Health Organization* 597 U.S. 215 (2022).

become legal in Ireland as a result of judicial interpretation. This concern was heightened due to the absence of specific constitutional protection for the unborn child.

As a result, a campaign began to amend the Constitution to prevent against abortion by explicitly ensuring that the right to life of the unborn child was protected in the text of the Constitution. On 27 April 1981, the Pro-Life Amendment Campaign was established to push for constitutional recognition of the right to life of the unborn.[108] As a referendum proposal can only be put to the people following a resolution of the Oireachtas, the campaign focused on the members of the Oireachtas. This was strengthened as a general election was called just six weeks later, ensuring that the abortion issue became part of the election rhetoric.[109] The campaign leading up to the referendum proposal, and the referendum campaign itself, was hugely divisive.[110] Eventually, the Eighth Amendment was passed, with 67 per cent of those voting in favour of the amendment. The wording inserted into the Constitution had been criticised as being too uncertain, which would create difficulty in future potential cases.[111] Among those raising concerns was the then Attorney General, Peter Sutherland, who noted that it could have "unforeseeable and perhaps undesirable consequences, and which could set an unfortunate precedent in other areas and ultimately even provide a means whereby the fundamental rights guaranteed in our Constitution could be undermined."[112] This proved to be prescient, with a series of cases that illuminated some of these difficulties, commencing with *Attorney General v X*.[113]

The *X* case concerned a 14-year-old girl who had been raped by a family friend and became pregnant as a result. She wished to travel to England to undergo an abortion and when this became known to the authorities investigating her rape, the Attorney General petitioned the High Court for an injunction preventing her travel by way of protecting the right to life of her unborn child. The injunction was granted by the

[108] J.A. Quinlan, "The Right to Life of the Unborn—An Assessment of the Eighth Amendment to the Irish Constitution" (1984) *Brigham Young University Law Journal* 371 at 383.

[109] J.A. Quinlan, "The Right to Life of the Unborn—An Assessment of the Eighth Amendment to the Irish Constitution" (1984) *Brigham Young University Law Journal* 371 at 384.

[110] T. Hesketh, *The Second Partitioning of Ireland? The Abortion Referendum 1983* (Dublin: Brandsma Books, 1990), p.386.

[111] T. Hesketh, *The Second Partitioning of Ireland? The Abortion Referendum 1983* (Dublin: Brandsma Books, 1990), p.388.

[112] P. Sutherland, Memoranda of Attorney General Peter Sutherland to Government of 15 February 1983 and 1 March 1983 (National Archives Ref 2013/100/557-569).

[113] [1992] 1 I.R. 1.

High Court. X appealed to the Supreme Court to have the injunction lifted. Counsel for X argued that the wording of the amendment required the court to balance the right to life of the unborn with the equal right to life of the mother. In this case, the mother was herself a child and was threatening suicide if she was refused the right to travel to access a treatment lawfully available in another jurisdiction. Finlay C.J. stated: "if it can be established as a matter of probability that there is a real and substantial risk to the life, as distinct from the health, of the mother, which can only be avoided by the termination of her pregnancy, such termination is permissible."[114] On this basis, the Supreme Court ruled that the injunction should be lifted.

That the Eighth Amendment could be interpreted in this way was certainly not something that those who had advocated for its inclusion had intended. Such was the consternation that the *X* case caused, that it resulted in three further constitutional referendums related to the abortion issue. The Twelfth Amendment to remove the exception for cases of suicide identified in the *X* case was defeated, but both the Thirteenth Amendment (on the right to travel) and the Fourteenth Amendment (on the right to distribute information relating to abortion services) were both accepted by the people. Once again, these referendums took place at a politically sensitive time, on the same day as a general election on 25 November 1992.

The next high-profile case to arise out of the Eighth Amendment and the interpretation given to it in the *X* case was *A and B v Eastern Health Board and C.*[115] In this case, a 13-year-old rape victim became pregnant and was in the care of the State. The agency responsible for her care, the Eastern Health Board, applied for and received permission from the District Court to enable C to travel to England for an abortion. C's parents, who had initially been supportive, appealed to the High Court to overturn the District Court decision. Similar to the *X* case, this case turned on the suicidality of C and, consequently, Geoghegan J. ruled that the real and substantial risk to her life entitled the Health Board to facilitate her travel.

Following the *C* case, an extensive review of the law was undertaken and the Interdepartmental Working Group on the issue reverted with seven different reform proposals.[116] Some years later, in 2002, another attempt to remove by referendum the suicide exception by means of the Twenty-fifth Amendment was again rejected. Five years later, in 2007,

[114] [1992] 1 I.R. 1 at 62.

[115] [1998] I.L.R.M. 464.

[116] Interdepartmental Working Group, *Green Paper on Abortion* (Dublin: Stationery Office, 1996).

the abortion issue came before the courts again.[117] Ms D was a 17-year-old girl in the care of the State who had an anencephalic pregnancy.[118] As a result, she sought permission from the Health Service Executive to travel to England to avail of an abortion. The High Court confirmed her right to travel, notwithstanding her position as a ward of the State.

Following the ruling of the European Court of Human Rights in *A, B and C v Ireland* in 2010,[119] the abortion issue came back on the political agenda. In *A, B and C* it was determined that where a woman's pregnancy posed a real and substantial threat to her life, the failure to provide access to a legal abortion within the country violated that woman's right to respect for her private and family life under Article 8 of the European Convention on Human Rights. The Government established an Expert Group to advise on how best to legislate to permit abortions to be carried out in Ireland within the limits of the *X* case precedent. This Group reported in November 2012.[120] Just prior to the publication of the report, yet another scandal ignited the public debate on abortion anew. Savita Halappanavar died in University Hospital Galway as a result of complications due to a miscarriage. The spark that caused the explosion of public outrage was the revelation that she had requested and had been denied a potentially life-saving termination procedure, which in the circumstances could have been lawful.[121]

It was in this highly charged atmosphere that the debates surrounding the passage of the Protection of Life During Pregnancy Act 2013 (the "2013 Act") took place. The 2013 Act outlined the circumstances when it would be legal to perform an abortion in Ireland. It restricted the availability of terminations in Ireland to situations when the life of the mother was imperilled. The 2013 Act did account for instances where the mother was suicidal but did not make provision for occasions where the unborn suffered from a fatal foetal abnormality, or where the pregnancy resulted from rape or incest. The inclusion of suicidality and the exclusion of the latter two factors was hugely controversial.[122]

117 *D (A Minor) v District Judge Brennan*, unreported, High Court, McKechnie J., 9 May 2007.

118 Anencephaly is the absence of a major portion of the brain, skull and scalp that occurs during embryonic development. Rarely do infants with this condition survive long after birth.

119 (2011) 53 E.H.R.R. 13.

120 *Report of the Expert Group on the Judgment in* A, B and C v Ireland (Dublin: Department of Health and Children, November 2012).

121 See R. Fletcher, "Silences: Irish Women and Abortion" (1995) 50(1) *Feminist Review* 44; J. Schweppe (ed.), *The Unborn Child, Article 40.3.3 and Abortion in Ireland: Twenty-five Years of Protection?* (Dublin: Liffey Press, 2008); M. Berer, "Termination of pregnancy as emergency obstetric care: the interpretation of Catholic health policy and the consequences for pregnant women. An analysis of the death of Savita Halappanavar in Ireland and similar cases" (2013) 21(41) *Reproductive Health Matters* 9.

122 R. Fletcher, "Contesting the cruel treatment of abortion-seeking women" (2014) 22(44) *Reproductive Health Matters* 10.

Since the enactment of the 2013 Act, the persistent lack of clarity as regards abortion became evident in the context of the treatment of NP.[123] NP was a woman who suffered brain death while pregnant. Against the wishes of her family, her doctors took the view that she ought to be kept artificially alive until her unborn baby could be successfully delivered. Her family brought proceedings to have the life-support treatment removed so that they could lay NP to rest. The High Court ruled in favour of the family and ordered the removal of the treatment.[124]

Since the introduction of the Eighth Amendment of the Constitution, much of the law reform in the context of abortion has resulted from moments of crisis—either a need to respond to a current pregnancy, with the resultant time pressures as in the *X*, *C*, and *D* cases, or heightened glare of publicity, scrutiny and outrage which cases like that of Savita Halappanavar created. Aside from these pivotal points of intense public pressure, the Eighth Amendment fulfilled the predictions of the Attorney General at the time of its introduction, Peter Sutherland, and introduced an uncertain and practically unusable position to Irish law.[125] Fletcher described the daily reality of life under the Eighth Amendment as "unlivable".[126] It overshadowed all pregnant people in Ireland, the healthcare professionals who cared for them, and the lawyers for the health service. It was felt most acutely by pregnant people who were forced to leave Ireland to access abortion services abroad.[127]

Following examination of the issue by the 2016–2018 Citizens' Assembly, a recommendation was made that the Eighth Amendment be replaced in order to enable the Oireachtas to legislate for termination of pregnancy.[128] This resulted in a close consideration of the matter by a special Joint Oireachtas Committee on the Eighth Amendment of the Constitution, who in addition to seeking its own legal advice, held public hearings including evidence from legal and health experts and ultimately

---

123 *PP v Health Service Executive* [2014] IEHC 622.

124 For a detailed analysis of the case, see A. Mulligan, "Maternal brain death and legal protection of the foetus in Ireland" (2015) 15 *Medical Law International* 182.

125 P. Sutherland, Memoranda of Attorney General Peter Sutherland to Government of 15 February 1983 and 1 March 1983 (National Archives Ref 2013/100/557-569).

126 R. Fletcher, "Making Law Liveable: Bringing Feminist Knowledge of Care into the Curriculum", Revaluing Care Research Network, 25 February 2015, quoted in M. Enright et al., "Abortion Law Reform in Ireland: A Model for Change" (2015) 5(1) *feminists@law* 1 at 3.

127 J. Mishtal, G. Zanani, S De Zordo, D. Clougher and C. Gerdts, "'To be vigilant to leave no trace': secrecy, invisibility and abortion travel from the Republic of Ireland" (2023) 25(7) *Culture, Health & Sexuality* 914.

128 2016–2018 Citizens' Assembly, *First Report and Recommendations of the Citizens' Assembly: The Eighth Amendment of the Constitution* (Dublin: Stationery Office, 2017), available at: *https://citizensassembly.ie/wp-content/uploads/2023/02/FirstReport_EIGHTAMENDMENT.pdf.*

recommended a simple repeal of the existing provision.[129] Ultimately, this led to a need for yet another referendum on the matter.

In 2018, a referendum resulted in the Thirty-sixth Amendment of the Constitution which repealed the Eighth Amendment and replaced it with other language on the issue of abortion. The language of the relevant constitutional section, 40.3.3°, had read as follows:

> "The State acknowledges the right to life of the unborn and, with due regard to the equal right to life of the mother, guarantees in its laws to respect, and, as far as practicable, by its laws to defend and vindicate that right.[130]
> This subsection shall not limit freedom to travel between the State and another state.[131]
> This subsection shall not limit freedom to obtain or make available, in the State, subject to such conditions as may be laid down by law, information relating to services lawfully available in another state."[132]

As a result of the Thirty-sixth Amendment, Article 40.3.3° of the Constitution now reads:

> "Provision may be made by law for the regulation of termination of pregnancy."

Therefore, the Oireachtas was empowered to legislate for abortion. Thus, the Health (Regulation of Termination of Pregnancy) Act 2018 (the "2018 Act") was introduced. In general, the 2018 Act maintains the previous position that abortion is a crime and it is, under s.23, an offence punishable by a fine or imprisonment of up to 14 years to intentionally end the life of a foetus outside the provisions of the Act.[133] The 2018 Act outlines four exceptions where abortion would be permissible:

1. where, following medical examination, two medical practitioners certify that there is a serious risk to the life or of serious harm to the health of a pregnant person (s.9 of the 2018 Act);

[129] Joint Oireachtas Committee on the Eighth Amendment of the Constitution, *Report of the Joint Committee on the Eighth Amendment of the Constitution* (Dublin: Houses of the Oireachtas, 2017), available at: *https://opac.oireachtas.ie/AWData/Library3/Report_of_the_Joint_Committee_on_the_Eighth_Amendment_web_version_091929.pdf.*

[130] Clause inserted into the Constitution following the Eighth Amendment in 1983.

[131] Clause inserted following the Thirteenth Amendment in 1992.

[132] Clause inserted following the Fourteenth Amendment in 1992.

[133] See further, F. de Londras, "'A Hope Raised and then Defeated'? The Continuing Harms of Irish Abortion Law" (2020) 124(1) *Feminist Review* 33.

2. where, following an examination by one medical practitioner, in cases of emergency, there is an immediate serious risk to the life of a pregnant person or of serious harm to their health (s.10 of the 2018 Act);
3. where two medical practitioners are of the opinion, formed in good faith, that there is present a condition affecting the foetus that is likely to lead to the death of the foetus either before, or within 28 days of, birth (s.11 of the 2018 Act);
4. where there has been a period of three days following a certification that the pregnancy has not exceeded 12 weeks (s.12 of the 2018 Act).

De Londras argues that the 2018 Act maintains the "foetocentric" approach to the regulation of abortion first adopted in Irish law following the introduction of the Eighth Amendment in 1983.[134] Notwithstanding the introduction of the 2018 Act, Irish law continues to construe abortion as an exceptional occurrence. It is an instance where the constitutional rights of pregnant people to make decisions about their bodies are limited.[135] As Enright notes, the 2018 Act establishes medical professionals as gatekeepers of the rights of pregnant people. It places upon the judgment of medical professionals the weight of determining whether a pregnant person "qualifies" for an abortion.[136]

The issue of abortion is, and has always been, divisive. In response to the US Supreme Court decision in *Dobbs v Jackson Women's Health Organization* to reverse *Roe v Wade*, in March 2024, the French Senate voted to include an explicit right to abortion within the text of Article 34 of the French Constitution.[137] The story of the evolution of law on this matter in Ireland directly reflects the impact of advocacy and activism. It demonstrates the power of the public to demand and achieve legal change, whether at the constitutional or legislative level.[138]

134 F. de Londras, "'A Hope Raised and then Defeated'? The Continuing Harms of Irish Abortion Law" (2020) 124(1) *Feminist Review* 33.

135 F. de Londras and M. Enright, *Repealing the 8th: Reforming Irish Abortion Law* (Bristol: Policy Press, 2018).

136 M. Enright, "Abortion Law in Ireland: Reflecting on Reform" in L. Black and P. Dunne (eds), *Law and Gender in Modern Ireland: Critique and Reform* (Oxford: Hart Publishing, 2019), pp.73–89.

137 S. Lecocq and G. Fuentes, "French Lawmakers Make Abortion a Constitutional Right", Reuters, 4 March 2024, available at: *https://www.reuters.com/world/europe/french-lawmakers-hold-vote-make-abortion-constitutional-right-2024-03-04/*.

138 For a more detailed analysis of the 2018 Act, see C. Murray and M. Donnelly, "Early Medical Abortion Care in Ireland: Conscientious Provision and the Role of Law" [Working Paper] (2023), available at: *https://hdl.handle.net/10468/14464*; L. Grimes et al., "'Still travelling': Access to abortion post-12 weeks gestation in Ireland" (2023) 98 *Women's Studies International Forum* 102709.

2. Strategic Litigation

8–36 Strategic litigation is a method that can bring about significant changes in the law, practice or public awareness via taking carefully selected cases to court. The case may create change either through the success of the action and its impact on law, policy or practice, or by publicly exposing injustice, raising awareness and generating broader change. It is important that strategic litigation be used as one part of a wider campaign, rather than being conceived of as an end in itself. The areas of law where strategic litigation can be useful are as broad as the law itself. Cases that have been litigated in Ireland for strategic purposes include: *McGee v Attorney General*,[139] which concerned the availability of contraception for married couples in Ireland; *de Burca v Attorney General*,[140] which challenged the exclusion of female jurors under the Juries Act 1927; and *Sinnott v Minister for the Environment*,[141] a case concerning the failure of the State to provide a mechanism to enable those with visual impairments to exercise their right to vote in secret in the European and Local Elections in 2014.

8–37 Strategic litigation has both advantages and disadvantages. When run well and in the right circumstances, strategic litigation can create significant systemic change that can have a positive impact on a large number of people. However, it is important to recall that litigation is not the only tactic nor indeed the most appropriate strategy in all circumstances. The advantages of strategic litigation include the precedential value that the judgment in such a case may create. This then, as in the *Foy v An tArd Chláraitheoir* series of cases,[142] can be used to maintain pressure on the Government and legislature to introduce legislative, and hence systemic, change. An added benefit of such cases is that the resultant media exposure raises awareness of the issue amongst the public and this can be more significant than the case itself. Such was obvious

[139] [1974] I.R. 284.

[140] [1976] I.R. 38.

[141] [2017] IEHC 214.

[142] *Foy v An tArd Chláraitheoir (No. 1)* [2002] IEHC 116; *Foy v An tArd Chláraitheoir (No. 2)* [2007] IEHC 470; *Foy v An tArd Chláraitheoir (No. 3)*, settled in 2014. The declaration of incompatibility issued in *Foy (No. 2)* and the failure of the Government to respond to it in a meaningful manner was the subject matter of proceedings in *Foy (No. 3)*, which were eventually settled in October 2014 on foot of the Government's statement to the High Court regarding its "firm intention" to enact the necessary laws "as soon as possible" in 2015. See M. Carolan, "Lydia Foy settles transgender birth cert case against State", *Irish Times*, 2 October 2014.

in the series of cases resulting in the marriage equality referendum and the introduction of marriage equality to Ireland. As a result of the *Norris* cases, homosexuality was decriminalised in Ireland.[143] This contributed to the change in public opinion regarding LGBT people in Ireland, assisted by the case of *Zappone v Revenue Commissioners*,[144] where the High Court refused to recognise the validity of a Canadian marriage contracted by the applicants. Ultimately, the social change was confirmed by the overwhelming support in favour of guaranteeing marriage equality in the Constitution following the referendum in May 2015[145] and the subsequent introduction of the Marriage Act 2015 which was officially signed into law on 29 October 2015.

8–38 However, strategic litigation can also be disadvantageous. As with all litigation, resort to the courts is a costly process and, should the litigant lose, they may be left with very large costs orders against them.[146] There

---

[143] *Norris v Attorney General* [1984] I.R. 36; *Norris v Ireland* (1991) 13 E.H.R.R. 186, where, in the latter case, the ECtHR found that the continued criminalisation of homosexual activity between consenting adults amounted to a violation of Article 8 of the European Convention on Human Rights. Five years later, the Criminal Law (Sexual Offences) Act 1993 was introduced, which decriminalised homosexuality.

[144] [2006] IEHC 404.

[145] 62% of voters voted in favour of the introduction of marriage equality. See *https://electionsireland.org/results/referendum/refresult.cfm?ref=201534R.*

[146] *O'Keeffe v Hickey* [2009] IESC 39 concerned the question of whether a person who had unsuccessfully sued the State should be forced to pay the legal fees of the State. The appellant successfully sued the first defendant who had sexually abused her when she was a child and he was her teacher. The appellant also sued the Minister for Education and the State for vicarious liability as the employers of her abuser. In other words, her argument was that the State, as the ultimate employer of her abuser, failed to protect her by adequately supervising and controlling his behaviour. The appellant lost her case against the State. She appealed that decision and also lost the appeal. Thus, the State sought costs against the appellant on the basis of the general principle that the losing party must pay the successful party's costs. The appellant argued in the Supreme Court that she should not have to meet these costs as her case was a test case and a significant number of cases were underway concerning the substantive question of the liability of the Minister for Education for the sexual abuse of pupils by primary school teachers who were salaried by the State. Drawing on the decision of Clarke J. in *Cork CC v Shackelton*, unreported, High Court, 12 October 2007, that where there are special circumstances, the court may exercise its discretion not to apply the general principle that costs follow the event, Murray C.J. held that such "exceptional circumstances" were present in this case. Thus, the appellant was not required to pay the costs of the State. It should be noted that while Louise O'Keeffe lost her case in the domestic courts regarding the liability of the State, she brought her case to the ECtHR, where it was held that the State had violated her rights under Article 3 (prohibition on torture, inhuman and degrading treatment) and Article 13 (right to an effective remedy before national authorities for violations of rights under the Convention) of the Convention by failing to protect her from abuse in primary school: *O'Keeffe v Ireland* (2014) 59 E.H.R.R. 15.

is no guarantee that the litigants will win the case. An example is the case of *CA v Minister for Justice and Equality*,[147] which sought to litigate strategically the system of direct provision for asylum seekers. The judge in that case was critical that the applicants' legal representatives utilised judicial review, rather than plenary hearing, where evidence could have been tested by cross-examination.[148] Similarly, the involvement of the media can be a double-edged sword. While positive publicity can assist to change public opinion, negative publicity can have the opposite effect. Finally, depending on the area of law, litigation may not be an option that is appropriate because it might not be possible to bring the particular dispute before the courts. Thus, it can be useful to consider alternative dispute resolution mechanisms such as ombudsmen.[149]

8–39 That said, strategic litigation can place an issue in the public spotlight. Argued properly, it can be an opportunity to place a reasoned view before the public, in opposition to any dominant political or corporate perspective. Coupled with media coverage, failed test cases can also often lead to legislative reform or increased awareness of an issue that may lead to long-term change, as occurred with *Norris* and *Zappone*. Thus, strategic litigation can result in legal, political and societal impact, regardless of the outcome of the case.

Box 8.4: Case Focus
***Doherty v Government of Ireland* [2011] 2 I.L.R.M. 516**

The applicant in this case was a sitting member of Seanad Éireann and had been chosen by the Sinn Féin party to contest the by-election in Donegal South West. The vacancy arose as the previous incumbent of the Dáil seat, Pat "The Cope" Gallagher, had been elected to the European Parliament on 6 June 2009, which necessitated the resignation of his Dáil seat.

A series of attempts had been made by opposition TDs to "move the writ" for the election—the formal process by which an election is called—all of which had been resisted by the Government. This resulted in the constituency of Donegal South West being under-represented in the Dáil, having only two serving TDs. Thus, the applicant claimed

[147] [2014] IEHC 532.
[148] See generally, L. Thornton, "*C.A. and T.A.*: The Direct Provision Case" (2014) 4 *Irish Journal of Family Law* 116.
[149] For more on ombudsmen, see Ch.10, Section D.

that the ratio of public representative to population far exceeded the constitutional maximum as set down in Article 16.2.2° and 16.2.3°.

The case happened at a politically sensitive time. In the midst of recession, the Government had a narrow majority and was attempting to push through unpopular reforms.[150] Unsurprisingly, the Government fought the case, relying on the separation of powers to argue that any order forcing the calling of the by-election would involve the court in political matters outside its remit.[151] However, the applicant was very careful to clarify that he did not seek an order requiring the holding of an election, merely a declaration that the 16-month delay in filling the vacant seat was unreasonable.[152]

Section 39(2) of the Electoral Act 1992 governs the holding of by-elections and seems to suggest that the timing of such elections is entirely a matter for the Dáil. It states:

> "Where a vacancy occurs in the membership of the Dáil by a person ceasing to be a member otherwise than in consequence of a dissolution, the Chairman of the Dáil ... shall, as soon as he is directed by the Dáil so to do, direct the Clerk of the Dáil to issue a writ to the returning officer for the constituency in the representation of which the vacancy has occurred directing the returning officer to cause an election to be held of a member of the Dáil to fill the vacancy mentioned in the writ."

In his judgment, Kearns P. stated that, in interpreting the section, the court had to be mindful of the provisions of Article 3 of Protocol 1 to the European Convention on Human Rights, which requires that elections are held "at reasonable intervals".[153] Then he found that the questions before him were whether there was an obligation to hold the by-election within a reasonable period of time, whether determining the length of time was entirely a matter for the Dáil, and whether the delay in this case was unreasonable.

Kearns P. concluded that the issue was not related to the internal workings of the Dáil, or to any matter of external politics, or to any socio-economic issue, and thus the court could consider the matter as it concerned the right to equality of political representation. On the question of whether a need to hold a by-election within a reasonable period of time could be read into s.39(2) of the Electoral Act 1992, Kearns

[150] For a discussion of this case, see E. O'Malley, "Is the Doherty Judgement Justified?", available at: *http://politicalreform.ie/2010/11/03/is-the-doherty-judgement-justified/*.

[151] [2011] 2 I.L.R.M. 516 at 520.

[152] [2011] 2 I.L.R.M. 516 at 528.

[153] [2011] 2 I.L.R.M. 516 at 538.

P. found that to interpret the subsection in any other manner would be offensive to Articles 5 and 16 of the Constitution. On whether the delay was unreasonable, he noted that "the Dáil has a 5 year term and the unprecedented delay in this instance—the longest in the history of the State—represents a significant proportion of the term of the current Dáil".[154] He also noted the proposal in the report of the Constitution Review Group that Article 16 be amended to require the filling of such vacancies within 90 days, while recognising that there should be a wide margin of appreciation extended to governments in this regard. Nonetheless, Kearns P. concluded:

> "I am satisfied that the delay in this case is so inordinate as to amount to a breach of the applicant's constitutional rights to such a degree as to warrant the Court granting some form of relief. Far from the Court 'tearing asunder' the provisions of the Constitution by adjudicating upon this application, it is the ongoing failure to move the writ for this by-election since June 2009 which offends the terms and spirit of the Constitution and its framework for democratic representation."[155]

As a direct result of the ruling in this case, the Government announced on 4 November 2010 that the by-election would be held on 25 November 2010 and Pearse Doherty was returned to the Dáil as the newly-elected TD. Not only did this case result in a positive outcome for Pearse Doherty and for his party, but it also led to much-needed legislative reform. Following on from the case, after the general election in February 2011, the Government introduced the Electoral (Amendment) Act 2011, which became law on 25 July 2011. Section 2 of the 2011 Act amended s.39 of the Electoral Act 1992 by the insertion of a new s.39(2A) to require the holding of a by-election within six months of the vacancy arising.

D. Conclusion

8–40 The ability to reform the law is essential to ensuring that laws remain relevant for an evolving society. According to King, the law reflects society and so the ability to reform the law is central to ensuring that justice is done.[156] Yet, to return to the quote that began this chapter,

[154] [2011] 2 I.L.R.M. 516 at 539.
[155] [2011] 2 I.L.R.M. 516 at 539.
[156] D.B. King, "The Law Reform Challenge" (1969) 3 *St Louis University Law Journal* 403.

Barnett comments that the actual process of law reform is complex. Law reform originates from both formal and informal mechanisms. In this chapter, we have considered the various devices that are employed to bring about reform of the law. Common to all the strategies is the presence of the public, whether formally or informally. Reflecting the fact that sovereignty in Ireland rests with the people, the State employs both direct and deliberative democratic means to keep the public engaged in law reform. The public are formally involved via public consultation, citizens' assemblies or referendums, or when represented by those who access justice through the courts. They are also formally involved when they elect a particular party to govern the country on the basis of its law reform agenda. They are informally involved when tribunals are established in response to public outrage at the discovery of certain events, and through advocacy and activism. The constant reform of the law, through both formal and informal mechanisms, is essential to ensuring that the law remains an effective tool for justice. This is demonstrated most particularly in the context of strategic litigation, which is important for compelling vindication of the rights of individuals, as in *Norris*;[157] society as a whole, as in *Doherty*;[158] and for upholding the rights of the politically powerless, as in *CA*.[159] As King notes:

> "Law reform captures the imagination of society, for the law can be an instrument of societal change ... The needs of individuals are better served when the law is reformed to meet their needs. The goals of justice are more nearly reached, there is greater harmony with other disciplines, and new knowledge and the law participate in modern social advances when law reform approaches actuality."[160]

[157] *Norris v Attorney General* [1984] I.R. 36; *Norris v Ireland* (1991) 13 E.H.R.R. 186.
[158] [2011] 2 I.L.R.M. 516.
[159] [2014] IEHC 532.
[160] D.B. King, "The Law Reform Challenge" (1969) 3 *St Louis University Law Journal* 403.

Chapter 9

The Irish Courts System and Alternative Dispute Resolution

"As to the objectives, it would probably be generally agreed that it is the duty of the State to provide the citizens with a system of civil and criminal justice that is accessible to all and which functions in a manner that is impartial, open and expeditious."

Keane C.J., "The Irish Courts System in the 21st Century: Planning for the Future" (2001) 6 *Bar Review* 321.[1]

In this chapter we:

- introduce the courts system in Ireland;
- identify the first-instance jurisdiction of the Irish courts;
- examine the appellate jurisdiction of the courts in Ireland;
- consider what foreign courts can have a role in the Irish legal system;
- analyse alternatives to court-based dispute resolution.

A. Introduction

9–01 The courts play a central and vital role in our legal system. This is a theme we have explored obliquely through the early chapters in this book. In Chs 3 and 4, we examined the role of the courts as interpreters of the law, as identified in both the Constitution[2] and legislation.[3] Chapter 5 focused on how the courts can participate in the evolution of law through the development of precedent. We discussed the impact that the decisions reached by courts might have on the legislative process

[1] This article derived from a lecture presented to the Student Law Society in University College Cork on 23 March 2001. However, see the opening quote of Ch.13.

[2] See further, Ch.3, Section D.

[3] See further, Ch.4, Sections C–H.

and consequent reform of the law in Chs 7[4] and 8.[5] However, we have yet to turn to a comprehensive consideration of the primary function of the courts as arbitrators of disputes. In this chapter, we will analyse the structure of the courts system in Ireland. We will uncover the legal basis underpinning the Irish courts and evaluate where and how cases are heard at first instance. We will also examine on what basis a party to a case may appeal the decision of a court, and the structure supporting the appellate courts in Ireland. However, litigation is not the only method by which parties may seek to resolve their disputes and thus this chapter will also analyse alternatives to the traditional resolution of disputes.[6]

B. The Domestic Courts

9–02 The Irish courts system is governed first and foremost by Articles 34–38 of the Constitution. The key components of our courts system are sketched in these Articles; the detail is then added in by legislation. In this section, we will consider the constitutional and legislative provisions relevant to the establishment and operation of our domestic courts system. The Article that structures this discussion is Article 34.1, which provides as follows:

> "Justice shall be administered in courts established by law, by judges appointed in the manner provided by this Constitution and, save in such special and limited cases as may be prescribed by law, shall be administered in public."

A number of important points and principles are contained in this provision. First, it requires that our courts must be established by law. There are two sources of law that do this: the Constitution itself, where certain courts are named and their establishment is required, and legislation which establishes these and other courts not named but envisaged by the Constitution. Article 34.1 also requires that justice should primarily be administered in public, although exceptions are permissible. These issues will be considered in turn. The appointment of judges will be considered in detail in Ch.11.[7]

---

4 See further, Ch.7, paras 7–18 to 7–20 and Ch.7, Section E.
5 See further, Ch.8, Section B.6.
6 For a consideration of administrative justice structures, see generally Ch.10.
7 See further, Ch.11, paras 11–25 to 11–31.

1. Courts Established by Law—the Constitutional Provisions

9–03 Article 34.2 requires the establishment of courts of first instance, a court of appeal, and a court of final appeal. A court of first instance is the court where the case is commenced and which has the ability or authority to hear the claim or case in question. An appellate court hears appeals from courts lower than it in the hierarchy of courts. Article 34.2 clearly establishes this chain of command, with courts of first instance at the bottom of the chain, and a single court of final appeal at the top. As we know from Chs 2 and 5,[8] a clear hierarchy of courts is essential for the rule of law and for the doctrine of precedent to operate.

9–04 The Constitution requires the establishment of two appellate courts. The Supreme Court is stated to be the "Court of Final Appeal" (Article 34.5.1°) and, as such, it is at the top of the domestic court hierarchy.[9] Next in line of authority is the Court of Appeal which has "appellate jurisdiction from all decisions of the High Court, and shall also have appellate jurisdiction from such decisions of other courts as may be prescribed by law".[10]

9–05 With regard to courts of first instance, only one court is specifically named. This is the High Court, and it is stated to be a court of first instance with "full original jurisdiction" (Article 34.3.1°). In addition to the High Court, the Constitution also permits the establishment of other first-instance courts with "local and limited jurisdiction". These courts, which are lower in the chain of command than the High Court, are not named in the Constitution. It was, however, envisaged when the 1937 Constitution was drafted that the existing system of District and Circuit Courts established by the Courts of Justice Act 1924 pursuant to the 1922 Constitution would continue. This was given effect by Article 58 of the 1937 Constitution which provided for the continuance of the Free State courts system until it was re-established under the terms of the 1937 Constitution.[11]

[8] See further, Ch.2, para.2–28 and Ch.5, para.5–20.

[9] Note that in this section we are focusing on the ranking of domestic courts. As will be further discussed in Section E, the Supreme Court's status as the final court of appeal was altered somewhat when Ireland became a member of the European Economic Community, as it then was, in 1972 and so became subject to the jurisdiction of the European Court of Justice, as established by the Treaty of Rome 1957. See Ch.6, paras 6–31 to 6–34.

[10] Article 34.2.1°.

[11] Article 58 was one of a number of transitory provisions that were deleted from the

9–06 The jurisdiction of the District and Circuit Courts is local because it is confined to particular geographic regions. In civil cases, the local jurisdiction requirement means that one of the parties must reside in/be based in the District or Circuit geographical area, or that the contract was concluded or action complained of occurred in that area. In criminal cases, it means that the crime must have occurred in the geographical area or the defendant must have been arrested there.[12] Their jurisdiction is limited because only the High Court has full original jurisdiction to hear all matters, pursuant to Article 34.3.1°. Unlike the High Court, the Court of Appeal and the Supreme Court, the District and Circuit Courts are created by statute and can be abolished without the requirement of a referendum.

9–07 It is important to note that although the District and Circuit Courts are known as the inferior courts, this designation is not pejorative. It is to distinguish them from the superior courts above them in the hierarchy, both legally and constitutionally. In fact, the District and Circuit Courts play a very important role in the Irish courts system, both in terms of convenience and cost. They are the most active courts in our system, as the following table illustrates:[13]

Table 9.1: Civil and Criminal Business by Court 2023

Court	Civil Matters		Criminal Matters	
	Incoming	Resolved	Incoming	Resolved
Supreme Court	175	147	41	45
Court of Appeal	325	368	2,701	1,847
High Court/Central Criminal Court	17,346	14,374	2,659	2,988
Special Criminal Court	N/A	N/A	35	55
Circuit Court	28,954	21,120	31,906	39,347
District Court	133,000	107,635	329,714	294,100

Constitution after the date the first President entered into office. See Ch.3, para.3–49. This re-establishment did not occur until the passage of two statutes in 1961. These will be discussed at para.9–10.

12 The one exception is if the case is a particularly notorious one in the area. In such a case, either the DPP or the accused can request that the trial be heard in the Dublin Central Criminal Court if it would be manifestly unjust to the accused for the trial to be heard in their own locality.

13 Taken from Courts Service, *Annual Report 2023* (Dublin: Courts Service, 2024), p.54 (civil) and p.55 (criminal). Criminal matters are based on a per offence basis.

9–08 The Constitution also permits the establishment of the Special Criminal Court. Article 38.3.1° provides:

> "Special courts may be established by law for the trial of offences in cases where it may be determined in accordance with such law that the ordinary courts are inadequate to secure the effective administration of justice, and the preservation of public peace and order."

Like the District and Circuit Courts, the Special Criminal Court is a creature of statute and it can only exist if and when the Government issues a proclamation that it is necessary to exist.[14] Indeed, it has been held that the Government's decision to establish the Special Criminal Court cannot be challenged.[15]

2. Courts Established by Law—the Statutory Provisions

9–09 In various Articles, the following phrases appear: "established by law", "as may be prescribed by law", "as determined by law" and "in accordance with law". These phrases bestow the legislature with an important role in the establishment and regulation of our courts system. Article 36 is particularly noteworthy in this context as it specifies that the legislature determines the number of judges each court has, the terms of their appointment, and their respective jurisdictions. The courts system is a very good example of how legislation builds on and develops the fundamental principles and institutions that are established by the Constitution.

9–10 Our courts were formally established by means of two pieces of legislation in 1961, namely the Courts (Establishment and Constitution) Act 1961 and the Courts (Supplemental Provisions) Act 1961. These two statutes largely re-established the courts structure of the Free State under the authority of the 1937 Constitution,[16] although they additionally

[14] This is because the legislation that created the Special Criminal Court gives the Government the power to establish the court: s.35(2) of the Offences against the State Act 1939.

[15] *Kavanagh v Ireland* [1996] 1 I.R. 321.

[16] These statutes were prompted by the Supreme Court's decision in *State (Killian) v Minister for Justice* [1954] I.R. 207 where it was held that Article 34.1 should be read as requiring the legislature to enact legislation to establish courts under the 1937 Constitution.

established the Court of Criminal Appeal, which ceased to exist when its jurisdiction was transferred to the Court of Appeal in 2014, subject to s.78 of the Court of Appeal Act 2014. This section allowed the Court of Criminal Appeal to continue to exercise jurisdiction over cases that had been initiated and had been heard in part or in full before it prior to the establishment of the Court of Appeal. Many of the provisions in the Courts of Justice Act 1924 were expressly carried over in the Courts (Supplemental Provisions) Act 1961, i.e. the 1924 Act is still largely in force.

9–11 Legislation also specifies the composition of our courts. Section 22 of the Courts and Civil Law (Miscellaneous Provisions) Act 2013 provides that there can be 10 Supreme Court judges, one of whom is the Chief Justice. There were reports that if the Court of Appeal was successful in clearing the backlog of cases that had built up, the number of Supreme Court judges may be reduced.[17] However, there has been no further political discussion on this issue in the intervening 10 years. The President of the High Court is an additional ex officio member of the Supreme Court. The former Chief Justice can also be an additional member, pursuant to s.5 of the Courts (No. 2) Act 1997. The Court of Appeal currently consists of a President and 18 ordinary judges pursuant to s.1A of the Courts (Establishment and Constitution) Act 1961, as amended by s.2 of the Courts, Civil Law, Criminal Law and Superannuation (Miscellaneous Provisions) Act 2024.[18] There are also two ex officio members: the Chief Justice and the President of the High Court.

9–12 Both appellate courts are collegiate courts, i.e. each case is heard by a panel of judges. Section 7 of the Courts and Court Officers Act 1995 (the "1995 Act") allows the Supreme Court to sit in multiple divisions concurrently. It also requires a panel of five judges to hear cases concerning the constitutional validity of a statute. The Court of Appeal Act 2014 provides that the Court of Appeal sits in panels of three judges. As the impetus to establish the Court of Appeal derived primarily from concerns about the significant backlog of civil cases awaiting

[17] R. Byrne, P. McCutcheon, L. Cahillane and E. Roche-Cagney, *Byrne and McCutcheon on the Irish Legal System*, 7th edn (Dublin: Bloomsbury Professional, 2020), para.4.60.

[18] This statute amends s.1A of the Courts (Establishment and Constitution) Act 1961, inserted by s.6 of the Court of Appeal Act 2014.

hearing before the Supreme Court,[19] it was initially determined that two of these panels would focus on civil appeals and one on criminal.[20] The reservation of criminal cases to one panel was intended to have the added benefit of establishing a dedicated cadre of judges who will consider criminal appeals, which would reduce the inconsistency that had developed in Court of Criminal Appeal precedents, where no such specialised panel existed.[21]

9–13 The ordinary first-instance courts are governed by the 1995 Act, as amended. There are currently 48 ordinary judges who sit in the High Court.[22] Three additional members of the High Court are the President of the High Court, the Chief Justice and the President of the Circuit Court. The latter two are ex officio members. Section 10 of the 1995 Act, as amended by s.5 of the Courts Act 2023 (the "2023 Act"), provides that there are 45 ordinary Circuit Court judges, excluding the President of the Circuit Court. The President of the District Court is an ex officio Circuit Court judge. The country is divided into eight circuits. Section 11 of the 1995 Act, as amended by s.6 of the 2023 Act, provides that the District Court consists of the President of the District Court and 71 ordinary judges. The country is divided into 24 districts. The District and Circuit Courts typically hear cases by means of a judge sitting alone, although in criminal cases the Circuit Court consists of a judge and jury. The High Court typically consists of a single judge; however, in cases of importance, the President of the High Court can convene a panel of three judges to hear the case, and it is known as the Divisional Court in such a capacity. When the High Court hears criminal cases, it assumes the name of the Central Criminal Court and it sits with judge and jury.

---

19 *Report of the Working Group on the Court of Appeal* (Dublin: Stationery Office, 2009), pp.40–46. This backlog will be discussed further at para.9–66.

20 R. Byrne, P. McCutcheon, L. Cahillane and E. Roche-Cagney, *Byrne and McCutcheon on the Irish Legal System*, 7th edn (Dublin: Bloomsbury Professional, 2020), para.4.68.

21 The Court of Criminal Appeal consisted of three judges nominated by the Chief Justice, one of whom was to be a Supreme Court judge and the other two High Court judges: s.3(2) of the Courts (Establishment and Constitution) Act 1961. For an example of criticism of the inconsistency of Court of Criminal Appeal judgments, see the Working Group on Jurisdiction of the Courts, *The Criminal Jurisdiction of the Courts* (Dublin: Stationery Office, 2003), para.639. This Group, however, did not recommend the abolition of the Court of Criminal Appeal, but that particular judges be assigned to hear criminal cases only.

22 Section 9 of the Courts and Court Officers Act 1995, as substituted by s.4 of the Courts Act 2023.

9–14 Finally, the Special Criminal Court was established pursuant to Pt V of the Offences against the State Act 1939. The current iteration of the Special Criminal Court was brought into existence in 1972. Special Criminal Court (No. 2) was established in October 2015 to respond to a 20-month backlog in cases.[23] There is a panel of 19 judges appointed to serve on the Special Criminal Court who are drawn from the High, Circuit and District Courts. It sits in panels of three judges. There is no jury.

Box 9.1: Ever-Increasing Judicial Numbers

In 1924, legislation permitted the appointment of 50 judges. In 2024, it allows for 196. On the bare metric of population, this looks good. The almost 400 per cent increase in judicial numbers over a 100-year period far exceeds the 21 per cent increase in population over roughly the same time frame.[24] However, when these figures are compared with other EU member states, the situation in Ireland looks less favourable. We have had the lowest number of judges per 100,000 in the EU for the past decade.[25] While there are differences between civilian and common law systems that might explain why there are more judges in civilian systems,[26] there is no such excuse for why Ireland has, for example, five times fewer High Court judges per head of population than England and Wales.[27] This matters, as the 2021 *Rule of Law Report* noted, because an insufficient number of judges risks reducing the efficiency of the courts to administer justice in a timely manner.[28] Not only does delay

23 Department of Justice and Equality, "Minister Fitzgerald confirms the setting up of a second Special Criminal Court" (28 October 2015), available at: *https://agsi.ie/articles/minister-fitzgerald-confirms-the-setting-up-of-a-second-special-criminal-court/*. The Special Criminal Court (No. 2) has been operational since 2016.

24 The population was recorded at 4.2 million in the 1926 Census and at 5.1 million in the 2022 Census. The Central Statistics Office estimated in April 2024 that the population stood at 5.38 million. See C. Ó Gráda, "The Population of Ireland 1700-1900: A Survey" [1979] *Annales de Démographie Historique* 281 at 283; Central Statistics Office, *Census of Population 2022 – Summary Results* (30 May 2023), available at: *https://www.cso.ie/en/releasesandpublications/ep/p-cpsr/censusofpopulation2022-summaryresults/* and CSO, Population and Migration Estimates 2024, available at: *https://www.cso.ie/en/statistics/population/populationandmigrationestimates/*.

25 R. Halpin, *Increasing the Number of Judges in Ireland*, Library and Research Service Note, Houses of the Oireachtas (17 May 2023), p.3. This remains the case as reported in the most recent figure: European Commission, *2024 EU Justice Scoreboard* (Luxembourg: Publications Office of the European Union, 2024), Figure 37, p.32.

26 OECD, *Modernising Staffing and Court Management Practices in Ireland: Towards a More Responsive and Resilient Justice System* (Paris: OECD Publishing, 2023), p.45.

27 *Shannon v Shannon* [2024] IEHC 291 at para.3 and para.15.

28 European Commission, *2021 Rule of Law Report – Country Chapter on the Rule of*

impact on the lives of individuals before the courts, most acutely in the areas of criminal justice, personal injuries and domestic violence,[29] it also renders Ireland liable to breaches of the European Convention on Human Rights.[30]

The 2023 Act was the first phase in a plan to bring judicial numbers in line with international norms by increasing the number of judges from 173 (pre the 2023 Act) to 217 (on completion of the second phase).[31] In its *Annual Report 2023*, the CEO of the Court Service observed that the appointment of these judges "had an instant impact, reducing backlogs and waiting times".[32] This plan was welcomed by the European Commission in the 2024 *Rule of Law Report.*[33] The increase in District Court and Circuit Court judges is particularly needed as previous increases in judicial capacity have focused on the superior courts. For example, in the last decade there has been a 76 per cent increase in the number of superior court judges but no increase in inferior court numbers.[34] In their submissions to the Judicial Planning Working Group, whose Report influenced the changes introduced by the 2023 Act, the Presidents of the District Court and Circuit Court said there was an urgent need for 18 and 8 additional judges respectively.[35] As these courts are our busiest,[36] it is no surprise that they are overburdened.

3. The Administration of Justice in Courts

9–15 The Constitution also requires, under Article 34.1, that justice be administered in courts. However, this Article must be read in tandem with

Law Situation in Ireland (Brussels, 20.7.2021, SWD(2021) 715 final), p.6, available at: *https://eur-lex.europa.eu/legal-content/EN/TXT/PDF/?uri=CELEX:52021SC0715.*

29 R. Halpin, *Increasing the Number of Judges in Ireland*, Library and Research Service Note, Houses of the Oireachtas (17 May 2023), p.9.

30 Ireland lost nine cases before the European Court of Human Rights for inadequacies in remedies for court delays between 2002 and 2018; R. Halpin, *Increasing the Number of Judges in Ireland*, Library and Research Service Note, Houses of the Oireachtas (17 May 2023), p.10.

31 R. Halpin, *Increasing the Number of Judges in Ireland*, Library and Research Service Note, Houses of the Oireachtas (17 May 2023), p.1.

32 Courts Service, *Annual Report 2023* (Dublin: Courts Service, 2024), p.16.

33 European Commission, *2024 Rule of Law Report – Country Chapter on the Rule of Law Situation in Ireland* (Brussels, 24.7.2024, SWD(2024) 807 final), p.7, available at: *https://commission.europa.eu/document/2987cf65-31e4-4746-bbd0-fabd15f515e3_en.*

34 R. Halpin, *Increasing the Number of Judges in Ireland*, Library and Research Service Note, Houses of the Oireachtas (17 May 2023), pp.2–3.

35 Judicial Planning Working Group, *Report of the Judicial Planning Working Group* (Department of Justice, December 2022), pp.60–61, available at: *https://www.gov.ie/en/collection/af6ff-judicial-planning-working-group-report/.*

36 See Table 9.1.

Article 37.1, which permits "the exercise of limited functions and powers of a judicial nature, in matters other than criminal matters, by any person or body of persons duly authorised by law". The effect of Article 37.1 is to validate some of the functions of bodies such as the Master of the High Court, Bord na Móna, tribunals of inquiry, the Adoption Authority of Ireland, etc. However, the courts have placed limits on the extent of the powers of non-courts and it has been determined that certain matters can only ever be heard before the courts. The features that such cases would have were considered in *McDonald v Bord na gCon (No. 2)*:

> "1. A dispute or controversy as to the existence of legal rights or a violation of the law;
> 2. The determination of the rights of a party, the imposition of liabilities, or the infliction of a penalty;
> 3. The final determination of legal rights/liabilities/penalties;
> 4. The enforcement of such rights/liabilities/penalties;
> 5. The making of an order that was traditionally made by the courts in this country."[37]

More recently in *Zalewski v Workplace Relations Commission*, the Supreme Court held that these five criteria should be viewed as "indicating general features which tend to show the administration of justice, rather than as a definite and prescriptive test."[38] The fifth criterion was downplayed, with O'Donnell C.J. holding:

> "The administration of justice is not, however, to be defined by, or limited to, those areas traditionally dealt with by the courts. The proper scope of the administration of justice is not determined simply by analogy with what was done by the courts as a matter of history, and still less by the form of orders traditionally made by them ... I would, therefore, be reluctant to give decisive weight to this feature, and would, in any event, take a reasonably broad view of what it requires."[39]

9–16 What constitutes "limited ... powers" was explored in *Re Solicitors Act 1954*.[40] In this case, which concerned a challenge to the power of

[37] [1965] I.R. 217 at 231.
[38] [2021] IESC 24 at para.92 per O'Donnell C.J.
[39] [2021] IESC 24 at para.96.
[40] [1960] I.R. 239.

the disciplinary committee of the Incorporated Law Society of Ireland to strike a solicitor off the roll of solicitors for malpractice, the Supreme Court identified the following test:

> "The test as to whether a power is or is not 'limited' in the opinion of the Court, lies in the effect of the assigned power when exercised. If the exercise of the assigned powers and functions is calculated ordinarily to affect in the most profound and far-reaching way the lives, liberties, fortunes or reputations of those against whom they are exercised they cannot properly be described as 'limited.'"[41]

Applying this test to the Solicitors Act 1954, the court determined that the consequences for a solicitor of being struck off the roll were far-reaching and, for this reason, the disciplinary committee could not take such a step. As a result of this decision, the legislature had to enact new legislation, namely the Solicitors (Amendment) Act 1960. As explored in detail in Ch.12, the disciplinary system for legal practitioners has changed significantly since then.[42] It should be noted that in subsequent cases, other bodies have been permitted to issue disciplinary measures similar to that disallowed in *Re Solicitors Act 1954*. Ryan suggests that the justification for this differential treatment may be due to the historical role that solicitors have played in the work of the courts.[43]

9–17 Bodies that deal with limited and non-criminal matters are required to exercise their powers in a judicial manner. This means that they must comply with the basic principles of fair procedure, including advance notice of proceedings and allowing both sides to present their case. These fair procedure principles are founded on common law principles of natural justice,[44] but they also have a constitutional basis, because the right to fair procedures in decision-making was held to be a personal unenumerated right under Article 40.3.1° in *Garvey v Ireland*.[45] O'Higgins C.J. stated:

[41] [1960] I.R. 239 at 264 per Kingsmill Moore J.

[42] The new regulatory and disciplinary system for solicitors and barristers provided for under the Legal Services Regulation Act 2015 is discussed in detail in Ch.12, paras 12–27 to 12–46.

[43] F. Ryan, *Constitutional Law*, 2nd edn (Dublin: Round Hall Ltd, 2008), pp.103–104.

[44] R. Byrne, P. McCutcheon, L. Cahillane and E. Roche-Cagney, *Byrne and McCutcheon on the Irish Legal System*, 7th edn (Dublin: Bloomsbury Professional, 2020), para.4.16.

[45] [1981] I.R. 75.

"[U]nder the Constitution powers cannot be exercised unjustly or unfairly. This applies as well to the Government as to any other authority within the State to which is given the power to take action which may infringe on the rights of others."[46]

4. The Administration of Justice in Public

9–18 Article 34.1 also requires that justice be administered in public. Historically, secret hearings allowed for the abuse of power and this is why the administration of justice in public is regarded as an important facet of a democracy.[47] As Walsh J. in *Re R. Ltd* noted:

"The actual presence of the public is never necessary but the administration of justice in public does require that the doors of the court must be open so that members of the general public may come and see for themselves that justice is done."[48]

However, Article 34.1 also permits exceptions to this general principle in "such special and limited cases as may be prescribed by law". The two exceptions are in camera proceedings and the occasional use of pseudonyms.

(a) In camera proceedings

9–19 When a court is not sitting in public, it is described as hearing the case in camera. Directly translated, in camera means "in a box", so it captures the sense of a court sitting in private/behind closed doors.[49] Where a case is heard in camera, members of the public and the media[50] are excluded from the courtroom, and attendance is limited to the judge, jury (where applicable), the court register or clerk, the parties to the proceedings and their legal representatives. Such restrictions are put in place in the interests of the privacy of individuals' lives and affairs and also to facilitate, at times, an urgent application. Thus, s.45(1) of the

46 [1981] I.R. 75 at 97.

47 R. Byrne, P. McCutcheon, L. Cahillane and E. Roche-Cagney, *Byrne and McCutcheon on the Irish Legal System*, 7th edn (Dublin: Bloomsbury Professional, 2020), para.4.24.

48 [1989] I.R. 126 at 134.

49 R. Byrne, P. McCutcheon, L. Cahillane and E. Roche-Cagney, *Byrne and McCutcheon on the Irish Legal System*, 7th edn (Dublin: Bloomsbury Professional, 2020), para.4.24, fn.49.

50 But see para.9–21.

Courts (Supplemental Provisions) Act 1961 provides for the hearing in camera of family law matters, cases involving the disclosure of a secret manufacturing process, habeas corpus proceedings and injunctions, in addition to other matters.

9–20 Sometimes the justice system has an interest in protecting the identities of victims, which can in turn lead to the protection of the identities of offenders, for example those accused of incest.[51] In other situations, limitations can be placed on what can be reported. An example is s.17 of the Criminal Procedure Act 1967 regarding the limitations on the right of reporting details once a person has been charged. The press can only report:

- the fact that X has appeared in court;
- the name and address of X;
- the charge brought against X.

However, once the case commences against the accused in court, the press can report on any evidence revealed therein as long as that evidence is heard in open court.

9–21 The secrecy that accompanies in camera proceedings has led to criticisms of family law matters in particular, with the Law Reform Commission noting in 1994 that "anecdote, rumour and myth inform the public's understanding of what goes on in the family courts".[52] As a result, inroads have been made in respect of the reporting of family law cases in an attempt to facilitate an understanding and awareness of the decisions of the courts. Pursuant to s.40(3) of the Civil Liability and Courts Act 2004 (the "2004 Act"), a barrister, solicitor, researcher or family law specialist can prepare reports on family law cases on maintenance issues and various orders under the Domestic Violence Act 2018, among other matters. More recently, family law cases involving children can be reported on, with the enactment of Pt 2 of the Courts and Civil Law (Miscellaneous Provisions) Act 2013. However, the publication of any details that would identify the parties involved in an in camera case, or the publication of any sensitive information, amounts to contempt of court and the relevant individual can be called before the court and

[51] Criminal Law (Sexual Offences) Act 2017 s.29.
[52] *Consultation Paper on Family Courts* (LRC CP 78-1994), para.7.09.

sanctioned accordingly. Such reporting is essential because it becomes possible to identify shortcomings in processes and procedures in the family law system and make evidence-based recommendations for reform.[53] Included in the Department of Justice *Family Justice Strategy 2022–2025* is a commitment to examine the feasibility of establishing a system for the public reporting of all types of family law cases.[54]

(b) The use of pseudonyms

9–22 The requirement that justice be administered in public also acts generally to prevent a person who is issuing proceedings from using a pseudonym in order to protect their identity. This was discussed in *Roe v Blood Transfusion Service Board*.[55] In this case, the plaintiff sought to sue the Blood Transfusion Service Board for negligently supplying her with contaminated blood which caused her to contract Hepatitis C, but she wished to use a pseudonym to keep her identity secret. Laffoy J. drew from Walsh J.'s statement of principle in the *Re R. Ltd* case and held:

> "In my view, in the context of the underlying rationale of Article 34, s.1, the public disclosure of the true identities of parties to civil litigation is essential if justice is to be administered in public. In a situation in which the true identity of a plaintiff in a civil action is known to the parties to the action and to the court but is concealed from the public, members of the general public cannot see for themselves that justice is done."[56]

---

[53] The work of the Child Care Law Reporting Project was particularly important in this regard. It commenced in 2012 as a precursor to the wider lifting of the in camera rule in family law cases and developed on the Family Law Reporting Pilot Project which had run from 2006–2008. See, e.g. M. Corbett and C. Coulter, *Findings and Observations for Reform from 10 Years' Attendance at Child Protection Proceedings* (Child Care Law Reporting Project, 19 June 2023), available at: *https://www.childlawproject.ie/publications/*. Unfortunately, funding for the project ran out in October 2024, despite concerns expressed by judges. See J. Power, "Judge expresses 'grave disappointment' after care watchdog shelved", *Irish Times* (12 October 2024), available at: *https://www.irishtimes.com/crime-law/courts/2024/10/12/judge-expresses-grave-disappointment-after-care-watchdog-shelved/*.

[54] Department of Justice, *Family Justice Strategy 2022–2025* (16 November 2022), p.32, available at: *https://www.gov.ie/en/collection/4790f-family-justice-strategy/*.

[55] [1996] 1 I.L.R.M. 555.

[56] [1996] 1 I.L.R.M. 555 at 559. Roe, who was Bridget Cole, subsequently died in 1997. Her case triggered the Lindsay Tribunal into how infected blood products were distributed by the Irish Blood Transfusion Board.

If this case were brought now, the plaintiff would be protected by s.27 of the Civil Law (Miscellaneous Provisions) Act 2008. Under this section, a person whose civil case revolves around their medical condition can apply to prohibit the publication of any details that would lead to their identification. This application will only be granted if the identification of the person would be likely to cause them distress.

9–23 For cases other than those involving medical conditions, the basic rule established in *Roe* still applies. In *Doe v Revenue Commissioners*, where the plaintiffs wanted to anonymously challenge the Revenue Commissioners' interpretation of the penalties section in the Taxes Consolidation Act 1997, Clarke J. stated that the only circumstance in which an individual can ask for anonymity in a court case, if not expressly provided for in a statute, is where the Constitution mandates it.[57] In his view, the only constitutional right that outweighs Article 34.1 is the right of an accused to a fair trial:

> "[The] rights [to privacy or to a good name] are not of the same weighty nature (in distinction to the right of an accused to a fair trial) such as could displace the clear obligation to conduct the administration of justice in public. To the extent, therefore, that the plaintiffs may have a general constitutional right to privacy which applies to such matters concerning their revenue affairs as may be deemed confidential by statute and where there is no other overriding requirement (such as the proper determination of litigation), those rights cannot interfere with the clear and weighty constitutional obligation to the effect that justice be administered in public."[58]

9–24 In family law, abbreviations are used to protect the anonymity of the parties, instead of pseudonyms, for example O'D for O'Donnell, McC for McCarthy, etc. Pseudonyms are permitted in cases involving minors, such as *Attorney General v X*, a case considered in Ch.8.[59] These anonymity protections can continue beyond the conclusion of the case by court order as another case involving minors illustrates. Following their convictions for the murder (Boy A and Boy B) and aggravated sexual

[57] [2008] 3 I.R. 328 at 338.
[58] [2008] 3 I.R. 328 at 342.
[59] [1992] 1 I.R. 1. See Ch.8, Box 8.3.

assault (Boy A) of Ana Kriégel in 2019, several people shared images of one/both boys on social media and/or named them. Eleven people were charged, 10 of whose cases were forwarded to the Circuit Court.[60] In his sentencing remarks in one of the cases for which sentencing information is available,[61] Judge Codd noted that "[p]eople have to understand they don't have to publish every opinion they hold into the world of social media ... the world doesn't need to know their views on all things."[62] Concerns about the misuse of social media during trials and its impact on the constitutional right to a fair trial have led to the introduction of a practice direction that bans live posts during trials apart from bona fide posts by journalists and lawyers.[63] However, where a child "ages out", i.e. becomes an adult, during their trial or in the period between conviction and taking an appeal, they can be named as long as there is not a court order in place prohibiting their naming.[64]

Box 9.2: Court Reporters

The difficulty experienced in finding out what happened in the Circuit Criminal Court cases taken against those who shared photographs/ names of the two teenage boys convicted in the Kriégel case exposes a major issue with the principle of open courts. In reality, most of us will not sit in on a court case unless we work in the legal sphere or the case is one that directly affects us or someone we know. We therefore depend on the media to attend court in our stead and report on what occurs to assure us that justice is being done. However, with declining

60 Six men and four women; T. Tuite, "10 accused of sharing pictures or naming boys who murdered Ana Kriegel", *The Journal* (28 October 2020).

61 Of the three Circuit Court cases for which information on sentence is available, sentences ranged from eight months suspended to 18 months. Three accused have been granted permission to challenge the decision to charge them before the Circuit Criminal Court rather than in the District Criminal Court; A. O'Loughlin, "Three accused of identifying boys who murdered Ana Kriegel get further appeal", *Irish Examiner* (2 May 2024). One accused had challenged the allocation of jurisdiction to the Circuit Court at High Court level but he is not listed in the Supreme Court appeal and information on whether his case has proceeded could not be found. The same is true of the remaining three accused whose cases were forwarded to the Circuit Court. The sole person charged before the District Court was fined €1,200.

62 E. Dodd, "Woman who identified one of Ana Kriégel's killers on Facebook escapes prison sentence", *Limerick Leader* (20 March 2024).

63 SC18 – Use of cameras and electronic devices in court (19 November 2018), available at: *https://www.courts.ie/content/use-cameras-and-electronic-devices-court.*

64 *People (DPP) v PB*, unreported, Court of Appeal, 19 January 2024. The Supreme Court has agreed to hear an appeal against this judgment; *People (DPP) v PB* [2024] IESCDET 41.

resources, due both to audiences moving away from traditional media and a collapse in advertising revenue since 2008,[65] media organisations have less money to hire dedicated court reporters and the ones they do have are typically not sent to report on cases being heard before the inferior courts. This matters because "[t]he fewer cases that are reported, the less aware the public is of the rule of law and the less informed they are as to whether justice is being administered in the way it should."[66]

In the *Report of the Future of Media Commission*, the "importance of comprehensive, professional and publicly accessible reports of court proceedings"[67] was acknowledged, as was the fact that it is costly to hire and train journalists with the requisite knowledge of legal processes. They accordingly recommended the setting up of a scheme that would fund court reporting at local, regional and national levels. In partial meeting of this recommendation, Coimisiún na Meán received €6 million in funding from the government to fund a pilot court reporting scheme for inferior courts and a scheme that will cover local authority hearings.[68] Both public interest journalism schemes were launched in July 2024, with an application deadline in September 2024, and regulated broadcast/print/online media outlets or skilled journalists who are affiliated with a regulated outlet can apply. The funding can be used to cover 100 per cent of the costs incurred to provide additional court reporting by hiring a new/freelance journalist or turning a part-time contract into a full-time one.[69] All material generated will be posted freely on An Coimisiún na Meán's website within seven days of being posted/printed by the media organisation. It must also be freely available on the media organisation's own website. After 12-months, An Coimisiún na Meán will review the operation, effectiveness, and impact of the scheme and submit a report to the Minister for Tourism, Culture, Arts, Gaeltacht, Sport and Media.

65 Future of Media Commission, *Report of the Future of Media Commission* (July 2022), p.94.

66 Coimisiún na Meán, *Courts Reporting Scheme* (10 July 2024), p.5, available at: *https://www.cnam.ie/wp-content/uploads/2024/07/20240710_CRS_v.01_AOB_Accessible.pdf*.

67 Future of Media Commission, *Report of the Future of Media Commission* (July 2022), p.172.

68 This was also a recommendation of the Future of Media Commission. See *Report of the Future of Media Commission* (July 2022), pp.170–171.

69 Coimisiún na Meán, *Courts Reporting Scheme* (10 July 2024), p.8, available at: *https://www.cnam.ie/wp-content/uploads/2024/07/20240710_CRS_v.01_AOB_Accessible.pdf.*

C. The First-Instance Jurisdiction of the Domestic Courts

9–25 A court is said to have original or first-instance jurisdiction when it is the first court with the ability or authority to hear the claim or case in question. In this section, we will consider the first-instance jurisdiction of Irish courts. Before doing so, it is important to note what principles and practices guide the assignation of jurisdiction to particular courts.

9–26 In civil cases, which court has jurisdiction is determined by one of two means. First, jurisdiction is based on the amount of damages being sought. The precise quantum amounts will be discussed later. Second, in cases where damages are not the primary focus of the case, the legislature has assigned certain categories of litigation to certain courts. In both instances, it is assumed that the more complicated the case or the greater the amount of damages being sought, then the more serious are the issues being raised. The capacity of each court to deal with serious issues increases as we move up the first-instance court hierarchy, with the least serious cases being heard by the District Court and the most serious by the High Court.

9–27 In criminal cases, jurisdiction is determined by the class of the offence. There are two types of offence: summary and indictable. Summary offences are also known as "minor" offences and can be tried without a jury, pursuant to Article 38.2 of the Constitution. Indictable offences are more serious offences and they usually carry with them the right to trial by jury. However, the Constitution does not explain how you can distinguish between a major and a minor offence. For that, you have to turn to case law, specifically the cases of *Melling v Ó Mathghamhna*[70] and *Conroy v Attorney General*.[71] In both of these cases, the Supreme Court indicated that two factors are important in determining whether a criminal offence is a minor one or not:

(a) the severity of the punishment prescribed for the offence; and
(b) the moral guilt involved.

[70] [1962] I.R. 1.
[71] [1965] I.R. 411.

9–28 The severity of the punishment is the primary consideration and it was noted in *Melling* that imprisonment over 12 months could change an offence from minor to major. In *Conroy*, a case where the accused argued that his disqualification from driving raised the offence from being a minor one to a serious one, a distinction was made between primary and secondary punishment:

> "In the opinion of this Court, so far as punishment is concerned, the punishment which must be examined for the purpose of gauging the seriousness of an offence is what may be referred to as 'primary punishment.' That is the type of punishment which is regarded as punishment in the ordinary sense and, where crime is concerned, is either the loss of liberty or the intentional penal deprivation of property whether by means of fine or other direct method of deprivation."[72]

In other words, although being disqualified from holding a driving licence can have very severe consequences for certain people, particularly those who drive for a living, it is not a primary punishment but a punishment whose punitive character differs according to the circumstances of the particular individual concerned. Accordingly, it can be disregarded for the purposes of evaluating the nature of the offence in question.

9–29 This distinction has been roundly criticised by Kelly, a leading, but now deceased, constitutional scholar:

> "Apart from the instinct which must protest against admitting … any distinction between 'primary' and 'secondary' punishment, it seems wrong to present a forfeiture, revocation or disqualification as a 'regulation' or 'withdrawal' of a statutory right. The truth, historically, in this State as any other, must be that once upon a time everyone was free to sell drink, lay bets or travel in a vehicle; only when the State perceived a potential public injury in this uncontrolled liberty … was it proposed to avert this injury, or reduce the risk of it, by a regime of licensing. This was … a general though conditional curtailment of freedom, though not a punishment. To make, however, in the case of an individual infringing one of

[72] [1965] I.R. 411 at 441.

the terms on which limited freedom was still allowed to him, a conditional liberty into an absolute deprivation of liberty ... is a real punishment."[73]

9–30 The second consideration is the moral quality of the offence. In *Melling*, not much time was spent on the moral quality of the crimes, apart from Lavery J. noting that moral blame can be imputed to those who violate the tax code on a commercial scale.[74] Kingsmill Moore J. agreed, suggesting that smuggling on a commercial scale involves moral delinquency.[75] *Conroy* is the more significant precedent on this point. In the High Court, it was determined that drunk driving was very morally wrong due to the potential for loss of life. The Supreme Court took a slightly different approach. Although the Supreme Court agreed that drunk driving is morally wrong, they noted that the moral guilt attaching to an offence can vary depending on the circumstances of that offence. Accordingly, the immorality of an accused's actions is only relevant if it is part of the definition of the offence in question. Walsh J. stated:

> "The fact that in many or even most cases the circumstances under which the offence is committed are of a character to create a considerable moral guilt is not relevant when those aggravating circumstances are not the necessary ingredients of the offence."[76]

However, he noted that some offences could never be minor ones because of their high levels of moral guilt:

> "But the moral quality of the acts necessary to constitute the offence as defined by law is a relevant consideration. For example, the offences of murder, manslaughter or rape as now legally defined are offences of such grave moral guilt as to make it impossible to consider them minor offences within the meaning of Article 38 of the Constitution, even if the punishment provided by law was minimal."[77]

[73] G. Hogan, G. Whyte, D. Kenny and R. Walsh, *Kelly: The Irish Constitution*, 5th edn (Dublin: Bloomsbury Professional, 2018), para.6.5.345. For an example of a recent decision exploring this, see *Carroll v A Judge of the District Court and the DPP* [2023] IECA 271, in particular paras 43–52.

[74] [1962] I.R. 1 at 15.

[75] [1962] I.R. 1 at 34.

[76] [1965] I.R. 411 at 435–436.

[77] [1965] I.R. 411 at 436.

As a result of comments made in these cases, the maximum prison sentence for a summary offence has generally been set at 12 months. Since 1994, offences with fines of up to €5,000 have also been regarded as minor offences.[78]

9–31 Tom O'Malley SC notes that, at times, there is "neither rhyme nor reason" to determining what offences are serious or less serious.[79] Focusing on sexual offences, O'Malley remarks:

> "Provided the indictment includes a rape or aggravated sexual assault charge, the case must be tried in the Central Criminal Court. Otherwise, it will be tried in the Circuit Court. So, if a person were accused of serial child abuse, but all the offences charged involved sexual assault, incest and/or so-called defilement (sexual intercourse with an underage person), he will be tried in the Circuit Court. On the other hand, a person charged with a single offence of rape must be tried in the Central Criminal Court. The Criminal Law (Sexual Offences) Act 2017 introduces many new sexual offences against children and persons with mental disabilities, and it amends the definitions of many others. Yet, all of these offences, despite the complexity of some of their definitions, will be triable in the Circuit Court."[80]

1. Supreme Court

9–32 The Supreme Court has original jurisdiction for two matters only. As it is the highest-ranking domestic court, it also has exclusive jurisdiction for these matters. The first is for an Article 26 procedure. This procedure is invoked where, having received a Bill for signature, the President refers the Bill to the Supreme Court as the President is concerned that the Bill or any provision of the Bill may be unconstitutional. There have been 16 Article 26 referrals up to September 2024.[81] The second matter is where

---

[78] R. Byrne, P. McCutcheon, L. Cahillane and E. Roche-Cagney, *Byrne and McCutcheon on the Irish Legal System*, 7th edn (Dublin: Bloomsbury Professional, 2020), para.5.116. For a recent exploration of this, again within the field of driving offences, see *People (DPP) v Coen* [2022] IECA 308, in particular paras 24–33.

[79] T. O'Malley, "The Allocation of Criminal Jurisdiction – Again" (2018), available at: *https://www.universityofgalway.ie/media/law/docs/The-Allocation-of-Criminal-Jurisdiction.docx.*

[80] T. O'Malley, "The Allocation of Criminal Jurisdiction – Again" (2018), p.5.

[81] The most recent referral was *Re Article 26 of the Constitution and the Judicial Appointments Commission Bill 2022* [2023] IESC 34.

a question as to the permanent incapacity of the President arises. This is provided for by Article 12.3.1.° The Supreme Court has never been called on to consider such a question to date.

2. High Court/Central Criminal Court

9–33 Any High Court judge is entitled to determine any case, whether civil or criminal. This is provided for by Article 34.3.1° of the Constitution:

> "The Courts of First Instance shall include a High Court invested with full original jurisdiction in and power to determine all matters and questions whether of law or fact, civil or criminal."

This means that the High Court possesses an inherent jurisdiction to hear all matters but, in practice, legislation has been enacted to devolve the consideration of certain matters to particular courts. It was, however, noted in *R v R* that even when legislation gives jurisdiction to another court, the High Court retains concurrent jurisdiction by virtue of Article 34.3.2°.[82]

9–34 Up until 1988, all personal injuries actions in the High Court were heard with a jury. That right to a jury has been limited, but cases where a jury is present include libel, slander, and false imprisonment.[83] In addition, the workload of the High Court has been reduced with the establishment of the Personal Injuries Resolution Board (Injuries Board) by the Personal Injuries Assessment Board Act 2003, as amended. In its 2023 Annual Report, the Injuries Board noted that it had awarded €170 million in claims that year,[84] a slight increase on the 2022 awards, which had been the lowest amount awarded in 16 years.[85] It was estimated that the use of the Injuries Board, rather than courts and associated litigation costs, resulted in €75 million of costs being avoided.[86] 2022 was the first full year that the Personal Injuries Guidelines were used[87]

82 [1984] I.R. 296.

83 The Defamation (Amendment) Bill 2024 proposed to remove the jury from defamation cases. This Bill lapsed with the dissolution of the Dáil in November 2024.

84 Injuries Board, *Annual Report 2023* (Dublin: Injuries Board, 2024), p.7.

85 Injuries Board, *Annual Report 2022* (Dublin: Injuries Board, 2023), p.7.

86 Injuries Board, *Annual Report 2023* (Dublin: Injuries Board, 2024), p.7.

87 The constitutionality of these guidelines, introduced by the Judicial Council Act 2019, was challenged in *Delaney v Personal Injuries Assessment Board* [2024] IESC 10. Although the issuing of the guidelines was held to be an unconstitutional breach of

and the average award was down by 34 per cent on previous years.[88] The Injuries Board deals with civil actions by employees against their employers for negligence or breach of duty arising in the course of the employee's employment with that employer; actions arising out of the ownership, driving or use of a mechanically propelled vehicle; and actions arising out of occupiers' liability, among others.

9–35 The High Court's civil jurisdiction commences when claims exceed €75,000. This is because of quantum limits imposed on the Circuit Court. There is no limit on the amount of damages that the High Court can award. Indeed Byrne et al suggest that it might be unconstitutional to set an upper limit.[89] Apart from quantum, exclusive jurisdiction has been given to the High Court for a number of matters, either by the Constitution or by the legislature. Article 34.3.2° confers exclusive jurisdiction on the High Court to determine the constitutional validity of any legislation.[90] It also has exclusive jurisdiction over challenges to Oireachtas election[91] and referendum[92] results. Other examples of exclusive jurisdiction include s.564 of the Companies Act 2014, which confers exclusive jurisdiction on the High Court over winding-up proceedings, and s.509 of that Act, which provides that only the High Court can appoint a company examiner for large companies.[93] The High Court also has exclusive jurisdiction where an individual is claiming bankruptcy, pursuant to the terms of the Bankruptcy Act 1988, as amended. The final example of civil jurisdiction that will be mentioned is s.14 of the Competition Act 2002, which provides that civil proceedings under that Act can be taken in the Circuit Court or the High Court. This is a change on the previous position whereby proceedings could only be initiated in the Circuit Court. The Competition Act 2002 was influenced by the report of the Competition and Mergers Review Group which considered that, because most competition cases

judicial independence, it was also determined that this breach had been remedied by s.30 of the Family Leave and Miscellaneous Provisions Act 2021. Future guidelines will be governed by the amendment of the 2019 Act by Pt 6 of the Courts, Civil Law and Superannuation (Miscellaneous Provisions) Act 2024.

88 Injuries Board, *Annual Report 2022* (Dublin: Injuries Board, 2023), p.5.

89 R. Byrne, P. McCutcheon, L. Cahillane and E. Roche-Cagney, *Byrne and McCutcheon on the Irish Legal System*, 7th edn (Dublin: Bloomsbury Professional, 2020), para.5.94.

90 However, this decision can be appealed to the Court of Appeal and/or the Supreme Court.

91 Electoral Act 1992 s.132.

92 Referendum Act 1994 s.42.

93 The same section provides that small companies can go before the Circuit Court.

are quite complex, even though they may appear comparatively simple, cases should be dealt with by specialist High Court judges.[94]

9–36 When the High Court hears criminal cases at first instance, it is known as the Central Criminal Court and these cases are tried by a judge and jury. A jury is required because the Central Criminal Court only hears very serious criminal matters and, pursuant to Article 38.5 of the Constitution, an accused is entitled to a jury in such circumstances. However, the vast majority of criminal cases are heard in the lower courts, and it is generally only the most serious crimes that are reserved for the Central Criminal Court, specifically cases where the accused is charged with encouraging, harbouring, or comforting persons found guilty of treason, any case where the accused is charged with usurping the functions of the Government, or where the accused is charged with murder or piracy.[95] Other examples of exclusive first-instance jurisdiction include various sexual offences under the Criminal Law (Rape) (Amendment) Act 1990, offences under the Genocide Act 1973, offences under the Geneva Conventions Act 1962, and offences contrary to the International Criminal Court Act 2006.

9–37 An interesting example of where exclusive jurisdiction is granted to the High Court based not on the seriousness of the offence but on its complexity is s.11 of the Competition Act 2002. This section provides that certain offences, namely under anti-competitive agreements, decisions or concerted practices (s.6) and abuse of a dominant position (s.7) can be tried summarily in the lower courts, but they may only be tried on indictment in the Central Criminal Court. This provision was enacted in response to a recommendation of the Competition and Mergers Review Group.[96]

9–38 Finally, in addition to civil and criminal original jurisdictions, the High Court has an important supervisory role over the lower courts, tribunals and administrative bodies. It has the power to review the decisions of inferior courts and tribunals by way of judicial review. Judicial review is

[94] *Report of the Competition and Mergers Review Group* (Dublin: Stationery Office, 2000), paras 4.4.26, 4.9.11.

[95] Courts (Supplemental Provisions Act) 1961 s.25(2).

[96] *Report of the Competition and Mergers Review Group* (Dublin: Stationery Office, 2000), paras 4.4.26, 4.9.11.

not strictly speaking an appellate function, as it is not concerned with how the law was applied in a case but with whether the court/body in question had the authority to make such a decision and/or with the procedures utilised by the court/body to make the decision.[97]

3. Circuit Court

9–39 The Circuit Court has no inherent jurisdiction; it only has whatever jurisdiction is conferred on it by statute. Subject to the concurrent jurisdiction of the High Court, the Circuit Court has been given exclusive jurisdiction over the more serious family law matters, such as divorce and judicial separation.[98] It also hears examinership petitions from small and medium-sized companies,[99] and various landlord and tenant issues.[100] It has also been given the power to hear all civil matters that the High Court can hear, subject to two important limitations. First, if the Constitution or the legislature has granted exclusive jurisdiction to other courts, then the Circuit Court cannot hear such cases. For example, the Circuit Court has no jurisdiction over constitutional law, company law, judicial review or bankruptcy matters.

9–40 Second, the legislature has set a monetary limit for damages that can be sought before the Circuit Court. Pursuant to s.14 of the Courts and Civil Law (Miscellaneous Provisions) Act 2013, the Circuit Court can hear cases where damages of up to €75,000 are sought. However, this quantum limit can be exceeded if both parties agree in writing that the court can do so.[101] A separate and lower limit of €60,000 is set for cases involving personal injuries claims.[102] This is to encourage claimants and respondents to deal with such issues before the Injuries Board.

---

[97] See further, Ch.10, paras 10–17 to 10–19 and Box 10.2.

[98] Section 38(2) of the Family Law (Divorce) Act 1996 will be substituted by s.83 of the Family Courts Act 2024 when it is commenced. This substitution will relocate cases where land value is less than or equal to €1 million to the District Court. Practitioners strongly opposed this, describing it as the creation of a "two-tier family justice system"; C. Kenna, "Family Courts Bill will create 'two-tier' system for divorce, say barristers: Cases where family home is worth less than €1m will be heard in District Court", *Irish Times*, 21 March 2024.

[99] Companies Act 2014 s.509.

[100] Landlord and Tenant (Amendment) Act 1980.

[101] Courts (Supplemental Provisions) Act 1961 s.22(1)(b).

[102] The Third Schedule to the Courts (Supplemental Provisions) Act 1961, as amended by s.17 of the Courts and Civil Law (Miscellaneous Provisions) Act 2013.

9–41 The Circuit Court has an extensive criminal jurisdiction. All indictable offences, except those reserved exclusively for the Central Criminal Court, are tried with a 12-person jury in the Circuit Court. This is because, as stated previously, Article 38.5 of the Constitution provides that all non-minor criminal offences must be heard with a jury.

4. District Court

9–42 The District Court is also a court of local and limited jurisdiction whose jurisdiction is delineated exclusively by statute. Its civil jurisdiction is limited to cases involving claims of up to €15,000. This quantum limit is set by s.15 of the Courts and Civil Law (Miscellaneous Provisions) Act 2013. However, as with the Circuit Court, if both parties consent, then damages in excess of this amount may be awarded.[103] The District Court also has jurisdiction over family law matters, such as maintenance or custody and access rights, but the major family law issues, such as divorce and judicial separation, are currently reserved for the Circuit[104] and High Courts. The District Court has also been granted exclusive jurisdiction for any contesting of the renewal of an intoxicating liquor licence.[105]

9–43 One of the more important functions that the District Court fulfils in its civil capacity is the operation of the Small Claims Court. The Small Claims Court is administered in the District Court by the District Court Clerk, known as the Small Claims Registrar. The Registrar acts to try to reach a compromise between the two parties involved, both of whom must live in or be based in Ireland,[106] and it can be accessed online via the *courts.ie* and the *citizensinformation.ie* websites. The service was originally only open to consumers, i.e. someone not acting in the course of a business, but since January 2010, businesses can institute small claims against each other before the Small Claims Court too. Claims arising in the following circumstances are excluded from the scheme: personal injuries, hire-purchase agreements, debts, and breaches of

[103] Courts Act 1991 s.4(c).

[104] But see fn.98 on possible changes here if the relevant section of the Family Courts Act 2024 is commenced.

[105] Courts (No. 2) Act 1986 s.4.

[106] If one of the parties resides in or is based in an EU member state, the relevant process is the European Small Claims Procedure. This process cannot be completed online and requires submitting the application to the Small Claims Registrar in your local District Court; see *https://www.citizensinformation.ie/en/justice/courts-system/european-small-claims-procedure/*.

leasing agreements.[107] A small claim is one that is under €2,000. There is a fee of €25 to avail of the service. If the claim is disputed by the respondent, the Registrar will try to negotiate a settlement between the parties. If one cannot be reached, then there is a formal hearing of the matter in the District Court. The decision of the District Court may be appealed to the Circuit Court. Although either side may engage the services of a solicitor, the service is designed to allow the parties to proceed without one.

9–44 With regard to the District Court's criminal jurisdiction, the District Court hears summary, i.e. non-jury, cases only. In addition, the District Court has jurisdiction to hear indictable offences triable summarily. These are hybrid offences that may be tried on indictment in one of the higher criminal courts but can also be heard summarily by the District Court where the Director of Public Prosecutions (DPP) directs and when the judge is satisfied that the offence is minor in nature. "Either way" offences are also offences that can be tried summarily or on indictment, but these offences are scheduled to the Criminal Justice Act 1951. If an "either way" offence is to be tried summarily, a number of conditions must be satisfied. Like hybrid offences, the District Court judge will consider whether the factual circumstances of the alleged offence make it a minor one. The accused must also have waived their right to be heard by a jury. For some specific offences, for example where damage caused to property is over a certain amount, the consent of the DPP is required.

9–45 Since 1 May 2002, the District Court becomes the Children Court[108] when it hears criminal charges against children, apart from rape, murder and manslaughter, or when hearing applications for orders relating to a child. There is a separate criminal court for children where proceedings are held in camera[109] because it is recognised that a child who commits a crime is not in the same position as an adult and, for this reason, it is appropriate to treat the child differently in the hope that they can be diverted from a life of crime. The requirement that the District Court must sit in a different building or room and on different days or times from any

[107] Order 53A r.1 of the District Court Rules, as substituted by the District Court (Small Claims) Rules 2009 (S.I. No. 519 of 2009).
[108] Established by Pt 7 of the Children Act 2001.
[109] See Section B.4(a).

other court when it exercises its jurisdiction as the Children Court[110] is an additional recognition of the increased trauma of the criminal justice experience for a child.

9–46 If the offence is a summary one, the Children Court can process the case in a way similar to that of an ordinary trial, but the court has options that an adult court does not. The court has the power to divert the juvenile either to the care of Tusla (Child and Family Agency),[111] where the child's needs will be assessed in a family welfare conference, or to the Probation Service,[112] where the juvenile will participate in a family conference the purpose of which is to prevent the recurrence of offending. This plan is subject to the supervision of the Children Court and, if the child does not comply with the plan, then criminal proceedings can be recommenced before the Children Court.

9–47 If the offence is indictable, s.75 of the Children Act 2001 provides that the Children Court may deal summarily with the offence, apart from the most serious offences such as rape, murder and manslaughter which are required to be tried by the Central Criminal Court. In such cases, the child will be prosecuted as an adult. It is "may" not "must" because children accused of an indictable offence have the right to trial by jury. Accordingly, they must consent to their case proceeding before the Children Court.

9–48 Finally, the District Court serves as the first port of call for serious offences. It is the court before which the book of evidence is presented and the District Court judge determines if there is a case to answer. If yes, the accused is sent to trial either to the Circuit Court or the Central Criminal Court.

5. Special Criminal Court

9–49 The final court that has a first-instance jurisdiction that we will consider in this chapter is the Special Criminal Court and, as its name

[110] In Dublin, the Children Court is housed in Smithfield and hears cases daily.
[111] Originally, the juvenile was diverted to the relevant health board pursuant to s.77 of the Children Act 2001. This became the Child and Family Agency by virtue of Sch.2 to the Child and Family Agency Act 2013.
[112] Children Act 2001 s.78.

suggests, it hears criminal cases only. These cases are special because, pursuant to Article 38.5, no jury is required. Article 38.3 explains that such a court can be created "where ... ordinary courts are inadequate to secure the effective administration of justice, and the preservation of public peace and order". We see this same language utilised in Pt V of the Offences against the State Act 1939 (the "1939 Act"), which established the Special Criminal Court for the first time in 1939. Section 35 of the 1939 Act provides that such a court can be established "whenever the Government is satisfied that the ordinary courts are inadequate to secure the effective administration of justice and the preservation of public peace and order".

9–50 The Executive has brought the Special Criminal Court into existence three times. The first time was in 1939 (and the court continued to exist until 1946) in response to concern that the IRA would compromise Irish neutrality during World War II; the second in 1961 (for nine months in response to an IRA border campaign);[113] and, finally, in 1972 in response to "The Troubles" in the North. The Special Criminal Court remains operational to date and it has been scaled up, with two courts hearing cases since 2016. A case can be sent to the Special Criminal Court No. 1 or No. 2 by one of two routes. First, the Government can designate offences as scheduled offences, pursuant to s.36 of the 1939 Act. Anyone who commits a scheduled offence must be tried in the Special Criminal Court unless the DPP directs otherwise. Second, the DPP is empowered under s.46 of the 1939 Act to require that a person be tried before the Special Criminal Court.[114]

9–51 Unlike the other trial courts, where verdicts are issued either by a judge sitting alone or by a jury, both Special Criminal Courts sit with a panel of three judges. Section 39 of the 1939 Act allows for judges to be drawn from the ranks of barristers and solicitors of seven years'

[113] Although it should be noted that a proclamation was not issued by the Executive on this occasion. The proclamation issued in 1939 had not been revoked so the Special Criminal Court was simply "revived" in 1961. R. Byrne, P. McCutcheon, L. Cahillane and E. Roche-Cagney, *Byrne and McCutcheon on the Irish Legal System*, 7th edn (Dublin: Bloomsbury Professional, 2020), para.5.140.

[114] Note that the 1939 Act specifies the Attorney General, but by virtue of s.3 of the Prosecution of Offences Act 1974, the DPP has been empowered to perform the functions of the Attorney General as provided for under any criminal law statute or statutory instrument, which would obviously include the 1939 Act.

standing, an officer of the Defence Forces with a rank of commandant or above, in addition to ordinary judges from the ranks of the District Court, Circuit Court and High Court. Since its re-establishment in 1972, only ordinary judges have sat on the Special Criminal Court. However, in both its first and second incarnations, all of the judges were members of the Defence Forces.[115] At present, and for some years past, the practice has been to appoint one High Court judge, one Circuit Court judge and one District Court judge. Currently, there is a panel of 19 judges drawn from these three courts who may sit as judges of the Special Criminal Court.

9–52 The continued existence of the Special Criminal Court since 1972, and its shift from hearing alleged paramilitary cases to those allegedly connected to organised crime, has been challenged unsuccessfully in courts[116] and has been criticised by various national and international human rights bodies. As Conway et al note, it is debatable that we can be said to be experiencing an emergency in excess of then-40 now-50 years.[117] However, the Government shows no sign of wishing to wind down the Special Criminal Court, most recently renewing a list of offences connected to organised crime that had been added to the 1939 Act Schedule by s.8 of the Criminal Justice (Amendment) Act 2009.[118]

9–53 This practice of scheduling offences was criticised in 2023 in the judge-led review of the Offences against the State Acts 1939–1998. Although there were significant points of disagreement between the authors of the majority and minority reports, both reports recommended that a decision on whether a case should be sent to the Special Criminal Court should be made on its merits rather than because the accused happens to be accused of committing a particular offence.[119] There was

[115] J.A. Andrews, *Human Rights in Criminal Procedure* (The Hague: M. Nijhoff, 1982), p.185.

[116] *Kavanagh v Ireland* [1996] 1 I.R. 321; *Dowdall v DPP* [2022] IESC 36.

[117] V. Conway, Y. Daly and J. Schweppe, *Irish Criminal Justice: Theory, Process and Procedure* (Dublin: Clarus Press, 2010), para.8.75.

[118] Department of Justice, "Oireachtas approves renewal of provisions to combat terrorism and organised crime" (27 June 2024), available at: *https://www.gov.ie/en/press-release/5a94c-oireachtas-approves-renewal-of-provisions-to-combat-terrorism-and-organised-crime/*.

[119] The majority recommended that this assessment be made by the DPP, the minority recommended that it be a judge as part of a pre-trial review of the evidence; Offences Against the State Acts Independent Review Group, *Report of the Majority* (May 2023), paras 4.58–4.62; Offences Against the State Acts Independent Review Group, *Report of the Minority* (May 2023), p.9.

also agreement that more measures should be put in place to protect jurors—the ostensible reason for the existence of the Special Criminal Court[120]—with the result that resort to the court would be rarer than it currently is. These measures would include:

- providing for juror anonymity;
- limiting access to the juror lists;
- screening jurors from public view;
- special protection measures for jurors during the trial; and
- locating jurors in a different place from where the trial is held, with communication via video link.[121]

It remains to be seen whether any of these recommendations will be followed or whether they and the reports that contain them will gather dust on the shelves alongside the Hederman J.-led review which issued similar recommendations in 2002.[122]

D. The Appellate Jurisdiction of the Domestic Courts

9–54 All of our domestic courts, bar the Special Criminal Court and the District Court, have an appellate function. Accordingly, in this section we will exclude those two courts from consideration. Appeals can be divided into three types:

(a) an appeal de novo;
(b) an appeal on a point of law; or
(c) an appeal on the facts.

[120] But see criticism of this argument in Irish Human Rights and Equality Commission, *Submission to the Independent Review Group on the Offences Against the State Acts* (November 2021), pp.25–36, available at: *https://www.ihrec.ie/documents/submission-to-the-independent-review-group-on-the-offences-against-the-state-acts/*. This criticism was dismissed in the majority report; Offences Against the State Acts Independent Review Group, *Report of the Majority* (May 2023), para.4.16. The minority report was critical of this dismissal; Offences Against the State Acts Independent Review Group, *Report of the Minority* (May 2023), pp.5–6.

[121] Offences Against the State Acts Independent Review Group, *Report of the Majority* (May 2023), paras 4.62–4.63; Offences Against the State Acts Independent Review Group, *Report of the Minority* (May 2023), pp.7–8.

[122] *Report of the Committee to Review the Offences Against the State Acts 1939–1998 and Related Matters* (October 2002), available at: *https://assets.gov.ie/236674/178286b1-3aa7-4acc-b6b6-84a68fc0f937.pdf.*

A de novo appeal is one where a party to the case applies for the case to be reheard in its entirety before a higher court. Such an appeal, in effect, erases the lower court hearing of the case and the case is heard as if for the first time. "De novo" translates as "afresh" or "beginning again". De novo appeals can be raised by parties to civil and criminal cases in the District Court or in the Circuit Court. The appeal is heard by the next court in the hierarchy of the courts, so the Circuit Court hears de novo appeals from the District Court and the High Court hears de novo appeals from the Circuit Court. There is no de novo appeal from the High Court to the Court of Appeal. The de novo court is constrained by the limits imposed on the original court, i.e. the appellate court cannot impose a penalty or liability greater than would have been possible in the lower court. The decision of the de novo court is generally final and not appealable.

9–55 An appeal on a point of law does not involve a rehearing of the case. Its focus is far more precise. The appellant argues that the trial judge in a civil or criminal case incorrectly applied the law on a particular issue, that a decision was made in ignorance of the relevant law, or that they incorrectly directed the jury as to the appropriate law. Opposing counsel therefore focus their attention on those specific legal issues.

9–56 The third category of appeal is an appeal on the facts. Such appeals are very rare, as witnesses do not re-testify on appeal. Instead, the appellate court relies on transcripts taken at the court of first instance. Accordingly, if the appellate court can find a logical foundation for various findings of fact made by the lower court, it will accept those findings. The reason is obvious: the lower court judge scrutinises the witnesses—considers how they compose themselves, how they answer the questions put to them—and deduces their credibility from these observations. This information is not available to the appellate judges.

9–57 However, an appellate court can overrule secondary findings of fact made by a first-instance court. Secondary findings are inferences drawn from the primary findings of fact, i.e. additional findings of fact based on a process of logical deduction from the primary facts that have been proved. Their significance is not determined by how credible or not a witness was. An example is the case of *Hanrahan v Merck Sharp*

& Dohme (Ireland) Ltd.[123] The plaintiff dairy farmers claimed that they, their farm animals, and plant life on the farm, had suffered severe injury and damage as a result of emissions from the defendant factory. In the High Court, Keane J. found that the scientific evidence provided by the defendant proved that the emissions were not to blame for the animals' illnesses and abnormalities, and that soil toxicity was within recommended guidelines. He also determined that insufficient evidence was presented to support claims in respect of the second plaintiff's respiratory illness.

9–58 The Supreme Court disagreed, with Henchy J. stating that the High Court judge should have given less weight to the abstract scientific evidence and more weight to the direct evidence of locals who testified as to the concurrence of the emission of toxic fumes and the plaintiffs' animals being in visible distress, and to the second plaintiff's doctor. He held:

> "[T]he scientific evidence ... given on behalf of the defendants ... even if accepted in full ... only shows what *could* or *should* have happened in the way of damage by toxic emissions. In the light of what did happen in the way of toxic damage, I consider that the defendants' evidence could not be held to rebut the plaintiffs' case. Theoretical or inductive evidence cannot be allowed to displace proven facts ... It would be to allow scientific theorising to dethrone fact to [allow otherwise]."[124]

1. Supreme Court

9–59 The Supreme Court is primarily an appellate court. This function is noted in the Constitution. Article 34.5 states that the Court of Final Appeal shall be called the Supreme Court. It has the power to hear appeals from the Court of Appeal, but it does so in limited circumstances. Article 34.5.3° provides:

> "The Supreme Court shall, subject to such regulations as may be prescribed by law, have appellate jurisdiction from a decision of the Court of Appeal if the Supreme Court is satisfied that—

[123] [1988] I.L.R.M. 629.
[124] [1988] I.L.R.M. 629 at 644–645 (emphasis in original).

i the decision involves a matter of general public importance, or
ii in the interests of justice it is necessary that there be an appeal to the Supreme Court."

9–60 There is also the possibility of a direct appeal from the High Court to the Supreme Court, as provided for by Article 34.5.4°:

> "Notwithstanding section 4.1° hereof, the Supreme Court shall, subject to such regulations as may be prescribed by law, have appellate jurisdiction from a decision of the High Court if the Supreme Court is satisfied that there are exceptional circumstances warranting a direct appeal to it, and a precondition for the Supreme Court being so satisfied is the presence of either or both of the following factors:
> i the decision involves a matter of general public importance;
> ii the interests of justice."

This category of appeal is known as a "leapfrog" appeal.

9–61 Both appeal routes require an appellant to identify how their case meets the threshold for being heard before the Supreme Court,[125] namely that their case raises an issue of general public importance or that it is in the interests of justice for the Supreme Court to hear it. The "general public importance" criterion was considered in *BS v DPP*, where it was noted that:

> "… it can rarely be the case that the application of well established principles to the particular facts of the relevant proceedings can give rise to an issue of general public importance. … [But this] does not, in and of itself, mean that the way in which such principles may be properly applied in different types of circumstances may not itself potentially give rise to an issue which would meet the constitutional threshold."[126]

In *Odum v Minister for Justice and Equality*, O'Donnell C.J. observed: "[t]he fact that the importance is described as both *general* and *public* suggests that the issue transcends the particular case and the private dispute of the parties."[127]

125 *Attorney General v Lee* [2016] IESCDET 93 at para.18.
126 [2017] IESCDET 134 at para.5.
127 [2023] IESC 3 at para.35 (emphasis in original).

9–62 In *Quinn Insurance Ltd v PricewaterhouseCoopers*, it was stated that the "interests of justice" criterion was best viewed as a residual category and that an error did not amount to injustice.[128] Although O'Donnell C.J. was reluctant to give specific examples, the examples he gave have been described as "reflect[ing] the Supreme Court's aim to ensure fairness as between both sides in litigation."[129] He wrote:

> "First, a point may be made by way of cross-appeal, which itself cannot amount to a matter of general public importance. Nevertheless it would be unjust to permit one party to appeal to the Supreme Court and restrict another party from cross-appeal because the respondent's appeal point was not itself of general public importance. Similarly a point may be raised in a case which itself may not be of general public importance but which is necessary to permit an appellant to argue, since otherwise determination of the issue of general public importance may not resolve the case. A further example may be where the point the applicant seeks to advance relates to something which occurred for the first time in the Court of Appeal. It might be said in such circumstances that the interests of justice would be served by permitting an appeal to the Supreme Court even though the matter itself was not itself of general public importance."[130]

9–63 There is an additional requirement for an appellant seeking to pursue the leapfrog route. They must establish that there are "exceptional circumstances" that warrant a direct appeal to the Supreme Court. This requirement establishes that the "default position"[131] is that appeals from the High Court should be to the Court of Appeal. This is because, as explained in *Fox v Mahon*[132] and *Wansboro v DPP*,[133] having an intermediate appeal clarifies the issues.

9–64 In *Barlow v Minister for Agriculture, Food and Marine*,[134] the Supreme Court noted that a leapfrog appeal would be appropriate in cases involving temporal urgency:

---

[128] [2017] IESC 73 at para.9.

[129] H. Biehler, D. McGrath, E. Egan McGrath, A. Beirne and G. Downey, *Delany and McGrath on Civil Procedure*, 5th edn (Dublin: Round Hall, 2023), para.23–42.

[130] [2017] IESC 73 at para.9.

[131] *Wansboro v DPP* [2017] IESCDET 115 at para.6.

[132] [2015] IESCDET 2.

[133] [2017] IESCDET 115 at para.6.

[134] [2015] IESCDET 8.

> "There clearly will be cases where … a clock in the real world is ticking. In such cases, even if there may be perceived to be some … advantage to … an intermediate appeal, the balance may favour a direct appeal to this Court, precisely because the downside of any delay … would be disproportionate in the circumstances of the case."[135]

Temporal urgency was also identified as an example of a factor that would tilt the Supreme Court in favour of granting a leapfrog appeal in *Wansboro v DPP*, along with the cost of taking two appeals where little would be gained from an intermediate appeal; whether the uncertainty in law caused by the appeal affects other cases; and whether, even after the refinement of the issue(s) by an intermediate appeal, there would still be a live issue or issues requiring a hearing before the Supreme Court.[136] This was a non-exhaustive list.

Figure 9.1: Appeals to the Supreme Court

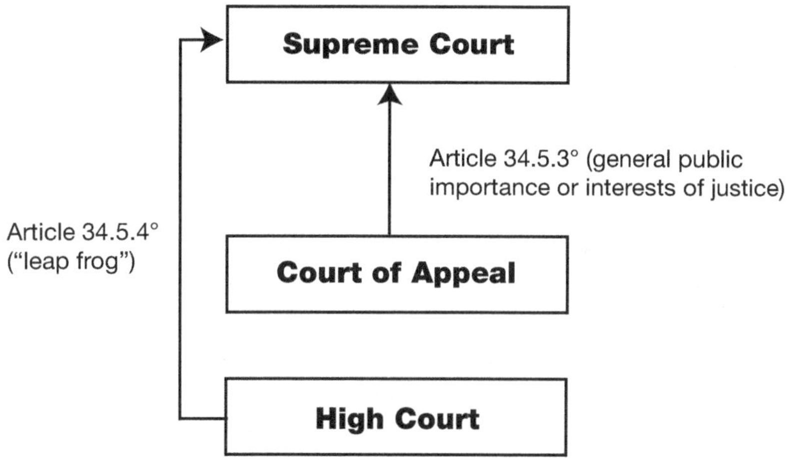

9–65 The changes inserted into the Constitution to require the establishment of the Court of Appeal have also introduced an appeal route, via the High Court, from the Circuit Court to the Supreme Court that did not exist before, as long as the issue(s) in the case meet(s) the constitutional threshold for an appeal. This is because Article 34.5.4° does not permit the legislature to exclude an appeal to the Supreme

[135] [2015] IESCDET 8 at para.17.
[136] [2017] IESCDET 115 at para.6.

Court. In *Pepper Finance Corporation (Ireland) DAC v Cannon*,[137] it was held that it was possible for an appeal to be taken from a decision of the High Court when it was exercising its appellate function for the Circuit Court. This was so despite s.39 of the Courts of Justice Act 1936 which provides that the decision of the High Court on an appeal under that part of the Act shall be "final and conclusive and not appealable".[138]

9–66 The revised Articles also mean that for the first time since its establishment, the Supreme Court decides for itself which cases it will hear. This, as Byrne et al note, is "a key change, bringing the Supreme Court into line with other comparable final courts of appeal in other jurisdictions, such as the UK Supreme Court and the US Supreme Court".[139] Prior to this, the Supreme Court operated as a final clearing house, and could not confine itself to questions of constitutional or public importance. This led to a significant backlog of up to four years before a non-urgent case could be heard before the Supreme Court.[140] Such a delay was obviously problematic in terms of the timely and effective administration of justice. Writing in 2019, Biehler observed that the constitutional reforms have had their desired result but that the transfer of jurisdiction of cases to the Court of Appeal has had the unsurprising result that delay has now become an issue for cases before the Court of Appeal.[141]

9–67 A second side-effect of the freeing-up of the Supreme Court's time has been its willingness to consider cases that previously it would have rejected for reasons of mootness, prematurity, or lack of standing. This, Casey and Doyle write, "illustrates its new role of providing clarification of legal principles as much as resolving disputes between parties."[142] Finally, the increasing length of Supreme Court judgments has been observed. This is both a positive and a negative. It is a positive because:

137 [2020] IESC 2.
138 [2020] IESC 2 at para.21.
139 R. Byrne, P. McCutcheon, L. Cahillane and E. Roche-Cagney, *Byrne and McCutcheon on the Irish Legal System*, 7th edn (Dublin: Bloomsbury Professional, 2020), para.7.26.
140 R. Mac Cormaic, "Supreme Court braced for a shake-up but reforms will leave important questions unanswered", *Irish Times*, 9 July 2013.
141 H. Biehler, "The Criteria for Appeals to the Supreme Court" (2019) 37(1) *Irish Law Times* 7 at 12.
142 C. Casey and O. Doyle, "Foreword: The Constitution under the New Supreme Court" (2024) 44(1) *Dublin University Law Journal* 5 at 33.

> "When we see judges moving in an intelligent, considerate, temperate way from one argument to the next, when we see judges navigating complexity and not skirting nuance, when we see judges arriving at wise, clear and reasoned conclusions, the whole legal system benefits from the seriousness and competence with which they engage in their work."[143]

The negative is that these careful, nuanced and lengthy judgments are harder to read, especially for students who are new to law,[144] so do not worry if you find them challenging. They are. Moreover, it could be argued that they raise rule of law concerns regarding the comprehensibility and precision of the law.[145]

2. Court of Appeal

9–68 The Court of Appeal came into being on 28 October 2014 when the Court of Appeal Act (the "2014 Act") was passed to give effect to the Thirty-third Amendment of the Constitution. The Court of Appeal can hear appeals from decisions on civil matters in the High Court, including those on the constitutionality of legislation.[146] The Court of Appeal held in *Collins v Minister for Justice, Equality and Law Reform* that when deciding an appeal from the High Court, it can overrule a High Court decision when the interests of justice dictate. Accordingly, it is not confined to overruling a High Court judgment when the lower court made an error in principle.[147]

9–69 The 2014 Act also gave the Court of Appeal the appellate function over criminal matters that was previously exercised by the Court of Criminal Appeal. These would include appeals by the DPP on the undue

[143] M. Cahill, "From *Cityview* to *NECI* and Judicial Virtues in Action: Afterword to the Foreword by Conor Casey and Oran Doyle" (2024) 44(2) *Dublin University Law Journal* 3 at 10.

[144] M. Cahill, "From *Cityview* to *NECI* and Judicial Virtues in Action: Afterword to the Foreword by Conor Casey and Oran Doyle" (2024) 44(2) *Dublin University Law Journal* 3 at 10–11.

[145] L. Cahillane and S. Enright, "Spring Cleaning in the Supreme Court and Potential Ripple Effects: Afterword to the Foreword by Conor Casey and Oran Doyle" (2024) 44(2) *Dublin University Law Journal* 13 at 19.

[146] Article 34.4.1°.

[147] [2015] IECA 27 at para.79.

leniency of a sentence[148] and on an acquittal.[149] A person convicted before the Circuit, Central Criminal or Special Criminal Courts can appeal their conviction or their sentence. The leave of the trial judge to appeal a conviction is no longer required.[150]

Figure 9.2: Appeals to the Court of Appeal

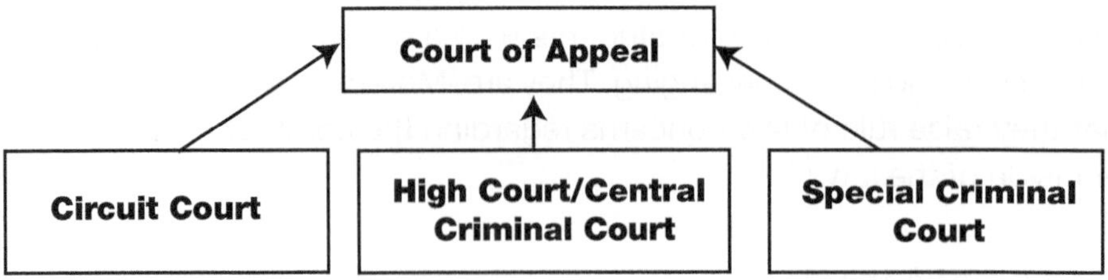

9–70 The Court of Appeal may also give a determination on any point of law referred to it by the Circuit Court by way of the case stated procedure. There are two types of case stated. One is where the final decision has been reached by the Circuit Court and the Court of Appeal is asked if it was the correct decision by means of a yes/no question.[151] The second, a consultative case stated, is where a final decision has not yet been made by the lower court and one party is seeking clarification on a point of law. Any party to a case that started in the Circuit Court can request that the Circuit Court judge refer a question of law to the Court of Appeal and the judge must forward the question on unless they regard it as frivolous. A refusal to forward the question can be subject to judicial review.

[148] Criminal Justice Act 1993 s.2.

[149] Criminal Procedure Act 1967 s.34, as amended by s.21 of the Criminal Justice Act 2006. However, such an appeal is one without prejudice to the accused who has been acquitted. The Court of Appeal's decision in such a case merely clarifies the law on a point for similar cases in the future.

[150] Criminal Procedure Act 2010 ss.31 and 32.

[151] See further, R. Byrne, P. McCutcheon, L. Cahillane and E. Roche-Cagney, *Byrne and McCutcheon on the Irish Legal System*, 7th edn (Dublin: Bloomsbury Professional, 2020), para.7.15.

Figure 9.3: Case Stated Appeals to the Court of Appeal

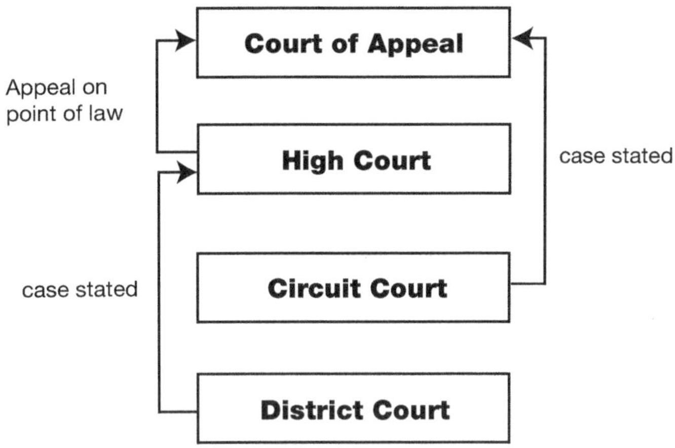

9–71 The Court of Appeal may also hear an appeal from a case that originated in the District Court where a question of law was referred to the High Court by means of the case stated procedure. In such instances, the Court of Appeal can hear an appeal from the decision of the High Court. This is provided for by s.8 of the 2014 Act.

3. High Court

9–72 The High Court can hear de novo appeals from all civil cases that originated in the Circuit Court. The High Court can also hear appeals from the District Court on a point of law through the case stated and consultative case stated procedures in civil and criminal cases. This appeal can be initiated by either party to the case. It may also hear appeals in certain other circumstances provided by statute, e.g. regarding decisions of the District Court on applications for bail. Finally, the High Court can hear appeals from decisions of other bodies, such as the Injuries Board. If either the claimant or the respondent is unhappy with the determination of the Injuries Board, then the Injuries Board will issue the party concerned the authorisation to proceed to the High Court.

Figure 9.4: Appeals to the High Court

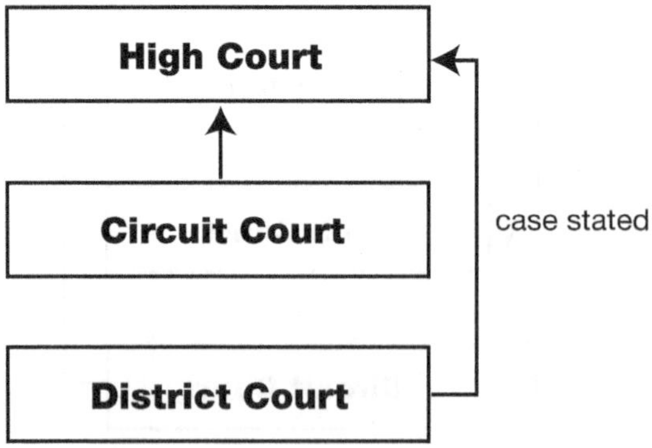

4. Circuit Court

9–73 In general, an appeal will lie from the District Court to the Circuit Court from civil and criminal matters. This appeal takes the form of a de novo appeal. The de novo decision of the Circuit Court is not appealable,[152] subject to the possibility of judicial review.[153] In criminal matters, the right to a de novo appeal from the District Court is limited to an accused who has been convicted.

E. Non-Domestic Courts

9–74 In addition to the domestic courts considered, there are two supranational courts that form part of our courts structure: the Court of Justice of the European Union (CJEU) and the European Court of Human Rights (ECtHR). The CJEU ranks higher than the Supreme Court in matters pertaining to European Union (EU) law. This alteration of the Supreme Court's status as the final court of appeal for such matters was made when Ireland joined the European Economic Community, as it then was, in 1972.[154] Ireland is a signatory to the European Convention on Human Rights (ECHR) and individuals can argue before the ECtHR that the signatory State is in breach of its obligations under the ECHR. The ECHR was adopted into Irish law at a sub-constitutional level by the

[152] Courts of Justice Act 1924 s.84, as amended by s.57 of the Courts of Justice Act 1936.

[153] *Tormey v Ireland* [1985] I.R. 289.

[154] Article 29.4.3°, as adopted by referendum on 8 June 1972.

European Convention on Human Rights Act 2003 (the "2003 Act").[155] We will now consider both courts briefly.

1. Court of Justice of the European Union

9–75 The CJEU, which is located in Luxembourg, comprises two courts: the Court of Justice and the General Court. We are concerned only with the Court of Justice as it is the court with primary responsibility for referrals from domestic courts, and it is the interaction between the Court of Justice and our domestic courts that is of interest to us.[156] The Court of Justice has 27 judges, all of whom hold office for six-year renewable terms.[157] The President of the court is elected by the judges of the court for a three-year term, which can also be renewed. The Court of Justice may sit as a full court or in a Grand Chamber of 15 judges if a Member State or a Union institution that is a party to the proceedings requests it, or if the case is particularly complex or important. It can also sit in chambers of three or five judges.

9–76 The Court of Justice is assisted in its decision-making by 11 Advocates General. The Advocate General reads and hears all the submissions made before the court and provides a detailed opinion as to what the outcome of the case should be. The court is not bound by their decision, but often follows it.[158] As Walsh notes, there is no equivalent counterpart to the Advocate General in the common law system.[159]

9–77 The Court of Justice's function is to ensure consistency and uniformity in the application of EU law across the Member States. Article 267 of the Treaty on the Functioning of the European Union provides that national courts and tribunals of a Member State may or must refer points of law to the Court of Justice depending on their ranking in the domestic system. Where the national court or tribunal is the final body

---

155 See further, Ch.6, paras 6–31 to 6–45 (EU law) and paras 6–87 to 6–91 (ECHR law).

156 For information on which preliminary references can be referred to the General Court, see Regulation (EU, Euratom) 2024/2019 of the European Parliament and of the Council of 11 April 2024 amending Protocol No 3 on the Statute of the Court of Justice of the European Union.

157 For information on the General Court, please refer to the CJEU website at: *http://curia.europa.eu/jcms/jcms/Jo2_7024/*.

158 D. Walsh, *Criminal Procedure* (Dublin: Thomson Round Hall, 2002), para.2–28.

159 D. Walsh, *Walsh on Criminal Procedure*, 2nd edn (Dublin: Thomson Reuters Round Hall, 2016), para.2–162, fn.456.

with authority to determine the matter, then it must refer the question to the Court of Justice. This would mean that any court exercising an appellate function from which no further appeal is typically allowed would be required to refer the question to the Court of Justice, i.e. the Supreme Court, the Court of Appeal, and the High and Circuit Courts when exercising their de novo appeal jurisdiction. If the national court or tribunal is not the final court of appeal, e.g. any court exercising a first-instance jurisdiction, it can still seek the Court of Justice's guidance. The general preference, however, is to try to decide cases without dealing with the European issue. This is, as Byrne et al note, very similar to the rule of self-restraint applied to constitutional issues which we considered in Ch.3.[160]

9–78 Once the question is answered by the Court of Justice, the case is returned to the national court or tribunal and the matter is decided by the national court or tribunal in accordance with the Court of Justice's ruling. The referral of a question to the Court of Justice is similar to the consultative case stated procedure that was outlined in the context of the domestic courts.[161]

2. European Court of Human Rights

9–79 The ECtHR derives its authority from the ECHR, which was enacted in 1950 in the wake of World War II. The ECHR is a document that seeks to provide international protection for various civil and political rights and freedoms. Any State that is a signatory to the ECHR agrees to adhere to its terms. One of the means of enforcing it is the ECtHR, which sits in Strasbourg.[162] Every signatory to the ECHR has a national judge sitting on the ECtHR, which means there are 46 judges elected to the ECtHR, all of whom hold office for a non-renewable period of nine years.[163] Cases that are found to be admissible are typically heard before committees of three judges or chambers of seven. In exceptional and appeal cases, a Grand Chamber of 17 judges will hear a case. Whenever a chamber or Grand Chamber hears a case, the judge who

[160] R. Byrne, P. McCutcheon, L. Cahillane and E. Roche-Cagney, *Byrne and McCutcheon on the Irish Legal System*, 7th edn (Dublin: Bloomsbury Professional, 2020), para.7.91.
[161] See paras 9–70 to 9–71.
[162] See further, Ch.6, paras 6–87 to 6–91.
[163] Article 23(1) ECHR.

was appointed by the respondent State will be an ex officio member of the bench to provide assistance to their peers in relation to the domestic legal system in question.[164] For cases heard before a committee, the domestic judge is empanelled only if necessary.[165]

9–80 In order to be heard before the ECtHR, the applicant must allege that one or more of their ECHR rights have been breached by a State, they must apply within four months of having exhausted their domestic avenues of redress, and they must have suffered a significant disadvantage. The application, submitted electronically, is first screened by the Court Registry and can be dismissed for administrative reasons, e.g. if the application is incomplete.[166] If the complaint clearly fails to meet the eligibility criteria outlined above, it is sent to a single judge who will issue an inadmissibility decision.[167] Approximately 80 per cent of applications to the ECtHR are disposed of in this manner.[168] If, after the preliminary screening, the complaint may have merit, it is sent to a committee of three judges (if it is a case that can be resolved with reference to established principles) or a chamber of seven (if it is a new or more complicated case) in order to determine if it should proceed. If it is determined that it is not admissible, the merits of the case are not considered and an inadmissibility decision is issued. No dissenting or concurring judgments are permitted.[169] If it is admissible, the committee or chamber will issue a judgment that engages with the admissibility and merits issues.[170] Committees are required to decide unanimously so only a single judgment will issue.[171] Concurring and dissenting judgments are permitted for cases heard by a chamber or Grand Chamber of judges.[172]

[164] Article 26(4) ECHR.

[165] Article 28(3) ECHR.

[166] J. Gerards, *General Principles of the European Convention on Human Rights*, 2nd edn (Cambridge: Cambridge University Press, 2023), para.2.51.

[167] These are usually no more than a page in length and are not published on the online HUDOC database; J. Gerards, *General Principles of the European Convention on Human Rights*, 2nd edn (Cambridge: Cambridge University Press, 2023), para.2.6.1.

[168] J. Gerards, *General Principles of the European Convention on Human Rights,* 2nd edn (Cambridge: Cambridge University Press, 2023), para.2.3.

[169] These decisions are published on the online HUDOC database as they are often "substantive in nature"; J. Gerards, *General Principles of the European Convention on Human Rights*, 2nd edn (Cambridge: Cambridge University Press, 2023), para.2.6.1.

[170] Only in cases involving an inter-State dispute will a separate admissibility decision be issued; J. Gerards, *General Principles of the European Convention on Human Rights*, 2nd edn (Cambridge: Cambridge University Press, 2023), para.2.5.2.

[171] Article 28(1) ECHR.

[172] Article 45(2) ECHR.

9–81 The judgment does not become final for three months, unless the parties declare that they will not seek a referral of the case to the Grand Chamber. If one of the parties does seek a referral, a panel of five judges will determine whether the referral should proceed.[173] If the State is found to be in violation of its ECHR obligations, the Committee of Ministers of the Council of Europe is informed and it confers with the State in order to determine how best to execute the ECtHR's judgment. Typically, amending legislation is proposed. A State that fails to give effect to the decision is in breach of the ECHR. The Committee of Ministers can request the ECtHR to reopen the case,[174] but this rarely occurs as the political pressure exerted by the Committee of Ministers is usually sufficient to result in change.[175]

9–82 As the 2003 Act adopted the ECHR at sub-constitutional level,[176] this means that any decisions of the ECtHR that conflict with any interpretations that have been given to constitutional provisions can be disregarded and that its decisions generally are not binding on Irish courts. However, ss.2 and 3 of the 2003 Act do provide ECtHR decisions with more weight before Irish courts than judgments issued by other non-domestic courts:

> "2—(1) In interpreting and applying any statutory provision or rule of law, a court shall, in so far as is possible, subject to the rules of law relating to such interpretation and application, do so in a manner compatible with the State's obligations under the Convention provisions.
>
> …
>
> 3—(1) Subject to any statutory provision (other than this Act) or rule of law, every organ of the State shall perform its functions in a manner compatible with the State's obligations under the Convention provisions.

[173] Article 43(2) ECHR.

[174] Article 46(4) ECHR.

[175] J. Gerards, *General Principles of the European Convention on Human Rights*, 2nd edn (Cambridge: Cambridge University Press, 2023), para.2.6.3. Gerards identifies just two cases where this referral resulted in a Court judgment: *Mammadov v Azerbaijan* (App. No. 15172/13), judgment of the ECtHR (Grand Chamber), 29 May 2019, and *Kavala v Turkey* (App. No. 28749/18), judgment of the ECtHR (Grand Chamber), 11 July 2022.

[176] Chapter 6, paras 6–92 to 6–98.

> (2) A person who has suffered injury, loss or damage as a result of a contravention of subsection (1), may, if no other remedy in damages is available, institute proceedings to recover damages in respect of the contravention in the High Court (or, subject to subsection (3) [regarding quantum], in the Circuit Court) and the Court may award to the person such damages (if any) as it considers appropriate."

9–83 Section 4 of the 2003 Act directs Irish courts to take notice of ECtHR decisions but this does not amount to a requirement to apply those decisions. Humphreys J. put it thus:

> "... s. 4 itself only requires the court to apply general principles and not to follow individual cases slavishly merely because certain facts might appear to overlap. Section 4 requires that judicial notice be taken of all Strasbourg judgments and decisions but goes on to say, 'a court shall, when interpreting and applying the Convention provisions, take due account of the principles laid down by those declarations, decisions, advisory opinions, opinions and judgments'. Thus it is the principles as set out in well-established case law that a court must follow, not any and every individual case however outlying."[177]

9–84 Finally, Irish courts can declare that a statutory provision is incompatible with the ECHR pursuant to s.5 of the 2003 Act. However, this declaration does not repeal the offending section; that task is left to the legislature. The first such declaration was made in the Lydia Foy case in 2007.[178] Foy is a transgender woman who argued that the Irish government's refusal to issue her with a new birth certificate, with her gender changed thereon from male to female, was contrary to her rights under the ECHR.[179] The passage of the Gender Recognition Act 2015 which ultimately resulted from her case is discussed in detail in Ch.7.[180]

[177] *Seredych v Minister for Justice and Equality (No. 2)* [2018] IEHC 307 at para.7.

[178] *Foy v An tArd Chláraitheoir (No. 2)* [2007] IEHC 470.

[179] The impugned legislation was s.4 of the Births and Deaths Registration Act (Ireland) 1880.

[180] See Ch.7, Section E.

F. Alternative Dispute Resolution

9–85 So far in this chapter we have examined the courts and considered how they operate as a forum for resolving disputes between parties. However, going to court is not the only option for parties seeking external help to resolve a disagreement between them. Indeed, the formal judicial process might not be the preferred option, especially in light of the delays, costs and publicity inherent in taking a case to court. The Law Reform Commission has noted that the inclusion and integration of alternative dispute resolution (ADR) processes is an essential aspect of ensuring the realisation of the fundamental right of access to justice within the Irish Constitution.[181] That the Constitution envisaged a broader "menu of choices"[182] for formal problem-solving is clear in Article 37.1:

> "Nothing in this Constitution shall operate to invalidate the exercise of limited functions and powers of a judicial nature, in matters other than criminal matters, by any person or body of persons duly authorised by law to exercise such functions and powers, notwithstanding that such person or such body of persons is not a judge or a court appointed or established as such under this Constitution."

In essence, this constitutional provision means that alternatives to litigation in the courts can be used to solve civil disputes between parties.

9–86 That the Constitution would envisage alternatives to the courts as a means of resolving disputes is unsurprising. This history of ADR is as old as the ability of people to fall out and disagree.[183] Dissatisfaction with the courts as a venue for dispute resolution is evident throughout history and literature is replete with examples of disputants seeking alternatives to, or displaying their unhappiness with, the courts system. Dick the butcher in Shakespeare's *Henry VI, Part II* famously suggests

---

[181] Law Reform Commission, *Report on Alternative Dispute Resolution: Mediation and Conciliation* (LRC 98-2010), para.1.02.

[182] Law Reform Commission, *Consultation Paper on Alternative Dispute Resolution* (LRC CP 50-2008), para.1.12.

[183] For an excellent discussion of ADR and peaceful practices for resolving conflict across the world, see J.T. Barrett and J. Barrett, *A History of Alternative Dispute Resolution: The Story of a Political, Social, and Cultural Movement* (New York: Wiley, 2004).

"first ... let's kill all the lawyers",[184] and Dickens's novel *Bleak House* centres around the interminable, fictional case of *Jarndyce v Jarndyce*, an inheritance dispute that takes so long to resolve, there is nothing left to inherit by the time the case concludes.[185] Barrett and Barrett, in their fascinating discussion of the history of ADR, note that Ireland introduced an arbitration law in 1632, and that a system of commercial arbitration underpinned the resolution of disputes throughout the British Colonies.[186] The Law Reform Commission noted in its *Consultation Paper on Alternative Dispute Resolution* that the majority of people will become involved in a dispute at least once in their lifetime.[187] Such is the inevitable by-product of living in society.[188] However, the vast majority of these disputes are not resolved and no action is taken. The Law Reform Commission suggests that there is a myriad of reasons for this, including that seeking resolution is "more trouble than it's worth".[189] Nonetheless, the Commission explains that "access to justice" should encompass a range of options so that disputants can select the resolution option that best suits their dispute,[190] or, as Sander put it, "let the forum fit the fuss".[191]

9–87 Such fora or options can include conciliation, mediation, arbitration and specialist quasi-judicial bodies such as administrative tribunals, tribunals of inquiry and ombudsmen. The more formal administrative processes—namely tribunals, inquiries and ombudsmen—are considered later in Ch.10. In this chapter, we examine those ADR processes where the parties meet with a professional third party who helps them resolve their dispute in a way that is less formal and often more consensual than is done in the courts. As such, we confine our consideration in this

184 W. Shakespeare, *Henry VI , Part II*, Act 4, scene 2.

185 C. Dickens, *Bleak House* (1852) (London: Penguin Classics, 2003).

186 J.T. Barrett and J. Barrett, *A History of Alternative Dispute Resolution: The Story of a Political, Social, and Cultural Movement* (New York: Wiley, 2004), Ch.1.

187 Law Reform Commission, *Consultation Paper on Alternative Dispute Resolution* (LRC CP 50-2008), para.1.02.

188 Law Reform Commission, *Consultation Paper on Alternative Dispute Resolution* (LRC CP 50-2008), para.1.02.

189 Law Reform Commission, *Consultation Paper on Alternative Dispute Resolution* (LRC CP 50-2008), para.1.11.

190 Law Reform Commission, *Consultation Paper on Alternative Dispute Resolution* (LRC CP 50-2008), paras 1.52–1.56.

191 F. Sander, "Varieties of Dispute Processing. National Conference on the Dissatisfaction with the Administration of Justice" (1976) 70(1) *Federal Rules Decisions* 79 at 112–113. See also, J. Lande and G. Herman, "Fitting the Forum to the Family Fuss" (2004) 42(2) *Family Court Review* 280; F. Sander and S. Goldberg, "Fitting the Forum to the Fuss: A User-Friendly Guide to Selecting an ADR Procedure" (1994) 10 *Negotiation Journal* 49.

chapter to the processes of conciliation, mediation and arbitration. Prior to engaging in that analysis, it is worth pausing to consider the merits of negotiation as a method of resolving disputes.

1. Negotiation

9–88 Abraham Lincoln famously advised young lawyers thus:

> "Discourage litigation. Persuade your neighbors to compromise whenever you can. Point out to them how the nominal winner is often a real loser—in fees, expenses, and waste of time."[192]

Prior to engaging in litigation, or any ADR, it is advisable that parties should attempt to negotiate a settlement. Many cases, although listed for hearing before the courts, are settled by negotiation prior to the court hearing taking place. Negotiation can be defined as "communication for the purpose of persuasion".[193] It is a process in which parties to a dispute discuss possible outcomes directly with each other. Parties exchange proposals and demands, make arguments, and continue the discussion until a solution is reached, or an impasse declared.

9–89 Ury and others have identified three different approaches to discussion-based dispute resolution.[194] Each approach can achieve a different outcome as the underlying focus and orientation diverges, depending on whether the approach is interests-based, rights-based or power-based.[195] The interests-based approach involves reorientation of the discussion from the position of the parties to the interests that each has in the dispute and possible outcomes. In this way, it is possible to identify a range of potential solutions that might end the dispute, as each party may have more than one interest underpinning the position

[192] Abraham Lincoln in *Notes for a Law Lecture, July 1 1850*, quoted in F.T. Hill, *Lincoln the Lawyer* (New York: The Century Company, 1912), p.102.

[193] S.B. Goldberg, F. Sander, N.H. Rogers and S.R. Cole, *Dispute Resolution: Negotiation, Mediation and other Processes*, 2nd edn (Boston: Little, Brown, 1992), p.597.

[194] W. Ury, J.M. Brett and S.B. Goldberg, *Getting Disputes Resolved: Designing Systems to Cut the Costs of Conflict* (Cambridge: Harvard University Project on Negotiation, 1993), Ch.1.

[195] R. Fisher, W. Ury and B. Patton, *Getting to Yes: negotiating an agreement without giving in*, 3rd edn (London: Random House Business, 2011), Ch.3; W. Ury, J.M. Brett and S.B. Goldberg, *Getting Disputes Resolved: Designing Systems to Cut the Costs of Conflict* (Cambridge: Harvard University Project on Negotiation, 1993), p.5.

they have adopted. An exclusive focus on the position each party has adopted might entrench views such that neither party is willing to shift their position, and thus the negotiation ends in stalemate. This in turn, Ury et al argue, may cause parties to turn to a position of insisting on their rights and seeking to enforce these by means of a court judgment. The power-based approach resorts to threats or violence as a means of coercing a conclusion to the dispute. Consequently, they conclude that negotiation based on the interests each party has in the dispute is most likely to result in a successful outcome.[196]

9–90 Negotiating a settlement can be as informal as the parties wish. There is no need to involve professionals if the parties are willing to compromise and agree a solution. In some cases, the parties may conduct such settlement negotiations through their solicitors. The benefits of successfully negotiating a settlement are that it costs less than litigation; the details of both the dispute and the settlement remain private; and the parties to the dispute control the negotiation process and the final settlement that is agreed. Where negotiation is impossible, the parties may wish to avail of one of the other ADR processes.

2. Conciliation

9–91 Conciliation is an ADR process whereby an independent person, called a conciliator, attempts to facilitate a settlement of the dispute between the parties. Both the Rules of the Superior Courts (Commercial Proceedings) 2004[197] and the Rules of the Superior Courts (Competition Proceedings) 2005[198] mention conciliation. Yet neither legislative enactment defines this term. The Law Reform Commission opined that despite the lack of a clear legislative definition, conciliation must be understood as a process separate from mediation.[199] They were proved correct with the introduction of the Mediation Act 2017, which governs mediation in Ireland, which we will consider below. For now, we will focus on conciliation which the Law Reform Commission defines as "an

[196] W. Ury, J.M. Brett and S.B. Goldberg, *Getting Disputes Resolved: Designing Systems to Cut the Costs of Conflict* (Cambridge: Harvard University Project on Negotiation, 1993), Ch.1.
[197] S.I. No. 2 of 2004.
[198] S.I. No. 130 of 2005.
[199] Law Reform Commission, *Report on Alternative Dispute Resolution: Mediation and Conciliation* (LRC 98-2010), para.2.40.

advisory, consensual and confidential process, in which parties to the dispute select a neutral and independent third party to assist them in reaching a mutually acceptable negotiated agreement".[200]

9–92 As an ADR process, conciliation is little used in Ireland, expect for in the construction sector.[201] However, within the construction industry, Bond notes that it "has evolved into a distinct, exceptionally successful low-cost method of resolving disputes".[202] Conciliators can involve themselves in the substantive negotiations between the parties and can issue formal recommendations and propose settlement options. Thus, conciliators play an active and interventionist role in seeking to resolve the dispute. Parties to conciliation are not bound to agree a settlement, nor to the resolution proposed by the conciliator. They are free to leave the process at any stage. Thus, those who engage in this type of assisted negotiation may resort to the courts, or arbitration, should the conciliation process fail. Section 6 of the Construction Contracts Act 2013 introduced a statutory right to refer payment disputes in construction contracts to adjudication. Bond noted that in the period between the passing of the 2013 Act and early 2014, 97 per cent of payment disputes relating to construction contracts had been successfully resolved by conciliation.[203] Therefore, in the construction contracts space, conciliation has proved to be a very successful ADR process due to the twin facts of being non-adversarial and low-cost.

3. Mediation

9–93 Mediation is an "interest-based dispute resolution process".[204] In essence this means that the mediator looks beyond the legal rights and focuses on clarifying the parties' real motivations or underlying interests in the dispute with the aim of reaching a mutually acceptable compromise

[200] Law Reform Commission, *Consultation Paper on Alternative Dispute Resolution* (LRC CP 50-2008), para.2.129 (emphasis in original).
[201] Chartered Institute of Arbitrators – Ireland Branch, "Conciliation", available at: *https://www.ciarb.ie/services/conciliation.234.html.*
[202] B. Bond, *Conciliation of Construction Industry Disputes* (Abingdon: Routledge, 2024), p.300.
[203] B. Bond, *Conciliation of Construction Industry Disputes* (Abingdon: Routledge, 2024), p.105.
[204] Law Reform Commission, *Report on Alternative Dispute Resolution: Mediation and Conciliation* (LRC 98-2010), para.2.22.

that meets the real interests of both parties.[205] Thus, mediators can also engage with the parties' emotions and seek creative solutions to the dispute. This differs from conciliation where the conciliator can be more focused on the parties' legal rights.

9–94 Cheevers notes that the Mediation Act 2017 (the "2017 Act") was introduced both to increase the importance of mediation within the Irish civil justice system and to regulate its practice.[206] Section 2(1) of the 2017 Act defines "mediation" as a confidential, facilitative and voluntary process in which parties to a dispute, with the assistance of a mediator, attempt to reach a mutually acceptable agreement to resolve the dispute. The emphasis on the voluntariness of mediation is restated under s.6(2) of the 2017 Act, and further supported by the provision under s.6(4)(a) that allows either party to "withdraw from the mediation at any time during the mediation". It is a process that is led by the parties, who determine the outcome of the mediation process.[207] The mediator is a facilitator who is obliged to "act with impartiality and integrity and treat the parties fairly".[208] It is important to note that parties to a mediation can be accompanied and assisted by a person (including a lawyer) who is not a party to the dispute[209] and retain the right to obtain independent legal advice at any time during the mediation.[210]

9–95 Section 8 of the 2017 Act outlines the role of the mediator. It obliges mediators to make reasonable enquiries to identify any potential conflict of interest in the matter.[211] If such a conflict exists, mediators are required to recuse themselves from acting as a mediator for this matter.[212] At the beginning of the mediation process, the mediator must also give to the parties proof of their qualifications to serve as a mediator,[213] and a copy of the code of practice to which the mediator

[205] Law Reform Commission, *Consultation Paper on Alternative Dispute Resolution* (LRC CP 50-2008), para.1.08.
[206] A. Cheevers, "The Irish Mediation Act 2017: Much Done, Much More to Do" (2020) 1(2) *Amicus Curiae* (Series 2) 143 at 143.
[207] Mediation Act 2017 s.6(9).
[208] Mediation Act 2017 s.8(2)(b).
[209] Mediation Act 2017 s.6(4)(b).
[210] Mediation Act 2017 s.6(4)(c).
[211] Mediation Act 2017 s.8(1)(a)(i).
[212] Mediation Act 2017 s.8(1)(a)(ii).
[213] Mediation Act 2017 s.8(1)(b).

subscribes.[214] Throughout the mediation process the mediator must, as outlined above, act with fairness and integrity.[215] They must remain vigilant for any potential conflict of interest that might emerge, declare this to the parties and, except for where the parties agree to continue with them as mediator, resign the role as mediator.[216] Mediators must ensure that the parties are aware of their right to seek independent legal advice.[217] Generally, mediators facilitate the parties to come to a conclusion of the mediation process and do not make proposals for how a dispute may be resolved.[218] However, where the parties request that the mediator make proposals to resolve the dispute, the mediator may do so, but the parties are not obliged to accept these proposals.[219]

9–96 Under s.12 of the 2017 Act, the establishment of the Mediation Council of Ireland is envisaged. The Schedule to the 2017 Act outlines the role and functioning of the Council. It will consist of 11 members. Five members will represent the interests of mediators, and six members will represent the public interest.[220] The Schedule lists the five core functions of the Council:

1. promotion of public awareness of mediation in Ireland;
2. development and maintenance of the standards for mediation, including offering continuing professional development;
3. preparation and oversight of the implementation of codes of professional practice for mediators;
4. establishment and maintenance of a register of mediators who have subscribed to an approved code of practice; and
5. advising the Minister for Justice on the development of a scheme and attendant information sessions for the use of mediation in family and succession law matters.[221]

Although the entire 2017 Act was formally commenced in January 2018,[222] the Council has not yet been established. In December 2023, in

[214] Mediation Act 2017 s.8(1)(c).
[215] Mediation Act 2017 s.8(2)(b).
[216] Mediation Act 2017 s.8(2)(a).
[217] Mediation Act 2017 s.8(2)(d).
[218] Mediation Act 2017 s.8(3).
[219] Mediation Act 2017 s.8(4).
[220] Mediation Act 2017 Sch., para.3.
[221] Mediation Act 2017 Sch., para.1.
[222] Mediation Act 2017 (Commencement) Order 2017 (S.I. No. 591 of 2017).

response to a written Dáil question, the Minister for Justice noted that the Department was working with the mediation section to support their work on its establishment.[223] In response to an additional Dáil question on this in June 2024, the Minister shared that matters progressed further with a plenary meeting of the sector in February 2024, followed by the convening of a Mediation Council Shadow Group by the Legal Aid Board, supported by the Department of Justice in May of that year. Finally, she noted that the establishment of a Mediation Council of Ireland remained an action in the scheduled work of the Department of Justice contained in the Justice Plan 2024.[224]

9–97 The 2017 Act contains a series of provisions to increase engagement with the mediation process in Ireland. Section 16 enables a court, either at its own instigation or following a request from one of the parties, to invite the parties to attempt to resolve their dispute by mediation.[225] Where parties to a case that has been diverted to a mediation process seek to bring the case back before the courts, under s.17 of the 2017 Act, the mediator is required to submit a report on the mediation process to the court. This report should include details such as whether the mediation took place, including a statement as to why it did not occur if relevant, and a statement as to whether a settlement of all or part of the dispute has been reached. There is a consequence for parties who have been invited by the court to enter a mediation and refuse to do so. Under s.21, a refusal to engage in mediation may impact the court's decision when determining the costs that each party should bear.

9–98 Thus, mediation seeks to be a process in which parties participate in a mostly voluntarily capacity (subject to potential consequences under the s.16 process), and over which they have considerable control and autonomy. The mediator is a facilitator who guides the process efficiently and flexibly in an open, transparent and ethical manner that preserves the confidentiality of the process. Reflecting on Cheevers' point that the purpose of the legislation is twofold, it does seem as if the 2017 Act has met its aim as it both regulates mediation practices in Ireland while also promoting increasing engagement with mediation as an ADR process.

[223] *https://www.oireachtas.ie/en/debates/question/2023-12-05/381/.*
[224] *https://www.oireachtas.ie/en/debates/question/2024-07-23/1502/.*
[225] Mediation Act 2017 s.16(1).

9–99 Mediation and conciliation have clear advantages above the litigation process. They encourage reconciliation between disputants and seek to maintain good relationships between them. Given the primarily voluntary nature of both mediation and conciliation, they ensure that disputants retain a sense of empowerment in the process. Any party can exit the process at any stage; thus, the disputants retain control of the process. As the Law Reform Commission notes, mediation and conciliation have clear benefits as regards time, cost, efficiency and confidentiality.[226]

9–100 Yet mediation and conciliation also have disadvantages. Where these interventions do not end the dispute, they can be viewed as little more than an additional layer of cost and delay in the litigation process.[227] Some cases do not lend themselves to resolution outside the courts, for example if the case involves public interest or allegations of impropriety.[228]

4. Arbitration

9–101 Having considered conciliation and mediation, this chapter now turns to an analysis of arbitration as an ADR mechanism.[229] Arbitration is a long-established form of dispute resolution. Arbitration differs in a fundamental manner from mediation and conciliation. All three mechanisms involve an independent third party. As discussed above, in mediation or conciliation, that third party facilitates or advises on the resolution of the dispute. In arbitration, by contrast, the third party, or arbitrator, adopts a role more similar to that of a judge in a formal court hearing. In other words, the independent arbitrator decides how the dispute will be resolved.

9–102 Arbitration clauses, requiring that parties attempt arbitration prior to instigating court proceedings, are often found in commercial contracts, particularly in the context of construction contracts, insurance contracts and holiday contracts. Consequently, recourse to arbitration

[226] Law Reform Commission, *Report on Alternative Dispute Resolution: Mediation and Conciliation* (LRC 98-2010), "Introduction".

[227] A. Kenneally and J. Tully, *The Irish Legal System* (Dublin: Clarus Press, 2013), p.347.

[228] A. Kenneally and J. Tully, *The Irish Legal System* (Dublin: Clarus Press, 2013), p.348.

[229] For a detailed analysis of the law on arbitration in Ireland, see A. Dowling-Hussey and D. Dunne, *Arbitration Law*, 3rd edn (Dublin: Round Hall, 2018).

proceedings may arise automatically from the terms of a contract that includes such an arbitration clause. Where an arbitration clause appears in a contract, any attempt to bring court proceedings rather than referring to arbitration must be stayed on the application of the other party.[230] In essence, the inclusion of an arbitration clause in a contract indicates that all parties have agreed that in the event of a dispute arising, it will be referred to an arbitrator and that the decision of the arbitrator will be binding and final.[231]

9–103 All arbitrations in Ireland, whether involving domestic or international disputants, are governed by the Arbitration Act 2010 (the "2010 Act"). This consolidating legislation repealed and replaced the previous Arbitration Acts from 1954, 1980 and 1998. The first two of these Acts concerned domestic arbitrations, while the final one, from 1998, adopted the United Nations Commission on International Trade Law (UNCITRAL) Model Law for use in international arbitrations,[232] and this is appended to the 2010 Act as its First Schedule.[233] All arbitrations are conducted according to the terms of each specific arbitration clause; nonetheless, Pt 2 of the 2010 Act establishes a baseline for arbitrations in Ireland. It outlines an array of conditions that underpin arbitration unless the parties elect in their arbitration agreement to opt out of them.

9–104 The first task that parties to arbitration must undertake is to appoint an arbitrator. Generally, the arbitration agreement will not identify a specific person but will outline how the arbitrator is to be chosen.[234] Where the parties are unable to agree, the court may appoint an arbitrator to the dispute under Article 11(5) of Sch.1 to the 2010 Act.

---

230 Article 8(1) of Sch.1 to the Arbitration Act 2010.

231 Article 54(1) of the Convention on the Settlement of Investment Disputes between States and Nationals of Other States 1965 contained in Sch.3 to the Arbitration Act 2010.

232 Resolution 31/98 adopted by the UN General Assembly on 15 December 1976, Arbitration Rules of the United Nations Commission on International Trade Law, as revised by UNCITRAL Rules on Transparency in Treaty-based Investor-State Arbitration 2013. For detailed analysis of the UNCITRAL Rules, see M. Rubino-Sammartano, *International Arbitration Law and Practice*, 3rd edn (New York: JurisNet, 2014).

233 The version of the UNCITRAL arbitration rules contained in Sch.1 to the 2010 Act is the UNCITRAL Model Law on International Commercial Arbitration, as adopted by UNCITRAL on 21 June 1985, with amendments as adopted by UNCITRAL at its thirty-ninth session on 7 July 2006.

234 Article 11(2) of Sch.1 to the Arbitration Act 2010.

Either party can challenge the appointment of a particular arbitrator.[235] A potential arbitrator is obliged to disclose any conflicts of interest that exist both prior to their appointment and if one should arise during the course of the arbitration.[236]

9–105 The function of the arbitrator is to conduct the arbitration in an efficient manner and to act reasonably, impartially and independently. The 2010 Act gives the arbitrator a number of powers to ensure the smooth running of the arbitration. Consequently, they can grant interim measures to preserve the status quo pending the decision;[237] they may direct that a witness give evidence under oath and administer oaths for that purpose;[238] they may award security for costs;[239] and they may order specific performance of a contract.[240] Article 16 of Sch.1 to the 2010 Act expressly recognises the competence of an arbitrator to rule on their own jurisdiction. This is designed to help reduce costs and avoid delays in the arbitration process. The arbitrator can rule on any allegation or challenge raised.[241] The High Court can only be asked to resolve an issue on jurisdiction where it has first been dealt with as a preliminary question by the arbitral tribunal.[242] An application cannot be brought after the final award has been granted by the arbitral tribunal.[243] Where an arbitrator becomes unable to carry out their functions for whatever reason, whether legal or factual, or where they cause undue delay, they may resign or be removed as arbitrator by agreement of the parties.[244] In such circumstances, a substitute arbitrator may be appointed.[245]

9–106 It is the arbitration agreement that determines the parameters of the arbitration. If, for example, an arbitration agreement specifically excludes a particular issue from resolution by arbitration, the arbitrator has no jurisdiction in relation to disputes that involve that issue. As stated above, where the arbitration agreement lacks detail in terms of

[235] Article 12 of Sch.1 to the Arbitration Act 2010.
[236] Article 12 of Sch.1 to the Arbitration Act 2010.
[237] Article 17 of Sch.1 to the Arbitration Act 2010.
[238] Section 14 of the Arbitration Act 2010.
[239] Section 19 of the Arbitration Act 2010.
[240] Section 20 of the Arbitration Act 2010.
[241] Article 16(2) of Sch.1 to the Arbitration Act 2010.
[242] Article 16(3) of Sch.1 to the Arbitration Act 2010.
[243] Article 16(3) of Sch.1 of the Arbitration Act 2010.
[244] Article 14 of Sch.1 to the Arbitration Act 2010.
[245] Article 15 of Sch.1 to the Arbitration Act 2010.

the conduct of arbitration proceedings, the default provisions contained in the 2010 Act apply. Arbitrations occur in private. In the course of the arbitration, the parties must be treated equally and the principles of natural justice apply to ensure there is no bias on the part of the arbitrator[246] and that both sides are permitted equal opportunity to present their arguments. Where one party to the dispute fails to appear at the arbitration or fails to produce documentary evidence, the arbitrator may continue the proceedings and make an award.[247] Should the parties agree a settlement prior to the conclusion of the arbitration proceedings, then the arbitration may be terminated.[248]

9–107 Article 31 of Sch.1 to the 2010 Act provides that an award must be in writing and signed by the arbitrator.[249] Unless the parties have agreed otherwise, the reasons for the decision must be recorded in the document recording the award.[250] The award must also be dated and state the place in which it is made.[251] A signed copy of the award must be given to each party.[252] Section 23 of the 2010 Act provides that an award made by an arbitrator is enforceable, and where leave is given by the High Court, judgment may be entered in the terms of the award. An award made pursuant to the 2010 Act shall be binding on the parties between whom it is made.[253] A dissatisfied party may challenge the award on specific, and limited, terms.[254] Such circumstances occur where:

(1) a party to the arbitration agreement was under some alleged incapacity or the arbitration agreement was not valid under the law to which the parties have subjected it or under the law of the State;
(2) the party making the application was not given proper notice of the appointment of the arbitrator or of the arbitral proceedings or was otherwise unable to present their case;

[246] Article 12 of Sch.1 to the Arbitration Act 2010.
[247] Article 25(c) of Sch.1 to the Arbitration Act 2010.
[248] Article 30 of Sch.1 to the Arbitration Act 2010.
[249] Article 31(1) of Sch.1 to the Arbitration Act 2010.
[250] Article 31(2) of Sch.1 to the Arbitration Act 2010.
[251] Article 31(3) of Sch.1 to the Arbitration Act 2010.
[252] Article 31(4) of Sch.1 to the Arbitration Act 2010.
[253] Section 23(2) of the Arbitration Act 2010.
[254] Article 34 of Sch.1 to the Arbitration Act 2010.

(3) the award contains decisions on matters beyond the scope of the submission to arbitration;
(4) the composition of the arbitral tribunal was not in accordance with the agreement of the parties;
(5) the arbitral procedure was not in accordance with the agreement of the parties;
(6) the award is in conflict with the public policy of the State; and/or
(7) the subject matter of the dispute is not capable of settlement by arbitration under the law of the State.

9–108 Section 9(1) of the 2010 Act provides that the High Court is the relevant court for applications under the 2010 Act. Section 11 provides that there is no right of appeal from the High Court in respect of applications under the 2010 Act. This means that the High Court's decision is final in respect of any application made to it, which could include: a stay application under s.11(a); an application to set aside an award under s.11(b)(i); and an application for recognition and enforcement of an arbitration award under s.11(b)(i) and s.11(c). The High Court has its usual powers for granting interim measures of protection and assistance in the taking of evidence,[255] although most interim measures may now also be granted by the arbitrator.[256] The High Court's powers are subject to s.10(2) of the 2010 Act, which provides that the High Court is not at liberty to order security for costs or discovery of documents unless otherwise agreed by the parties. This emphasises the autonomy of the arbitrator.

9–109 The advantages of agreeing to engage in arbitration are many: the parties can choose their own arbitrator; they have control over the location and time of the proceedings; arbitrations occur in private; they may be more time and cost-efficient; arbitration proceedings are flexible and offer tailor-made remedies; and awards are enforceable by the courts. Yet arbitration is not without its disadvantages. There is no system of precedent in arbitration and the grounds of appeal are very limited. The rules of evidence are also considerably relaxed when compared to court proceedings. Nonetheless, the inherent flexibility and efficiency of arbitration, taken together with the fact that an independent

[255] Articles 9, 17J and 27 of Sch.1 to the Arbitration Act 2010.
[256] Article 17 of Sch.1 to the Arbitration Act 2010.

party decides the outcome, makes it an attractive alternative to pursuing a case before the courts.

G. Conclusion

9–110 In this chapter, we have considered the courts system in Ireland. We have examined the composition and operation of the courts both at first instance and on appeal. We have also, briefly, discussed the court-based options outside of Ireland. Finally, we have examined alternatives to the courts for resolving disputes. As discussed above, the Law Reform Commission has noted that the inclusion and integration of ADR processes is an essential aspect of ensuring the realisation of the fundamental right of access to justice within the Irish Constitution.[257] We can see that the increased use of conciliation, albeit within a very specific sector of industry, and the introduction of a legislative basis for mediation enables the flourishing of these alternative dispute mechanisms in the Irish legal landscape. The support that the legal system gives to arbitration is evident in the limited circumstances in which the High Court can interfere in determinations by arbitrators. As envisaged by the Law Reform Commission, an integrated system of access to justice has been strengthened by placing mediation on a legislative footing and can be further strengthened by doing the same with conciliation.

[257] Law Reform Commission, *Report on Alternative Dispute Resolution: Mediation and Conciliation* (LRC 98-2010), para.1.02.

Chapter 10

Law, Administration and the Irish State

> "We nod approvingly today when someone tells us that, whereas the State used to be merely policeman, judge and protector, it has now become schoolmaster, doctor, house-builder, road-maker, town-planner, public utility supplier and all the rest of it."
>
> C. Carr, *Concerning English Administrative Law* (Oxford: OUP, 1941), p.10.

In this chapter we:

- introduce the Irish administrative state and administrative law;
- consider non-court decision-making in Ireland, including the concept of judicial review;
- reflect on the role and remit of the Public Service Ombudsman in Ireland;
- critique the role of public inquiries in Ireland.

A. Introduction

10–01 Law plays an essential role in the organisation of the State. Law often touches upon the activities of government, state institutions and society more broadly. Courts and judges play a fundamental role in the adjudication of societal disputes.[1] However, courts are not the only bodies in the State that have decision-making functions in determining the rights and obligations that people may have. Within all modern democratic states, there exists state architecture to provide, deliver and decide rights and obligations. Generally, this is established by law. In Part B of this chapter, we introduce the Irish administrative state and explain the concept and remit of administrative law. In Part C, we highlight examples of administrative decision-making in the Irish legal system. This includes a brief overview of judicial review of administrative

[1] This is discussed in more detail in Ch.11, paras 11–02 to 11–09.

decision-making bodies, with a case study on the law of homelessness in Ireland. In Part D, the role of the Ombudsman within Ireland is discussed. Finally, in Part E, after explaining the role of public inquiries in Ireland, we cast a critical eye on how they operate.

B. The Irish Administrative State and Administrative Law

10–02 As the opening quote to this chapter suggests, the administrative state is viewed as "ever expanding", but what is the Irish administrative state? It is difficult to come across any agreed-upon definition. In decisions of the Irish superior courts, the focus is on the remit and limits of non-court bodies' decision-making functions, along with limited delegation of legislative powers by the Oireachtas to other bodies.[2] Article 34 of the Constitution requires justice to be administered by courts, but Article 37 recognises that limited functions and decisions of a judicial character may be taken by a person or persons in a body who are not judges.[3] This is done because placing decision-making in the hands of a specialised body "enables persons to have their legal rights determined at a lower cost, with less formality, and with greater expedition than through the court system."[4]

10–03 However, the administrative state does more than adjudicate. Hardiman, MacCarthaigh and Scott have attempted to classify the varying functions of the Irish administrative state.[5] As Hardiman and

---

[2] *Náisiúnta Leictreach Contraitheoir Éireann Cuideachta Faoi Theorainn Ráthaíochta v Minister for Justice* [2021] IESC 36 at para.53 per Charleton J.; *Costello v Government of Ireland* [2022] IESC 44 at para.178 per MacMenamin J.; *Kirwan v O'Leary* [2023] IESC 27 at para.91 per Murray J. See too, Ch.4, Section B.2(b).

[3] For a much more substantive exploration of the interplay between Article 34 and Article 37, see T. Hickey, "*Zalewski* and the Future of Irish Public Law" (2024) 87(2) *Modern Law Review* 466.

[4] *Lee v Revenue Commissioners* [2021] IECA 114 at para.13 per Murray J.

[5] N. Hardiman, M. MacCarthaigh and C. Scott, *The Irish State Administration Database*, available at: *http://www.isad.ie*. See also, N. Hardiman and M. MacCarthaigh, "Organising for Growth: Irish State Administration 1958–2008" (2010) 41(3) *The Economic and Social Review* 367; N. Hardiman and C. Scott, "Governance as Polity: An Institutional Approach to the Evolution of State Functions in Ireland" (2010) 88(1) *Public Administration* 170; N. Hardiman and C. Scott, "Ordering Things: The Irish State Administration Database" (2012) 27(1) *Irish Political Studies* 1. For a fascinating exploration of the administrative state up to 1936, see J. Biggins, M. MacCarthaigh and C. Scott, "Priming the state: continuity and junctures in the foundation of the Irish

MacCarthaigh note, "[p]ublic administration is integral to the political, economic and social life of the state".[6] Hardiman and Scott explore the publicness of institutions, their function, the policy arenas that these public bodies exercise domain within, and the legal status of these public bodies.[7] The legal form of the institutions may be as ministerial departments, local government, executive agencies, statutory or non-statutory bodies, and public or private limited companies.[8] Functions of such institutions may include "legal" or "quasi-legal" adjudicatory bodies that make decisions on the rights or obligations that a person may have. In addition, some of these institutions also include bodies/organisations responsible for formulating or advising on policy issues; collecting taxes; service provision for people living in Ireland; and the licensing of certain professions. All these functional bodies may have roles within one or more policy domains, such as agriculture and fisheries, housing, child protection, environmental protection, social welfare, public order, defence of the State, and the arts. The Irish State Administration Database classifies how the Irish State is organised and seeks to analyse how "public power is exercised to achieve different kinds of policy objectives".[9] As of 2023, it identifies 359 units of state administration in Ireland. This provides some indication of the number of different bodies and organisations that exist in the State that are tasked, to one degree or another, with administering the Irish State. Overall, understanding the make-up of the State (beyond just focusing on the executive, ministerial offices and the courts system) provides us with a framework to consider and reflect upon state activity within a given policy domain or legal area.

administration" (2024) 39(2) *Irish Political Studies* 162, *https://doi.org/10.1080/07907184.2024.2334489* and J. Biggins, M. MacCarthaigh and C. Scott, "Greening the Irish State: early legislative and administrative dynamics" (2024) 39(2) *Irish Political Studies* 187, *https://doi.org/10.1080/07907184.2024.2334490*.

6 N. Hardiman and M. MacCarthaigh, "Organising for Growth: Irish State Administration 1958–2008" (2010) 41(3) *The Economic and Social Review* 367 at 386. For an outstanding graphic that maps the Irish administrative state, see Zero-G, *A Map of the Irish State* (2015), available at: *http://state.zero-g.ie/*.

7 N. Hardiman and C. Scott, "Ordering Things: The Irish State Administration Database" (2012) 27(1) *Irish Political Studies* 1 at 8–11. In deciding whether a body was "public" for the purposes of this study, the authors considered public ownership status, funding models, whether a public (including ministerial) appointment process was utilised, and whether this was based on statutory or executive powers.

8 See further, N. Hardiman, M. MacCarthaigh and C. Scott, *The Irish State Administration Database*, available at *http://www.isad.ie*.

9 N. Hardiman and C. Scott, "Ordering Things: The Irish State Administration Database" (2012) 27(1) *Irish Political Studies* 1 at 6.

10–04 Many government departments "house" other statutory or non-statutory agencies. Let us take two examples. The Department of Children, Equality, Disability, Integration and Youth is the "home" department of Tusla, the Child and Family Agency. The powers of Tusla are established in legislation in the Child and Family Agency Act 2013 (the "2013 Act"), as amended. The vast functions of Tusla are established by s.8 of the 2013 Act; these include child protection, supporting and encouraging the effective functioning of families, and offering advice to the Minister for Children. Unlike Tusla, the Irish Prison Service (IPS), established in 1998 to administer prisons and care for prisoners, does not have a statutory/legislative basis. Rather, the Minister for Justice has delegated the day-to-day management of prisons to the IPS.[10] The administrative state includes not only the machinery of state that is tasked with making a decision on rights and obligations, but also has systems in place to determine whether, for example, a person can qualify for a particular benefit, be issued a taxi licence, or whether a person must pay tax.

10–05 In addition, a variety of state bodies, statutory and non-statutory, carry out significant state functions. This may be in the arena of service delivery, such as the International Protection Accommodation Services (IPAS), a non-statutory body tasked with providing accommodation to international protection applicants.[11] The State also has a role in the regulation of the legal and medical professions.[12] With regard to the medical profession, the State has put in place systems to monitor State/private care, disability services and health services by the Health Information and Quality Authority.[13] Bodies such as the Ombudsman are tasked with ensuring quality administration, discussed below. A key function of the Irish Human Rights and Equality Commission and the Ombudsman for Children is to advise the government on protection of human rights, and protection of the rights of the child, respectively.[14]

[10] There is a proposal to place the IPS on a statutory footing; see Draft General Scheme of an Irish Prison Service Bill 2023.

[11] European Communities (Reception Conditions) Regulations 2018 (S.I. No. 230 of 2018). IPAS is a division of the Department of Children, Equality, Disability, Integration and Youth, and does not have a statutory basis.

[12] For the legal profession, see Ch.12. For medical practitioners, see the Medical Practitioners Act 2007 (as amended).

[13] Health Act 2007 (as amended) and a multitude of statutory instruments.

[14] Irish Human Rights and Equality Commission Act 2014 (as amended) and Ombudsman for Children Act 2002 (as amended).

This type of state machinery can be labelled as being part of the Irish administrative state.

10–06 When speaking about the administrative state, it would be remiss not to acknowledge the central role of politics and political ideologies in its operation. The administrative state only exists due to political choices tied in with political preferences about what the role of the State is or ought to be. "Red light theorists"[15] argue that the primary, if not sole, function of administrative law is to ensure that the State does not exercise excessive power. Red light theorists are suspicious of states that seek to redistribute wealth, that overly regulate economies within the State, or that are thought to cede control to unelected bodies/agencies. On the other hand, there are "green light theorists"[16] who see the administrative state as playing a fundamental role in regulating activities perceived as harmful, in licensing and standard-setting for certain categories of employment, and in providing some modicum of support to people in the form of the welfare state.[17] As Hogan, Morgan and Daly suggest, the administrative state and administrative law came about due to "socio-economic developments".[18] Such developments included greater protection for workers' rights, the creation and expansion of the welfare state, regulating the relationship between landlords and tenants, and identifying taxation obligations. These developments necessitated the establishment of processes and systems to determine individuals' rights and duties within a state. These legal and political tensions as regards what the role of the State *is*, or what the role of the State *ought to be*, are inherent within discussions of state administration and the law.

10–07 As is clear from the Irish State Administrative Database, there is a large number of state agencies and organisations within the Irish

[15] For a full exploration of "red light theories" on the exercise of state power, see C. Harlow and R. Rawlings, *Law and Administration*, 4th edn (Cambridge: CUP, 2021), pp.32–40, and F. Donson and D. O'Donovan, *Law and Public Administration in Ireland* (Dublin: Clarus Press, 2015), paras 1–21 to 1–27.

[16] For a full exploration of "green light theories" on the exercise of state power, see C. Harlow and R. Rawlings, *Law and Administration*, 4th edn (Cambridge: CUP, 2021), pp.32–40, and F. Donson and D. O'Donovan, *Law and Public Administration in Ireland* (Dublin: Clarus Press, 2015), paras 1–28 to 1–32.

[17] For an overview of the Irish welfare state, its formation and operation, see M. Cousins, *Explaining the Irish Welfare State: An Historical, Comparative and Political Analysis* (Lewiston: Edwin Mellen Press, 2005).

[18] G. Hogan, D.G. Morgan and P. Daly, *Administrative Law in Ireland*, 5th edn (Dublin: Round Hall, 2019), paras 1–12 to 1–13.

administrative system. In the next section, we will focus on non-court decision-making. All these agencies must act strictly within their powers, i.e. they must act constitutionally, within the limits of their legislative or non-legislative remit and functions, and can be subject to judicial review by the superior courts. We therefore need to understand what is meant by "administrative law". Hogan, Morgan and Daly define administrative law as "the law regulating the organisation, composition, functions and procedures of public authorities; their impact on the citizen; and the restraints to which they are subject."[19] Parker views administrative law as being concerned with "(a) the powers and duties of public authorities and (b) judicial control of the exercise of those powers and the performance of those duties."[20] An aspect of administrative law that we will turn to below engages with "legal doctrines developed by the domestic courts for the purpose of overseeing the activities of public administration."[21] This is called judicial review.[22] One only has to examine the table of contents of texts on administrative law to realise what an exceptionally broad field it is. For example, the leading Irish text on administrative law by Hogan, Morgan and Daly contains 22 chapters. These chapters encompass the organisation of the Irish State, the Ombudsman, public inquiries, decision-making tribunals, judicial review of public bodies, procedural law, fair procedures, and local government law.[23] So all that can be done in this chapter is to provide readers with a flavour of aspects of administrative law in Ireland.

C. Administrative Decision-Making

1. Administrative Decision-Making and Administrative Justice

10–08 Not all decisions on civil legal rights, wrongs, obligations or entitlements are made by courts. This would be impractical. Legislation (usually) establishes the legal entitlement or obligation that a person has.

[19] G. Hogan, D.G. Morgan and P. Daly, *Administrative Law in Ireland*, 5th edn (Dublin: Round Hall, 2019), para.1–01.

[20] C. Parker, *Administrative Law: Cases and Materials* (Windhoek: University of Namibia Press, 2019), p.8.

[21] J. Bell, *The Anatomy of Administrative Law* (Oxford: Hart, 2020), p.1.

[22] Another form of judicial review, where judges consider the constitutionality of a Bill or a statute, was considered in Ch.3.

[23] G. Hogan, D.G. Morgan and P. Daly, *Administrative Law in Ireland*, 5th edn (Dublin: Round Hall, 2019).

This is a policy decision usually made by the Oireachtas. This legislation will establish the criteria for determining whether a person is eligible for the right or has an obligation imposed on them. The legislation, or secondary legislation, may set out the processes by which a decision is to be reached, and who will make the decision. It may or may not include a right of appeal to a different body, which may be called "Tribunal" or "Office" or "Board", or indeed to a court. This of course is subject to judicial review by the superior courts. Many administrative bodies exercise decision-making functions within a range of fields, of which we will outline just a small number of examples: social welfare law, landlord and tenant law, mental health law, education law, revenue law, and international protection law. Each of these areas provide examples of where state bodies and administrative agencies can impact fundamentally on the rights and obligations of people within Ireland. It is important to note that all the decision-making bodies that are discussed below, whether or not they are considered to be exercising limited judicial powers in the sense of Article 37.1 of the Constitution,[24] must act in accordance with constitutional justice, including the right to a fair determination and non-bias in the exercise of administrative function.[25] This is broadly known as "administrative justice". As this is a general text, only a broad-brush stroke overview will be provided. Additional resources are cited in the footnotes if you are interested in learning more.

(a) Social welfare law[26]

10–09 An individual may make an application for a particular social assistance or social security benefit. On the basis of completing an application form, a decision will be made on whether a person qualifies for this payment.[27] This decision will first be made by a deciding officer in

[24] The law in this area has changed significantly. The Supreme Court has adopted a new test for determining whether a body is exercising limited functions and powers of a judicial nature. See T. Hickey, "*Zalewski* and the Future of Irish Public Law" (2024) 87(2) *Modern Law Review* 466.

[25] For a thorough review of requirements for constitutional justice and fair procedures, see F. Donson and D. O'Donovan, *Law and Public Administration in Ireland* (Dublin: Clarus Press, 2015), Chs 10 and 11; G. Hogan, D.G. Morgan and P. Daly, *Administrative Law in Ireland*, 5th edn (Dublin: Round Hall, 2019), Chs 12–16.

[26] See, generally, the Social Welfare Consolidation Act 2005 (as amended). For a much deeper analysis of adjudication of social welfare applications and decisions on social welfare appeals, see M. Cousins and G. Whyte, *Social Security Law in Ireland*, 4th edn (Alphen aan den Rijn: Wolters Kluwer, 2024), pp.368–396.

[27] Under the Social Welfare Consolidation Act 2005 (as amended), there is a wide variety

the Department of Social Protection. Where a person believes that they have been wrongly denied a payment, they may request an independent internal review, i.e. the file is handed over to another decision maker who re-examines whether a person qualifies for payment.[28] If an individual is still unsatisfied with this decision, and feels that they are entitled to the social assistance or social security payment, they may appeal to the Social Welfare Appeals Office (SWAO).[29] An appeals officer in the SWAO may then, on the basis of a paper review, or where an oral hearing is requested, uphold, modify or vacate the initial decision on the basis of all evidence (including new circumstances) that may pertain to the application for the social security or social assistance payment.[30] In certain circumstances, the Chief Appeals Officer of the SWAO may review a decision and, at their discretion, may refer a question only on a point of law to the High Court, i.e. how a certain legislative provision within the Social Welfare Consolidation Act 2005 should be interpreted.[31] An appeal on a point of law[32] may also be taken to the High Court by an individual who is not satisfied with a decision by an appeals officer or the Chief Appeals Officer.[33] The SWAO has never made a reference to the High Court on a point of law.[34]

(b) Landlord and tenant law (residential tenancies)[35]

10–10 The Residential Tenancies Acts 2004–2024 establish the rights and obligations of landlords and tenants. Disputes that arise between landlords and tenants may include setting of rent above the market rent,

of social security (contributory) and social assistance (non-contributory) payments that a person may be entitled to. Examples of such payments include child benefit, one-parent family payment, unemployment allowance/assistance, maternity benefit, occupational injuries benefits, and carer's allowance.

[28] Sections 299–303 of the Social Welfare Consolidation Act 2005 (as amended).

[29] Sections 304–321 of the Social Welfare Consolidation Act 2005 (as amended). However, for significant criticisms and an outline of core weaknesses with the Irish social welfare appeals processes, see S. Brady/FLAC, *Not Fair Enough: Making the Case for the Reform of the Social Welfare Appeals System* (Dublin: Printwell, 2012).

[30] Section 313 of the Social Welfare Consolidation Act 2005 (as amended).

[31] Sections 307–311 of the Social Welfare Consolidation Act 2005 (as amended).

[32] For an explanation of what an appeal on a point of law is, see Ch.9, para.9–52.

[33] Section 327 of the Social Welfare Consolidation Act 2005 (as amended).

[34] *Petecel v Minister for Social Protection* [2020] IESC 25 at para.51.

[35] Residential Tenancies Acts 2004–2024. For commentary on and analysis of this area of law, see Ú. Cassidy and J. Ring, *Landlord and Tenant Law: the Residential Sector*, 2nd edn (Dublin: Round Hall, 2020) and N. McGrath, *Lyall on Land Law*, 5th edn (Dublin: Round Hall, 2023), Ch.20.

eviction, withholding of deposits, and a myriad of other rights breaches. Where disputes arise, the Residential Tenancies Board can determine the legality of the actions of the landlord and/or tenant.[36] If mediation between the landlord and tenant is either not utilised or is unsuccessful, an adjudicator will issue a decision.[37] If the decision of the adjudicator is accepted by both parties, then the three-person Tenancy Tribunal[38] will issue a determination order. If the adjudicator's decision is not accepted by one or both parties, then, upon payment of the requisite fee, an appeal can be forwarded to the Tenancy Tribunal. The Tenancy Tribunal will hear the case and come to a decision, issuing a determination order that will rule on the dispute.[39] One or both parties must then comply with the determination order, and if they do not, court proceedings can follow. The District Court has the power to require a party to a dispute to comply with the determination order,[40] unless the initial decision reached was unfair in terms of procedures followed, new information has come before the District Court, and/or the decision was "manifestly erroneous".[41]

(c) Mental health law[42]

10–11 A person suffering from a mental disorder may be detained, and this detention is subject to review.[43] Where a person is an involuntary

---

[36] Residential Tenancies Act 2004 Pt 6. This body was previously known as the Private Residential Tenancies Board, but the name was changed to the Residential Tenancies Board by virtue of s.13 of the Residential Tenancies (Amendment) Act 2015. See also the Residential Tenancies (Amendment) Act 2015 (Commencement of Certain Provisions) (No. 2) Order 2016 (S.I. No. 151 of 2016).

[37] The Residential Tenancies Board provides an easy-to-understand dispute resolution process; see RTB, Dispute Resolution Services, *https://www.rtb.ie/dispute-resolution-services.*

[38] Residential Tenancies Act 2004 s.103 and s.121, the latter as substituted/amended by Residential Tenancies (Amendment) Act 2015 s.55(a) and (b), and Planning and Development (Housing) and Residential Tenancies Act 2016 s.48(1)(a)–(d). Planning and Development (Housing) and Residential Tenancies Act 2016 s.44 is not yet commenced. If it is commenced, it will permit the Tenancy Tribunal to be composed of one member in relation to most disputes before the Tenancy Tribunal.

[39] Residential Tenancies Act 2004 ss.104–108.

[40] Residential Tenancies Act 2004 s.124(2).

[41] Residential Tenancies Act 2004 s.124(3).

[42] See, generally, the Mental Health Act 2001. For commentary and critique of aspects of Irish mental health law, see C. O'Mahony, "The reform of Irish mental health law: Aligning with human rights obligations?" (2024) 95 *International Journal of Law and Psychiatry* 102004, *https://www.sciencedirect.com/science/article/pii/S0160252724000530?via%3Dihub* and references cited therein.

[43] Mental Health Act 2001 Pt 3.

patient in a prescribed mental health institution, and is suffering from a mental disorder,[44] they have an entitlement to have their detention reviewed periodically. A person detained has a right to request a review of the detention decision every three months, if they so choose.[45] The Mental Health Commission, a statutory body established under the Mental Health Act 2001, will form a Mental Health Tribunal composed of a lawyer as chairperson, a consultant psychiatrist and a layperson who will determine the lawfulness (or otherwise) of the involuntary detention of the patient.[46] The patient will have representation provided by a solicitor, independent of the Mental Health Tribunal, who will represent their interests. The Mental Health Tribunal will then make a decision as to whether continued detention of the involuntary patient is appropriate.[47] A patient who is not successful at the Mental Health Tribunal in securing release may appeal to the Circuit Court.[48]

(d) Education law[49]

10–12 A student in an approved higher education provider may be entitled to a grant if they satisfy financial and other eligibility criteria.[50] A student will fill in the requisite application form, enclosing appropriate evidence of eligibility for this grant.[51] If the student's grant application

44 The term "mental disorder" has a precise legal definition; see s.3 of the Mental Health Act 2001.

45 Section 15(3) of the Mental Health Act 2001, as substituted by s.4 of the Mental Health (Renewal Orders) Act 2018. This change occurred due to the Court of Appeal declaration that parts of s.15(3) of the Mental Health Act 2001 (as enacted) were unconstitutional. See *AB v Clinical Director of St Loman's Hospital* [2018] IECA 123.

46 Mental Health Act 2001 ss.31–55.

47 For more on the Mental Health Commission, its processes, procedures and modes of operation, see *http://www.mhcirl.ie.*

48 Mental Health Act 2001 s.19.

49 Education law is a very wide area, dealing with such matters as admissions to and exclusions from educational institutions, and supports the State must (but often does not) provide to children to enable them to exercise their constitutional right to education. For a more general exposition of this area of law, see D. Glendenning, *Education and the Law*, 3rd edn (Dublin: Bloomsbury Professional, 2023).

50 Student Support Act 2011 s.16. The particulars of qualification for a grant are outlined in statutory instruments, with the monetary rates of grants and qualifying institutions announced each year by the Minister for Further and Higher Education, Research, Innovation and Science, with approval from the Minister for Public Expenditure, National Development Plan Delivery and Reform. See the Student Support Regulations 2024 (S.I. No. 104 of 2024) and the Student Grant Scheme 2024 (S.I. No. 103 of 2024). See also ss.7–8 of the Student Support Act 2011.

51 The full particulars of the application process are outlined on SUSI's website, *www.susi.ie.*

is refused, the student can request that this decision be reviewed by a Student Universal Support Ireland (SUSI) appeals officer.[52] If a student is not satisfied with this decision, then they can appeal this decision to the Student Grants Appeal Board.[53] The Student Grants Appeal Board will then determine afresh the application for a student grant and come to an ultimate decision. An appeal on a point of law to the High Court is permitted under the Student Support Act 2011.[54]

(e) Revenue law[55]

10–13 The initial calculation of tax liability will be made by the Revenue Commissioners, either automatically or as part of a self-assessment of tax to be paid. Where a person disputes the calculation of tax liability made by the Revenue Commissioners, there is an appeals mechanism in place for a person to appeal the Revenue Commissioners' decision. The Finance (Tax Appeals) Act 2015 streamlines the tax appeals system. The Tax Appeals Commission can hear appeals on practically all tax liability decisions, including income tax, gift tax and inheritance tax, corporation tax, value added tax, residential property tax and certain customs and excise duties that the State can impose.[56] Previously, it had been possible for either the Inspector of Taxes or a taxpayer to appeal a tax liability decision to the Circuit Court. The Circuit Court had then been able to hear the case afresh.[57] However, under the Finance (Tax Appeals) Act 2015, this right of appeal to the Circuit Court has been removed.[58] Now a member of the Tax Appeals Commission may utilise a case stated procedure, i.e. seek a decision of the High Court on a point of law only.[59]

---

52 Student Support Act 2011 s.20.

53 Student Support Act 2011 s.21 and the Student Support Act 2011 (Student Grants Appeals Board) (Establishment Day) Order 2011 (S.I. No. 451 of 2011).

54 Student Support Act 2011 s.21(6).

55 There are a significant number of revenue and taxation statutes that impose tax liability on people; see, generally, the Taxes Consolidation Act 1997 (as amended). See also, P. Mulcahy (ed.), *Irish Taxation: Law and Practice*, 22nd edn (Dublin: Irish Tax Institute, 2024).

56 See s.34 of the Finance (Tax Appeals) Act 2015, which inserts s.949A into the Taxes Consolidation Act 1997. See also *http://taxappeals.ie* for more information on rules and procedures before the Tax Appeals Commission.

57 See former s.942 of the Taxes Consolidation Act 1997 (as amended).

58 See generally s.35 of the Finance (Tax Appeals) Act 2015.

59 See former s.942 of the Taxes Consolidation Act 1997 (as amended). For further discussion on the two types of case stated procedure, see Ch.9, para.9–70. See now s.29 of the Finance (Tax Appeals) Act 2015.

(f) International protection law

10–14 A person who applies for international protection is known as an "international protection applicant".[60] The phrase "asylum seeker" is also often used and both mean the same thing. "International protection" consists of two forms of protection status: refugee status and subsidiary protection status.[61] Both forms of protection status are highly legalised concepts,[62] and definitions have specialised legal meanings that may not necessarily correlate with how we might ordinarily use or understand those words.[63] A person is a refugee where they have left their country of origin and if returned to that country would be persecuted for reasons of their race, religion, nationality, membership of a particular social group, and/or political opinion.[64] Where a person does not meet this strict legal definition of refugee, and are non-EU nationals, they may nonetheless be entitled to subsidiary protection. Subsidiary protection is where they face a substantial risk of serious harm if returned to their country of origin. Serious harm is defined as being subject to the death penalty; torture, inhuman and degrading treatment or punishment; and/or danger to their lives due to indiscriminate violence during international or internal armed conflict.[65]

10–15 A person must make an application for international protection at a port of entry, or in person at the International Protection Office in Dublin. A preliminary interview will be undertaken.[66] This preliminary interview must identify why the person is claiming international protection. Subsequent to this, the applicant will be called to a personal interview.[67]

---

60 International Protection Act 2015 s.2(1).

61 These should not be confused with the status of temporary protection for people who are fleeing Russia's illegal war in Ukraine. See International Protection Act 2015 s.60. The practicalities and qualification criteria for who is entitled to temporary protection are set out in an information note: Immigration Service Delivery, "Information on Temporary Protection for People fleeing the conflict in Ukraine", available at: *https://www.irishimmigration.ie/information-on-temporary-protection-for-people-fleeing-the-conflict-in-ukraine/.*

62 The definition of refugee is set out in international law, European Union law and Irish law.

63 For a detailed exploration of this area of law, see C. Hughes and S. Hughes, *International Protection Act 2015: Annotated* (Dublin: Clarus Press, 2020). More generally, the rule on technical or legal language in statutes is set out in Ch.4, Section E.2.

64 International Protection Act 2015 s.2.

65 International Protection Act 2015 s.2 and s.15.

66 International Protection Act 2015 s.13.

67 See full particulars of this personal interview, see International Protection Act 2015 ss.34–40.

This interview will take place with an international protection officer. Once the interview is complete, the international protection officer prepares a report for the Minister for Justice. This "section 39" report must include a recommendation as to whether an applicant should be granted refugee status[68] or a subsidiary protection declaration,[69] or whether the application for international protection should be rejected.[70] By virtue of s.40 of the International Protection Act 2015, the Minister informs the applicant of the outcome, along with procedures for appealing the recommendation of the international protection officer. An applicant who is refused protection status may appeal to the International Protection Appeals Tribunal (IPAT).[71] The applicant has the right to an oral hearing.[72] IPAT is a more judicialised and formalised process for determining entitlement to protection. IPAT may affirm the decision of the international protection officer not to grant the applicant a refugee[73] or subsidiary protection declaration.[74] Alternatively, IPAT may determine that the applicant be declared a refugee[75] or a person entitled to subsidiary protection status.[76] There is one IPAT member allocated to each appeal, who is responsible for delivering a decision as to whether an appeal from a recommendation of an international protection officer should be upheld or set aside. There is no appeal from the decision of IPAT to a court.

(g) Concerns around impact of administrative bodies

10–16 The role and impact of all these bodies (and other bodies not discussed) on the lives of individuals should not be understated. Decisions taken can potentially result in a person being without a social welfare payment for a significant period of time; being without housing, if a person or family can be removed from a residential rented property; facing torture or other serious threats if removed from Ireland; being required to pay a significant tax liability; or being refused an educational

[68] International Protection Act 2015 s.39(3)(a).
[69] International Protection Act 2015 s.39(3)(b).
[70] International Protection Act 2015 s.39(3)(c).
[71] See generally International Protection Act 2015 Pt 10.
[72] However, as stated in s.42(3) of the International Protection Act 2015, "an appeal may be determined without an oral hearing", although this is subject to a rider: "except where otherwise provided".
[73] International Protection Act 2015 s.46(2)(a).
[74] International Protection Act 2015 s.46(3)(a).
[75] International Protection Act 2015 s.46(2)(b) and s.46(3)(b). See also s.46(5).
[76] International Protection Act 2015 s.46(3)(c). See also s.46(5).

grant. These are decisions that impact on the lives of people in a fundamental manner. Let us explore in more detail the field of social welfare law.

Box 10.1: Legal Insight
Social Welfare Law: Decisions, Appeals and People[77]

In 2022, the Department of Social Protection spent over €22 billion on social protection supports for people.[78] As highlighted above, a whole decision-making structure is in place to determine whether applicants for a social welfare payment meet the legislative entitlement conditions.[79] In 2022, deciding officers determined entitlement to social welfare payments in about 2 million decisions.[80] About 85 per cent of all applications for a social welfare payment are approved internally within the Department of Social Protection. In 2022, the Social Welfare Appeals Office (SWAO) finalised 24,267 appeals.[81] In just over 6,700 of appeals lodged, the matter was resolved in favour of the person who made the appeal, due to revision of a decision by a deciding officer.[82] Appeals officers in the SWAO resolved over 16,128 appeals, with over 5,900 appeals determined in favour of appellants. 1,411 appeals were withdrawn by appellants.[83] So, in total, 54.8 per cent of all appeals lodged—over 1 in every 2 appeals to the SWAO—had a favourable outcome for appellants.[84]

For a portion of these decisions, the appellant may provide new information to deciding officers permitting them to revise their decision, or new information to permit the SWAO to allow their appeal. Keep in mind that around 85 per cent of social welfare claims made in any one year will be approved. However, an administrative system that operates

77 For discussion of some broader concerns surrounding the independence of decision makers in the Department of Social Protection, and the independence of the Social Welfare Appeals Office, see G. Hogan, D.G. Morgan and P. Daly, *Administrative Law in Ireland*, 5th edn (Dublin: Round Hall, 2019), paras 6–95 to 6–117.

78 Department of Social Protection, *Statistical Information on Social Services Annual Report 2022* (2023), p.12.

79 See para.10–09.

80 Social Welfare Appeals Office, *Annual Report 2022* (Dublin: Social Welfare Appeals Office, 2023), p.18.

81 Social Welfare Appeals Office, *Annual Report 2022* (Dublin: Social Welfare Appeals Office, 2023), p.18.

82 Social Welfare Appeals Office, *Annual Report 2022* (Dublin: Social Welfare Appeals Office, 2023), p.19.

83 Social Welfare Appeals Office, *Annual Report 2022* (Dublin: Social Welfare Appeals Office, 2023), p.20.

84 Social Welfare Appeals Office, *Annual Report 2022* (Dublin: Social Welfare Appeals Office, 2023), p.25.

on the basis of success for more than half of all appeals does raise questions around good administrative decision-making by deciding officers in the Department of Social Protection. While Brady's analysis of these issues is over 13 years old, it does give a sense of how long-standing concerns have been surrounding first-instance decision-making. Brady stated:

> "In 2011, the rate of negative decisions by the Social Welfare Appeals Office exceeded the number of successful appeals, but the success rate still remained high at almost 43 per cent. However, prior to 2010 more than half of the appeals processed by the Social Welfare Appeals Office consistently had positive outcomes, *emphasising the need for better first instance decision-making*."[85]

Decision makers determining entitlement, or not, to a social welfare payment exercise significant power. Whelan, a leading welfare state scholar, reminds us of the reality of engaging with the social welfare system for *some* who need to make an application for a welfare payment.[86] Whelan has conducted a study on lived experiences of those engaging with processes for claiming benefits and their engagement with the administrative justice system. Feelings of fear and being under scrutiny within such systems can cause people significant distress. This comes from the claimant's own feelings of inadequacy at having to engage with a complex system to determine entitlement. One claimant reflected:

> "[E]very individual must prove that she is worthy of public money ... Every aspect of their life and mindset is rendered fair game for scrutiny."[87]

Engaging as a claimant with the social welfare system can be taxing in terms of level of form-filling required. As one jobseeker's allowance recipient in Whelan's study highlighted:

> "I had to fill in about 10 fucking forms. Now this is all information they already have ... Nothing is going to change in my life ... oh here, fill that in ... ."[88]

[85] S. Brady/FLAC, *Not Fair Enough: Making the Case for Reform of the Social Welfare Appeals System* (Dublin: FLAC, 2012), p.52 (emphasis added).

[86] J. Whelan, "We have our dignity, yeah? Scrutiny under suspicion: Experiences of welfare conditionality in the Irish social protection system" (2021) 55(1) *Social Policy Administration* 34.

[87] J. Whelan, "We have our dignity, yeah? Scrutiny under suspicion: Experiences of welfare conditionality in the Irish social protection system" (2021) 55(1) *Social Policy Administration* 34 at 39.

[88] J. Whelan, "We have our dignity, yeah? Scrutiny under suspicion: Experiences of

Another claimant for One Parent Family Payment spoke about the intrusive nature of questions that can be (lawfully) asked, and commented on their feelings of being investigated and having to disclose deeply personal issues. When asked why she was not getting maintenance from the biological father of her child, she had to answer questions such as:

> "[W]here is he? What's his name? How do we know you're telling the truth ... All this kind of stuff ... And you're just like I don't know ... I barely know the fella."[89]

2. Judicial Review

10–17 Where a decision maker or appeals body/tribunal, or even a lower court, determines rights or obligations that impact an individual, the superior courts may not be able to interfere with the merits of that decision unless it is established in primary legislation that an appeal lies to a court.[90] A judicial review is not an appeal.[91] Judicial review in administrative cases is generally concerned with how a decision was reached. One would have to prove, for example, that the decision maker did not have legal authority to make the decision. Alternatively, that the manner in which the decision was reached was "unreasonable", which in essence means that a decision maker had taken leave of their senses and no other decision maker could have arrived at that decision.[92] Although, when considering matters that impact on human or fundamental rights, courts will explore the proportionality of the decision reached.[93] O'Donnell C.J. in *Burke v Minister for Education and*

welfare conditionality in the Irish social protection system" (2021) 55(1) *Social Policy Administration* 34 at 40.

89 J. Whelan, "We have our dignity, yeah? Scrutiny under suspicion: Experiences of welfare conditionality in the Irish social protection system" (2021) 55(1) *Social Policy Administration* 34 at 41.

90 See the discussion of appeal mechanisms in the preceding section.

91 There are other grounds of review; for a full outline of the law of judicial review in Ireland, see G. Hogan, D.G. Morgan and P. Daly, *Administrative Law in Ireland*, 5th edn (Dublin: Round Hall, 2019), Chs 10–19, and F. Donson and D. O'Donovan, *Law and Public Administration in Ireland* (Dublin: Clarus Press, 2015), Chs 9–14.

92 *Burke v Minister for Education and Skills* [2021] IECA 67 at paras 224–226.

93 This was first established in the Supreme Court decision of *Meadows v Minister for Justice, Equality and Law Reform* [2010] 2 I.R. 701, in particular Murray C.J.at 723–728; Denham J. at 741–745. For a succinct summary of the relationship between unreasonableness and proportionality in Irish law, see *Singh v Minister for Business, Enterprise and Innovation* [2023] IEHC 332 at paras 31–37.

Skills stated that "the principle of proportionality could be employed in the analysis and resolution of cases raising issues as to the impact of decisions on fundamental rights."[94] An appellant could also point to some procedural irregularity in how the decision was come to. Decision makers must arrive at their decision fairly, not be biased, and must hear from all parties to the issue. There are other grounds for review that we do not need to discuss. If a judicial review is successful for the applicant, then the superior court does not then proceed to make a decision. Rather, the matter is sent back to the body/person that has the legal authority to make the decision, for a fresh determination by a different decision maker.

10–18 Judicial review can only ever be commenced in the High Court. Some judicial reviews relate to matters of great importance. Other judicial reviews do not. Twomey J. in *Shannon v Shannon*[95] outlined the problems that can occur with the law requiring persons to take any and all judicial reviews to the High Court. This overburdens the High Court, when proportionally Ireland has five times fewer judges per head of population than in England and Wales.[96] There has been no review of jurisdiction of the various courts in decades. The number of District and Circuit Courts in Ireland has reduced significantly, with 400 per cent fewer District Courts now contrasted with 1961.[97] Despite judicial attempts to highlight the costs of litigating in Ireland, these issues have been ignored by government.[98] Twomey J. then provided a number of examples where the issues to be determined by the High Court in judicial reviews, if legislatively permitted, could have been taken before a lower court. This included the High Court having to determine if a €500 rental deposit had to be returned to a tenant,[99] and hearing a dispute relating to an €80 clamping release fee.[100] Where judges try to persuade a litigant to

[94] [2023] 2 I.R. 1 at 51–52.

[95] [2024] IEHC 291. With thanks to Anthony Kerr SC for bringing this decision to our attention.

[96] [2024] IEHC 291 at para.3 and para.15. See Ch.9, Box 9.1 on recent increases to judicial numbers.

[97] [2024] IEHC 291 at paras 13–17.

[98] [2024] IEHC 291 at paras 19–23.

[99] *Abeyneh v Residential Tenancies Board* [2023] IEHC 81, as cited in *Shannon v Shannon* [2024] IEHC 291 at para.26, fn.16.

[100] *Irish Times*, 18 October 2022, as cited in *Shannon v Shannon* [2024] IEHC 291 at para.26, fn.17.

utilise a lower court (where this is possible), the litigant can still choose to proceed in the High Court rather than be required to use a lower court.[101]

10–19 To provide a more tangible understanding of judicial review, we will explore one area of Irish law: housing law and judicial review.

Box 10.2: Legal Insight
Housing Law and Judicial Review

Irish government policy on housing has been subject to significant debate over decades. Hearne argues that the lack of housing availability, high rents, and extraordinarily poor quality of some rented properties in Ireland is

> "... not a 'natural' disaster or an accident of policy. [The housing crisis] ... results from the specific neoliberal housing and economic policies pursued by government and the interlocking effects of growing social inequality and financialisaton."[102]

Housing law consists of a complex body of legislation, case law and policy directions. The key thing to remember is that we are not, as such, concerned with the ins and outs of this field, but rather decision-making on housing entitlement in select areas. Our key focus is to explain how judicial review operates regarding the exercise of powers by local authorities in relation to (i) allocation of one form of social housing, and (ii) homelessness. In Ireland, local authorities are responsible for a number of housing functions. When exercising housing functions, local authorities are known as "housing authorities". Turning first to allocation of social housing, we are focusing on one type of social housing: what is colloquially known as "council housing".[103] This is where the housing authority owns the property and rents it to a person who meets the strict conditions for entitlement to social housing.[104] In *Keenan v Clare County Council*, Bradley J. succinctly summarised the role of Irish courts as regards judicial review of housing authority decisions:

[101] *O'Keeffe v Commissioner of An Garda Síochána* [2023] IECA 332 as cited in *Shannon v Shannon* [2024] IEHC 291 at para.26.

[102] R. Hearne, *Housing Shock: The Irish Housing Crisis and How to Solve It* (Bristol: Policy Press, 2020), p.11.

[103] Housing (Miscellaneous Provisions) Act 2009 s.19(2)(a).

[104] This includes, amongst other things, meeting an income threshold test, having a housing need as assessed by the housing authority, along with a range of other conditions. Housing authorities also must adopt a prioritisation scheme.

> "Unless a clear error in the decision-making process is established by a disappointed applicant for housing or re-housing, the courts may not intervene and quash a decision that has led to that disappointment."[105]

So, just because an individual disagrees with a decision of the housing authority as regards allocation of council housing, this is not grounds for a successful judicial review. Case law in this area has overwhelmingly seen the courts emphasising that they will not interfere with decisions on social housing made by housing authorities. An applicant must prove to the court that (non-exhaustive): the housing authority made a "clear error";[106] there was an absence of "fair procedures";[107] the decision reached was "self-evidently irrational";[108] and/or the housing authority failed to have regard to relevant considerations or took into account irrelevant considerations.

The applicants in *Mulhare v Cork County Council*[109] were a person with cerebral palsy and her mother. The applicants were residing in very poor quality accommodation that did not meet their needs, some 40km away from Cork University Hospital. The applicants sought the High Court to require Cork County Council to provide social housing for them within a five-mile radius of Cork University Hospital (for medical reasons). The reason that Cork County Council did not provide accommodation to the applicants was because there was no accommodation within a five-mile radius of the hospital. The Court of Appeal emphasised that there is no obligation on housing authorities to have at their disposal accommodation that can immediately meet the housing needs of people in the applicants' situation,[110] or to provide the precise type of accommodation the applicant wishes to have.[111] The vast majority of case law in this area results in similar court decisions.

Let us consider one example where the decision of the housing authority was quashed. In *Agamah v South Dublin County Council*,[112] the applicant had suffered abuse and intimidation, including damage to property from other housing authority tenants. This included a hammer

[105] [2023] IEHC 598 at para.37(vii), relying on *Mulhare v Cork County Council* [2018] IECA 206 at para.34.

[106] *Mulhare v Cork County Council* [2018] IECA 206 at para.34.

[107] *Mulhare v Cork County Council* [2018] IECA 206 at para.22.

[108] *Agamah v South Dublin County Council* [2015] IEHC 424. This judgment does not utilise paragraph numbers; this point is made on page 3 of the decision, as accessed on *courts.ie*.

[109] [2018] IECA 206 at paras 2–5.

[110] [2018] IECA 206 at paras 18–21.

[111] [2018] IECA 206 at para.17.

[112] [2015] IEHC 424.

attack on the applicant for which there was a successful prosecution of the assailant, and a fire being deliberately set on his property. The applicant wished to transfer to another property. The housing authority stated that the applicant did not come within the terms of being prioritised for a transfer. Kearns P. in the High Court emphasised that, "in reviewing decisions of expert administrative bodies the courts are required to have regard to the doctrine of curial deference and should be slow to interfere with such decisions." In making its decision to refuse the applicant's transfer request, the housing authority relied exclusively on the observations of a Garda Chief Superintendent who was of the view that the attacks were not racist in character. The housing authority did not engage with the applicant's testimony or evidence that the abuse and criminal actions directed to him were due to his race (as a Ghanaian man). From a natural justice viewpoint, Kearns P. held that this was deeply problematic. While the housing authority could take into account the views of the Gardaí, it could not in essence delegate the decision to the Gardaí and adopt their analysis of the situation without carrying out any assessment of its own. In quashing the decision of the housing authority, Kearns P. determined that the applicant suffered a violent attack, the attacker was moved from the housing complex as a priority transfer, but the applicant was not. This, the court determined, was "self evidently irrational". With the decision quashed, the housing authority now had to make a fresh determination (by a different decision maker) on the applicant's request to transfer to other council housing. Ultimately, this decision was one for the housing authority to make and was not within the remit or mandate of the High Court to determine if a transfer should be provided to the applicant. However, Kearns P. did "express the wish" that the Council would facilitate the transfer of the applicant as a priority.

Local authorities also have responsibility for the housing needs of those without homes. At the end of June 2024, there were over 14,000 people, including children and families, who were homeless in Ireland.[113] The Irish government has committed to "working towards" eradicating homelessness by 2030.[114] Just like housing authority powers regarding

[113] Department of Housing, Local Government and Heritage, *Monthly Homelessness Report* (June 2024). Up-to-date homelessness figures can be accessed at: *https://www.gov.ie/en/collection/80ea8-homelessness-data/#homelessness-data.*

[114] Government of Ireland, *Housing for All: Pathway to Eradicating Homelessness, Increasing Social Housing Delivery and Supporting Social Inclusion* (2021), available at: *https://www.gov.ie/en/campaigns/dfc50-housing-for-all/.* Ireland has also signed the Lisbon Declaration on the European Platform on Combatting Homelessness (European Commission, 2021). This (non-legally binding) Declaration commits its signatories to working towards ending homelessness by 2030.

social housing, courts are very reluctant to interfere with decisions of housing authorities as to whether a person is "homeless", and if so, what the housing authority *may* do to alleviate homelessness under s.10 of the Housing Act 1988.[115] Once an offer of homelessness support is made, and where a homeless person does not take up or accept this offer, then their "homelessness has ended."[116] In *C v Galway County Council*,[117] the applicant and her five children were rendered homeless after their lease on private rental property came to an end. The Council granted the applicant emergency accommodation in a hotel and subsequently offered her a property. She refused this offer as the property was over 100km away from Galway City and one of C's children needed ongoing and constant medical treatment in Galway City. This was the only property in the housing authority's housing stock that could accommodate the family. O'Regan J. held that the withdrawal of emergency homeless accommodation to C and her family was reasonable. In coming to her decision, O'Regan J. emphasised that housing authorities have limited resources and it is for the housing authority to best balance the needs of the individual in light of needs of a large number of others also entitled to support.[118]

There is only rarely an obligation ("must") upon housing authorities to exercise powers to provide assistance, accommodation or financial support to a person who is homeless. In very extreme circumstances, the housing authorities' powers under s.10 of the Housing Act 1988 become mandatory. In *O'Donnell v South Dublin County Council*,[119] the Supreme Court held that the fourth-named applicant, who was disabled, was subject to treatment that was inhuman and degrading. This treatment was caused in part by the housing authority's refusal to exercise its powers under s.10 of the Housing Act 1988. The Supreme Court held that the housing authority, who had full knowledge of the applicant's living conditions, breached her constitutional right to bodily autonomy. MacMenamin J. highlighted that this was a truly exceptional case.

An application for judicial review of a housing authority's decision must be made to the High Court. The judicial review cannot be heard at

---

115 Housing Act 1988 s.2 (definition of homelessness) and s.10 (powers that local authorities may exercise).

116 *Doherty v South Dublin County Council* [2007] 2 I.R. 696 at 712. See also *Fingal County Council v Gavin* [2007] IEHC 444.

117 [2017] IEHC 784.

118 [2017] IEHC 784 at para.22.

119 [2015] IESC 28, discussed in L. Thornton, "Socio-Economic Rights and Ireland" in S. Egan (ed), *International Human Rights: Perspectives from Ireland* (London: Bloomsbury, 2015), para.9.31 et seq.

the level of the District Court or Circuit Court. So, persons will have no choice other than challenging the decision before the High Court, which brings us back to the concerns of Twomey J.[120] This may be a prime area whereby courts other than the High Court could first determine whether the decision of the housing authority was made fairly.

D. Ireland's Ombudsman Offices

10–20 The formal administrative decision-making bodies outlined and discussed above provide only a partial picture of the Irish administrative state. This is complemented by ombudsman offices that can review actions of state administrative bodies. Their core task is to hold government departments and other state bodies to account for maladministration. There exists a range of ombudsman offices in Ireland. The Financial Services and Pensions Ombudsman is tasked with dealing with public complaints as regards financial services institutions and pensions, through "mediation and, where necessary, by investigation and adjudication", and resolves grievances between customers, financial institutions and pension providers.[121] The Ombudsman for the Defence Forces, who is independent of the Defence Forces,[122] investigates complaints from current and former members of the armed forces on a number of set grounds[123] after the complainants have exhausted internal complaint mechanisms. The Garda Síochána Ombudsman Commission (GSOC) can investigate complaints and conduct investigations relating to alleged garda misconduct or misbehaviour.[124] GSOC is shortly to be

[120] See para.10–18.

[121] Financial Services and Pensions Ombudsman Act 2017.

[122] Ombudsman (Defence Forces) Act 2004. See also: *http://www.odf.ie.*

[123] Section 4(2) of the Ombudsman (Defence Forces) Act 2004 outlines the functions of this Ombudsman. The Defence Forces Ombudsman may investigate actions that adversely affect the complainant, where such actions were "(i) taken without proper authority, (ii) taken on irrelevant grounds, (iii) the result of negligence or carelessness, (iv) based on erroneous or incomplete information, (v) improperly discriminatory, (vi) unreasonable, notwithstanding consideration of the context of the military environment, (vii) based on undesirable administrative practice, or (viii) otherwise contrary to fair or sound administration" (Ombudsman (Defence Forces) Act 2004 s.4(2)(b)).

[124] Garda Síochána Act 2005 Pts 3 and 4. For a robust analysis of the effectiveness of GSOC, see V. Conway, "A Sheep in Wolf's Clothing? Evaluating the Impact of the Garda Síochána Ombudsman Commission" (2009) 43 *Irish Jurist* 109; V. Conway and D. Walsh, "Current Developments in Police Governance and Accountability in Ireland" (2011) 55(2–3) *Crime, Law and Social Change* 241.

renamed the Office of the Police Ombudsman.[125] The Ombudsman for Children[126] and the Irish Human Rights and Equality Commission[127] also enjoy ombudsman-like functions. In this part of the chapter, we consider the role of the Public Service Ombudsman, given the wide scope of review powers that this Ombudsman has, as well as this Ombudsman being the longest established office of its kind in Ireland.

1. The (Public Service) Ombudsman

10–21 Taking legal action will not always be feasible, may not be legally possible, or may not be appropriate in order to correct poor administrative decision-making or other practices by public bodies. The Ombudsman is not responsible for overturning a decision of a body, but for determining whether proper and adequate information and decision-making processes were in place. The Ombudsman Acts 1980–2012 provide for the establishment of the Office of the Ombudsman.[128] The Ombudsman is to act independently of Government,[129] is appointed by the President after a resolution is passed in both Houses of the Oireachtas for a period of six years (renewable),[130] and can only be removed from their office for stated misbehaviour and after a vote of the Oireachtas.[131] The Ombudsman's salary and allowances are the same as a judge of the High Court.[132]

(a) What can be investigated?

10–22 The remit of the Ombudsman's investigatory powers are provided for in s.4(2)(b) of the Ombudsman Acts 1980–2012.[133] Where

[125] Policing, Security and Community Safety Act 2024 Pt 5. At the time of writing, this Act had not been commenced.

[126] See the Ombudsman for Children Act 2002, as amended.

[127] See the Irish Human Rights and Equality Commission Act 2014, as amended.

[128] Ombudsman Act 1980 s.2(1). For a comprehensive overview and consideration of the role of the Ombudsman in Ireland, see G. Hogan, D.G. Morgan and P. Daly, *Administrative Law in Ireland*, 5th edn (Dublin: Round Hall, 2019), Ch.9.

[129] Ombudsman Act 1980 s.4(1).

[130] Ombudsman Act 1980 s.2(2).

[131] Ombudsman Act 1980 s.2(3), as amended by ss.3(4) and 6 of the Ombudsman (Amendment) Act 2012.

[132] Ombudsman Act 1980 s.3(1), as amended by s.3 of the Ombudsman (Amendment) Act 2012.

[133] Ombudsman Act 1980 s.4, as amended by ss.6 and 7 of the Ombudsman (Amendment) Act 2012.

a person has been adversely affected by the actions[134] of certain state bodies, institutions and/or administrative agencies,[135] the Ombudsman may investigate where the actions of such organisations are:[136]

(i) taken without proper authority;
(ii) taken on irrelevant grounds;
(iii) the result of negligence or carelessness;
(iv) based on erroneous or incomplete information;
(v) improperly discriminatory;
(vi) based on an undesirable administrative practice;
(vii) a failure by an agency or organisation to provide reasonable assistance in a fair and timely manner to an individual where that organisation is determining a right, privilege, obligation, liability or some penalty that may benefit/be imposed upon an individual, in light of available resources of that organisation;
(viii) otherwise contrary to fair or sound administration.

The totality of these grounds for complaint is known as maladministration. The Ombudsman's Office also has a role regarding appeals against refusal of freedom of information requests. When the Ombudsman exercises this function, they are generally called the Information Commissioner.[137]

10–23 As well as having a complaint on the grounds of maladministration, a tentative complainant must first ensure that they utilise all internal grievance mechanisms so as to get a resolution within the organisation to which the complaint relates, before complaining to the Ombudsman.[138]

[134] Defined in s.1(1) of the Ombudsman Act 1980, as amended by s.3 of the Ombudsman (Amendment) Act 2012, as including a decision, a failure to act or an omission by bodies covered by the Acts.

[135] The full list of the bodies, institutions and agencies (or certain functions therein) not subject to the jurisdiction of the Ombudsman is set down in Sch.2 to the Ombudsman Act 1980, as substituted by the Ombudsman (Amendment) Act 2012. The Minister for Justice may, after consultation with the Ombudsman, designate certain entities exercising public functions to be subject to the Ombudsman's jurisdiction; see s.4(10)(a) of the Ombudsman Act 1980. See also s.1A of the Ombudsman Act 1980, as inserted by s.4 of the Ombudsman (Amendment) Act 2012. This is discussed further below.

[136] This, of course, includes persons acting in an official role within these organisations, and civil servants; see s.1(1) and (2) of the Ombudsman Act 1980.

[137] Freedom of Information Act 2014 (as amended), Pt 6.

[138] Ombudsman Act 1980 s.4(5)(b)(iii), as amended by ss.6 and 7 of the Ombudsman (Amendment) Act 2012.

In addition, a complaint must not be "trivial or vexatious",[139] and the complainant must have a sufficient interest in the matter complained about.[140] The Ombudsman is statutorily prohibited from investigating a complaint where civil legal proceedings are under way or have been concluded, or a complaint in respect of which a complainant may appeal to a court or has some other grievance mechanism provided for by law.[141] Other exclusions also apply, as fully outlined in s.5 of the Ombudsman Acts 1980–2012, including where the action relates to military activities or national security, the recruitment and appointment process for employing specified public and civil service positions, or to the immigration or international protection system in Ireland.[142]

(b) Which state agencies can be subject to investigation?

10–24 An individual (or representative on their behalf) can make a complaint to the Ombudsman's Office and this will be determined on the basis of the published procedures of the Ombudsman's Office.[143] The Ombudsman endeavours to acknowledge receipt of a complaint within seven days.[144] Once a complaint is deemed admissible, the Ombudsman will cause the complaint to be investigated. The First Schedule to the Ombudsman Act 1980, as replaced by the Ombudsman (Amendment) Act 2012, lists the reviewable state bodies and agencies against which a complaint under s.4 of the Ombudsman Act 1980, as amended, can be taken. This includes government departments, any entity established to administer a public statutory or non-statutory scheme, a company where the Government is the majority shareholder (including subsidiaries and whether controlled directly or indirectly by Government), any agency that is a creature of statute, higher education institutions, and an entity "that immediately prior to the enactment of the Ombudsman (Amendment)

[139] Ombudsman Act 1980 s.4(5)(b)(i), as amended by ss.6 and 7 of the Ombudsman (Amendment) Act 2012.

[140] Ombudsman Act 1980 s.4(5)(b)(ii), as amended by ss.6 and 7 of the Ombudsman (Amendment) Act 2012.

[141] Ombudsman Act 1980 s.5, as substituted by s.8 of the Ombudsman (Amendment) Act 2012.

[142] Since April 2017, the Ombudsman has the remit to investigate complaints relating to the provision of services by the International Protection Accommodation Services (IPAS). See *www.ombudsman.ie* for several reports on the system of direct provision. (Note, the work of IPAS had previously been conducted by the Reception and Integration Agency.)

[143] See generally, *https://www.ombudsman.ie/making-a-complaint/make-a-complaint/.*

[144] Client Service Charter of the Office of the Ombudsman.

Act 2012" was subject to the review of the Ombudsman.[145] Part II of the First Schedule excludes a number of bodies from oversight or review by the Ombudsman, including the Adoption Authority of Ireland when exercising its powers as regards intercountry adoptions;[146] the Nursing and Midwifery Board of Ireland, except for matters relating to the maintenance of a register of nurses and midwives, and the recognition of foreign qualifications; clinical judgments of professionals working in the Health Service Executive; and the Legal Aid Board's decisions to provide legal advice or representation.[147] The Second Schedule contains an exhaustive list of exempt agencies, whereby individuals cannot complain about maladministration, in the sense defined under s.4(2)(b) of the Ombudsman Act 1980, as amended. This includes bodies such as Coimisiún na Meán, public transport providers, the Criminal Assets Bureau, the Irish Human Rights and Equality Commission, the Judicial Appointments Advisory Board, the National Asset Management Agency, the Office of the Ombudsman itself, the Office of the Ombudsman for Children, the International Protection Office, the International Protection Appeals Tribunal, and the Voluntary Health Insurance Board.

10–25 In 2023, the Ombudsman received 4,465 complaints.[148] Of these complaints, 1,175 related to the actions/operations of the civil service within government departments, 1,430 related to actions of local authorities, while the remainder concerned the Health Service Executive, universities and other regulatory bodies and a wide array of other agencies.[149] As regards the actions of civil servants within government departments, the vast majority of complaints in 2023 related to the Department of Social Protection, which had 636 complaints.[150] The Annual Reports and previously the Case Books of the Ombudsman provide a rich source of examples of actions that the Ombudsman has the jurisdiction to investigate.[151]

[145] Ombudsman Act 1980 First Schedule, Pt 1, para.(i), as substituted by the Ombudsman (Amendment) Act 2012.
[146] Adoption Act 2010.
[147] As regards the system of civil legal aid in Ireland, see generally, Ch.13, paras 13–35 to 13–39.
[148] Office of the Ombudsman, *Annual Report 2023* (Dublin: Ombudsman, 2024), pp.18–19.
[149] Office of the Ombudsman, *Annual Report 2023* (Dublin: Ombudsman, 2024), p.18.
[150] Office of the Ombudsman, *Annual Report 2023* (Dublin: Ombudsman, 2024), p.20.
[151] These can be accessed online at: *https://www.ombudsman.ie/en/.*

(c) Remedies provided

10–26 Unlike a court, the findings of the Ombudsman do not have legal force. The Ombudsman only has the power to recommend that the state body take a specific action. The Ombudsman cannot compel the body against which a negative determination is made to carry out the recommendation. The Ombudsman may recommend that the public body must further consider the matter,[152] "remedy, mitigate or alter the adverse effect of the action",[153] and/or request the public body to explain why the particular course of action had been taken.[154] If the Ombudsman is not satisfied with the response of the public body, then they may "cause a special report on the case" to be laid before the Houses of the Oireachtas.[155] From time to time, controversy has erupted due to public bodies not following the recommendations of the Ombudsman.[156]

10–27 The best outcomes are when the public body does follow the recommendations, such as one example from the 2023 Annual Report.[157] We noted above that courts are very reluctant to review decisions of housing authorities as regards their housing duties. The Ombudsman received a complaint from a family in Cork. The parents worked but lost their housing due to their landlord selling their property. The family were offered homeless accommodation. Cork County Council offered the family permanent social housing some 40km away from the area where they lived, where their children went to school, where both parents were in employment, and where they had based their lives. When the family rejected this offer on the basis of distance, Cork County Council threatened to withdraw the homeless accommodation and to report the parents to Tusla (the Child and Family Agency) for "putting the children at risk". Cork County Council then provided them with details of a small property that they could rent, but then distanced themselves by saying they could not recommend the property because it would legally result in overcrowding given how small the property was. But for the intervention

[152] Ombudsman Acts 1980–2012 s.6(3)(a).
[153] Ombudsman Acts 1980–2012 s.6(3)(b).
[154] Ombudsman Acts 1980–2012 s.6(3)(c).
[155] Ombudsman Acts 1980–2012 s.6(5) and (7).
[156] For a discussion of some of the core controversies, see F. Donson and D. O'Donovan, *Law and Public Administration in Ireland* (Dublin: Clarus Press, 2015), paras 4–56 to 4–69.
[157] Office of the Ombudsman, *Annual Report 2023* (Dublin: Ombudsman, 2024), pp.35–36.

of the Office of the Ombudsman, the family would have been removed from their homeless accommodation. The Ombudsman conducted an investigation. The Ombudsman severely criticised the actions of Cork County Council in relation to their threats to the parents that Tusla would be involved if they did not accept the property 40km away. The Ombudsman further criticised the Council for providing information on a wholly inadequate property and then threatening them with the withdrawal of homeless accommodation. The outcome for the family was that the Council had to apologise to the family. The Council did not accept that the offer of their accommodation was unreasonable in light of the housing stock available, but provided "further assistance" to the family and located a suitable property nearer to their work and their school.

E. Public Inquiries

10–28 Inquiries have a long history in Ireland.[158] Tribunals of inquiry and commissions of investigation can be seen as "machinery for investigation"[159] that may be established due to some perceived or actual crisis of confidence in state action or inaction surrounding a particular event or series of events.[160] Usually such inquiries will be established to consider how and why particular "disasters, accidents, policy failures or scandals"[161] occurred, and what can be learned from them so as to prevent reoccurrence. These forms of inquiries have the potential to subject governments to scrutiny[162] where, for a variety of reasons, parliaments may not be deemed the proper forum for establishing facts, learning from past events, and holding persons or organisations

[158] For a discussion on inquiries, labelled "decision inquiries", where decisions may be made as regards removal of staff members from certain employments, within the realm of aircraft investigations, compulsory purchase orders and certain matters relating to planning, see G. Hogan, D.G. Morgan and P. Daly, *Administrative Law in Ireland*, 5th edn (Dublin: Round Hall, 2019), paras 8–01 to 8–03.

[159] C. Harlow and R. Rawlings, *Law and Administration*, 3rd edn (Cambridge: CUP, 2009), p.571.

[160] C. Harlow and R. Rawlings, *Law and Administration*, 4th edn (Cambridge: CUP, 2022), p.641.

[161] R. Sulitzeanu-Kenan, "Scything the Grass: Agenda-setting Consequences of Appointing Public Inquiries in the UK. A Longitudinal Analysis" (2007) 35(4) *Policy and Politics* 629 at 630.

[162] For more on the accountability of the State and the role of public inquiries, see P. Sales, "Accountability of Government via Public Inquiries" (2004) 9(3) *Judicial Review* 173.

accountable for administrative or policy failures.[163] Therefore, such inquiries can "arouse intense controversy. They may tap into political passions and prejudices."[164] Let us turn first to consider parliamentary inquiries, before exploring tribunals of inquiry and commissions of investigation.

1. Parliamentary Inquiries

10–29 In *Maguire v Ardagh*,[165] the applicants were members of An Garda Síochána who were compelled to appear before an Oireachtas sub-committee investigating the death of a man at Abbeylara, Co. Longford.[166] The "Abbeylara incident" related to the shooting dead of John Carthy after a stand-off with Gardaí in April 2000.[167] The Oireachtas, utilising legislative powers,[168] sought to call named members of the Gardaí who were involved in the operation that led to Carthy's death. A key issue was whether the Oireachtas could conduct inquiries that could make findings of fact, including a finding of unlawful killing, against members of An Garda Síochána.[169] A majority of the Supreme Court determined that the Oireachtas (and any committees established by the Oireachtas) does not have powers to make findings of fact against named individuals where there is a potential to damage the good name of that person.[170] Murray J., in rejecting the arguments of the respondents (who were all members of the Oireachtas sub-committee on Abbeylara) that there was an implied power within the Irish Constitution that permitted the Oireachtas to hold inquiries, declared:

[163] G. Howe, "The Management of Public Inquiries" (1999) 70(3) *The Political Quarterly* 294. For a discussion on this in the Irish context, see P. Rabbitte, "A Tribunal of Enquiry or an Investigation by Dáil Committee?" (1999) 4(3) *Bar Review* 114.

[164] P. Sales, "Accountability of Government via Public Inquiries" (2004) 9(3) *Judicial Review* 173.

[165] [2002] 1 I.R. 385.

[166] For a succinct overview of the matters of controversy that the Oireachtas sub-committee sought to investigate, see Denham J.'s summations: [2002] 1 I.R. 385 at 552–554.

[167] [2002] 1 I.R. 385 at 552.

[168] Committees of the Houses of the Oireachtas (Compellability, Privileges and Immunities of Witnesses) Act 1997.

[169] See [2002] 1 I.R. 385 at 585 for Murray J.'s summation of the powers of the Oireachtas sub-committee.

[170] The right to the protection of one's "good name" is guaranteed under Article 40.3.2° of the Irish Constitution.

> "[I]f the Oireachtas is to exercise the power to establish committees of inquiry so as to make findings of fact and reach conclusions involving personal culpability of individual citizens for alleged wrongdoing of the gravest kind and thereby impugning the good name of a citizen, that power must be found in the Constitution."[171]

10–30 In 2011, a constitutional amendment was proposed that would have enabled the Oireachtas to "determine, with due regard to the principles of fair procedures, the appropriate balance between the rights of persons and the public interest for the purposes of ensuring an effective inquiry".[172] The Irish Council for Civil Liberties, one of the most outspoken groups against the amendment, argued that, if passed, it would "delete the rule of law".[173] The amendment was rejected by the people in a referendum.[174] With the referendum defeated, the Houses of the Oireachtas (Inquiries, Privileges and Procedures) Act 2013 (the "2013 Act") was introduced instead and it establishes the limited inquiry functions of the Oireachtas and its committees. The 2013 Act permits five types of Oireachtas inquiry. First, an inquiry that will record evidence and report the evidence.[175] This type of inquiry cannot make findings of fact, unless those facts "are not contradicted by any witness or other person giving evidence".[176] Second, the committee may conduct "an inquiry relating to the exercise of one or more than one of the legislative functions of the House or, if the committee is a joint committee, both Houses, including whether there is a need for new legislation".[177] Third, the 2013 Act fleshes out details on when the Oireachtas may conduct inquiries into the removal of judges or the President in a constitutionally appropriate manner.[178] Fourth, an inquiry may be established on the conduct of a member of the Houses of the Oireachtas.[179] Fifth, an

---

171 [2002] 1 I.R. 385 at 607. See also the judgment of McGuinness J. ([2002] 1 I.R. 385 at 642–657), Denham J. ([2002] 1 I.R. 385 at 554) and Hardiman J. ([2002] 1 I.R. 385 at 672–678).

172 Thirtieth Amendment of the Constitution (Houses of the Oireachtas Inquiries) Bill 2011.

173 Irish Council for Civil Liberties, "Government's Kangaroo Court Proposals 'Delete Rule of Law' says NO campaign", 26 October 2011.

174 See further, E. O'Leary, "Oireachtas Inquiries Referendum" (2014) 29(2) *Irish Political Studies* 318.

175 Houses of the Oireachtas (Inquiries, Privileges and Procedures) Act 2013 s.7.

176 Houses of the Oireachtas (Inquiries, Privileges and Procedures) Act 2013 s.7(2).

177 Houses of the Oireachtas (Inquiries, Privileges and Procedures) Act 2013 s.8.

178 Houses of the Oireachtas (Inquiries, Privileges and Procedures) Act 2013 s.9, as amended by s.77 of the Online Safety and Media Regulation Act 2022 and s.290 of the Policing, Security and Community Safety Act 2024.

179 Houses of the Oireachtas (Inquiries, Privileges and Procedures) Act 2013 s.10.

inquiry may be established to hold Government or certain office-holders in public employment to account.[180] The 2013 Act establishes, in some detail, the procedures that must be utilised for each type of inquiry, the compellability of persons to attend an Oireachtas inquiry, and the fair procedure and good name rights that persons benefit from under the 2013 Act.[181]

10–31 Constitutionally, members of the Oireachtas have immunity for any utterances they make in parliament.[182] Committees of the Oireachtas do not necessarily enjoy the same extent of protection. In *Kerins v McGuinness*,[183] the appellant, Kerins, was invited to provide evidence on specified matters before the Public Accounts Committee (PAC), a committee of the Oireachtas. Members of the PAC ventured well beyond the remit of the invitation, making serious and sustained accusations against the appellant through aggressive questioning and grandstanding soliloquies. The key question that arose in this case was whether a committee of the Oireachtas enjoys the same privileges as the Oireachtas itself. The appellant's health and well-being was impacted in the most severe manner, so she declined to further attend the PAC. The PAC's application to compel Kerins to provide evidence under the 2013 Act was rejected by the Oireachtas Committee on Privileges and Procedure.[184] The seven-judge Supreme Court determined that while the PAC did enjoy a high degree of constitutional protection, this was not unlimited. Rather, "[PAC] has a constitutional obligation to keep within that remit. Where, as here, a committee has strayed very far beyond the boundaries of its remit ... it is appropriate for the Court to intervene."[185] In this case, the PAC had acted significantly outside of its terms of reference and the conditions upon which the appellant had been invited to give evidence before the Committee. The manner in which the PAC meeting was conducted meant that the views of individual members of

[180] Houses of the Oireachtas (Inquiries, Privileges and Procedures) Act 2013 s.11.
[181] For a full review of these issues, see F. Donson and D. O'Donovan, *Law and Public Administration in Ireland* (Dublin: Clarus Press, 2015), paras 2–94 to 2–124. For an analysis of the limitations of the 2013 Act as regards the Oireachtas Banking Inquiry, see F. Donson and D. O'Donovan, "Designing Effective Parliamentary Inquiries: Lessons Learned from the Oireachtas Banking Inquiry" (2016) 39(2) *Dublin University Law Journal* 303.
[182] Article 15.13 of the Constitution, discussed in depth in *O'Brien v Clerk of Dáil Éireann* [2019] IESC 12.
[183] [2019] IESC 11. See also [2019] IESC 42.
[184] [2019] IESC 11 at paras 2.16–2.17.
[185] [2019] IESC 11 at para.10.11.

the PAC could be ascribed to the committee as a whole. The Supreme Court also emphasised that the appellant had no remedy available to her.[186] Therefore, the Supreme Court simply declared that the actions of the PAC were unlawful.[187]

10–32 Given the limited powers of the Oireachtas to hold persons and organisations to account (often for very good reason, as the treatment of Kerins before the PAC illustrates), tribunals of inquiry and commissions of investigation are said to provide some mechanisms for investigating public controversies and maladministration. In the next sections we will explore tribunals of inquiry and commissions of investigation. Both methods of inquiry are posited as having a number of purposes.[188] First, the investigation or inquiry may be a fact-finding exercise. Second, whatever the type of inquiry, its purposes may be a method of learning about institutional or systemic failures within the realms of law, policy, provision of state services or political decision-making. Third, the inquiry may make recommendations on how best to avoid the occurrence of similar issues in the future. Fourth, the inquiry may potentially hold persons to account for their actions. Fifth, persons who have been impacted by the events that led to the inquiry may be provided with some relief at having their story told by a body established by the State.

2. Tribunals of Inquiry

10–33 Tribunals of inquiry may be established by the Oireachtas to investigate a "definite matter ... of urgent public importance".[189] The Oireachtas must agree on the terms of reference of a tribunal of inquiry, which set out the issue or issues that a tribunal must investigate.[190] The core purpose of a tribunal of inquiry is not necessarily to apportion

---

[186] [2019] IESC 11 at para.15.2 and [2019] IESC 42 at para.3.1. In *Kerins v Dáil Éireann* [2024] IESC 24, the Supreme Court dismissed the appellant's attempts to be provided with documentation from the Dáil in discovery for her damages action.

[187] [2019] IESC 42 at paras 6.1–6.4. For further insight and analysis, see T. Hickey, "Judges and the Political Organs of State" in D.M. Farrell and N. Hardiman (eds), *The Oxford Handbook of Irish Politics* (Oxford: OUP, 2022) and B. Murray, "Kerins v McGuinness (Nos 1 and 2) [2019] IESC 11 & 42 and O'Brien v Clerk of Dáil Éireann [2019] IESC 12" (2020) 2 *Irish Supreme Court Review* 175.

[188] See generally, K. Walshe, "Understanding and Learning from Organisational Failure" (2003) 12(2) *Quality and Safety in Health Care* 81; A. Hegarty, "Government of Memory: Public Inquiries and the Limits of Justice in Northern Ireland" (2002) 26 *Fordham International Law Journal* 1148, from which these five principles are drawn.

[189] Tribunals of Inquiry (Evidence) Acts 1921–2011 s.1(1).

[190] Tribunals of Inquiry (Evidence) Acts 1921–2011 s.1(1).

blame, but to engage in a "fact-finding operation".[191] It will be for each individual tribunal of inquiry to determine the precise standard of proof required—civil or criminal or somewhere in between these standards. Donson and O'Donovan note:

> "Although it might be concluded that a criminal standard is not applicable to an inquisitorial fact-finding process, conversely the consequences of an adverse finding by an inquiry might suggest that the balance of probability standard was also inappropriate."[192]

Murray C.J. in *Lawlor v Planning Tribunal*[193] provided an overview of the different standards of proof that had been applied by various tribunals of inquiries. In the Morris Tribunal and the Commission of Investigation into Child Abuse,[194] the civil standard of the balance of probabilities was utilised.[195] The Beef Tribunal worked on the basis of the criminal standard of proof, while the Blood Transfusion Tribunal, although not explicitly stating the standard of proof it required, "employed terminology consistent with the more stringent criminal requirement".[196] Other tribunals approached the question of burden of proof on a "sliding scale", depending on the seriousness of the allegations at issue or matters for decision; either a balance of probabilities approach, a beyond reasonable doubt approach, or somewhere in between both of these standards of proof was utilised.[197] Ultimately, Murray C.J., with whom other members of the Supreme Court agreed, concluded that "[t]he findings made [in a tribunal of inquiry] must clearly be proportionate to the evidence available. Any such findings of grave wrongdoing should in principle be grounded upon cogent evidence."[198]

10–34 Tribunals of inquiry are not considered to be administering justice, in the sense of Article 34.1 or Article 37.1 of the Constitution.[199] Tribunals

[191] *Goodman v Hamilton* [1992] 2 I.R. 542 at 588 per Finlay C.J.

[192] F. Donson and D. O'Donovan, *Law and Public Administration in Ireland* (Dublin: Clarus Press, 2015), para.5–62. See further, F. Donson and D. O'Donovan, "Public Inquiries and Administrative Justice" in M. Hertog et al (eds), *The Oxford Handbook of Administrative Justice* (Oxford: OUP, 2020).

[193] [2010] 1 I.R. 170.

[194] This Commission was established under the Commission to Inquire into Child Abuse Act 2000.

[195] [2010] 1 I.R. 170 at 178.

[196] [2010] 1 I.R. 170 at 178.

[197] [2010] 1 I.R. 170 at 178.

[198] [2010] 1 I.R. 170 at 186.

[199] *Goodman v Hamilton* [1992] 2 I.R. 542 at 590 per Finlay C.J.

of inquiry will generally be held in public, unless the chairperson of the tribunal decides it is in the public interest, relating to the subject matter of the inquiry or the nature of the evidence to be given by a witness, for it to be in private.[200] Significant case law has emerged as regards the process, procedure and conduct of tribunals of inquiry in Ireland. Fair process and procedures within tribunals are essential.[201] The chairperson of a tribunal of inquiry has similar powers to a High Court judge to enforce the attendance of witnesses and compel an individual or organisation to produce documentation. Witnesses are provided with legal privilege against defamation.[202]

10–35 All recent tribunals of inquiry have been chaired by serving or retired judges of the High Court, Court of Appeal or Supreme Court.[203] Generally, tribunals of inquiry have fallen out of favour due to their high costs, as well as the significant delays in producing final reports.[204] In the preceding 30 years, several tribunals of inquiry were established in Ireland. These tribunals investigated matters relating to corruption by politicians,[205] planning,[206] policing matters (discussed below), and alleged state collusion in the murders of policemen in Northern Ireland.[207] Invariably, recommendations were provided by each of the tribunals of

200 Tribunals of Inquiry (Evidence) Acts 1921–2011 s.2(a).

201 *Goodman v Hamilton* [1992] 2 I.R. 542, in particular at 565 per Costello J.

202 Tribunals of Inquiry (Evidence) Acts 1921–2011 s.1(1) and (3), and s.4 of the Tribunals of Inquiry (Evidence) (Amendment) Act 1979. For judicial interpretation of these sections, see *Lawlor v Flood* [1999] 3 I.R. 107.

203 For a full list of inquiries, see Law Reform Commission, *Consultation Paper on Public Inquiries including Tribunals of Inquiry* (LRC CP 22-2003), pp.317–318. There are two updates to this list. First, the Smithwick Tribunal inquiring into collusion between members of An Garda Síochána and the IRA as regards the murder of two members of the Royal Ulster Constabulary (RUC) in 1989, report published in 2013. Second, the Disclosures Tribunal, whose six reports were published between 2017 and 2023.

204 See Comptroller and Auditor General, *Special Report: Tribunals of Inquiry* (December 2008) and 581 *Dáil Debates* Cols 911–922 (4 March 2004), where the then Minister for Justice, in introducing the Commissions of Investigation Bill 2003, noted the need to have more effective, efficient and timely public inquiries. We discuss commissions of investigation below.

205 Inquiry into Payments to Politicians and Related Matters (the Moriarty Tribunal), *https://moriarty-tribunal.ie/*.

206 Inquiry into Certain Planning Matters and Payments (the Mahon Tribunal), *https://www.planningtribunal.ie/*.

207 Inquiry into Suggestions that Members of An Garda Síochána or Other Employees of the State Colluded in the Fatal Shootings of RUC Chief Superintendent Harry Breen and RUC Superintendent Robert Buchanan on the 20th March 1989 (the Smithwick Tribunal), *https://www.smithwicktribunal.ie*.

inquiry. Whether or not those recommendations are implemented is a matter for the political/governmental sphere of the state.

10–36 We are now going to explore two tribunals. It is important to emphasise that these two examples are highly unusual because their report findings have subsequently been set aside. In the recent past, two tribunal of inquiry reports have effectively been set aside: the Kerry Babies Tribunal and the Stardust Tribunal. The Kerry Babies Tribunal was established to investigate allegations by the Hayes family relating to their supposed confessions to the murder of two babies and their ill-treatment in Garda custody in Kerry. The "confessions" were to a "murder" they simply could not have committed. Yet the Tribunal did not focus on how this could have happened. Instead, Joanne Hayes was subject to the most disgraceful questioning about the most minute and intimate details of her private and sexual life. She was heavily sedated for a portion of her testimony due to the line of questioning employed by barristers and permitted by Mr Justice Lynch. The Tribunal branded the Hayes family as unreliable, never really exploring how members of the family all separately confessed to murders that they could not have committed. In essence, it was disbelieved that they suffered ill-treatment at the hands of the Gardaí.[208] Throughout the sitting of the Tribunal, there were significant protests by the local community and others in support of Joanne Hayes and her family. Many knew just how wrong the treatment of the family was at the time of the Tribunal. In 2020, the Irish State and An Garda Síochána apologised to Joanne Hayes and the Hayes family. The findings of the Kerry Babies Tribunal were set aside. The State agreed that the findings of the Tribunal were unfounded and incorrect. The appalling treatment that Joanne Hayes and her family suffered at the hands of institutions of the Irish State was acknowledged to be in gross breach of their constitutional rights.[209]

[208] For a much more piercing overview and analysis of how this Tribunal operated and its bizarre findings, see Y. Daly, "Commentary on The Report of the Tribunal of Inquiry into 'The Kerry Babies Case'" and Dr Vicky Conway's excoriating critique of the Kerry Babies Tribunal in M. Enright et al. (eds), *Northern/Irish Feminist Judgments: Judges' Troubles and the Gendered Politics of Identity* (Oxford: Hart, 2017), pp.195–228, and V. Conway, *Policing Twentieth Century Ireland: A History of An Garda Síochána* (London: Routledge, 2014), pp.172–173.

[209] See *Report of the Tribunal of Inquiry into the "Kerry Babies Case"* (Dublin: Stationery Office, 1985) and the High Court Order of 18 December 2020 in *Hayes v Commissioner of An Garda Síochána* (2019 No. 1800 P), both available at: *https:///opac.oireachtas.ie/Data/Library3/Documents%20Laid/2021/pdf/DOJdocslaid090321_090321_172959.pdf*.

10–37 In March 2024, the State similarly apologised for the treatment of survivors and families of the deceased of the Stardust tragedy by the Stardust Tribunal, with An Taoiseach Simon Harris acknowledging "that State processes heaped misery upon tragedy for the Stardust families".[210] On Valentine's night in 1981, 41 young people died and many more were injured at a nightclub, "Stardust", in Artane, Dublin. The Stardust Tribunal, chaired by Mr Justice Ronan Keane, was established within days of the fire occurring and concluded in 1982 that the owners of the Stardust had acted in "reckless disregard" for the safety of the patrons of the nightclub, including the purposeful locking of fire exit doors.[211] The owners of the Stardust nightclub received almost IRL£600,000 in compensation in 1983, as O'Hanrahan J. was satisfied that the damage was caused by arson. This was based on Mr Justice Keane's finding that the fire was "probably" started by arson,[212] declaring that there had been a joint enterprise by persons unknown and for reasons unknown to start a fire, resulting in deaths and injuries.[213] This finding caused huge distress to the families of the deceased and survivors of the fire as it was viewed as casting aspersions on the characters of the deceased and survivors by labelling them arsonists, responsible for their own misfortune. In 2008, a report by Paul Coffey SC recommended to the government that the findings of the Tribunal in this regard should be repudiated.[214] Fresh inquests were ordered in 2021 to determine the cause of deaths of the 41 people who had died.[215] In April 2024, the inquest concluded that they had been unlawfully killed.[216]

See also, Radio Kerry, "High Court Settlement and new State apology to the Hayes Family", 18 December 2022, and N. Michael, "Joanne Hayes and family to be awarded €2.5m over treatment during Kerry Babies scandal", *Irish Examiner*, 17 December 2020.

210 Volume 1052 Col. 72, *Dáil Debates*, Thursday 28 April 2024.

211 *Report of the Tribunal of Inquiry on the Fire at the Stardust, Artane, Dublin on the 14th of February 1981* (Dublin: Stationery Office, 1982), Ch.9, para.9.42.

212 *Report of the Tribunal of Inquiry on the Fire at the Stardust, Artane, Dublin on the 14th of February 1981* (Dublin: Stationery Office, 1982), Ch.3, para.3.207 and Ch.9, para.9.14.

213 *Report of the Tribunal of Inquiry on the Fire at the Stardust, Artane, Dublin on the 14th of February 1981* (Dublin: Stationery Office, 1982), Ch.6, para.6.205.

214 Paul Coffey SC, *Report of the Independent Examination of the Stardust Victims Committee's Case for a Reopened Inquiry into the Stardust Fire Disaster* (January 2008), Ch.3.

215 Coroner for the Dublin District Court, Dr Myra Cullinane, *In re the Stardust Fire Inquests: Ruling on Scope of the Inquests*, 13 August 2021.

216 Department of Justice, "Statement from Minister Helen McEntee on Verdict of Unlawful Killing at Stardust Inquest", 18 April 2024; C. Hunt, "Verdicts of unlawful killing returned

10–38 The Kerry Babies Tribunal and Stardust Tribunal examples were selected for discussion because they both illustrate an important point about the class dynamics in Irish law, politics and society. Joanne Hayes spoke of her treatment at the Tribunal, the alien nature of the proceedings, and the accents and tones of the barristers, indicating the difference in social class between them.[217] Catherine Connolly TD, during the Dáil statements on the Stardust apology, neatly encapsulates what was at play in both tribunals:

> "[The Kerry Babies] tribunal was set up to investigate gardaí, but instead we got a narrative about Joanne Hayes and her family. They have received an apology and the survivors of the Stardust have received an apology, but the establishment has learned absolutely nothing. The powerful protect the powerful. *What happened here was absolutely class distinction*. If the Government does not face that and begin to learn from it, then we will have learned nothing."[218]

10–39 With these exceptional examples, we can see how, conducted improperly, findings of tribunals can have devastating consequences. Now let us turn to examples where findings of tribunals made significant positive changes to policing in Ireland, even if some concerns remain.

Box 10.3: Legal Insight
Tribunals and Policing in Ireland

Public confidence in policing is essential. The Gardaí as "guardians of the peace" have a rather unenviable responsibility for ensuring public safety and the security of the State. Section 7 of the Garda Síochána Act 2005[219] lists the functions of the force. These include: preserving

at Stardust inquests", RTÉ News, 18 April 2024. Families of the deceased created pen portraits to provide insights into the lives of each of the victims unlawfully killed in the Stardust fire; see RTÉ, Stardust: The Pen Portraits, available at: *https://www.rte.ie/history/stardust/#panel-pen-portraits-the-stardust-victims-remembered.*

217 J. Hayes and J. Barrett, *My Story: Joanne Hayes* (Kerry: Brandon/Mount Eagle Publications, 1985), p.165.

218 Volume 1052 Col. 72, *Dáil Debates*, Thursday 28 April 2024 (emphasis added). See also the contribution of Mick Barry TD, Solidarity/People Before Profit: "Some people say Ireland does not have a class system. That is not true and never was true. If anyone out there ever doubts it, just look at the story of the Stardust. This was about social class from beginning to end."

219 As substituted by the National Vetting Bureau (Children and Vulnerable Persons) Act

peace and public order, protecting life and property, vindicating human rights, preventing crime, protecting the security of the State, bringing offenders to justice, and road safety. This necessitates the Gardaí having significant, although in no way unrestricted, powers to meet these functions. Hamilton and Black, exploring policing and public confidence, note that in Ireland, confidence in the police is very high.[220] In 2022, the Garda Public Attitudes Survey found that 75 per cent of people were "very satisfied" or "quite satisfied" with Garda service in their local communities.[221] Ninety per cent of people trust An Garda Síochána.[222] Hamilton and Black describe this as "puzzling" given the recent (and not so recent) scandals that have engulfed the Gardaí.[223] Conway captures some of these issues succinctly:

> "Allegations have related to the policing of protests, removal of Roma children from families, reports of institutionalised racism, abuse of penalty points systems, poor investigation of serious crime, improper use of computer systems, recording of phone calls into police stations, poor treatment of victims, poor treatment of whistle-blowers, mass inflation of breath test figures, misappropriation of funds in the training college and data quality issues, including homicide figures."[224]

In 2002, a joint resolution passed by the Oireachtas established the Morris Tribunal to consider serious allegations of Gardaí misconduct in Donegal in the mid to late 1990s.[225] Mr Justice Frederick Morris, a former President of the High Court, was the sole member of the Tribunal of Inquiry and he made the following findings:[226]

2012 s.25. The 2005 Act will be repealed by the Policing, Security and Community Safety Act 2024 once it is commenced; see s.5 and Sch.1 of the 2024 Act.

220 C. Hamilton and L. Black, "'Strikingly and Stubbornly High'": Investigating the Paradox of Public Confidence in the Irish Police" (2023) 3(1) *Journal of Contemporary Criminal Justice* 38 at 40.

221 An Garda Síochána, "Garda Public Attitudes Survey 2022" (November 2023), pp.30–36.

222 An Garda Síochána, "Garda Public Attitudes Survey 2022" (November 2023), pp.22–24.

223 C. Hamilton and L. Black, "'Strikingly and Stubbornly High'": Investigating the Paradox of Public Confidence in the Irish Police" (2023) 3(1) *Journal of Contemporary Criminal Justice* 38 at 46–47.

224 V. Conway, "Near or Far Away: Local Police Governance in Ireland" (2019) 16(5) *European Journal of Criminology* 515 at 523.

225 Established pursuant to the Tribunals of Inquiry (Evidence) Act 1921 (Establishment of Tribunal) Instrument 2002 (S.I. No. 175 of 2002). The full extent of Garda deception and illegality that led to the establishment of the Morris Tribunal will not be outlined here; for that, see V. Conway, *The Blue Wall of Silence: the Morris Tribunal and Police Accountability in Ireland* (Dublin: Irish Academic Press, 2010). All reports of the Morris Tribunal can be accessed at: *http://www.morristribunal.ie/index.htm.*

226 For a summary of the findings of the Morris Tribunal, see V. Conway, *The Blue Wall of*

i. certain members of the Gardaí were involved in planting explosives;
ii. the death of Richie Barron was most likely in a hit-and-run and Frank McBrearty Jnr, Mark McConnell and Michael Peoples were harassed and falsely arrested in relation to this death;
iii. Michael Peoples and his wife, Charlotte Peoples, and several more individuals were unlawfully arrested; and
iv. members of the Travelling Community were unlawful arrested.

Conway, an expert on policing issues in Ireland, described the Morris Tribunal Report as the first occasion that "schemes of corruption and abuse [in An Garda Síochána] have been exposed beyond an individual level and recognised as institutional".[227] Prior to the completion and publication of the Morris Tribunal Report, but no doubt disturbed by the potential for abuse of office by members of An Garda Síochána, the Garda Síochána Ombudsman Commission (GSOC) was established to investigate, inter alia, complaints about the Gardaí from members of the public. The early reports that emerged from the Morris Tribunal, it has been argued, may have been the impetus for the passing of the Garda Síochána Act 2005.[228] Somewhat belatedly,[229] and albeit not a direct recommendation within the Morris Tribunal Report, a Policing Authority was established on 1 January 2016. The Policing Authority is responsible for monitoring the performance of the Gardaí in institutional and structural matters (i.e. the Policing Authority does not have a role in considering public complaints),[230] and in the appointment, and possible removal, of the Garda Commissioner and other senior members of An Garda Síochána.[231]

Silence: the Morris Tribunal and Police Accountability in Ireland (Dublin: Irish Academic Press, 2010), Ch.3.

227 V. Conway, *The Blue Wall of Silence: the Morris Tribunal and Police Accountability in Ireland* (Dublin: Irish Academic Press, 2010), p.173.

228 V. Conway, *The Blue Wall of Silence: the Morris Tribunal and Police Accountability in Ireland* (Dublin: Irish Academic Press, 2010), p.123.

229 Garda Síochána (Policing Authority and Miscellaneous Provisions) Act 2015.

230 Garda Síochána (Policing Authority and Miscellaneous Provisions) Act 2015. See also *https://www.policingauthority.ie/*. While not explicitly recommended in the Morris Tribunal reports, calls for a policing authority formed the backdrop of political discussions post the publication of the findings of the Morris Tribunal. See, for example, Motion on Morris Tribunal by Senator Joanna Tuffy, 18 *Seanad Éireann Debates* Col. 1770 (15 June 2005), and contributions by various TDs during the Second Stage of the Garda Síochána (Policing Authority and Miscellaneous Provisions) Bill 2015 *(Dáil Debates*, 24 September 2015).

231 Garda Síochána (Policing Authority and Miscellaneous Provisions) Act 2015 Pt 2. There are significant changes relating to the Gardaí, Garda oversight and scrutiny that will come into force post the publication of this text; see Department of Justice, "Minister

The "avalanche of scandal and controversy" in Irish policing continued, leading to the establishment of various investigations in the 2010s. This included the establishment of the Disclosures Tribunal in 2017 which led to the resignations of two Garda Commissioners, two government ministers and two Secretaries General of the Department of Justice, before and during the Tribunal.[232] The initial impetus for the Disclosures Tribunal related to cancellation by members of the Gardaí of fixed penalty speeding fines for people, as well as providing incorrect data on roadside breath tests.[233] A Garda whistleblower, Sergeant Maurice McCabe, who brought these matters to political and public attention was subject to a campaign of vilification by a former Garda Commissioner and the then Garda Press officer. This included serious, untrue and wholly unsubstantiated claims regarding sexual abuse, albeit this emerging from an incorrect Tusla report.[234] The Disclosures Tribunal found that Garda Sergeant McCabe was motivated by the public interest in making these disclosures, and suffered a heavy price for this. Focusing on the structural issues with the organisation and management of An Garda Síochána, Mr Justice Peter Charleton concluded that all organisations tend to go into "protective" mode so as to avoid confronting systemic issues. Mr Justice Charleton remarked that there would not have been any need for the Disclosures Tribunal if Sergeant McCabe's concerns were first addressed and dealt with by the Gardaí.[235]

These tribunals have nonetheless meant that significant governance and oversight reforms have occurred and are occurring in An Garda Síochána, in particular from recommendations of the Commission on the Future of Policing in Ireland (concluded in the midst of the Disclosures Tribunal).[236] There is a clear government commitment to implementing at least some of the Commission's recommendations, in particular through the Policing, Security and Community Safety Act 2024 (the "2024

McEntee commences landmark reform of An Garda Síochána and oversight bodies", 15 October 2024, available at: *https://www.gov.ie/en/press-release/62c4f-minister-mcentee-commences-landmark-reform-of-an-garda-siochana-and-oversight-bodies/.*

232 C. Hamilton and L. Black, "'Strikingly and Stubbornly High'": Investigating the Paradox of Public Confidence in the Irish Police" (2023) 3(1) *Journal of Contemporary Criminal Justice* 38 at 47.

233 See A. Mulcahy, "Parking Tickets and Police Reform: an Analysis of the Development and Impact of Police Scandals" (2021) 31(2) *Policing and Society* 161.

234 Disclosures Tribunal, *Third Interim Report of the Tribunal of Inquiry into Protected Disclosures Made under the Protected Disclosures Act 2014 and Certain Other Matters* (11 October 2018).

235 Disclosures Tribunal, *Third Interim Report of the Tribunal of Inquiry into Protected Disclosures Made under the Protected Disclosures Act 2014 and Certain Other Matters* (11 October 2018), p.294.

236 Commission on the Future of Policing in Ireland, *Future of Policing in Ireland* (2018).

Act").[237] In a May 2024 report, the Irish Council for Civil Liberties (ICCL) provided an overview of the changes that will result from the 2024 Act, once it is commenced.[238] The report notes that some recommendations of the Commission on the Future of Policing in Ireland remain to be implemented, or have only been partially implemented.[239] The ICCL concluded:

> "[W]hile there has been progress made on recommendations that have less of a direct impact on human rights, such as those requiring non-legislative change, the recommendations directly concerning the oversight bodies and the transparency and accountability of An Garda Síochána have not been fully implemented. This is incredibly concerning given the history of weak external accountability of Gardaí, [and] the historical practice of politicians and Garda management denying problems (including corruption) within the organisation ...".[240]

Such analysis is not to be dismissed lightly. At the same time, there is at least progress towards ensuring matters uncovered by the Morris and Disclosures Tribunals will not occur again. Only with time will we know if this is the case.

3. Commissions of Investigation

10–40 A commission of investigation can differ significantly from a tribunal of inquiry. As explored below, a commission of investigation can sit in private—something that can only be done in exceptional circumstances for a tribunal of inquiry. A commission of investigation can limit the use of legal representation, and overall is supposed to permit a greater degree of flexibility that will ensure timely conclusion of the commission of investigation. Therefore, at least in theory, a commission

[237] See also, Department of Justice, *A Policing Service for Our Future: Implementing the Report of the Commission on the Future of Policing in Ireland October 2020 to March 2022* (March 2022).

[238] ICCL, *Human Rights in Irish Policing: Analysing the Implementation of the Recommendations from the Commission on the Future of Policing in Ireland* (May 2024).

[239] ICCL, *Human Rights in Irish Policing: Analysing the Implementation of the Recommendations from the Commission on the Future of Policing in Ireland* (May 2024), pp.45–53.

[240] ICCL, *Human Rights in Irish Policing: Analysing the Implementation of the Recommendations from the Commission on the Future of Policing in Ireland* (May 2024), p.32.

of investigation is to be more inquisitorial, compared to the adversarial nature of a tribunal of inquiry. Whereas a tribunal of inquiry is vested with the powers of a High Court judge, a commission of investigation only has powers as set down in its primary statute.

10–41 The Commissions of Investigation Act 2004 (the "2004 Act") provides that, with the approval of the Minister for Public Expenditure and Reform, the Government may by order establish a commission of investigation "to investigate any matter considered by the Government to be of significant public concern",[241] and to publish a report on this issue.[242] The 2004 Act permits the investigation of issues of public concern that arose prior to the passage of the 2004 Act.[243] Such commissions of investigation are to be established after the Government places a draft of the proposed order before both Houses of the Oireachtas,[244] and this draft proposed order is approved by both Houses.[245] If the commission of investigation is not permitted to set its own terms of reference, the terms of reference for the commission of investigation are to be set down by a specified Government Minister in consultation with "any persons".[246] The specified terms of reference must relate "to the events, activities, circumstances, systems, practices or procedures to be investigated",[247] and accompanied by an estimate of costs for the commission of investigation.[248]

10–42 The terms of reference may be amended in specified circumstances.[249] One or more members of the commission of investigation may be appointed by Government, subject to the requirements that the person or persons appointed should have "appropriate experience, qualifications, training or expertise".[250] Part 3

[241] Commissions of Investigation Act 2004 s.3(1)(a), as construed in light of the Finance (Transfer of Departmental Administration and Ministerial Functions) Order 2011 (S.I. No. 418 of 2011).
[242] Commissions of Investigation Act 2004 s.3(1)(b).
[243] Commissions of Investigation Act 2004 s.3(4).
[244] Commissions of Investigation Act 2004 s.3(2)(a).
[245] Commissions of Investigation Act 2004 s.3(2)(b).
[246] Commissions of Investigation Act 2004 s.4.
[247] Commissions of Investigation Act 2004 s.5(1).
[248] Commissions of Investigation Act 2004 s.5(2).
[249] Under s.6 of the Commissions of Investigation Act 2004, the specified Minister may amend the terms of reference with the agreement of, or upon request by, the commission of investigation.
[250] Commissions of Investigation Act 2004 s.7. Section 7 of the 2004 Act also sets down

of the 2004 Act establishes the procedural operation of commissions of investigation. Significantly, commissions of investigation are generally held in private,[251] and they can limit the presence of legal representatives (subject to this being in the interests of justice and of the investigation to do so).[252]

10–43 While the commission of investigation must endeavour to facilitate the voluntary attendance and cooperation of any witness,[253] the 2004 Act contains powers of compellability, whereby a refusal to cooperate may be a criminal offence.[254] All commissions of investigation are under a statutory duty to observe fair procedures.[255] Once a report is in draft form, any person who is identified in the report has an opportunity to make submissions to the commission of investigation.[256] Where this person raises concerns that fair procedures have not been followed, then they may request the report to be changed.[257] The member or members of the commission of investigation may accede to this request, apply to the High Court for directions on how to deal with the request, or submit the report to the specified Government Minister, without making amendments.[258] The specified Government Minister is under a statutory duty to publish the report (or any interim report),[259] unless the Government Minister is of the view that the report may prejudice any criminal proceedings.[260] The Government Minister may seek High Court directions concerning the publication of the report.[261]

10–44 As of 2024, 14 commissions of investigation have been established under the 2004 Act. These commissions of investigation

procedures for multi-member commissions of investigation, the appointment of a chairperson, and specifies what is to occur when a member (or members) is/are unable to continue with their duties.

251 Section 11(1)(a) and (b) of the 2004 Act permits the commission of investigation to hear evidence in public where (i) it is requested by a particular witness, and (ii) the commission is satisfied that it is in the interests of the investigation and fair procedures to hear the witness in public.

252 Commissions of Investigation Act 2004 s.11(2).

253 Commissions of Investigation Act 2004 s.10.

254 Commissions of Investigation Act 2004 s.16.

255 Commissions of Investigation Act 2004 s.15(1).

256 Commissions of Investigation Act 2004 ss.34 and 35.

257 Commissions of Investigation Act 2004 s.35(1).

258 Commissions of Investigation Act 2004 s.35(3).

259 Commissions of Investigation Act 2004 s.38.

260 Commissions of Investigation Act 2004 s.38(2).

261 Commissions of Investigation Act 2004 s.38(2).

have related to the Dublin and Monaghan bombings of 1974;[262] the role of members of An Garda Síochána as regards the investigation and prosecution of crimes and the use of force;[263] a death in prison;[264] child sex abuse scandals;[265] Mother and Baby homes;[266] the operation of a named nursing home;[267] and the operation of and activities relating to the banking sector in Ireland.[268] The findings of various commissions of investigation have sometimes led to some structural or policy changes to state administrative and accountability mechanisms. Other commissions of investigation sought to bring closure to persons who suffered from abuse, by providing a narrative of what had happened and why it had happened. However, the extent that this narrative reflects the lived experience of people can, at times, be questioned. We now turn to consider the Mother and Baby Homes Commission of Investigation.

Box 10.4: Legal Insight
The Mother and Baby Homes Commission of Investigation: "Historical" Narratives

"Unmarried mothers" were seen as an existential threat to Irish society.[269] The supposed violation of social mores that children should only be born within married families led to the establishment of several institutions known as "Mother and Baby Homes". These were established mainly by religious orders and funded by the State. The alleged purpose of

[262] Commission of Investigation (Dublin and Monaghan Bombings) Order 2005 (S.I. No. 222 of 2005).

[263] Commission of Investigation (Dean Lyons Case) Revised Order 2006 (S.I. No. 69 of 2006), the Commission of Investigation (Ronan MacLochlainn) Order 2014 (S.I. No. 346 of 2014), Commission of Investigation (Certain Matters relative to An Garda Síochána and other persons) Order 2014 (S.I. No. 192 of 2014), and Commission of Investigation (Certain Matters relative to the Cavan/Monaghan Division of the Garda Síochána) Order 2015 (S.I. No. 38 of 2015).

[264] Commission of Investigation (Death of Gary Douch in Mountjoy Prison) Order 2007 (S.I. No. 371 of 2007).

[265] Commission of Investigation (Child Sexual Abuse) (Amendment) Order 2009 (S.I. No. 117 of 2009).

[266] Commission of Investigation (Mother and Baby Homes and certain related Matters) Order 2015 (S.I. No. 57 of 2015).

[267] Commission of Investigation (Leas Cross Nursing Home) Order 2007 (S.I. No. 304 of 2007).

[268] Commission of Investigation (Banking Sector) (Amendment) Order 2010 (S.I. No. 590 of 2010).

[269] L. Earner-Byrne, "The Irish Family: Blame, Agency and the 'Unmarried Mother Problem', 1980s to 2021" (2023) 32 *Contemporary European History* 270 at 273–276. See above for the discussion of the Kerry Babies Tribunal, paras 10–35 to 10–38.

these institutions was to care for unmarried mothers and their children, albeit for many mothers their children were adopted, sometimes without any real consent.[270] In 2014, Irish historian Catherine Coreless published information regarding 786 deceased children buried in a septic tank of a former Mother and Baby Home in Tuam, Co. Galway. This led to a commission of investigation whose terms of reference were to examine the creation and operation of certain Mother and Baby Homes, the use of children in vaccine trials, illegal adoptions, and the high death rates of children born into these institutions, amongst several other matters.[271] There were three members of this Commission: Judge Yvonne Murphy (chairperson), Dr William Duncan and Professor Mary E. Daly. The Commission sat in private. Survivors of Mother and Baby Homes provided testimony of their experiences to a confidential committee to which the Commission members were to have regard. In January 2021, the Commission of Investigation published its final report. The findings of the Commission included the following:[272]

- Over 56,000 women and 57,000 children spent time in Mother and Baby Homes. While similar institutions existed in other countries, the numbers of those confined to these institutions in Ireland were some of the highest in the world.
- There were very high infant mortality rates in Mother and Baby Homes.
- Women in these institutions suffered from emotional abuse by the religious congregations running these institutions.
- There was an acknowledgement that many women in these institutions did not have a real choice other than to give their children up for adoption. However, the Commission refused to recognise this as forced adoption.

The narrative adopted by the Commission of Investigation attracted widespread criticism.[273] Condon states that the Commission, while

[270] P.M. Garrett, "'Unmarried Mothers' in the Republic of Ireland" (2016) 16(6) *Journal of Social Work* 708.

[271] Commission of Investigation (Mother and Baby Homes and certain related Matters) Order 2015 (S.I. No. 57 of 2015).

[272] Commission of Investigation into Mother and Baby Homes and Related Matters, Executive Summary, available at: *https://www.gov.ie/en/publication/316d8-commission-of-investigation/*.

[273] M. Enright and A. O'Donoghue (eds), *Mother and Baby Homes Commission of Investigation Report: Draft Alternative Executive Summary* (July 2021); J. Gallan, "Institutions and Ireland: Mother and Baby Homes and Transitional Justice" (2022) 52(1) *Irish University Review* 103; K. O'Donnell, "Commission to Inquire into Ireland's Mother and Baby Homes: An Epistemology of Ignorance" in P. Giladi and N. McMillan

acknowledging the wrong (to an extent) done to women and children in these institutions, utilised language to try to limit this reality. The Commission spoke of how all women in Irish society were treated harshly.[274] The Commission placed the blame for the existence of Mother and Baby Homes on the fathers of the children and on the families of the women.[275] In essence, the Commission report, at least to a degree, seemed to paint religious orders and the State as almost the saviours of "rejected women". In responding to testimony of survivors speaking about the work they had to conduct in these institutions, the Commission stated that this was "generally doing the sort of work that they would have done at home."[276] The confidential committee report on the work that women warehoused in Mother and Baby Homes had to do, based on several similar descriptions from survivors, would suggest otherwise:

> "Some referenced scrubbing as an inescapable part of their lives in the homes - saying that, while working, they were frequently and very closely supervised by a nun, some of whom would slap or punch them if they were judged not to be working hard or fast enough."[277]

On de facto forced adoptions, one witness to the confidential committee described how she came to be adopted in the late 1940s:

> "A witness born in 1949 who had been adopted to the USA from the mother and baby home successfully traced her birthmother in later life ... Her birthmother said that her adoption had been organised entirely by correspondence, through 'Catholic Charities' – and that the adopters had never been to Ireland. Her parents, she said, had paid $1500 to adopt her ... It was 'by accident' she discovered she was adopted. She said she had 'grave concerns'

(eds), *Epistemic Injustice and the Philosophy of Recognition* (London: Routledge, 2022); Clann Project, "Irish High Court Declares that Mother and Baby Home Commission of Investigation Treated Survivors Unlawfully", 17 December 2021, available at: *https://kodlyons.ie/wp-content/uploads/2021/12/Clann-Press-Release_17-12-21.pdf*; R. Condon, "Narrativized Discursive Legitimation: Comment on the Mother and Baby Homes Report" (2022) 30(2) *Irish Journal of Sociology* 196.

274 R. Condon, "Narrativized Discursive Legitimation: Comment on the Mother and Baby Homes Report" (2022) 30(2) *Irish Journal of Sociology* 196 at 198.

275 R. Condon, "Narrativized Discursive Legitimation: Comment on the Mother and Baby Homes Report" (2022) 30(2) *Irish Journal of Sociology* 196 at 199.

276 Commission of Investigation into Mother and Baby Homes and Related Matters, Executive Summary, para.15.

277 *Report of the Confidential Committee to the Commission of Investigation into Mother and Baby Homes* (June 2020), p.41.

that her birthmother was not aware [of] what she was signing when completing the paperwork as she was illiterate at the time."[278]

The Commission found limited value in the testimony provided by survivors of these institutions. As Enright and others expertly outline, the Commission failed in any manner to highlight the legal obligations of the Irish State as existed while Mother and Baby Homes operated, including constitutional rights or other legislative rights. This failure is deeply concerning.[279] The Commission members declined to appear before an Oireachtas Committee to discuss their findings. Judge Murphy on behalf of the Commission responded: "[t]he independence of the commission cannot simply be abandoned because its findings are not acceptable to some at a political level."[280]

F. Conclusion

10–45 One cannot understand administrative law as a legal concept without appreciating the political choices that have created the Irish administrative state.[281] Political choices are inherent in creating welfare rights for people, providing protections for tenants, enabling persons to seek and enjoy protection, setting down obligations of taxation, and entitlement to a third-level grant.[282] While courts have no role in determining the level of taxation, the amount of a welfare payment, or the exercise of powers of housing authorities, courts do supervise the exercise of powers of these bodies through their judicial review function.[283] Within these multiple legal fields, political choices were made to provide a level of entitlement/obligation. We may agree or disagree with the existence of a right or obligation, but it is the democratically-made decision of the Oireachtas.

10–46 We contend that administrative law is ultimately about people. In a modern liberal democratic state like Ireland, legislation is a reflection

[278] *Report of the Confidential Committee to the Commission of Investigation into Mother and Baby Homes* (June 2020), pp.90–91.

[279] M. Enright and A. O'Donoghue (eds), *Mother and Baby Homes Commission of Investigation Report: Draft Alternative Executive Summary* (July 2021), pp.83–85.

[280] J. Bray, "Murphy hits back hard at critics over mother and baby home report", *Irish Times*, 11 June 2021.

[281] See paras 10–02 to 10–07.

[282] See paras 10–08 to 10–16.

[283] See Box 10.1 and Box 10.2, along with paras 10–17 to 10–18.

of political decisions; legislation may create a state architecture to deliver upon political policy objectives, and may enable decision-making bodies to consider rights and obligations of people. All these bodies are supervised via the High Court's judicial review function. In the field of housing law, for example, we highlighted what the role of judicial review is. It is not to supplant the superior court's decision for that of the original decision maker. Judicial review is a means and method of determining whether a decision or action of a body was legally proper. For decision-making bodies, the overwhelming majority of these decisions are well made, apply the particular law and/or policy, and deliver a reasoned outcome. This is not to say there are no structural issues with some decision-making bodies, as we have highlighted in the field of social welfare law.

10–47 Ombudsman offices provide a forum to interrogate the State's legal and policy preferences, and how these are implemented. This allows relevant public bodies to reflect on the quality, or otherwise, of their interpretation and implementation of law and policy in a variety of fields.[284] We considered in some detail the functions of the Public Service Ombudsman, who is responsible for ensuring quality administration of most public bodies.[285] So while the Ombudsman cannot order a public body to comply with its recommendations, most public bodies do so.

10–48 Administrative law offers a potential conduit for reflection on failures of the State, politics, law, policy, administration and indeed wider society.[286] Tribunals of inquiry and commissions of investigation are a product of political, or more precisely, governmental choice. These bodies seek to establish truth and where necessary may make recommendations for reform, if that of course is required. The aim of such reflection is ultimately to ensure that the State or institutions of the State function better, learn from past mistakes and prevent something similar happening again. For example, and not without some reservation, we noted how tribunals have positively led to structural and legal reforms to the Gardaí. We have been quite critical of the Kerry Babies and Stardust Tribunals of Inquiry. We have documented the significant concerns expressed about the final report of the Mother and

[284] See para.10–26.
[285] See paras 10–20 to 10–27.
[286] See Section E of this chapter.

Baby Homes Commission of Investigation. We focused on these to give you a sense of how law can create an official narrative that may be some distance from what actually occurred. At least with the Kerry Babies and Stardust Tribunals, there has been, very belatedly and with Stardust after much family campaigning, an acknowledgment of how the findings of these tribunals were wrong.

10–49 The field of administrative law, as we now know it, is based on how Irish society has developed since the early twentieth century. Administrative law is a reflection, at least to a degree, of political choice. Ultimately, we contend that without a sense of how the Irish State operates, the role of politics, policy and law, one cannot fully appreciate the field of administrative law.

Chapter 11

The Judiciary

"Being a judge is undoubtedly a responsible job, and it is a privilege to be given the job, but ultimately it is just a job. The idea that it is a 'sacred office', i.e. connected with some god or dedicated to a religious purpose, and so deserving of veneration, is ... fanciful."

White v Bar Council of Ireland [2016] IEHC 406 at para.7 per Barrett J.

"A person appointed as a judge under the Constitution is appointed as the holder of judicial office. He or she is an office holder in the judicial arm of Government ... Article 35.2 of the Constitution stipulates 'All judges shall be independent in the exercise of their judicial functions and subject only to this Constitution and the law'. It is a fundamental misconception to consider being a judge to be 'just a job'."[1]

White v Bar Council of Ireland [2016] IECA 363 at para.54 per Finlay Geoghegan J.

In this chapter we:

- explore the role of judges in Ireland and consider the function of judges;
- assess the importance of judicial independence in the Irish legal system, and consider select aspects of the tensions between judicial independence, judicial criticism and judicial pay;
- outline the constitutional requirements and legislative rules and mechanisms for appointing judges in Ireland. This will include a reflection on the ,role of politics, the concept of merit in judicial appointment, and the issue of judicial diversity;
- examine judicial (mis)conduct and the legislative framework for reprimanding judges under the Judicial Council Act 2019;
- discuss the constitutional requirements and political realities of the removal of judges from office.

---

[1] For a discussion of this decision, see J. O'Dowd, "'Sacred Office' or 'Just a Job'? The Status of Irish Judges under Scrutiny" in E. Carolan (ed.), *Judicial Power in Ireland* (Dublin: Institute of Public Administration, 2018).

A. Introduction

11–01 As noted in Ch.2, one of the essential principles for the rule of law to operate is protection of and respect for an independent judiciary.[2] As Llewellyn notes, "[f]or some (perhaps most for judges) membership in The Legal System lends per se a tremendous power".[3] The judicial interpretive role is particularly significant in difficult policy issues because the legislature is often reluctant to do anything for fear of electoral reprisal—hence the superior courts having to hear cases about abortion, or assisted suicide, or frozen embryos—which is where the political values of judges may be determinative.[4] Judges are one of the most central actors in the Irish legal system. Ensuring impartial and independent determination of legal disputes is central to the role of a judge. The Irish public have high levels of confidence in the independence of the courts and the judiciary. The EU Barometer Survey on public perception of judicial independence in 2024 ranked Ireland as seventh in the EU for faith in the independence and impartiality of judges.[5] Judicial independence is protected by Article 35.2 of the Constitution: "[a]ll judges shall be independent in the exercise of their judicial functions and subject only to this Constitution and the law." It is also a key feature of a society governed by the rule of law, with judges being independent and "free from political influence in the performance of their judicial function".[6] When discussing the judiciary, we need to engage with a complex web of law, both constitutional and legislative, as well as judicial and political practice or convention, and tease out tensions surrounding the interrelationships between judges, the executive, the legislature and wider society. It is these issues that are core to this chapter.

[2] See Ch.2, paras 2–41 to 2–43. See also *Curtin v Dáil Éireann* [2006] 2 I.R. 556 at 617.

[3] K.N. Llewellyn, "The Normative, the Legal and the Law-Jobs": The Problem of Juristic Method" (1939–40) 49(8) *Yale Law Journal* 1355 at 1381.

[4] D. Feenan, "Judicial Appointments in Ireland in Comparative Perspective" (2008) 8(1) *Judicial Studies Institute Journal* 37 at 55.

[5] Eurobarometer Report, *Perceived independence of the national justice systems in the EU among the general public*, February 2024.

[6] *Re Article 26 and the Judicial Appointments Commission Bill 2022* [2023] IESC 34 at para.69.

B. Judges and the Judicial Function

1. Judges in Ireland

11–02 Ireland has one of the lowest number of judges per capita when contrasted with member states of the Council of Europe.[7] In 2022, the European Judicial Systems Report noted that Ireland has 3.3 judges per 100,000 people.[8] This contrasts with 25 judges per 100,000 in Germany, 38.1 judges per 100,000 in Serbia, and 5.2 per 100,000 in Azerbaijan. The amount of money invested in the Irish judicial system was not calculated for this 2022 report, but the European average was 0.35 per cent of Gross Domestic Product (GDP).[9] There are 196 judges[10] in Ireland's courts system at the time of writing.[11] The Supreme Court consists of nine ordinary judges and the Chief Justice (10).[12] The Court of Appeal comprises 18 ordinary judges and the President of the Court of Appeal (19).[13] There are 48 ordinary High Court judges and the President of the High Court (49).[14] There are 45 ordinary Circuit Court judges and the President of the Circuit Court (46).[15] In the lowest court, the District

7 The Council of Europe is not the European Union but has 47 member states. This includes all member states of the European Union plus 20 other countries, including the United Kingdom; Department of Justice, *Report of the Judicial Planning Working Group* (2022), p.55. For a full breakdown of judicial numbers in Ireland from 2000–2022, see p.56. The Working Group obtained their statistics from the Council of Europe, *European Judicial Systems CEPJR Evaluation Report, Part 1 2022 Cycle* (CEPJR).

8 CEPJR, p.48.

9 CEPJR, p.20.

10 This chapter is only concerned with civilian courts; for military courts, see the Defence Act 1954 and the Defence (Amendment) Act 2007.

11 For a discussion on the jurisdiction of the various courts in Ireland, see Ch.9, Sections C–D.

12 Courts (Establishment and Constitution) Act 1961 s.1(2)(b), as substituted by s.22 of the Courts and Civil Law (Miscellaneous Provisions) Act 2013.

13 Court of Appeal Act 2014 s.6, inserting s.1A into the Courts (Establishment and Constitution) Act 1961, as amended by Courts Act 2023 s.2 and as further amended by Courts, Civil Law, Criminal Law and Superannuation (Miscellaneous Provisions) Act 2024 s.2.

14 Courts Act 2015 s.1, substituting s.9 of the Courts and Court Officers Act 1995, as amended by Civil Law (Miscellaneous Provisions) Act 2021 s.8, as substituted by Courts Act 2023 s.4. It is possible for one additional judge to be appointed to the High Court by virtue of s.8 of the Civil Law (Miscellaneous Provisions) Act 2021, which amends s.9 of the Courts and Court Officers Act 1995.

15 Courts and Court Officers (Amendment) Act 2007 s.3, amending s.10 of the Courts and Court Officers Act 1995, as amended by Assisted Decision-Making (Capacity) (Amendment) Act 2022 s.98 and Courts Act 2023 s.5. For specialist Circuit Court judges in the personal insolvency field, see s.191 of the Personal Insolvency Act 2012, which inserts s.10A into the Courts and Court Officers Act 1995.

Court, there are 71 ordinary District Court judges and the President of the District Court (72).[16] The Special Criminal Court[17] is composed of judges already appointed. The Special Criminal Court is constituted by one member each of the High Court, Circuit Court and District Court. The Presidents of the Court of Appeal and of the High Court sit ex officio on the Supreme Court.[18] The Chief Justice and the President of the Circuit Court both sit ex officio in the High Court.[19] The President of the District Court sits ex officio in the Circuit Court.[20] The Chief Justice and Presidents of the other courts highlighted the significant problems with Ireland's low number of judges in 2022: significant delays in progressing court business, increase in legislation that requires judicial resolution of disputes in criminal and civil fields, and the complexity of legal issues, in particular but not exclusively, heard by the superior courts.[21] The Judicial Planning Working Group recommended that, by 2024, the following should be the number of judges at each court level:[22]

Court	Current Judges (Nov. 2024)	Recommended Level
Supreme Court	10	10 (achieved)
Court of Appeal	19	20 (almost achieved)
High Court	49	56 (not yet achieved)
Circuit Court	46	52 (not yet achieved)
District Court	72	78 (not yet achieved)

11–03 Legislative amendments throughout 2023 and 2024 have come exceptionally close to implementing the recommendations of the Judicial

[16] Civil Law (Miscellaneous Provisions) Act 2008 s.32, amending s.11 of the Courts and Court Officers Act 1995, as substituted by Courts Act 2023 s.6.

[17] See further, Ch.9, Section C.5. For a fascinating exploration of the history of this court, see F. Davis, *The History and Development of the Special Criminal Court, 1922–2005* (Dublin: Four Courts Press, 2007). A majority expert report recommended the retention of the Special Criminal Court in 2023; see Independent Review Group, *Offences against the State Acts* (2023). A minority report recommended the abolition of the Special Criminal Court.

[18] Court of Appeal Act 2014 s.6, inserting s.1A into the Courts (Establishment and Constitution) Act 1961.

[19] Courts (Establishment and Constitution) Act 1961 s.2(3) (Chief Justice) and s.2(4) of the same Act (President of the Circuit Court).

[20] Courts and Court Officers Act 1995 s.33.

[21] For a much more detailed outline of the challenges faced by courts, see Department of Justice, *Report of the Judicial Planning Working Group* (2022), pp.57–62.

[22] Department of Justice, *Report of the Judicial Planning Working Group* (2022), p.81.

Planning Working Group. Of note has been the recommendation by the Working Group for further reviews of judicial numbers in 2025 and 2028.[23] The aim is to ensure that judicial resources are available to deal with court business in a timely and efficient manner. It is also worth pointing out that the Working Group recommended that the Department of Justice "critically analyse existing legislation which involves enforcement by Courts to establish if other administrative means could be employed".[24]

2. The Judicial Function

11–04 The Irish judiciary in 2014 noted:

> "Single judges make judgments on married people, young judges make decisions about older people, gay judges make decisions about heterosexuals, female judges make judgments about men, atheists and agnostics make decisions about believers and in each case, and obviously, vice versa. This is how it should be."[25]

Judges make decisions in all manner of criminal and civil cases. The decision that a judge may make can have a profound impact on an individual, family, business, and on the administration of the State. The type of decision made by a judge will depend on the court to which they are appointed. Here are some common areas in which a judge in Ireland will have to decide:

- whether an individual is guilty of a criminal offence;[26]
- which party (if any) is liable for the commission of a tort;[27]
- whether the State has vindicated the constitutional rights of an individual;[28]

---

23 Department of Justice, *Report of the Judicial Planning Working Group* (2022), pp.81–82.

24 Department of Justice, *Report of the Judicial Planning Working Group* (2022), p.82. On administrative justice mechanisms, see Ch.10.

25 Submission by Irish judges, *Preliminary Submission to the Department of Justice and Equality's Public Consultation on the Judicial Appointments Process* (2014), para.50.

26 In the District Court, judges will often decide such issues themselves. For more on the role of the judge in criminal cases, see T.J. McIntyre, S. McMullan and S. Ó Toghda, *Criminal Law* (Dublin: Round Hall, 2012).

27 B. McMahon and W. Binchy, *Law of Torts*, 4th edn (Dublin: Bloomsbury Professional, 2013).

28 Consider the case of *Re a Ward of Court (Withholding Medical Treatment) (No. 2)* [1996] 2 I.R. 79.

- who should have sole or part custody of a child;[29]
- whether a violent partner should be barred from the family or shared home;[30]
- whether decisions of administrative (and other) tribunals have been made in accordance with law and within their competence;[31]
- whether a company should be protected for a period from its creditors and be permitted to enter the examinership process;[32]
- whether laws passed by the Oireachtas are constitutional;[33]
- whether an individual is lawfully detained.[34]

11–05 In addition to these "traditional" judicial roles, the abilities of judges are also used in other areas of State adjudication and administration. Judges have other significant roles within the legal and political system. A five-judge Supreme Court can decide whether the President is incapacitated.[35] A judge can chair a Committee of Privileges to resolve disputes as to whether a Bill before the Oireachtas is a Money Bill.[36] High Court, Court of Appeal and Supreme Court judges also have ceremonial roles, witnessing the President making the constitutional declaration to "maintain the Constitution of Ireland and uphold its laws".[37] The Electoral Commission is responsible for, inter alia, explaining to the public the subject matter of a referendum, Dáil and local authority constituency reviews, awareness-raising on the electoral process and

---

[29] A judge will be responsible for considering this issue and the legal principles set down in legislation; see the Guardianship of Infants Act 1964 (as amended).

[30] A District Court judge will have to decide whether such an order is made for married couples or civil partners, as well as for cohabiting couples; see, generally, the Domestic Violence Act 2018 and the Civil Partnership and Certain Rights and Obligations of Cohabitants Act 2010.

[31] For an example of this in the immigration sphere, where a judge struck down the decision of the Refugee Appeals Tribunal due to factual inconsistencies in how the decision-maker came to his decision, see *P v Refugee Appeals Tribunal* [2013] IEHC 448. For further discussion on administrative justice and judicial review, see Ch.10, paras 10–17 to 10–19 and Box 10.2.

[32] See Pt 10 of the Companies Act 2014 and T.B. Courtney et al., *Bloomsbury Professional's Guide to the Companies Act 2014* (Dublin: Bloomsbury Professional, 2015).

[33] Such a case may come before judges as an Article 26 reference or where the constitutionality of certain legislative provisions is called into question during litigation. For a discussion on the Article 26 procedure, see Ch.3, paras 3–22 and 3–52 and Ch.9, para.9–32.

[34] Article 40.4.2° of the Constitution.

[35] Article 12.3.1° of the Constitution.

[36] Article 22.3 of the Constitution.

[37] Article 12.8 of the Constitution.

how persons can get involved in political life, as well as protecting the integrity of the electoral process in Ireland.[38] The Chief Justice appoints a judge to chair the Electoral Commission.[39] To date, the President of the Law Reform Commission[40] has, as a matter of convention, always been either a serving or retired superior court judge. Judges, or retired judges, have always been appointed as chairs of tribunals of inquiry[41] and, in some cases, of non-statutory inquiries.[42] All these issues can potentially involve questions of political controversy and can involve judges in the rough and tumble of politics.

3. Delivering Justice though the "Heavens Fall"[43]

11–06 The precise function of a judge has been debated for millennia. Aristotle, the Greek philosopher, stated in his work on *Ethics* that the "nature of the judge is some sort of living justice".[44] A former Chief Justice of the Supreme Court, Thomas Finlay, observed that there are three fundamental roles or functions of a judge:[45] first, ensuring justice in a dispute; second, deciding issues fairly, and for these issues to be seen by others as having been decided fairly; and finally, ensuring justice be done, regardless of the consequences, in particular in political, social or religious fields. The decisions taken may impact significantly on the lives of those before the court, be it in a civil or criminal matter.

11–07 The issue of the independence and impartiality of judges is significant, in that a judge is supposed to disregard the social and/or

---

38 Electoral Reform Act 2022 s.30.

39 Electoral Reform Act 2022 s.9(2)(b). The current chair of the Electoral Commission is Baker J. of the Supreme Court.

40 For more on the function and composition of the Law Reform Commission, see Ch.8, Section B.3. See s.3 of the Law Reform Commission Act 1975. The current chairperson is the former judge of the Supreme Court and Chief Justice, Mr Justice Frank Clarke.

41 See the Tribunals of Inquiry (Evidence) Acts 1921–2011. For more on tribunals of inquiry, see Ch.10, paras 10–33 to 10–39 and Box 10.3.

42 G. Hogan, D.G. Morgan and P. Daly, *Administrative Law in Ireland*, 5th edn (Dublin: Round Hall, 2019), para.8–06. For example, the appointment of the retired Supreme Court judge and former Chief Justice, Ms Justice Susan Denham, to conduct a non-statutory review of the actions of Woulfe J., discussed at paras 11–76 to 11–79.

43 This comes from the maxim *fiat justitia ruat caelum* (let justice be done though the heavens fall).

44 Aristotle, *Nicomachean Ethics* (Book V), B, p.4, translated by W.D. Ross, available at: *http://classics.mit.edu//Aristotle/nicomachaen.html*.

45 T. Finlay, "The Role of the Judge" (2005) 5(1) *Judicial Studies Institute Journal* 1 at 1–2.

political power or influence of those before them.[46] This is acknowledged in the judicial oath, set out in Article 34.5.1° of the Constitution, which every person appointed judge must make:

> "In the presence of Almighty God, I do solemnly and sincerely promise and declare that I will duly and faithfully and to the best of my knowledge and power execute the office of Chief Justice (or as the case may be) without fear or favour, affection or ill-will towards any man, and that I will uphold the Constitution and the laws, May God direct and sustain me."

Yet, Parliament, when passing legislation, can engage with many representative and civil society bodies, such as business representative organisations, trade unions, trade associations, companies, agricultural representative bodies and human rights organisations. Posner, a legal theorist and a retired US judge, argues that judges are insulated (to a degree) from political pressure from such interest groups.[47] However, he does criticise those judges who he sees as overstepping their judicial role, who go beyond their role as "agents in application" of law.[48] A major task for judges is in interpreting legislation.[49] According to Posner:

> "If judges would only read legislation carefully, sensitively, with a disposition to help rather than hinder the legislative thrust—to complete rather than thwart the enterprise set on foot by the legislation—they would be able to bring about a result both 'intended' by the legislature in a meaningful but not confining sense and good in its own right as expressing and fostering the social optimum to which legislation in a democratic society could be expected to conduce."[50]

---

46 For discussion of the concept of impartiality and the Judicial Council Act 2019, see B. Barry, "Judicial Impartiality in the Judicial Council Act 2019: Challenges and Opportunities" (2022) 6(1) *Irish Judicial Studies Journal* 38.

47 Posner fully outlines his arguments on the role of pragmatism in judicial and legislative actions in R. Posner, "What Has Pragmatism to Offer Law?" (1990) 63 *Southern California Law Review* 1653, in particular at 1656–1659. On this aspect, Ronald Dworkin also agrees with Posner; see R. Dworkin, *A Matter of Principle* (Harvard: Harvard University Press, 1986), p.28.

48 R. Posner, "Legislation and Its Interpretation: A Primer" (1989) 68 *Nebraska Law Review* 431 at 439.

49 See Ch.4, Sections C–G for a full discussion on this issue.

50 R. Posner, "Legislation and Its Interpretation: A Primer" (1989) 68 *Nebraska Law Review* 431 at 434.

11–08 Rules of statutory interpretation, precedent, distinguishing cases on the facts, legal reasoning, analogy, and having regard to how judges in other jurisdictions have dealt with a similar case or interpreted similar legislative measures, are all core parts of the judicial function. However, an understanding of the role of judges has to go beyond merely some computational, formalistic understanding of legal interpretation. All individuals have sympathies, prejudices and preferences for certain codes of conduct or certain behaviours. Legal realists reject legal formalism, i.e. judges being impartial umpires, instead embracing the "indeterminate"[51] nature of law and legal reasoning of rules. For former US Supreme Court judge, Oliver Wendell Holmes, "[t]he life of the law has not been logic, it has been experience".[52] So we acknowledge that judges should be fair in their determination of disputes before them. Indeed, Posner suggests that the role of judges goes beyond mere formalism in resolving a dispute; their decision may be influenced by their politics, their views on life, or simple pragmatism.[53]

11–09 Hogan J., writing prior to his appointment to the Supreme Court, highlights the dilemma that can be caused due to following the "scientific" method of judging, deciding without fear or favour regardless of the impact their decision may have, or any consequences spurring from the decision.[54] Hogan J. explores examples where, in spite of very significant pressure from others, judges have refused to do what might be perceived as "popular".[55] Judges, he argues, "are better guided by the application of principle rather than any endeavour to peek behind the blinds of justice and to seek to anticipate the consequences of their decisions and to work backwards in their reasoning."[56] Hogan J. contrasts his thinking with that of Humphreys J., an Irish High Court judge. Humphreys J., writing extrajudicially, argued that in interpreting law, in

[51] For a more in-depth examination of the ideas surrounding legal realism (in particular, American legal realism), see J.P. McCutcheon, "American Legal Realism" in T. Murphy (ed.), *Western Jurisprudence* (Dublin: Round Hall, 2004), p.214.

[52] O.W. Holmes, *The Common Law*, edited by P. Pereira and D. Beltran (Toronto: University of Toronto Law School Typographical Society, 2011), p.5.

[53] See further, R. Posner, "The Role of the Judge in the 21st Century" (2006) 86 *Boston University Law Review* 1049.

[54] G. Hogan, "Should Judges Be Neutral?" (2021) 74(1) *Northern Ireland Legal Quarterly* 63 at 69.

[55] G. Hogan, "Should Judges Be Neutral?" (2021) 74(1) *Northern Ireland Legal Quarterly* 63 at 69–75.

[56] G. Hogan, "Should Judges Be Neutral?" (2021) 74(1) *Northern Ireland Legal Quarterly* 63 at 88.

particular constitutional law, it is essential for judges to acknowledge the social consequences of their decisions.[57] In making this argument, Humphreys J. notes the often slow response of the government and Oireachtas in reacting to a decision of a court that highlights antiquated legislation, or interpretation of legislation that may have unintended consequences.[58] Humphreys J. contends that judges should reject the "dangerous nonsense" of the maxim *fiat justitia ruat caelum* (let justice be done though the heavens fall). For him, cold and rational assessment should be taken of potential consequences of decisions in judging.[59] In order to do this, judges should engage with the text of the legal instrument, and the surrounding circumstances of its passage, to ensure a democratically legitimate means of legal interpretation.[60]

C. Judicial Independence in Ireland

1. Understanding Judicial Independence

11–10 Judicial independence in Ireland has been described by the Supreme Court as a "fundamental constitutional requirement"[61] that protects adherence to the rule of law.[62] Judicial independence is constitutionally protected, embraces institutional independence, and incidentally protects individual judges.[63] Gallagher succinctly identifies the core aspects of judicial independence.[64] First, a judge must be able to reach a decision in a case before them without any external

57 R. Humphreys, "The Constitution and Law as Living Instruments for a Living Society" (2017) 40(2) *Dublin University Law Journal* 45.

58 R. Humphreys, "The Constitution and Law as Living Instruments for a Living Society" (2017) 40(2) *Dublin University Law Journal* 45 at 53.

59 R. Humphreys, "The Constitution and Law as Living Instruments for a Living Society" (2017) 40(2) *Dublin University Law Journal* 45 at 69.

60 R. Humphreys, "The Constitution and Law as Living Instruments for a Living Society" (2017) 40(2) *Dublin University Law Journal* 45 at 70.

61 *Re Article 26 and the Judicial Appointments Commission Bill 2022* [2023] IESC 34 at para.163. For broader exploration of the Irish judiciary and the Constitution, see G. Hogan, G. Whyte, D. Kenny and R. Walsh, *Kelly: The Irish Constitution*, 5th edn (Dublin: Bloomsbury Professional, 2018), Part 6. For a discussion of judicial independence, see J. O'Dowd, "'Sacred Office' or 'Just a Job'? The Status of Irish Judges under Scrutiny" in E. O'Carolan (ed.) *Judicial Power in Ireland* (Dublin: Institute of Public Administration, 2018), in particular pp.309–312.

62 *Curtin v Dáil Éireann* [2006] 2 I.R. 556 at 617.

63 *Curtin v Dáil Éireann* [2006] 2 I.R. 556 at 617.

64 P. Gallagher, "Challenges to the Rule of Law in 21st Century Ireland" in E. Carolan (ed.), *Judicial Power in Ireland* (Dublin: Institute of Public Administration, 2018), p.274.

interference or influence from outside parties. Second, the independence of the judiciary must be specially protected to ensure no influence by government or the Houses of the Oireachtas.[65] Huchhanavar neatly categorises three aspects of judicial independence:[66]

- Institutional judicial independence: Judges being able to reach a lawful decision without external influence from government, parliament or any other external public or private body. We will consider aspects of institutional judicial independence below, in particular when we discuss judicial appointments, judicial removal and judicial salary.
- Internal judicial independence: Judges act independently and impartially, have the competence to perform their duties, and make decisions without fear or favour. This includes judges reaching a decision without bias, which we will discuss shortly. It can also include areas pertaining to sanctions for judicial misconduct, examined below.
- Individual judicial independence: The European Court of Human Rights decision in *Tadić v Croatia* summarises this as meaning that judges are free from pressure exerted by other judges, and by court administrators, including presidents of the courts.[67] We explore this below when discussing the Sheedy affair.

The Council of Europe in its recommendations on judicial independence, efficiency and responsibilities highlights the importance of these forms of judicial independence.[68]

11–11 The importance of judicial independence for a society governed by the rule of law has come to the fore within certain member states of the European Union, namely Hungary and Poland, in the last decade. Judgments of the Court of Justice of the European Union have

[65] Restated most recently in *Re Article 26 and the Judicial Appointments Commission Bill 2022* [2023] IESC 34 at para.163. This was established decades previously in *Buckley v Attorney General* [1950] I.R. 67.

[66] S.S. Huchhanavar, "Conceptualising Judicial Independence and Accountability from a Regulatory Perspective" (2022) 9(2) *Oslo Law Review* 110, in particular 110–120.

[67] *Tadić v Croatia* (App. No. 25551/18), judgment of the European Court of Human Rights (Second Section), 28 November 2023, para.71.

[68] Recommendation CM/Rec (2010)12 of the Committee of Ministers to Member States on judges: independence, efficiency and responsibilities adopted by the Committee of Ministers on 17 November 2010, in particular Chs I–V. This Recommendation is explicitly identified in the long title to the Judicial Appointments Commission Act 2023.

emphasised the centrality of the rule of law and judicial independence in the resolution of legal disputes. As Pech and Jaraczewski convincingly argue, the European Commission has been found wanting for not challenging the lack of judicial independence more forcefully.[69] The "rule of law breakdown" and attacks on judicial independence in Poland were so serious that MacMenamin J. of the Irish Supreme Court took part in a silent march in Poland, along with other judges from several EU member states, in 2020.[70]

11–12 O'Donnell C.J., writing extrajudicially,[71] discusses further aspects of judicial independence. The government is responsible for judicial appointment and setting the remuneration of judges, which ordinarily cannot be reduced during their term of office. The constitutionally-ascribed role of the Oireachtas in judicial removal has the potential, and only the potential, to impact on judicial independence. Accordingly, judges may not be members of the Oireachtas or hold any other paid position.[72] Judicial independence is a key factor in ensuring the protection of citizens from arbitrary use of government power and in having a system for the impartial resolution of disputes between individuals, or between individuals and the State. Therefore, judges occupy a central role in the Irish legal and constitutional systems. Given the extent of this power and its ramifications for society, this means judges fulfil an important law-making function.[73] Gallagher notes that in common law liberal democracies such as Ireland, judges have significant power to

---

[69] L. Pech and J. Jaraczewski, "Systematic Threat to the Rule of Law in Poland: Updated and New Article 7(1) TEU Recommendations", UCD Sutherland School of Law, Working Paper No. 13/2023, available at: *https://papers.ssrn.com/sol3/papers.cfm?abstract_id=4326932*. For a broader EU discussion on systematic judicial independence concerns, see U.A. Kos, "Signalling in European Rule of Law Cases: Hungary and Poland as Case Studies" (2023) 23(4) *Human Rights Law Review* 1, available at: *https://doi.org/10.1093/hrlr/ngad035.* For a review of the Court of Justice of the European Union's jurisprudence on judicial independence, see *Re Article 26 and the Judicial Appointments Commission Bill 2022* [2023] IESC 34 at paras 94–97 and 104–110. The European Court of Human Rights (ECtHR) has also identified the obligations on states under the European Convention on Human Rights to have an independent judiciary; see, e.g. *Żurek v Poland* (App. No. 39650/18), judgment of the ECtHR (First Section), 16 June 2022, and case law cited therein.

[70] Law Society of Ireland, "Judges march in solidarity with Polish judiciary", 8 January 2020.

[71] D. O'Donnell, "Some Reflections on the Independence of the Judiciary" in E. Carolan (ed.), *Judicial Power in Ireland* (Dublin: Institute of Public Administration, 2018), Ch.13.

[72] Article 35.3 of the Constitution.

[73] For a discussion on common law, see Ch.5, paras 5–02 to 5–05.

ensure accountability of government.[74] Constitutional interpretation, for example, can result in significant changes to social objectives that in theory should be left for the Oireachtas to determine and for the Government to implement.[75]

11–13 The Judicial Council has published Guidelines on Conduct and Ethics[76] for judges that further identify the substance of judicial independence: impartiality, integrity, equality, propriety, competence and diligence.[77] Focusing on the principle of impartiality, or objectivity, the Guidelines restate long-established jurisprudence that a judge should recuse themselves if a reasonably informed and independent bystander would apprehend a lack of objectivity.[78] To sustain a claim of subjective bias, a litigant would have to prove "that the judge had deliberately set out to hold against [them]".[79] There have been a number of instances where decisions of a judge had to be set aside due to objective bias. This has included previous non-judicial involvement with a particular cause or issue, or for the potential for financial conflicts of interest.[80] It

[74] M. Gallagher, "Politics, the Constitution and the Judiciary" in J. Coakley, M. Gallagher, E. O'Malley and T. Reidy (eds), *Politics in the Republic of Ireland*, 7th edn (Abingdon: Routledge, 2024), Ch.3. See also, Ch.3, Section D for an analysis of constitutional interpretation.

[75] M. Gallagher, "Politics, the Constitution and the Judiciary" in J. Coakley, M. Gallagher, E. O'Malley and T. Reidy (eds), *Politics in the Republic of Ireland*, 7th edn (Abingdon: Routledge, 2024), pp.74–77 outlines some key constitutional decisions that resulted in significant political change.

[76] The legal basis for the Judicial Council being required to issue guidelines on judicial conduct and ethics is found in Judicial Council Act 2019 s.43(3)(d). The Judicial Council is discussed in detail in Section E of this chapter.

[77] Judicial Council, *Guidelines for the Judiciary on Conduct and Ethics*, 1 June 2022. These draw upon the United Nations Bangalore Principles of Judicial Conduct, UN Doc. ECOSOC 2006/23. The 2022 Guidelines expand on each of these six principles in some detail.

[78] Judicial Council, *Guidelines for the Judiciary on Conduct and Ethics*, 1 June 2022, Principle 2: Impartiality. See *Bula Ltd v Tara Mines (No. 6)* [2000] 4 I.R. 412 at 440–441 per Denham J. See also the decision of McGuinness J., [2000] 4 I.R. 412 at 478–486, which synthesises the key legal principles applicable to determining objective bias.

[79] *Adigun v McEvoy* [2018] IECA 229 at para.91. For an example of the High Court overturning a decision of a member of the then Refugee Appeals Tribunal due (in part) to the court's finding that the Tribunal Member simply did not like the appellant, see *AAMO [Sudan] v Refugee Appeals Tribunal* [2014] IEHC 49 at para.23. This decision is discussed in detail in *Fundamentals of the Irish Legal System*, 1st edn (Dublin: Round Hall, 2016), para.10–16.

[80] In *Dublin Wellwoman Centre Ltd v Ireland* [1995] 1 I.L.R.M. 408, the Supreme Court held that Carroll J. should have recused herself from a hearing on issues relating to abortion, as she had made a submission to the government in her extrajudicial capacity as Chairwoman of the Commission for the Status of Woman. This case is

is for the party to the litigation claiming bias to prove that this exists.[81] In general, a judge's past academic writings, conference contributions or prior representation of a litigant are not in and of themselves a basis for substantiating a claim of bias.[82] There must be "something more".[83] What exactly constitutes "something more" can be difficult to pinpoint. Dignam J. in *Campbell v O'Doherty* stated that this "something more" may be:

> "... a long, recent and varied connection between the judge (former barrister) and the party, or where an issue in the previous proceedings is a live issue in the current proceedings, or where the previous proceedings involved a detailed attack on a party's credibility. This is not intended to be exhaustive."[84]

2. Criticism of Judges

11–14 Judges and judicial decisions should not be immune from criticism. In the Oireachtas, politicians should generally not criticise a judge or their rulings, should not praise a particular judge, lest a different opinion be expressed, nor make "charges relating to the political affiliations of district justices".[85] While judges are often criticised in the popular press for decisions made, open public criticism of judges for their decisions and determinations in the Oireachtas is rare.[86] In 1994, a former Fine Gael TD, Jim Mitchell, attacked the independence of the then President of the High Court, stating:

discussed in F. O'Brien, "*Nemo Iudex in Causa Sua*: Aspects of the No-Bias Rule of Constitutional Justice in Courts and Administrative Bodies" (2011) 2(2) *Irish Journal of Legal Studies* 26 at 43–44. See also *Goode Concrete v CRH plc* [2015] IESC 70, where the Supreme Court set aside a decision of Cooke J., as he had failed to disclose shareholdings in the CRH group, who were defendants in the original trial. See further, F. Donson and D. O'Donovan, *Law and Public Administration in Ireland* (Dublin: Clarus Press, 2015), Ch.11.

81 *Commissioner of An Garda Síochána v Penfield Enterprises Ltd* [2016] IECA 141 at para.37.

82 *Burke v An Adjudication Officer* [2023] IEHC 225, in particular paras 3–8.

83 *Campbell v O'Doherty* [2024] IEHC 320 at paras 26–29.

84 [2024] IEHC 320 at para.27. See also paras 34–43 for further discussion of the test of objective bias.

85 Dáil Éireann, *Salient Rulings of the Chair*, 4th edn (February 2021), Rulings 457–464.

86 For a discussion of public criticism of the judiciary and matters of contempt of court, see M. Kotsonouris, "Criticising Judges in Ireland" (2001) 2(1) *Judicial Studies Institute Journal* 79.

"The President of the High Court is an illustrious judge ... For such promotion [to Chief Justice] he is depending on the nomination of the present Ministers, some of whom have a vested interest in his findings as sole member of the Tribunal of Inquiry into the Beef Industry."[87]

The following day, Mr Mitchell apologised for these remarks, adding:

"[T]he President of the High Court, as I said yesterday, is an illustrious judge. I will go further and say that he is a judge of the highest standing and held in the utmost respect. He matches up to the highest judicial standards internationally."[88]

The leader of the opposition in 2017, Micheál Martin TD, criticised Whelan J. by name as not being as distinguished or competent as other named (only male) judges.[89] This did not result in a press release being issued by the Association of Judges of Ireland (AJI), as was the case in a 2020 judicial criticism incident.

11–15 In 2020, the former TD Bríd Smith stated in response to a decision of Simons J. on aspects of employment law, that the decision was "a war on workers and it is time for workers to fight back".[90] In Facebook and other social media posts, Deputy Smith labelled Simons J. a "right-wing judge" and "upper class". The AJI[91] stated that this attack was "extraordinary", "wholly unjustified", and expressed concern that these comments were made by a member of Dáil Éireann. The AJI continued, stating that "[s]uch rhetoric endangers the rule of law. Fortunately, that has never been a feature of political discourse in this State and it would be very regrettable if it were to be considered acceptable now." Deputy Smith labelled the response of the judges and others as "hysterical",

[87] 440 *Dáil Debates* Cols 1112–1113 (23 March 1994).

[88] 440 *Dáil Debates* Col. 1490 (24 March 1994). See also, *Report of the Committee on Procedure and Privileges on Disorderly Remarks Made by a Member of the Dáil about the President of the High Court, the Attorney General and the Judiciary Generally* (15 April 1994).

[89] See para.11–32.

[90] Deputy Bríd Smyth, Offences against the State (Amendment) Act 1998 and Criminal Justice (Amendment) Act 2009: Motions, *Dáil Debates*, 24 June 2020.

[91] Association of Judges of Ireland, "Statement by the Association of Judges of Ireland in response to recent comments made by Ms Bríd Smyth TD", 25 June 2020. See also, C. Keena, "'Personalised attack' on High Court judge strongly criticised", *Irish Times*, 25 June 2020.

saying that her comments on the judgment and the judge were to highlight the class bias of a judiciary composed of a very small segment of Irish society.[92]

11–16 Internationally, there has been more direct political criticism of judges, sometimes for decisions that are seen as impacting on government policy, othertimes because of an aspect of a judge's identity. An example of the former is an incident in 2003 when Collins J. in the High Court of England and Wales ruled that government policy that enforced destitution on some asylum seekers was inhuman and degrading, in violation of the UK's obligations under the Human Rights Act 1998 and, in particular, Article 3 of the European Convention on Human Rights.[93] In an interview on BBC Radio 4, the then Labour Party Home Secretary, David Blunkett MP, responding to this decision, stated: "[f]rankly, I'm personally fed up with having to deal with a situation where Parliament debates issues and the judges then overturn them."[94] However, the High Court decision was upheld by the Court of Appeal and the House of Lords.[95]

11–17 In Australia, a Liberal Senator, Mr Bill Heffernan, in the Australian Senate, accused a then serving High Court judge, Kirby J., in 2002 of using a state car service to go in search of male sex workers in Sydney.[96] At the end of the speech, Mr Heffernan made it clear that he was referring to Kirby J. The "evidence" that Mr Heffernan had was in fact false. Several days later, Mr Heffernan lost his position as Parliamentary Secretary and was censured by the Senate. Mr Heffernan also apologised to Kirby J. In response, Kirby J. stated: "I accept Senator Heffernan's apology and reach out my hand in a spirit of reconciliation. I hope that my ordeal will show the wrongs that hate of homosexuals can lead to."[97] In November

92 O. O'Donnell, "Smith says reaction to comments on court ruling 'hysterical'", *RTÉ News*, 26 June 2020.

93 *R. (Q) v Secretary of State for the Home Department* [2003] EWHC 195 (Admin).

94 See L. Morris, *Asylum, Welfare and the Cosmopolitan Ideal: A Sociology of Rights* (Abingdon: Routledge, 2010), in particular pp.52–56. See also, BBC News, "Blunkett to fight asylum ruling", 20 February 2003.

95 *R. (Limbuela, Tesema and Adam) v Secretary of State for the Home Department* [2004] Q.B. 1440; *R. v Secretary of State for the Home Department, Ex p. Adam, Limbuela and Tesema* [2006] 1 A.C. 396.

96 Senator Heffernan, Australian Senate, *Hansard*, 12 March 2002, pp.555–557.

97 "Kirby accepts Heffernan's apology", *The Age*, 20 March 2002, available at: *https://www.theage.com.au/*.

2016, the English *Daily Mail* published a headline "Enemies of the People" with pictures of judges who decided that the British Government had to seek the consent of the British Parliament to give notice of its exit from the European Union.[98] The *Daily Mail* initially identified one of the judges as "an openly gay ex-Olympic fencer". This was subsequently removed by the *Daily Mail*, a newspaper that continues to be hostile to the LGBTQI+ community. Finally, in 2018, an Irish judge, Donnelly J., faced a barrage of homophobic attacks against her from government-friendly right-wing media in Poland. This occurred because Donnelly J. referred questions of law to the Court of Justice of the European Union regarding the rule of law in Poland.[99]

3. Judicial Pay

11–18 Non-reduction of judicial salary while in office is an important element of judicial independence, as it may be seen as having an impact on how a judge would decide a case.[100] Prior to 2011, Article 35.5 of the Constitution stated: "[t]he remuneration of a judge shall not be reduced during his continuance in office." In essence, this prevented a government, for whatever reason, from lowering judicial income.[101] The meaning of Article 35.5 was considered in the case of *O'Byrne v Minister for Finance*.[102] Prior to this case, in 1950, a number of judges wrote to the Taoiseach (through the Office of the Chief Justice) stating that their salaries were immune from reduction by way of general taxation.[103] The Supreme Court had to decide whether Article 35.5.1° prohibited the State from imposing income tax on judicial salaries. Mrs O'Byrne was the widow of a former High Court and Supreme Court judge. She was the executrix of Mr Justice O'Byrne's estate after his death. Mrs O'Byrne challenged the reduction of her husband's income. Dixon J. noted that similar protections regarding reduction of income applied to former British colonies (that now had dominion status). This was a core

---

98 *R. (on the application of Miller) v Secretary of State for Exiting the European Union* [2016] EWHC 267 (Admin).

99 Association of Judges of Ireland, Press Release, 15 March 2018.

100 For an historical overview of non-reduction in judicial pay, see *O'Byrne v Minister for Finance* [1959] I.R. 1 at 7.

101 See discussion of this by Lavery J. in the Supreme Court decision in *O'Byrne v Minister for Finance* [1959] I.R. 1 at 39–42 and of Kingsmill Moore J. [1959] I.R. 1 at 63–65.

102 [1959] I.R. 1.

103 See mention of this in the Supreme Court decision of Kingsmill Moore J. in *O'Byrne v Minister for Finance* [1959] I.R. 1 at 59–60.

principle of the US Constitution and had been recognised in the 1922 Constitution of the Irish Free State.[104] The remuneration of judges in the Irish Free State was set down in the Courts of Justice Act 1924 as a fixed sum, but was silent as to whether this sum was liable for income tax that would be applicable to all others on the same income. After considering case law from the United States,[105] South Africa[106] and Australia,[107] Dixon J. found that the constitutional prohibition on reduction of judicial remuneration during time in office did not render judges immune from having to pay income tax:

> "A non-discriminatory tax of general application is a reasonable guarantee of its legitimate purpose: a discriminatory tax of limited application might not be conclusive, but would be some indication, of an improper purpose."[108]

11–19 Mrs O'Byrne then appealed to the Supreme Court. In a 3:2 decision, the Supreme Court dismissed the appeal. The Supreme Court noted that the object of Article 35.2 was "to secure the independence of the judges and the impartial administration of justice".[109] This did not grant some sort of immunity to judges not to pay income tax. Kingsmill Moore J. noted:

> "Any discrimination by tax or otherwise against a judge or judges as a body, having the effect of reducing his or their salary would be equally objectionable. But I fail to see how a tax which is non-discriminatory against judges can assail the judicial independence. It is not and cannot be imposed by way of punishment to the judiciary for an assertion of independence. With certain exceptions, it is common to all. It is an unfortunate vicissitude of life from which the judiciary cannot claim to be immune."[110]

[104] [1959] I.R. 1 at 8.

[105] For discussion by Dixon J. of *Evans v Gore* 253 U.S. 245, *O'Malley v Woodrough*, 307 U.S. 277, and *Baker v Commissioner of Internal Revenue* 4 Tax Cases No. 39, 149 Fed. Rep. (2nd series), see *O'Byrne v Minister for Finance* [1959] I.R. 1 at 13–18.

[106] *Krause v Commissioner for Inland Revenue* (1929) So. Afr. R. (A.D.) 286, considered in *O'Byrne v Minister for Finance* [1959] I.R. 1 at 18–20.

[107] *Cooper v Commissioner of Income Tax for the State of Queensland* (1907) 4 C.L.R. 1304, considered in *O'Byrne v Minister for Finance* [1959] I.R. 1 at 17–18.

[108] [1959] I.R. 1 at 25.

[109] [1959] I.R. 1 at 64.

[110] [1959] I.R. 1 at 64.

11–20 The economic crash, starting from 2007, impacted significantly on issues relating to the pay of employees in Ireland.[111] In 2008 and 2009, measures were introduced to expand the tax base, in particular through the imposition of income levies and pension levies. The pension levy applied to those who were civil or public servants or who otherwise enjoyed entitlement to a State pension. This pension levy was not imposed on the judiciary, as it was a tax that was only imposed on a certain class of worker—public and civil servants who pay into a State pension—and not private sector workers. The Attorney General expressed concerns as to whether the imposition of this levy onto the judiciary would be constitutionally permissible.[112]

11–21 In reaction to public concern regarding the exclusion of judges from the pension levy, the then Chief Justice, John Murray, negotiated measures with the Revenue Commissioners whereby judges could voluntarily opt to pay the pension levy. By 2011, the vast majority of judges had voluntarily done so.[113] However, the voluntary nature of this scheme was seen as politically unsatisfactory. In 2011, an amendment to the Constitution was successfully passed with an almost 80 per cent vote in favour.[114] The newly amended Article 35.5 reads as follows:

> "1° The remuneration of judges shall not be reduced during their continuance in office save in accordance with this section.
>
> 2° The remuneration of judges is subject to the imposition of taxes, levies or other charges that are imposed by law on persons generally or persons belonging to a particular class.
>
> 3° Where, before or after the enactment into law of this section, reductions have been or are made by law to the remuneration of persons belonging to classes of persons whose remuneration is paid out of public money and such law states that those reductions are in the public interest, provision may also be made by law to make reductions to the remuneration of judges."

---

111 Financial Emergency Measures in the Public Interest Acts of 2009–2013.

112 For political discussion on attempts to extend the generally applicable pension levy to judges, see 657 *Dáil Debates* Cols 463–465.

113 Revenue Commissioners, *Headline Results for 2010*, p.2. See also, P. Duncan, "22 judges failed to pay voluntary pension levy", *Irish Times*, 7 January 2011.

114 Twenty-Ninth Amendment of the Constitution (Judges' Remuneration) Act 2011.

11–22 The Irish judiciary issued a memorandum[115] that was critical of the proposed referendum. This memorandum was initially placed on the Courts Service website but removed after complaints from the Minister for Justice. The judges, while accepting that the issue was one for the people, stated that they had an issue with how the reduction should be achieved, rather than with whether a reduction should be implemented.[116] The judges categorised the referendum as a potential threat to the rule of law,[117] noting the strong, long-standing protection pre and post the 1937 Constitution given to judicial independence, including the principle of not reducing judicial pay.[118] Alleged "fundamental flaws" with the wording were highlighted, and the judges criticised the failure to provide for "an in-built mechanism for an independent review of the levels of the reduction of judicial pay".[119] The judiciary also expressed concern that a finding by an "international court" or "observations by an international organisation" that judicial independence had been compromised by this referendum "would have huge reputational implications for Ireland and for confidence in our legal system".[120]

11–23 The immediate impact of the passage of this amendment was that the public service pension levy was applicable to judges. Some have suggested that the amendment is so loosely worded that the Oireachtas could simply cut judicial pay at a whim or by reference to other small classes of public servant.[121] Any reduction in judicial pay must be imposed by law, either on persons generally or applicable to a certain class of public servant. The legislation must state that this

[115] *Re: Proposed Referendum on Article 35.3 of the Constitution: Memorandum on the Proposed Amendment.* The text of this memorandum is on file with the authors and does not appear to be online. For a discussion on the contribution of sitting judges to the referendum campaign, see J. O'Dowd, "Judges in Whose Cause? The Irish Bench after the Judges' Pay Referendum" (2012) 2 *Irish Jurist* 102.

[116] *Re: Proposed Referendum on Article 35.3 of the Constitution: Memorandum on the Proposed Amendment*, para.1.

[117] *Re: Proposed Referendum on Article 35.3 of the Constitution: Memorandum on the Proposed Amendment*, para.28.

[118] *Re: Proposed Referendum on Article 35.3 of the Constitution: Memorandum on the Proposed Amendment*, paras 2–5.

[119] *Re: Proposed Referendum on Article 35.3 of the Constitution: Memorandum on the Proposed Amendment*, para.26.

[120] *Re: Proposed Referendum on Article 35.3 of the Constitution: Memorandum on the Proposed Amendment*, para.29.

[121] See, in particular, P. McMahon, "How (Not) to Draft a Constitutional Amendment" (2011) 29 *Irish Law Times* 194, and F. de Londras, "The Judicial Pay Referendum in Its Broader Context of Dáil Empowerment" (2011) 29 *Irish Law Times* 202.

taxation or levy is "in the public interest" and must be proportionate. One could argue that Article 35.5 of the Constitution does not permit the Oireachtas to capriciously single out or distinguish the judiciary for cuts or reductions to salaries that could not be imposed more generally. However, even taking into account criticisms of the amendment, it is worth remembering that the amended Article will have to be read in conjunction with other Articles in the Constitution that protect judicial independence. The dissent of La Forest J. in the Canadian case of *Provincial Judges Reference* is instructive here.[122] He noted:

> "Judges, in my opinion, are capable of ensuring their own independence by an appropriate application of the Constitution ... [J]udges are able to distinguish between changes to their remuneration effected for a valid public purpose and those designed to influence their decisions."[123]

In other words, judges are perfectly capable of taking a case to the courts where they feel that a particular reduction is designed to compromise their independence.

11–24 The issue is still very much a sensitive one for the judiciary. Several weeks after the passage of the referendum, the Association of Judges of Ireland was formed.[124] In its 2014 submission on judicial appointments, the issue of judicial pay was raised on several occasions. Concerns were raised as regards the cumulative impact of levies and income tax rises impacting on new judicial appointments.[125] This was seen as potentially deterring excellent candidates from applying for judicial office.[126] The judges also referred to levies imposed on any pre-existing private pensions as "penal taxation provisions".[127] O'Donnell J. noted that judges appointed after 2010 are subject to a significant decrease in net take home pay and what he terms "penal" changes to pension entitlements for judges.[128] This, he argues, may impact on the quality of

[122] [1997] 3 S.C.R. 3.
[123] [1997] 3 S.C.R. 3 at 196.
[124] You can access the website of the Association of Judges of Ireland at *www.aji.ie.*
[125] *Judges' Submission*, para.43.
[126] *Judges' Submission*, para.179.
[127] *Judges' Submission*, para.180.
[128] D. O'Donnell, "Some Reflections on the Independence of the Judiciary" in E. Carolan (ed.), *Judicial Power in Ireland* (Dublin: Institute of Public Administration, 2018), pp.269–272.

judges who are appointed going forward given that legal practitioners often take a very steep pay cut to become a judge. According to a 2024 report of the European Commission for the Efficiency of Justice, judges in Ireland were some of the most highly paid judges in Europe, but also the most overworked.[129]

D. Judicial Appointments: the Interaction of Law and Politics

Box 11.1
Designing a Judicial Appointments System

Before reading this part of the chapter, if you were to design a system of judicial appointments (ignoring constitutional/legislative requirements in Ireland for one moment):

(a) What do you think should be the professional experience requirements to be appointed a judge?
(b) Would you limit judicial appointments just to legal practitioners? If so, why? If not, why not?
(c) Who do you believe should make the decision on who to appoint to the bench? Do you believe it should, for example, be made by the government? Should the Oireachtas have any role? Should it be a decision just for those who are currently serving and/or former judges?

1. The Constitution and Legislation

11–25 A key question interlinked with the discussion of judicial independence above is: who should appoint judges to the courts? The Irish Constitution provides a clear answer to this question. All judges "shall be appointed by the President". This is limited by Article 13.9 of the Constitution, where the President must exercise their judicial appointment power "only on the advice of the Government". Therefore, in reality, the government makes the appointment of judges to courts.[130]

[129] European Commission for the Efficiency of Justice (Council of Europe), *European Judicial Systems 2024 Edition* (2022 Data) (Strasbourg: COE, 2024), p.77.

[130] See *State (Walshe) v Murphy* [1981] I.R. 275 at 284 per Finlay P., who describes the constitutional approach to the issue of judicial appointments as being firmly in the hands of the executive.

Past political practice was that a name was brought before the cabinet, and the decision to appoint was approved rather than voted on.[131] In essence, the Taoiseach and the Minister for Justice discussed the issue before bringing a name to cabinet for approval. Depending on the political make-up of government at any given time, this may have involved the Tánaiste, if they are from a different political party, and the leaders of any smaller coalition parties in government. The system for appointing judges changed on 1 January 2025 with the commencement of all the necessary provisions of the Judicial Appointments Commission Act 2023 (the "2023 Act").[132]

11–26 It is first necessary to understand the previous system for judicial appointments that had been established in Pt IV of the Courts and Court Officers Act 1995, as amended (the "1995 Act").[133] This had been the first occasion where there was input from anybody other than the government of the day in making judicial appointments. The 1995 system, in place for almost 30 years, was subject to much critique. The table below provides a core overview of how judges are appointed in the Irish legal system, under the 1995 Act and the 2023 Act. In this section of the chapter, we want to briefly consider the development of a judicial appointments system in the 1990s, and the pathway to reform of judicial appointments from 2012 onwards that ultimately culminated in the passing of the 2023 Act. The President referred the 2023 Act to the Supreme Court under Article 26 of the Constitution, with the Supreme Court finding that it was constitutional.[134] With this key overview of how judges are appointed under both systems, a more in-depth exploration of certain issues related to judicial appointments is required. In the main, this will focus on the 2023 Act, with appropriate reference to the 1995 Act, if necessary.

---

[131] J. Carroll MacNeill, *The Politics of Judicial Selection in Ireland* (Dublin: Four Courts Press 2016), p.102; see also p.136.

[132] Department of Justice, "Minister McEntee announces establishment of the Judicial Appointments Commission", 17 October 2024. For a detailed explanation of the 2023 Act, see L. Cahillane, "Judicial Appointments Commission Act 2023: Annotated", *Irish Current Law Statutes Annotated* (Dublin: Round Hall, 2024), Release 207, October 2024, accessible on Westlaw IE (with subscription).

[133] For a comprehensive overview of judicial appointments under the 1995 Act, see *Fundamentals of the Irish Legal System*, 1st edn (Dublin: Round Hall, 2016), Ch.11, paras 11–08 to 11–16.

[134] *Re Article 26 and the Judicial Appointments Commission Bill 2022* [2023] IESC 34.

2. Development of a Judicial Appointments System in Ireland 1995–2025

(a) The prompt for the 1995 Act

11–27 Until 1995, there had been no legislative system in place that structured, at least in part, how a government would appoint a judge. So, prior to 1995, judges were appointed without any input from any other body, other than the government of the day. This changed due to a political scandal in the 1990s—the Brendan Smyth affair—relating to the extradition of a pedophile priest from Ireland to Northern Ireland.[135] It had been a long-standing practice (or convention) that the Attorney General of the day[136] be offered first refusal on a vacant judicial office. The then Attorney General, Harry Whelehan, informed the then Taoiseach, Albert Reynolds (Fianna Fáil), that he was interested in appointment as President of the High Court. There was significant public disquiet about how Whelehan, as Attorney General, had failed to deal with extradition requests from Northern Ireland relating to Brendan Smyth. The Labour Party (in coalition with Fianna Fáil) made it clear that it would not support Whelehan for appointment as President of the High Court. The Fianna Fáil ministers in the coalition government proceeded to appoint Whelehan as President of the High Court. This was despite the Labour Party leader and then Tánaiste, Dick Spring, stating publicly that the appointment of Whelehan was "totally unacceptable".[137] A few days after his appointment, Whelehan, who was now the President of the High Court, was accused by the Taoiseach of giving a "seriously misleading"[138] account of what he knew about the Brendan Smyth extradition.[139] The Taoiseach continued: "I now accept that the reservations voiced by the Tánaiste are well founded and I regret the appointment of the former Attorney General as President of the High Court."[140] Whelehan resigned

[135] Much more detail on this issue is provided in *Fundamentals of the Irish Legal System*, 1st edn (Dublin: Round Hall, 2016), pp.372–374.

[136] An Taoiseach, Mr Albert Reynolds TD, *Confidence in Government: Motion*, 447 *Dáil Debates* Cols 317–318 (16 November 1994). See further, paras 11–73 to 11–75. See also, *Irish Times* editorial, "Picking the Judges", *Irish Times*, 21 September 1994.

[137] P. McGarry, "London court told of strains in coalition over appointment of Harry Whelehan", *Irish Times*, 15 October 1996, p.6.

[138] This statement was used by the Taoiseach, Mr Albert Reynolds, when attempting to save the Government from collapse; see *Confidence in Government: Motion*, 447 *Dáil Debates* Col. 318 (16 November 1994).

[139] J. Maher, "Controversial end to 28-year climb to the top of the legal tree", *Irish Times*, 18 November 1994, p.9.

[140] An Taoiseach, Mr Albert Reynolds TD, *Confidence in Government: Motion*, 447 *Dáil Debates* Col. 319 (16 November 1994).

as President of the High Court after six days (and after two court hearings),[141] having refused to delay his swearing in.

(b) The 1995 Act and the necessity for reform and the 2023 Act

11–28 The particulars of the 1995 Act and how it differs from the 2023 Act are set out in the table below. However, a 2007 report by the Irish Council for Civil Liberties (ICCL), *Justice Matters*, set out the main criticisms of the process for appointment of judges under the 1995 Act. The ICCL made several reform recommendations, including that:

- the appointments process should be transparent, with well-defined and clear criteria that applicants would have to meet to be appointed a judge;
- minority or under-represented status should be treated as a component of competence;
- the Judicial Appointments Advisory Board should recommend only three persons for appointment, rather than the seven recommendations under the 1995 Act;
- consideration should be given by the government to publishing a statement as to why a particular judge was appointed, focusing on skills and competences of that individual.[142]

11–29 From December 2013 to January 2014, the then Minister for Justice and Equality, Alan Shatter TD, conducted a public consultation on judicial appointments in Ireland.[143] The reform initiative was predicated on the basis that there would be no constitutional change as regards judicial appointments.[144] Judges,[145] the professions[146] and civil

[141] See C. Newman, "Whelehan leaves with regret and an appeal for family privacy", *Irish Times*, 18 November 1994, p.8; J. Maher, "Controversial end to 28-year climb to the top of the legal tree", *Irish Times*, 18 November 1994, p.9.

[142] Irish Council for Civil Liberties, *Justice Matters* (Dublin: ICCL, 2007), p.97.

[143] Department of Justice and Equality, "Minister Shatter announces consultations on the process of judicial appointments", 6 December 2013.

[144] Department of Justice and Equality, "Minister Shatter announces consultations on the process of judicial appointments", 6 December 2013.

[145] Submission by Irish judges, *Preliminary Submission to the Department of Justice and Equality's Public Consultation on the Judicial Appointments Process* (January 2014) (hereinafter, *Judges' Submission*).

[146] Bar Council of Ireland, *Submissions on the Procedures for Appointment as a Judge* (January 2014) (hereinafter, *Bar Council Submission*), and Law Society of Ireland, *Submission on the Consultation on the Review of Procedures for Appointing Judges* (January 2014) (hereinafter, *Law Society Submission*).

society organisations[147] engaged with this consultation. On the format of the public consultation on appointments, the judges stated: "[i]t is regrettable that there has been no prior consultation with the judiciary on the methodology and structure of this consultation process in advance of public advertisement."[148] It was also noted that the judiciary play a fundamental role in the administration of justice more generally.[149] The judges stated that a high-level group should have been appointed to consider any submissions and make any recommendations. This was proposed due to the "process itself ... being initiated by a member of the Executive, and will apparently be decided upon by the Executive without further discussion".[150] Similar concerns were expressed by the Bar Council, who stated that the discussion on the appointments process must not be overly influenced by government.[151] Neither the Law Society, the Free Legal Advice Centres (FLAC) nor the ICCL commented on the perceived problematic nature of public consultation on judicial appointments.

11–30 In the 2017 and 2021 Programmes for Government,[152] reforming judicial appointments was identified as a matter that the respective governments would address urgently. In 2017, the Minister for Justice published the Judicial Appointments Commission Bill 2017. The 2017 Bill was never enacted. The then Attorney General, Séamus Woulfe, described the 2017 Bill as a "dog's dinner",[153] based on two factors: one, the Attorney General would no longer have any role within the proposed Judicial Appointments Commission; and two, several of the legislative provisions were (in the Attorney General's view) unconstitutional. Concerns were also raised by the Council of Europe's Group of States against Corruption (GRECO) regarding the 2017 proposal that the

[147] Free Legal Advice Centres, *Preliminary Submission on the Review of Procedures for Appointment as a Judge* (January 2014) (hereinafter, *FLAC Submission*), and Irish Council for Civil Liberties, *Review of Procedures for Appointment as a Judge* (February 2014) (hereinafter, *ICCL Submission*).

[148] *Judges' Submission*, para.29.

[149] *Judges' Submission*, paras 27–28.

[150] *Judges' Submission*, para.29.

[151] *Bar Council Submission*, paras 6–9.

[152] Government of Ireland, *A Programme for Partnership Government* (2017), p.151, and Government of Ireland, *Programme for Government: A Shared Future* (2021), p.85.

[153] Ingrid Miley, "New judicial appointments bill a 'dogs' dinner' – Attorney General", *RTÉ News*, 23 March 2018.

Judicial Appointments Commission (JAC) would have a lay majority,[154] as well as the lack of consultation with the judiciary.[155] Under the 2017 Bill, the Chief Justice would not have been chair of JAC, which caused significant disquiet.[156] The Judicial Appointments Commission Bill 2022 dealt with the majority of these concerns, ensuring that there would be a judicial majority on JAC appointment panels, that the body would be chaired by the Chief Justice, and ensuring that all appointments, including promotions and appointments/elections to international courts, would be within the remit of JAC. The Chief Justice, Donal O'Donnell, criticised the exclusion of representatives of the Law Society and Bar of Ireland from JAC.[157] In addition, the Chief Justice expressed concern in relation to the equal number of judges and laypersons on JAC, four each, with the Attorney General as a non-voting member.[158] In December 2023, the Supreme Court upheld the constitutionality of the 2023 Act, rendering it immune from subsequent constitutional challenge. In the table below, we outline the core structures of the judicial appointments system in Ireland. We contrast the now-repealed judicial appointments provisions of the 1995 Act with the judicial appointments process in place today.

3. The Politics of Judicial Appointments

11–31 When discussing the politics of judicial appointment, it can be challenging to communicate just how non-politically contentious most judicial appointments have been in the last three decades. This does not mean that the judicial appointments process has not legitimately been subject to critique, and in this section we will focus on a few controversies that have arisen and provide some context for that critique.

[154] GRECO, "GRECO urges Ireland to ensure judiciary's independence on appointments and promotion of judges", 5 July 2018.

[155] GRECO, *Fourth Evaluation Round: Corruption, prevention in respect of members of parliament, judiciary and prosecutors* (Council of Europe, adopted 25 September 2020), paras 29–33.

[156] RTÉ Radio One, "Judicial Appointments Bill a 'kick in the teeth for the Chief Justice'", interview with retired Supreme Court Judge, Catherine McGuinness, *News at One*, 27 June 2017, available at: *https://www.rte.ie/radio/radio1/clips/21193838/*. See also, Micheál Martin T.D. (then leader of the opposition, albeit supporting the minority government), *Dáil Debates*, Leaders' Questions, Tuesday 27 June 2017.

[157] Donal O'Donnell, Chief Justice, "Address on the theme of 'Judicial Dialogue'", Association of Law Teachers' Spring Discourse, 24 May 2022, pp.10–11, available at: *https://services.courts.ie/docs/default-source/default-document-library/supreme-court/speeches/o'donnell-cj_judicial-dialogue-(iatl-spring-discourse).pdf.*

[158] Donal O'Donnell, Chief Justice, "Address on the theme of 'Judicial Dialogue'", Association of Irish Law Teachers' Spring Discourse, 24 May 2022, p.8.

Table 11.1 Core Requirements for Judicial Appointment in Irish Law

Judicial Appointments	Courts and Court Officers Act 1995 (as amended)	Judicial Appointments Commission Act 2023 (as amended)
Who is eligible for appointment?	District Court: 10 years practice as a solicitor or barrister. Circuit Court: 10 years practice as a solicitor or barrister. Superior Courts: 12 years practice as a solicitor or barrister.	District Court: 10 years practice as a solicitor or barrister. Circuit Court: 10 years practice as a solicitor or barrister. Superior Courts: 12 years practice as a solicitor or barrister. Legal academics: May be appointed to the courts where they continuously practised as a barrister or solicitor for at least four years, and who have been an academic for a period of at least 12 years.
Composition of appointment body.	**Judicial Appointments Advisory Board (JAAB)**: 11 members. **Judicial (5)**: Chief Justice, who is chair of JAAB, along with the Presidents of the District Court, Circuit Court, High Court and Court of Appeal. **Attorney General (1).** **Practice and Professional (5)**: a practising barrister nominated by the Bar Council, a practising solicitor nominated by the Law Society of Ireland, and not more than three appointments by the Minister for Justice of persons, who in the Minister's opinion, have engaged in or have knowledge of commerce, finance, administration or who are consumers of services provided by the courts.	**Judicial Appointments Commission (JAC)**: 9 members. **Judicial (4)**: Chief Justice, President of Court of Appeal*, two members elected by the Judicial Council. **Attorney General (1)**: Non-voting member. **Lay Members (4)**: Appointed through Public Appointments Service (PAS). Must not have ever been a judge or a practising solicitor/barrister. *The President of the Court of Appeal is replaced by the relevant president of the other courts, where appointments are being made by these courts. Structures are in place to replace judicial members where judicial offices are vacant or where a judge on JAC may need to recuse themselves.

Table 11.1 ***(continued)***

Judicial Appointments	**Courts and Court Officers Act 1995 (as amended)**	**Judicial Appointments Commission Act 2023 (as amended)**
When will the appointments system be used?	Government can decide whether to promote a judge to a higher court, without having to go through this JAAB process. JAAB makes their recommendations to the Minister for Justice. JAAB includes a list of all those who applied for the vacancy. JAAB has no role in the appointment of Chief Justice or Presidents of other courts. JAAB has no role in recommending judges for appointment or election where this is to a court outside the State (e.g. EU judicial offices, European Court of Human Rights, International Criminal Court, etc).	The system must be used for all judicial appointments within the State, including promotion and filling vacancies in the offices of Chief Justice and Presidents of other courts. JAC provides their recommendation to the Minister for Justice. JAC provides a list of all those who applied for the vacancy. JAC must recommend the appointment (or ability to go forward for an election) of applicants to the: European Union: Court of Justice, Advocate General to the Court of Justice, and General Court. Council of Europe: European Court of Human Rights (election). United Nations: International Criminal Court (election). The Minister for Foreign Affairs is the responsible Minister to whom this recommendation must be made for appointments/election to courts outside of the State.
Seeking applicants for judicial office.	Advertised publicly. This will restate required factors JAAB must consider (see below).	Advertise publicly. This will also direct potential applicants to a website, where a judicial selection statement will be available for each appointment.
Are interviews of applicants for judicial appointment required?	Power to conduct interviews in law, but this power has never been used by JAAB.	JAC, once determining eligibility and suitability for judicial office, must interview these applicants prior to making recommendations to the relevant Minister.

Table 11.1 ***(continued)***

Judicial Appointments	**Courts and Court Officers Act 1995 (as amended)**	**Judicial Appointments Commission Act 2023 (as amended)**
Required factors that appointment body *must* consider.	(1) The applicant complies with minimum practice requirements as regards appointment as a judge of the particular court they are applying to. (2) The applicant has displayed probity and competence in their professional practice. (3) The applicant is "suitable on the grounds of character and temperament" and is tax-compliant. (4) The applicant provides an undertaking to conduct judicial training, if directed. (5) If applying for a vacancy before the High Court, Court of Appeal or Supreme Court, the applicant has appropriate knowledge of decisions, procedure and practice before those courts, and JAAB shall have regard to the degree to which they practised before these courts.	(1) A judicial selection statement will be prepared. JAC must consult with relevant persons and the public as to what precisely a selection statement as regards knowledge and selection procedures (broadly) should include. JAC is obliged to consult with presidents of each courts. JAC may consult the public. JAC must send the draft statement to the relevant Minister and take into account their views on the draft statement. (2) JAC must publish the judicial selection statement (if required). (3) The applicant complies with minimum practice requirements as regards appointment as a judge of the particular court they are applying to. (4) The applicant possesses the requisite knowledge, skills and attributes for the judicial office that is outlined in the judicial selection statement, which will be different depending on the judicial office and court to which the applicant seeks appointment. (5) The applicant has appropriate practice before the court to which the applicant is seeking to be appointed. (6) The applicant must undertake specified judicial training or education.
Other required considerations.	Not applicable.	A diversity statement must be published by JAC within two years of its operation. This statement must outline how JAC will consider recommendations for judicial appointment based on merit,

Table 11.1 ***(continued)***

Judicial Appointments	Courts and Court Officers Act 1995 (as amended)	Judicial Appointments Commission Act 2023 (as amended)
Other required considerations. *(continued)*	Not applicable.	coupled with diversity requirements. This may include identification of barriers and removing these (where appropriate) within the population who are under-represented in the judiciary. Recommendations for judicial appointment to be based on merit, with reference to three specific requirements, so that, to the greatest extent feasible and possible: (a) judiciary in each court should comprise equal numbers of men and women; (b) reflect the diversity of the population as a whole; (c) include judges proficient in the Irish language.
Number of applicants that can be recommended to Government.	**One judicial appointment**: JAAB can recommend up to seven names for appointment to the Minister for Justice where one judicial vacancy arises (or is about to arise). Where fewer than seven people apply for the position, then all names are forwarded to the Minister for Justice. **More than one judicial appointment for same court**: JAAB must inform the Minister for Justice of the names and qualifications of all applicants, and recommend at least seven persons for each vacancy.	**One judicial appointment**: A maximum of three persons will be recommended for appointment. Where applicants do not qualify for judicial appointment and/or there are fewer than three applicants, JAC may recommend fewer than three persons to the Minister. **More than one judicial appointment for the same court**: JAC must recommend three persons and two persons for each second and subsequent vacancy.
Powers of Government to advise the President to appoint.	Only obligation on Government is to "first consider" JAAB recommendations. No requirement to appoint person(s) recommended by JAAB. Government may appoint persons outside the JAAB system.	The Government must only consider JAC-recommended persons for appointment. The Government may recommence the appointment process if they do not wish to appoint any of the applicants recommended by JAC for judicial office.

11–32 We start with Mick Barry TD's scathing assessment of the judicial appointments process:

> "The story of the Irish Judiciary and of the judicial appointments system is a story of class privilege and establishment political interests from start to finish ... the bulk of these politically connected judges are connected to Fianna Fail and Fine Gael ... of course there are some Labour Party judges."[159]

Leading scholars find some truth to this. Writing about the pre-2023 Act judicial appointments systems, Cahillane found that political favouritism played a part, and not an insignificant one, in appointing judges.[160] Elgie and others, in analysing whether there was evidence of party political partisanship in Supreme Court judgments, premised this by acknowledging that many Supreme Court judges were likely appointed, at least in part, due to their closeness to a particular political party.[161] Carroll-MacNeill outlines that in the 1980s to the early 1990s, judicial appointments were "typified by the sharing of judicial appointments between coalition parties on roughly agreed rotations".[162] She identifies how, following the introduction of the Courts and Court Officers Act 1995, JAAB was mainly used for appointment of District and Circuit Court judges. These courts, as she notes, are where "government members receive the greatest lobbying for positions and there is the greatest incentive to reward local political involvement".[163] Political connections, therefore, may be important as regards who may be selected to be a judge, with this becoming of lesser significance, according to Carroll MacNeill, for appointments to the superior courts.[164] Being known

[159] Deputy Mick Barry (Solidarity/People Before Profit), *Dáil Debates*, Wednesday 21 June 2017.

[160] L. Cahillane, "Judicial Appointments in Ireland: The Potential for Reform" in L. Cahillane, J. Gallen and T. Hickey (eds), *Judges, Politics and the Irish Constitution* (Manchester: Manchester University Press, 2017), p.125. See also, D. O'Donnell, "Some reflections on the independence of the judiciary in Ireland" in E. Carolan (ed.), *Judicial Power in Ireland* (Dublin: Institute of Public Administration, 2018), p.261, for a discussion on this point

[161] R. Elgie, A. McAuley and E. O'Malley, "The (not-so-surprising) non-partisanship of the Irish Supreme Court" (2018) 33(1) *Irish Political Studies* 88 at 89.

[162] J. Carroll MacNeill, *The Politics of Judicial Selection in Ireland* (Dublin: Four Courts Press, 2016), p.67.

[163] J. Carroll MacNeill, *The Politics of Judicial Selection in Ireland* (Dublin: Four Courts Press, 2016), p.102; see also pp.134–135.

[164] J. Carroll MacNeill, *The Politics of Judicial Selection in Ireland* (Dublin: Four Courts Press, 2016), p.102; see also pp.137–138.

personally or professionally is also a significant factor in determining who should be appointed.[165]

11–33 Lesser significance does not, however, mean that political connections were of no significance in the appointment of superior court judges. Carroll noted that 48 per cent of superior court judges had some involvement with political parties, either as a student, making financial donations, or by acting in some advisory role for a political party.[166] Other judges admitted to having previously canvassed for a party, or to having been known as a supporter of a political party. Judges in their 2014 submission on judicial appointments did appear to accept that individuals may be appointed for reasons other than simple merit, and party political considerations may play a role.[167] Indeed, Byrne and others report that appointments have been delayed until the government was presented with what it considered to be a suitable list of candidates.[168]

11–34 There have, accordingly, been adverse comments on the method of selecting superior court judges over many decades.[169] In the 1970s, Thomas O'Higgins was appointed, first as a judge of the High Court, and then as the Chief Justice of the Supreme Court very shortly afterwards. Mr O'Higgins was a former Fine Gael minister and a candidate for the Presidency on two occasions. Several law lecturers in Trinity College Dublin reacted to O'Higgins C.J.'s appointment in a letter to the *Irish Independent*, stating:

> "The making of judicial appointments on the basis of political patronage is deplorable, and doubly so when practised by a Government some of whose members used frequently to proclaim the need to get away from this practice."[170]

165 J. Carroll MacNeill, *The Politics of Judicial Selection in Ireland* (Dublin: Four Courts Press, 2016), p.102; see also p.154. On this, see R. Mac Cormaic, *The Supreme Court* (Dublin: Penguin Ireland, 2016), Ch.17, which outlines the political leanings of a number of judges appointed to the Supreme Court in the late 1990s/early 2000s.

166 See J. Carroll, "You Be the Judge: Part 1—A Study of the Backgrounds of Superior Judges in Ireland 2004" (2005) 10(5) *Bar Review* 153 at 170–171. See also, J. Carroll, "You Be the Judge: Part II" (2005) 10(6) *Bar Review* 182.

167 *Judges' Submission*, paras 34–41 and 130–137.

168 R. Byrne, P. McCutcheon, L. Cahillane and E. Roche-Cagney, *Byrne and McCutcheon on the Irish Legal System*, 7th edn (Dublin: Bloomsbury Professional, 2020), para.4-123.

169 C. Allen, "Is this the way to pick a judge?", *Sunday Independent*, 22 November 1970, p.14.

170 K. Asmal, J. Casey, W. Duncan and Y. Scannell, "Judicial appointments", *Irish Press*, 26 October 1974. The *Irish Independent* also carried an editorial which stated:

The issue also cropped up from time to time in the 1980s.[171] In 1989, the then Chief Justice, Thomas Finlay, a former Fine Gael TD, was originally appointed to the High Court by a Fianna Fáil government and subsequently to the Chief Justice position by a Fine Gael/Labour government. Finlay C.J. stated:

> "[S]omebody must be accountable for the standard and type of judiciary that is appointed. There is a significant amount to be said for making politicians accountable for it. They are the ones to whom the people in general can turn if bad judicial appointments are being made. If appointments are made by some body of people who are relatively anonymous then there is no one to turn to and to blame."[172]

11–35 In the early 1990s, then Workers Party TD and spokesman on justice (and subsequently a judge of the Circuit Court), Pat McCarten, called for "independent selection procedures" to be put in place to select judges.[173] It was only due to the Whelehan scandal in 1994 that the judicial appointments process was placed on a legislative footing.[174] Yet still allegations of cronyism were made. Commenting on Mr Justice Adrian Hardiman's appointment to the Supreme Court directly from the Bar in 2000, Gene Kerrigan quipped:

> "Adrian was one of the top performers in the Law Library and his admirers stress that even had he not been a founding member of the PDs [Progressive Democrats], a failed Fianna Fáil election candidate, and a friend of [then Tánaiste] Mary Harney, he would have got the gig on merit."[175]

"Mr O'Higgins is now chief justice, mainly because of political patronage." *Irish Independent*, 27 October 1974.

171 C. Glennon, "Coalition balance in judicial appointments", *Irish Independent*, 16 January 1985, p.1.

172 "Appointments and their link to politics", *Irish Independent*, 28 January 1989.

173 "Second woman judge for the High Court", *Irish Times*, 12 April 1991. See also, G. Kennedy and Special Correspondent, "The mystery of judicial nominations", *Irish Times*, 11 April 1991, where it was stated: "Judges are quite openly appointed predominantly from among active party supporters of the party in power. This is admitted and accepted."

174 See paras 11-27 and 11–73 to 11–75 and *Fundamentals of the Irish Legal System*, 1st edn (Dublin: Round Hall, 2016), pp.372–374.

175 G. Kerrigan, "Pass the hat round for a judge's sacrifice", *Sunday Independent*, 6 February 2000, p.72.

11–36 Mac Cormaic, in his fascinating book *The Supreme Court*, offers interesting vignettes of lobbying for the position of Chief Justice in 2011 (this under the 1995 Act being an exclusive decision for government). A sitting Supreme Court judge knocked on TDs' doors in Mayo informing them of his suitability to be appointed Chief Justice, in the hope they might have a word with the then Taoiseach, himself from Mayo, Enda Kenny. This judge even had his wife approach the wife of a then senior government minister in a supermarket, noting how excellent a chief justice her husband would be.[176] Another judge contacted the government press office complaining that his name had not been included in an *Irish Times* report as a likely candidate. The Chief Justice who was appointed, Denham C.J., was not the person visiting Mayo or accidentally on purpose bumping shopping trolleys. There was nevertheless still some concern expressed by her judicial colleagues who, according to Mac Cormaic, were "critical" of what they perceived to be her "getting too close" to the then Minister for Justice.

11–37 In 2017, the appointment of the then Attorney General, Máire Whelan, to the Court of Appeal caused some public disquiet. Post the Brendan Smyth affair, no attorney general had been directly appointed to judicial office. Whelan had not applied to be appointed a judge under the 1995 Act; rather, her appointment was approved by government while Whelan remained in the room.[177] In a Dáil Debate on Whelan J.'s appointment, Brendan Howlin, Labour Party TD, stated that there was a "whiff of misogyny" around concerns about this appointment. He stated this in response to a Dáil deputy stating: "[Whelan] is a member of the Deputy's party."[178] The then leader of the opposition, Micheál Martin TD, said: "[t]his was an insider appointment and it stinks to high heaven."[179] Deputy Martin then continued: "Máire Whelan is no Frank Clarke, no Adrian Hardiman and no Donal O'Donnell."

11–38 In July 2020, Séamus Woulfe, who had replaced Whelan J. as Attorney General in 2017, was appointed to the Supreme Court, after

[176] R. Mac Cormaic, *The Supreme Court* (Dublin: Penguin Ireland, 2016).

[177] See P. Hosford, "How did the appointment of a judge threaten to bring the government down?", *The Journal*, 22 June 2017.

[178] Appointment to the Judiciary Nomination Procedure: Statements, *Dáil Debates*, Wednesday 21 June 2017.

[179] Leaders Questions, Deputy Micheál Martin TD, *Dáil Debates*, 20 June 2017.

being recommended by JAAB.[180] The Government stated that the appointment was "completely independent of Government formation talks [between Fianna Fáil, Fine Gael and the Green Party]". Cahillane and Kenny note that this appointment "was subject to little comment at the time".[181] This lack of controversy may have been due to the Dáil's summer recess and the Covid-19 pandemic still being to the forefront of minds. However, "Golf-gate", discussed in more detail below, renewed focus on issues relating to judicial appointments and judicial conduct.

11–39 Yet, to repeat the point made above, most judicial appointments are not politically contentious. Indeed, it could be argued that the political nature of the judicial appointments process is unavoidable as it is the Constitution itself that makes judicial appointment subject to political regulation. Moreover, Morgan has suggested that it is appropriate for the Government to retain some influence in the judicial appointments process. This is because the judiciary have power under the Constitution to strike down legislation on the grounds that it is unconstitutional. Such decisions do not always relate to such technical issues as legal interpretation. Sometimes, "subjective factors like the view of the judge as to what is in the public interest"[182] is just as important when a decision on unconstitutionality is determined. Finally, even if there is an element of political choice and preference for who is appointed a judge, this does not mean that decisions made by judges will be perceived as favourable to the political party that may have had an influence, or that championed their appointment. Elgie and others, in examining thousands of judicial decisions, concluded that even where judges may have been associated with a political party, this did not impact the decision they reached, as it was likely to be the same decision as would be made by a judge associated with a different political party.[183] That being said, reform was needed and we will consider some of the improvements introduced under the 2023 Act in the next sections.

---

[180] Minister for Justice, Helen McEntee, "Statement by the Minister for Justice on the appointment of Mr Séamus Woulfe SC as a judge of the Supreme Court", 26 November 2020.

[181] L. Cahillane and D. Kenny, "The Séamus Woulfe controversy and the deficiencies in Ireland's judicial appointments process" (2023) 74(1) *Northern Ireland Legal Quarterly* 22 at 32.

[182] D.G. Morgan, "Selection of Superior Judges" (2004) 22 *Irish Law Times* 42 at 44.

[183] R. Elgie, A. McAuley and E. O'Malley, "The (not-so-surprising) non-partisanship of the Irish Supreme Court" (2018) 33(1) *Irish Political Studies* 88 at 99.

4. Merit and Limiting Political Choice under the 2023 Act

11–40 In advertising for a new position (or to fill an existing one), the Judicial Appointments Commission (JAC), post consultation with the Presidents of the courts, the Courts Service as regards the needs of Irish language users, and potentially a broader range of stakeholders,[184] are required to publish a judicial selection statement.[185] The judicial selection statement must identify how a candidate for judicial office is to be selected and the requisite knowledge, skills and attributes for appointment to judicial office. The key criterion in selecting a judge is "merit". Section 39(1) states that judicial appointment "shall be based on merit" but does not define the term.

11–41 In the Article 26 reference on the constitutionality of the 2023 Act, counsel argued that the concept of merit was "wholly vague and incapable of clear and consistent application".[186] The failure on the part of the Oireachtas to define merit, it was argued, was an impermissible legislative delegation to JAC.[187] They drew from Kenny who has argued that the concept of merit is "filled with content that is invariably political" given the makeup of those who qualify to be judges.[188] The Supreme Court examined Kenny's arguments in the Article 26 reference, but stated that this "philosophical" or "ideological" debate did not impact on the constitutionality of what is now the 2023 Act.[189] They also noted that the legislation had requirements regarding:

(1) the nature of an applicant's legal practice and experience;
(2) appropriate procedural knowledge as relevant to the court to which an applicant is seeking appointment;
(3) professionalism, competency and probity in practice, or as an academic;

---

[184] Judicial Appointments Commission Act 2023 s.56.

[185] Judicial Appointments Commission Act 2023 s.57.

[186] *Re Article 26 and the Judicial Appointments Commission Bill 2022* [2023] IESC 34 at para.211.

[187] *Re Article 26 and the Judicial Appointments Commission Bill 2022* [2023] IESC 34 at para.209.

[188] D. Kenny, "Merit, diversity and interpretive communities: the (non-party) politics of judicial appointments and constitutional adjudication" in L. Cahillane, J. Gallen and T. Hickey (eds), *Judges, Politics and the Irish Constitution* (Manchester: Manchester University Press, 2017), p.148.

[189] *Re Article 26 and the Judicial Appointments Commission Bill 2022* [2023] IESC 34 at para.223.

(4) upskilling, should the applicant be appointed to a court that was outside their area of prior practice;
(5) awareness of the needs of lay litigants;
(6) the diversity of society; and
(7) professional development.[190]

JAC would, according to the Supreme Court, ensure that the judicial selection statement would be "consonant with and governed by" these legislative requirements.[191] This, therefore, would not be a usurpation of the legislative function of the Oireachtas.[192]

11–42 It is possible to refer to international norms and standards to assist in understanding what is meant by merit. The European Network of Councils for the Judiciary adopted the "Dublin Declaration", which outlines what European judges regard as best practice for judicial appointment. In part, it provides that:

> "1. Judicial appointments should only be based on merit and capability ...
> 2. Selection competencies should include intellectual and personal skills of a high quality, as well as a proper work ethic and the ability of the candidates to express themselves.
> 3. The intellectual requirement should comprise the adequate cultural and legal knowledge, analytical capacities and the ability independently to make judgments.
> 4. There should be personal skills of a high quality, such as the ability to assume responsibility in the performance of his/her duties as well as qualities of equanimity, independence, persuasiveness, sensibility, sociability, integrity, unflappability and the ability to co-operate."[193]

[190] *Re Article 26 and the Judicial Appointments Commission Bill 2022* [2023] IESC 34 at para.219.
[191] *Re Article 26 and the Judicial Appointments Commission Bill 2022* [2023] IESC 34 at para.219.
[192] *Re Article 26 and the Judicial Appointments Commission Bill 2022* [2023] IESC 34 at paras 224–225.
[193] European Network of Councils for the Judiciary, *Dublin Declaration on Standards for the Recruitment and Appointment of Members of the Judiciary* (May 2012), pp.3–5.

In England and Wales, as Cahillane outlines, there are six features of merit: intellectual capacity, personal qualities, fairness, authority and communication, efficiency, and leadership and management skills.[194]

11–43 Regarding limiting political choice, s.51(1) of the 2023 Act provides:

> "In advising the President in relation to the appointment of a person to a judicial office in the State, the Government shall only consider for appointment those persons who have been recommended by the Commission."

Section 51(2) of the 2023 Act permits the Government, if advising the President to appoint a person to judicial office, to seek confirmation from JAC that this person is eligible to be appointed a judge. In the Article 26 reference, counsel argued that the Oireachtas sought to impermissibly limit the constitutional authority and discretion of government as to who to appoint as a judge.[195] In rejecting this argument, the Supreme Court highlighted that government discretion on who to appoint is already limited by the Oireachtas, such as legislative eligibility/practice requirements.[196] The Supreme Court noted that s.47(5) of the 2023 Act, like under the 1995 system, requires JAC to forward the names of all those who applied for a judicial vacancy.[197] Just because three names are recommended does not place an obligation on the government to appoint any of these recommendations. The government may ask JAC to advertise the post again, should they not wish to make a judicial appointment on the recommendations before them.[198]

[194] L. Cahillane, "The Application of Merit and Diversity Criteria after Re Article 26 and the Judicial Appointments Commission Bill 2022", Trinity College Dublin School of Law, Legal Studies Research Paper No. 03/2023. See also, K. O'Neill, "Judged on Its Merits: The Judicial Appointments Commission Bill 2022" (2023) 23 *Dublin University Law Journal* 58 and D. Kenny, "Merit, diversity and interpretive communities: the (non-party) politics of judicial appointments and constitutional adjudication" in L. Cahillane, J. Gallen and T. Hickey (eds), *Judges, Politics and the Irish Constitution* (Manchester: Manchester University Press, 2017), Ch.9.

[195] *Re Article 26 and the Judicial Appointments Commission Bill 2022* [2023] IESC 34 at para.183.

[196] *Re Article 26 and the Judicial Appointments Commission Bill 2022* [2023] IESC 34 at paras 195–197.

[197] *Re Article 26 and the Judicial Appointments Commission Bill 2022* [2023] IESC 34 at para.176.

[198] *Re Article 26 and the Judicial Appointments Commission Bill 2022* [2023] IESC 34 at paras 180–181 and para.207.

5. Does Diversity in the Judiciary Matter?

11–44 Subject to the recommendation of JAC being on "merit", s.39(2) of the 2023 Act requires JAC to consider, where it is "feasible and practicable", objectives relating to judicial diversity. These objectives are specified in s.39(2) of the 2023 Act as follows:

(a) An equal number of men and women as judges. Although not specified in s.39(2) of the 2023 Act itself, non-binary persons can also be appointed based on merit and are not excluded from appointment by the 2023 Act's specification of equal (binary) gender diversity.[199]
(b) Judges should reflect the diversity of the Irish population.
(c) A significant number of judges competent in running court proceedings through the Irish language.

JAC, no later than 1 January 2027, will have to publish a diversity statement.[200] This statement must set out the measures JAC will take to achieve the objectives specified under s.39(2) of the 2023 Act. This is in essence a process-based duty, requiring JAC to assist in removing barriers to applicants for judicial office who are under-represented.

11–45 In the Article 26 reference, counsel who challenged the constitutionality of the Bill stated that the concept of diversity was "so inherently uncertain that it could never be the subject of any meaningful scrutiny".[201] The Attorney General, arguing for the constitutionality of the Bill, highlighted that merit was the peremptory requirement, and that JAC could not recommend a less meritorious applicant on the basis of their ethnicity, gender or on other grounds.[202] This is the reading the Supreme Court adopted to this aspect of the Bill. The court highlighted that the totality of the Bill privileged merit. JAC could not select a candidate due to their race, ethnicity, social class, disability, etc. who did not merit appointment.[203]

[199] *Re Article 26 and the Judicial Appointments Commission Bill 2022* [2023] IESC 34 at para.250.
[200] Judicial Appointments Commission Act 2023 s.28.
[201] *Re Article 26 and the Judicial Appointments Commission Bill 2022* [2023] IESC 34 at para.230.
[202] *Re Article 26 and the Judicial Appointments Commission Bill 2022* [2023] IESC 34 at para.231.
[203] *Re Article 26 and the Judicial Appointments Commission Bill 2022* [2023] IESC 34

11–46 Yet diversity is still a relevant factor. So why is the issue of diversity important when we discuss the make-up of the Irish judiciary? In her 2005 article, Carroll noted that the person who is most likely to be a judge in the superior courts in Ireland is:

> "... male, was born in Dublin and grew up in an urban setting ... He did not necessarily come from a legal family background. He attended a private secondary school and studied at University College Dublin ... His first self-supporting job was a barrister and he has never worked in any other capacity."[204]

This analysis remains true today; however, the judiciary is certainly less male. Most Irish judges have attended private fee-paying schools.[205] It is hardly the fault of any judge regarding the secondary school that their parents or guardians chose for them. Nonetheless, given that a tiny proportion of students in Ireland attend private fee-paying secondary schools, this is a legitimate issue to discuss. Rooney calculated that 62 per cent of all Irish Supreme Court judges since the foundation of the State attended fee-paying schools. To highlight just how stark this finding is:

> "The accumulative number of Supreme Court judges from three fee-paying schools—Belvedere College, Clongowes Wood College, and Blackrock College—is only two less than the total number of all Supreme Court judges known to have never attended any fee-paying school."[206]

11–47 This of course assumes that one's class background, and not one's current social class, would somehow impact on how they would judge. Cahillane argues that one's background, educational attainment and life experiences do impact on how a judge may determine a

at paras 240–244. The Supreme Court also noted the role of JAC in encouraging applicants from under-represented groups under s.28 of the 2023 Act.

204 J. Carroll, "You Be the Judge: Part 1—A Study of the Backgrounds of Superior Judges in Ireland 2004" (2005) 10(5) *Bar Review* 153 at 166. See also, D. Feenan, "Judicial Appointments in Ireland in Comparative Perspective" (2008) 8(1) *Judicial Studies Institute Journal* 37.

205 J. Rooney, "Judges, Education and Class in Ireland" (2023) 7(3) *Irish Judicial Studies* Journal 92.

206 J. Rooney, "Judges, Education and Class in Ireland" (2023) 7(3) *Irish Judicial Studies* Journal 92 at 96.

particular case before them.[207] In their submission on reforms to the judicial appointments process in 2014, the Irish judges commented:

> "Among the issues raised in the consultation has been the question of diversity. This appears to be an echo of a larger debate in other jurisdictions particularly the United Kingdom and the United States. It appears that the demand for diversity in the appointment process in those jurisdictions is a reflection of particular conditions in those societies. It is not apparent that the same conditions necessarily apply in Ireland or in relation to entry to the legal profession and appointment to the judiciary. Certainly the degree of commentary in relation to diversity within the judiciary does not appear to be commensurate with that in other jurisdictions. If there are indeed problems of integration of any group they appear societal rather than specific to the judicial appointment process and accordingly the remedy, if any, may lie at the level of society or at the point of entry to the legal profession."[208]

Contrast this with Cahillane's pointed (and in our view wholly correct) analysis:

> "It is easy for Irish judges to talk about neutrality and objectivity when they are generally drawn from a very narrow section of society where the experiences, education and backgrounds may be so similar so as to limit the emergence of 'different' views."[209]

11–48 The homogeneity of Irish judges is problematic, particularly when one thinks of the criminal justice system. Study after study has shown that the majority of those who come before the Irish courts on criminal charges tend to be from seriously economically and socially deprived areas with low levels of educational attainment.[210] By way of contrast, although the judges themselves were reluctant to classify themselves as upper class in Carroll's 2005 study, 52 per cent self-identified as middle-class. Yet, as one judge said, it is difficult to think of

[207] L. Cahillane, "Judicial Diversity in Ireland" (2016) 6(1) *Irish Journal of Legal Studies* 1.
[208] *Judges' Submission*, para.46.
[209] L. Cahillane, "Judicial Diversity in Ireland" (2016) 6(1) *Irish Journal of Legal Studies* 1 at 14.
[210] See, e.g. Irish Penal Reform Trust, *The Vicious Circle of Social Exclusion and Crime: Ireland's Disproportionate Punishment of the Poor* (Dublin: IPRT, 2012), pp.5–9.

more upper class than a senior counsel.[211] (One can also make the exact same point around tenured legal academics, at least those of us within the professorial ranks.) The class background of judges can only ever start to change by tackling the sustained and systemic disadvantages of a significant portion of the Irish population regarding educational attainment. This is a wider political and societal issue, given decades of lack of interest in fully tackling educational disadvantage in Ireland for working class students. People from working class backgrounds are least likely to attend higher education, albeit this is improving. Nonetheless, participation by working-class students in higher education remains well below the national average.[212] What this means is that the characteristics of the population of those being judged are very different from the characteristics of those doing the judging. The question becomes: what impact might these very different lives have on the ability of a judge to understand the reasons why a person broke the law? Might a judge be so far removed from the experiences of those they judge that they are unable to judge them fairly? Analysis of differentiated decision-making on the basis of (previous) social class would be difficult to quantify. A key area where there has been much more discussion is whether a judge's gender makes a difference to how they will resolve a case.

11–49 Baroness Hale (formerly of the UK Supreme Court) argues that in a real democracy, judges can no longer claim legitimacy solely on the basis of their legal expertise and social superiority. They must reflect the fact that "they are servants of a diverse society all of whose members are valued equally".[213] In relation to more gender diversity on the bench, relying on comments made by the female Chief Justice of Canada, Hale makes four arguments in favour of having different gender perspectives on the bench:

(i) it ensures public confidence in the judicial system;
(ii) it would symbolise democratic commitments to equality and fairness;

[211] J. Carroll, "You Be the Judge: Part I—A Study of the Backgrounds of Superior Judges in Ireland 2004" (2005) 10(5) *Bar Review* 153 at 169–170.

[212] See generally, M. Scanlon, P. Leahy, H. Jenkinson and F. Powell, "'My biggest fear was whether or not I would make friends': working-class students' reflections on their transition to university in Ireland" (2020) 44(6) *Journal of Further and Higher Education* 753, in particular 753–755.

[213] B. Hale, "Making a Difference? Why We Need a More Diverse Judiciary" (2005) 56 *Northern Ireland Legal Quarterly* 281.

(iii) it would represent sound use of human resources, so as to utilise the academic expertise of (over) half the population who happen to be female; and
(iv) women will bring different perspectives to judging than men.[214]

The final ground regarding different female perspectives is controversial. Legal education is premised on the idea that all judges, regardless of race, gender and social class, adjudicate impartially and neutrally. Resnick argues that the composition of the judiciary is a subject that merits much examination.[215] She notes that most judges in the UK are overwhelmingly white, male and from a narrow social and educational background. It is therefore essential, Resnick argues, that those choosing judges would come from a diverse background.

11–50 Baroness Hale came back to the issue of judging and gender in the case of *Radmacher (formerly Granatino) v Granatino*.[216] This case revolved around ante-nuptial agreements. Ante-nuptial agreements are agreements between parties before entering into marriage, as regards how assets of both parties should be spilt (or otherwise) post a marriage breakdown. In this case, rather unusually, the ante-nuptial agreement would have had a more detrimental impact on the former husband to the relationship. The UK Supreme Court in this case, by a majority of 8:1, held that decisive weight can be provided to ante-nuptial agreements freely entered by the parties to a marriage, as regards asset division in the event of a breakdown. Baroness Hale began her dissenting judgment by noting that "there is a gender dimension to the issue which some may think ill-suited to decision by a court consisting of eight men and one woman".[217] She noted that on such a complex issue, Parliament should have a final say as regards what impact, if any, ante-nuptial and other such agreements should have before the courts.[218] While Baroness Hale did not exclude the fact that the agreement should have some weight on the court, it should not be decisive.[219]

[214] B. Hale, "Making a Difference? Why We Need a More Diverse Judiciary" (2005) 56 *Northern Ireland Legal Quarterly* 281 at 287–290.
[215] J. Resnik, "Composing a Judiciary: Reflections on Proposed Reforms in the United Kingdom on How to Change the Voices of and the Constituencies for Judging" (2004) 24 *Legal Studies* 228.
[216] [2011] 1 A.C. 534.
[217] [2011] 1 A.C. 534 at 577.
[218] [2011] 1 A.C. 534 at 576.
[219] [2011] 1 A.C. 534 at 585–589.

11–51 In 2013, a new duty was enshrined obliging the Lord Chancellor and Lord Chief Justice of England and Wales to "take such steps as that office-holder considers appropriate for the purpose of encouraging judicial diversity".[220] Whether such judicial diversity makes an actual difference in decision-making and the "art" of judging is an issue of debate.[221] One gets a sense that judges are extraordinarily uncomfortable in admitting that their life experiences influence their decisions. It is fanciful to think that one's class background, gender, gender identity, race, ethnicity, sexuality and the many other intersections of one's identity and experiences do not impact how a judge might decide a decision. The Northern/Ireland Feminist Judgments Project offers us insights into how this could potentially occur.

Box 11.2
Legal Insight: the Northern/Irish Feminist Judgments Project

(i) Feminist Judging

Feminist judgments projects, where academics rewrite decisions of courts, can be viewed as a form of "academic activism". They critique judging by showing that alternative ways of thinking about legal issues could sometimes result in the same decision being reached by a different method and in others in an entirely different outcome. As Ms Justice Aileen Donnelly notes:

> "[Feminist] judgments make us think about the process we are engaged in, they remind us of the importance of what we do for the individuals before us and those not before us, that the language we use consciously or subconsciously reflects a history of legal and societal norms which can be contested and that even the most apparently straightforward decision can be reached by a variety of paths."[222]

McCandless, Enright and O'Donoghue, in the first chapter to *Northern/Irish Feminist Judgments*, highlight that the project sought to further question the supposed "neutrality" of judging and judgment.[223] Those who rewrote judgments within this collection had to ask questions as

[220] Constitutional Reform Act 2005 s.137A, as inserted by item 11 of Sch.13 to the Crime and Courts Act 2013.

[221] In this regard, see R. Hunter, "More than Just a Different Face? Judicial Diversity and Decision-making" (2015) 68(1) *Current Legal Problems* 119.

[222] A. Donnelly, "Book Review: Northern/Irish Feminist Judgments: Judges Troubles' and the Gendered Politics of Identity" [2017] *Irish Judicial Studies Journal* 90 at 92.

[223] M. Enright, J. McCandless and A. O'Donoghue (eds), *Northern/Irish Feminist Judgments: Judges' Troubles and the Gendered Politics of Identity* (Oxford: Hart, 2017).

to whether law and judges are as impartial and as neutral as can be incessantly claimed. Law claims objectivity and neutrality, yet judges are people, and all people will bring their life experiences to bear on decisions. However, feminist judgments projects subject themselves to only applying the law and legal rules and social knowledge that existed at the time a judgment was delivered. So those engaging in rewriting judgments from a feminist perspective had to adhere to rules of law, precedent and legal custom. Often feminist judgments will utilise ignored knowledge and seek to embrace less adversarial and less abstract approaches to judicial reasoning. Feminist judging, as the authors note, is not exclusively about asking "the woman question", as it can illuminate the impacts of legal interpretation and gendered effects of seemingly objective laws, which challenge the liberal legal constructs of law as "neutral".

Feminist judging technique is not without criticism. The leading feminist and prison abolition campaigner, Professor Angela Davis, speaking about law, and its utility and limits, states:

> "I don't know that I would give the law that much power. It seems that in instances where there have been major victories ... those victories have in many, if not most instances been produced by mass movements, so I don't see the law operating within a vacuum."[224]

Therefore, by working with the law as it is, it can be argued that feminist judgment projects simply enhance the structures of law that oft ignore those of whom are marginalised. They also, by restricting themselves to then-existing legal doctrines and legal interpretation, often apply rules developed before democracy, before women had a right to vote, and where widespread societal discrimination was part and parcel of the state. Yet, even accepting these arguments, feminist judging does highlight the value-laden nature of judging.

Here we will focus on just one example: the feminist judgment, from the Northern/Irish Feminist Judgments Project, of "Chief Justice" Lucy Ann Buckley[225] in the decision of *Re Article 26 and the Matrimonial Homes Bill, 1993*.[226]

---

[224] Interview with Angela Y. Davis: Law and resistance in the prisons of empire (2004), available at: *https://www.academia.edu/11098730/Interview_with_Angela_Y._Davis_Law_and_resistance_in_the_prisons_of_empire.*

[225] The author of this feminist judgment is Prof. Lucy Ann Buckley, Full Professor of Commercial Law, University of Limerick. For Buckley's judgment, along with expert commentary from Prof. Louise Crowley, see M. Enright, J. McCandless and A. O'Donoghue (eds), *Northern/Irish Feminist Judgments: Judges' Troubles and the Gendered Politics of Identity* (Oxford: Hart, 2017), Ch.8.

[226] [1994] 1 I.R. 305.

(ii) The Context

A spouse who does not own the family home, and so ownership rests with one spouse, must give permission for the sale of the family home. If a spouse does not give such permission, a court may dispense with this consent. This has been the case in Ireland since the Family Home Protection Act 1976.

Article 41.1.2° of the Irish Constitution guarantees that the State will protect the "constitution and authority" of the marital family.

Article 41.2 of the Irish Constitution provides:

> "1° In particular, the State recognises that by her life within the home, woman gives to the State a support without which the common good cannot be achieved.
> 2° The State shall, therefore, endeavour to ensure that mothers shall not be obliged by economic necessity to engage in labour to the neglect of their duties in the home."

This is a much-criticised provision, but a recent attempt to remove this from the Constitution was unsuccessful for a variety of reasons.[227]

Even if one fundamentally disagrees with this Article, it nonetheless highlights a key issue: why do judges "discover"' derived constitutional rights within one constitutional article, but disregard them in another constitutional article such as Article 41.2.2°?

There was one attempt by a High Court judge, Barr J., to utilise Article 41.2.2° to provide substantive and enforceable rights for women in the case of *L v L*.[228] Mr L had purchased the family home from his own money. His wife, Mrs L, had not contributed financially to the purchase of the home. Mrs L was subject to continuous domestic violence from her husband, with the husband also engaging in adultery. Mrs L sought a judicial separation from her husband (divorce was not legal in Ireland at this time), along with orders that would determine her interests in the family home. The Married Women's Status Act 1957 permitted courts to determine the title to or the possession of any property. Barr J. noted that past case law had determined that child-rearing and caring for the family did not establish any interest in the family home for a wife who did

227 The Citizens' Assembly in 2021 recommended that the provision be deleted and replaced; Citizens' Assembly, *Report of the Citizens' Assembly on Gender Equality* (June 2021), available at: *https://citizensassembly.ie/wp-content/uploads/2023/02/report-of-the-citizens-assembly-on-gender-equality.pdf*. A weaker variation of this proposal was put forward for referendum in March 2024 and this watering down of the proposal, in addition to concerns that there had been insufficient parliamentary time allocated for scrutiny of the text and that it reinforced ableism, are all believed to have had a role in its rejection by the people.

228 [1989] I.L.R.M. 528.

not contribute financially to the purchase of the family home. However, Barr J. said that those cases had not considered Article 41.2.2°, as the plaintiffs in those cases did not raise it in legal argument. After considering Article 41.2.2°, Barr J. held:

> "[A] mother who adopts that concept and devotes herself entirely to the family after marriage, has a special place in society which should be buttressed and preserved by the State in its laws."[229]

In this case, Barr J. held that Mrs L's beneficial interest in the home was 50 per cent of the total value of the property, i.e. the husband holds in trust for Mrs L the 50 per cent value.[230]

The Supreme Court overturned this decision,[231] stating that Article 41.2.2° was a direction to the State, including the judiciary, but could not be interpreted as providing a wife, who had not contributed to the purchase of the family home (or any portion by way of mortgage payments), with an entitlement to a 50 per cent beneficial interest in the family home for following the constitutionally prescribed values.

(iii) The Matrimonial Homes Bill 1993 and the Article 26 Reference

Partly in response to this decision, the Oireachtas passed the Matrimonial Homes Bill 1993. The then President, Mary Robinson, sought a decision from the Supreme Court on its constitutionality under Article 26 of the Constitution.[232] The 1993 Bill sought to create an automatic statutory right for a non-owning spouse of the family home to acquire a 50 per cent equitable share in the family home, unless, of course, both spouses equally owned the property. This would apply from 25 June 1993, irrespective of whether the property had been purchased before 25 June 1993. There were provisions in the Bill providing that a non-owning spouse, after taking independent legal advice, could in writing renounce such 50 per cent equitable ownership. This, in effect, would have reinstated the decision of Barr J. in the High Court. The Oireachtas, in passing this legislation, decided it had a role to play in protecting women in the home who may be economically vulnerable. The Oireachtas sought to use the State's ability to limit property rights based on the common good. The Oireachtas determined that it was in the common good that the non-owning spouse would have an automatic 50 per cent share in the family home.

[229] [1989] I.L.R.M. 528 at 533.
[230] [1989] I.L.R.M. 528 at 534.
[231] [1992] 2 I.R. 77.
[232] *Re Article 26 and the Matrimonial Home Bill, 1993* [1994] 1 I.R. 305.

The Supreme Court determined that the 1993 Bill was repugnant to Article 41 of the Constitution. The court did so for several reasons, the key reason being that this was unwarranted State interference with the constitutional authority of the family to determine the property-owning arrangements. The 1993 Bill, according to Finlay C.J., "constitute[d] a failure by the State to protect the authority of the family".[233]

(iv) The Feminist Judgment of Buckley C.J.

Buckley C.J.'s feminist judgment argues that the 1993 Bill could have been deemed constitutional. Just as the actual Supreme Court judgment relied on law and interpretation, Buckley deals head on with the key question: why is it that male home ownership can be seen as a "personal preference" and "mutual choice" between spouses? Engaging with the case of *McGee v Attorney General*, which established the derived right of marital family privacy, Buckley held that this did not mean the State could never interfere with family choices.[234] Marital partnership, fairness and equality could, according to Buckley, "justify state intervention to ensure that both spouses have some measure of economic security and share in the fruits of the marriage".[235]

Buckley also engaged with an argument, put forward by counsel in the Supreme Court decision, but not addressed by the Supreme Court, as regards the "private property" arguments. Buckley centres the constitutional respect for property rights subject to the "common good". As per Article 43 of the Constitution (protection of private property), the State may regulate private property rights "by the principles of social justice." For Buckley C.J., the Oireachtas, as the elected body, is best-placed to legislate on what precisely the principles of social justice are, once of course these comply with other constitutional rights. Therefore, the key question for Buckley C.J. was whether the Oireachtas's desire to regulate ownership of property between spouses was excessive, arbitrary or disproportionate. Considering this, Buckley C.J. held:

- There was an objective basis for the Oireachtas seeking to regulate property ownership between spouses, which would potentially contribute to marital stability and broader general protection of the family as per Article 41 of the Constitution.[236]

[233] *Re Article 26 and the Matrimonial Home Bill, 1993* [1994] 1 I.R. 305 at 322.

[234] M. Enright, J. McCandless and A. O'Donoghue (eds), *Northern/Irish Feminist Judgments: Judges' Troubles and the Gendered Politics of Identity* (Oxford: Hart, 2017), p.167.

[235] M. Enright, J. McCandless and A. O'Donoghue (eds), *Northern/Irish Feminist Judgments: Judges' Troubles and the Gendered Politics of Identity* (Oxford: Hart, 2017), p.171.

[236] M. Enright, J. McCandless and A. O'Donoghue (eds), *Northern/Irish Feminist Judgments: Judges' Troubles and the Gendered Politics of Identity* (Oxford: Hart, 2017), p.165.

- A non-owning spouse, who would receive a beneficial equitable 50 per cent share of the family home, had a mechanism whereby she (and it would usually be she) could receive independent legal advice. She could then declare in writing that she did not wish to benefit from this legislative right.[237]
- The owning spouse was not entitled to financial compensation under the Bill; this, Buckley argued, was fundamentally different from where the State compulsorily acquires land and is obliged to pay compensation. Since the Constitution recognises the importance of "work within the home", the 1993 Bill restricted who benefits from the legal change to ownership: the benefit being to the person to whom the owning spouse is married and has entered into a lifelong partnership, where "contributions of each partner are of equal value and are equally essential to the well-being of the family as a whole".[238]

Box 11.3
Time to Reflect

- Does it really matter that judges in Ireland tend to come from a relatively small geographical area, are of a certain socio-economic background, and mainly are of one gender?
- Do you believe that judges (at least in certain "controversial" areas) could be more guided by their life philosophy/ideology in reaching a decision?
- Should not the only concern be that the individual appointed approaches matters in the spirit of impartiality, gives both sides in a case a fair hearing, comes to a decision by considering relevant issues and laws, and excludes irrelevant considerations and laws?
- We advise that you explore other "judgments" in the *Northern/Irish Feminist Judgments* text and consider examples where the feminist judgment agreed with the result reached in the original case but used different reasoning processes to come to the same result.

[237] M. Enright, J. McCandless and A. O'Donoghue (eds), *Northern/Irish Feminist Judgments: Judges' Troubles and the Gendered Politics of Identity* (Oxford: Hart, 2017), p.175.

[238] M. Enright, J. McCandless and A. O'Donoghue (eds), *Northern/Irish Feminist Judgments: Judges' Troubles and the Gendered Politics of Identity* (Oxford: Hart, 2017), p.175.

E. Judicial (Mis)Conduct

11–52 Not all poor behaviour by a judge reaches the requisite constitutional requirement for their removal from office. Until the 2022 commencement of complaints mechanisms established by the Judicial Council Act 2019 (the "2019 Act"), there had been no formal route for the public, legal practitioners or indeed other judges to complain about the behaviour of a member of the judiciary. Prior to the enactment of the 2019 Act, there was a limited investigation system in place for District Court judges. Under now-repealed provisions of the Courts (Supplemental Provisions) Act 1961,[239] the Chief Justice had the power to interview a judge of the District Court privately and inform the District Court judge of their view that the administration of justice is being brought into disrepute.[240] The President of the District Court could investigate a District Court judge whose conduct was "prejudicial to the prompt and efficient discharge of the business" of the court.[241] Under s.21 of the Courts of Justice (District Court) Act 1946 (now repealed), the Minister for Justice could request the Chief Justice to appoint a judge of the Supreme Court or the High Court to:

> "(a) investigate the condition of health, either physical or mental, of a Justice, or
> (b) to inquire into the conduct (whether in the execution of his office or otherwise) of a Justice, either generally or on a particular occasion".[242]

That provision had been used on (at least) two occasions.[243]

11–53 A number of reports had recommended the establishment of a Judicial Council.[244] This resulted in the drafting of legislative proposals

[239] Judicial Council Act 2019 s.3, brought into force by the Judicial Council Act 2019 (Commencement) Order 2022 (S.I. No. 489 of 2022).
[240] Courts (Supplemental Provisions) Act 1961 s.10(4).
[241] Courts (Supplemental Provisions) Act 1961 s.36(2).
[242] Courts of Justice (District Court) Act 1946 s.21(i). The Chief Justice could have appointed a judge of the High Court, with the consent of the President of the High Court.
[243] For a full exploration of this, see L. Cahillane, "Disciplining Judges: The Special Position of District Court Judges" (2009) 5 *Irish Law Review* 14.
[244] *Working Group on a Courts Commission: Sixth Report* (November 1998), Ch.VIII, in particular paras 8.12–8.13, and All-Party Oireachtas Committee on the Constitution, *Fourth Progress Report: The Courts and the Judiciary* (1999), p.15.

in 2010[245] and the operation of a non-statutory interim Judicial Council in 2012, which focused on education and training only. The 2019 Act established the (statutory) Judicial Council, which has been in place since 2020. The ability to provide for sanctions short of impeachment, i.e. some form of reprimand/punishment for stated misbehaviour, commenced in October 2022.[246]

Box 11.4
Legal Insight: The Judicial Council—Core Overview

In this chapter, we are only exploring the role of the Judicial Council as it pertains to complaints on the behaviour of judges. Every judge in the District Court, Circuit Court, High Court, Court of Appeal and the Supreme Court is a member of the Judicial Council. The Board of the Judicial Council[247] is tasked with delivering upon the functions of the Council.[248] The functions of the Judicial Council are much broader than simply hearing and determining complaints. Section 7 of the 2019 Act obliges the Judicial Council to promote and maintain, amongst other things:

- excellence in a judge's exercise of their judicial functions (the concept of "excellence" is undefined);
- high standards of probity in judicial conduct;
- judicial education and training;[249]
- the importance of respect for the independence of judges; and,
- public confidence in the judiciary and the administration of justice.[250]

---

[245] General Scheme of the Judicial Council Bill 2010.

[246] For a more detailed background to the introduction of the Judicial Council Act 2019, see *Fundamentals of the Irish Legal System*, 1st edn (Dublin: Round Hall, 2016), paras 11–41 to 11–43 and 11–53 to 11–58.

[247] Judicial Council Act 2019 s.11.

[248] Membership of the Board of the Judicial Council comprises the Chief Justice and the Presidents of the other courts, one judge elected by their judicial colleagues from each court and one additional judge. Per s.12 of the Judicial Council Act 2019, this was a Supreme Court judge until 2024, currently a Court of Appeal judge until 2028, a High Court judge from 2032 and so on.

[249] Charleton J. (of the Supreme Court) acts as Director of the Judicial Studies Committee. For more on this, see Judicial Council, *Annual Report 2023*, pp.16–21. See also, Judicial Council Act 2019 s.30(3) regarding the establishment of Judicial Support and Welfare Committees; see Judicial Council, *Annual Report 2023*, pp.29–30.

[250] Section 7(2) of the 2019 Act identifies precise matters the Judicial Council must do, including adopting Personal Injuries Guidelines and Sentencing Guidelines. The constitutionality of the Personal Injuries Guidelines issued by the Judicial Council were upheld in *Delaney v Personal Injuries Assessment Board* [2024] IESC 10.

11–54 Judges, like us all, can be rude, abrasive, impatient and stubborn-minded. It is unusual for a judge, in particular in the superior courts, to evidence this in a written judgment. However, we have two examples where this occurred. Baker J., in her Supreme Court decision in *Serėdych v Minister for Justice and Equality*, noted that there are mutual obligations of professionalism and courtesy expected between legal practitioners and judges.[251] In criticising Humphreys J. of the Irish High Court for "offensive and humiliating" comments against two named barristers, Baker J. said: "[i]t is no part of the judge's role to be personally insulting to the lawyers who appear before him or her."[252] Baker J. acknowledged that the decision reached by Humphreys J. was "lucid, reasoned, elegant and intelligent";[253] however, the judge had made "quite remarkable and personally insulting comments regarding the competence and trustworthiness of counsel for the State[254] and the professional competence of both senior counsel".[255]

11–55 This was not the first time that Humphreys J. had engaged in similarly insulting and derogatory remarks directed towards a barrister. Humphreys J., in his decision in *IE v Minister for Justice and Equality*, said that a leading text, *The Law of Refugee Status*,[256] adopted "the crusading spirit of a social justice campaigner" rather than providing a dispassionate analysis of law.[257] Marc de Blacam SC published an article critiquing Humphreys J.'s comments in *IE (Nigeria)*.[258] De Blacam stated that Humphreys J.'s "onslaught" on the text indicated a "parochial" approach to interpretations of Irish refugee law, divorced from the wider international refugee legal contexts.[259] Subsequently, in the case of *LF (South Africa) v International Protection Appeals Tribunal*,[260] de Blacam invited Humphreys J. to consider a particular argument made by the authors of *The Law of Refugee Status*. In his written judgment, Humphreys J. vigorously protested what he saw as his arguments in *IE*

251 [2020] IESC 62 at para.9.
252 [2020] IESC 62 at para.99.
253 [2020] IESC 62 at para.101.
254 Now Phelan J., a colleague of Humphreys J. in the High Court.
255 [2020] IESC 62 at para.94.
256 J.C. Hathaway and M. Foster, *The Law of Refugee Status*, 2nd edn (Oxford: OUP, 2014).
257 [2016] IEHC 85 at para.29.
258 M. de Blacam, "In Defence of the Textbook" (2018) 41(1) D.U.L.J. 175.
259 M. de Blacam, "In Defence of the Textbook" (2018) 41(1) D.U.L.J. 175 at 183–184.
260 [2019] IEHC 512.

being misstated by de Blacam in his article. Humphreys J. stated that he had derived "assistance" from *The Law of Refugee Status* previously.[261] Humphreys J., reflecting overall on de Blacam's article, said that those who read the article had to "[endure] a choking-on-one's-organic-muesli tone of modish umbrage adopted by Mr. de Blacam in this ululating exercise in social justice warfare."[262]

11–56 The 2019 Act defines judicial misconduct as:

(i) constituting a "departure" from "acknowledged standards of judicial conduct", such as those outlined in the Guidelines for the Judiciary on Conduct and Ethics;[263] *and*
(ii) that brings the administration of justice into disrepute.[264]

The Judicial Council published the Guidelines for the Judiciary on Conduct and Ethics in 2022, just as the complaints procedures under the 2019 Act commenced.[265] The Judicial Conduct Committee (JCC) is a committee of the Judicial Council. The function of the JCC is to:

> "... promote and maintain high standards of conduct among judges, having regard to the principles of judicial conduct requiring judges to uphold and exemplify judicial independence, impartiality, integrity, propriety (including the appearance of propriety), competence and diligence and to ensure equality of treatment to all persons before the courts."[266]

11–57 There are 13 members of the JCC:[267] the Chief Justice and Presidents of the other courts, three judges elected by the Judicial Council, and five laypersons appointed through the Public Appointments System process. The Registrar to the JCC is responsible for the proper administration of the JCC. This includes considering complaints against a sitting judge[268] regarding actions occurring only after 3 October 2022, determining admissibility, referring these complaints to an informal or

[261] [2019] IEHC 512 at para.13.
[262] [2019] IEHC 512 at para.14.
[263] See para.11–13.
[264] Judicial Council Act 2019 s.2, s.7(1)(b) and s.43(2) (emphasis added).
[265] Judicial Council Act 2019 (Commencement) Order 2022 (S.I. No. 489 of 2022).
[266] Judicial Council Act 2019 s.43(2).
[267] Judicial Council Act 2019 ss.44–45.
[268] Judicial Council Act 2019 s.42. If a judge retires, then the complaint process ends.

formal resolution process, and/or undertaking investigations regarding the conduct of a judge.[269] The actions complained of must generally have occurred within three months prior to the complaint being made to the Registrar of the JCC.[270] There are several potential stages in the complaints process, which will be considered in turn.

11–58 Power of the JCC to Initiate/Continue Investigations for Judicial Misconduct: The JCC may refer any matter to a Panel of Inquiry where they are satisfied that prima facie evidence exists for judicial misconduct and this is required to ensure the proper administration of justice.[271]

11–59 Admissibility: The judge against whom a complaint is made must be informed of the complaint, providing them with the name of the complainant and the particulars of the misconduct claim.[272] In this regard, s.53 of the 2019 Act requires that the person who is making the complaint must have been directly affected or witnessed the alleged misconduct.[273] The complaint must be made in line with the Complaints Procedures.[274] In addition, the complaint must not be frivolous or vexatious, or simply a means to express dissatisfaction about a decision a judge has reached in a case in which they were involved. The Registrar of the JCC determines whether the complaint is admissible, and this decision can be reviewed if requested by the complainant. The Complaints Review Committee will then determine admissibility.[275] Of the 222 complaints made in 2023, the vast majority (196) were inadmissible.[276] Of these 222 complaints, 53 were made by the same person. The vast majority of inadmissible complaints were from people unhappy with the outcome

[269] Judicial Council Act 2019 s.43(3).
[270] Judicial Council Act 2019 s.51. Under s.51(3) of the 2019 Act, the JCC may extend this three-month time period where it is "just and equitable" to do so.
[271] Judicial Council Act 2019 s.59, as substituted by s.84 of the Courts and Civil Law (Miscellaneous Provisions) Act 2023.
[272] Judicial Council Act 2019 s.50(5).
[273] Judicial Council Act 2019 s.50. The Law Society of Ireland or the Bar of Ireland may make complaints on behalf of solicitors and barristers, respectively.
[274] Judicial Council Act 2019 s.52. The precise particulars are outlined in: Judicial Conduct Committee, "Complaints procedures specified for the purposes of s.52", as updated on 22 May 2023.
[275] Judicial Council Act 2019 s.49.
[276] Judicial Conduct Committee, *Annual Report 2023* (included within Judicial Council, *Annual Report 2023*), p.39.

of a court decision.[277] In 2023, the Registrar found one complaint to be admissible. Of the 62 referrals to the Complaints Review Committee, none were determined to be admissible.[278] To date, the JCC has not determined any complaints. Where the JCC itself makes a referral, this will not be subject to an admissibility determination.

11–60 Informal Resolution: The JCC may refer the complaint for informal resolution where the complainant and the judge against whom the complaint is made agree to this (and where this is appropriate).[279] A designated judge (or judges) will be involved in the informal resolution. Neither the 2019 Act nor the JCC's complaints procedures identify what exactly the role of the designated judge is in this process.

11–61 Panel of Inquiry: If an informal resolution was not used, had failed, or where it was not appropriate to use this, a Panel of Inquiry will be established.[280] A Panel of Inquiry will consist of two judicial members and one lay member.[281] The Panel of Inquiry has significant powers to compel witnesses and seek documentation or other materials akin to a High Court judge. The Panel of Inquiry, after completing its work, must prepare a report for the JCC, which should include recommendations as to whether the complaint is upheld (in whole or in part) or whether the complaint is not proven.[282] The Panel may recommend the action that the JCC should take regarding reprimanding a judge.[283] The Panel of Inquiry takes place in private.[284]

---

[277] Judicial Conduct Committee, *Annual Report 2023*, p.38.

[278] Judicial Conduct Committee, *Annual Report 2023*, p.38.

[279] Judicial Council Act 2019 s.73, and Judicial Conduct Committee, "Complaints procedures specified for the purposes of s.52", section 13.

[280] For what occurs where a judge or complainant does not engage with the JCC, see Judicial Conduct Committee, "Complaints procedures specified for the purposes of s.52", section 16 (complainant); the inquiry will discontinue. For a judge (section 17), the Panel of Inquiry must make a mandatory recommendation to the JCC regarding reprimanding the judge for their failure to engage.

[281] Judicial Council Act 2019 ss.67–69, and Judicial Conduct Committee, "Complaints procedures specified for the purposes of s.52", sections 14–18.

[282] Judicial Council Act 2019 s.77. Prior to this, a draft of the report will be sent to the complainant and the judge for their comment; see Judicial Conduct Committee, "Complaints procedures specified for the purposes of s.52", section 23. It is possible for the Panel of Inquiry to amend this report if it is appropriate to do so pursuant to s.78 of the 2019 Act.

[283] On a Panel of Inquiry relating to the health of a judge, see Judicial Council Act 2019 s.72 and Judicial Conduct Committee, "Complaints procedures specified for the purposes of s.52", section 18.

[284] A range of criminal offences exist for failure to cooperate with an investigation; see

11–62 Determination of Complaint by the JCC: A complainant and the judge will have a further opportunity to make submissions in relation to the Panel of Inquiry's report.[285] There then will be (yet another) in camera hearing, where the JCC will have all the powers of the Panel of Inquiry.[286] The JCC then must determine whether the complaint is upheld or has not been substantiated. The JCC determines whether its decision will or will not be published.[287]

11–63 The Complaint Outcome: If a complaint is deemed admissible or prior to the issuance of a decision of the JCC, a judge may consent to receiving a reprimand. The JCC may issue a reprimand where a complaint has been proven. The reprimand of the judge by the JCC may involve one or more of the following: issuing advice; recommending the judge take a course of action; and/or issuing an admonishment.[288] The judge concerned must then inform the JCC of actions (if any) that they have taken in order to comply with the conditions of the reprimand.

11–64 Potential of Referral to the Minister for Justice: The JCC may refer any matter for consideration to the Minister for Justice where it is determined that judicial removal from office may be appropriate in the circumstances (whether this emerged from a complaint or otherwise).[289] Any statement or submission a judge may have made to the Panel of Inquiry or JCC will not be admissible in the Oireachtas Committee (or Oireachtas) who are examining the issue of removal of a judge. The issue of judicial removal is considered in detail in the next section.

11–65 Given that regulation of judicial conduct is new to Ireland, how then can we understand the importance of the 2019 Act? Drawing on the work of Scott, we should think more deeply about whether the 2019

generally, Judicial Council Act 2019 s.69 (protection of witnesses and evidence); s.82 (prohibition of JCC members and others from disclosing information).

[285] Judicial Council Act 2019 s.75, and Judicial Conduct Committee, "Complaints procedures specified for the purposes of s.52", section 24.1.

[286] Judicial Council Act 2019 s.79, and Judicial Conduct Committee, "Complaints procedures specified for the purposes of s.52", section 24.

[287] Judicial Council Act 2019 s.79, and Judicial Conduct Committee, "Complaints procedures specified for the purposes of s.52", section 25.

[288] Judicial Conduct Committee, "Complaints procedures specified for the purposes of s.52", section 25.

[289] Judicial Council Act 2019 s.80, and Judicial Conduct Committee, "Complaints procedures specified for the purposes of s.52", section 26.

Act ensures effective regulation of judicial conduct.[290] To a degree, the 2019 Act as understood considering the Guidelines for the Judiciary on Conduct and Ethics, does allow us to understand what actions (or inactions) may constitute judicial misconduct. The mechanisms for detecting misconduct, be it by complaint or on the JCC's own motion, create a convoluted regulatory system. This may be the price to pay for ensuring the protection of judicial independence. However, given that most complaints of misconduct will never reach the level of removal from judicial office, it must still be questioned just how the investigation and recommendation/decision process will operate in practice. The sanctions available to the JCC at least now provide a formal mechanism for reprimanding a judge and, in the most serious situations, allow for a recommendation to the Minister for Justice that the judge should be removed from office.

F. Removal from Judicial Office

11–66 Under Article 36 of the Constitution, provision may be made in law for the age of retirement of judges. The retirement age of judges is the same as that of the general population (66); however, judges must retire by the age of 70.[291] Outside normal retirement, judges may be removed from office in only the most exceptional of circumstances. In the seventeenth century, judges held offices "at the will and pleasure" of the monarch. Judges were dismissed for bringing in decisions unfavourable to the King. Later, Parliament defeated the King in the mid-seventeenth century civil war, known as the Glorious Revolution, and Parliament later enacted a provision limiting these powers,[292] which is replicated in Article 35.4.1° of the Constitution. Since the Act of Settlement 1701 in Britain, and since 1782 in Ireland,[293] judges were guaranteed security of judicial office and security of judicial pay for life.

[290] C. Scott, "Regulating Judicial Conduct Effectively" in E. Carolan (ed.), *Judicial Power in Ireland* (Dublin: Institute of Public Administration, 2018), Ch.18.

[291] See generally, ss.47 and 47A of the Courts and Court Officers Act 1995 (s.47A inserted by s.18 of the Court of Appeal Act 2014). It should be noted that for judges appointed prior to 1995, the retirement age is 72. For Circuit Court judges, see Courts (Supplemental Provisions) Act 1961 s.18, and for District Court judges, see Courts (Supplemental Provisions) Act 1961 s.30.

[292] Act of Settlement 1701.

[293] 21 & 22 Geo. III c.11 re-enacted by s.13 of the Supreme Court of Judicature Act (Ireland) 1877. See also, R. Grimes and P. Horgan, *Introduction to Law in the Republic of Ireland* (Dublin: Wolfhound Press, 1982), p.134.

11–67 Article 35.4.1° provides:

> "A judge of the Supreme Court, the Court of Appeal or the High Court shall not be removed from office except for stated misbehaviour or incapacity, and then only upon resolutions passed by Dáil Éireann and Seanad Éireann calling for his removal."

Circuit Court[294] and District Court judges[295] enjoy the same protection, albeit this being granted by legislation rather than the Constitution.[296] To date, no judge in Ireland has been removed for "stated misbehaviour" or "incapacity" under the Constitution, neither phrase being defined in the Constitution or in legislation. A majority of votes by the Oireachtas would be required to remove a judge for stated misbehaviour or incapacity. The Supreme Court in *Curtin v Dáil Éireann* emphasised that any such removal via a resolution must not be "an irrational or irresponsible" abuse of power by the Oireachtas. The Oireachtas must not act in "bad faith", such as a reaction to an unpopular judicial decision.[297] Fair procedures should be observed, requiring members of the Oireachtas to come to a personal decision, whereby the party whip cannot be applied, and where members of the Oireachtas would not make public comments on how they would vote.[298]

11–68 The Houses of the Oireachtas (Inquiries, Privileges and Procedures) Act 2013 establishes what is to occur in the Houses of the Oireachtas where an investigation is taking place on the removal of a sitting judge from office.[299] If a judge challenged their removal, it would be likely that all the Oireachtas Committee could do would be to record and report evidence for the benefit of the Houses of the Oireachtas.[300] The Supreme Court decision in *Kerins v McGuinness*[301] may also be instructive. Albeit not examining Article 35.4.1°, it was held that it

294 Courts of Justice Act 1924 s.39.

295 Courts of Justice (District Court) Act 1946 s.20.

296 See Courts (Supplemental Provisions) Act 1961 s.49 (Circuit Court) and Courts (Supplemental Provisions) Act 1961 s.38 (District Court).

297 [2006] 2 I.R. 556 at 627.

298 *Maguire v Ardagh* [2002] 1 I.R. 385 at 656.

299 Section 9 of the Houses of the Oireachtas (Inquiries, Privileges and Procedures) Act 2013, as amended by s.72 of the Court of Appeal Act 2014.

300 Houses of the Oireachtas (Inquiries, Privileges and Procedures) Act 2013 s.9(2)(a) and (b).

301 [2019] IESC 11 at para.11(2).

is a requirement for any Oireachtas Committee to act strictly within their powers and to observe procedural fairness and natural justice. It would then be for a majority of members of the Dáil and the Seanad to exercise their powers under Article 35.4.1° of the Constitution, and if a resolution is passed in both Houses, for the President to remove the judge from office. In light of *O'Brien v Clerk of Dáil Éireann*, any "utterances" made in the Houses of the Oireachtas by parliamentarians on a resolution to remove a judge for stated misbehaviour or incapacity would not, in and of themselves, be a matter subject to judicial review.[302] Clarke C.J., delivering judgment for the Supreme Court in *O'Brien*, emphasised that "matters which are immune from review by the courts are questions which relate indirectly or collaterally to utterances made in the Houses."[303] If the resolutions are passed, then the Taoiseach informs the President, and the President "shall" remove the judge from office.[304] While no judge has ever been removed from office under Article 35.4.1°, there have been occasions where there had at least been some potential for this process to have been engaged. We now turn to consider these, under the headings of criminal conviction, accusations of criminality, and where there was public and political disquiet regarding the conduct of judges. It is to the credit of the overall quality of those who have been appointed as judges that, despite the historical flaws in our judicial appointments system, there have been so few cases.

1. Criminal Conviction

11–69 In November 2012, Judge Heather Perrin[305] was convicted before the Dublin Circuit Criminal Court of deception, in trying to bequeath half of an elderly man's estate to her own children. The then Minister for

[302] Article 15.12 of the Constitution provides that "[a]ll official reports and publications of the Oireachtas or of either House thereof and utterances made in either House wherever published shall be privileged." See *O'Brien v Clerk of Dáil Éireann* [2019] IESC 12.

[303] [2019] IESC 12 at para.11.5.

[304] Article 35.4.2° and 35.4.3° of the Constitution.

[305] See generally, "Man never agreed to leave half of his estate to judge's children, court hears", *Irish Times*, 13 November 2012; F. Gartland, "Judge found guilty of deceiving elderly man over his will", *Irish Times*, 21 November 2012; F. Gartland, "Impeachment process: first judge convicted of serious crime", *Irish Times*, 21 November 2012; Statement of Minister Alan Shatter, "Resignation of Judge Heather Perrin", Department of Justice and Equality, 27 November 2011; Statement of Minister Alan Shatter, "Conviction of former District Judge Heather Perrin", Department of Justice and Equality, 28 November 2011.

Justice, Alan Shatter, indicated after the guilty verdict that impeachment would ensue. However, Perrin resigned.[306] In December 2023, Judge Gerard O'Brien of the Circuit Court was found guilty of attempted rape and sexual assault.[307] On 5 January 2024, Judge O'Brien resigned.[308] In May 2024, O'Brien was sentenced to four years imprisonment. Had neither former judge resigned, it would have been likely that Article 35.4.1° would have been deployed.

2. Accusations of Criminality

11–70 In November 2002, Judge Brian Curtin[309] was charged with possession of child pornography. This charge was ultimately dismissed in April 2004, due to a legally defective search warrant.[310] On 3 June 2004, the then Minister for Justice, Michael McDowell, in the Dáil, and leader of the Seanad, Mary O'Rourke, laid down motions for the removal of Judge Curtin from office.[311] A number of legislative changes were made, including ensuring that Committee members or Judge Curtin would not be criminally liable for possession of child pornography relating to the investigation.[312] Other legislative measures were introduced to make Judge Curtin compellable before the Joint Oireachtas Committee that had been charged with taking evidence on issues relating to the discovery of child pornography on Judge Curtin's personal computer.[313] Judge Curtin

[306] Subsequently, Mrs Perrin was convicted of another offence relating to the conduct of her solicitors practice and was jailed for a term of two years, to run concurrently with the November 2012 sentence. See: "Ex-judge has two years added to term but will not serve added time", *Irish Times*, 14 March 2013.

[307] O. O'Donnell, "Gerard O'Brien: From role model to disgraced former judge", *RTÉ News*, 1 June 2024.

[308] D. MacRedmond, "McEntee confirms resignation of Judge Gerard O'Brien following sexual assault conviction", *TheJournal.ie*, 6 January 2024.

[309] See *Report of the Joint Oireachtas Committee on Article 35.4.1° of the Constitution and section 39 of the Courts of Justice Act 1924* (14 November 2006), and L. Cahillane, "Judicial Discipline: Where Do We Stand? A Consideration of the Curtin Case" (2009) 27 *Irish Law Times* 26.

[310] RTÉ News, "Trial of Judge Curtin Collapses", 26 April 2004.

[311] *Report of the Joint Oireachtas Committee on Article 35.4.1° of the Constitution and section 39 of the Courts of Justice Act 1924* (14 November 2006), paras 1–5.

[312] Child Trafficking and Pornography (Amendment) Act 2004 s.1.

[313] Section 3A of the Committees of the Houses of the Oireachtas (Compellability, Privileges and Immunities of Witnesses) Act 1997, as inserted by the Committees of the Houses of the Oireachtas (Compellability, Privileges and Immunities of Witnesses) (Amendment) Act 2004. See Appendix 1 of the *Report of the Joint Oireachtas Committee on Article 35.4.1° of the Constitution and section 39 of the Courts of Justice Act 1924* (14 November 2006).

challenged the work of the Joint Oireachtas Committee on a number of grounds, including on the basis of the separation of powers, the power of the Committee to compel him to appear before it, and the use of illegally obtained evidence for purposes other than the criminal trial.[314]

11–71 The Supreme Court, upholding the decision of the High Court, dismissed Judge Curtin's challenge to the constitutionality of the amending legislation and the procedures of the Committee. Keane C.J., delivering judgment of the court, noted that while Article 35.4.1° of the Constitution was silent on the process that the Oireachtas could use to make a decision to remove a judge, "[t]he Constitution is clear. A judge may be removed from office only by means of a resolution of both Houses and by no other means whatever."[315] After this decision and prior to the re-commencement of the Committee hearings, on 13 November 2006, Judge Curtin resigned.[316] This negated the need for any resolution of the Dáil and Seanad to remove Curtin from office.

3. Public and Political Disquiet

11–72 Public discussion surrounding removal of judges from office is rare. On only two occasions has there been significant political, media and public interest in this issue.

(a) Sheedy affair

11–73 In October 1997, Phillip Sheedy[317] was convicted of causing the death of Anne Ryan, while intoxicated. Sheedy was sentenced to four years imprisonment. In October 1998, Judge Hugh O'Flaherty met Sheedy's sister while out walking and a discussion took place on the sentencing of Sheedy. O'Flaherty J. suggested that, based on a previous

314 *Curtin v Dáil Éireann* [2006] 2 I.R. 556. For a full examination of the arguments put forward by Judge Curtin, see [2006] 2 I.R. 556 at 602–608.

315 *Curtin v Dáil Éireann* [2006] 2 I.R. 556 at 626.

316 *Report of the Joint Oireachtas Committee on Article 35.4.1° of the Constitution and section 39 of the Courts of Justice Act 1924* (14 November 2006), pp.2–4.

317 For a more detailed examination of all the key facts and dates, and sequence of events, see, L. Hamilton, *Report on the Role of the Judiciary* (14 April 1999); Department of Justice, Equality and Law Reform, *Report Arising from the Early Release from Prison of Phillip Sheedy* (20 April 1999); Chief State Solicitor's Office, *Report on the involvement of the Chief State Solicitor's Office in relation to the case of the DPP-v-Sheedy* (23 April 1999). See also, R. Byrne, P. McCutcheon, L. Cahillane and E. Roche-Cagney, *Byrne and McCutcheon on the Irish Legal System*, 7th edn (Dublin: Bloomsbury Professional, 2020), paras 4-145–4-158.

case over which he had presided in the Court of Criminal Appeal, *DPP v McDonald*,[318] Sheedy may benefit from a reduced sentence. Shortly after this conversation, O'Flaherty J. contacted the County Registrar, Michael Quinlan, to see if there was a process at the Circuit Court level to have Sheedy's case relisted and his sentencing reopened. A series of events then occurred whereby Sheedy's new solicitor was contacted by Quinlan and asked if he would like to relist the case for reconsideration of the sentence. At all times, it was stated that it would be for the sitting Circuit Court judge to decide whether this would be possible, and if the term of imprisonment would be reduced. The original sentencing judge, Judge Matthews, was not available so Judge Cyril Kelly, who had originally heard the case but did not pass sentence in the case, was to hear the relisted case in November 1998. On the day of the hearing, the Chief State Solicitor's Office was informed that the case was number 19 on the list of cases. The case subsequently came before Judge Kelly as case number 9. Therefore, the Chief State Solicitor's Office was not present.[319] Before any arguments could be heard by Judge Kelly, he suspended the remainder of Sheedy's sentence, stating that he had read the psychology report (which had been before the original sentencing judge, Judge Matthews). After this hearing, Judge Kelly asked Sheedy's solicitors to place an updated psychology report on the court file. Post this hearing date, Judge Kelly was appointed to the High Court. In the meantime, the Director of Public Prosecutions sought to quash Judge Kelly's order for release. However, Sheedy consented to the quashing of this order and was returned to prison.

11–74 Once this series of events became known, there was significant public concern with the actions of all judges and the country registrar involved in this case.[320] The case almost brought down the Fianna Fáil and Progressive Democrats coalition after it emerged that the then Taoiseach, Bertie Ahern, had made representations on behalf of Sheedy.[321] Subsequently, O'Flaherty J., Judge Kelly (then of the High

[318] This decision was an ex tempore judgment delivered by O'Flaherty J. in the Court of Criminal Appeal on 29 July 1998.

[319] Chief State Solicitor's Office, *Report on the involvement of the Chief State Solicitor's Office in relation to the case of the DPP-v-Sheedy* (23 April 1999), paras 10–12.

[320] For a selection of comment, see B. Dowling, "Sheedy political fallout rekindles controversy", *Irish Independent*, 27 April 1999, p.8, and G. Kerrigan, "Now answer the questions Cyril", *Sunday Independent*, 25 June 2001, p.72.

[321] RTÉ News, "Taoiseach denies concealing role in Sheedy affair", 2 May 1999; G.

Court) and County Registrar Quinlan resigned.[322] It seemed likely that if moves had been made to impeach both judges before Dáil Éireann, the impeachment would have succeeded. However, the resignations ensured that no such vote would take place.[323] In light of the Sheedy affair, the Government drafted the Twenty-second Amendment of the Constitution Bill. This Bill would have provided for constitutional recognition of an investigatory procedure for judges in office, as well as permitting "provision to be made in law" for the establishment of a body to investigate judges in office who "engaged in conduct constituting misbehaviour or were affected by incapacity".[324] This body was to be composed mainly of judges and "one or more persons who are not judges or former judges".[325] In addition, further particulars were set down on how an impeachment motion should be investigated by either the Dáil or any other body appointed by the Dáil, including a right for the judge under threat of impeachment to have the right to appear and be represented at any such hearing. However, the Twenty-second Amendment was never put before the people, due to opposition concerns with the structure and wording of the amendment.[326]

11–75 Subsequent to the resignation of the judges involved in the Sheedy affair, the Oireachtas passed legislation protecting the pension entitlements of former judges O'Flaherty and Kelly, along with the county registrar.[327] A challenge to this legislation was deemed "frivolous and vexatious" by the High Court and the Supreme Court.[328] O'Flaherty was subsequently nominated for appointment as vice-president of the European Investment Bank; however, he subsequently withdrew from this contest, causing some political turmoil.[329] O'Flaherty J. was

McKenna, "Apology ends the standoff", *Irish Independent*, 5 May 1999, p.11; RTÉ News, "Taoiseach denies improper actions in Sheedy affair", 5 May 1999.

322 "Resignation statement of Mr. Justice Hugh O'Flaherty", *Irish Times*, 17 April 1999; "Mr. Justice Cyril Kelly's statement", *Irish Times*, 21 April 1999; K. Humphries, "Two judges, registrar resign following Chief Justice's report", *Irish Times*, 24 April 1999.

323 M.M. Tynan, "Dáil may impeach judges if they refuse to resign", *Irish Times*, 17 April 1999.

324 Proposed Article 35.4.1°.

325 Proposed Article 35.4.5°.

326 See also Ch.3, para.3–84.

327 Courts (Supplemental Provisions) (Amendment) Act 1999.

328 *Farley v Ireland* [2000] 5 JIC 2602.

329 G. Kennedy, "Major drop-in support for FF, FG", *Irish Times*, 16 June 2000; D. Coghlan, "Government stands over O'Flaherty nomination", *Irish Times*, 28 August 2000; F. O'Toole, "Historic defeat for cronyism as Hugh O'Flaherty bows out", *Irish Times*, 20 September 2000.

subsequently appointed to the Arbitration Board for the gardaí with little or no fuss in 2007,[330] and was appointed to the Civil Service Arbitration Board in 2011.[331]

(b) "Golf-gate"

11–76 On 5 November 2022, the then Chief Justice Frank Clarke wrote to Mr Justice Séamus Woulfe, stating that it was his view and the unanimous view of all other members of the Supreme Court that "[y]ou should resign".[332] On 9 November 2022, Woulfe J. replied: "I have come to the conclusion that I should not resign." Woulfe J. continues to be a member of the Supreme Court. So how did a situation come about where the Chief Justice believed a recently appointed judge of the Supreme Court should resign? The answer to this lies in the actions and reactions of Woulfe J. to a public scandal commonly known as "Golf-gate".

11–77 To summarise, Woulfe J., a sitting Supreme Court judge, attended a golf event hosted by the Oireachtas Golf Society during the Covid-19 Pandemic.[333] The Golf Society was made up of mainly former, but some current, members of the Oireachtas. Given that Woulfe J., prior to his appointment to the Supreme Court, was Attorney General, it is hardly surprising that he socialised with those who work or worked in the Oireachtas. Woulfe J. had additionally informed the Chief Justice that he would attend the event, although did not mention that there would be a dinner. The event included an 81-person dinner, more than the 50 persons legally permitted to be in a room together at that time. However, the organisers stated that there were in fact two rooms, and a partition was removed for speeches. The day before the event, the Government announced that the maximum number of persons permitted at events

330 M. Brennan, "Resigned judge brought back", *Irish Independent*, 12 July 2007.

331 Department of Public Expenditure and Reform, Written Answers, Question 29, *Dáil Éireann Debate*, 3 July 2012.

332 RTÉ News, "Letters between Chief Justice and Seamus Woulfe", 10 November 2022.

333 For a detailed exploration of "Golf-gate" from socio-legal and political perspectives, see L. Cahillane and D. Kenny, "The Séamus Woulfe controversy and the deficiencies in Ireland's judicial appointments process" (2023) 74(1) *Northern Ireland Legal Quarterly* 22; L. Cahillane and D. Kenny, "Lessons from Ireland's 2020 judicial conduct controversy" (2022) 51(1–2) *Common Law World Review* 24; and C. Casey and E. Daly, "Political Constitutionalism under a Culture of Legalism: Case Studies from Ireland" (2021) 17(2) *European Constitutional Law Review* 202.

like this would be six; however, this announcement was not given legal effect for several days afterwards. Once this event was reported in the media, a government minister resigned, several politicians lost the party whip, and it played a part in the resignation of the then EU Commissioner for Trade. The 2019 Act had not yet been commenced, so a non-statutory review by former Chief Justice, Ms Justice Susan Denham, ensued aimed at resolving whether Woulfe J. should have attended the golf event (yes), the post-golf dinner (no), whether any Covid-related legal obligations were breached (no), and in effect should Woulfe J. resign (no).[334]

11–78 Denham C.J. in September 2022 concluded that Woulfe J.'s resignation would be "unjust and disproportionate".[335] The finding that Woulfe J. should not have attended the dinner (but could have attended the golf) due to issues of judicial propriety is rather illogical. The distinction between why one was proper but not the other is difficult to understand. Both involved engagement with current Oireachtas deputies. Denham C.J. did note that as a new judge of the Supreme Court, Woulfe J. did not benefit from an induction programme, and there were no guidelines or rules on judicial conduct. It was when the transcript of Woulfe J.'s meetings with Denham C.J. were released that further controversy ensued.[336] Woulfe J. expressed concern that his golf handicap could have gone down due to Covid and so he was very pleased to receive an invitation.[337] Earlier in the interview, Woulfe J. bizarrely stated he was

> "... appalled at the kind of media treatment of the [golf] society event and ... it's presented, in some way it's like a Ku Klux Klan now, because on that day and both times there was a friendly social atmosphere."[338]

---

334 Ms Justice Susan Denham, *Report* (Denham Report), available at: *https://judicialcouncil.ie/assets/uploads/documents/report-1-10-20.pdf.* For a discussion on law-making during Covid-19, see Ch.2, Box 2.2.

335 Denham Report, p.28.

336 C. Casey and E. Daly, "Political Constitutionalism under a Culture of Legalism: Case Studies from Ireland" (2021) 17(2) *European Constitutional Law Review* 202 at 204–207.

337 Transcript, Denham C.J and Woulfe J., p.53, available at: *https://judicialcouncil.ie/assets/uploads/documents/Appendix%20D%20Transcript%208th%20September%202020.pdf.*

338 Transcript, Denham C.J. and Woulfe J., p.47. Woulfe J. offers further criticism of the media "lies" at p.108.

Woulfe J. was aghast at the lack of "fair procedures" that seemingly the media and politicians owed him.[339] He expressed his amazement that as a former Attorney General and sitting Supreme Court judge, he was regarded as "part of the elite".[340] The tone-deafness of this and other comments Woulfe J. made only added to the deep concerns regarding his suitability for office. As stated in *Curtin*, "judges themselves [must] behave in conformity with the highest standards of behaviour, both personally and professionally."[341]

11–79 Due to illness, Woulfe J. was unable to meet Clarke C.J. until November 2022. Clarke C.J. made it clear that all members of the Supreme Court believed it would be appropriate for him to resign. Clarke C.J. stated that if he had the power to, he would have reprimanded Woulfe J. Woulfe J. stated that he would not resign but accepted the reprimand and agreed that he would not be allocated cases until February 2023. Woulfe J. also donated his salary for this time period to a nominated charity.[342] Ultimately, while there were government and political discussions on whether Woulfe J. would be impeached, the matter was left to rest.[343] Cahillane and Kenny argue:

> "This is a borderline case ... it is clearly not outside the constitutional standard, and if the Oireachtas determined in good faith that these actions ... constituted misbehaviour, this might well be within the constitutional standard."[344]

This then raises the thorny issue of who exactly should be the arbiter of what is or is not stated misbehaviour. Under the Constitution, this is for the legislature to determine. Apparently the threshold was not reached in this case, despite politicians from across the political spectrum expressing deep concerns regarding the actions of Woulfe J. and how he responded to this entire issue, seeking to blame everybody but himself.[345]

---

339 Transcript, Denham C.J. and Woulfe J., p.110.
340 Transcript, Denham C.J. and Woulfe J., p.110.
341 *Curtin v Dáil Éireann* [2006] 2 I.R. 556 at 618.
342 RTÉ News, "Letters between Chief Justice and Séamus Woulfe", 10 November 2022.
343 See C. Casey and E. Daly, "Political Constitutionalism under a Culture of Legalism: Case Studies from Ireland" (2021) 17(2) *European Constitutional Law Review* 202 at 206–207, and L. Cahillane and D. Kenny, "Lessons from Ireland's 2020 judicial conduct controversy" (2022) 51(1–2) *Common Law World Review* 24 at 38–39.
344 L. Cahillane and D. Kenny, "Lessons from Ireland's 2020 judicial conduct controversy" (2022) 51(1–2) *Common Law World Review* 24 at 39.
345 See para.11–78.

G. Conclusion

11–80 The judiciary play a fundamental role within the Irish legal system. In any modern liberal democratic society, judges have the unenviable task of resolving disputes. Whether that dispute impacts on a small or large number of persons, the Irish legal system is premised on the notion that a judge will determine issues fairly and impartially and without fear or favour. This judicial ideal does not mean that decisions of judges should be immune from critique or criticism. Throughout the chapter, we have highlighted the (healthy) tension that exists between the three branches of government. The judiciary is but one government branch, albeit the branch that determines matters of legal interpretation of laws passed by the Oireachtas, or acts done by the Executive. There must be some final arbiter on all issues of law, with that being tasked ultimately to the Supreme Court. In the last decade or so, tensions between judges and other branches of government on judicial pay and pensions, judicial appointments and judicial conduct came to the fore.

11–81 The issuing of judgments is not a value-free nor ideologically-free zone. Depending on the decision a court must make, a judge's ideology may impact on the outcome, albeit this is really only likely in constitutional decisions, or other decisions whereby there may be more than one reasonable decision that could be reached. We do not use the word "ideology" here in any sort of derogatory manner; we all have ideologies that shape our engagement with, understanding of, and our place in society. The Northern/Irish Feminist Judgments Project was also an expression of ideology. We think that the Project provides us with a lens through which we can understand judging and the process of judgment. In this chapter, we have only focused on aspects of social class and gender; however, other identities and experiences could also impact on judging and judgment. Law is not a science nor is there any scientific method to judging.

11–82 Protestations that there were barely any links between politics and judicial appointment were, in our analysis, not based on reality.[346] The new manner of appointment of judges, at least in part, is aimed at taking

[346] See D. O'Donnell, "Some reflections on the independence of the judiciary in Ireland" in E. Carolan (ed.), *Judicial Power in Ireland* (Dublin: Institute of Public Administration, 2018) p.255.

political preference out of judicial appointment decisions. It remains to be seen how precisely the judicial appointments system under the 2023 Act will operate in practice. The 2023 Act withstood an Article 26 reference. The 2023 Act does limit governmental choice in who to appoint. Of course, as we have indicated above, nothing prevents the government from rejecting these recommendations from the Judicial Appointments Commission. Although, were this to become routine, it would likely result in political and public disquiet. Constitutionally, the government may not appoint persons recommended by the Commission. This is because, ultimately, it is the Constitution that provides the government with the power to "advise" the President on who is to be appointed as a judge.

11–83 The new judicial conduct and reprimand system under the 2019 Act is still in its infancy. It could prove to be a useful regulatory system for identifying and, where appropriate, sanctioning a judge for their misconduct. Only time will tell if the system is delivering on what it is designed to achieve. As we have outlined, the system and process for coming to a determination that misconduct has occurred is somewhat laborious. This, however, needs to be understood in terms of the importance of judicial independence. No judge has ever been removed from judicial office under Article 35.4.1°. This in fact should not be surprising. In any event, in some of the situations we discussed above, most judges against whom Article 35.4.1° could have been deployed, ultimately resigned. "Golf-gate", which did not result in the resignation or removal of Woulfe J., was an extraordinary and public spat amongst judges, in which the Oireachtas ultimately did not want to get involved.

Chapter 12

Legal Practitioners in Ireland

> "Contemporary lawyer images are not just about winning landmark cases, championing unpopular causes, representing the unrepresented ... [T]hey are also about earning money, acquiring material possessions, about following the agenda of a large organisation ... and about choosing among morally ambiguous and difficult alternatives."
>
> C.J. Menkel Meadow, "Can a Law Teacher Avoid Teaching Legal Ethics?" (1991) 41 *Journal of Legal Education* 3 at 4–5.

In this chapter we:

- consider the role of the legal professions in Ireland;
- review the role and functions of the Legal Services Regulatory Authority, the Law Society of Ireland and the Bar of Ireland;
- explore the role of solicitors and barristers, including an overview of the qualification criteria to act as a solicitor or barrister in Ireland. This will include an overview of proposals for significant reforms in this area;
- understand the complaints and disciplinary mechanisms for solicitors and barristers in Ireland under the Legal Services Regulation Act 2015;
- briefly sketch the roles of the Attorney General, Chief State Solicitor and Director of Public Prosecutions in the Irish legal system.

A. Introduction

12–01 With law deemed necessary to regulate public and private conduct, it is unsurprising that there would be a need for persons qualified in the language, interpretation and practice of law. A "legal practitioner" in Ireland is defined as "a person who is a practising solicitor or a practising barrister and a reference to a solicitor includes a reference to a firm of solicitors."[1] Legal practitioners in Ireland are solicitors who have practising certificates[2] and barristers entered onto the Roll of Practising Barristers.[3] The Law Society of Ireland, the Honorable Society of King's Inns, the Bar of Ireland (previously called the Bar Council), and the Legal Services Regulatory Authority (LSRA) all have significant roles in select fields relating to the admission, education and representation of the professions; the practice of law; and the discipline of legal practitioners in Ireland. Legal practitioners have obligations to act with integrity, probity and trustworthiness.[4] A long-running discussion amongst public commentators and legislators is the continued distinction between solicitors and barristers in the Irish legal system. As with many other aspects of our legal system, this distinction was transplanted from the English legal system, and was subsequently maintained upon independence.[5] The Irish system of a bifurcated legal profession can be viewed as "an ideology imposed on British colonies".[6] Ireland has maintained this split in legal professions, whilst other former British colonies have not, most notably India and New Zealand. The LSRA recommended in 2020 that there should not be a unification of the two legal professions at this time.[7] The rationale was based on the coming into force of various reforms to legal services, and the LSRA wished to review the impact of these changes prior to revisiting the question of (re)unification of the legal professions. The LSRA is due to review this position again in 2025.

1 Legal Services Regulation Act 2015 s.2.

2 Legal Services Regulation Act 2015 s.2 and Solicitors Act 1954 s.9, as amended by s.65 of the Solicitors (Amendment) Act 1994.

3 Legal Services Regulation Act 2015 s.133.

4 See *Carroll v Law Society of Ireland* [2016] IESC 49 at paras 69–70 and *Law Society of Ireland v Herlihy* [2017] IEHC 122 at paras 36–41.

5 For Ireland, see generally, C. Kenny, *King's Inns and the Kingdom of Ireland: The Irish 'inn of court' 1541–1800* (Dublin: Irish Academic Press, 1992), and E. Hall and D. Hogan, *Portrait of a Profession: The Law Society of Ireland 1852 to 2002* (Dublin: Four Courts Press, 2002). For a brief discussion of the emergence of solicitors and barristers in England (and Wales), see D. Kelly, *Slapper and Kelly's English Legal System*, 20th edn (Oxon: Routledge, 2024), pp.650–659.

6 A. Boon, "Introduction" in A. Boon (ed.), *International Perspectives on the Regulation of Lawyers and Legal Services* (Oxford: Hart, 2017), p.6.

7 LSRA, *Greater than the sum of its parts? Consideration of Unification of the Solicitors' Profession and the Barristers' Profession* (Dublin: LSRA, 2020). See, in particular, the Executive Summary, pp.3–10, for an outline of why the LSRA did not make a recommendation to the Minister for Justice to unify the professions.

12-02 Law for many people has an aura of mystique—the language of law can be complex, convoluted and at times indecipherable.[8] As Bingham notes, "few people are competent to assess the strength of a claim and conduct litigation without professional help".[9] The insistence on ignorance of the law as no excuse is faced with the reality that most people are not versed in law to the extent that legal practitioners will be. Therefore, there will be a reliance on legal practitioners, who will require payment. Legal practice is, first and foremost, a business. Outside criminal legal aid and civil legal aid,[10] seeking legal advice, legal services and/or legal representation is costly. At the same time, viewing law as exclusively a marketable commodity[11] fails to capture significant aspects of legal practice in Ireland and elsewhere.

12-03 While some have noted sceptically that "[t]he model of altruistic lawyer seeking to promote the public good—a bastion against individualism and materialism—is likely to produce a hollow laugh in most circles",[12] the role of the legal profession in protecting the rule of law in a state should not be under-emphasised.[13] Often, the first task of despots and dictators is to fundamentally alter the rule of law, with lawyers and an independent judiciary the first line of attack. Yet, even within democratic states, lawyers can be targeted for supporting politically and socially unpopular groups who utilise law to hold legislators and government to account. The Council of Bars and Law Societies in Europe (CCBE) documented threats and attacks on lawyers based on who they represented, including politicians seeking to undermine the work and role of lawyers.[14] Willing clients, with the assistance and support of

8 See Ch.4, Section H.

9 T. Bingham, *The Rule of Law* (London: Penguin, 2011), pp.86–87.

10 See Ch.13.

11 L. Bugatti, "Towards a New Era for the Legal Profession" (2019) 27(1) *European Review of Private Law* 83 at 89.

12 J. Herring, *Legal Ethics*, 2nd edn (Oxford: OUP, 2017), p.50.

13 See Ch.2 and L.S. Terry, S. Mark and T. Gordan, "Adopting Regulatory Objectives for the Legal Profession" (2012) 80(6) *Fordham Law Review* 2685.

14 See CCBE, *Contribution for the 2023 Rule of Law Report*, 16 February 2023, and CCBE, *Contribution for the 2024 Rule of Law Report*, 14 February 2024. In terms of attacks on lawyers by government in Ireland, see United Nations press release, "Committee against Torture hears response of Ireland", 24 May 2011 (stating that lawyers representing international protection applicants were involved in a "legal racket"). The Minister for Health stated that lawyers were "licking their lips" when a few firms offered to represent persons whose sensitive medical information was made publicly available; see P. Ryan, "Health Minister Stephen Donnelly criticised for lawyers 'licking their lips' comment after HSE cyber attack", *Irish Independent*, 21 March 2021.

activist lawyers, have challenged Irish laws in several (arguably) publicly unpopular causes. Select examples of public interest lawyering in Ireland[15] include the decriminalisation of sexual relations between gay men;[16] the easing of restrictions on the right to access contraception;[17] the rights of women to access abortion;[18] and the rights of members of the Traveller community in the field of housing.[19] Throughout this book, we have already seen examples of public interest lawyering, including the rights of children with disabilities to a needs assessment (Ch.2) and the rights of persons seeking international protection (Ch.6 and Ch.8). Lawyering in the public interest is of course a political act—seeking to achieve an outcome that may, for example, enhance the rights of a politically weak societal group. This does, of course, cause some tension, given that lawyers' focus should be on the interests of their client, rather than wider societal injustices. For others, public interest lawyering evidences the political nature of law in and of itself.[20]

12–04 This view of the legal profession as indispensable to uphold the rule of law, and thus needing to be (somewhat) independent of state control and regulation, resulted in resistance from the legal profession as

15 For a comprehensive exploration of public interest lawyering in Ireland, see G. Whyte, *Social Inclusion and the Irish Legal System: Public Interest Law in Ireland*, 2nd edn (Dublin: IPA, 2015) and I. Bacik and M. Rogan, *Legal Cases that Changed Ireland* (Dublin: Clarus Press, 2016). The Public Interest Law Alliance (PILA), a project of FLAC, seeks to build momentum for public interest lawyering in Ireland; see *www.pila.ie*. See also, Ch.8, Section C.2.

16 Compare *Norris v Attorney General* [1984] 1 I.R. 36 with the decision of the European Court of Human Rights in *Norris v Ireland* (1991) 13 E.H.R.R. 186. The Criminal Law (Sexual Offences) Act 1993 ultimately abolished any rule of law that criminalised anal sex (otherwise known as buggery).

17 *McGee v Attorney General* [1974] I.R. 284.

18 See *Attorney General v X* [1992] 1 I.R. 1, and more recently, *A, B and C v Ireland* (2011) 53 E.H.R.R. 13, which was partly responsible (along with the death of Savita Halappanavar) for the introduction of the Protection of Life During Pregnancy Act 2013. See further, C. O'Sullivan, J. Schweppe and E. Spain, "Article 40.3.3° and the Protection of Life During Pregnancy Bill 2013: The Impetus for, and Process of, Legislative Change" (2013) 3(3) *Irish Journal of Legal Studies* 1. With the removal of Article 40.3.3° of the Irish Constitution, access to abortion services is now regulated by the Health (Regulation of Termination of Pregnancy) Act 2018.

19 See, in particular, *Clare County Council v McDonagh* [2022] IESC 2 and *O'Donnell v South Dublin County Council* [2015] IESC 28, the latter discussed in L. Thornton, "Socio-Economic Rights and Ireland" in S. Egan (ed.), *International Human Rights: Perspectives from Ireland* (Dublin: Bloomsbury Professional, 2015), pp.178–180.

20 A. Batesman, "Lawyers Who Want to Make the World a Better Place: Scheingold and Sarat's Something to Believe In" in D. Newman (ed), *Leading Works on the Legal Profession* (London: Routledge, 2023), Ch.15.

the Irish State moved away from the historical position where the legal profession was self-regulated towards more State regulation.[21] The legal profession in Ireland had been self-regulated to some degree since the late 1400s.[22] The Honorable Society of King's Inns was the body established for the education of barristers in Ireland in 1541.[23] Many centuries ago, the legal profession was a more unified body containing barristers as advocates and also draftsmen and attorneys.[24] Due to differences in work practices, the work of the legal professions separated over time. In the nineteenth century, there was a complete separation of the professions of barristers and solicitors. The Law Society of Ireland was founded in 1830 and incorporated by royal charter in 1852.[25] Post independence, the solicitor's profession was extensively self-regulated, albeit with legislative underpinning. The catalyst for the shift to State regulation was the onset of the 2008 recession and Ireland's entry to and exit from a structured economic adjustment (bailout) programme between 2010 and 2013. Although the Troika (European Central Bank, European Commission and the International Monetary Fund) exited the country without any substantial reform of the legal professions,[26] the passage of the Legal Services Regulation Act 2015 (the "2015 Act") ultimately emerged from their requirements to bail out the Irish State. There was much resistance from the Law Society and Bar of Ireland to the 2015 Act, with the then-President of the Law Society, Donald Binchy, arguing that the Irish legal system would be comparable to legal systems in China, Gambia and Iran if the 2011 Bill, as initiated, became law.[27]

---

[21] A. Boon and N. Semple, "Still Special After All These Years? Fundamental Questions in Legal Services Regulation" in R. Abel et al (eds), *Lawyers in 21st-Century Societies* (Oxford: Hart, 2022), p.2.

[22] See G. Hogan and W.N. Osborough (eds), *Studies in Irish Legal History* (Dublin: Four Courts Press, 1999), Ch.7.

[23] See generally, C. Kenny, *King's Inns and the Kingdom of Ireland: The Irish 'inn of court' 1541–1800* (Dublin: Irish Academic Press, 1992).

[24] R. Grimes and P. Horgan, *Introduction to Law in the Republic of Ireland: Its History, Principles, Administration and Substance* (Dublin: Wolfhound Press, 1981), pp.46–48 and 137–140.

[25] R. Grimes and P. Horgan, *Introduction to Law in the Republic of Ireland: Its History, Principles, Administration and Substance* (Dublin: Wolfhound Press, 1981), pp.46–48.

[26] See further, M. Hosier, "The Legal Profession in Troikaland: Before and After the Irish Bailout" (2015) 22(2) *International Journal of the Legal Profession* 193; A. Cahill, "IMF denies undermining Irish legal system", *Irish Examiner*, 26 March 2014; I. Yates, "Farewell again to the Troika and to our chances of the real reform we desperately need", *Irish Independent*, 20 November 2014.

[27] D. Binchy, "A Call to Action" (2011) 105(10) *Law Society Gazette* 1.

Hosier rightly described the reaction of the Irish legal professions to changes that came about as a result of the 2015 Act as "hysterical".[28]

B. Legal Services and Legal Practitioners

1. The Legal Services Regulation Act 2015 and the Legal Services Regulatory Authority

12–05 Recommendations for reform of the legal profession and legal services go back decades, and in all likelihood only came about due to external pressures.[29] Rights of audience for solicitors before the superior courts, optional wearing of wigs for barristers, case management issues and limited direct access for certain groups to barristers, have all been introduced. The abolition of the Irish language competency requirement,[30] permitting barristers to become solicitors,[31] and reform of practices that did not permit the switching of barristers in a case until the previous barrister had been paid are further reforms.[32] The core function of the LSRA is to "regulate the provision of legal services by legal practitioners and shall ensure the maintenance and improvement of standards in the provision of such services".[33] Section 13(4) of the 2015 Act provides that, in carrying out its functions, the LSRA must have regard to protecting and promoting the public interest, promoting competition and "encouraging an independent, strong and effective legal profession".[34] In addition, the LSRA must promote and maintain adherence amongst the legal profession to "professional principles".[35]

---

[28] M. Hosier, "Éire: The Lawyers of the Celtic Phoenix" in A. Boon (ed.), *International Perspectives on the Regulation of Lawyers and Legal Services* (Oxford: Hart, 2017), p.71. For an outline of these concerns, see *Fundamentals of the Irish Legal System*, 1st edn (Dublin: Round Hall, 2016), paras 12–21 to 12–22 and 12–25 to 12–26.

[29] See para.12–04. For an outline of critiques of legal services regulation in Ireland before the 2015 Act, see *Fundamentals of the Irish Legal System*, 1st edn (Dublin: Round Hall, 2016), paras 12–21 to 12–22. For a more recent evaluation, see M. Hosier, "Éire: The Lawyers of the Celtic Phoenix" in A. Boon (ed.), *International Perspectives on the Regulation of Lawyers and Legal Services* (Oxford: Hart, 2017), p.71. Not all aspects of the 2015 Act can be considered; for the role of the Legal Costs Adjudicator, see ss.138–167 of the 2015 Act.

[30] Legal Practitioners (Irish Language) Act 2009.

[31] See "Essentials of Legal Practice—The Inaugural Course" (2008) 102(8) *Law Society Gazette* 49 and *www.lawsociety.ie*.

[32] See Bar of Ireland, *Code of Conduct for the Bar of Ireland* (2024), paras 12.1–12.7.

[33] Section 13(1) of the 2015 Act.

[34] Section 13(4)(e) of the 2015 Act.

[35] Section 13(4)(f) of the 2015 Act.

These professional principles include independence and integrity of legal practitioners, legal practitioners acting in their clients' best interests and maintaining their confidentiality, and legal practitioners maintaining proper standards of work with regard to court appearances, as an officer of the court.[36]

12–06 Day-to-day functioning of the LSRA is in the hands of a chief executive[37] and other staff who are obliged to carry out the LSRA's statutory duties.[38] The LSRA has a supervisory responsibility ensuring legal practitioners' compliance with their statutory obligations under the 2015 Act, as well as other legal obligations upon the legal practitioner.[39] Section 13(2) of the 2015 Act enumerates a number of non-exhaustive functions vested in the LSRA, including the ability, or the obligation, to review and make recommendations as to educational standards and practices for legal professionals;[40] regulate the inspection of legal practitioners; professional indemnity insurance requirements for members of the legal profession; receive and investigate complaints;[41] advise the Minister for Justice on issues within the LSRA's remit; and promote public awareness of the functions of the LSRA. In line with its legislative obligations, and following public consultation, the LSRA has produced reports on professional legal education for those wishing to qualify as solicitors and barristers.[42] As noted previously, it recommended to the Minister for Justice in 2020 that there not be a fusion of the legal professions at that time.[43] In 2023, the LSRA recommended that a profession for conveyancers should not be created at present.[44]

---

36 Section 13(5) of the 2015 Act.

37 For a review of the role and powers of the chief executive, see s.24 of the 2015 Act.

38 Under s.25 of the 2015 Act, the LSRA can appoint staff (subject to agreement of the Minister for Public Expenditure and Reform). Section 26 of the 2015 Act permits the LSRA "to give appropriately qualified staff of the Law Society or the Bar Council an option to transfer to the Authority".

39 See generally ss.37–44 of the 2015 Act. Under s.44 of the 2015 Act, information or documents obtained during the inspection may be admitted in evidence under any complaints procedure or disciplinary hearing conducted under the 2015 Act.

40 See Box 12.2.

41 This is discussed in detail in Section D below.

42 Section 34(1)(a) of the 2015 Act. This report under s.34(3) of the 2015 Act must include recommendations, amongst other issues, as regards the appropriate standards of education and training for legal practitioner qualifications, and minimisation of duplication where a person has already undertaken aspects of a third-level law degree; see para.12–26 and Box 12.2 for a discussion of this report.

43 See para.12–01; this power is exercised pursuant to s.34(1)(b) and s.34(4) of the 2015 Act.

44 Section 34(1)(c) and (d) of the 2015 Act. As regards the creation of a profession for

12–07 When legislation on legal services regulation was initially introduced as the Legal Services Regulation Bill 2011,[45] the Government had significant discretion in determining who was to be appointed to the LSRA. This was subject to criticism from the Law Society of Ireland,[46] the Bar of Ireland,[47] and the Free Legal Advice Centres (FLAC).[48] The then Minister for Justice and Equality, Alan Shatter, committed to ensuring that the lay members of the LSRA would be appointed in a transparent manner, which would not give rise to accusations of ministerial interference.[49] These changes are evidenced in the 2015 Act. In line with the 2015 Act, the LSRA is composed of 11 Authority members, at least four women and at least four men.[50] The majority of the LSRA members are required to be laypersons.[51] The Law Society can nominate two solicitors,[52] the Bar Council and King's Inns may nominate one person each,[53] and the Legal Aid Board may nominate a solicitor.[54] The lay members of the LSRA are nominated by a number of bodies, who each may make one nomination. The bodies capable of making appointments

conveyancers, see s.34(5) of the 2015 Act. In 2023, the LSRA issued this report to the Minister for Justice: LSRA, *Consideration of a New Profession of Conveyancer: Authority Report to the Minister for Justice* (November 2023). Ultimately, the LSRA proposed a series of reforms regarding technological innovations, price transparency and consumer awareness campaigns on conveyancing services offered by solicitors. The LSRA did not recommend, at this stage, the introduction of a separate profession of conveyancer.

45 For a review of the many concerns of various bodies in relation to the now 2015 Act, see *Fundamentals of the Irish Legal System*, 1st edn (Dublin: Round Hall, 2016), paras 12–21 to 12–26. See cl.8(2)(a) of the 2011 Bill (as initiated).

46 Further concerns about appointment processes and the make-up of the LSRA were voiced by the Law Society; see D. Binchy, "The Good, the Bad and the Ugly" (2011) 105(10) *Law Society Gazette* 8. See also comments of the (then) Irish Human Rights Commission, *Submission on the Legal Services Regulation Bill 2011* (February 2012), pp.11–13.

47 Bar Council, *Initial Submission on the Legal Services Regulation Bill 2011* (December 2011), p.25. See now s.10(3) of the 2015 Act.

48 FLAC, *Submission on the Legal Services Regulation Bill 2011* (February 2012), p.9.

49 A. Shatter, "Speech on Legal Services Regulation Bill 2011", Law Society Annual Conference 2012. See also, C. Coulter, "Legal Bill amendments considered", *Irish Times*, 14 April 2012.

50 The 2015 Act also regulates the terms of appointment (s.10(1) and (2)); the ability of re-appointment for a maximum of eight years (s.10(5)); and disqualification and removal from the LSRA (ss.11–12 respectively).

51 Section 9(4)(a) of the 2015 Act. A "lay person" is defined in s.2 of the 2015 Act as a person who is not a practising solicitor or barrister, including a person who may have previously practised law as a solicitor or barrister, but who has not done so for a period of at least five years.

52 Section 9(4)(e) of the 2015 Act.

53 Section 9(4)(b) and (d) of the 2015 Act.

54 Section 9(4)(c) of the 2015 Act.

are: the Citizens Information Board, the Higher Education Authority, the Competition and Consumer Protection Commission, the Irish Human Rights and Equality Commission, the Institute of Legal Costs Accountants and the Consumers' Association of Ireland.[55] In making nominations, these bodies have to take account of criteria within s.9(3) of the 2015 Act,[56] which sets down the different skills and competencies desired for the LSRA. These skills and competencies include, amongst others, knowledge of financial management, the maintenance of professional standards and dealing with complaints, the legal profession and legal education, competition law and policy, and the needs of consumers of legal services.[57] Once the nominations of the various bodies are made, then these nominees are appointed as members of the LSRA by the Government, with a resolution approving these appointments having passed in Dáil Éireann and Seanad Éireann.[58] The Government chooses the lay member who will be chairperson of the LSRA.[59] One of the key functions of the LSRA is the oversight of legal practitioners, in particular as regards complaints against legal practitioners.

12–08 Semple provides a clear, if reductive, description of the tasks of legal practitioners: "advice about the law, preparation of instruments with legal effect, representation of another before a court or tribunal."[60] Kruse's conception adds to this understanding further, better embracing the more nuanced role of a lawyer. For Kruse, "lawyering" involves: (a) the identification of laws/rules at issue; (b) putting these laws/rules into their societal context; and (c) lawyers operating within the constraints of these laws/rules, while reflecting on wider societal implications for actions.[61] While not fully reflective of all legal work or services, these summations of the lawyer role indicate some significant aspects of legal work with which practitioners in Ireland will engage. There are

55 Section 9(4)(a) of the 2015 Act. See also s.9(5)(a) of the 2015 Act which directs nominating bodies to nominate a primary candidate of one sex, and a substitute candidate of the other sex. As regards the Law Society, one of its nominees must be female and one of its nominees must be male.

56 This obligation upon the nominating bodies is set out under s.9(5)(b) of the 2015 Act.

57 Section 9(3)(a) of the 2015 Act.

58 Section 9(2)(a) of the 2015 Act.

59 Section 9(2)(b) of the 2015 Act. For a list of current members of the LSRA, see: *https://www.lsra.ie/about-us/authority-members/*.

60 N. Semple, *Legal Services Regulation at the Crossroads: Justitia's Legions* (Cheltenham: Edward Elgar, 2015), p.13.

61 K.R. Kruse, "Professional Role and Professional Judgment: Theory and Practice in Legal Ethics" (2011) 9(2) *University of St Thomas Law Journal* 250 at 254.

distinctions in the precise roles of solicitors and barristers in the Irish legal system, which will be highlighted below. At the end of 2023, there were 11,871 solicitors holding practising certificates.[62] Since 2015, the majority of practising solicitors have been female.[63] This trend continued in 2023, where a majority (6,320) of solicitors were women.[64] The majority of trainee solicitors have been women for quite some time.[65] Of the 3,051 practising barristers at the end of 2023, just over 36 per cent were female. Just 21 per cent of all senior counsel barristers are women.[66]

Box 12.1: Over 100 Years of Women in Legal Practice

It is now over 100 years since women have been permitted to practise as solicitors and barristers. Both the Bar of Ireland and the Law Society marked this centenary-milestone. Providing biographies of some of the early female entrants, their fascinating projects highlight just how far women's representation in law has come.[67] Research has, however, indicated that gender inequality continues to exist. Professor Margaret Thornton notes the inflexibility of (some areas of) legal practice wherein women often take prime responsibility for caring within families.[68] It is worth providing some background to how women were excluded from the legal professions. This highlights something we have explored in other parts of this text: how societal norms impact upon the supposed neutrality of law.

---

62 Law Society of Ireland, *Annual Report and Accounts 2023/2024*, p.8.

63 T. Kelly, "Profession's Perfect Parity" (2015) 109(1) *Law Society Gazette* 20–21.

64 Law Society of Ireland, *Annual Report and Accounts 2023/2024*, p.9. Thirty-seven solicitors did not declare their gender.

65 LSRA, *Pathways to the Professions: Annual Report on Admission Policies of Legal Professions 2023* (Dublin: LSRA, 2024), p.51.

66 LSRA, *Pathways to the Professions: Annual Report on Admission Policies of Legal Professions 2023* (Dublin: LSRA, 2024), p.3; Bar of Ireland, "Mark of Legal Excellence: 27 Members Called to the Inner Bar", 10 October 2024.

67 Bar of Ireland, *Trailblazers: 1919–2019: 100 Years of Women at The Bar* (2021). In 2023, the Law Society published biographies of the first 100 women who practised as solicitors in Ireland; see Law Society of Ireland, *Celebrating a Century of Equal Opportunity Legislation: The first 100 women solicitors* (Dublin: Law Society, 2023). Law Society of Ireland, *Annual Report and Accounts 2022/2023*, p.26.

68 Although Professor Thornton's work is focusing on Australia, her arguments reflect key worldwide debates on women in legal practice; see M. Thornton, "Who Cares? The Conundrum for Gender Equality in Legal Practice" (2020) 43(4) *University of New South Wales Law Journal* 1473. For an Irish focus on gender and the legal profession, see I. Bacik, C. Costello and E. Drew, *Gender Injustice: Feminising the Legal Professions?* (Dublin: Trinity College Dublin Law School, 2003) and for a discussion of gender at the Bar, see N. Howlin, *Barristers in Ireland: An Evolving Profession Since 1921* (Dublin: Four Courts Press, 2023), pp.74–75 and Ch.9.

Women were formally excluded from the legal professions until 1919 in Ireland.[69] Attempts made by women through the courts to be admitted to the roll of solicitors and to the Bar prior to 1919 had failed.

Ms Bebb[70] had applied to the Law Society of England and Wales to be permitted to sit preliminary examinations so that she may (eventually) practise as a solicitor. Women had not previously been admitted as solicitors, so the Law Society refused Ms Bebb's application. Section 48 of the Solicitors Act 1843 (the "1843 Act") provided that "every Word importing the Masculine Gender only shall extend and be applied to a Female as well as a Male".

Counsel for Bebb argued that s.48 of the 1843 Act,[71] properly construed, meant that unmarried women suffered no disability under the common law to be admitted to the Law Society and act as solicitors. In response, the Law Society argued that the 1843 Act did not confer any new rights on women and, in line with practice "for hundreds of years", women suffered a disability at common law and were unable to act as solicitors before the court.[72]

Joyce J. dismissed this action at first instance but permitted an appeal to the Chancery Division of the Court of Appeal. In upholding Joyce J.'s decision, the Court of Appeal held that as no other woman had applied to become, or been admitted as, a solicitor (or previously as an attorney at law), the court was "loath to depart" from this practice.[73] Cozens-Hardy M.R. stated that if changes were to be made to this common law practice disbarring women from even being permitted to apply to become solicitors, it would be for Parliament to rectify.[74] All judges referred to the views and opinions of Lord Coke[75] from three centuries previously in coming to this decision.[76] Coke was of the view that "[f]ems ne poient estre attorneyes".[77]

---

69 Sex Disqualification (Removal) Act 1919.

70 For a fascinating background and subsequent study of Gwyneth Bebb's action and a feminist perspective on law, gender and the "legal story", see R. Auchmuty, "Whatever Happened to Miss Bebb? *Bebb v The Law Society* and Women's Legal History" (2011) 31(2) *Legal Studies* 199.

71 Along with s.1 of the Interpretation Act 1889, which provided that, in interpreting statutes, words importing the masculine gender also apply to those of the female gender (unless, of course, a particular statute states otherwise): *Bebb v Law Society* [1914] 1 Ch. 286 at 289.

72 [1914] 1 Ch. 286 at 289 and 291.

73 [1914] 1 Ch. 286 at 294 per Cozens-Hardy M.R.

74 [1914] 1 Ch. 286 at 294 per Cozens-Hardy M.R.

75 A.D. Boyer, *Sir Edward Coke and the Elizabethan Age* (Stanford: Stanford University Press, 2003).

76 [1914] 1 Ch. 286 at 293–294 per Cozens-Hardy M.R.; 295–296 per Swinfen Eady L.J.; 297–298 per Phillimore L.J.

77 [1914] 1 Ch. 286 at 296. Translates as "women cannot be lawyers".

This case is interesting from a number of perspectives. From a literalist approach[78] to the legislation, the arguments of Bebb appeared most convincing. However, straightforward legal argument based on the interpretation of statutory provisions was no match for ingrained prejudices of law towards women in the early decades of the twentieth century. The case also highlights the very limited argument that was being made by Bebb, described in the case report as a "spinster", whose legal team went to great pains not to question the continuing legal disabilities (including exclusion from the profession) that would apply to married women,[79] or to women seeking to become barristers.[80]

Eventually, the Sex Disqualification (Removal) Act 1919 (the "1919 Act") was passed by the British Parliament and removed the common law legal disqualification of women as solicitors and barristers. While the Law Society of England and Wales sought to adopt measures before this to permit women to practise as solicitors,[81] the Bar Council had still sought to exclude women.[82] In Ireland, prior to the coming into force of the 1919 Act, a challenge took place before the then-Irish Court of Appeal which had to determine whether a woman could act as a Clerk of Petty Sessions.[83] The Clerk of Petty Sessions would have been, in some ways, similar to the now District Court clerk, i.e. recording decisions of the District Court judge and other related functions.[84] The Irish Court of Appeal decided, by a 2:1 majority, that because she was a woman, Frost could not act as a Clerk of Petty Sessions. Lord Chancellor Shandon (who by the time of judgment had resigned as Lord Chancellor, but with agreement of the parties provided a judgment), would have held in favour of Frost. The case then went to the House of Lords.[85] By the time the case came for hearing, the 1919 Act had become law. Lord Birkenhead in the House of Lords, during an adjournment, noted that since the 1919 Act was now in force, Frost was no longer under a legal disability from acting as Clerk of Petty Sessions.[86] During the

78 See Ch.4, Section D.

79 [1914] 1 Ch. 286 at 289. See also the discussion of married women acting as solicitors by Phillimore L.J.: [1914] 1 Ch. 286 at 299.

80 [1914] 1 Ch. 286 at 291.

81 R. Auchmuty, "Whatever Happened to Miss Bebb? *Bebb v The Law Society* and Women's Legal History" (2011) 31(2) *Legal Studies* 199 at 221–222.

82 R. Auchmuty, "Whatever Happened to Miss Bebb? *Bebb v The Law Society* and Women's Legal History" (2011) 31(2) *Legal Studies* 199 at 222.

83 *Frost v The King* [1919] 1 I.R. 81. For a review and discussion of this litigation, see P. de Bhaldraithe, "Sixmilebridge Clerks of Petty Sessions", available at: *http://www.maths.tcd.ie/~pwaldron/frost.pdf.*

84 Court Officers Act 1926 s.46.

85 P. de Bhaldraithe, "Sixmilebridge Clerks of Petty Sessions", pp.4–5. See also, K. Donovan, "An unlikely pioneer", *Irish Times*, 27 April 2000, p.13.

86 P. de Bhaldraithe, "Sixmilebridge Clerks of Petty Sessions", p.5.

adjournment, representations were made, and Frost's appointment was approved retrospectively. De Bhaldraithe notes that Frost continued as Clerk of Petty Sessions in Sixmilebridge, Co. Clare, until her retirement in 1922.[87] Christian Kyle and Averil Deverell were the first women called to the Bar in 1921,[88] while Mary Dorothea Heron became the first female solicitor in Ireland in 1923.[89]

2. Solicitors

12–09 Solicitors have a variety of functions within the legal system, and in engaging in these forms of legal practice, ethical behaviour and professionalism are core unifying features.[90] Solicitors can be used in a variety of non-contentious issues, such as the provision of general legal advice to the public, purchase of land (conveyancing), mergers and acquisitions of companies, and the creation of a will. Solicitors can provide advice to individuals about the legal rights (or wrongs) of a given issue, be it related to criminal law, personal injuries, health and safety law, immigration law, commercial law or company law. The day-to-day work of a solicitor will be varied, depending on the type of practice they engage in, be it as a sole practitioner or within a community law centre, medium-size firm or a large internationally focused legal practice. As of the end of 2023, there are 3,139 solicitors firms,[91] employing 11,871 solicitors.[92] 3,019 solicitors work in firms that employ 1 to 10 solicitors, while 5,227 solicitors work in 120 law firms that employ between 11 and 400 solicitors.[93] Over the last number of years, there have been some changes to the business model of solicitors. Solicitors may now form a Limited Liability Partnership (LLP) which ensures solicitors will not be

[87] P. de Bhaldraithe, "Sixmilebridge Clerks of Petty Sessions", pp.5–6.

[88] I. Bacik, C. Costello and E. Drew, *Gender Injustice: Feminising the Legal Professions?* (Dublin: Trinity College Dublin Law School, 2003), p.56. For a discussion of gender at the Bar, see N. Howlin, *Barristers in Ireland: An Evolving Profession Since 1921* (Dublin: Four Courts Press, 2023), pp.74–75 and Ch. 9.

[89] I. Bacik, C. Costello and E. Drew, *Gender Injustice: Feminising the Legal Professions?* (Dublin: Trinity College Dublin Law School, 2003), p.55. The Law Society of Ireland in 2023 published biographies of the first 100 women who practised law in Ireland; see Law Society of Ireland, *Celebrating a Century of Equal Opportunity Legislation: The first 100 women solicitors* (Dublin: Law Society, 2023).

[90] D.L. Rhode, "Ethical Perspectives on Legal Practice" (1984–1985) 37(2) *Stanford Law Review* 589; K.R. Kruse, "Professional Role and Professional Judgment: Theory and Practice in Legal Ethics" (2011) 9(2) *University of St Thomas Law Journal* 250.

[91] Law Society of Ireland, *Annual Report and Accounts 2023/2024*, p.9.

[92] Law Society of Ireland, *Annual Report and Accounts 2023/2024*, p.8.

[93] Law Society of Ireland, *Annual Report and Accounts 2023/2024*, p.8.

personally liable for any debts or liabilities.[94] Other forms of business models that are permitted under the 2015 Act include Legal Partnerships (LPs) and the yet-to-be-introduced Multi-Disciplinary Practices (MDPs).[95]

12–10 Solicitors also perform a litigation function, where they may prepare a case and sometimes represent a client before the courts and administrative tribunals. With the introduction of s.17 of the Courts Act 1970, solicitors have rights of audience before all courts in Ireland. In general, in issues relating to minor criminal offences, public house licensing issues and other minor legal disputes before the District Court and the Circuit Court, solicitors often receive direct instruction from their clients and advocate for their clients before these courts. Despite solicitors having a general right of audience before the superior courts (the High Court, Court of Appeal and Supreme Court), the majority of client advocacy before these courts tends to be carried out by barristers. Since 2020, solicitors in Ireland can apply to be recognised as Senior Counsel. This is discussed below.[96] Globalisation[97] too will continue to impact the role, regulation, education and societal status of solicitors in Ireland and wider afield.[98] Globalisation already impacts the method of delivery of legal services to the public and business. The extent of this impact remains much debated.[99] Whether globalisation or generative artificial intelligence will impact the future role and work of lawyers remains to be seen.[100]

---

[94] For an overview of the Limited Liability Partnership (LLP), see B.J. Doherty and P. Langan, "Limited Liability Partnerships Insight" (2020) 114(3) *Law Society Gazette* 48–51 and F. Meenan, *Employment Law*, 2nd edn (Dublin: Round Hall, 2023), paras 2–147 to 2–153. A full list of LLPs is available on the LSRA's website: *https://www.lsra.ie/for-law-professionals/limited-liability-partnerships/.*

[95] For LPs, see Legal Services Regulation Act 2015 s.100, Legal Services Regulation Act 2015 (Legal Partnerships) Regulations 2024 (S.I. No. 489 of 2024) and LSRA, "About legal partnerships", available at: *https://www.lsra.ie/for-law-professionals/about-legal-partnerships/.* For MDPs, these have not yet been commenced. See Legal Services Regulation Act 2015 s.102, which has yet to be commenced at the time of writing. The LSRA provided recommendations to the Minister for Justice on MDPs in September 2017; see LSRA, *Multi-Disciplinary Practices: Further Report to the Minister for Justice and Equality* (2017).

[96] See paras 12–17 to 12–18.

[97] There is much dispute as to what precisely is meant by the term "globalisation"; however, in essence, globalisation can be understood as a more interconnected world that impacts all facets of life.

[98] J. Faulconbridge and D. Muzio "Legal Education, Globalization, and Cultures of Professional Practice" (2009) 21 *Georgetown Journal of Legal Ethics* 1335.

[99] R. Susskind, *Tomorrow's Lawyers: An Introduction to Your Future* (Oxford: OUP, 2013).

[100] See, for example, D. Hunter, "The Death of the Legal Profession and the Future of Law"

12–11 For solicitors, the Law Society of Ireland[101] exercises a number of functions under the Solicitors Acts.[102] The Solicitors Acts are supplemented by the Law Society's own rules and regulations. The Law Society maintains the roll of solicitors who are entitled to practise in the State.[103] The Law Society's current functions include responsibility for the qualifying criteria and education of solicitors,[104] certain disciplinary matters regarding client accounts,[105] and other matters relating to a solicitor's practice.[106] The Law Society is also the representative body for solicitors in Ireland. The Law Society is currently governed by a President, a Council, a Director General and a directorate that provides support and assistance in the realisation of the Law Society's functions.[107] The President is often viewed as the public face of the Law Society for their term of office. The President will represent the views of the Law Society in the media, in conferences and other fora, and will represent the views of solicitors on issues that may affect the role of solicitors in the Irish legal system. The Council comprises a number of nominated solicitors, past presidents and elected solicitors who carry

(2020) 43(4) *University of New South Wales Law Journal* 1199 and K. Benyekhlef and J. Zhu, "The Judicial System and the Work of Judges and Lawyers in the Application of Law and Sanctions Assisted by AI" in M. Garcia-Murillo, I. MacInnes and A. Renda (eds), *Handbook of Artificial Intelligence at Work: Interconnections and Policy Implications* (Cheltenham: Edward Elgar, 2024), Ch.13. For a discussion of generative artificial intelligence, see Ch.16.

[101] The Law Society of Ireland was founded as the Incorporated Law Society of Ireland in 1830, received a Royal Charter in 1852, and was given control of the education and training of solicitors in Ireland under the Solicitors (Ireland) Act 1898.

[102] The Solicitors Acts have been amended on a number of occasions. The primary legislation is the Solicitors Act 1954. This has been amended by the Solicitors (Amendment) Act 1960, the Solicitors (Amendment) Act 1994, the Solicitors (Amendment) Act 2002 and s.58 of the Civil Law (Miscellaneous Provisions) Act 2011 and Pt 13 of the Legal Services Regulation Act 2015.

[103] Section 9 of the Solicitors Act 1954, as amended by s.65 of the Solicitors (Amendment) Act 1994.

[104] Part IV of the Solicitors Act 1954 (as amended).

[105] Section 51(6) of the 2015 Act and Solicitors Accounts Regulations 2023 (S.I. No. 118 of 2023). For an explanation of this, see, e.g. Chairperson of the Solicitors Disciplinary Tribunal, *Report 2021*, pp.4–7. For a review of the powers of the Solicitors Disciplinary Tribunal, see *Fundamentals of the Irish Legal System*, 1st edn (Dublin: Round Hall, 2016), para.12–29.

[106] Such as payment of fees to the Law Society of Ireland (s.66 of the Solicitors (Amendment) Act 1994) and restriction on the withdrawal of a solicitor from a case (s.77 of the Solicitors (Amendment) Act 1994).

[107] It is for the Law Society of Ireland to manage its representative functions and a full explanation of internal governance can be found on *www.lawsociety.ie*. The Law Society's annual report provides a comprehensive overview of the role and tasks conducted each year. Annual reports can be accessed on *www.lawsociety.ie*.

out a number of statutory and non-statutory functions "for the better rule and government of the Society, and for the better direction and management of the concerns thereof".[108]

12–12 The functions of the Council relate to the protection of solicitors' clients, admission and education of those wishing to become solicitors, along with a wide range of other tasks. A number of committees have been established by the Council to advise and make recommendations to the Council on best practice in relation to a number of areas as diverse as client complaints, human rights, family law, professional indemnity insurance, and arbitration and mediation. The Director General of the Law Society, as well as having some statutory functions under the Solicitors Acts, is the full-time chief executive of the Law Society. Like the President, the chief executive is often in the media discussing issues relevant to the solicitor profession. The Director General of the Law Society is responsible for the day-to-day running of the Law Society and is assisted by a number of administrative departments.

3. Barristers

12–13 The role of a barrister is that of an advocate before the courts in criminal and civil proceedings, mainly before the Circuit Court, High Court, Court of Appeal and Supreme Court. However, many junior barristers also conduct work in criminal matters in the District Court.[109] In court, when acting as an advocate, some barristers choose to wear a horsehair wig. However, since 1995 the wearing of the wig is not mandatory.[110] A barrister's work does not solely relate to litigation. Much of their time is spent on drafting pleadings, delivering opinions to solicitors on legal issues, and providing ad hoc expert advice to solicitors. Solicitors will often contact barristers who may have specialised knowledge in a number of legal fields, who can advise the solicitor on how to proceed.

12–14 Barristers cannot be approached directly by members of the public to represent them. In *Bond v Dunne*, the defendants wished to

[108] Law Society of Ireland, Charter of 1852; see *www.lawsociety.ie*.
[109] For a greater expansion on the role of junior barristers in Ireland, see S. Reid and A. Grealish, *The Devil's Handbook*, 3rd edn (2023).
[110] Courts and Court Officers Act 1995 s.49.

instruct a barrister directly, without going through a solicitor.[111] This barrister was not a member of the Bar of Ireland, but a member of an organisation called the Association of Barristers in Ireland. The barrister argued that there was no legal basis for preventing individuals from instructing them directly.[112] Gilligan J. dismissed the argument that the High Court had an inherent jurisdiction to permit an individual to instruct a barrister directly. The basis for this dismissal relied on the structure of the Irish courts system, whereby solicitors had to complete certain acts that barristers could not, e.g. file documents, issue notice of motions, etc.[113] Accordingly, barristers must await instructions from a solicitor to represent a client. Since 2019, barristers who are employees of an organisation can provide legal services to their employer,[114] including appearing in court on behalf of their employer.[115] Prior to September 2024, direct professional access to barristers was limited to non-contentious advice to certain pre-approved registered organisations.[116] Since September 2024, barristers may provide non-contentious legal services to any person, without needing a solicitor to instruct the barrister.[117]

12–15 In September 2024, the LSRA issued a code of conduct for barristers pursuant to s.22 of the 2015 Act. This code outlines the legal knowledge, legal skills, professional competencies and personal attributes required of practising barristers. The Code requires barristers to act independently, with integrity, and in the interests of their clients.[118] The Code notes barristers' obligations in the event of a conflict of interest, how barristers are to conduct themselves vis-à-vis solicitors and clients, as well as the conduct that a barrister must comply with in a criminal trial. The Code does not replace the codes of conduct/required

[111] [2017] IEHC 646 at paras 1–6.

[112] [2017] IEHC 646 at paras 12–14.

[113] [2017] IEHC 646 at paras 23–30. See also, *Houston v Barniville* [2019] IEHC 601.

[114] Section 212 of the 2015 Act and Legal Services Regulation Act 2015 (Commencement of Certain Provisions) (No. 2) Order 2019 (S.I. No. 502 of 2019).

[115] Section 212(2) of the 2015 Act prohibits a professional body from adopting any code of practice that would seek to limit this right.

[116] The current list of organisations is available at: *https://www.lawlibrary.ie/legal-services/dpa/list-of-approved-dpa-bodies/*.

[117] Whether a barrister chooses to provide direct professional access or not is their decision. A list of barristers who do provide direct access is available at: *https://www.lawlibrary.ie/find-a-barrister/*. See Legal Services Regulation Act 2015 (Commencement of Certain Provisions) Order 2024 (S.I. No. 477 of 2024), art.3(c) and (d).

[118] LSRA, *Code of Conduct for Practising Barristers*, 26 September 2024, paras 3.1–3.8.

competencies issued by the Bar of Ireland or King's Inns.[119] However, where there is a conflict between the codes, the LSRA's code applies.

12–16 The Honorable Society of King's Inns was founded in the sixteenth century during the reign of Henry VIII and is the oldest legal educational establishment on the island of Ireland. Initially solicitors and barristers were a unified profession, but over time different attorneys' roles had diverged to such an extent that the profession split into solicitors and barristers.[120] The functions of King's Inns are not set down by legislation. King's Inns operates as a voluntary society, headed by Benchers of the Honorable Society of King's Inns. Benchers consist of all High Court, Court of Appeal and Supreme Court judges and elected barristers. King's Inns is mainly responsible for the education of prospective barristers in Ireland. Once admitted as a barrister and after completing one year of devilling,[121] an individual joins the Bar of Ireland (also known as the Law Library) if they so wish.[122] The Bar of Ireland, which is located in Dublin, has rules that practising barristers in Ireland must follow.[123] Barristers who pay requisite library fees will have access to office space and legal texts either near the Four Courts or adjacent to the main courthouse in Cork. Previously, the Bar of Ireland had a role in disciplining barristers.[124] As is explored in detail below, the Bar of Ireland no longer has a role in barrister discipline.

4. Senior Counsel: Barristers and Solicitors

12–17 The separation of barristers into Junior Counsel and Senior Counsel (SC) is long-standing. For barristers who are Senior Counsel, they become members of the Inner Bar. The SC designation is seen as a mark of distinction, a recognition of the abilities of a barrister. Previously the SC designation was restricted to barristers only,[125] but was extended

[119] Bar of Ireland, *Code of Conduct for the Bar of Ireland*, as adopted on 22 July 2024, and King's Inns, *Statement of the Required Competencies of a Barrister*, 11 November 2020.

[120] W.N. Osborough, *Studies in Irish Legal History* (Dublin: Four Courts Press,1999), Ch.7.

[121] See para.12–25.

[122] Bar of Ireland, *Constitution of the General Council of the Bar of Ireland*, as adopted on 25 July 2022.

[123] Bar of Ireland, *Code of Conduct for the Bar of Ireland*, as adopted on 22 July 2024.

[124] For a review of this, see *Fundamentals of the Irish Legal System*, 1st edn (Dublin: Round Hall, 2016), paras 12-30 to 12-33.

[125] For further background, see *Fundamentals of the Irish Legal System*, 1st edn (Dublin: Round Hall, 2016), paras 12–09 to 12–11.

to solicitors by the 2015 Act. Focusing on barristers first, prior to Irish independence, the power to grant an individual the status of King's Counsel (the colonial precursor to SC) was on the basis of the royal prerogative.[126] Post independence, the stated basis for the appointment of SC was s.2 of the Executive Powers (Consequential Provisions) Act 1937.[127] Under this old system, individual barristers were appointed as SC on the basis of a recommendation by an advisory committee, whose membership included the Chief Justice, the Attorney General and the Chairman of the Bar Council.[128] This committee issued patents of precedence. The 2015 Act brought about fundamental reforms relating to the issuance of patents of precedence. Since 2020, solicitors, as well as barristers, may be issued with patents of precedence, and may then use SC after their name.[129] Most persons recommended for patents of precedence continue to be (male) barristers.[130] An advisory committee recommends to Government whether to grant patents of precedence.[131] The Government then grants patents of precedence on the basis of the advisory committee's recommendation.[132]

12–18 The advisory committee consists of the Chief Justice, the President of the High Court, the Attorney General, the President of the Law Society and the Chairperson of the Bar Council, and a lay member of the LSRA appointed by the Minister for Justice.[133] Section 173 of the 2015 Act provides that the advisory committee has the power to establish criteria for the grant of patents of precedence. Since 2020,

[126] For a more detailed discussion on the non-applicability of this principle in Ireland, see G. Hogan, D.G. Morgan and P. Daly, *Administrative Law in Ireland,* 5th edn (Dublin: Round Hall, 2019), Ch.22. During the reign of Queen Elizabeth II, the title would have been Queen's Counsel (QC). All QCs became King's Counsel upon the accession of King Charles III to the British throne and Commonwealth realms.

[127] 521 *Dáil Debates* Cols 191–192 (13 June 2000).

[128] Special Group on Public Service Numbers and Expenditure Programmes, *Report of the Special Group on Public Service Numbers and Expenditure Programmes, Vol II: Detailed Papers* (Dublin: Department of Finance, 2009), p.209.

[129] Section 171 of the 2015 Act. Section 176 of the 2015 Act also provides that where a barrister had previously been granted the title of Senior Counsel, but may have then become a solicitor, that individual is entitled to use the designation of Senior Counsel.

[130] See the LRSA's annual reports since 2021. The annual reports outline the number of applications received for the grant of patents of precedence, and those they recommend the government to grant.

[131] Section 172 of the 2015 Act.

[132] Section 171(1) of the 2015 Act.

[133] Section 172(2) of the 2015 Act. Appointments are initially for periods "not exceeding 3 years", and persons are eligible for re-appointment. The lay member must continue to be a member of the LSRA if re-appointment occurs.

the LSRA has issued yearly guidance for applicants regarding the grant of a patent of precedence.[134] In making a decision on the grant of a patent of precedence, the advisory committee must be satisfied that the legal practitioner's temperament, professional competency as a legal practitioner, professional independence, tax compliance, and their possession of recognised advocacy skills, specialised litigation practice and/or some specialist knowledge of law, meet the standards to be expected of a SC.[135] The 2015 Act also permits the advisory committee to revoke patents of precedence,[136] where the High Court has directed the LSRA to make an application for a revocation of a patent of precedence.[137] It is for the advisory committee to determine whether it will recommend revocation to the Government.[138] An individual who has their patent of precedence revoked may appeal to the High Court within a specified time period of 30 working days.[139] This process has not yet been utilised.

C. Qualifying as a Legal Practitioner in Ireland

12–19 Only persons who qualify as solicitors or barristers have audience before the Irish courts, other than litigants representing themselves. Since 2019, the LSRA has published annual reports on admissions of persons to King's Inns and the Law Society. The Pathways to the Professions reports provide fascinating statistical insights into who is seeking to qualify as a legal practitioner in any given year.[140] There are different qualification routes in Ireland in order for persons to become solicitors and barristers. Part IV of the Solicitors Act 1954, as amended by Pt V of the Solicitors (Amendment) Act 1994, along with a significant

[134] For the 2024 guidelines, see LSRA, *Guidance for Applicants for the Grant of Patents of Precedence 2024*.

[135] Section 173(2) of the 2015 Act. The LSRA in its Guidance for Applicants for the Grant of Patents of Precedence 2024 provides that in determining whether to grant a patent of precedence, the professional experience, professional independence, integrity and honesty, excellence in advocacy and specialist knowledge in area(s) of law, are considered by the advisory committee.

[136] Section 175(2) of the 2015 Act. This power has not been exercised to date.

[137] Section 85(7)(g) of the 2015 Act.

[138] Section 175(2)(b) of the 2015 Act.

[139] Section 175(9) of the 2015 Act. The High Court will either affirm or revoke the decision of the advisory committee under s.175(10) of the 2015 Act.

[140] The Pathways to the Professions reports can be accessed at *https://www.lsra.ie/*.

number of statutory instruments,[141] establishes the criteria for qualifying as a solicitor in Ireland.

12–20 For applicants without prior legal practice experience, there are four stages of entry into the Law Society for the purpose of undertaking professional education and practice so as to be admitted as a solicitor. Stage one consists of the preliminary examination.[142] This preliminary examination consists of three papers on English, Irish government and politics, and general knowledge. Those with a primary university degree (in any discipline) from Ireland and the United Kingdom are exempt from having to undertake this examination.[143] Graduates from outside Ireland and the UK can also apply for an exemption to the Education Committee of the Law Society of Ireland. Those who are law clerks or legal executives may also apply for an exemption from the preliminary examination on the basis of experience (10 years or more) or a combination of a professional qualification (Diploma in Legal Studies) coupled with five years of on-the-job experience.

12–21 Once a person passes or is exempt from the preliminary exam, they must then complete the Law Society's Final Examination.[144] The Final Examination consists of two stages: Final Examination 1 (FE-1) and the Professional Practice Course (PPC).[145] Prior to 1995, law graduates were exempt from the FE-1.[146] Those law students who commenced their undergraduate degrees from the 1996–1997 academic year onwards have had to complete the FE-1 prior to entry onto the PPC.[147] The FE-1

[141] See generally, the Solicitors Acts 1954 to 1994 (Apprenticeship and Education) Regulations 2001 (S.I. No. 546 of 2001), as amended up to the Solicitors Acts 1954 to 2011 (Apprenticeship and Education) (Amendment) Regulations 2019 (S.I. No. 503 of 2019).

[142] Solicitors Act 1954 s.41, as amended by s.50 of the Solicitors (Amendment) Act 1994.

[143] Solicitors Act 1954 s.41, as amended by s.50 of the Solicitors (Amendment) Act 1994.

[144] Law Society of Ireland, "Summary of regulations and procedures relating to the Final Examination-first part" (January 2020).

[145] Prior to 2023, the PPC course consisted of two stages: PPC-1 and PPC-2. This has now been condensed into one three-semester course; see *Fundamentals of the Irish Legal System*, 1st edn (Dublin: Round Hall, 2016), para.12–15. For a summation of the new PPC, see "Fusion Reaction" (2022) 116(6) *Law Society Gazette* 46–49. For a discussion on the background impetus to these changes, see G. Brennan, "Irish Professional Legal Education" (2020) 54(1) *The Law Teacher* 149–157, in particular at 153.

[146] See *Bloomer v Incorporated Law Society of Ireland* [1995] 3 I.R. 14 (HC); (1997) 6 I.J.E.L. 220 (SC).

[147] *Abrahamson v Law Society of Ireland* [1996] 2 I.R. 403.

currently consists of eight exams in company law, constitutional law, contract law, criminal law, equity, European Union law, the law of real property (land law) and tort law. These exams are usually held twice yearly in March/April and October. The FE-1 syllabus, exam rules and past examination papers are available on the Law Society of Ireland's website.[148] Since January 2020, candidates seeking to sit the FE-1 may sit any number of examinations, subject to completing all examinations within a period of "not more than seven years".[149] Previously, only degree-holders could sit the FE-1;[150] however, any person who proceeds into the second year of their university degree may now sit the FE-1. If the examination is passed, then the result is provisional until the candidate is awarded their degree.[151]

12–22 Once a candidate has passed these eight exams, and if the candidate has a traineeship (apprenticeship) with a practising solicitor[152] of over four years' standing, the candidate will then attend the PPC in Blackhall Place in Dublin.[153] In the past, this was split into PPC-1 and PPC-2. Now a trainee solicitor completes the PPC in one year either in person or as a hybrid offering.[154] The PPC provides trainee solicitors with education in a wide variety of fields, including (but not limited to) conveyancing, land law, trusts, criminal law and procedure, family law, litigation, professional training, court processes and procedures, professional ethics and client counselling. Trainees on this course must also complete certain in-house training with their solicitors' firms for two years in total (this can include some time period prior to official

148 The Law Society website is *www.lawsociety.ie*.

149 Regulation 12 of the Solicitors Acts 1954 to 1994 (Apprenticeship and Education) Regulations 2001 (S.I. No. 546 of 2001), as substituted by reg.4 of the Solicitors Acts 1954 to 2011 (Apprenticeship and Education) (Amendment) Regulations 2019 (S.I. No. 503 of 2019).

150 For a review of past entry requirements, see *Fundamentals of the Irish Legal System*, 1st edn (Dublin: Round Hall, 2016), paras 12–14 to 12–15.

151 Regulation 12A of the Solicitors Acts 1954 to 1994 (Apprenticeship and Education) Regulations 2001 (S.I. No. 546 of 2001), as inserted by reg.5 of the Solicitors Acts 1954 to 2011 (Apprenticeship and Education) (Amendment) Regulations 2019 (S.I. No. 503 of 2019).

152 A solicitor qualified to practise is defined in s.54 of the Solicitors Act 1954, as amended by s.62 of the Solicitors (Amendment) Act 1994.

153 See s.40 of the Solicitors Act 1954, as amended by s.49 of the Solicitors (Amendment) Act 1994, and the Solicitors Acts 1954 to 2011 (Apprenticeship and Education) Regulations 2001–2019.

154 See Law Society of Ireland, Professional Practice Course (PPC) Hybrid, available at: *https://www.lawsociety.ie/education--cpd/Trainees/PPC-Courses/ppc-hybrid.*

entry into the PPC course). Once a trainee has completed the PPC and in-house training, and once their indentures have expired, they can apply for admission to the Law Society of Ireland as a solicitor. The final stage that must be satisfied relates to the candidate being a "fit and proper person" to be admitted as a solicitor. In *Carroll v Law Society of Ireland*,[155] McGuinness J. in the High Court stated that a crucial object and purpose set down by the Oireachtas in the Solicitors Acts was "that persons qualifying to fulfil the crucial role of solicitors in our legal system should not only be academically qualified but should also be persons of integrity, probity and good conduct".[156] Once an individual meets all the requirements, the President of the High Court will then admit the person to the roll of solicitors. This individual can now practise as a solicitor in Ireland.

12–23 Different rules apply for qualified barristers wishing to become solicitors.[157] Section 50 of the Solicitors (Amendment) Act 1994 provides that those holding the Barrister-at-Law degree from King's Inns or those with a "professional qualification prescribed as being equivalent thereto" are also exempt from the FE-1. Those who are qualified lawyers in other European Union Member States[158] or from other jurisdictions have to complete certain examinations known as the Qualified Lawyers Transfer Test.[159] Solicitors from Northern Ireland, England and Wales do not have to complete any such steps and may be added automatically to the roll of solicitors in Ireland.[160]

12–24 Turning to qualification as a barrister, for those applicants with an approved law degree,[161] an entry examination into the Barrister-at-Law

155 [2003] 1 I.R. 284. For a more substantive background to this case, see *Incorporated Law Society of Ireland v Carroll* [1995] 3 I.R. 145.

156 [2003] 1 I.R. 284 at 296.

157 Solicitors (Amendment) Act 1994 s.41.

158 See the European Communities (Freedom to Provide Services) (Lawyers) Regulations 1979 (S.I. No. 58 of 1979); the European Communities (Freedom to Provide Services) (Lawyers) (Amendment) Regulations 1981 (S.I. No. 197 of 1981); and the European Communities (Lawyers' Establishment) Regulations 2003 (S.I. No. 732 of 2003).

159 See, for example, the Solicitors Acts 1954 (Section 44) Regulations 2009 (S.I. No. 35 of 2010), which outline the conditions for certain attorneys/solicitors from other non-European Union jurisdictions to practise as a solicitor in Ireland.

160 Solicitors Act 1954 (Section 44) (Northern Ireland) Order 2020 (S.I. No. 742 of 2020) and Solicitors Act 1954 (Section 44) (England and Wales) Order 2020 (S.I. No. 741 of 2020).

161 King's Inns, *Schedule of Approved Qualifications*, available at: *https://www.kingsinns.ie/education/entrance-examination*; and King's Inns, *Education Rules* (as adopted in June 2021), Part II, rule 4.

degree is held every August. This degree has to include passed subjects in Irish land law (including the law of succession), company law, equity and trusts, law of the European Union, jurisprudence and administrative law. For mature applicants, or for students with an approved non-law degree, King's Inns has a two-year part-time Diploma in Legal Studies, where applicants study a range of legal subjects. Once a student from either of these cohorts successfully completes the Diploma in Legal Studies, they are eligible to sit the entry examination for the Barrister-at-Law degree course.[162] For qualifying applicants, the relevant exams are in contract law, criminal law, Irish constitutional law, the law of tort and the law of evidence.[163] Upon passing the King's Inns entrance examination, students may then be admitted to the Barrister-at-Law degree, which can be taken in one year (full-time) or over two years (part-time). In the degree programme, students undertake a range of subjects and practical exercises on remedies and quantum, legal practice and procedure, legal skills and advocacy, ethics and professional practice, and moots, and are given an opportunity to study a number of specialised areas of law.

12–25 Once a student successfully completes the educational aspect of their degree, they are then called to the Bar by the Chief Justice.[164] Those intending to practise must apply to the LSRA for admission to the roll of practising barristers.[165] If an individual wishes to practise at the Bar, and become a member of the Law Library, then they must undertake at least one year of a pupillage.[166] A pupillage, more commonly called "devilling", is an informal apprenticeship whereby the newly qualified barrister must work, without pay, for a barrister who has been practising for at least seven years. In this time, the devil must assist their master in all facets of their professional practice. Once a devil finishes the apprenticeship period, they may then become a member of the Law Library, receive instructions from solicitors, and be an advocate before any Irish court. Barristers may be self-employed and may form a legal practice, be this

[162] King's Inns, *Education Rules*, Part II, rules 2 and 3.
[163] King's Inns, *Education Rules*, Part III, rule 6.
[164] King's Inns, *Education Rules*, Part I, rule 1.
[165] Section 134 of the 2015 Act, as substituted by s.64 of the Courts and Civil Law (Miscellaneous Provisions) Act 2023. Barristers who decide not to practise are obliged to inform the LSRA of this as soon as possible; see s.135 of the 2015 Act, as amended by s.65 of the Courts and Civil Law (Miscellaneous Provisions) Act 2023.
[166] See further, S. Reid and A. Grealish, *The Devil's Handbook*, 3rd edn (2023).

with other barristers, or between a solicitor and barrister.[167] However, there is no obligation to be a member of the Law Library in order to practise as a barrister, albeit the vast majority of barristers in Ireland are members of the Law Library.

12–26 The LSRA also has the power, after consultation with relevant regulatory bodies and any other persons, to exempt qualified solicitors and barristers from "unnecessary" admission requirements, to enable legal practitioners to move between both branches of the profession, i.e. for a qualified solicitor to become a barrister, and vice versa. This to date has not occurred.[168] Precise regulations will be necessary in order to give effect to this provision, and it does not prevent the LSRA from ordering those seeking to move between the different branches from completing certain educational or examination requirements.[169] The most profound changes may come to the entry requirements for trainee solicitors and barristers, to which we now turn.

Box 12.2: Potential Changes to Professional Legal Education and Training in Ireland

The 2015 Act obliged the LSRA to produce a report on professional legal education for solicitors and barristers as regards the appropriate standards of education and training for legal practitioner qualifications, and to minimise duplication where a person has already undertaken aspects of a third level law degree.[170] A commissioned report by Hook Tangaza, a research consultancy firm, on legal practitioner education and training was published in 2018.[171] This review sought submissions from a wide variety of stakeholders, current providers of education and training, students, universities, the legal sector and others. Subsequent to this independent report, the LSRA produced its recommendations

[167] See para.12–14. See further, Legal Services Regulation Act 2015 (Legal Partnerships) Regulations 2024 (S.I. No. 489 of 2024). These Regulations outline specific requirements to establish a legal partnership. The first Legal Partnership established in Ireland was Simmons & Simmons (Ireland) LLP, operating a solicitor-barrister legal practice.

[168] The concept of "unnecessary" is further defined in s.217(4) of the 2015 Act.

[169] Section 217(2) of the 2015 Act.

[170] Section 34(1)(a) of the 2015 Act. See further particulars that must be considered by the LSRA in s.34(3) of the 2015 Act.

[171] Hook Tangaza, *Review of Legal Practitioner Education and Training* (September 2018) and LSRA, *Report on the Education and Training of Legal Practitioners* (September 2018).

to the Minister for Justice published in November 2020.[172] This *Setting Standards* report made a significant number of reform proposals, including the establishment of a Legal Practitioner Education and Training (LPET) Committee.[173] The establishment of the LPET Committee as part of, but independent from, the LSRA would require legislative amendment to the 2015 Act, which to date has not occurred.[174] Of particular interest is the three core tasks of the proposed LPET Committee.[175] First, establishing a Competency Framework for Legal Practitioners. Second, ensuring that the educational and training roles of the Law Society, King's Inns and new providers map onto the competency framework. Third, removing barriers to education and training, including increasing and promoting diversity in the legal profession. The *Setting Standards* report was only the first step to making recommendations for changes to legal education and training. The *Breaking Down Barriers* report followed in 2024, which sought to provide more detailed recommendations. The *Barriers Report* details pathways to removing the obstacles that exist for those wishing to qualify as a legal practitioner. Of particular note is that there is no proposal to end the FE-1 examinations for solicitors nor the entrance exams for King's Inns.[176] The *Barriers Report* proposes 32 core recommendations. These recommendations are grouped into qualification and information barriers,[177] early career challenges,[178] and diversity and "connections".[179]

---

[172] LSRA, *Setting Standards: Legal Practitioner Education and Training* (September 2020). For background on discussion prior to the publication of this report, see G. Brennan, "Pending Reform of Irish Legal Education" (2020) 54(2) *The Law Teacher* 308–319.

[173] LSRA, *Setting Standards: Legal Practitioner Education and Training* (September 2020), p.87.

[174] The composition of the proposed LPET committee would be a lay member of the LSRA nominated by the Minister for Justice, along with six other members recruited through a public appointments process. The *Setting Standards* report also recommends that all members "should be able to demonstrate independence from all of the providers of legal education and training." See LSRA, *Setting Standards: Legal Practitioner Education and Training* (September 2020), pp.88–89.

[175] The three core tasks are supplemented by other interrelated roles and objectives, including ongoing monitoring of educational and training provision, encouraging innovation within legal practitioner education, and review of education and training by providers on an ongoing basis; see LSRA, *Setting Standards: Legal Practitioner Education and Training* (September 2020), p.88.

[176] LSRA, *Breaking Down Barriers: Addressing the challenges facing early career legal professionals*, January 2024 (*Barriers Report*). The LSRA has also produced an implementation plan: *Breaking Down Barriers: Implementation Plan*, September 2024 (*Implementation Plan*).

[177] *Barriers Report*, pp.3–11.

[178] *Barriers Report*, pp.12–17.

[179] *Barriers Report*, pp.18–20.

(1) Competency Framework for Legal Practitioners. This competency framework, drafted by the LPET Committee, would "define the core knowledge, skills and aptitudes required by competent legal practitioners".[180] This would be a statement of skills and aptitudes expected of competent legal practitioners.

(2) Who should offer professional legal education? Once the competency framework is completed, the LPET committee would then define the competencies for admission to legal practitioner education. Legal practitioner education and training is currently monopolised by the Law Society for solicitors and King's Inns for barristers. The issue of monopoly on professional legal education has been raised for over three decades, with recommendations for reforms that have not been followed through.[181] The *Setting Standards* report recommends that the LPET Committee would review the education and training provision of the Law Society and King's Inns,[182] while also permitting new providers to offer qualification as a solicitor and/or barrister. If new legal practitioner education and training providers were permitted to offer qualification routes, the ability to provide this would be assessed by the LPET Committee. This would include measuring the financial viability of the new provider to offer practitioner education, assessing whether this new offering meets competencies set by the LPET committee, and ensuring that it provides outreach to underrepresented groups and fair and transparent admission requirements.[183] The *Barriers Implementation Plan* does not contain any recommendations regarding the establishment and approval for new providers of education and training for barristers and solicitors. The Plan does indicate that there will be further oversight of the Law Society and King's Inns' educational offerings for those entering the professions.[184]

(3) Removing barriers for entry to legal practitioner education and training. For those who graduate with a law degree from a third level institution, the *Setting Standards* report recommends the removal of entrance examinations in order to enter legal practitioner education

[180] LSRA, *Setting Standards: Legal Practitioner Education and Training* (September 2020), p.91.
[181] LSRA, *Setting Standards: Legal Practitioner Education and Training* (September 2020), p.84.
[182] LSRA, *Setting Standards: Legal Practitioner Education and Training* (September 2020), pp 92–93.
[183] LSRA, *Setting Standards: Legal Practitioner Education and Training* (September 2020), p.93.
[184] *Implementation Plan*, pp.7–8.

and training.[185] This would be subject to an application by third-level education providers to evidence how their degree programmes meet the standards required for admission to professional education and training.[186]

The *Barriers Implementation Plan* indicates the potential for significant changes to entry to the professions in the coming years. The LSRA has recommended that the Law Society and King's Inns "enhance and expand" online training, synchronous and asynchronous, along with hybrid educational training.[187] The Plan also recommends that King's Inns review its code of conduct to assess whether the devilling requirement is fit for purpose.[188] However, most recommendations in the Plan focus on ameliorating difficulties faced by newly-qualified barristers. This includes a commitment by the LSRA to review challenges in finding a Master, in particular outside Dublin, and the lack of pay during the period of the pupillage.[189] Issues of pay and terms and conditions for trainee solicitors will also be explored.[190]

Those with connections due to their educational background, social class, and even due to the educational/professional achievement of parents, may have social capital already in place to be in a better position than others to build their career. The LSRA acknowledges this issue as follows:

> "There is a perception that the legal profession lacks diversity and is heavily reliant on prior connections and networks, which may discourage candidates from underprivileged and underrepresented backgrounds from considering the profession as a career."[191]

The LSRA recommends collecting aggregate data to identify persons entering/in the professions who have a legally protected characteristic,[192]

---

185 LSRA, *Setting Standards: Legal Practitioner Education and Training* (September 2020), p.94.

186 The LSRA recommend that for a defined period, those providing professional qualification education and training would be permitted, if they so choose, to continue operating further entry requirements, be that by means of an examination, interview, or simply permitting LPET Committee-accredited third-level degree programmes to be the entry route; see LSRA, *Setting Standards: Legal Practitioner Education and Training* (September 2020), p.94.

187 *Implementation Plan*, p.10.

188 *Implementation Plan*, p.8.

189 *Implementation Plan*, p.11.

190 *Implementation Plan*, pp.12–13.

191 *Implementation Plan*, p.28.

192 Under employment and equal status law, the nine protected characteristics are: gender, marital status, family status, age, disability, sexual orientation, race, religion and membership of the Traveller community. While there have been recommendations for "socio-economic status" to be a protected equality ground, the legislature has

and a non-legally protected characteristic: socio-economic status (social class). We discussed the issue of social class and judges in some detail in Ch.11.[193] In the context of perceived and real barriers making it more difficult for those with diverse backgrounds to enter the professions, the lack of diversity in our judges is now less surprising. This of course also requires universities to provide a variety of pathways into degree programmes. Interestingly, by 2026, the LSRA will submit proposals to the Minister for Justice on the potential for an apprenticeship pathway into the solicitors profession.

The *Barriers Implementation Plan* identifies the need for the legal professions to create a joint disability action plan to be agreed on by the end of 2025, as well as to agree a Diversity Charter.[194] These measures may, if implemented, at least provide a starting point to a much deeper reflection of diversity, social class and the professions. The holistic approach of exploring all barriers in the round ensures that all issues impeding access to the professions can be considered.

Even if the recommendations in the *Setting Standards* report are ultimately adopted, in whole or in part, it may be many years before the entry route(s) to legal practitioner education and training are reformed, and new education and training providers are established.

D. Complaints, Investigations and Sanctions

12–27 The need for legal practitioners to be held to the highest of standards was put eloquently by Collins J. in the Court of Appeal in *Law Society of Ireland v Doocey:*

> "[W]hile membership of the solicitors' profession may bring many benefits, those benefits come at the price of being held to exacting standards of honesty, integrity and trustworthiness. The continuing vitality of such standards is essential to the maintenance of trust and confidence in the solicitor's profession, which is an essential component in the administration of justice and the rule of law."[195]

While focusing on solicitors in this case, this statement is equally applicable to barristers. Prior to the coming into force of complaints and

not acted on these recommendations to date. See, e.g. Irish Human Rights and Equality Commission, *Policy Statement on Socio-Economic Status as a Ground of Discrimination under the Equality Acts* (April 2024).

[193] See Ch.11, paras 11–44 to 11–48.

[194] *Implementation Plan*, p.29.

[195] [2022] IECA 2 at para.23.

investigatory procedures under the 2015 Act on 7 October 2019, the Law Society of Ireland and the Bar of Ireland, as well as representing the interests of their respective legal practitioners, also had a disciplinary role.[196] For all complaints regarding legal practitioners post 7 October 2019, the LSRA is the main body that has investigatory and sanction powers relating to legal practitioners. The Solicitors Disciplinary Tribunal and the Barristers' Professional Conduct Tribunal (BPCT)[197] previously conducted the role that now resides with the LSRA and the Legal Practitioners Disciplinary Tribunal. A number of complaints relating to matters pre-7 October 2019 are still being determined within the old disciplinary systems.[198] There is one important exception to this for solicitors, that being where a solicitor is alleged to have breached obligations relating to client accounts, the Law Society may investigate this and forward a complaint to the Solicitors Disciplinary Tribunal.[199]

12–28 One of the core aspects of the 2015 Act is the wholescale reform of complaints and investigatory procedures for solicitors and barristers in Ireland.[200] The LSRA can receive complaints relating to three areas: (i) the provision of inadequate legal services, (ii) charging of excessive costs, and (iii) misconduct. The High Court has the exclusive power to strike a solicitor off the roll of practising solicitors, and barristers from the roll of practising barristers.[201] Complaints on inadequate legal services and/or on costs of legal services may be made by a client, or a person acting on

[196] For a full explanation of the investigation and complaints procedures, along with disciplinary sanctions, pre-7 October 2019, see *Fundamentals of the Irish Legal System*, 1st edn (Dublin: Round Hall, 2016), paras 12–27 to 12–33.

[197] For barristers, there was an appeal to the Barristers Professional Conduct Appeals Board (BPCAB), and in the final instance, the Disciplinary Committee of the Benchers of King's Inns.

[198] For solicitors, see Chairperson of the Solicitors Disciplinary Tribunal, *Reports 2019–2021*, available at: *https://www.distrib.ie/annual-reports/*. Since 2024, the Solicitors Disciplinary Tribunal is required to publish its determinations; see LSRA, *Annual Report 2023*, p.7. The Law Society maintains a register of all findings that can be accessed at: *www.lawsociety.ie/Public/disciplinarysearch.* For barristers, complaints were investigated in private, and no public acknowledgement of wrongdoing by barristers would have been made public, except for the disbarment of barristers; see *Fundamentals of the Irish Legal System*, 1st edn (Dublin: Round Hall, 2016), para.12–33.

[199] Section 51(6) of the 2015 Act and Solicitors Accounts Regulations 2023 (S.I. No. 118 of 2023). For an explanation of this, see e.g. Chairperson of the Solicitors Disciplinary Tribunal, *Report 2021*, pp.4–7. For a review of the powers of the Solicitors Disciplinary Tribunal, see *Fundamentals of the Irish Legal System*, 1st edn (Dublin: Round Hall, 2016), para.12–29.

[200] See, generally, Pt 6 of the 2015 Act.

[201] See paras 12–45 to 12–46.

behalf of a client, to the LSRA.[202] In the case of misconduct, anybody may make a complaint about a legal practitioner.[203] The Bar of Ireland, King's Inns or the Law Society, on their own motion, can make a complaint to the LSRA.[204] Since the commencement of this new complaints regime, the vast majority of complaints relate to solicitors, given that solicitors have engagement with clients in a manner that barristers do not.[205] The LSRA publishes a report on their website every six months that contains information on complaints and their outcome.[206]

12-29 Part 6 of the 2015 Act and regulations[207] outline the functions of the LSRA in considering a complaint. A complaint against a legal practitioner must have occurred after 7 October 2019 and must generally be made within three years, except for a misconduct complaint, which can be made at any time.[208] The LSRA will conduct a preliminary review of the complaint to determine its admissibility.[209] The LSRA will notify a legal practitioner of a complaint.[210] A complainant or practitioner must provide the LSRA with any further information relating to a complaint within 21 days.[211] After conducting the preliminary review, the LSRA may

[202] Section 51(1) of the 2015 Act. The complaint can be made online, via email or by post; reg.3 of the Legal Services Regulation Act 2015 (Complaints Procedures) Regulations 2019 (S.I. No. 573 of 2019) (the "2019 Regulations"). Where a complaint is received by the Bar of Ireland, King's Inns or the Law Society, these are to be referred to the LSRA; s.52 of the 2015 Act.

[203] Section 51(2) of the 2015 Act.

[204] Section 52(4) of the 2015 Act. For the Law Society, see also reg.4 of the 2019 Regulations.

[205] For example, between September 2020 and March 2021, of the 805 complaints received by the LSRA, 783 related to solicitors and 22 to barristers; see LSRA, *Complaints about Solicitors and Barristers: Report 1 of 2021*, p.13. Between September 2022 and March 2023, the LSRA received 595 complaints, 576 related to solicitors and 19 regarding barristers; see LSRA, *Complaints about Solicitors and Barristers: Report 1 of 2023*, p.15. From September 2023 to March 2024, the LSRA received 637 complaints, 607 related to solicitors and 30 to barristers; see LSRA, *Complaints about Solicitors and Barristers: Report 1 of 2024*, p.17.

[206] This is required under s.73 of the 2015 Act. All reports can currently be accessed at: *https://www.lsra.ie/publications/reports-and-laws/*.

[207] Legal Services Regulation Act 2015 (Complaints Procedures) Regulations 2019 (S.I. No. 573 of 2019).

[208] See s.58(7) and (8) of the 2015 Act for calculation of the reckonable three-year period. Complaints regarding legal practitioner conduct pre-October 2019 can be made to the Law Society or Bar Council.

[209] Section 57 of the 2015 Act.

[210] Regulation 5 of the 2019 Regulations. This will also be sent to the legal practitioner's employer (if they have one).

[211] Regulation 7 of the 2019 Regulations.

deem the complaint to be admissible,[212] inadmissible,[213] or may pause consideration of the complaint due to ongoing civil or criminal proceedings that await a final determination.[214] A complaint will be inadmissible where it is vexatious, frivolous, without substance or foundation,[215] or where the particular complaint is the same or substantially the same as a complaint previously considered.[216] Where the LSRA determines a complaint to be admissible, and where the complaint relates to allegations of an excessive charge of costs by the legal practitioner, the legal practitioner cannot issue civil proceedings against the complainant or continue with civil proceedings until the complaint is determined. This is unless, on notice to the LSRA, a court orders otherwise.[217] The complaints process differs as to whether the subject matter of the complaint relates to: (1) inadequate legal services and excessive costs, or (2) misconduct. Each mechanism is now considered.

1. Inadequate Legal Services and Excessive Costs

12–30 Inadequate legal services are defined as any act or omission by the legal practitioner where the legal services provided "were not of the quality that could reasonably be expected".[218] Legal practitioners are under a duty to provide an estimate of costs for legal services to a client.[219] Where it is not possible to provide the precise costs for legal services, then the legal practitioner must set out the basis upon which costs will be calculated (a bill of costs).[220] The complaint as to costs can only relate to whether this bill of costs has been implemented by

---

[212] Section 57(5)(a) of the 2015 Act.

[213] Section 57(5)(b) of the 2015 Act.

[214] This ground is set down in s.58(6)(a) of the 2015 Act.

[215] Section 58(2) of the 2015 Act.

[216] Section 58(3) of the 2015 Act. This ground of inadmissibility also applies to complaints that had been previously considered by the High Court, Law Society disciplinary mechanisms, the Barristers' Professional Conduct Tribunal or King's Inns, or any other court proceedings (civil or criminal) against legal practitioners, that had been resolved in favour of the legal practitioner (s.58(4) and (5) of the 2015 Act).

[217] Section 61(9) of the 2015 Act.

[218] Section 49(2)(a)(i) and (ii) of the 2015 Act.

[219] Section 150(2)(a) of the 2015 Act. For barristers, see s.49(2)(a)(i) of the 2015 Act and D. Hand, "Barrister Fees and Section 150 Notices" (2019) 24(6) *Bar Review* 154–157. For solicitors, see s.49(2)(a)(ii) of the 2015 Act and J. Elliot, "New Legal Costs Regime under the LSRA" (2019) 113(7) *Law Society Gazette* 26–27. Notification of legal costs for solicitors was previously contained in s.68 of the Solicitors (Amendment) Act 1994.

[220] Section 150(2)(b) of the 2015 Act.

the practitioner.[221] Whether the costs are unreasonable or excessive is a matter exclusively for the Legal Costs Adjudicator.[222] Since October 2019, between 30 and 40 per cent of complaints to the LSRA relate to complaints of inadequate legal services or excessive costs.[223] The role of the complaints procedure relating to costs is exclusively whether the costs set down in the bill of costs tallies with what a complainant was charged. Key features of complaints on these grounds made to the LSRA since 2019 have been that most complaints are inadmissible, are resolved prior to or soon after a complaint is deemed admissible, or they have been withdrawn or resolved prior to the LSRA having to decide. Informal resolution is at the heart of the legal practitioners' complaints regime, hence it is not all that surprising that the vast majority of complaints do not proceed to any form of investigation. Even prior to an admissibility determination, the LSRA encourages the complainant and legal practitioner to resolve an issue between themselves if possible.[224]

12–31 One important aspect of the 2015 Act that applies to the investigatory elements of complaints is that the LSRA,[225] the Complaints Committee and the Legal Practitioners Disciplinary Tribunal[226] may request the Law Society to "carry out an investigation" under the Solicitors Acts "into any matter that is relevant" to the complaint.[227] Once the Law Society receives such a request, it must comply with the request and furnish a report, interim or final, to the referring body within one month, unless a later period is specified by the referring body.[228] Any such report is admissible for the complaint proceedings.[229]

---

221 Section 49(2)(b) of the 2015 Act.

222 Section 160 of the 2015 Act. For a clear explanation of this distinction, see *LL v Legal Services Regulatory Authority* [2023] IEHC 315 at paras 55–60 and *Kenny v Legal Costs Adjudicator* [2023] IEHC 391 at para.6.

223 Taking two examples to illustrate this, between March 2021 and September 2021, of the 673 complaints, 193 (29%) related to inadequate legal services, while 37 (5%) related to excessive costs; see LSRA, *Complaints about Solicitors and Barristers: Report 2 of 2021*, p.13. Between September 2023 and March 2024, of the 637 complaints, 134 complaints related to inadequate legal services and alleged excessive costs; see LSRA, *Complaints about Solicitors and Barristers: Report 1 of 2024*, p.18.

224 For an outline on the modalities of informal resolution/mediation, see LSRA, *Guidelines for the resolution of complaints by mediation or informal means* (March 2024).

225 Section 59(1) of the 2015 Act.

226 Section 59(2) of the 2015 Act.

227 Section 59(1) and (2) of the 2015 Act.

228 Section 59(3) of the 2015 Act.

229 Section 59(4) of the 2015 Act.

(a) Informal resolution

12–32 If a complaint is admissible, and without resolution at this stage, the complainant and legal practitioner will be invited to undergo informal resolution by the LSRA.[230] By agreeing to take part in the informal resolution of the complaint, the legal practitioner is not deemed to be admitting liability.[231] In addition, any statements made during the course of the informal resolution "may not be used in any disciplinary, civil or criminal proceedings".[232] Engaging in informal resolution is of course subject to the agreement of all parties to the complaint.[233] Where the complainant and legal practitioner choose to engage with the informal resolution process, the LSRA Complaints and Resolution Unit, staffed by trained mediators, attempt to resolve the dispute. Where the informal resolution is either not utilised or is not successful,[234] the LSRA may proceed, after receiving statements of the respective positions of the complainant and legal practitioner, to determine the complaint.[235]

(b) LSRA determination

12–33 If the LSRA determines that the legal services provided by the practitioner were "of an inadequate standard",[236] then the LSRA can direct the practitioner to do one or more of the following:

- rectify the matter at their own expense;
- undertake any other action that the LSRA may specify;[237]
- transfer relevant documents relating to the subject matter of the complaint to another person or body; and/or
- pay the complainant a sum not exceeding €3,000.[238]

---

[230] See, generally, s.60 of the 2015 Act, which relates to informal resolution of complaints as regards adequacy of services. Section 61 of the 2015 Act relates to resolution of complaints as regards excessive costs.

[231] Section 66 of the 2015 Act.

[232] Section 65(1) of the 2015 Act.

[233] Section 60(5) of the 2015 Act and s.61(2) of the 2015 Act.

[234] In this regard, where the LSRA determines that a reasonable amount of time has passed in order to allow the complainant and legal practitioner to resolve the issue in an informal manner, the LSRA will give notice that it is to determine the complaint. The LSRA may not determine the complaint, after providing notice, for a period of at least 30 days; see s.60(3) of the 2015 Act and s.61(6) of the 2015 Act.

[235] Section 60(5) of the 2015 Act.

[236] Section 60(6) of the 2015 Act.

[237] Under s.60(6)(d), this is subject to a €3,000 limit for the practitioner or, for solicitors, their firm.

[238] Section 60(6)(a)–(d) of the 2015 Act. Such a payment is "without prejudice to any legal right of the client"; see s.60(11) of the 2015 Act.

If the LSRA determines that the legal practitioner charged excessively,[239] it may direct the legal practitioner to refund all or part of the costs charged, or waive, in whole or in part, the right of the legal practitioner to recover costs.[240] As a snapshot, between September 2021 and March 2022, the LSRA issued 29 determinations. In 11 of these determinations, the complaints were not upheld. In the 18 complaints that were upheld, some of the directions issued by the LSRA required practitioners to refund fees, pay compensation, transfer a file to a client or another solicitor, or require the legal practitioner to waive all or part of fees charged to a complainant.[241]

(c) Review Committee

12–34 Either the complainant or the practitioner may request a review of the LSRA's determination by the Review Committee.[242] The Review Committee, comprising three persons drawn from the Complaints Committee—only one of whom is a legal practitioner[243]—must then reach an outcome whether to confirm the determination of the LSRA, remit the matter to the LSRA for reconsideration, or amend the determination of the LSRA, e.g. increasing or decreasing compensation or requiring additional actions to be completed by the legal practitioner.[244] Exploring again the period between September 2021 and March 2022,[245] of the 12 Review Committee outcomes, eight confirmed the determinations of the LSRA and one confirmed the determination of the LSRA but reduced

239 In this regard, the informal resolution mechanisms for excessive costs are set out in s.61 of the 2015 Act; however, they mirror closely the informal resolution mechanisms for allegations of acts and omissions.

240 Section 61(6) of the 2015 Act. Detail on the determinations of the LSRA are contained in the statistical analysis of complaints within their six-monthly reports.

241 LSRA, *Complaints about Solicitors and Barristers: Report 1 of 2022*, pp.27–28. This trend has continued; see LSRA, *Complaints about Solicitors and Barristers: Report 2 of 2024,* p.31. See p.27 of this report for a case study on excessive costs.

242 Section 62 of the 2015 Act.

243 Members of the Review Committee are appointed from persons who are members of the Complaints Committee (s.62(4) of the 2015 Act); the functions of this body will be considered below. If the complaint under review relates to a solicitor, then a solicitor will sit on the Review Committee. Where the complaint under review relates to a barrister, then a barrister sits on the Committee; see s.62(3)(a) and (b) of the 2015 Act. Details of the decisions of the Review Committee are contained in the LSRA Complaint Reports. The Complaints Committee composition is discussed at paras 12–39 to 12–40.

244 Section 62(5) of the 2015 Act.

245 LSRA, *Complaints about Solicitors and Barristers: Report 1 of 2022*, p.29.

the compensation payable to the client from €3,000 to €2,500. Three outcomes were remitted to the LSRA for a fresh determination.

(d) Appeal to the High Court

12–35 Either the complainant or the legal practitioner may appeal the determination of the Review Committee to the High Court within 21 days.[246] The appeal is on the basis that the Review Committee had made an error or a series of errors.[247] After the 21-day period has expired, and if no appeal to the High Court is exercised, then the determination of the Review Committee becomes "absolutely binding" on the client and the legal practitioner.[248] Refusal to comply with the determination of the Review Committee can constitute an offence under the 2015 Act.[249] In *LL v Legal Services Regulatory Authority*,[250] L appealed the decision of the Review Committee. The appellant had complained that her solicitor failed to provide adequate legal services and failed to notify her of the costs of taking a complicated family law issue. The solicitor informed the appellant about the costs, as well as fees for certain actions (interim applications, notification of costs for experts, etc.).[251] The LSRA and Review Committee determined that the legal services provided were adequate and the costs were not excessive in light of the complexity of the legal issues.[252] In dismissing the appellant's claim, Barr J. noted the sum of the appellant's arguments, being "the unhappy ending of her marriage and the separate land dispute between her husband and his brothers, in arriving at the conclusion that she has been greatly injured in life and that it was all the fault of the solicitor."[253]

12–36 On L's allegation that the solicitor provided inadequate legal services—a bare allegation without any proof—and that the solicitor had conspired to prolong the litigation in order to increase their fees, the court held that there had been ample evidence before the Review Committee to make the findings that it did. The solicitor subject to the

246 Section 63(1) of the 2015 Act.
247 Confirmed in *LL v Legal Services Regulatory Authority* [2023] IEHC 315 at paras 42–44.
248 Section 63(2) of the 2015 Act.
249 Section 63(4) of the 2015 Act.
250 *LL v Legal Services Regulatory Authority* [2023] IEHC 315.
251 [2023] IEHC 315 at paras 7–12.
252 [2023] IEHC 315 at paras 27–30.
253 [2023] IEHC 315 at para.41.

complaint was diligent in the conduct of the legal proceedings, clearly explained the basis for legal costs, and had kept the appellant updated on the legal proceedings throughout.[254] On the excessive costs issue, the High Court noted that the Review Committee does not have a role in determining whether the legal fees charged were unreasonable; this is for the Office of the Legal Costs Adjudicator.[255]

2. Misconduct

12–37 Section 50(1) of the 2015 Act outlines 14 grounds whereby an act or omission by a legal practitioner will constitute misconduct. In summary, this includes:

a) fraud or dishonesty;
b) legal services that are "to a substantial degree" inadequate (this indicates a standard over and above "mere" inadequacy per s.49 of the 2015 Act);
c) whether the practitioner continues to be a "fit and proper" person to provide legal services;
d) committing a breach of the 2015 Act and/or an offence under the 2015 Act. For solicitors, this includes a breach of, or an offence under, the Solicitors Acts 1954–2015;
e) a solicitor or barrister bringing the profession into disrepute;
f) commission of an arrestable offence, including outside of Ireland;
g) grossly excessive costs; and/or
h) a legal practitioner withdraws from a case, where their client is in custody, without first obtaining permission of the court.

The vast majority of complaints to the LSRA have been allegations of solicitor misconduct.[256] Like inadequate services and legal costs, the

[254] [2023] IEHC 315 at paras 46–50.

[255] [2023] IEHC 315 at paras 46–50. See also, *Connolly v Legal Services Regulatory Authority* [2023] IECA 252, in particular para.65 onwards.

[256] For example, between 7 October 2019 and 6 March 2020, 342 (54%) of the 638 total complaints related to misconduct; see LSRA, *Complaints about Solicitors and Barristers: Report 1 of 2020*, p.9. Between March 2023 and September 2023, of the 665 total complaints, 427 (65%) related to allegations of misconduct; see LSRA, *Complaints about Solicitors and Barristers: Report 2 of 2023*, p.15. Between March 2024 and September 2024, of the 740 complaints, 611 of these alleged misconduct of some descriptions; see LSRA, *Complaints about Solicitors and Barristers: Report 2 of 2024*, p.31.

majority of legal practitioner misconduct allegations are found to be inadmissible or, if admissible, do not proceed to a determination by the Review Committee.

(a) Informal resolution

12–38 Like inadequate legal services or costs complaints, the LSRA will determine admissibility. Where a complaint of misconduct is admissible, then the complainant and legal practitioner are invited to informally resolve the issue.[257] However, this agreement does not prevent the LSRA from continuing to consider or investigate the complaint.[258] Where a resolution is reached by the complainant and the legal practitioner, or where the legal practitioner sought to achieve an informal resolution, but ultimately the matter came before the Complaints Committee, Legal Services Disciplinary Tribunal or the High Court, this must be given "due regard" in determining the sanction, if any, to be imposed on the legal practitioner.[259]

(b) Complaints Committee

12–39 The Complaints Committee examines complaints of misconduct. The Complaints Committee is composed of 27 members, appointed by the LSRA, the majority of whom are lay persons.[260] Of these 27 persons, eight are nominated by the Law Society, each of whom must be practising solicitors of at least 10 years' standing.[261] The Bar Council must nominate four persons, each of whom must be barristers of at least 10 years' standing.[262] The Complaints Committee must sit in divisions of either three members or five members,[263] with a majority of lay members on each divisional complaints committee.[264] Depending on whether a complaint relates to a barrister or a solicitor, the composition

[257] Section 64(1) of the 2015 Act.
[258] Section 64(2) of the 2015 Act.
[259] Section 64(3) of the 2015 Act.
[260] Section 69 of the 2015 Act. Members of the Complaints Committee hold office for at least four years, and are eligible for re-appointment on one further occasion under s.69(2) of the 2015 Act. For the criteria the LSRA must consider in appointing lay members, see s.69(4) of the 2015 Act.
[261] Section 69(3)(b) of the 2015 Act.
[262] Section 69(3)(c) of the 2015 Act.
[263] Section 69(5) of the 2015 Act and reg.10 of the 2019 Regulations.
[264] Section 69(7) of the 2015 Act. In addition, the chairperson of the Divisional Committee must be a lay person by virtue of s.69(8) of the 2015 Act.

of the Divisional Complaints Committees will change.[265] The Divisional Complaints Committee has the power to request relevant information from the LSRA and the legal practitioner on the complaint[266] and, if necessary, require the complainant and the legal practitioner to appear before the Divisional Committee for the purposes of investigating the complaint.[267] The Divisional Complaints Committee is under a general duty to keep the complainant informed of any decisions taken on the complaint,[268] and to act expeditiously and proceed in a timely manner with its investigation of complaints.[269] All deliberations are in private and neither the identity of the complainant nor the legal practitioner can be disclosed, although the LSRA will provide broad information on determinations of the Complaints Committee.

12–40 Once the complaint is considered, the Divisional Complaints Committee may dismiss the complaint, or where misconduct by the legal practitioner is proved, can order the legal practitioner to undertake a number of measures.[270] Depending on the nature of the complaint, the Divisional Complaints Committee may specify the following sanctions (if any) for the legal practitioner:

(i) perform or complete a legal service that relates to the subject of the complaint;
(ii) undertake professional legal training;
(iii) waive fees, in whole or in part;
(iv) undertake any other action "in the interests of the client that the Committee may specify";
(v) comply with an undertaking to be given to another legal practitioner or any other person or body;
(vi) withdraw or amend an advertisement;

[265] Where the complaint is against a solicitor, then a solicitor will sit on a three-member Divisional Committee, or two solicitors in a five-member Divisional Committee (s.69(10) of the 2015 Act). Where the complaint is against a barrister, then a barrister will sit on the three-member Divisional Committee, or two barristers in a five-member Divisional Committee (s.69(11) of the 2015 Act).

[266] See, generally, s.70 of the 2015 Act, which includes provisions relating to where the legal practitioner does not furnish the required information to the Divisional Committee.

[267] Section 70(9) of the 2015 Act.

[268] Section 70(13)(a) of the 2015 Act.

[269] Section 70(13)(b) and (c) of the 2015 Act.

[270] For a full list of the measures that the Divisional Complaints Committee can specify, see s.71 of the 2015 Act.

(vii) pay up to €5,000 to a client who suffered due to the inadequacy of legal services provided;

(viii) pay the LSRA up to €5,000 to defray costs (in whole or in part) for investigating the complaint;

(ix) pay the LSRA up to €2,500 where the legal practitioner has "refused, neglected, or otherwise failed, without reasonable cause" to respond to the Divisional Complaints Committee's request for information, or failed to comply with a properly issued written direction from the Divisional Complaints Committee;[271] and/or

(x) impose a restriction on the practitioner's legal practice, with the Law Society or the Bar of Ireland (as appropriate) being informed of this restriction.[272]

Between September 2023 and March 2024, the Complaints Committee considered 136 complaints of misconduct. Excluding complaints that were discontinued, withdrawn or resolved, the Committee made seven referrals to the Legal Practitioners Disciplinary Tribunal, upheld 16 complaints issuing directions to legal practitioners, and did not uphold 45 complaints.[273]

(c) Appeal of Complaints Committee determination to the High Court

12–41 The LSRA[274] or the legal practitioner[275] concerned, but not the complainant, may appeal the decision of the Divisional Complaints Committee within 21 days to the High Court.[276] The High Court has the power to confirm, set aside or modify the sanctions imposed by the Divisional Complaints Committee.[277] This can include an appeal of

---

[271] Section 71(5) of the 2015 Act.

[272] Section 71(6) of the 2015 Act. The legal practitioner must notify the Complaints Committee of its agreement to abide by a practising restriction within 21 days, otherwise the matter will be referred to the Legal Practitioners Disciplinary Tribunal per s.71(8) of the 2015 Act.

[273] LSRA, *Complaints about Solicitors and Barristers: Report 2 of 2023*, p.19 and pp.43–44.

[274] Section 72(2) of the 2015 Act. This includes the ability of the LSRA to appeal a determination by the Divisional Complaints Committee not to refer the complaint to the Legal Practitioners Disciplinary Tribunal.

[275] Section 72(1) of the 2015 Act.

[276] Section 72(1) of the 2015 Act. It is not clear why the complainant does not have an appeal right, and this issue was not considered during the parliamentary debates for the Legal Services Regulation Bill 2011.

[277] Section 72(3) of the 2015 Act.

the Complaints Committee's determination to refer, or not, the subject matter of the complaint to the Legal Practitioners Disciplinary Tribunal. At the time of writing, there have been no published decisions of the High Court relating to appeals of Complaint Committee determinations.

3. Legal Practitioners Disciplinary Tribunal

12–42 Where, in the view of the Divisional Complaints Committee, the act or omission that is the subject of the complaint "is of a kind that is more appropriate for consideration by the Legal Practitioners Disciplinary Tribunal", then an application can be made to hold an inquiry under s.81 of the 2015 Act.[278] An application for an inquiry to the Legal Practitioners Disciplinary Tribunal (the "Disciplinary Tribunal") may also be made where, within 21 days after the imposition of any of the specified measures discussed above, the legal practitioner fails to agree to the specified measures imposed by the Divisional Complaints Committee.[279] Section 74 of the 2015 Act establishes the Disciplinary Tribunal.[280] Members of the Disciplinary Tribunal were appointed in November 2020;[281] however, only since 2021, with the passing of regulations,[282] has the Tribunal become operational. The Disciplinary Tribunal is independent of the LSRA, however the support staff for the Tribunal are employees of the LSRA.[283] The Disciplinary Tribunal is composed of "not more than 33 members".[284] The majority of members must be lay persons, with lay members of the Tribunal acting as Chairperson within divisions of a three-member Disciplinary Tribunal,[285] with a majority of each divisional tribunal being a lay member. At least 40 per cent of members must be

[278] The LSRA may appeal to the High Court the determination of the Divisional Complaints Committee that the subject matter of the complaint should not be sent to the Legal Practitioners Disciplinary Tribunal.

[279] Section 71(8)(c) of the 2015 Act.

[280] The website of the Disciplinary Tribunal is: *https://www.gov.ie/en/campaigns/64443-legal-practitioners-disciplinary-tribunal/.*

[281] President of the High Court, Justice Mary Irvine, "Legal Practitioners Disciplinary Tribunal Statement", 20 November 2020.

[282] Legal Practitioners Disciplinary Tribunal Regulations 2021 (S.I. No. 786 of 2021) (the "2021 Regulations"). The 2021 Regulations outline in detail the process and procedures before the Disciplinary Tribunal, such as the procedure for an inquiry into misconduct (Part 2), and general powers of the Tribunal, including in-person and remote inquiries. The Schedule to the 2021 Regulations provides requisite forms that must be completed when misconduct is referred to the Disciplinary Tribunal.

[283] LSRA, *Annual Report 2022*, p.7.

[284] Section 75(1) of the 2015 Act.

[285] Section 75(1)(a) and reg.2 of the 2021 Regulations.

male and at least 40 per cent of members must be female.[286] Six of the members are nominated by the Law Society, and six members by the Bar of Ireland.[287] A solicitor will sit on the divisional tribunal where a solicitor is before it, and a barrister will sit if it is a barrister before it. Lay members are appointed by the President of the High Court, on nomination by the Minister for Justice. The Minister for Justice makes their nomination after public competition.[288]

12–43 Matters will only come before the Disciplinary Tribunal where the Complaints Committee, or the Law Society (only as regards client accounts),[289] (i) considers the complaint before it to be of such gravity that it merits an inquiry by the Disciplinary Tribunal, or (ii) a legal practitioner before the Complaints Committee does not consent to the measures imposed on them.[290] The Disciplinary Tribunal is empowered to make a determination as to whether the misconduct alleged has or has not occurred, or whether the sanction imposed by the Complaints Committee on the legal practitioner should be upheld or modified.[291] The Disciplinary Tribunal has significant powers as regards the enforcement of attendance of witnesses[292] and compelling of discovery of relevant documents to a complaint.[293] The standard of proof required to make a finding of misconduct is the criminal standard, i.e. beyond reasonable doubt.[294]

12–44 Under s.81 of the 2015 Act, the Disciplinary Tribunal must arrange an inquiry which must be in public, unless the Disciplinary Tribunal is satisfied that it would be in the interests of justice to have

[286] Section 75(1)(d) of the 2015 Act.
[287] Section 75(1)(c) and (d) of the 2015 Act.
[288] For a full list of members of the Disciplinary Tribunal, see: *https://www.gov.ie/en/campaigns/64443-legal-practitioners-disciplinary-tribunal/*.
[289] Section 77(a) of the 2015 Act for referrals by the Complaints Committee; s.77(b) of the 2015 Act for referrals by the Law Society. The referrals by the Law Society will relate to the Solicitors Accounts Regulations 2023 (S.I. No. 118 of 2023); see, in particular, reg.39(8) of the 2023 Regulations.
[290] Regulation 2 of the 2021 Regulations.
[291] Section 81(8) of the 2015 Act.
[292] A witness before the Disciplinary Tribunal has, under s.80(8) of the 2015 Act, the "same immunities and privileges as if he or she were a witness before the High Court"; see also reg.10 of the 2021 Regulations.
[293] For this and other powers of the Disciplinary Tribunal, see s.80 of the 2015 Act. For the offence of not appearing as a witness, after being summoned, see s.80(7) and (9) of the 2015 Act.
[294] Regulation 15(2) of the 2021 Regulations.

the hearing in private.[295] The Disciplinary Tribunal can make an order recommending that the High Court impose one or more sanctions on the legal practitioner on the part of whom misconduct is found.[296] The sanctions that can be imposed include: advice; admonishment; censure; directions that the legal practitioner undertake training; payment of all or part of the costs of the subject matter of the complaint; a direction for the legal practitioner to take rectifying action on the subject matter of the complaint; payment of a sum of not more than €15,000; payment of the costs (in whole or in part) of the Disciplinary Tribunal; and/or the imposition of conditions on the professional activities that a practitioner may engage in, as regards their role as a solicitor or barrister. The LSRA, the Law Society or the legal practitioner concerned may, within 28 days, appeal the determination of the Disciplinary Tribunal to the High Court.[297] The High Court has the power to confirm the determination of the Disciplinary Tribunal or determine that the act or omission the subject of the inquiry did not constitute misconduct.[298] The High Court has the power to confirm the sanctions that were imposed, or impose additional sanctions that could have been imposed by the Disciplinary Tribunal.[299] The 2015 Act confers the power of striking off a barrister or solicitor from the practising rolls exclusively upon the High Court.[300]

4. The High Court and Strike-Off

12–45 The power of the High Court to strike off solicitors has been in place for decades.[301] Previously, barristers could only be disbarred by the Disciplinary Committee of the Benchers of King's Inns.[302] At the time of writing, there has been one High Court decision to strike off a legal practitioner, following a Disciplinary Tribunal recommendation under

[295] Section 81(2) and (3) of the 2015 Act. Pursuant to reg.8 of the 2021 Regulations, it is for the divisional tribunal to determine whether the inquiry will be held "otherwise than in public", where this is in the interests of justice.

[296] For a full review of the sanctions, see s.82(1)(a)–(m) of the 2015 Act.

[297] Section 83 of the 2015 Act. The jurisdiction vested in the High Court is to be exercised by the President of the High Court, pursuant to s.86 of the 2015 Act, or may be exercised by an ordinary judge of the High Court, if the President of that court so directs.

[298] Section 84(4) of the 2015 Act.

[299] Section 85(4)(a) of the 2015 Act and s.85(7) of the 2015 Act.

[300] Section 85(7)(e) and (f) of the 2015 Act.

[301] See *Fundamentals of the Irish Legal System*, 1st edn (Dublin: Round Hall, 2016), para.12–29.

[302] See *Fundamentals of the Irish Legal System*, 1st edn (Dublin: Round Hall, 2016), paras 12–32 and 12–33, where we noted the significant issues pertaining to the non-statutory system for barrister complaints.

the 2015 Act.[303] If the High Court exercises this particular power, then a notice must be published in *Iris Oifigiúil*.[304] A final appeal on striking off, by either the LSRA or the practitioner concerned, which may not have suspensive effect,[305] lies with the Court of Appeal.[306] The case law discussed here, while under the "old" disciplinary system and relating just to solicitors, nonetheless provides key insights into when the courts would or would not strike off a legal practitioner under the 2015 Act.[307] Kelly P. in *Law Society of Ireland v D'Alton*[308] stated there are five considerations the courts should examine in determining whether it is appropriate to prevent legal practitioners from practising. First, the protection of the public. Second, the maintenance of the reputation of the solicitors' profession. Third, the punishment of the misconduct of the legal practitioner. Fourth, to act as a deterrent to other solicitors who may be considering acting in a manner that constitutes misconduct. Fifth, the sanction imposed on the solicitor must be appropriate and proportionate.[309] In *D'Alton*, Kelly P. decided not to strike off this solicitor from the roll due to their "dreadful ill-health", despite their having a history of previous adverse disciplinary findings, and the application for strike-off related to client funds.[310] Kelly P. noted that all client monies were repaid and he imposed several conditions on D'Alton's continued practice. The judgment concluded with Kelly P. emphasising that this decision was unusual, stating this should not be interpreted as "any relaxation of the court's obligation to continue to ensure that public confidence in the integrity of the solicitors' profession is maintained."[311]

303 In December 2023, a solicitor consented to being struck off the roll. See S. Phelan, "Tribunal recommends ex-TD's solicitor daughter be struck off for misconduct", *Irish Independent*, 15 September 2023, and the newspaper report of Barniville P.'s decision: A. O'Loughlin, "Daughter of former Fianna Fáil TD John Ellis struck off roll of solicitors", *Irish Examiner*, 4 December 2023. See also, Legal Practitioners Disciplinary Tribunal, *Annual Reports 2020–2023* (2024), p.12.

304 Section 88(2) of the 2015 Act.

305 Unless the High Court or Court of Appeal determines otherwise under s.87 of the 2015 Act.

306 Section 86 of the 2015 Act.

307 See, in particular, the decisions of Donnelly and Collins JJ. in *Law Society of Ireland v Doocey* [2022] IECA 2, where reference was made to the 2015 Act and the disciplinary and sanctions processes.

308 [2019] IEHC 177.

309 [2019] IEHC 177 at para.33. In outlining these five factors, Kelly P. relied on previous court decisions, including *Law Society of Ireland v Enright* [2016] IEHC 151, the Supreme Court decision in *Carroll v Law Society of Ireland* [2016] IESC 49, and the English decision of *Bolton v Law Society* [1994] 2 All E.R. 486.

310 [2019] IEHC 177 at paras 37 and 39.

311 [2019] IEHC 177 at para.45.

12–46 The courts have stated on several occasions that dishonesty of a solicitor, in particular as regards client funds, will usually result in the solicitor being struck off the roll. In *Law Society of Ireland v Doocey*, Irvine P. acknowledged that being struck off the roll is "harsh"; however, she stated that neither claims of inexperience by a solicitor nor mitigating circumstances such as illness of a family member will act as a bar to the High Court imposing the most severest of sanction.[312] Doocey appealed to the Court of Appeal, which upheld the decision of Irvine P.[313] Collins J., in his separate concurring opinion in the Court of Appeal, focused on the need for exacting standards for solicitors given the necessity for the public to have trust and confidence in the profession.[314] The issue of mitigating circumstances was again raised in *Law Society of Ireland v Corrigan*.[315] The respondent Corrigan was in arrears on his mortgage, his wife had been diagnosed with a life-limiting condition, and he was the sole provider for the family. Corrigan had utilised client monies to cover professional and personal debts.[316] The Solicitors Disciplinary Tribunal did not propose to strike off Corrigan from the roll, imposing other sanctions and restrictions on his practice instead.[317] The Law Society applied to the High Court to have Corrigan struck off. Barniville P. was "just about persuaded" not to strike the solicitor off the roll, in light of the serious mitigating circumstances.[318] Barniville P., in coming to this decision, again emphasised that the usual sanction for dishonesty with client accounts is striking off a solicitor from the roll.[319] Barniville P. highlighted that it was not possible to outline all potential mitigating factors that may be taken into account in determining if a strike-off should occur.[320] In *Corrigan*, his immediate admissions, ensuring client monies were paid back, lack of any previous disciplinary sanctions against him, and the toll that this had taken on him, meant that a strike-off would be disproportionate.[321]

[312] [2020] IEHC 581 at paras 37–41. This decision was upheld by the Court of Appeal: [2022] IECA 2.
[313] [2022] IECA 2.
[314] [2022] IECA 2 at paras 20–23, relying on the decision of Bingham M.R. in *Bolton v Law Society* [1994] 2 All E.R. 486.
[315] [2023] IEHC 389.
[316] [2023] IEHC 389 at paras 10–16.
[317] [2023] IEHC 389 at paras 36–39.
[318] [2023] IEHC 389 at para.90.
[319] [2023] IEHC 389 at para.66.
[320] [2023] IEHC 389 at para.65.
[321] [2023] IEHC 389 at para.89.

E. The Attorney General, Chief State Solicitor, and Director of Public Prosecutions

12–47 Solicitors and barristers may also act in a variety of State offices provided for either under the Constitution or by legislation. This section of the chapter very briefly highlights the offices of the Attorney General,[322] the Chief State Solicitor, and the Director of Public Prosecutions. Under Article 30.1 of the Irish Constitution, the Attorney General is described as "the adviser of the Government in matters of law and legal opinion, and shall exercise and perform all such powers, functions and duties as are conferred or imposed on him by this Constitution or by law". The Attorney General is appointed by the President "on the nomination of the Taoiseach",[323] and holds office at the pleasure of the Taoiseach.[324] The Attorney General retires when the Taoiseach calls an election; however, they remain in office until a new Taoiseach is appointed.[325] While the Attorney General often attends cabinet meetings, they are not a member of the Government.[326] The Attorney General is an ex officio member of the Council of State.[327] In addition, where the Supreme Court is hearing an Article 26 reference—which is when the President refers a Bill to the Supreme Court because they have doubts as to its constitutionality—the Supreme Court must hear arguments from the Attorney General, or a representative of the Attorney General.[328]

12–48 There is no constitutional prohibition on the Attorney General being a TD; however, only one TD to date, and only for a period of two months, has simultaneously exercised the functions of the Attorney General.[329] The Attorney General has always been a senior counsel and will usually, but not always, have had a previous affiliation with

[322] For a more detailed exploration of the Attorney General and their role, see G. Hogan, G. Whyte, D. Kenny and R. Walsh, *Kelly: The Irish Constitution*, 5th edn (Dublin: Bloomsbury Professional, 2018), paras 5.4.01–5.4.72.

[323] Article 30.2 of the Irish Constitution.

[324] Under Article 30.5 of the Irish Constitution, the Taoiseach may request, "for reasons which to him seem sufficient", the resignation of the Attorney General. Where the Attorney General refuses to resign, the President, on the advice of the Taoiseach, can terminate the Attorney General's appointment.

[325] Article 30.5.4° of the Irish Constitution.

[326] Article 30.4 of the Irish Constitution.

[327] Article 31.2.i of the Irish Constitution.

[328] Article 26.2.1° of the Irish Constitution.

[329] See *https://www.gov.ie/en/organisation/office-of-the-attorney-general/* and Office of the Attorney General, *Annual Report 2023* (2024).

the Government party (or one of the parties) in power. Section 6 of the Ministers and Secretaries Act 1924 (as amended) provides that the functions of the Attorney General include:

> "... the administration and business generally of public services in connection with the representation of the Government ... and of the public in all legal proceedings for the enforcement of law, the punishment of offenders and the assertion or protection of public rights and all powers ...".[330]

12–49 As regards this power, the Attorney General has occasionally acted independently of the Government. The most notable example of this was in *Attorney General v X*.[331] In this case, X was a pregnant 14-year-old girl who had been raped. X and her parents wanted to travel to the United Kingdom to obtain an abortion. While X was in the United Kingdom, the Attorney General obtained an injunction ex parte from the High Court which sought to prevent X from obtaining an abortion. X and her parents returned to Ireland. The Supreme Court ultimately decided that Article 40.3.3° (which at that time prohibited abortion in Ireland) of the Constitution did not prevent, amongst other issues, X from travelling abroad to obtain an abortion. The High Court[332] and Supreme Court[333] emphasised that the Attorney General had acted appropriately in seeking to vindicate the life of the "unborn" under Article 40.3.3°. The exercise of this "protection of public rights" power has not been utilised by any Attorney General to date, for example, where local authorities were in clear breach of the European Convention on Human Rights Act 2003 in how local authority tenants were removed.[334] The role of "defender

[330] Ministers and Secretaries Act 1924 s.6, as amended by s.28 of the Civil Service Regulation (Amendment) Act 2005. Sections 2(2) and 28 of the National Treasury Management Agency (Amendment) Act 2000 also confer specific powers on the Office of the Attorney General.

[331] [1992] 1 I.R. 1.

[332] [1992] 1 I.R. 1 at 9, where Costello J. stated that the Attorney General was "an especially appropriate person to invoke the jurisdiction of the court in order to vindicate and defend the right to life of the unborn".

[333] [1992] 1 I.R. 1 at 77, where McCarthy J. stated that where "the termination of pregnancy is imminent, and the prospective mother is leaving or has left the jurisdiction for that purpose, in my view the Attorney General is constitutionally entitled to apply to the court to make such order as is necessary and appropriate. It is a power, function and duty imposed on him by the Constitution."

[334] See, for example, *Donegan v Dublin City Council* [2012] 3 I.R. 600 (discussed in detail in S. Kingston and L. Thornton, *A Report on the European Convention on Human Rights Act 2003 and the EU Charter of Fundamental Rights: Evaluation and Review*

of public rights" may be delegated to a private individual taking a case by means of a "relator action".[335] The Supreme Court has indicated that these powers should only be used in "exceptional circumstances".[336] Activities of the Attorney General have, on occasion, come under intense public scrutiny, such as the Brendan Smyth affair,[337] as regards the retirement of a former Garda Commissioner, Martin Callinan,[338] and due to certain events, the former Attorney General, Séamus Woulfe (then appointed to the Supreme Court) having a "hazy" knowledge of Covid-19 regulations that his office had drafted.[339]

12–50 The Office of the Parliamentary Counsel to the Government and the Office of the Chief State Solicitor are both located within the Office of the Attorney General.[340] The Office of the Parliamentary Counsel to the Government drafts Bills on behalf of the Government and Government ministers. The core duty of the Chief State Solicitor's Office is to act as solicitor for the Attorney General, the State and Government departments. This includes acting for the State within all civil legal matters.[341] Until 1974, criminal charges were brought in the name of the Attorney General; however, these functions, as permitted by Article 30.3 of the Constitution, are now exercised by the Director of Public Prosecutions (DPP). The DPP "shall perform all the functions capable of being performed in relation to criminal matters"[342] that had previously been exercised by the Attorney General. This generally relates to a decision on whether a person should be charged with certain offences, after having received a file on this from An Garda Síochána. The DPP

(Dublin: Law Society, 2015), pp.95–98, where the Attorney General as notice party appealed a decision of the High Court, where there were clear indications from the jurisprudence of the European Court of Human Rights—*Connors v United Kingdom* (2005) 40 E.H.R.R. 189—that the statutory system for removing local authority tenants was a clear breach of Article 6 of the European Convention on Human Rights.

335 Further details on this are available at: *https://www.gov.ie/en/organisation/office-of-the-attorney-general/*. For an example of the Attorney General declining to permit a relator action (by Sligo County Council), see *Walsh v Sligo County Council* [2013] IESC 48 at para.39.

336 *Attorney General v Lee* [2000] 4 I.R. 298 at 303–304 per Keane C.J.

337 Discussed in detail in Ch.11, para.11–27.

338 *Report of the Fennelly Commission* (March 2017). See also, Ch.10, Box 10.3.

339 See Ch.11, paras 11–76 to 11–79.

340 For a full review of the functions and services offered by this office, see: *www.gov.ie/en/organisation-information/5a2c7-office-of-the-parliamentary-counsel-opc/*.

341 For a full overview of the functions of the Chief State Solicitor's Office, see: *www.gov.ie/en/organisation/chief-state-solicitors-office/*.

342 Prosecution of Offences Act 1974 s.3(1).

must exercise their functions independently[343] and must exercise their powers "subject to the constitutional requirement of fair procedures" when determining if a prosecution is warranted.[344] Since 2008, the Office of the DPP provides reasons for its decisions not to prosecute in cases involving the death of a victim.[345] For all other cases, the relevant policy was adopted in 2015. However, these policies place limits on the circumstances in which reasons for not prosecuting will be given, such as excluding cases where the sharing of such information would cause injustice.

F. Conclusion

12–51 Often maligned, legal practitioners play a fundamental role in the Irish legal system, be it in private practice, or within offices of State. Fundamentally, practising solicitors and barristers ensure that individuals and businesses have access to justice. Those in State offices contribute to the operation of the State within the framework of the rule of law. For most solicitors and barristers in Ireland, the needs of the (paying) client are to the fore when conducting legal business. This is not to say, of course, as we see in the next chapter, that this fee for justice arrangement is unproblematic, but law, and provision of legal advice and representation, is mainly a business for which persons must be paid. The 2015 Act has had an impact on practising solicitors and barristers. Whether other more significant changes will occur, in particular as regards unification of both professions or trainee entrance requirements, remains to be seen. The 2015 Act is positive in that it has subjected the regulatory bodies for solicitors and barristers in the State to a period of well-overdue scrutiny. The independence of the complaints and investigations mechanisms has to be welcomed.

12–52 While this chapter was concerned with the role, functions and regulation of legal practitioners, it is important to emphasise that studying for a law degree does not confine you to legal practice. A legal diploma

[343] Prosecution of Offences Act 1974 s.2(5).

[344] *Carlin v DPP* [2010] 3 I.R. 547 at 550 per Denham J. See also, DPP, *The Decision Whether to Prosecute* (Dublin: Office of the DPP, 2010).

[345] DPP, *Policy on the Giving of Reasons for Decisions Not to Prosecute* (Dublin: Office of the DPP, 2008). See also, DPP, *Discussion Paper on Prosecution Policy on the Giving of Reasons for Decisions* (Dublin: Office of the DPP, 2023).

or law degree equips you with a wide variety of skills, and enables you, sometimes after further study, to engage in a diverse number of careers. This may be as entrepreneurs in business, becoming elected representatives and legislating for the country, becoming involved in policy and analysis in civil society organisations, as an academic lawyer in colleges or universities shaping the legal minds of the future, as accountants, tax consultants, legal executives, paralegals, news reporters for local, regional or national press, or as television reporters and presenters for national or international broadcasters. Legal practice, although important, is but one career path for those studying law.

Chapter 13

Access to Justice in Ireland

> "I remain very concerned that there are cases where persons or entities have suffered from wrongdoing but where those persons or entities are unable effectively to vindicate their rights because of the cost of going to court. That is a problem to which solutions require to be found. It does seem to me that this is an issue to which the legislature should give urgent consideration."
>
> *SPV Osus Ltd v HSBC Institutional Trust Services (Ireland) Ltd* [2019] 1 I.R. 1 at 7–8 per Clarke J.

In this chapter we:

- examine access to justice in Ireland;
- consider the current schemes of criminal and liberty legal aid and engage in an analysis of why these exist, their effectiveness and proposals for reform;
- describe the system of civil legal aid, reflecting on its purpose, role and function, noting potential reforms;
- invite you, throughout the chapter, to question whether the inability to pay should impact on an individual's right to access justice.

A. Introduction

13–01 Access to justice forms a core component of a society living under the rule of law. As the former United Nations Special Rapporteur on the Independence of Judges and Lawyers notes, access to justice "represents an important safeguard that contributes to ensuring the fairness and public trust in the administration of justice."[1] Unfortunately, seeking to enforce legal rights through courts is expensive, leading to a

1 G. Knaul, *Report of the Special Rapporteur on the independence of judges and lawyers, Gabriela Knaul* (March 2013), presented to the United Nations Human Rights Council, UN Doc. A/HRC/23/43, p.3.

courts system that is "alien to many and truly accessible to increasingly few."[2] The expense of taking legal action in Ireland is summed up by Twomey J. as follows:

> "The problem with this high level of costs is not only that a defendant could be 'ruined' if he is sued by an impecunious plaintiff, but also that it is arguable that justice is denied to a citizen (whether a plaintiff or defendant) on the average income in the State (or anything close to it), but who cannot afford to 'gamble their home' on the outcome of a case."[3]

13–02 There is nothing to prevent persons from representing themselves before courts and tribunals in Ireland. Legal complexity, lack of knowledge of legal rules and court procedures and court fees[4] and, potentially, negative attitudes of judges towards lay litigants, all mitigate against many people ever attempting to represent themselves, in particular before the superior courts.[5] For this reason, those who cannot afford to hire lawyers to represent them often turn to criminal and civil legal aid. However, the adequacy or otherwise of these systems continues to be debated and is something you should reflect upon when reading this chapter. First, this chapter considers criminal and related legal aid, and its importance within a modern democratic liberal state. Second, consideration turns to civil legal aid, and its necessity in a society governed by the rule of law.[6]

---

2 *Traynor v Guinness UDV Ireland* [2015] IEHC 732 at para.1 per Barrett J.

3 *McEvaddy Property Ltd v National Asset Loan Management DAC (No. 2)* [2021] IEHC 125 at para.32. See also, European Commission, *2023 Rule of Law Report: Ireland* (SWD(2023) 807 final), p.2 and p.5, which criticises the lack of progress made in reducing the costs of litigation in Ireland.

4 See, generally, the Court Fees Orders (numbering 97 at the time of writing) on the Irish Statute Book website (*www.irishstatutebook.ie*) that establish fees for motions, filing appeals, setting a case down for trial, appearances, etc. The precise rates are set by the Minister for Justice. For a substantive exploration of issues relating to fees, costs, etc. of legal services, see the Kelly Report, *Review of the Administration of Civil Justice* (2020), in particular Ch.9.

5 For more on self-represented litigants, and the ability of such litigants to have a "McKenzie friend" to provide assistance and advise them in a court, see *McKenzie v McKenzie* [1971] 3 W.L.R. 472 and *D v McGuinness* [1999] 2 I.R. 141.

6 For more on the rule of law and access to justice, see Ch.2, para.2–13 and Section C.3.

B. Criminal and Liberty Legal Aid

13–03 There are a number of differing criminal and liberty legal aid schemes in Ireland, each coming into play at different stages of contact with the criminal justice system. These include:

1. legal advice and solicitor representation at garda stations;
2. criminal legal aid at the trial stage;
3. custody issues and proceedings related to the Criminal Assets Bureau.

13–04 At the time of writing, there is no one piece of legislation that brings together legal aid schemes that relate to criminal justice (or lack of liberty). As the Supreme Court noted in *Minister for Justice and Equality v O'Connor*, the various schemes are "piecemeal" and cause confusion for "lawyers, litigants and judges."[7] While the Supreme Court stated that it may be valuable to have all schemes on a statutory footing, this is a matter for the Oireachtas.[8] As discussed below, there is now a broad proposal for all criminal and liberty legal aid schemes to be contained in one legislative enactment.[9] Criminal legal advice and representation is provided to persons in Ireland by private solicitors and barristers, paid set fees by the State for delivering this service, once registered for the criminal legal aid schemes. This differs significantly from the public defender model most notably used in the United States, where lawyers are employees of the state, provided to an accused without choice.[10] In 2013, the European Union introduced a directive on the right of access to a lawyer in criminal proceedings.[11] Ireland has not to date exercised an opt-in to this directive, so the rights established in this directive form no part of Irish law.[12]

---

7 [2017] IESC 21 at para.25.

8 [2017] IESC 21 at para.25.

9 See paras 13–25 to 13–28.

10 Introducing a public defender scheme was discussed, but not recommended: see First Report by the Criminal Legal Aid Committee, *An Examination of the Feasibility of Introducing a Public Defender System for Ireland* (2000). The Committee, chaired by Judge Buchanan, found that the system as it operates in Ireland was the most equitable and cost-effective.

11 Directive 2013/48/EU of the European Parliament and of the Council of 22 October 2013 on the right of access to a lawyer in criminal proceedings and in European arrest warrant proceedings, and on the right to have a third party informed upon deprivation of liberty and to communicate with third persons and with consular authorities while deprived of liberty [2013] OJ L294/1.

12 For more on the concept of "opt-in", see *Minister for Justice and Equality v Mocek (No. 1)* [2021] IEHC 404 at para.31 and *DPP v Doyle* [2018] 1 I.R. 1 at 196.

1. Legal Advice and Solicitor Representation at Garda Stations

13–05 In the criminal arena, the need for legal advice for an accused can occur well before the commencement of any trial. The gardaí will have to investigate if a crime has occurred and may, under various legislative enactments, detain a suspect for questioning for certain offences, often for a significant period of time.[13] As is explored below, it took a considerable period of time for Irish practice and policy to recognise the right of a person accused of a crime to have their solicitor present during questioning. Before considering the current law and practice relating to legal advice and solicitor representation at garda stations, it is important to provide some historical context to this issue.

13–06 The treatment of suspects in garda stations has, from time to time, given rise to some disquiet, although not necessarily widespread public concern.[14] The actions of the garda "heavy gang" in the 1970s;[15] the garda investigation relating to the "Kerry babies" and the treatment of the Hayes family in the 1980s;[16] the Dean Lyons case, where a vulnerable young man confessed to a crime that he simply could not have committed;[17] and the treatment of several families in Donegal by members of An Garda Síochána, including an alleged confession by

---

[13] See, for example, s.4 of the Criminal Justice Act 1984 and s.42 of the Criminal Justice Act 1999 (maximum period of detention: 24 hours/1 day); s.30 of the Offences against the State Act 1939 (maximum period of detention: 72 hours/3 days); and s.2 of the Criminal Justice (Drug Trafficking) Act 1996 and s.50 of the Criminal Justice Act 2007 (maximum period of detention: 168 hours/7 days).

[14] See V. Conway, *The Blue Wall of Silence: The Morris Tribunal and Police Accountability in Ireland* (Dublin: IPA, 2010), in particular pp.13–17. See also, Ch.10, Box 10.3.

[15] In this regard, see the *Irish Times* special investigation from 14 and 15 February 1977 by Don Buckley, Renagh Holohan and Joe Joyce on the garda "heavy gang". These reports contained serious allegations of garda brutality against those suspected of involvement with terrorist activities in Northern Ireland.

[16] For a socio-legal exploration of the Kerry babies case, see N. McCafferty, *A Woman to Blame: The Kerry Babies Case* (Cork: Cork University Press, 2010). V. Conway, in *The Blue Wall of Silence: The Morris Tribunal and Police Accountability in Ireland* (Dublin: IPA, 2010), p.23, notes: "[i]n the Kerry Babies case, the evidence of police ill-treatment of the suspects was played down and the inconsistencies in the statements of the Hayes family were highlighted, reaffirming the legitimacy and power of the police." Only in 2020, settling a High Court action, the Irish State apologised to the Hayes family for the treatment they suffered: see A. O'Faolain, "'Suffering and stress of this ordeal is finally behind us' - Joanne Hayes issues statement following State apology over the Kerry babies case", *Irish Independent*, 18 December 2020.

[17] G. Birmingham SC, *Report of the Commission of Investigation (Dean Lyons Case)* (September 2006). For discussion on commissions of investigation, see Ch.10, paras 10–40 to 10–44.

Frank McBrearty Jnr to a non-existent murder,[18] all raised significant questions about the conduct of policing in Ireland. Nicky Kelly, convicted by the Special Criminal Court of the Sallins Train robbery (which included a judge who was asleep for a large portion of the trial),[19] described his treatment by gardaí as follows:

> "(Garda A) rammed my head off the locker door. Some of the Brits treatment. Spreadeagled. Jabbed in ribs, slapped in face, legs kicked. Lights switched off. Placed behind door. Spreadeagled. Door pushed in. Collision. Ended up on ground. Once on floor refused to get up. Hair pulled. Hit on back. Frightened more than hurt. Taken upstairs by (Garda A). Smell of drink off him. Corner of cell. Toilet. Grabbed by hair. 'Tomorrow—long day'. Shoved head five–six times down toilet, didn't wet face. Taken out of cell by (Garda A). To wall—out of sight of cell. Short delay. Knee in groin. Caught in thigh. Spat in face. Back to cell. Five minutes there. (Garda A): 'eventually you'll talk'."[20]

13–07 Despite legislative provision for the audio-recording of interviews with detainees since 1984,[21] for many years, facilities for audio-visual recording were not available in garda stations. In 2003, after many years of having to consider excuses on the part of the State and gardaí as to why audio-visual recordings of interviews would not be utilised as a matter of course, the Supreme Court made it clear that excuses would no longer be tolerated. Hardiman J. stated:

---

[18] V. Conway, *The Blue Wall of Silence: The Morris Tribunal and Police Accountability in Ireland* (Dublin: IPA, 2010), Ch.3. For discussion on this, see Ch.10, Box 10.3.

[19] M. McAleese, "The Strange Case of Nicky Kelly", *Irish Times*, 11 August 1984, p.12, where Mary McAleese (who would go on to become the eighth President of Ireland) noted: "seven out of eight most senior judges in this country found as a matter of fact that Judge O'Connor (who presided over Kelly and Co.'s first, and incomplete trial) was fully capable of adjudicating on the guilt or innocence of the accused, despite incontrovertible evidence that the man fell asleep many times during the trial."

[20] Senator Joe Costello, 130 *Seanad Éireann Debates* Cols 111–112 (23 October 1991), quoting evidence of Nicky Kelly during his trial accused of participation in the Sallins Train Robbery. Nicky Kelly was released from prison on "humanitarian grounds" in 1984 and was pardoned by President Mary Robinson, on the advice of Government, in 1992. For a detailed account of Nicky Kelly's miscarriage of justice, see P. McGarry, *While Justice Slept: The True Story of Nicky Kelly and the Sallins Train Robbery* (Dublin: Liffey Press, 2006).

[21] Criminal Justice Act 1984 s.27. Regulations were not made as regards audio-visual recordings until 1997, some 13 years later; see the Criminal Justice Act, 1984 (Electronic Recording of Interviews) Regulations 1997 (S.I. No. 74 of 1997).

> "It is clear from the history of legal and legislative concern with uncorroborated confessions over a period of nearly two decades that legislators and judges alike have emphasised the importance of the audio-visual recording of interviews ... The time cannot be remote when we will hear a submission that, absent extraordinary circumstances (by which we do not mean that a particular Garda station has no audio-visual machinery or that the audio-visual room was being painted), it is unacceptable to tender in evidence a statement which has not been so recorded."[22]

In *People (DPP) v Power*, the Supreme Court stated that the more widespread introduction of audio-visual recordings of suspect interviews has been "of very significant assistance in dealing with allegations by accused persons that alleged admissions were fabricated."[23]

13–08 This right of reasonable access to a solicitor for persons questioned in garda stations was recognised in *People (DPP) v Madden*[24] in the late 1970s. This right had to be requested, and there was no obligation for gardaí to inform the accused of their entitlement to consult a solicitor.[25] This often meant that where attempts to reach an accused's solicitor were not successful, interrogation would and could continue.[26] Only in the most exceptional of circumstances, such as where the gardaí recommended a solicitor to an accused knowing that the particular solicitor would be unable to come to the station in a timely manner, would the interrogation of questioning of an accused have to cease.[27] Prior to 2014, there was a constitutional right for an accused to be provided with *reasonable* access to a solicitor during detention.[28] This right to consult did not entitle a solicitor to be present

---

22 *People (DPP) v Connolly* [2003] 2 I.R. 1 at 17–18.

23 [2020] 2 I.L.R.M. 279 at 303. The Supreme Court accepted that this did not fully remove the concerns over the reliability of confessions, however it is for the accused to evidence that the confession has been improperly induced or obtained.

24 [1977] I.R. 336.

25 [1977] I.R. 336 at 355.

26 See *People (DPP) v Healy* [1990] 2 I.R. 73 at 82 per Finlay J., approved in *People (DPP) v Buck* [2002] 2 I.R. 268 at 279 per Keane C.J.

27 *People (DPP) v O'Brien* [2005] 2 I.R. 206.

28 See, in particular, *People (DPP) v Healy* [1990] 2 I.R. 73 and *People (DPP) v Buck* [2002] 2 I.R. 268. For a review of the right of access to a solicitor in garda custody prior to 2000, see A. Ryan, "Arrest and Detention: A Review of the Law" (2000) 17(1) *Irish Criminal Law Journal* 2.

at the interview.[29] Until 2001, there was a limited legislative right to consult a solicitor.[30] However, this right was one an accused had to self-fund regardless of their means. This changed in 2001 when the non-statutory Garda Station Legal Advice Scheme provided that a person in receipt of social welfare, or with an income less than €20,315, was eligible to receive a number of consultations with a solicitor, paid for by the State.[31] In 2011, the administration of this scheme was taken over by the Legal Aid Board. In *DPP v Ryan*,[32] the Court of Criminal Appeal decided that once an accused had requested a solicitor, barring any exceptional circumstances, questioning of the accused should not commence until they had the opportunity to consult a solicitor. In *People (DPP) v Gormley*,[33] the Supreme Court had to consider whether statements made by the accused, after he had requested a solicitor, but before the solicitor was available for consultation, were admissible in evidence. Departing from previous jurisprudence, with reference to the approach of the European Court of Human Rights (ECtHR),[34] the US Supreme Court[35] and other common law jurisdictions,[36] Clarke J. held:

> "There would be little point in giving constitutional recognition to a right of access to a lawyer while in custody if one of the principal purposes of that custody in many cases, being the questioning of the relevant suspect, could continue prior to legal advice being obtained."[37]

---

[29] *Lavery v Member in Charge, Carrickmacross Garda Station* [1999] 2 I.R. 390 at 396 per O'Flaherty J.

[30] Criminal Justice Act 1984 s.5.

[31] The number of paid consultations depended on the statutory ground for detaining an accused, varying from three consultations up to 11 consultations. For precise information, see *Garda Station Legal Advice Scheme* (14 February 2001), para.5.

[32] [2011] IECCA 6.

[33] [2014] 1 I.L.R.M. 377. The Supreme Court also decided that there was no requirement for gardaí to await the presence of a solicitor where, under operation of law, a forensic sample (i.e. blood, saliva, etc.) was requested. See further, *People (DPP) v McDonald* [2022] IESC 29.

[34] [2014] 1 I.L.R.M. 377 at 390–395. The Supreme Court in particular discussed the case of *Salduz v Turkey* (2009) 49 E.H.R.R. 19, where the ECtHR held: "Article 6 will normally require that the accused be allowed to benefit from the assistance of a lawyer ... at the initial stages of police interrogation."

[35] [2014] 1 I.L.R.M. 377 at 395–396.

[36] [2014] 1 I.L.R.M. 377 at 396–398, including a review of the legal frameworks as regards rights of detained persons to seek the assistance of a lawyer in Canada and New Zealand.

[37] [2014] 1 I.L.R.M. 377 at 402.

Clarke J. noted that the Constitution is a "living document".[38] Clarke J. stated:

> "The right to a trial in due course of law encompasses a right to early access to a lawyer after arrest and the right not to be interrogated without having had an opportunity to obtain such advice. The conviction of a person wholly or significantly on the basis of evidence obtained contrary to those constitutional entitlements represents a conviction following an unfair trial process."[39]

13–09 While not argued in *Gormley*, Clarke J. did note obiter[40] that the jurisprudence of the ECtHR and the US Supreme Court "recognises that the entitlements of a suspect extend to having the relevant lawyer present".[41] Rather than wait for a definitive pronouncement from the Supreme Court,[42] the Director of Public Prosecutions initiated a scheme permitting solicitors to be present during questioning by gardaí in May 2014.[43] In August 2014, the Legal Aid Board published the Garda Station Legal Advice Revised Scheme. This scheme sets out the rates payable to solicitors who offer advice on a consultation basis to a detained person and rates payable to a solicitor who is present during questioning.[44] Those who are entitled to a social welfare payment or

[38] [2014] 1 I.L.R.M. 377 at 400.

[39] [2014] 1 I.L.R.M. 377 at 405.

[40] *People (DPP) v Doyle* [2018] 1 I.R. 1 at 14 per Denham C.J. Denham C.J. characterised Clarke J.'s analysis of a right to have a lawyer present during questioning as obiter because the matter was not the precise issue the Supreme Court had to consider in *Gormley*.

[41] [2014] 1 I.L.R.M. 377 at 404–405, Hardiman J. concurring with this assessment at 419, stating: "[f]or many years now judicial and legal authorities have pointed to the likelihood that our system's option for the very widespread questioning of suspects who are held in custody for that purpose, was very likely to attract a right on the part of such suspects, not merely to be advised by lawyers before interrogation, but to have lawyers present at the interrogation, and enabled to intervene where appropriate."

[42] The Department of Justice had appeared to recognise that such a decision was likely to come in any event. See *Final Report of the Working Group to Advise on a System Providing for the Presence of a Legal Representative During Garda Interviews* (July 2013). The Working Group noted, at pp.2–3, that "the trend in the case law of the European Court of Human Rights suggests that Ireland's policy of not permitting solicitors to be present during interviews will come under pressure in the medium term."

[43] E. Doocey and J. O'Neill, "Right of Access to Solicitor in Garda Interviews" (2014) 7 *Irish Criminal Law Update* 1.

[44] Legal Aid Board, *Garda Station Legal Advice Revised Scheme* (August 2014), para.3. While the scheme was issued in August 2014, the rates payable to solicitors who were present during questioning was backdated to 7 May 2014, the date the DPP issued a practice direction stating that solicitors may be present during garda questioning. Rates of payment for solicitors are set down in para.5 of the scheme.

whose gross salary is under €20,316 per annum are eligible to benefit from consultation with, and/or the presence of, a solicitor during garda questioning.[45] Those surpassing these income limits must self-fund any solicitor consultation and solicitor presence during questioning.

13–10 In *People (DPP) v Doyle*,[46] the Supreme Court determined that there was no constitutional right of an accused to have their solicitor physically present during questioning. The appellant was convicted of murder in 2012 on the basis of a confession made in 2009. The confession came during his fifteenth interview with gardaí, and after the accused had consulted his solicitor on a number of occasions. Doyle at no stage requested that his solicitor be present, which, as MacMenamin J. noted, would not have been surprising as "the prevailing position at the relevant time was that there was no right to have a solicitor present during interview."[47] Seeking to rely on Clarke and Hardiman JJ.'s analysis in *Gormley*, Doyle argued that he had an entitlement to have his solicitor present during questioning and that the gardaí had an obligation to permit this, regardless of his not requesting this. On this retrospective application issue, MacMenamin J. stated:

> "The appellant must face the fact that the logic of what is sought to be applied here is a retrospective recognition and application of a then unrecognised constitutional right to have a lawyer present throughout interviews."[48]

MacMenamin J. was prepared to accept that Article 38.1 now required, if requested by a suspect, their lawyer to be present during questioning, but this did not apply retrospectively.[49] The majority of the Supreme Court in *Doyle* stated that the constitutional right to have access to a lawyer did not extend to having a lawyer physically present during interview.[50] The

[45] Legal Aid Board, *Garda Station Legal Advice Revised Scheme* (August 2014), para.4. It should be noted that entitlement to a solicitor under the scheme does not automatically entitle a person to benefit from criminal legal aid at the trial stage.

[46] [2018] 1 I.R. 1. For a full analysis of this decision, see C. Duff, "DPP v Doyle – 'The Road not Taken'" (2018) 28(1) *Irish Criminal Law Journal* 10.

[47] [2018] 1 I.R. 1 at 61–62.

[48] [2018] 1 I.R. 1 at 110.

[49] [2018] 1 I.R. 1 at 112.

[50] [2018] 1 I.R. 1, see e.g. per Denham C.J. at 12–15, O'Donnell J. at 18–23, and Charleton J. at 153–163. O'Malley J. at 184–188, concurring with the majority, stated that the determination of the issue may have been different if it related to inferences drawn from an accused exercising their right to silence (see 187).

court engaged with an extensive review of US and ECtHR jurisprudence in assessing whether constitutional guarantees to a fair trial under Article 38.1 now included a right to have a solicitor present during the interview of a suspect. The case law of the US Supreme Court on the right to have a lawyer present during questioning was contextualised by O'Donnell J. as emerging from endemic racism within the US, as well as interrogation practices that were the norm when the US court reached its decision in *Miranda*.[51] The majority of the Supreme Court concluded that the jurisprudence of the ECtHR did not (at the time of this judgment) clearly indicate that a suspect had a right to have a lawyer present during interrogation.[52] The court in its analysis of ECtHR jurisprudence highlighted that the European Convention on Human Rights (ECHR) is concerned with the entire fairness of the investigatory process, which had to at least include access to legal advice throughout detention for interrogation. Dissenting, McKechnie J. would have allowed the appeal of Doyle on this (and other) grounds. McKechnie J. held that the Irish constitutional position, in light of international and European developments, had crystallised to such a degree in 2009 that the failure to permit a solicitor to be present during interview violated Doyle's constitutional rights, rendering the subsequent trial unfair.[53]

13–11 In August 2019, the ECtHR delivered its judgment in *Doyle v Ireland*[54] and determined on the specific facts of this case that there had been no such unfairness within the trial so as to breach Article 6 of the ECHR. The ECtHR noted that Doyle was in contact with his solicitor throughout his interrogation, albeit that his solicitor was not physically present. Connected with representation at trial, along with the Irish courts' careful consideration of appeals against his conviction, Article 6 was not violated. However, the ECtHR did state that the majority of the Supreme Court "failed to recognize that the right of an accused to have access to a lawyer extended to having that lawyer physically

51 *Miranda v Arizona* (1966) 384 U.S. 436. See [2018] 1 I.R. 1 at 21. See also Charleton J. at 160–163.

52 [2018] 1 I.R. 1, see e.g. per O'Donnell J. at 19–20 and MacMenamin J. at 112–118.

53 [2018] 1 I.R. 1 at 61–93. McKechnie J. stated: "[w]hilst the right which I suggest exists has been solely attached to Article 38 of the Constitution, this is reflective of how the argument was presented and the submissions made. In so doing, I am not necessarily, nor indeed at all, to be taken as suggesting that the right may not be found in, nor its breach have consequences pursuant to, other constitutional provisions."

54 Application No. 51979/17, decision of the ECtHR (fifth section), 23 May 2019.

present during police interviews."[55] Conway and Daly categorise the *Doyle* decision of the Supreme Court as "surprising" and argue, echoing McKechnie J.'s dissent, that the majority failed to recognise the position of inequality that suspects are in when garda questioning occurs.[56] There is also the issue that the entitlement to have a lawyer present during questioning in Ireland has no statutory basis, deriving solely from a letter issued by the DPP. Daly and Conway are critical of this because "[t]he circular does not establish a legal or constitutional right, and ... [lacks] clarity."[57] Hence, from a rule-of-law perspective, it is concerning that the Oireachtas has not seised itself of this issue thus far, although this may change.[58] The Supreme Court decision in *Doyle* did not impact on the DPP's decision to permit solicitors to be present during questioning. The Supreme Court in *Doyle* determined there is no constitutional right to have a solicitor present during questioning. However, the ECtHR held in its *Doyle* decision that Article 6 of the ECHR does protect this right. Article 6 is indirectly applicable in Irish law.[59]

2. Criminal Legal Aid at Trial

13–12 The Criminal Justice (Legal Aid) Act 1962 (the "1962 Act") establishes the statutory entitlement of accused persons to legal aid at the trial stage.[60] In order to qualify for criminal legal aid before a court,[61] or if an individual is taking an appeal against conviction,[62] a judge must

55 *Doyle v Ireland* at para.101.

56 V. Conway and Y. Daly, "From Legal Advice to Legal Assistance: Recognising the Changing Role of the Solicitor in the Garda Station" (2019) 3 *Irish Judicial Studies Journal* 103 at 111–112. See further, V. Conway and Y. Daly, *Criminal Defence Representation at Garda Stations* (Dublin: Bloomsbury Professional, 2023).

57 Y. Daly and V. Conway, "Selecting a Lawyer: the Practical Arrangement of Police Station Legal Assistance" (2021) 48(4) *Journal of Law and Society* 618 at 626.

58 In light of decisions relating to the Custody Issues Scheme, discussed in more detail at para.13–20, there is likely no obligation on the Oireachtas to legislate in light of *Minister for Justice and Equality v O'Connor* [2017] IESC 21. However, see reform discussion at paras 13–23 to 13–28.

59 See Ch.6, paras 6–92 to 6–97.

60 A person must be charged with an offence before there is an entitlement to criminal legal aid. A request by gardaí for a person to attend court on a certain date in the expectation of being charged with criminal offences, but where no charges are in fact brought, does not permit the District Court to grant criminal legal aid, as there is no trial: see *McEntaggart v DPP* [2019] 2 I.R. 314.

61 Sections 2 and 3 of the 1962 Act. The 1962 Act has been amended and extended by a large number of other Acts. You are advised to consult the Legislation Directory entry on the Irish Statute Book website for the precise amendments.

62 Sections 4 and 6 of the 1962 Act. Legal aid may also be granted under s.4 where it relates to a case stated from a lower court to a superior court.

be satisfied that the defendant's financial means are insufficient for him to employ counsel[63] and, due to the gravity of the charge or other exceptional reasons, "it is essential in the interests of justice that he should have legal aid in the preparation and conduct of his defence".[64] An application for criminal legal aid on each specified criminal charge must be made.[65] A key question that arises from the legislative entitlement to criminal legal aid is: what precisely constitutes a charge of such gravity to enable a person, who satisfies the other criteria, to benefit from criminal legal aid? This issue was determined in *State (Healy) v Donoghue*,[66] where the Supreme Court held that an accused had to be informed of their right to access the criminal legal aid scheme.

Box 13.1: Case Focus
***State (Healy) v Donoghue* [1976] I.R. 325**

Healy had been convicted of a number of offences before the District Court in 1974 and 1975.[67] On 12 June 1974, Healy was convicted of breaking and entering and theft by a District Court judge. The matter was adjourned on a number of occasions, and Healy was sentenced to three months' imprisonment on 15 January 1975. Healy had not been informed by the District Court judge of the existence of the criminal legal aid scheme, so was not represented by legal counsel. On 13 December 1974, Healy was convicted of a separate offence relating to theft of a car. Prior to sentencing, on 30 December 1974, Healy applied for and was granted legal aid on this second conviction. Due to a dispute between the Department of Justice and solicitors and barristers as regards fees payable under the criminal legal aid scheme, Healy was not represented by counsel (as regards the sentencing element of his December 1974 conviction) on a number of occasions in January 1975 when sentence was to be imposed. On 29 January 1975, the District Court judge imposed sentence despite objections from Healy.

63 See ss.2(1)(a), 3(2)(b), 4(2)(b), 5(2)(b) and 6(2)(b) of the 1962 Act.
64 In this regard, the practice has been that where a person is charged with murder, they will not have to satisfy this second limb, as it is presumed to be in the essential interests of justice that where a defendant cannot afford representation, it is in the interests of the defendant to be represented.
65 See *Cully v DPP* [2020] IEHC 438 and *King v DPP* [2022] IEHC 74.
66 [1976] I.R. 325.
67 For a full outline of the facts relating to Healy, and the other prosecutor in this case, see the High Court decision of Gannon J. in *State (Healy) v Donoghue* [1976] I.R. 325 at 330–333.

Key issues that had to be determined by the High Court, and eventually the Supreme Court, were whether the right to criminal legal aid under the 1962 Act had been respected, and whether Healy's constitutional and statutory rights had been properly vindicated. Healy argued that an accused had (1) the right to be informed of the existence of criminal legal aid, and (2) the right to be granted criminal legal aid, with the accused's representation paid out of public monies. In making this argument, counsel for Healy relied on provisions of the Constitution,[68] as well as constitutional jurisprudence from the US Supreme Court. The respondents argued that in providing a system of criminal legal aid under the 1962 Act, the Oireachtas was entitled to limit this to those who (i) required and (ii) applied for criminal legal aid. The respondents stated that the Irish Constitution differed significantly from the Sixth Amendment to the Constitution of the United States, which provides: "[i]n all criminal prosecutions, the accused shall ... have the assistance of counsel for his defense." The respondents argued that both convictions and periods of imprisonment should be affirmed.

In the High Court, Gannon J. held that the December 1974 conviction should be quashed.[69] However, he held that there was no right, legislative or constitutional, for an accused to be informed of the right to apply for criminal legal aid.[70] Therefore, the May 1974 conviction and subsequent sentence stood. However, the Supreme Court held that both convictions should be quashed. O'Higgins C.J. noted that the Irish Constitution makes it mandatory "that every criminal trial shall be conducted in accordance with the concept of justice, that the procedures applied shall be fair, and that the person accused will be afforded every opportunity to defend himself".[71] O'Higgins C.J. stated that where a person's liberty is at stake, or where other serious or personal consequences may result in a conviction on a criminal charge, criminal legal aid must be provided and a person must be told of their right to apply for criminal legal aid.[72] Standards of fairness in criminal trials are not fixed, and may change depending on the development of society.[73] Were an accused not informed of the statutory scheme of criminal legal aid and their right to apply for this, Henchy J. stated that

[68] Counsel referred to Article 38.1 of the Constitution ("No person shall be tried on any criminal charge save in due course of law"), coupled with Article 40.3.1° ("The State guarantees in its laws to respect, and, as far as practicable, by its laws to defend and vindicate the personal rights of the citizen").

[69] [1976] I.R. 325 at 340–342.

[70] [1976] I.R. 325 at 339.

[71] [1976] I.R. 325 at 349.

[72] [1976] I.R. 325 at 350.

[73] [1976] I.R. 325 at 347.

this would be a "hollow and specious expression of the constitutional guarantee".[74] Reference was made to the difficulties faced by those not versed in the language of law, court process and evidentiary rules in being able to conduct a proper defence.[75]

13–13 The right to criminal legal aid is for the benefit of the applicant in order to ensure that they receive a fair trial.[76] The constitutional significance of *Healy* should not be underestimated. It situates criminal legal aid as a constitutional right, which exists independently of the 1962 Act. In *Carmody v Minister for Justice, Equality and Law Reform*, the Supreme Court described this as follows: "the right to legal aid does not stem from a statute. It is a constitutional right. The Act of 1962, to the extent that it does make provision for legal aid, is merely a means of vindicating that right."[77] This right extends to having a choice of legal representative, albeit that they have to be on the criminal legal aid panel.[78] There have been many challenges to decisions of District Court judges relating to the grant of criminal legal aid certificates under the 1962 Act. A number of key judicial principles emerge from these cases, including:

a) judges can only grant criminal legal aid when an application is made;
b) judges cannot fetter their discretion in granting criminal legal aid;
c) there is a right to criminal legal aid even where a judge is not minded to impose a custodial sentence; and
d) there is generally no right to "equality of arms" between a defendant and the State in criminal trials unless the exceptional circumstances of the case dictate otherwise.

(a) Criminal legal aid only granted on application

13–14 Both *Cully v DPP*[79] and *King v DPP*[80] related to whether a District Court judge could, of their own motion, provide criminal legal aid

74 [1976] I.R. 325 at 355.
75 See, in particular, the decision of Kenny J. in *State (Healy) v Donoghue* [1976] I.R. 325 at 364–365.
76 *King v DPP* [2022] IEHC 74 at para.15.
77 [2010] 1 I.R. 635 at 653.
78 *Mulhall v O'Donnell* [1989] I.L.R.M. 367 at 368.
79 [2020] IEHC 438.
80 [2022] IEHC 74.

certificates to an accused on multiple charges, despite an application being made on just one of those charges. It might seem unusual that this would be challenged; after all, a person would likely want representation on all charges. The factual context of both cases illuminates the low fees paid to lawyers to represent clients. In both *Cully* and *Doyle*, solicitors applied for a legal aid certificate to cover one charge only, despite both having multiple charges that the District Court would have to determine.[81] The High Court in both cases determined that since an application was made on one charge only, a District Court judge could not, of their own motion, grant a legal aid certificate for all charges.[82] Underlying both decisions was the recognition that significantly less fees would be paid to legal representatives if a legal aid certificate was granted on all charges, rather than on a charge-by-charge basis.[83] Meenan J. in *Cully* highlighted the level of work required to provide proper representation to an accused before a court, e.g. consulting with the client, engaging with the prosecuting garda, disclosure of evidence. Meenan J. stated that he would "very much doubt that a credible case could be made that these fees are reasonable remuneration for the professional work and responsibility involved."[84] Phelan J. in *King* noted that decisions on financing of the criminal legal aid system and levels of fees involved are a matter for the political branches of government.[85] Although it was not relevant to this case, if it could be proven that the system "is failing to ensure effective representation for accused persons remanded in custody",[86] the courts could intervene to uphold an accused's entitlement to representation.

13–15 In *Ward v Minister for Justice and Equality*,[87] three co-accused all wished to be represented by the same solicitor at the Circuit Court level. The solicitor had no objection to representing the three accused

---

81 In *Cully v DPP* [2020] IEHC 438 at paras 1–2, the accused had four charges against them, with a legal aid certificate applied for on only one of the four charges. In *King v DPP* [2022] IEHC 74 at paras 5–10, the accused had two charges against them, in addition to a bench warrant for failing to attend court for sentence on a previous occasion.

82 [2020] IEHC 438 at paras 5–7 and *King v DPP* [2022] IEHC 74 at para.17.

83 Regulation 7(4) of the Criminal Justice (Legal Aid) Regulations 1965 (S.I. No. 12 of 1965).

84 [2020] IEHC 438 at para.3.

85 [2022] IEHC 74 at para.24.

86 [2022] IEHC 74 at para.24.

87 [2019] 2 I.R. 565.

persons, however 1978 Regulations[88] meant that the solicitor would only receive the same fee as if he represented just one of the accused. The solicitor declined to represent the two applicants in *Ward*, as they were already representing the third co-accused. The Minister for Justice argued that the Regulations should be interpreted as setting the fee at zero for solicitors who represent more than one co-accused during the same Circuit Court trial.[89] Baker J. held that while the Minister had the power to set fees pursuant to s.10 of the 1962 Act, the Oireachtas could not have intended to grant a power to the Minister to set and amend fees from time to time down to zero.[90] This interfered with the right of the accused to choose their own solicitor.[91] Furthermore, within the District Court, a fee, albeit at a lower rate, would be paid where a solicitor represents co-accused; it was irrational then for the Circuit Court fee to be set at zero.[92] On foot of this decision, the Minister amended the offending Regulations, providing for the payment of a fee in the Circuit Court to support the representation of more than one co-accused.[93]

(b) Judges cannot fetter their discretion

13–16 In determining whether or not to grant criminal legal aid, judges should not adopt fixed or rigid policies that fetter their discretion. For example, in *Whelan v Fitzpatrick*,[94] Budd J. quashed a decision of a District Court judge who refused to grant the applicant a legal aid certificate. In this case, the applicant had been refused legal aid as regards a drink driving offence on the basis that the judge "did not give legal aid in driving cases".[95] This was determined to be an irrelevant factor, as the District Court judge simply had to concern himself with the legislative provisions on criminal legal aid, rather than imposing his own principles and policies for denying criminal legal aid.[96] Not only was this in the interests of justice, it was also a statutory requirement by virtue

88 Criminal Justice (Legal Aid) (Amendment) Regulations 1978 (S.I. No. 33 of 1978).
89 Regulation 3(1)(g) of the 1978 Regulations.
90 [2019] 2 I.R. 565 at 578–579.
91 [2019] 2 I.R. 565 at 575–576.
92 [2019] 2 I.R. 565 at 580.
93 Regulation 2 of the Criminal Justice (Legal Aid) (Amendment) Regulations 2018 (S.I. No. 579 of 2018), amending reg.3(1)(g) of the 1978 Regulations. Fee payments were backdated to 1 November 2017, the date Baker J. made the decision in *Ward*.
94 [2008] 2 I.R. 678.
95 [2008] 2 I.R. 678 at 683.
96 [2008] 2 I.R. 678 at 694–695.

of s.2 of the 1962 Act, whereby the District Court judge "shall" grant criminal legal aid once an applicant meets the legislative criteria.[97]

(c) The right to criminal legal aid even where an individual is not at risk of a custodial sentence

13–17 In *Tighe (A Minor) v Haughton*,[98] the applicant pleaded guilty to engaging in threatening, abusive or insulting behaviour towards a member of An Garda Síochána contrary to s.6 of the Criminal Justice (Public Order) Act 1994 (as amended). The District Court judge noted that the applicant was "not at risk", a term used to signify that the applicant was not in danger of incarceration. The District Court judge refused to grant the applicant criminal legal aid for the subsequent probation report hearing. Challenging this refusal by way of judicial review, Hanna J. noted that the applicant was represented throughout the trial, up until the judge ordered a probation report. Since the applicant was not at risk of a custodial sentence, and his circumstances were not so exceptional that legal aid had to be granted in order to conclude sentencing (which would not involve a custodial sentence), Hanna J. held that the District Court judge did not err in law in refusing to grant the applicant criminal legal aid.[99] Three months after this decision, the Supreme Court had to consider a very similar legal issue. In *Joyce v Brady*,[100] somewhat similar facts to *Tighe* were under scrutiny by the Supreme Court. Joyce was on trial for theft; it was his first offence before the District Court. In assessing Joyce's entitlement to criminal legal aid, the District Court judge asked a garda whether Joyce was "at risk", i.e. in danger of getting a custodial sentence, to which the garda stated that Joyce was not "at risk".[101] Unlike in *Tighe*, such actions on behalf of the District Court judge came in for adverse comment by the Supreme Court. Donnelly J. noted:

> "There is something more than odd in a court deciding the entitlement to legal aid by inviting a member of An Garda Síochána to consider if an accused is at risk that another court will or may impose a custodial sentence on the accused if convicted."[102]

[97] [2008] 2 I.R. 678 at 689–690.

[98] [2011] IEHC 64. There are no paragraph numbers to enable direct reference to precise parts of the judgment.

[99] Relying in particular on *O'Neill v Butler* [1979] I.L.R.M. 243 and *Costigan v Brady* [2004] IEHC 16, where a similar decision was reached.

[100] [2011] 3 I.R. 376.

[101] [2011] 3 I.R. 376 at 381.

[102] [2011] 3 I.R. 376 at 383. This is closely linked with the requirement that a judge should

In finding that Joyce should have been granted legal aid, the Supreme Court emphasised (in light of *Healy*) that criminal legal aid is a constitutional right, given statutory form in the 1962 Act.[103] In deciding whether or not to grant criminal legal aid, a District Court judge must consider the constitutional objective in ensuring a trial in due course of law is achieved.[104] Noting that this was the first occasion that Joyce had appeared before a court, he was likely to be unfamiliar with court processes. By refusing to grant legal aid, the District Court judge had placed Joyce's right to defend himself "at its lowest".[105] It appears that where there is a mere possibility that a custodial sentence or any other "severe penalty" will be imposed that can impact on a defendant's welfare or livelihood, an impecunious individual must be informed of their right to apply for legal representation under the 1962 Act, and criminal legal aid should be granted.[106]

(d) Entitlement to "equality of arms" in criminal trials in exceptional circumstances

13–18 While an individual has a right to be provided with criminal legal aid, this does not mean a person is entitled to "equality of arms" with the State prosecutor. This touches upon the question of whether, for example if the State (as prosecutor) has a solicitor and a barrister presenting a case, the accused also has to be provided with a solicitor and a barrister. This issue arises as regards entitlement to counsel (barristers) mainly at the District Court level. In *Carmody v Minister for Justice, Equality and Law Reform*, the plaintiff had been charged with 42 criminal offences relating to improper record-keeping of cattle, their movements, and failure to register control of certain cattle.[107] If convicted of these offences, the plaintiff could have faced a significant monetary fine or up to two years' imprisonment.[108] The plaintiff was granted legal aid in the District Court

not fetter their discretion, and seemingly make a decision to grant legal aid on the basis of the opinion of another in the court.

[103] [2011] 3 I.R. 376 at 386–388.

[104] [2011] 3 I.R. 376 at 387.

[105] [2011] 3 I.R. 376 at 388.

[106] See, generally, *O'Neill v Butler* [1979] I.L.R.M. 243; *Cahill v Reilly* [1994] 3 I.R. 547; *McSorley v Governor of Mountjoy Prison* [1996] 2 I.L.R.M. 331; *Clarke v Kirby* [1998] 2 I.L.R.M. 30; *Leonard v Garavan* [2003] 4 I.R. 60. It is for an accused's legal representative to place information before a judge on application regarding financial means of an accused: see *King v Coghlan* [2015] IEHC 300.

[107] [2010] 1 I.R. 635 at 640–641.

[108] [2010] 1 I.R. 635 at 641.

so as to instruct a solicitor to represent him in these criminal proceedings. However, the State sought to utilise both a solicitor and junior counsel in prosecuting the case.[109] At that time, a District Court judge could only grant a defendant a legal aid certificate that limited representation to a solicitor. Carmody argued that his constitutional rights and his rights under Article 6 of the ECHR to criminal legal aid were violated due to the disparity in representation between him and the State.[110] The Supreme Court proceeded to consider the constitutional question only.[111] Murray C.J. for the Supreme Court noted: "[s]ometimes simplistic and unthinking comments surface in the public arena suggesting that fairness and fair procedures at a criminal trial only exist for the benefit of criminals."[112] The court noted that the number of imprisonable offences now tried at the District Court level had increased dramatically since the introduction of criminal legal aid in Ireland in 1962.[113] Rather than finding s.2 of the 1962 Act unconstitutional, the court stated:

> "[T]he absence of a right to apply for legal aid to include counsel in appropriate cases [in the District Court] must properly be considered as stemming from a failure of the State to make, by one means or another, specific provision for such legal aid rather than from any provision, in particular any prohibition, in the Act of 1962."[114]

The Supreme Court therefore held that it would be unjust and contrary to Article 38.1 of the Constitution (right to a fair trial) if the prosecution were to proceed while the applicant did not have the opportunity to apply for legal aid to include a solicitor and a barrister.[115] The Supreme Court held that the State had to put in place a scheme (be it on a legislative or administrative basis) that provided the applicant with an opportunity to

[109] [2010] 1 I.R. 635 at 641.
[110] [2010] 1 I.R. 635 at 645–646.
[111] In this regard, the Supreme Court noted that if it accepted the plaintiff's contention that s.2 of the 1962 Act was incompatible with Ireland's obligations under the ECHR, then the only remedy open to the plaintiff would be a declaration of incompatibility (s.5 of the European Convention on Human Rights Act 2003), which would not resolve the issue before the court, as it would ultimately be for the Oireachtas to determine how to remedy the alleged breach of Ireland's obligations under the ECHR. The court therefore decided to consider the constitutional question first; see further, [2010] 1 I.R. 635 at 649–651.
[112] [2010] 1 I.R. 635 at 662.
[113] [2010] 1 I.R. 635 at 658–660.
[114] [2010] 1 I.R. 635 at 667.
[115] [2010] 1 I.R. 635 at 668.

apply for legal aid to include both a solicitor and counsel.[116] In light of the *Carmody* decision, an Ad-Hoc District Court (Counsel) Scheme came into force in October 2009, on the date the Supreme Court delivered its decision in *Carmody*.[117] The non-statutory Ad-Hoc Scheme[118] can also apply to appeals from the District Court to the Circuit Court.[119] In order to be granted a right to have counsel, in addition to meeting the requirements for criminal legal aid at trial outlined previously, the solicitor for the accused must show that:

> "... the gravity of the charge and complexity of the case, as well as any other exceptional circumstances make it essential in the interests of justice that he or she should have the assistance of counsel in the preparation and conduct of his or her defence."[120]

13–19 The prosecution, if it so desires, may make submissions to the District Court judge as to whether the request for counsel should be granted or not.[121] The decision of the District Court judge is "final and shall not be appealable".[122] In *Ward v Judge Reynolds*,[123] O'Malley J. had to consider a legal challenge to the Ad-Hoc Scheme. In this case, the applicant, Ward, claimed that the Ad-Hoc Scheme was ultra vires the 1962 Act[124] and was unconstitutional.[125] Ward had been charged with a variety of offences under the Road Traffic Acts, including driving without a licence or insurance, dangerous driving, and driving while intoxicated.[126] In dismissing Ward's challenge, O'Malley J. noted:

[116] [2010] 1 I.R. 635 at 669. The court also noted that the remedy afforded to Carmody in this case adequately protected his right to criminal legal aid, be it under the Constitution or the ECHR, and so there was no need to consider whether a declaration of incompatibility should be granted under the European Convention on Human Rights Act 2003. On declarations of incompatibility, see further, Ch.6, para.6–97.

[117] Courts Policy Division, Department of Justice, *Procedures Governing the Payment of Criminal Legal Aid Fees* (2019), paras 16.1–16.3.

[118] Ad-Hoc District Court (Counsel) Scheme (October 2009) (on file with author).

[119] Ad-Hoc District Court (Counsel) Scheme, para.2.

[120] Ad-Hoc District Court (Counsel) Scheme, para.1(1)(b).

[121] Ad-Hoc District Court (Counsel) Scheme, para.1(3).

[122] Ad-Hoc District Court (Counsel) Scheme, para.1(2). However, O'Malley J. in *Ward v Judge Reynolds* [2015] IEHC 783 at paras 65–66 noted that nothing prevented a Circuit Court judge (on appeal) from finding that counsel is necessary for an accused if there is a "material change of circumstances" and it is "essential in the interests of justice" to now provide counsel for the accused under the criminal legal aid scheme. See also, *Brett v District Judge Coughlan* [2011] IEHC 540.

[123] [2015] IEHC 783.

[124] [2015] IEHC 783 at paras 47–52 and 66–67.

[125] [2015] IEHC 783 at paras 50–52 and 72.

[126] [2015] IEHC 783 at para.5.

> "Charges under the Road Traffic Acts constitute a very significant proportion of the case-load of the District Court. I do not say that they are not capable of giving rise to complex legal issues but there is nothing to suggest complexity of any sort in the instant case."[127]

Ward's challenge was therefore dismissed as there was nothing exceptional or complex, or mandated in the interests of justice, for him to have counsel in his legal team.[128]

3. Custody Issues Scheme and Criminal Assets Bureau

13–20 A number of other non-statutory legal aid schemes exist within the criminal justice/liberty field. The Custody Issues Scheme (CIS)[129] provides legal aid for superior court bail applications, extradition and European arrest warrant procedures, or an application for habeas corpus. A person will only have access to the CIS upon a recommendation from a court,[130] subject to meeting the financial criteria. Since 1 June 2012, the Legal Aid Board is responsible for the administration of this scheme.[131] The CIS does not currently have a statutory basis,[132] but rather operates as published operational guidance. The Supreme Court has held in *Minister for Justice and Equality v O'Connor*,[133] a European arrest warrant decision, that the non-statutory nature of the CIS does not breach European Union law. Its non-statutory nature also does

[127] [2015] IEHC 783 at para.70.

[128] [2015] IEHC 783 at para.72.

[129] Legal Aid Board, *Legal Aid – Custody Issues Scheme: Scheme Provisions and Guidance Document* (June 2013), available at: *https://www.legalaidboard.ie/en/our-services/criminal-legal-aid/guidance-documents/*.

[130] Legal Aid Board, *Legal Aid – Custody Issues Scheme: Scheme Provisions and Guidance Document* (June 2013), para.9. The recommendation by a judge that the CIS applies comes at the end of proceedings: see *Cerkovska v Minister for Justice and Equality* [2014] IEHC 258. In *Winters v Legal Aid Board* [2024] IEHC 744, the applicant was injured on an Irish Prison Service transport vehicle between a court and his return to prison. The applicant received damages. The applicant also sought payment for pre-litigation correspondence sent by his solicitor to the Department of Justice. At paras 11–16, Bolger J. rejected an argument that the CIS could be used for personal injuries litigation; the terms of the CIS were clearly limited to the actions listed.

[131] For a history of the emergence of this scheme, see *Fundamentals of the Irish Legal System*, 1st edn (Dublin: Round Hall, 2016), para.13–19, *O'Shea v Legal Aid Board* [2020] IESC 51 at paras 12–30, and *M v Director of Oberstown Children Detention Centre* [2021] IECA 260 at paras 11– 17.

[132] However, see discussion of the General Scheme of the Criminal Justice (Legal Aid) Bill 2023 at paras 13–23 to 13–28.

[133] [2017] IESC 21, on appeal from *Minister for Justice and Equality v O'Connor* [2015] IECA 227.

not render it unconstitutional. O'Donnell J., delivering the judgment of the court, in essence held that the CIS scheme is a constitutional imperative.[134] While rejecting the appellant's core legal claims, O'Donnell J. did state that:

> "... [the] piecemeal development and combination of sources may only lead to confusion, and litigants, lawyers and judges should not have to read a series of reported cases to understand the circumstances in which legal aid may be made available [under the CIS] ... there may be merit in placing the entire area on a comprehensive statutory footing."[135]

13–21 In *O'Shea v Ireland*,[136] the applicant's judicial review, challenging the constitutionality of criminal sentencing requirements, had failed. The trial judge had recommended that the applicant's costs be covered under the CIS.[137] Counsel for the Legal Aid Board were invited to make submissions to the High Court on the applicability of CIS to this case. The Legal Aid Board had not instructed counsel to make submissions as to whether costs under the CIS should be granted.[138] Counsel did note that the applicant had sought an injunction, while CIS only covered reliefs of certiorari, mandamus and prohibition.[139] The Legal Aid Board then declined to pay O'Shea's legal costs arising from the failed constitutional challenge. The Legal Aid Board argued that where a judge made a recommendation that the CIS should be used for an individual's legal costs, this is subject to the Legal Aid Board ensuring the type of proceedings came within the CIS so as to pay legal fees.[140] In the High Court, Simons J. after reviewing the text of the CIS held that it was solely for a judge within proceedings to determine eligibility.[141] Simons J. determined that the Legal Aid Board sought, in essence, to overrule a decision by a judge, which "would be an affront to the dignity of the court", against the spirit of the CIS, and concerning from the perspective of legal certainty.[142] In making this decision, Simons J. further held that even if he

[134] [2017] IESC 21, in particular at para.15 and para.17.
[135] [2017] IESC 21 at para.25.
[136] [2017] IEHC 9.
[137] *O'Shea v Legal Aid Board* [2019] IEHC 385 at para.12.
[138] [2019] IEHC 385 at para.12.
[139] [2019] IEHC 385 at para.11.
[140] [2019] IEHC 385 at para.17.
[141] [2019] IEHC 385 at paras 35–39.
[142] [2019] IEHC 385 at para.43.

was mistaken on that point, O'Shea would succeed on a narrower ground in that if he had been successful, this potentially would have resulted in him serving a concurrent rather than consecutive sentence.[143] Since the outcome touched upon the applicant's liberty, seeking to deny access to the CIS on rather technical grounds was not in keeping with the spirit of the CIS.[144] The Legal Aid Board, while now accepting the applicant came within the CIS on the narrower ground of Simons J.'s decision, appealed to the Supreme Court. The Supreme Court did not go as far as Simons J. in stating that, in all situations of a recommendation by a court, the Legal Aid Board must abide by this recommendation as if it were a court order.[145] While rejecting the High Court's analysis that the Legal Aid Board's refusal to follow a recommendation would be an "affront to the dignity of the court", Baker J. did assert that "it is hard to envisage circumstances in which the recommendation of the court would not bear very significant weight in the decision, and may be in most cases dispositive."[146] So, this decision does leave it open in future cases to permit the Legal Aid Board to refuse payment of counsel fees. Where it does so, the Legal Aid Board's decision must be "rational and lawful".[147]

13–22 While not falling into the realm of "criminal law", the Proceeds of Crime Act 1996 permits the High Court (after investigation and the bringing of an application by the Criminal Assets Bureau (CAB))[148] to dispose of the assets obtained from crime proceeds.[149] In 1998, the Department of Justice introduced an ad-hoc legal aid scheme, administered by the Courts Policy Division, for those who were subject to various proceedings under the Proceeds of Crime Act 1996. In January 2014, responsibility for the administration of the CAB Scheme

[143] [2019] IEHC 385 at para.78.
[144] [2019] IEHC 385 at paras 63–69.
[145] *O'Shea v Legal Aid Board* [2020] IESC 51 at paras 63–79.
[146] [2020] IESC 51 at para.94.
[147] [2020] IESC 51 at para.96.
[148] Criminal Assets Bureau Act 1996. For an exploration of the Proceeds of Crime Act 1996 and CAB, see L. Campbell, "Theorising Asset Forfeiture in Ireland" (2007) 71 *Journal of Criminal Law* 441, and L. Campbell, "Taxing Illegal Assets: The Revenue Work of the Criminal Assets Bureau" (2006) 24 *Irish Law Times* 316.
[149] The CAB Scheme also applies when a Circuit Court judge orders forfeiture of cash under s.34 of the Criminal Justice Act 1994 where the "cash directly or indirectly represents any person's proceeds of, or is intended by any person for use in, drug trafficking". The CAB Scheme also applies where a member of CAB is a respondent or defendant in certain social welfare (Social Welfare Consolidation Act 2005 s.307) and taxation appeals.

came under the remit of the Legal Aid Board, where it remains.[150] Unlike the CIS, legal aid under the CAB Scheme has to be granted by a judge at the commencement of proceedings. The CAB Scheme cannot be applied for retrospectively.[151] Legal aid under the CAB Scheme will be provided where it comes within its scope, the applicant's means are insufficient to enable him to fund legal representation, and "by reason of exceptional circumstances it is essential"[152] that the applicant have assistance in the preparation and conduct of the case.[153] In *Murphy v GM*,[154] Hardiman J. for the Supreme Court noted that litigation relating to the seizure of the proceeds of crime can often be more complex than criminal litigation. In *Murphy v Gilligan*,[155] the Supreme Court accepted that in the right circumstances, which were not present in this case,[156] the CAB Scheme could cover the provision of a forensic accountant to present evidence that the financial means of an applicant did not come about through criminal involvement. In *Criminal Assets Bureau v DW and CW*,[157] the High Court admitted both respondents to the CAB Scheme on the basis of their means, as well as it being in the interests of justice to do so given the complexity of issues. CAB appealed this decision to the Court of Appeal arguing that the means of the respondents were sufficient to pay for their own representation, albeit that these means were alleged to come from the proceeds of crime.[158] CAB further argued that there was nothing exceptional in this case requiring legal representation to be provided to the respondents.[159] Whelan J., delivering judgment for the Court of Appeal, rejected both of CAB's arguments. She noted

[150] Legal Aid Board, *Criminal Assets Bureau Ad-hoc Legal Aid Scheme* (January 2014), para.2. For discussion on the legislative proposal to place the CAB Scheme on a statutory footing, see paras 13–23 to 13–28.

[151] Legal Aid Board, *Criminal Assets Bureau Ad-hoc Legal Aid Scheme* (January 2014), para.3.

[152] As regards exploring what is meant by "essential", see the decision of O'Higgins J. in *MFM v WFB* [1999] 1 I.R. 112.

[153] Legal Aid Board, *Criminal Assets Bureau Ad-hoc Legal Aid Scheme* (January 2014), para.5. A person seeking to benefit from the CAB Scheme must provide the High Court with information to enable the court to determine the applicant's financial means.

[154] [2001] IESC 33.

[155] [2014] IESC 43.

[156] The Supreme Court noted that the matters that Gilligan sought to gain a forensic accountant for (so as to prove that his wealth came from significant gambling success, rather than proceeds of crime) had already been extensively litigated (see *Murphy v Gilligan* [2009] 2 I.R. 271 and *Murphy v Gilligan* [2011] IEHC 62).

[157] [2021] IECA 295.

[158] [2021] IECA 295 at paras 24–30.

[159] [2021] IECA 295 at paras 31–38.

that the trial judge examined the current income of the respondents, who strenuously denied that their historical income derived from the proceeds of crime. Whether their income was from the proceeds of crime had yet to be determined substantively.[160] Whelan J. further examined the complexity of the litigation, spanning financial transactions over a number of decades, involving complex assessments of income, property ownership and other various transactions.[161] The trial judge had carefully considered this issue and had reached a decision on the balance of probabilities that the complexity of the issues involved mandated entry of the respondents to the CAB Scheme. Whelan J. further noted that, at any stage, CAB could seek to re-enter proceedings to get a fresh determination of Scheme entitlement if new information was made available to the trial court.

4. Reform of the Criminal Legal Aid System

13–23 Ensuring effective access to justice is expensive. It can often be unpopular, socially and politically, to seek to defend the right to criminal legal aid for those accused of crime. The political system, in particular when societal concerns about incidents of crime may be high, can often argue for limitations and restrictions on criminal legal aid, with a particular focus on "repeat offenders".[162] Successive Ministers for Justice have often responded by highlighting that criminal legal aid is a constitutional right, whose overarching aim is to ensure due process.[163] As outlined in Table 13.1, the cost of criminal legal aid between 2018 and 2022 was almost €365 million.

---

160 [2021] IECA 295 at paras 83–87.

161 [2021] IECA 295 at paras 88–97 and 114.

162 For indicative examples of this, see the following questions that TDs have posed to Ministers for Justice: Bernard Durkan TD asked the Minister for Justice, Helen McEntee TD, about her plans to "review ... the criminal legal aid programme, with particular reference to its application to repeat offenders" (*Dáil Debates* (unrevised), Written Answer No. 551, 11 July 2023); and Peter Burke TD asked the Minister "if she has addressed the matter of free legal aid being granted to repeat offenders" (*Dáil Debates* (unrevised), Written Answer No. 593, 1 March 2022).

163 See, e.g. Minister for Justice, Helen McEntee TD's response in *Dáil Debates* (unrevised), Written Answer No. 551, 11 July 2023 and Minister of State, Hildegarde Naughton TD in *Dáil Debates* (unrevised), Written Answer No. 1366, 27 July 2021.

Table 13.1: Criminal Legal Aid Schemes Expenditure 2018–2022[164]

Scheme/Year	2018	2019	2020	2021	2022
Criminal Legal Aid (1962 Act and CIS – Bail)	€60.014 million (m)	€60.135m	€55.872m	€65.275m	€78.781m
Garda Station Legal Advice Scheme	€1.948m	€1.715m	€1.983m	€1.888m	€4.1m
Custody Issues Scheme (CIS – non-bail)	€2.7m	€3.2m	€4.3m	€6m	€6.281m
Criminal Assets Bureau Scheme	€147,000	€42,000	€69,000	€410,059	€42,245
Total Yearly	**€64.809m**	**€65.092m**	**€62.192m**	**€73.573m**	**€89.204m**

13–24 Until January 2025, the rates of payment provided to barristers under the criminal legal aid scheme had not increased since 2011.[165] This issue arose from time to time in the Dáil.[166] The increase in fees followed a concerted campaign by barristers, including withdrawal of services on particular days in 2023 and 2024.[167] While the immediate issue of rates of pay has been resolved on this occasion, to what extent could low payment rates for legal practitioners impact on an accused's constitutional right to a fair criminal trial? Phelan J. in *King v DPP*, while stating that the level of fees is a matter for the political branches of government, nonetheless observed:

[164] Statistical sources: Office of the Auditor and Comptroller General, *Appropriation Accounts 2023* (September 2024), p.596; *Appropriation Accounts 2021* (September 2022), p.545; *Appropriation Accounts 2020* (September 2021), p.482; *Appropriation Accounts 2019* (September 2020), p.478; *Appropriation Accounts 2018* (September 2019), p.451. For all other schemes, see Legal Aid Board, *Annual Report 2022* (2023), pp.36–39.

[165] Department of Justice, "Criminal Legal Aid fees increase comes into effect", 1 January 2025. This had been announced in October 2024 when Budget 2025 was announced in the Dáil.

[166] See, e.g. response to question asked by Aodhán Ó Ríordáin TD, *Dáil Debates*, Question 26, 25 July 2023 and response to written questions nos. 123, 124, 125, 133 and 154 from several TDs on this issue on 3 July 2024.

[167] Mary Carolan, "Barristers step up protests over 'pitiful' criminal legal aid fees", *Irish Times*, 14 July 2023 and Bar of Ireland, "Ball is in your court, Criminal barristers tell Government, in advance of nationwide to withdrawal service", 8 July 2024.

> "Should practice before the Courts demonstrate that the system is failing to ensure effective representation for accused persons remanded in custody, it will inevitably result in the Court being mandated to intervene where the evidence before the Court establishes that the constitutional interest in the proper administration of justice and the duty to vindicate personal rights so requires."[168]

13–25 For over two decades, reform of the criminal justice legal aid schemes has been discussed.[169] Promises to reform criminal legal aid were made in the Programmes for Government of 2016 and 2020.[170] This included a commitment to examine the feasibility of a public defender system, i.e. moving away from the current system to criminal legal advice and representation being provided by State employees. The 2020 Programme for Government stated that a report would be completed on this matter within six months of the Government coming to power. The Minister for Justice in 2021 stated that the terms of reference were being drafted for an expert review of this matter.[171] In July 2023, the Department of Justice published the Draft General Scheme of Criminal Justice (Legal Aid) Bill 2023 (the "2023 Scheme").[172] Head 6 of the 2023 Scheme proposes the repeal of the 1962 Act. The 2023 Scheme will place on a legislative footing the current non-statutory Garda Advice Scheme, to be renamed "Custody Advice", and the Criminal Assets Bureau Scheme.[173] The Custody Issues Scheme (CIS), to be renamed "Custody Aid", is also proposed to be given a statutory footing.[174] This responds fairly directly to concerns of courts regarding the non-legislative nature of these three schemes.[175] These schemes will continue to be administered by the Legal Aid Board.[176] The 2023 Scheme lapsed with the dissolution of the Oireachtas in November 2024. In January 2025,

[168] [2022] IEHC 74 at para.24.
[169] *Fundamentals of the Irish Legal System*, 1st edn (Dublin: Round Hall, 2016), para.13-23.
[170] *A Programme for a Partnership Government* (Dublin: Department of An Taoiseach, 2016), pp.97–98, and *Programme for Government: Our Shared Future* (Dublin: Department of An Taoiseach, 2020), p.85.
[171] See *Dáil Debates*, Written Answer No. 153, 1 December 2021.
[172] Department of Justice, "Means tested Criminal Legal Aid can be withdrawn or cut from applicants under reforms" (19 July 2023).
[173] See Heads 45 and 46 of the 2023 Scheme.
[174] Head 27 and Schedule 2 of the 2023 Scheme.
[175] See para.13–20.
[176] Head 39 of the 2023 Scheme.

a new government was formed. The new Programme for Government commits to reforming the operation of the criminal legal aid system. This includes a commitment to enact "a [criminal] Legal Aid Bill to ensure financial assessment of means with powers to restrict legal aid or claw it back."[177] Given that Fianna Fáil and Fine Gael continue to be the main government partners, the 2023 Scheme may still be the core proposal for reforming the criminal legal aid system. With that in mind, we now consider aspects of the 2023 Scheme.

13–26 If the current government maintains the key proposals outlined in the 2023 Scheme, it will move responsibility for the administration of criminal legal aid, under the current 1962 Act, from the Department of Justice to the Legal Aid Board.[178] During pre-legislative scrutiny, the Joint Committee on Justice expressed concerns with this transfer. Experts who appeared before the Committee had noted how well the scheme is administered by the Department of Justice and that the process of applying for a criminal legal aid certificate under the 2023 Scheme is too convoluted.[179] The 2023 Scheme will continue to oblige a court to inform an accused, to be known as a "specified person" under the Scheme, of their right to make an application for criminal legal aid.[180] An application will be made to the court in writing or electronically and subsequently on a specified person's appearance in court.[181] A court can grant legal aid, where it is in the interests of justice to do so, and where a specified person does not have the ability to pay the costs of their defence before the court.[182] The concept of interests of justice is defined within Head 17 of the 2023 Scheme to include taking into account the following matters: complexity; where there are a large number of offences; the seriousness of the charges; the impact of conviction, including risk of imprisonment

[177] Department of An Taoiseach, *Programme for Government 2025: Securing Ireland's Future*, p.120.

[178] Heads 37 and 38 of the 2023 Scheme.

[179] Joint Committee on Justice, *Report on Pre-Legislative Scrutiny of the General Scheme of the Criminal Justice (Legal Aid) Bill 2023* (December 2023), pp.15 and 33–34.

[180] Head 11 of the 2023 Scheme. A "specified person" in essence includes a person charged with a criminal offence before Irish courts, including where they exercise a right of appeal or the court action results from a case-stated referral: see Head 10. Head 10(vii) includes a person "the subject of another proceeding of a criminal nature", to possibly act as a saver for any other matter not explicitly covered in the 2023 Scheme. Being a Scheme, it would not be unusual for the subsequent Bill to provide clarity on what precisely might be meant by that phrase.

[181] Head 12 of the 2023 Scheme.

[182] Head 15(2) of the 2023 Scheme.

and/or the effect of a conviction on a specified person's livelihood or welfare; and any "exceptional circumstances". It will be for the court to determine what constitutes exceptional circumstances.

13–27 On the second requirement for a grant of criminal legal aid, a specified person will have to provide a Statement of Financial Circumstances to the court.[183] The Minister for Justice is tasked with introducing regulations outlining the type of financial information an applicant for legal aid will have to supply.[184] It is proposed, under Head 14(5) and Head 15(4) of the 2023 Scheme, that where an applicant's disposable income or capital (to be specified in regulations) is above certain monetary amounts, the court must refer the issue to the Legal Aid Board. The Legal Aid Board may then, on the basis of the Statement of Financial Circumstances, or a Statement of Financial Means that can be requested by the Legal Aid Board,[185] recommend to the court whether criminal legal aid be granted, including whether a person could make a financial contribution to the cost of criminal legal aid.[186] Ultimately, it is for the court to determine whether, in light of the interests of justice and financial means, criminal legal aid will be granted. Any recommendation from the Legal Aid Board on financial means is just that: it does not bind the hands of the court from coming to its own decision. It is proposed that where a specified person knowingly provides false information in seeking a grant of legal aid, they will be liable to be convicted and sentenced to a term of imprisonment of six months and/or a fine.[187]

13–28 The 2023 Scheme will therefore introduce some further complexities to the grant of criminal legal aid. Arguably, this will create more work for legal practitioners in applying for legal aid and decisions on criminal legal aid may take longer if matters have to be referred to the Legal Aid Board by the courts. This may add significantly to the workload of the Legal Aid Board, who, as will be discussed in the next section, have sufficient difficulties in meeting their statutory obligations to provide civil legal aid. That said, the 2023 Scheme will bring a more

[183] Head 13 of the 2023 Scheme.

[184] Head 14 of the 2023 Scheme.

[185] See Head 22 of the 2023 Scheme. The means assessment differs from the Statement of Financial Circumstances. It can probably be understood as an even deeper evaluation of an applicant's financial position.

[186] Head 21 of the 2023 Scheme. Under Head 23 of the 2023 Scheme, calculation of potential contributions is to be set out in regulations.

[187] Head 31 of the 2023 Scheme.

structured decision-making process. A Criminal Legal Aid Oversight Committee is proposed to be established under the 2023 Scheme.[188] This Committee will be responsible for advising the Minister for Justice on the operation and implementation of the changed criminal legal aid system, advising on best practice implementation and experiences from other jurisdictions, technological improvements, and collaboration of all stakeholders with responsibility for implementation of the 2023 Scheme. If this Scheme is revived by the current government, it may still take a number of years before any of these changes will become operational given the complexity of the proposals under the Scheme.

C. Civil Legal Aid

1. Introduction

13–29 While the provision of criminal legal aid in Ireland has received significant legislative attention, coupled with somewhat intensive court scrutiny, arguably the same cannot be said of civil legal aid. As a person's liberty is not at stake, it could be argued that the State should not have to fund an individual's legal disputes with private parties in areas relating to tortious liability and family law, including divorce and separation and property rights. Similarly, it could be argued that the State should not fund (essentially against itself) challenges as regards education provision, social welfare entitlement or enforcing other statutory or constitutional rights. However, accessing legal mechanisms, in the form of courts, tribunals or even mediation, to defend or vindicate legal rights and entitlements is costly, and individuals may have no choice but to defend their actions before a court. The idea of equal access to justice is itself "fairly new".[189] Civil legal aid, at least in the not-too-distant past, was interlinked with the creation of the welfare state.[190]

[188] Head 39 of the 2023 Scheme. Membership of this Committee will comprise the Minister for Justice (or their representative), the Attorney General, the Chief State Solicitor, legal practitioner representatives, the Legal Aid Board, the DPP, the Garda Síochána and the Courts Service.

[189] L. Friedman, "Claims, Disputes, Conflicts and the Modern Welfare State" in M. Cappelletti (ed.), *Access to Justice and the Welfare State* (The Hague: Kluwer, 1981), p.244. Friedman traces the history of the access to justice movement, noting how in times past, individuals unable to afford access to justice had to rely on the charity of lawyers.

[190] T.H. Marshall and T. Bottomore, *Citizenship and Social Class* (London: Pluto Press, 1992), pp.29–44.

2. Establishing Civil Legal Aid in Ireland 1968–1995

13–30 The campaign for state-funded civil legal aid in Ireland commenced in the late 1960s after dedicated law student activism.[191] In 1971, the High Court rejected an attempt to recognise a right to civil legal aid as a constitutional right in *O'Shaughnessy v Attorney General*.[192] O'Kelly P. dismissed a constitutional challenge to the Criminal Justice (Legal Aid) Act 1962. O'Shaughnessy argued that the failure of the Oireachtas to make provision for civil legal aid in that statute rendered it unconstitutional.[193] O'Kelly P. emphasised that the courts did not have a role in rectifying legislation for perceived deficits. It is the role of the Oireachtas to decide whether any form of civil legal aid should be provided for or not. Eventually in 1979, the Government established the Pringle Committee to inquire into and to make recommendations on the statutory provision of legal advice and aid in civil matters.[194] After 89 meetings of the Pringle Committee and 15 sub-committee meetings, a comprehensive scheme of civil legal aid and advice was proposed in December 1977.[195] The Pringle Committee's report contained radical proposals to cover all civil legal matters, subject to a means test and a merits test. The Pringle Committee recognised that:

> "[t]he underprivileged often see [law] as an instrument of oppression rather than a statement of rights ... Solicitors in centres will be in a special position to assess where and how existing law fails to meet the real needs of the underprivileged."[196]

Despite significant support for the findings within civil society groups like the Free Legal Advice Centres (FLAC) and the professions, the radical

[191] For a much more detailed historical analysis of the introduction of civil legal aid in Ireland, see *Fundamentals of the Irish Legal System*,1st edn (Dublin: Round Hall, 2016), paras 13-25–13-31 and sources cited therein, which examined the tentative beginnings of civil legal aid up to the Civil Legal Aid Act 1995.

[192] Unreported, High Court, O'Kelly P., 16 February 1971.

[193] See further, G. Whyte, *Social Inclusion and the Legal System: Public Interest Law in Ireland*, 2nd edn (Dublin: IPA, 2015), pp.403–404.

[194] Report to the Minister for Justice, *Committee on Civil Legal Aid and Advice* (December 1977) (hereinafter, "Pringle Committee Report"), pp.4–5. For a more detailed discussion on the Pringle Committee Report, see *Fundamentals of the Irish Legal System*, 1st edn (Dublin: Round Hall, 2016), pp.473–474.

[195] Concerns were expressed in the Dáil as regards the non-time-limited nature of the Pringle Committee. In December 1974, the then Minister for Justice, Patrick Cooney TD, expressed his confidence that the Pringle Committee, given the urgency of the task, would report in a short time frame; Oral Answers: Legal Aid Committee, 276 *Dáil Debates* Cols 641–643 (3 December 1974).

[196] Pringle Committee Report, para.4.11.

suggestions for such a comprehensive civil legal aid scheme did not have governmental support. Only the most limited form of civil legal aid was eventually introduced, and this did not happen until Josie Airey took a case to the ECtHR.

Box 13.2: Case Focus
***Airey v Ireland* (1979–80) 2 E.H.R.R. 305**

Josie Airey lived in Cork and was living apart from her abusive husband. Airey sought to gain a decree of judicial separation from the High Court. At that time, Ireland had a constitutional prohibition on divorce.[197] Gaining a judicial separation from the High Court was cumbersome and expensive, potentially costing up to IR£1,200, and beyond the financial means of Airey, who was earning IR£39.99 per week.[198] A core issue that had to be determined by the ECtHR was whether the lack of financial means to gain a civil remedy (judicial separation) had violated Airey's rights under the ECHR.

Airey argued that Article 6(1) of the ECHR had been violated. Article 6(1) in its relevant parts provides: "[i]n the determination of ... civil rights and obligations ... everyone is entitled to a fair and public hearing within a reasonable time by an independent and impartial tribunal established by law." Airey further argued that Ireland failed to protect her right to private and family life under Article 8(1) of the ECHR, by failing to provide practical legal assistance that would enable her to access the legal remedy of judicial separation before the High Court.199

Ireland argued that Airey enjoyed access to the High Court since she was free to appear before the court without a lawyer. In addition, Ireland stated that Airey had "nothing to gain from a judicial separation".[200] Ireland noted that if the ECtHR were to accept Airey's argument, it would have profound consequences because it would require the provision of legal aid to those without means for the determination of any civil right by a domestic court.[201] This, Ireland argued, would have the effect of

[197] (1979–80) 2 E.H.R.R. 305 at 306–311. On divorce and separation in Irish law, see further, D. Fitzpatrick, "Divorce and Separation in Modern Irish History" (1987) 114 *Past & Present* 172.

[198] (1979–80) 2 E.H.R.R. 305 at 310 and 316. The ECtHR noted that in order to gain a judicial separation, it could cost Josie Airey as much as IR£1,200, depending on the complexity of the case.

[199] (1979–80) 2 E.H.R.R. 305 at 314–315.

[200] (1979–80) 2 E.H.R.R. 305 at 313.

[201] (1979–80) 2 E.H.R.R. 305 at 317. Ireland also noted that it had an express reservation to Article 6(3)(c) of the ECHR. Article 6(3)(c) provides: "[e]veryone charged with a criminal offence has the following minimum rights: to defend himself in person or through legal assistance of his own choosing or, if he has not sufficient means to

interpreting the ECHR in a manner that provides for socio-economic rights, something that the original contracting parties could not have envisaged.[202]

The ECtHR held that Ireland had violated Airey's rights under Articles 6 and 8 of the ECHR. The ECtHR noted that Article 6 guarantees the right to effective access to the courts in civil, as well as criminal, matters.[203] This did not mean that civil legal aid had to be granted in every instance. Due to the complexity of a legal dispute and the particular personal characteristics of a potential litigant, state support in accessing justice may be required, including through the provision of a lawyer.[204] The ECtHR emphasised that rights protected under the ECHR had to be "practical and effective" rather than merely "theoretical or illusory".[205] Stating that Airey was not prevented from arguing the case before the High Court herself, without the assistance of a lawyer, failed to take into account Airey's low means and her lack of formal education, which could disadvantage her in arguing for a judicial separation from her husband.[206]

The ECtHR rejected the argument that it was transforming the object and purpose of the ECHR, from protecting civil and political rights to that of protecting social and economic rights.[207] The ECtHR held that while the ECHR protects what are essentially civil and political rights, many of these rights have implications of a socio-economic nature.[208] The ECtHR also found that Airey had her rights under Article 8 (right to private and family life) violated by Ireland's failure to have an accessible legal procedure for recognition of Airey's de facto separation from her husband.[209]

---

pay for legal assistance, to be given it free when the interests of justice so require … ." Ireland's reservation (still in effect) attempted to limit the impact of Article 6(3)(c) to "free legal assistance … [that] … is now provided in Ireland". At the time of the reservation (1953), free legal assistance in criminal law was available solely in capital murder and murder cases.

202 (1979–80) 2 E.H.R.R. 305 at 316.

203 (1979–80) 2 E.H.R.R. 305 at 317.

204 (1979–80) 2 E.H.R.R. 305 at 317.

205 (1979–80) 2 E.H.R.R. 305 at 314.

206 (1979–80) 2 E.H.R.R. 305 at 315. The ECtHR noted the complexity of procedures before the High Court, and the difficult legal case that had to be proved in gaining judicial separation in Ireland at that time.

207 For an accessible exploration of the definition of social and economic rights, see L. Thornton, "An Introduction to Economic, Social and Cultural Rights" in Constitutional Convention, *Eighth Report of the Constitutional Convention: Economic, Social and Cultural Rights* (March 2014), pp.8–12. For a review of social and economic rights law in Ireland, see L. Thornton, "Socio-Economic Rights and Ireland" in S. Egan (ed.), *International Human Rights: Perspectives from Ireland* (Dublin: Bloomsbury, 2015).

208 (1979–80) 2 E.H.R.R. 305 at 316.

209 (1979–80) 2 E.H.R.R. 305 at 319.

13–31 Dillon argues that the establishment of the non-statutory scheme of civil legal aid in Ireland came about as a "forced response" to the decision of the ECtHR in *Airey*.[210] On 2 May 1979, a number of months after the *Airey* decision, the Government announced its intention of putting in place a non-statutory civil legal aid and advice scheme.[211] Then Senator Mary Robinson expressed deep concerns at the method by which the scheme was to be introduced, noting that "an attempt to implement such a scheme by administrative action would deprive the Houses of the Oireachtas of their proper jurisdiction in the matter".[212] The Government proceeded to introduce civil legal aid and advice on an administrative basis only, with this scheme coming into force in 1980.[213] When introducing the non-statutory civil legal aid scheme in 1980, the then Minister for Justice noted:

> "No scheme could or should put the poor person into the position of the rich man who can afford the best brains at the Bar. The Scheme of Civil Legal Aid and Advice puts the poor person into the position of a person with modest means ... and such people have to think twice before engaging in legal action. There is no reason in justice why poor people should be different."[214]

13–32 Although now introduced over 40 years ago, placed on a legislative footing in 1995 (discussed below), and with some important changes and caveats, the Civil Legal Aid Act 1995 in essence adopts the model of civil legal aid and advice provided for in the 1980 Scheme.[215] Whyte sums up neatly its limitations:

> "The Scheme of Civil Legal Aid and Advice ... was very restrictive ... it was not comprehensive as significant areas of unmet legal need, such as representation before Tribunals, were excluded from its remit and its strict financial provisions restricted the category of

[210] B. Dillon and Combat Poverty Agency, *A Review and Recent History of the Coolock Community Law Centre* (Dublin: CPA, 1989), p.8.

[211] For the full press release announcing the scheme, see Private Member's Motion: Civil Legal Aid Scheme, Mary Robinson, 92 *Seanad Debates* Col. 464 (20 June 1979).

[212] Private Member's Motion: Civil Legal Aid Scheme, Mary Robinson, 92 *Seanad Debates* Col. 464 (20 June 1979).

[213] *Scheme of Civil Legal Aid and Advice* (Dublin: Stationery Office, 1979).

[214] Minister for Justice, Mr Gerry Collins TD, 319 *Dáil Debates* Col. 1784 (22 April 1980).

[215] For a review of the Scheme's merits and means tests, and contributions, see *Fundamentals of the Irish Legal System*, 1st edn (Dublin: Round Hall, 2016), paras 13-28–13-32.

persons eligible for its services ... [F]or much of its existence, the Scheme was hopelessly underfunded ... [and] there were invariably lengthy waiting lists for appointments to see solicitors."[216]

13–33 In *MC v Legal Aid Board*,[217] the applicant, represented by FLAC, claimed that the delay in the then non-statutory Legal Aid Board determining her application for legal advice and aid for nullity proceedings violated her constitutional right of access to the courts.[218] The Legal Aid Board admitted that due to MC's lack of financial means, she would (probably) meet the criteria to be granted civil legal aid.[219] However, due to the financial constraints and inadequacy of staffing levels at the Athlone Legal Aid Board centre, no decision could be taken as to when and if the applicant would receive legal advice (and, if necessary, legal aid).[220] The Legal Aid Board, while accepting that there was a delay in determining whether the applicant should benefit under the scheme, noted that no disadvantage or unfairness accrued to the applicant, given that the nullity proceedings had not yet commenced.[221] Gannon J. held that the only obligation on the Legal Aid Board and the State was "to ensure that the scheme is implemented fairly to all persons and in a manner which fulfils its declared purpose".[222] There was no broad requirement for the State to fund litigation in private disputes.[223] Gannon J., however, did grant a declaration that the Legal Aid Board is obliged to consider a legal aid and advice application within a reasonable time and, in this case, the Board had fettered its inherent discretion in failing to consider whether the applicant's legal aid and advice should be prioritised.[224] The issue of limited civil legal aid scope and delay in accessing Legal Aid Board services continues, as will be explored below, to be a significant barrier to accessing justice in Ireland.

[216] G. Whyte, *Social Inclusion and the Legal System: Public Interest Law in Ireland*, 1st edn (Dublin: IPA, 2002), p.293. See further, G. Whyte, "And Justice for Some ..." (1984) 6 *Dublin University Law Journal* 88, and for an updated assessment, G. Whyte, *Social Inclusion and the Legal System: Public Interest Law in Ireland*, 2nd edn (Dublin: IPA, 2015), in particular pp.512–514.
[217] [1991] 2 I.R. 43.
[218] For an outline on the law of nullity, see L. Crowley, *Family Law* (Dublin: Round Hall, 2008), Ch.2. On the applicant's claims, see *MC v Legal Aid Board* [1991] 2 I.R. 43 at 47–48.
[219] [1991] 2 I.R. 43 at 46.
[220] [1991] 2 I.R. 43 at 46.
[221] [1991] 2 I.R. 43 at 50–51.
[222] [1991] 2 I.R. 43 at 55.
[223] [1991] 2 I.R. 43 at 55.
[224] [1991] 2 I.R. 43 at 45 and 56–57.

3. The Civil Legal Aid Act 1995 (as amended)

13–34 In 1995, the right to civil legal aid and advice was placed on a statutory footing. The Civil Legal Aid Act 1995 (the "1995 Act") permits the Legal Aid Board to provide legal advice and representation[225] in select fields of civil law. The 1995 Act placed the Legal Aid Board on a statutory footing,[226] established the criteria for the granting of legal aid and advice, including financial eligibility,[227] and provided for the location of law centres[228] and other ancillary matters.

(a) The Legal Aid Board

13–35 Section 3 of the 1995 Act established the Legal Aid Board on a statutory footing. The Board comprises 13 members,[229] at least five men and five women,[230] one chairperson, and 12 ordinary members. All members of the Board, including the Chairperson, are appointed by the Minister for Justice.[231] Of the 13 Board positions, four members must be practising barristers and solicitors (two of each) for not less than seven years; two members of the Board are chosen by staff of the Board; and the remainder at the (structured) discretion of the Minister for Justice. In deciding upon who to appoint, the Minister is statutorily obliged to consider the knowledge and experience that the appointee may have in court processes and procedures, finance, administration, consumer or social affairs, "or of any subject, which would, in the opinion of the Minister, be of assistance to the Board in the performance of its functions".[232] Since November 2014, where the Minister for Justice seeks to make a new appointment to the Board, this must go through the Public Appointments Service (PAS) for at least eight of the 13 Board members.[233] The PAS process does not apply to the staff Board

[225] Sections 24–28 of the 1995 Act (as amended).
[226] Sections 3–15 of the 1995 Act (as amended).
[227] Section 29 of the 1995 Act, as amended by s.80 of the Civil Law (Miscellaneous Provisions) Act 2008.
[228] Section 30 of the 1995 Act, as amended by s.81 of the Civil Law (Miscellaneous Provisions) Act 2008.
[229] Section 4(1) of the 1995 Act.
[230] Section 4(3)(b)(v) of the 1995 Act.
[231] Section 4(2)(a) of the 1995 Act.
[232] Section 4(3)(a) of the 1995 Act.
[233] See generally, Department of Public Expenditure and Reform, "Government agrees publication of protocol on the application of the new State Boards appointments process to NewERA companies" (10 February 2015). See further, *www.stateboards.ie* and for a list of current Legal Aid Board membership, see *https://membership.stateboards.ie/*.

members, nor to representatives of government departments who sit on the Board from the Departments of Justice, Social Protection and Public Expenditure. Legislatively, the power of appointment remains with the Minister.[234] It is unlikely, in light of past controversies, that the Minister would ignore the appointee recommendation of PAS.[235] The principal functions of the Board are, subject to resource and statutory limitations, to provide legal aid and advice as well as the power to provide family mediation services.[236] This is supplemented by a statutory obligation that the Board, "to such an extent and in such a manner as it considers appropriate", disseminate information about the services offered.[237] Attempts to augment these provisions to provide for a public duty to inform people about their rights and obligations, and a duty to conduct research in legal need,[238] were not included in the enacted legislation. However, the Minister for Justice, pursuant to s.6 of the 1995 Act, may confer additional functions on the Board that are "incidental to or consequential on" the Board's core functions to provide legal advice and aid. The Minister for Justice may also, under s.7 of the 1995 Act, issue general directives relating to legal advice and aid with which the Board must comply.[239]

(b) Scope of services provided by the Legal Aid Board

13–36 An applicant who satisfies a merits and means test can apply for civil legal advice and aid.[240] When providing legal advice, only the financial eligibility requirements are considered.[241] Many of the restrictions on access to civil legal aid in the non-statutory scheme continued under the

---

[234] Section 4(1) of the 1995 Act. For background to the controversy that led to the new process for State and other public board appointments, albeit not related to the Legal Aid Board, see Leaders Questions, *Dáil Debates* (unrevised), 1 October 2014; P. Melia, "John McNulty resigns from IMMA board with immediate effect", *Irish Independent*, 25 September 2014; and G. Griffin, "State board appointments to be professionalised under new rules", *Irish Times*, 5 February 2015.

[235] See, for example, O. Ryan, "Joan Burton faces motion of no confidence as second state board appointment emerges", *TheJournal.ie*, 19 January 2016.

[236] Section 5(1) of the 1995 Act, as substituted by s.54 of the Civil Law (Miscellaneous Provisions) Act 2011.

[237] Section 5(2) of the 1995 Act.

[238] See G. Whyte, *Annotated Civil Legal Aid Act 1995* (Dublin: Round Hall, 2000), para.95-32.15.

[239] Section 7 of the 1995 Act.

[240] Section 1 of the 1995 Act, as substituted by s.25(a) of the Courts and Civil Law (Miscellaneous Provisions) Act 2013.

[241] See discussion of the financial eligibility requirements at paras 13–42 to 13–45.

1995 Act.[242] Legal advice is defined as any oral or written advice, short of instituting legal proceedings,[243] given by a solicitor employed by, or a solicitor/barrister engaged by, the Legal Aid Board. This advice must relate to the application of Irish law[244] to the circumstances of the Legal Aid Board client, and any steps the client "might appropriately take" having regard to the law of Ireland to their particular circumstances. Legal aid means representation by a solicitor employed by the Legal Aid Board,[245] or a solicitor or barrister engaged by the Legal Aid Board, in coroners inquests[246] and in all civil proceedings conducted before the District Court, Circuit Court, High Court, Court of Appeal and/ or Supreme Court.[247] The Minister for Justice, with the consent of the Minister for Public Expenditure and Reform, can prescribe other courts and tribunals within which legal aid can be provided.[248] To date, the International Protection Appeals Tribunal is the only body prescribed

242 See now ss.26(2) and 29(9) of the 1995 Act (as amended).

243 Section 25 of the 1995 Act. This in essence replicates the definition of legal advice provided for in the non-statutory scheme; see *Scheme of Civil Legal Aid and Advice* (Dublin: Stationery Office, 1979) (as amended), paras 3.1.1–3.1.2.

244 There is an exception to this under s.26(4) of the 1995 Act, where the Legal Aid Board may provide guidance or assistance to a client as regards the law of another state if the Legal Aid Board deems this to be appropriate.

245 By virtue of the Civil Legal Aid Act 1995 (Section 11) Order 2014 (S.I. No. 237 of 2014), solicitors on permanent contracts were designated as civil servants in the civil service of the State. For an exploration of the importance of this designation more generally, see D.G. Morgan, G. Hogan and P. Daly, *Administrative Law in Ireland*, 5th edn (Dublin: Round Hall, 2019), Chs 3 and 4.

246 Section 24A of the 1995 Act, as inserted by s.25(b) of the Courts and Civil Law (Miscellaneous Provisions) Act 2013. The Supreme Court in *Magee v Farrell* [2009] 4 I.R. 703 found that there was no constitutional right to be provided with legal aid at an inquest, as it was an inquisitorial rather than adversarial process to determine the cause of death. Magee instituted proceedings against Ireland before the ECtHR. Ireland reached a friendly settlement with Magee, making a payment of €10,000 in respect of non-pecuniary loss and over €128,000 in legal costs for domestic court actions before the High Court and Supreme Court. The friendly settlement also resulted in the enactment of s.25 of the Courts and Civil Law (Miscellaneous Provisions) Act 2013, which inserted s.24A into the 1995 Act which provides for legal advice and (potentially) legal aid for individuals at inquests. The request for legal aid has to be made by a coroner and the person must satisfy the financial criteria set down in s.29 of the 1995 Act. See further, *Communication from Ireland concerning the case of Teresa Magee against Ireland* (Application No. 53743/09), Council of Europe, COE Doc. DH-DD(2013)1363 (18 December 2013), and Committee of Ministers, Resolution CM/ResDH(2014)79 (5 June 2014). The Civil Legal Aid Regulations 2021 (S.I. No. 248 of 2021) provide for legal representation at inquests for all families whose loved ones perished in the Stardust disaster. These families do not have to meet the means test.

247 Section 27 of the 1995 Act, as substituted by s.25(d) of the Courts and Civil Law (Miscellaneous Provisions) Act 2013.

248 Section 27(2)(b) of the 1995 Act.

where applicants for international protection may be provided with legal advice and aid by the Legal Aid Board.[249]

13–37 An applicant for civil legal advice or aid must be a natural person as opposed to a legal person. In *Friends of the Irish Environment CLG v Legal Aid Board*,[250] the appellant was a body corporate/legal person. It had applied for legal aid to the Legal Aid Board in order to seek a judicial review of aspects of the Government's National Development Plan.[251] Friends of the Irish Environment argued that the 1995 Act did not restrict legal advice and aid to natural persons. The core of this aspect of the decision in this case boiled down to questions of statutory interpretation.[252] Section 18 of the Interpretation Act 2005 defines "person" as both a natural and legal (corporate) person.[253] If s.18 of the 2005 Act were read in isolation, this would clearly have established the appellant's entitlement to apply for civil legal aid.[254] However, s.4 of the 2005 Act requires legislation to be read in context and as a whole, in order to evaluate whether the Oireachtas had a contrary intention, i.e. restricting civil legal aid to natural persons only. The Court of Appeal, upholding the decision of the High Court,[255] focused on those aspects of the 1995 Act that were highly indicative that only natural persons could benefit from civil legal advice and aid.[256] It was determined that it was the intention of the Oireachtas to exclude legal/corporate persons from its remit.[257] The framing of entitlement under the 1995 Act laid stress on such matters as

[249] Civil Legal Aid (International Protection Appeals Tribunal) Order 2017 (S.I. No. 81 of 2017). This replaces previous statutory instruments that provided for legal advice and aid before the former Refugee Appeals Tribunal.

[250] [2023] IECA 19.

[251] The substantive matter proceeded, with the Supreme Court referring questions to the Court of Justice of the European Union in 2022: see *Friends of the Irish Environment CLG v Ireland* [2022] IESC 42 at paras 1–10. The Board also relied on s.29(9)(a) of the 1995 Act in coming to its decision.

[252] See Ch.4, Section F.2(a).

[253] The appellant also had other unsuccessful grounds of challenge under aspects of European Union law ([2023] IECA 19 at paras 74–79) and international law ([2023] IECA 19 at paras 90–93).

[254] [2023] IECA 19 at para.23.

[255] [2020] IEHC 454.

[256] In doing so, Murray J., delivering the decision of the Court of Appeal, focused in particular on "the language, subject matter and context of the Act" as being "decisively probative" of the Oireachtas' intention: [2023] IECA 19 at para.41. The Court of Appeal's exploration of the context of the introduction of the 1995 Act, and the prior non-statutory scheme, would have been inconclusive, hence the key focus on the 1995 Act: [2023] IECA 19 at paras 44–47.

[257] [2023] IECA 19 at paras 55–60.

the grant of legal aid and advice to a person of insufficient means,[258] with no provisions stating how this would be assessed for a body corporate like the appellant.[259] The object and purpose of the exclusion of test cases/representative actions for individuals from the grant of civil legal advice and aid would have indicated that the Oireachtas was minded to exclude non-governmental organisations (be they corporate bodies or unincorporated entities) from utilising the 1995 Act to litigate in the public interest.[260] Another unsuccessful argument proffered by the appellant related to whether EU environmental law and the EU Charter of Fundamental Rights required the 1995 Act to be interpreted so as to oblige the Legal Aid Board to provide the appellant with legal advice or aid.[261] The Court of Appeal, in a subsequent related decision, refused to transmit questions to the Court of Justice of the European Union on whether Article 47 of the Charter required a legal aid scheme (one outside the strictures of the 1995 Act) for environmental issues.[262]

13–38 As discussed above, the Legal Aid Board is responsible for administering various legal aid schemes, the Custody Issues Scheme, the Garda Station Legal Aid Scheme and the CAB Ad-hoc Scheme.[263] In addition, the Legal Aid Board provides family mediation services.[264] The Legal Aid Board is responsible for providing legal advice to a person who may be a victim of human trafficking[265] and to complainants in a

258 [2023] IECA 19 at paras 61–64.
259 [2023] IECA 19 at para.65.
260 [2023] IECA 19 at paras 68–70. The Court of Appeal did find that the High Court should not have referred to regulations introduced contemporaneously with the 1995 Act on the basis that, "[i]f the interpretation of legislation urged by a sponsoring Minister before parliament is inadmissible to construe the legislation, it must follow that his or her opinion of the scope of the legislation following its enactment is similarly irrelevant to the process of construction." See Ch.4, Section F.2(c).
261 [2023] IECA 19 at paras 86–89.
262 *Friends of the Irish Environment CLG v Legal Aid Board* [2023] IECA 63. The reasons for this refusal related to how the appellant had structured its case; it had not made this particular argument before the courts so that "the answers to the questions it is proposed should be referred would not affect in any way the outcome of the case actually before the Court".
263 Discussed at paras 13–20 to 13–22.
264 Family Mediation Services offer mediation to married and non-married couples (opposite and same-sex) as regards seeking amicable separation or divorce of married couples and civil partners. See ss.36A and 36B of the 1995 Act, inserted by Pt 16 of the Civil Law (Miscellaneous Provisions) Act 2011. For further information on this service, see Legal Aid Board, *Family Mediation* (Dublin: Legal Aid Board, 2023), available at *www.legalaidboard.ie*.
265 Section 26(3B) and (8) of the 1995 Act, as inserted by s.3 of the Civil Law (Miscellaneous Provisions) Act 2011.

prosecution for a range of sexual offences.[266] The Money Advice and Budgeting Service, in co-operation with several other bodies and the Legal Aid Board, operates the Abhaile (Home) Scheme for those who are insolvent and at risk of losing their homes due to mortgage arrears. This includes the provision of legal advice and, where appropriate, representation from panels of private solicitors on legal issues that arise for persons and families in danger of losing their homes.[267] Since April 2023, the Legal Aid Board also has legislative obligations to provide legal advice and/or aid in certain matters for persons who may require assistance in making decisions or co-decisions, advanced healthcare directives, enduring powers of attorney, and discharge from wardship.[268]

13–39 A person cannot be granted legal advice or aid for any matter that is within the field of criminal law (unless it is advice on how to access criminal legal aid or a person is a victim of human trafficking or sexual offences).[269] The Legal Aid Board is *generally* prohibited from offering legal advice or legal aid to an applicant on a number of excluded grounds, including: defamation,[270] disputes concerning rights and interests over land,[271] conveyancing,[272] civil matters within the jurisdiction of the small claims procedure,[273] licensing,[274] election petitions,[275] or where the legal advice or aid is part of a "test case" strategy.[276] Section 29(b) and (c)

---

266 Section 26(3A) of the 1995 Act, as inserted by s.78 of the Civil Law (Miscellaneous Provisions) Act 2008.

267 See generally, Legal Aid Board, *Terms and Conditions: Abhaile Scheme*, available at: *www.legalaidboard.ie.*

268 Section 52 of the Assisted Decision-Making (Capacity) Act 2015 (as amended) and s.57A of the 2015 Act (as inserted by s.48 of the Assisted Decision-Making (Capacity) (Amendment) Act 2022). For analysis of these Acts, see M. Donnelly and C. Gleeson (eds), *The Assisted Decision-Making (Capacity) Act 2015: Personal and Professional Reflections* (Dublin: Health Service Executive, 2021).

269 Section 26(2)(a) of the 1995 Act. See also, *O'Connor v Legal Aid Board* [2022] IECA 216.

270 Section 28(9)(a)(i) of the 1995 Act. However, s.28(9)(b) of the 1995 Act permits the Legal Aid Board to grant a legal aid certificate if the court action involves the making of a counterclaim for defamation.

271 Section 28(9)(a)(ii) of the 1995 Act. However, see s.29(9)(c)(vi) of the 1995 Act and the Abhaile Scheme.

272 Section 28(9)(a)(v) of the 1995 Act. Under s.29(9)(c)(vi) of the 1995 Act, if a conveyancing matter is ancillary to other reasons for the grant of legal advice and/or aid, then the Legal Aid Board may provide such advice and/or aid.

273 Section 28(9)(a)(iii) of the 1995 Act.

274 Section 28(9)(a)(iv) of the 1995 Act.

275 Section 28(9)(a)(vi) of the 1995 Act.

276 Section 28(9)(a)(viii) and (ix) of the 1995 Act.

of the 1995 Act relaxes the general prohibition on offering legal advice and aid in a number of respects,[277] so that in family law proceedings, where issues of rights and interests over land may come to the fore, the Legal Aid Board can offer advice and aid.[278] Where advice or aid relates to an individual's "home", and an applicant has suffered some form of duress or undue influence or fraud in relation to a transaction involving the home, advice and aid may be provided where "a refusal to grant legal aid would cause hardship to the applicant".[279] The courts have held that there is no constitutional or statutory obligation for the civil legal aid scheme to represent those appearing before administrative tribunals.[280]

(c) Qualifying for civil legal aid and advice

13–40 A person will only be granted legal aid or advice where they make an application, including providing all relevant documentation required or requested by the Legal Aid Board.[281] As Costello J. held in *JS v MS* regarding civil law, "[i]t is not open to this court to grant legal aid to any litigant. That is a matter solely within the competence of the Legal Aid Board ...".[282] The legal matter must not come within one of the excluded grounds set out above. The applicant must satisfy the merits test and the means test under the 1995 Act. An applicant, if granted legal aid, has no entitlement to choose a solicitor, be they an employee of the Legal Aid Board or in private practice.[283] Where an applicant is not satisfied with the initial decision reached by the Legal Aid Board, they may appeal this decision to the Appeals Committee.[284] In 2022, there were 115 appeals

---

[277] For a full review of all qualifications to the general excluded areas, see G. Whyte, *Annotated Civil Legal Aid Act 1995* (Dublin: Round Hall, 2000), para.95-32.49.

[278] Section 29(9)(c)(i)–(iv) of the 1995 Act.

[279] Section 29(c)(iii)(II) of the 1995 Act.

[280] *Corcoran v Minister for Social Welfare* [1991] 2 I.R. 175; *Barry v Sentence Review Group* [2001] 4 I.R. 167; *Ms A v Child and Family Agency* [2015] IEHC 679. This issue is explored further below in the context of reforming civil legal aid.

[281] Section 28(4)(d) of the 1995 Act. As outlined in *Lopes v Legal Aid Board* [2023] IECA 164, the Legal Aid Board is entitled to refuse to process an application for legal aid where an applicant refuses to provide necessary information to enable a decision to be made as to entitlement.

[282] [2021] IECA 204 at para.45. This relates to civil matters and not to any of the custody/liberty issues discussed above. See also, *Beades v Ireland* [2019] IESCDET 5 at para.9(iii).

[283] *Mannion v Legal Aid Board* [2019] IECA 42, approving *Mannion v Legal Aid Board* [2007] IEHC 413.

[284] Generally, see reg.12 of the Civil Legal Aid Regulations 1996–2021.

to the Appeals Committee, with nine appeals allowed.[285] A person who receives legal aid will only be able to bring proceedings in the lowest court that would have jurisdiction in the case.[286]

(i) The merits test

13–41 Section 24 of the 1995 Act establishes a merits test that an applicant for legal aid and advice must satisfy, in addition to financial eligibility under s.29 of the 1995 Act. There are two limbs to this merits test: first, whether "a reasonably prudent person" would seek such advice and aid at their own expense, even if this did present some financial obstacle, but did not cause undue hardship;[287] second, whether a "solicitor or barrister acting reasonably" would likely advise such a reasonably prudent person to obtain legal services at their own expense.[288] In addition to these grounds, s.28(2) of the 1995 Act further provides, subject to ss.24 and 29, that: the applicant has reasonable grounds for instituting (or defending) legal proceedings; the applicant "is reasonably likely to be successful in the proceedings"; the proceedings are "the most satisfactory means (having regard to all the circumstances in the case, including the probable cost to the applicant)" of achieving the outcome sought; and, having regard to all other circumstances, it is reasonable for the Legal Aid Board to grant legal aid. In all child care proceedings[289] or proceedings regarding sex offender orders,[290] the Legal Aid Board cannot consider the likelihood of success, and once a person satisfies the financial eligibility criteria, they should be granted legal aid. In inquests, where a coroner has made a request that a person with an interest in the inquest should be provided with legal advice or

285 For a full review of the number and grounds of appeals from 2018–2022, see Legal Aid Board, *Annual Report 2022* (Dublin: Legal Aid Board, 2023), p.28.

286 Section 28(8) of the 1995 Act. This allows for an exception where the legally aided applicant is obliged to defend the action in a higher court.

287 Section 24(a) of the 1995 Act.

288 Section 24(b) of the 1995 Act.

289 As regards child care and welfare proceedings, this section was most likely in response to *MF v Legal Aid Board* [1993] I.L.R.M. 797 at 805, where the Supreme Court stated that in child care proceedings, on issues such as access, custody, etc., the (then non-statutory) Legal Aid Board had to consider: (1) whether there was a "reasonable likelihood" that the submissions of the parent should be amongst the material available to a judge tasked with the decision on the care of the child; and (2) whether the making of submissions would be of "benefit to the applicant" (para.3.2.3(6) of the non-statutory scheme).

290 Section 28(3)(b) of the 1995 Act, as substituted by s.24 of the Sex Offenders Act 2001.

aid, then this interested person must only satisfy the financial eligibility requirements.[291]

13–42 The case of *Sugg v Legal Aid Board*[292] is one of the few cases that explores the "merits" requirement set down in s.24 of the 1995 Act.[293] In *Sugg*, the applicant made an application for legal aid in order to proceed with a medical negligence appeal in the Supreme Court. The applicant met the means test; however, his application for legal aid was refused on the basis that the Legal Aid Board believed that the applicant was unlikely to be successful in his appeal of the High Court medical negligence action to the Supreme Court.[294] The applicant contended that his Supreme Court action could have succeeded (it was dismissed) if legal aid had been provided. Feeney J. in the High Court, in striking out the applicant's claim for damages against the Legal Aid Board, stated: "this Court can identify no basis, either in fact or logic, to support a claim that the Legal Aid Board was wrong or committed a wrongful act in holding that Mr. Sugg's claim was unlikely to succeed." Once the Legal Aid Board explores the case, unless there is some exceptional evidence of bad faith or a failure by the Legal Aid Board to consider relevant considerations, it is unlikely that any court would find it exercised its statutory powers to consider the merits of a given case unlawfully or irrationally.

(ii) The means test

13–43 Upon applying for civil legal aid and advice, an applicant must complete the form "Application for Financial Services: Civil Legal Aid and Advice".[295] Section 29 of the 1995 Act sets down the general parameters of the means test. This calculation is made on the basis of the disposable income[296] and disposable capital[297] of an applicant for

[291] Section 28(2A) of the 1995 Act, as inserted by s.25(e) of the Courts and Civil Law (Miscellaneous Provisions) Act 2013.

[292] For an examination of the "merits" test under the non-statutory civil legal aid and advice scheme, see *MF v Legal Aid Board* [1993] I.L.R.M. 797.

[293] [2009] IEHC 348. There are no paragraph numbers in this decision, so precise point reference is not possible.

[294] The express basis for this refusal by the Legal Aid Board lay in s.24(a) and (b), and s.28(2)(b), (c) and (e) of the 1995 Act.

[295] This form is available from *www.legalaidboard.ie*. Different forms must be completed depending on the particular scheme administered by the Legal Aid Board.

[296] Section 29(3) and (4) of the 1995 Act.

[297] Section 29(3) and (5) of the 1995 Act.

civil legal advice and aid. The precise financial criteria that applicants for legal aid and advice have to satisfy in order to qualify are provided for in regulations, which have remained substantially the same since 2006.[298] In general, applicants must have a disposable income of €18,000 or less and disposable capital of €100,000 or less. "Disposable income" is regarded as net income,[299] earned in the 12-month period prior to the application for legal aid or advice,[300] minus certain living allowances and expenses that are disregarded for the purpose of calculating disposable income.[301] As well as meeting the income requirements, an applicant must have a disposable capital of less than €100,000.[302] "Disposable capital" is the market value of every capital resource, excluding the family home[303] and "tools of the applicant's trade".[304] Examples of disposable capital provided in the regulations include farmland (excluding the family home) and business machinery and equipment, including any other land, minus any charge, loan, mortgage or debt that can be deducted from the capital value.[305]

[298] Civil Legal Aid Regulations 1996–2021. The Legal Aid Board provides an informal consolidation of these regulations on its website: *www.legalaidboard.ie*.

[299] Defined in reg.15(1)(a)–(e) of the Civil Legal Aid Regulations 1996–2021 as any wage, salary, profit from business, money received in the form of social security and social assistance payments and "any other benefits or privileges". Under reg.16(d) and (e) and reg.16(h) and (j), this is calculated as income after deduction of income tax, social insurance, universal social charge, and other deductions made on foot of s.2 of the Financial Emergency Measures in the Public Interest Act 2009 and s.2 of the Financial Emergency Measures in the Public Interest Act 2013.

[300] Civil Legal Aid Regulations 1996–2021 reg.15(2).

[301] See reg.16(1) for a full list of disregards. This includes a disregard of €3,500 per annum for the applicant's spouse (if any), €1,600 for each of the applicant's dependants, up to €6,000 for child care, €8,000 per annum in accommodation costs, and certain social assistance payments (child benefit, carer's benefit and allowance and foster care benefit). Previously, persons in receipt of Housing Assistance Payment (HAP) and other state housing payments had this calculated as part of their means. In June 2021, post the commencement of a judicial review, the Legal Aid Board changed its interpretation of accommodation costs, so that state-funded housing costs are now excluded from the calculation of means: see Legal Aid Board, "Important Notice re: Treatment of Housing Assistance Payments (HAP) in assessments of financial eligibility of persons seeking civil legal services" (28 May 2021) and Department of Justice, "Minister Naughton announces changes to Civil Legal Aid eligibility" (28 May 2021).

[302] Civil Legal Aid Regulations 1996–2021 reg.13(4).

[303] Civil Legal Aid Regulations 1996–2021 reg.18(3). As regards family home on farmland, see reg.19(1)(a) of the Civil Legal Aid Regulations 1996–2021.

[304] Civil Legal Aid Regulations 1996–2021 reg.18(4).

[305] Civil Legal Aid Regulations 1996–2021 reg.19(1). Motor vehicles and legally enforceable debts that fall to be paid to the applicant are deemed to be disposable capital for the purpose of these regulations.

13–44 An applicant must strictly meet the disposal income and disposable capital limits; even a small amount over these limits disentitles an individual to civil legal aid. In *Monahan v Legal Aid Board*,[306] the applicant applied for legal aid and advice. The applicant lived with her sister and adult nephew. The adult nephew had severe obsessive-compulsive disorder.[307] The applicant contended that her sister and nephew were dependants for the purposes of the Civil Legal Aid Regulations 1996–2006.[308] The Legal Aid Board decided in February 2007 (on appeal) that the applicant's sister and nephew were not dependants, and so no income disregard was applied. Due to this, the applicant was €217 over the €18,000 limit for access to legal aid.[309] After interventions from FLAC, the Legal Aid Board accepted that it had not properly considered the applicant's appeal in February 2007, and so reconsidered this in December 2007. The applicant was now found to be €536.95 over the €18,000 disposable income threshold.[310] The applicant challenged this decision before the High Court with the assistance of FLAC.

13–45 There were two core issues to be determined by Edwards J. in the High Court. First, did the definition of dependant include the applicant's sister and nephew? Second, did the Legal Aid Board have discretion to waive or disregard the income limit of €18,000 for legal aid? In answering both questions in the negative, Edwards J. held that the applicant's sister and nephew were not dependants for the purposes of the 1995 Act and regulations.[311] The definition of dependant in reg.16(3) of the Civil Legal Aid Regulations 1996–2006 provided:

> "'Dependants' for the purpose of paragraph (1)(b) shall include ... dependent relatives or other persons permanently residing with the applicant, who are supported by the applicant and who do not have available to them independent means of support."

306 [2009] 3 I.R. 458.
307 [2009] 3 I.R. 458 at 461.
308 Civil Legal Aid Regulations 1996–2006 reg.16(1)(b). There is no change from the current regulations in force.
309 [2009] 3 I.R. 458 at 463.
310 [2009] 3 I.R. 458 at 465–469.
311 [2009] 3 I.R. 458 at 479–480.

Relying on a literal interpretation of the 1995 Act and relevant regulations,[312] the applicant's sister and nephew had "independent means of support", as the applicant's sister was entitled to the One-Parent Family Payment.[313] Therefore, the Legal Aid Board was correct in finding that the applicant's sister and nephew were not "dependants".[314] On the second basis of challenge, as to whether the Legal Aid Board had discretion to waive the income requirements, Edwards J. noted that s.29(2) of the 1995 Act provides that the Legal Aid Board may, "in accordance with regulations, provide legal aid or legal advice to an applicant without reference to his or her financial resources". The Civil Legal Aid Regulations 1996–2006 did not provide the Legal Aid Board with the power to disregard the means test.[315] This power could only be provided for in regulations, which to date have not been adopted. Edwards J. held: "I consider that until such time as the Minister provides for the grant of legal aid irrespective of financial resources by way of regulation, the [Legal Aid Board] does not have the power to exercise the power provided for in s.29(2) of the Act."[316]

(d) Conditions for grant of legal aid and applicant contributions

13–46 Once an applicant has satisfied the means test and merits test, they can be subject to further conditions as regards the grant of legal aid, including withdrawal of entitlement to civil legal aid in certain instances.[317] The Legal Aid Board has the power to refuse to grant a legal aid certificate even where the applicant satisfied the means test and the merits test. This includes where the applicant could be provided with legal representation by "a body or association of which he or she is a member or any other source";[318] had failed to abide by instructions or directions as regards the terms upon which a previous grant of legal advice and/or legal aid certificate had been granted;[319] the contribution to be paid upon receiving legal advice or a legal aid certificate is less

312 [2009] 3 I.R. 458 at 471–479.
313 [2009] 3 I.R. 458 at 480. One-Parent Family Payment is provided for under Pt 3, Ch.7 (ss.172–178) of the Social Welfare Consolidation Act 2005 (as amended).
314 [2009] 3 I.R. 458 at 480.
315 [2009] 3 I.R. 458 at 484.
316 [2009] 3 I.R. 458 at 484.
317 For a comprehensive examination of this, see s.28(4) and s.28(6)–(8) of the 1995 Act (as amended), reg.4(5)–(7) and reg.9 of the Civil Legal Aid Regulations 1996–2021.
318 Section 28(4)(a) of the 1995 Act.
319 Section 28(4)(b) of the 1995 Act.

than engaging a solicitor or barrister in private practice;[320] or where the applicant fails to provide sufficient information to the Legal Aid Board on whether to grant a legal aid certificate.[321] The Legal Aid Board can instruct an applicant to comply with "such requirements as it reasonably considers expedient" in order for the applicant to continue to receive legal aid.[322] Decisions of the Legal Aid Board to revoke a legal aid certificate are not appealable. They are only subject to being judicially reviewed. As Phelan J. in *BA v Legal Aid Board* explains, this means an individual evidencing some improper decision-making process, such as proper procedure not followed or that the decision reached was unreasonable and irrational.[323] In *Prendergast v Legal Aid Board*,[324] the applicant sought to judicially review the Legal Aid Board's revocation of his legal aid certificate. The applicant was seeking leave of the High Court to bring judicial review proceedings.[325] Simons J. granted the applicant leave to take a judicial review. There was a statable argument that the Appeals Committee had not provided sufficient reasons for the revocation of the applicant's legal aid certificate.[326]

4. The Future of Civil Legal Aid in Ireland

(a) Denying justice?

13–47 The Pringle Committee Report of the 1970s had a number of radical proposals for a civil legal aid system, including representation rights, community law centres, and education provision, which were never enacted. The 1995 Act did not substantially affect the way in which legal aid provision has operated since the early 1980s. Community legal education is not promoted in any coherent manner. The overwhelming nature of the Legal Aid Board's work relates to family law issues.[327] While there have been some important extensions in the scope of the legal services provided by the Legal Aid Board since the 1995 Act, the scheme for civil legal aid in Ireland has not changed significantly since the 1980s.

---

320 Section 28(4)(c) of the 1995 Act.
321 Section 28(4)(d) of the 1995 Act.
322 Section 28(6) of the 1995 Act and reg.9(3) of the Civil Legal Aid Regulations 1996–2013.
323 [2023] IEHC 569 at para.32.
324 [2024] IEHC 265.
325 [2024] IEHC 265 at paras 1–5.
326 [2024] IEHC 265 at paras 28–34.
327 Legal Aid Board, *Annual Report 2022* (Dublin: Legal Aid Board, 2023), p.25.

At the end of 2021, 1,297 persons were on a waiting list to access the Legal Aid Board's services.[328] By the end of 2022, there were 950 persons on the Legal Aid Board's waiting lists to access legal aid. This represents a significant achievement, given that there were over 5,000 people on waiting lists to access legal aid in 2014.[329] As the Chief Executive of the Legal Aid Board has stated, "it is not optimal to have people waiting for services in circumstances where they may be experiencing considerable upheaval in their lives."[330] The average number of weeks persons will wait for their first appointment with the Legal Aid Board varies considerably, depending on the Legal Aid Board office responsible. At the end of 2022, the waiting time for a first consultation with the Legal Aid Board in Athlone was six weeks. Contrast this to 2021, where the waiting time in Athlone had been over one year.[331] For time-sensitive matters, relating to domestic violence, child care proceedings and child abduction, these waiting times would have been significantly less.[332] While there is no constitutional entitlement to civil legal aid, an individual who qualifies for civil legal aid is entitled to receive this in a relatively reasonable time frame.[333] In *O'Donoghue v Legal Aid Board*, Kelly J. awarded damages to the applicant, who experienced a 25-month delay in accessing services provided by the Legal Aid Board.[334] Kelly J. held that once an individual comes within the scope of the civil legal aid scheme, then the right to civil legal aid is "constitutionalised", in the sense that the civil legal aid scheme must be administered fairly and fulfil its core purpose.[335] While accepting that the staff of the Legal Aid Board were not negligent, and had simply too much work, it is not enough to set up a scheme to provide legal advice to a needy individual, but then render it meaningless for a long time. The legislature was entitled to define reasonable limits to the right to civil legal aid. The Legal Aid Board's own target of attempting to

---

328 Legal Aid Board, *Annual Report 2021* (Dublin: Legal Aid Board, 2022), pp.28–29.

329 See, e.g. Legal Aid Board, *Annual Report 2013* (Dublin: Legal Aid Board, 2014), p.20 (5,000 people on waiting lists); Legal Aid Board, *Annual Report 2014* (Dublin: Legal Aid Board, 2015), p.22 (3,412 on waiting lists); Legal Aid Board, *Annual Report 2016* (Dublin: Legal Aid Board, 2017), pp.22–23 (1,864 on waiting lists); Legal Aid Board, *Annual Report 2020* (Dublin: Legal Aid Board, 2021), pp.23–24 (1,588 on waiting lists).

330 Legal Aid Board, *Annual Report 2021* (Dublin: Legal Aid Board, 2022), p.22.

331 Legal Aid Board, *Annual Report 2021* (Dublin: Legal Aid Board, 2022), p.30 and Legal Aid Board, *Annual Report 2022* (Dublin: Legal Aid Board, 2023), p.28.

332 Legal Aid Board, *Annual Report 2021* (Dublin: Legal Aid Board, 2022), p.29.

333 *O'Donoghue v Legal Aid Board* [2006] 4 I.R. 204.

334 [2006] 4 I.R. 204 at 227.

335 [2006] 4 I.R. 204 at 234, approved by the Supreme Court in *Magee v Farrell* [2009] 4 I.R. 703 and *MIH v Minister for Justice and Equality* [2021] IESC 32 at para.26.

provide an initial appointment with a solicitor within 2–4 months was said to be reasonable.[336] Kelly J. awarded the plaintiff €8,991.60 for the denial of her right to be provided with civil legal aid, despite being entitled to it, for a period of 25 months.[337]

13–48 For over 40 years, FLAC have advocated for a significantly expanded system of civil legal aid.[338] They have continuously argued for increased funding so as to ensure legal aid is received in a prompt manner. FLAC have also set out the case for the extension of the remit of the Legal Aid Board, in particular as regards social welfare, housing, property and employment law. These calls have been ignored by successive governments. The FLAC report, *Accessing Justice in Hard Times*,[339] lays down the stark reality of the impact of austerity on the Irish system of civil legal aid. Persons who needed legal advice or representation on personal debt,[340] housing,[341] employment[342] and social welfare[343] were, due to the limits of the 1995 Act or Legal Aid Board practice, denied access to an adequate state-funded legal aid system. The core reason for this, on a reading of FLAC's report, seems to be the political disinterest in the legal needs of the poor and vulnerable within Irish society. On the basis of a detailed analysis of the Legal Aid Board's statistics, and a comparison of these with public requests for information on FLAC's delivery of legal advice, FLAC concluded:

> "[T]here is a substantial need for access to legal aid and advice in areas other than family and child law. While many of these issues are well within the mandate of the Legal Aid Board, there is either no public awareness of the Board's services in these areas, or some people are informally discouraged from applying for legal assistance in areas other than family law."[344]

[336] [2006] 4 I.R. 204 at 237.
[337] See reporter's note: [2006] 4 I.R. 204 at 238.
[338] See, e.g. FLAC, *Access to Justice: A Right or a Privilege?* (Dublin: Printwell, 2005); Community Law & Mediation, *Recommendations on the Lack of Legal Support Available to Borrowers Facing Repossession of Their Family Home* (Dublin: Community Law & Mediation, 2015).
[339] FLAC, *Accessing Justice in Hard Times: The Impact of the Economic Downturn on the Scheme of Civil Legal Aid in Ireland* (Dublin: Printwell, 2016).
[340] FLAC, *Accessing Justice in Hard Times* (2016), pp.7–8.
[341] FLAC, *Accessing Justice in Hard Times* (2016), pp.8–10.
[342] FLAC, *Accessing Justice in Hard Times* (2016), pp.10–11.
[343] FLAC, *Accessing Justice in Hard Times* (2016), pp.11–12.
[344] FLAC, *Accessing Justice in Hard Times* (2016), p.32.

FLAC argues that the failure to promote access to justice during the recession was due to the lack of political respect for the rights of the poor and the vulnerable. Avoiding prolonged delays in accessing a statutory right to civil legal aid is essential. As the former Director General of FLAC, Dr Noeline Blackwell, has stated:

> "You don't need to be a lawyer to know that we don't have that system in Ireland. Everyone knows of cases where people could not get the legal advice or the court representation they needed and deserved simply because they could not afford it. People challenging the authorities to vindicate their rights have felt the freezing 'chill factor' of potentially enormous legal costs."[345]

13–49 Successive United Nations human rights treaty bodies[346] have expressed significant concerns on Ireland's system of civil legal aid.[347] This includes the lack of rights-compliance with UN human rights treaties regarding waiting times to access civil legal aid and the impact of lack of legal aid for vulnerable groups such as survivors of domestic violence, Travellers and Roma, and persons living in poverty. The exclusion of legal aid for social welfare law, employment law and housing law significantly impacts an individual's ability to truly gain access to justice. The Kelly Report, *Review of the Administration of Civil Justice*, recommended in 2020 that "the Department of Justice and Equality give consideration to initiating a review of the criteria governing access to civil legal aid and the likely resourcing implications of any modification of those criteria."[348]

---

345 N. Blackwell, "All society is damaged when some can't access the legal system", *Irish Examiner*, 25 February 2016.

346 For a full overview of these international treaty supervisory bodies and their relationship with Irish law, see L. Thornton, "Socio-Economic Rights and Ireland" in S. Egan (ed.), *International Human Rights: Perspectives from Ireland* (Dublin: Bloomsbury, 2015), in particular paras 9.15–9.18.

347 Committee on the Rights of the Child, *Concluding Observations on the Combined Fifth and Sixth Periodic Reports of Ireland*, UN Doc. CRC/C/IRL/CO/5-6 (28 February 2023), para.27(g); Committee on the Elimination of Racial Discrimination, *Concluding Observations on the Combined Fifth to Ninth Reports of Ireland*, UN Doc. CERD/C/IRL/CO/5-9, paras 43–44; Committee against Torture, *Concluding Observations on the Second Periodic Report of Ireland*, UN Doc. CAT/C/IRL/CO/2 (31 August 2017), paras 11–12 and paras 31–32; Committee on the Elimination of All Forms of Discrimination against Women, *Concluding Observations on the Combined Sixth and Seventh Periodic Reports*, UN Doc. CEDAW/C/IRL/CO/6-7 (9 March 2017), paras 28–29; Committee on Economic, Social and Cultural Rights, *Concluding Observations on the Third Periodic Report of Ireland*, UN Doc. E/C.12/IRL/CO/3 (19 June 2015), para.8.

348 Kelly Report, *Review of the Administration of Civil Justice* (2020), p.348. This report

(b) Reforming civil legal aid in Ireland

13–50 In June 2022,[349] the Minister for Justice announced the first comprehensive review of Ireland's civil legal aid system in 40 years.[350] Chaired by former Chief Justice of Ireland, Frank Clarke, the Civil Legal Aid Review Group comprises 11 persons with knowledge and expertise in civil legal aid.[351] The Review Group is tasked with making recommendations regarding the delivery of civil legal aid, financing and operational matters, and the level of financial contribution beneficiaries of civil legal aid should pay.[352] As important will be the Review Group's analysis of the categories of civil law that legal aid should cover, income thresholds for the grant of legal aid, and the appropriateness of extending civil legal aid to quasi-judicial bodies, e.g. the Workplace Relations Commission and Social Welfare Appeals Office.[353] The Review Group launched a consultation, receiving submissions from a number of organisations to input into their analysis and recommendations for reform of civil legal aid.[354] A large array of suggestions were detailed throughout these submissions. The importance of a well-resourced, rights-focused system of civil legal aid was highlighted in all submissions for its role in protecting the rule of law, upholding human rights, and ensuring the most vulnerable in society have access to legal services. Civil legal aid cannot be viewed as a form of charity, but as a bedrock in democratic societies.

---

did note the varying income thresholds that exist in EU member states and the United Kingdom for accessing civil legal aid (pp.334–350).

[349] For a background to the establishment of the Review Group, see Department of Justice, *Justice Plan 2021*, p.23, and FLAC, "43 NGOs and advocates join FLAC's call on Justice Minister to ensure Ireland's vulnerable and marginalised individuals, families and communities can access Civil Legal Aid" (29 July 2021).

[350] Department of Justice, "Minister announces review of Civil Legal Aid Scheme" (2 June 2022).

[351] Civil Legal Aid Review Group, *Issues Paper to Guide Submissions on the Review of the Civil Legal Aid Scheme* (2023).

[352] Civil Legal Aid Review Group, *Terms of Reference* (2022), para.1, para.2(h) and para.5.

[353] Civil Legal Aid Review Group, *Terms of Reference* (2022), para.2.

[354] The submissions examined for the purpose of analysis are: Bar Council, *Submission to the Civil Legal Aid Review Group* (February 2023); Citizens Information Board (CIB), *Review of the Civil Legal Aid Scheme* (February 2023); Community Law and Mediation (CLM), *Submission on the Review of the Civil Legal Aid Scheme* (February 2023); Free Legal Advice Centres (FLAC), *Stakeholder Submission to the Review of the Civil Legal Aid Scheme* (February 2023); Irish Human Rights and Equality Commission (IHREC), *Submission to the Independent Review of Civil Legal Aid Scheme* (March 2023); Law Society of Ireland, *Submission to the Civil Legal Aid Review Group* (February 2023); and Mercy Law Resource Centre (MLRC), *Submission to the Civil Legal Aid Review Group* (February 2023).

There was significant agreement within the professions' and civil society submissions on the need to expand the areas the Legal Aid Board could offer advice and aid in. While acknowledging the necessity of legal aid and advice within family and child law, and the limited funding provided to the Board, concerns were expressed that the Legal Aid Board was seen as mainly just a family and child law legal service.[355]

13–51 Submissions to the Review Group acknowledged that not all legal disputes are so complex as to need legal representation. Nonetheless, these submissions emphasised that legal complexity arises in exceptionally important, currently excluded, legal areas. Quasi-judicial bodies[356] decide upon a range of disputes, rights, entitlements and responsibilities. Often, there is no appeal to courts from these decisions (although this is not always the case), other than potentially seeking judicial review, which, if successful, would result in a fresh re-determination of the issue.[357] This then gives rise to key questions regarding the ability of persons to realise their rights within such significant areas, such as residential tenancies and housing law,[358] entitlement to social welfare,[359] and employment rights.[360] The Bar of Ireland notes:

> "Merit should not be framed simply in terms of success or failure. Cases which appear at first instance to be unwinnable often throw up novel points of law which may ultimately result in success or, if not successful, assist in the evolution of legal principles which is to the benefit of the civil justice system as a whole."[361]

13–52 FLAC and the Irish Human Rights and Equality Commission (IHREC) argue that only cases adjudged to be "manifestly ill-founded"

[355] CIB, p.4; CLM, p.5; FLAC, p.54; IHREC, p.59; Law Society of Ireland, pp 7–8; MLRC, p.7.
[356] See Ch.10, paras 10–08 to 10–16.
[357] See Ch.10, paras 10–17 to 10–20.
[358] Bar Council, p.11; CIB, p.5; CLM, pp.20–21; FLAC, pp.52–53; IHREC, p.20; Law Society of Ireland, p.47; MLRC, pp.8–9.
[359] Bar Council, p.6; CLM, p.20; FLAC, pp.145–152; IHREC, pp.22–23; Law Society of Ireland, p.16.
[360] Bar Council, pp.7–10; CIB, p.5; CLM, pp.7–8; FLAC, pp.64–65; IHREC, pp.18–19; Law Society of Ireland, pp.13–16.
[361] Bar Council, pp.16–17. A similar argument is proffered by CLM, pp.27–28, in particular as regards public interest cases.

should be denied on the basis of merit.[362] Both rely on the ECtHR jurisprudence that focuses on, amongst other things, the importance of what is at stake, legal complexity, and the capacity of a person to represent themselves.[363] Determining the merits of a case is something that will continue to be complex. As regards financial means, all submissions agreed that the current means tests are in no way reflective of the costs of living in Ireland, with the means test generally not amended since 2006. The approach recommended by the IHREC, Community Law & Mediation (CLM) and FLAC is for any reformulated means test to adopt a yearly revised "reasonable cost of living" approach, whereby the actual costs of housing and life necessities should generally be excluded in calculating means.[364] In addition, some submissions to the Review Group stated that financial contributions should either not apply or that there should be some method on a case-by-case basis for the Legal Aid Board to waive any contribution.[365] The Review Group has not yet published its report. Therefore, we do not know whether any of the recommendations discussed above will feature in the Review Group report. In June 2024, the Minister for Justice noted their expectation that the Review Group would "conclude its work in the near future".[366] The same response was provided in January 2025.[367] There was no mention of the civil legal aid system in the 2025 Programme for Government.[368]

5. Provision of Civil Legal Advice and Aid outside the 1995 Act

13–53 Outside the 1995 Act, the IHREC has the power to provide "legal assistance", defined as legal advice and/or legal representation,[369] on matters involving the protection of human rights, including rights

[362] FLAC, pp.80–84, drawing upon the test utilised by the ECtHR, see pp.36–39. See also, IHREC, pp.39–41. The Law Society highlighted in its submission, p.31, that the purpose of the merits test is "to deter frivolous/vexatious actions".

[363] See further, D. Harris, M. O'Boyle, E. Bates and C. Buckley, *Law of the European Court of Human Rights* (Oxford: Oxford University Press, 2023), pp.401–403.

[364] CLM, pp.22–26; FLAC, pp.73–79; IHREC, pp.33–37.

[365] See, e.g. Law Society, p.32; IHREC, pp.42–44.

[366] Deputy James Lawless to the Minister for Justice, Question 245 Written Answers, 18 June 2024.

[367] Deputy James Lawless to the Minister for Justice, Question 245 Written Answers, 22 January 2025.

[368] Department of An Taoiseach, *Programme for Government 2025: Securing Ireland's Future* (2025).

[369] Irish Human Rights and Equality Commission Act 2014 s.40(10).

protected under the European Convention on Human Rights Acts 2003 and 2014, employment rights and equality rights.[370] This includes instituting proceedings before courts or quasi-judicial bodies in order to vindicate the rights of a person.[371] Prior to providing legal assistance, the IHREC must evaluate whether legal assistance could be granted under the criminal or civil legal aid schemes, or by any other person or body.[372] In order to grant legal assistance, the IHREC must consider whether the issue is one of legal principle, or whether it would be unreasonable to expect the person seeking legal assistance to bring the legal challenge themselves due to the complexity of issues. In 2023, the IHREC granted legal advice to 94 clients, and approved advice and representation for 53 clients.[373] Of particular note is that within the areas of disability rights, housing rights, employment law, immigration law and social welfare law, the IHREC's interventions resulted in settlement of legal proceedings before a decision of a court or quasi-judicial body had to be taken.[374] Independent Law Centres[375] are non-profit organisations who provide clients with legal advice and representation across a range of different legal fields such as social welfare law, housing law, rights of Travellers and Roma, protected disclosures and refugee and immigration law. As non-profit organisations, the ability to assist all with a legal need can be limited. The Citizens Information Board provides information, and at times advocacy, to individuals on their legal entitlements; however, this does not constitute legal advice or representation.[376]

D. Conclusion

13–54 While the system of criminal legal aid is far from perfect, it has maintained a focus on ensuring that those facing the prosecutorial power of the State can have representation from solicitors and, if necessary, barristers. It remains to be seen how the proposed transfer

[370] Irish Human Rights and Equality Commission Act 2014 s.10(2)(f) and s.40.

[371] Section 41 of the 2014 Act.

[372] Section 40(3) of the 2014 Act.

[373] IHREC, *Annual Report 2023* (2024), p.15. The IHREC did not grant advice and/or representation for 73 applicants. Ten applicants withdrew their request.

[374] See IHREC, *Annual Report 2022* (2023), pp.19–29 and IHREC, *Annual Report 2023* (2024), pp.16–27.

[375] Regulation 4 of the Solicitors Acts, 1954 to 2002 (Independent Law Centres) Regulations 2006 (S.I. No. 103 of 2006).

[376] Citizens Information Board, *Annual Report 2023* (2024).

of responsibility for all criminal legal aid schemes to the Legal Aid Board will operate. In the sphere of civil legal aid, only those with miniscule incomes and who are exceptionally poor in Irish society are capable of qualifying for civil legal aid. The system of civil legal aid that Ireland currently has emerged in the 1980s. Whether the current review of the civil legal advice and aid scheme will open up the possibility of adopting a more rights-embracing model or will simply become another dusty report on a shelf remains to be seen.

Part III

Legal Skills

Chapter 14

Researching Law

> "Legal research no longer requires beginning with knowledge of the law because the emphasis of electronic research is on facts and keywords, not legal concepts. Research now is truly a mechanical process of entering factual words into a database or search engine and retrieving results. These research results appear to support the realists' claims that law has no internal consistency."
>
> B. Bintliff, "Context and Legal Research" (2007) 99(2) *Law Library Journal* 249 at 266.

In this chapter we:

- discover how to research the law;
- describe how to use a law library;
- explore how to use some online legal databases;
- reflect on how best to record our research;
- consider how to use our research to advance a legal argument.

A. Introduction

14–01 This final sequence of chapters examines the skills that you will need when studying the law. Lawyers are professional communicators. We read, discuss and write about the law every day. The next two chapters will discuss how to read the law[1] and how to write about the law.[2] Before we can engage in either of those two activities, we need to be able to find the law, and for this we need to engage in legal research.

14–02 In its narrowest interpretation, legal research is the skill of finding the law. However, true research is the gathering of data, information and facts for the advancement of knowledge and, in the context of law, it is

[1] See further, Ch.15.
[2] See further, Ch.16.

about gathering information pertaining to the law and then examining it. Thus, there are two aspects to legal research: identifying what the law is, and questioning why the law is this way.[3] The second of these two aspects—the "why" question—is the one that moves reading, writing and researching about the law from the description phase towards the critical evaluation or critical analysis phase that is expected from all those students who, throughout their degree, wish to excel in their studies.

14–03 In either case, before you can identify or critique the law, you need to be able to locate it. This chapter focuses on the skills that are necessary to find the law. As discussed throughout this book, law is recorded in written form. The image of a lawyer as one surrounded by dusty tomes and ancient leather bound books is an accurate stereotype. Thus, where you find the law has not changed in centuries: primarily it is found in statutes and case reports. What has evolved over time is how you access these sources. In this chapter, we will consider how to navigate the law library and where the sources of law can be found online.

B. The Law Library

14–04 Famously, Christopher Columbus Langdell, Dean of the Harvard Law School from 1870–1895, identified the library as the key learning and working space of the lawyer, comparing it to a scientist's laboratory.[4] Traditionally, the law library was the place where lawyers researched, read and wrote about the law. In modern times, the advent of online legal databases has reduced the need for law students to visit the library. Yet the library remains an excellent resource for the research of the law. Most usefully, all good law libraries will have librarians who can help you to navigate both the physical library and the online databases. Law librarians are an invaluable aid to conducting legal research. They have general knowledge about law and legal sources and can be enormously helpful when it comes to rooting out difficult-to-locate sources and secondary commentaries. In addition, they have lots of advice and tips

3 A.T.H. Smith, *Glanville Williams: Learning the Law*, 13th edn (London: Sweet & Maxwell, 2006), p.210.

4 C.C. Langdell, quoted in Harvard Law School Association, *The Centennial History of the Harvard Law School, 1817–1917* (Cambridge, Mass.: The Harvard Law School Association, 1918), p.97.

on how to use the physical library and databases to which the library subscribes to yield the best results for your research.

14–05 When studying the law you need to become familiar with the layout of your law library. This will ensure that when you are engaged in legal research you can swiftly and easily find the sources you require. The big advantage in researching hard copies in the library is the manner in which items are shelved. Thus, once you go to the shelf where the contract law books are located, for example, you will find not only the core text you have been assigned but other contract law texts. A quick flick through some of these other books might enrich your research. Most law libraries hold not only the leading Irish student textbooks on contract law but those from England and Wales as well. You may find an alternative explanation of a principle in one of those texts that makes it easier for you to grasp that principle, or indeed a new way of doing things in that jurisdiction that might be a useful suggested reform of Irish law. In this way, your research has enhanced your knowledge.

14–06 There are a number of areas in the library where law students might find themselves. Obviously you will become accustomed to the shelves where the law books are held. These will include subject areas collections and shelves where you will find hard copies of legislation, law reports and academic journals. Another area of the library that will become familiar to you is the Official Publications. Here you will find all publications by the State, the EU or other international organisations such as the United Nations, the World Bank, the Organisation for Economic Co-operation and Development (OECD) and others. While many of these official reports can now be sourced online, some of the older publications are accessible in hard copy only and these can be located in this section of the library. Your study may take you outside the official "law" shelves of the library. There are many areas of law that overlap with other subjects or disciplines such as politics, history, sociology, medicine, ethics and so on. Consequently, you may on occasion venture into these unexplored terrains in order to locate a particular book that is of interest to you. Thus, you need to become familiar with the library catalogue and the layout of the library as a whole.

14–07 Law libraries will also hold extensive collections of reported cases, legislation and legal periodicals. Much of this information is also available online. Yet not all of it is. Before you despair of locating a particular case report or journal article, it is advisable to check out the online library catalogue to ascertain whether the hard copies of the relevant report series or journal predate those available online. The availability of online material is a relatively recent innovation. The physical collections of most libraries will contain items that are much older than those available via the online databases. Thus, it may be possible to access the hard copy of the source you require by a simple visit to the library.

1. The Library Catalogue

14–08 Most libraries employ the Dewey Decimal Classification system. Introduced by Melvil Dewey in 1876,[5] the system aims to organise books based on the subject. Thus, books on law are all found near each other. This is called the relative location principle. Before this system was introduced, books were simply placed on the shelves in the order in which they were acquired by the library. The reform introduced by Dewey facilitates readers in their research by grouping together books on a related subject. Broad subject areas are identified by three digits and these are further refined by numbers after the decimal point which enables increased specification and identification of a particular book. This system makes it very easy to locate and return a particular book to the shelves. The system itself is constantly updated to account for new subject specialisations, most recently, the 23rd edition of the hardcopy book in 2011, although there are continuous micro-updates being made online. Once you type the name of the author or title of the book you seek into the library catalogue, it will give you the catalogue number of the book using this system, which will tell you on what exact shelf in the building you can find the book.

Box 14.1: Skills Insight
Dewey Decimal Categories

Under the Dewey Decimal system, there are 10 broad classes of subject. These are broken down as follows:

[5] M. Dewey, *A Classification and Subject Index for Cataloguing and Arranging the Books and Pamphlets of a Library* (1876) (Project Gutenberg eBook).

- 000 – General works, computer science and information
- 100 – Philosophy and psychology
- 200 – Religion
- 300 – Social sciences
- 400 – Language
- 500 – Pure science
- 600 – Technology
- 700 – Arts and recreation
- 800 – Literature
- 900 – History and geography

According to this system, law is a social science. Thus, it is a sub-category that begins with the numbers "34". Law books are categorised as follows:

- 340 Law generally
- 341 International law
- 342 Constitutional and administrative law
- 343 Public law, including tax law, commercial law, international trade and media law
- 344 Social law, including employment, social service, environmental law and medical law
- 345 Criminal law
- 346 Private law, including contract, company, equity and trusts, and property
- 347 Procedure and courts, including law of evidence, alternative dispute resolution and rules of court
- 348 Legislation, regulations, cases
- 349 Law of specific jurisdictions, for example, French law and German law

Thus, under this system, if we are searching for Irish textbooks on contract law, we know that we need to look at the shelves beginning with "346". While each library has its own slight variations, we can predict with relative certainty that the books on Irish contract law are gathered together on shelf 346 and, within that, are organised alphabetically by author surname.

Once we understand this system, it is a simple matter to locate the book we want (providing someone else has not checked it out before we got there).

14–09 All libraries have a complete catalogue of everything they hold. These are now available online and are also accessible via dedicated computers throughout the library. These catalogues are very user-friendly and usually you can search the collection by author name, title of book and/or keyword. In addition to the information regarding shelf location, library catalogues provide other useful information about the book you seek. They will tell you how many copies of a particular title are in the collection, whether these are long or short-term loans or whether they are desk reserve copies that cannot be removed from the library. Furthermore, the catalogue will inform you of the status of each copy of the title: which are currently checked out, which are on hold for another reader, and which are currently on the library shelf. Occasionally, the catalogue will inform you that the book you want is not available in your own library. In these circumstances, it might be possible to order it on inter-library loan.

2. Inter-Library Loans

14–10 Most libraries will operate an inter-library loan service. If a title you want is not available in your own library, the library can borrow the book from another library on your behalf. There may be a small fee for this service depending on where your library can source the book you require. It usually takes time for a book ordered in this manner to become available for you to read. Presuming the library that owns the book has it in stock, it may only take a few days, but if the book is out on loan from that library, it may take months for a copy to get to you. Thus, it is best to talk to the librarian and discover the likelihood of your getting the book in time for your research purposes. You can then make an informed decision on whether to proceed with the inter-library loan.

C. Online Databases

14–11 Having discussed the library as a research tool, we now turn to a consideration of the online legal databases that might be of use when conducting research. Much of the information that we need when conducting research on a particular topic can be sourced online via various databases. Some of these databases are freely available to anyone, others are based on subscription to the material they contain.

We will now examine some of the databases that you might find useful when you are researching a particular question. It may be useful, when reading this section of the chapter, to follow the steps outlined on your computer.

1. Freely Available Databases

(a) Irish Statute Book: www.irishstatutebook.ie

14–12 This is an excellent resource for locating legislation in Ireland. It includes all legislation passed by the Oireachtas, whether primary legislation or delegated legislation.[6] It also includes sections for older legislation introduced prior to Irish independence. These pre-1922 Acts, some of which may still be in force, are available by clicking on the tab called "Legislation" in the menu running along the top of the screen, under the title bar.

14–13 When you visit the home page of this site, you will see underneath the title bar five tabs, which are shortcuts to the collection sorted in various ways. Four of these shortcuts will allow you to search the site quickly; the fifth brings you back to the home page. The collection of Acts of the Oireachtas, the collection of pre-1922 Acts discussed earlier, and the collection of statutory instruments are all grouped together under the "Legislation" tab. The current version of the Irish Constitution can be found under the "Constitution" tab. There are also tabs for "External Resources" and "FAQ".

14–14 If you click into the legislation tab, and then click on "Acts of the Oireachtas", you can see that you have the option to search for the legislation you require based on year of publication. The drop-down menus are organised by decade and within this you can choose which exact year you wish to browse and call up all the legislation passed in that year. The legislation is listed in alphabetical order. Once you have the title of the legislation you require, you simply click on it and you are brought to the landing page for that legislation. Here you can see hyperlinks to each section of the Act and can jump directly to the section you wish to read by clicking on it. Once reading a section, you

---

[6] For more on primary and secondary legislation, see Ch.4, Section B.

can navigate to the next or the previous section using the arrow buttons in the bottom right-hand corner of the screen. At any stage you can view the Act in its entirety by clicking on the "View Full Act" button which will be located at both the top and the bottom of the section on the left. After the "View Full Act" button, you will see "Bill History". Clicking on this will provide access to the history of the Act, including the original text of the Bill, the explanatory memorandum, amendments made by the Dáil and/or Seanad, and finally debates on the legislation. More detail on this is discussed in the next section. You can also choose to jump through to the Legislation Directory entry for the section by clicking on the button entitled "Amendments, Commencement, SIs made under the Act". You navigate the statutory instruments in a similar manner. A very important addition to the website over the last number of years is the inclusion of the Law Reform Commission "Revised Act". A Revised Act is a codification of all amendments made to an Act. Revised Acts are prepared by the Law Reform Commission. Not all legislation will have a Revised Act, which is why you also need to be able to navigate and understand the Legislation Directory.

14–15 One of the most useful facilities that this website offers is the Legislation Directory. Here you can check to see whether legislation has been amended since it was enacted, or whether it has been repealed and is no longer in force. There are search engines for both primary and secondary legislation. You will note the warning that the secondary legislation facility is not complete and thus you will need to perform additional checks to be certain of the continued relevance of any provision.

14–16 As regards primary legislation, the Legislation Directory entry gives you a wealth of information about the particular Act, including the commencement date and any secondary legislation that has resulted from the Act, with hyperlinks to the relevant statutory instruments. This will also tell you, on a section-by-section basis, what primary legislation has impacted the legislation you are researching. You can follow the hyperlink through to the section that introduced this amendment and see what words were inserted or deleted or if the entire section has been repealed and replaced. This is a handy tool to check that a particular section of a particular Act remains in force.

(b) www.oireachtas.ie

14–17 This is the website of the Houses of the Oireachtas. It is useful to legal researchers for a number of reasons. First, it enables us to trace through the changes in drafts of legislation as it progressed through the Oireachtas. Second, it enables us to research the Dáil and Seanad debates on any legislation.

14–18 Once you land on the home page you will see a series of buttons across the top of the page. The first of these is "Bills & Acts". You will be presented with a screen that offers you a series of search boxes. The first of these on the top left enables you to search for either enacted legislation, "Acts", or not yet enacted draft legislation, "Bills". The second, to the right, enables a search by keyword. The third, on the left, enables a search by year. Once you have selected the legislation you wish to view from the search results by clicking on the "View Act" or "View Bill" button, you are brought to the home page for that legislation. Here you can see the history of the legislation. There will be a callout box informing you of the present status of the legislation: signed into law, stage of progress through either Dáil or Seanad, or lapsed. Under that is a ribbon with a timeline indicating the current stage of progress of the legislation. As stages of the legislative journey are completed, the numbers of the stages will be replaced by tick marks. Underneath that are a series of tabs. The first, "Act and Bill Text", links to the differing versions of the legislative text as it progresses through the Oireachtas. Any of this text can be downloaded by clicking on the PDF icon button on the right. The next tab, "Related Documents", brings you to the explanatory memorandum for this legislation. The third tab, "Amendments", brings you to the proposed amendments to the legislation made at each stage of its journey. The final tab, "Debates", brings you to the transcripts of the Dáil/Seanad debates at each stage of the progress of this legislation through the Oireachtas. Thus, it is possible to trace the evolution of legislation in its entirety, from the formal text, to the initial intention of the drafters as expressed in the explanatory memorandum, through all the proposed amendments and to the debates that took place as the legislation was being drafted by the Oireachtas.

(c) www.irlii.org / www.bailii.org

14–19 These two sites are interrelated and are part of the World Legal Information Institute (worldlii) network. They provide indexes and links to full-text judgments from the Irish courts, the courts of England and Wales, Jersey, Scotland, Northern Ireland, the United Kingdom, the Court of Justice of the European Union and the European Court of Human Rights. You can search these databases by case name, by court and year, by legislation or by keyword. On the Irish site, *www.irlii.org*, you can also search by leading case. A particularly useful feature available on the UK site, *www.bailii.org*, is that if you select a UK Supreme Court judgment in a case, in the top right-hand corner of the screen there is a hyperlink that will bring you through to the Court of Appeal decision from which the present appeal to the UK Supreme Court originates. In a similar fashion, the Court of Appeal judgment enables you to trace back to the High Court decision (from the hyperlink in the top left-hand corner). Thus, you can easily track the progress of a case through the courts. This feature is not yet available via the *www.irlii.org* site.

14–20 One useful feature on the Irish site is the "journals" button at the top of the page. This page is an index of all Irish legal periodicals from 1997 to the present. The page does not provide links to the full text of the articles, with the exception of those where the copyright holder so permits. It does enable users to search for an article on a given topic from all the Irish legal journals, albeit you may have to source the article from elsewhere. Nonetheless, from the perspective of completing a thorough search of Irish academic commentary on the law, this site is an excellent resource for the researcher. In addition, the page includes some limited listings for open access (i.e. freely available) book chapters that focus on Irish law.

(d) www.courts.ie

14–21 This is the website of the Courts Service. Here you will find all sorts of information about the courts, including court fees, court forms, court rules, information on jury service, probate and the legal diary. You can also find information on the history of the courts in Ireland, descriptions of the work of each court and lists of all the judges of the various courts. Once you land on the home page, there are a range of options as to how to navigate from here. To find case law and judgments, choose the "Judgments" option, which will enable you to search judgments by court or by year of decision. Via the *courts.ie* website, you can locate judgments from the Supreme Court since 2001, the Court of Appeal since 2014 and the High Court since 2004. This is also where you will find Supreme Court determinations. These are where the Supreme Court gives the reasons for its determination or decision as to whether it will hear an appeal from the Court of Appeal or whether it will hear an appeal directly from the High Court, in essence leapfrogging the Court of Appeal. It is via this website that you can also locate judgments of the Court of Criminal Appeal, the Courts-Martial Appeal Court, the Central Criminal Court, the Circuit Court and judgments of the District Court in child care cases.

(e) www.europa.eu and EUR-Lex

14–22 The official website of the European Union is *www.europa.eu*. Once you have selected the language in which you wish to conduct your research, you are brought through to the relevant home page of the site. Here you can follow the links to uncover a wealth of information about the EU. By following the logical progression of the links, you can search both the legislation and case law of the EU. If you select the "find case-law" option from the drop-down menu, you encounter a simple interface that retrieves the full text of judgments from the Court of Justice of the European Union website. You can search simply by keyword in the search box. Alternatively, the "Advanced search form" hyperlink brings you directly to the search page at the Court of Justice of the European Union website where you can conduct a quite sophisticated search through its archives.

14–23 EUR-Lex provides dedicated access to all legal measures within the EU, including treaties, case law, regulations, directives and decisions. Here you will find a series of boxes: EU Law, EU case law, Information, National law and case law. Each of these boxes contains a series of headings that enable you to click through a chain to identify the material for which you are searching. In this way you can search for treaties, legislation, preparatory documents and case law.

(f) Council of Europe: www.echr.coe.int

14–24 This site enables you to search the human rights documents of the Council of Europe, including judgments of the European Court of Human Rights. Follow the links for case law and you are brought to the welcome page for the HUDOC database. On this page you will find user guides to assist you with your research using the database. Next to the logo in the text on the right you will see a hyperlink to the "HUDOC Database" itself. If you click on this, you will be brought to a chronological list of all decisions, determinations and judgments of the European Court of Human Rights. In the top right-hand corner is a simple search button where you can search by keyword. For a more sophisticated search, the advanced search link underneath the simple search box will open the more detailed search form. Here you can search using a variety of ways, including by the case name, the member state, the application number, date and other useful modifiers.

(g) www.lawreform.ie

14–25 This is the website of the Law Reform Commission and through this site you can locate its consultation papers, issues papers, working papers and reports. These can prove a useful resource for critique of the law. To access these materials, simply click on the "Search our Publications" button at the top of the page, and you can search under any of the headings that appear in a series of buttons on the page. The Law Reform Commission is responsible for the maintenance of the "Legislation Directory" which is accessible via the *irishstatutebook.ie* site. The Commission home page includes a link to this service. In addition, the Commission maintains a list of classified legislation, i.e. Acts currently in force, as part of its mandate to keep the law under review. You can click on the relevant button to be brought to the home page for this work, where you can download the most up-to-date list of Acts currently in force. The Revised Acts button brings you to the page where the Commission gathers all the information on consolidated legislation. A Revised Act is an administrative consolidation of that Act. It brings together in a single text all amendments and changes to an Act, making the law more accessible for all users. The Commission was given the responsibility for this administrative function in 2006 and the revised legislation can be accessed through this page. If you would like to read the law as it currently is in a particular area, without needing to cross-reference many different pieces of amending legislation, this is where you will find such information. One limitation of the Commission's website is that it does not have a search function. If you are not certain exactly what it is you seek, you will, unfortunately, have to trawl through the site to seek what it is you need.

(h) scholar.google.com

14–26 Google Scholar is an online search engine that indexes scholarly literature across an array of publishing formats and disciplines. Its index includes many peer-reviewed journals from Europe's and America's largest scholarly publishers, plus scholarly books and other non-peer reviewed journals. It is important to note that while Google Scholar can facilitate the identification of potentially useful sources—particularly secondary critique—it does not include access to full-text articles from commercial publishers that require subscription. In such cases, you may simply need to note the citation of the article and then search for it using the online databases that your library subscribes to and/or locate it on the physical shelves of your library.

14–27 One notable feature of Google Scholar is that it also traces the citation information relating to each article. Thus, you can grab the citation information of the article you are reading for export into EndNote, Zoterro or another electronic citation management system you employ. Google Scholar also includes a "cited by" feature that enables you to research those articles that refer to the one you are currently reading. This feature enables you to click through and read the abstract, if not the entire text, of an article that cites the one you are reading. Finally, Google Scholar includes a "related articles" feature that presents a list of articles closely related to the one you are currently reading. It ranks these suggestions based on how similar they are to the one you are consulting and in light of the relevance of each article.

(i) www.ssrn.com

14–28 The Social Science Research Network (SSRN) is a repository of new and forthcoming scholarship in a number of disciplines, including law. Its aim is to provide widespread dissemination of research and to facilitate rapid communication between researchers. Anyone may subscribe to SSRN as an author and upload their work there for others to download and read. There is no subscription fee. The site is often used as a space to pre-publish working papers and so it can be a good space from which to access the most up-to-date commentary on legal developments. You do not need an SSRN account in order to search the repository. Guests on the site may view abstracts of all papers and may download some full-text papers without registering, although some papers may be available as full text to account holders only. Once you land on the home page, you can search by subject area using the "First Look", "New Networks" or "Research Disciplines" boxes with hyperlinks. This will enable you to search through the various research paper series collected in the database. Alternatively, you can search by keyword by clicking on the magnifying glass icon in the top right-hand corner. A more detailed search facility is available in the "Advanced Search" section of the page, where you can search for a term in the title of the work, or in the abstract and keywords. In addition, this enables you to search by author's name. It is also possible to narrow your search by limiting the dates within which material was posted online using the "Date" drop-down menu.

(j) www.academia.edu

14–29 *Academia.edu* is a social networking site for academics. Similar to SSRN, it offers a repository where academics in all disciplines, including law, can share their research and post their papers online. In order to access *Academia.edu*, you need to sign up using your email address, Google sign-in or your Facebook account. You can search for papers by inserting a keyword into the search box at the top of the page. How useful your search results are depends on how well contributors have tagged both their work and their profiles. So, while you may find something very current in terms of commentary, this is not the most useful of places to begin researching a topic. It may be useful if you are searching for a particular article by a particular author, as they might have an electronic copy freely available on this site, or they may have a pre-published working draft available here or indeed another paper on a closely related topic that may be of interest to you.

Box 14.2: Skills Insight
Tips to Improve the Accuracy of Searching via Online Fora

Your ability to return search results that assist you with your research can be enormously enhanced by knowledge of a few tips that can help to narrow and refine the focus of that research. These tips are not special to any particular database but are applicable across search engines and search functions which can aid the return of useful and relevant resources to assist with your research. These tools are known as Boolean operators.

Inverted commas “”
The use of inverted commas will ensure that you can search for a precise term or a very specific phrase. It will search for this phrase exactly as it appears between the inverted commas, in the precise word order you have typed between the inverted commas. Thus, if you are researching the development of the principle of a duty of care in tort law, for example, you can put the key phrase “duty of care” in inverted commas into the search box and this will return all sources that contain this exact phrase. By corollary, it will also omit any results that do not feature the phrase. Without the inverted commas, the search could return any document that features any of the words in any combination. Consequently, the use of the inverted commas reduces the amount of resources through which you must sift in order to properly research the topic.

+
Ordinarily, common words such as “and” and “the” or “a” are ignored by search engines. If you particularly wish to ensure that such a common word forms part of the search you can either surround the word with inverted commas as above, or you can use the plus sign, +. This will ensure that your ordinarily ignored common word is included in the search.

–
In a similar way, the minus sign, –, will exclude a word that might otherwise be included. For example, if you wish to search for “duty of care” without any reference to the seminal case of *Donoghue v Stephenson*, then if you put the case name in inverted commas with the minus sign in front it, –“Donoghue v Stephenson”, all resources that reference that particular case will be excluded from the search.

OR

Using the word "OR" (uppercase) enables you to search for more than one word at a time. The word requires that at least one of the keywords is in the page/document which the search returns. Thus, use of the operator "OR" broadens the parameters of your search.

AND

By contrast, the use of "AND" (uppercase) as an operator requires that all of the terms you employ as keywords must be in the page or document returned. This narrows the search.

AND NOT

This operator excludes the words that follow it. Consequently, it can be useful in narrowing previously conducted searches. You should be careful when using "AND NOT" as it eliminates many pages and may exclude from the results resources that would be of use to you, due to other related information the page/document contains. For example, if you search for "duty of care" AND "Donoghue v Stephenson" AND NOT "third party", you will be presented with results containing the first two terms but excluding any page/document containing "third party", which may eliminate some resources that would have been useful.

NEAR

This operator requires that both terms be found within the document/page and that they occur in close proximity to each other. Although this is similar to AND, it will return fewer results because of the necessity that the keywords are close together. Please note that not all databases use the NEAR operator.

w/

Similarly, or alternatively, the "w/" operator enables you to determine how closely connected the two keywords must be. Thus, if you input "duty of care" w/5 "Donoghue v Stephenson", it will return results where the keywords occur within five words of each other. You can determine how closely the words should occur together by changing the digit following the "w/" operator. Another alternative is to employ "w/p", and this will search for the words within the same paragraph. Some databases use \ rather than / and others dispense with the need for "w", and so "/10" will suffice. Spending a very short time playing with the different options on each database will confirm which of these operators works best for that site.

( )
This operator requires that the terms and operators that occur within the brackets are searched first. Please note that you *must* use brackets to group terms when using the operators OR and NEAR when there is a second or further Boolean operator forming part of the search—for example, ("duty of care" OR "Donoghue v Stephenson") AND ("third party" NEAR "solicitor"). This should return a range of results building on the precedent of *Donoghue v Stephenson* which discuss the issue of the duty of care that a solicitor might owe to third parties.

Wild cards
Sometimes you might not know exactly what it is you are searching for and in these instances wild cards can be enormously useful. Many search engines support what is called a "wild card" search: basically, this means you can substitute the asterisk symbol * for a word or part of a word within a key phrase, essentially telling the search engine that you would like it to search for a word that is commonly associated with another word that you specify. For example, searching for negligen* will search for any word with this as a root and you will see pages/documents containing the words "negligence", "negligent", "negligently" or any other such variation. Similarly, if you were to search for "duty*care", you will be returned results that contain variations on this, such as "duty of care" and "duty to care".

An alternative wild card is the question mark, ?. This enables you to search for small variations in spelling—in essence, it accounts for differing American English and British/Irish English spellings of words and enables you to search for both variations at once. For example, "critici?e" will return results that contain both "criticise" and "criticize".

Please note that the wild card characters may vary from database to database.

2. Subscription Databases

14–30 The following databases require that you have a subscription in order to access the information they contain. Most of these sites will be accessible through your institution. You may need to enter some log-in information, particularly if you are accessing the site off campus. This is not an exhaustive list of subscription databases but an introduction to some of the ones you might find most useful in conducting your research. There are other databases, not included in the table below, that you may find useful in researching law, but which do not have law as their primary focus. You should become very familiar with your institution's library and the online services available to you via its catalogue. As noted above, most libraries will have a law librarian.[7] They will also have other subject librarians whose expertise you can draw from if and when needed.

Database	Most useful for:	Also has:
vLex Justis	Precedent Map—identify the cases that informed the decision and also how the instant case impacted upon subsequent cases. Key passages feature—identifies the most-quoted passages of a judgment	Irish case law, especially the *Irish Reports* (IR), but not full reports for the *Irish Law Reports Monthly* (ILRM). Online Proficiency test so you can test your skills at conducting online legal research.
Westlaw IE	Consolidated, updated legislation - selected legislation is brought together here so that you can read what the law is at the moment you are undertaking the research, by checking how it has been amended and updated since enactment. This subscription service can be more up-to-date than the free service provided by the Law Reform Commission.	Irish law reports (not including the *Irish Reports* (IR)). Good selection of Irish journals. Also available are the full text of a selection of the titles produced by Round Hall.
Westlaw UK	Irish case law—although note it does not provide links to the full text of all judgments. Index of Legal Terms—this is a searchable database of three leading legal dictionaries which is interlinked, cross-referenced and regularly updated.	UK legislation. UK Law reports including *All England Reports* (All ER), *Appeals Cases* (AC), *King's Bench* (KB), *Queen's Bench* (QB). Extensive list of journals providing either abstracts or full-text articles. Selected legal texts published by Sweet & Maxwell are also available.
Lexis-Nexis	UK case law International comparative material—especially case law from the United States and US journals.	Extensive collection of full-text journals, both international and US-based.

[7] See para.14–04.

D. Generative Artificial Intelligence

14–31 In recent years there has been an explosion in the field of Artificial Intelligence (AI). The development of machine learning algorithms and deep learning techniques have enabled AI systems to develop more lifelike generative models.[8] In other words, there now exist computer programmes that can create content, such as text, which could be used to support study. However, using such tools should be approached with caution. Koos and Wachsmann identify a number of advantages to engaging generative AI processes as part of studying law: (1) it may support the writing process by improving linguistic quality; (2) it may speed up the writing process by generating draft text; (3) it may provide novel insights; (4) it may free up time for gathering information to enable a focus on understanding, analysis and critical thinking; (5) it may facilitate collaboration and peer feedback by generating discussion points, posing questions and counterarguments.[9]

14–32 There are also significant limitations to generative AI that must be acknowledged. It can create inaccurate or incomplete information. In particular, it is important to understand that generative AI can produce content that seems plausible but in fact is entirely made up. These instances are known as "hallucinations".[10] Another limitation is that there is no in-built fact-checking in generative AI, therefore if using this tool, it is advisable to do thorough independent research to verify that everything produced by the programme is accurate. In addition, while generative AI can create human-like responses, it is not good at engaging with complex, specialised or nuanced tasks.[11] Furthermore, as Koos and Wachsmann note, overreliance on generative AI may stunt the critical thinking and problem-solving skills that assignments are

[8] K. Wach, C.D. Duong, J. Ejdys, R. Kazlauskaite, P. Korzynski, G. Mazurek, J. Paliszkiewicz and E. Ziemba, "The dark side of generative artificial intelligence: A critical analysis of controversies and risks of ChatGPT" (2023) 11(2) *Entrepreneurial Business and Economics Review* 7–30.

[9] S. Koos and S. Wachsmann, "Navigating the Impact of ChatGPT/GPT4 on Legal Academic Examinations: Challenges, Opportunities and Recommendations" (2023) 6(2) *Media Juris* 255–270.

[10] J. Schiller in D. Yücel, "Künstliche Intelligenz: Der plappernde Papagei im Netz" (2023), available at: *https://www.tagesspiegel.de/kunstliche-intelligenz-der-plappernde-papagei-im-netz-9381044.html.*

[11] S. Koos and S. Wachsmann, "Navigating the Impact of ChatGPT/GPT4 on Legal Academic Examinations: Challenges, Opportunities and Recommendations" (2023) 6(2) *Media Juris* 255–270.

specifically designed to develop.[12] Finally, using generative AI may raise concerns regarding ethical research, plagiarism and academic integrity. Universities have policies on plagiarism that may prohibit or limit use of AI. You should always check with your lecturer the extent that you may use, or not, AI.[13]

14–33 Generative AI is learning and changing very rapidly. While there are advantages to using it as a tool to support your study, there are also very significant disadvantages. For it to be an effective tool, you need to have a very solid foundational knowledge of the topic so that you can properly evaluate the accuracy and relevance of the information created by AI. Therefore, you should think of and employ generative AI programmes as a supplementary research tool rather than as a replacement for traditional research methods, or a shortcut for writing essays.

E. How to Effectively Record Your Research

14–34 When conducting your research you should keep detailed contemporaneous notes. This will enable you to keep track of what you have read and to pull together a grounded legal analysis at a later date. As you read a source, you should note the citation and sum up the main arguments that the writer advances. Once you have completed your research, you can return to these notes and determine whether you agree or disagree with the various points made in the sources you have researched. Keeping accurate and detailed notes will make writing up your research much easier, as you will not need to hunt down a reference or citation and can accurately write and cite as you go. As will be discussed in Ch.16, for any analysis you conduct to be compelling and persuasive, it must be constructed on a depth of research such that your deductions and critiques are the inevitable and logical conclusion.

[12] S. Koos and S. Wachsmann, "Navigating the Impact of ChatGPT/GPT4 on Legal Academic Examinations: Challenges, Opportunities and Recommendations" (2023) 6(2) *Media Juris* 255–270.

[13] O. Bakiner, "What do academics say about artificial intelligence ethics? An overview of the scholarship" (2023) 3 *AI & Ethics* 513–525; B.L. Frye and ChatGPT, "Should Using an AI Text Generator to Produce Academic Writing Be Plagiarism?" (2023) 33 *Fordham Intellectual Property, Media and Entertainment Law Journal* 947.

1. Beginning Your Research

14–35 At the outset you need to refine exactly what the question is that you are researching. This will very much depend on how a piece of coursework is formulated, or whether you are engaging in examination revision. Most lecturers will provide a reading list, which will be your starting point on researching a particular topic. You should always begin your research by reading some of the core textbooks and going over your lecture notes to get a feel for the topic. Within these textbooks, you may be referred to other reading materials. You should keep detailed notes of each resource you consult as part of this process. This should include detailed citations for any references, the original author(s) consulted that you think is/are particularly relevant and that you may wish to consult yourself at a later stage. Once this is complete, you will be in a position to identify the issues, ideas and keywords that you need to employ in an initial search.

2. Researching in Earnest

14–36 Now that you have a good general idea of the area you are researching, you should conduct an extensive trawl for materials using all of the information in the library and online via the various databases that are available to you. Inevitably, you will have many resources to sift through and determine whether these should be set aside for further consultation or discarded as irrelevant. This can be easily achieved by a very quick reading where you read and note all the headings and see how useful the resource might be. A second method of swiftly assessing a resource, particularly if you have access to a digital copy of the resource, is to search through it for a precise word or term (on a keyboard, pressing the "Ctrl" key in addition to the "F" key will enable you to "find" all instances of that word). Conducting this kind of quick scan of a resource will enable you to determine how crucial it is to your research. Prior to discarding a resource completely, you should note down the title, author and citation information lest you need to locate it again as you progress with your work.

14–37 If you decide that a source is worth reading, then your first step is to note the usual bibliographic information accurately. Then you read the resource through in its entirety more than once. This first reading is to gain an overall impression of the resource and to familiarise yourself with the general arguments and analysis it contains. A second, more detailed reading will enable you to focus more precisely on those aspects of the resource that are most relevant to your work. The third time you read the source, you should attempt to summarise in your own words the points that the author makes. This will not only help you to recall the detail of the resource later on, but also it will provide useful material in terms of building your own legal analysis.

3. Using Your Research

14–38 Once you have thoroughly researched the topic, you then need to turn your thoughts to a consideration of how you intend to present the results of your work. Usually, on a practical note, you now need to begin to write your assignment. This will be considered in more detail in Ch.16, but, in essence, you should break down your ideas into three or four points and then use your research to assist you to explore each point in turn. It is now that your summaries will come in useful. You can discuss the ruling in a case and contrast what the dissenting judge had to say with the findings of the majority. You can consider which perspective has been more widely accepted and why. Using your summaries, you can note what the various commentators have to say about the case and include your own thoughts as to which argument you find most compelling. In this way, you will present work that both displays the breadth and depth of your research and is formed against a background of considered knowledge. Thus, your work will be compelling and persuasive.

14–39 The more you practise this kind of research, the better you will get at it. You should take some time to complete the template below as you conduct each research assignment. The most important aspect of this in order to improve as a researcher is to undertake an honest and critical reflection of the process you completed each time. In this way, you can begin to identify what worked and what did not. You will see how to improve your technique and learn how to become a more efficient and effective researcher. Above all, you need to remember that good research cannot be rushed; it takes time. Thus, you must ensure that you allocate sufficient time to undertake the task before you.

Box 14.3: Skills Insight
Sample Research Record Template

1. Identify key issues:
   a. List bibliographic information for each introductory source consulted.
   b. Note key concepts / resources to consult later in more depth.
2. Identify keywords, phrases and terms to use in the database search.
3. List resources shortlisted.
4. For each resource consulted, note the following:
   a. Bibliographic information.
   b. Summarise each point.
5. Compile your research notes in an orderly fashion.
6. Write your assignment / revision notes.
7. Critically reflect on your process:
   a. Note those things you did that were effective.
   b. Note those things you did that were not effective.
   c. How will you change your approach in future?

F. Conclusion

14–40 In this chapter we have considered how to conduct effective legal research. We have discussed how you can use the library to facilitate your investigation of a particular subject. We have also explored the options for researching online and identified those sites, both commercial and open access, where you can find the law and retrieve reliable critiques of the law. We completed our discussion of legal research by examining how you might best use the results of your research to conduct your own effective legal analysis. Ultimately, we have found that good research requires a detailed and planned approach from the outset. As Hurston famously noted, "[r]esearch is formalized curiosity. It is poking and prying with a purpose."[14]

[14] Z.N. Hurston, *Dust Tracks on a Road* (New York: Harper Collins, 1996), p.143 (original publication 1942).

Chapter 15

Reading Law

"The library is to us what the laboratory is to the chemist and the museum is to the naturalist."

C.C. Langdell, quoted in Harvard Law School Association, *The Centennial History of the Harvard Law School, 1817–1917* (Cambridge, Mass.: Harvard Law School Association, 1918), p.97.

In this chapter we:

- examine how to read legislation;
- discover how to effectively read a case;
- consider how to read commentary on the law by legal academics and others.

A. Introduction

15–01 In the simple statement with which we began this chapter, Christopher Columbus Langdell, Dean of Harvard Law School, summed up what is at the core of the modern approach to teaching law. It is through the legislative pronouncements recorded in statute and by reading the judgments of judges who interpret the law that we discover what the law is. We learn about the law by reading the law, while acknowledging that law does not exist in a societal vacuum. By reading law, we can become lawyers and expert communicators of legal knowledge.

15–02 In order to be an effective and efficient student of law, you have to be able to read the law and read about the law. This chapter focuses on how to develop this skill. It identifies the various parts of statutes and explores the various aspects of written judgments so that these become easier to read. It also considers, briefly, how to read what others have written about the law in a way that is effective and useful for you.

B. Reading Legislation

15–03 Legislation involves the formal drafting of laws in written form. As was discussed in Chs 2[1] and 7,[2] legislation is the second highest ranking source of law in Ireland. The Constitution, in Article 15.2.1°, provides that "[t]he sole and exclusive power of making laws for the State is hereby vested in the Oireachtas: no other legislative authority has power to make laws for the State." So it is politicians, our elected officials in both the Dáil and Seanad, who make our laws. The vast majority of legislation considered by the Oireachtas is initiated by the Government, but Oireachtas procedures also allow members of opposition parties or independent members to introduce their own Bills. As discussed in Ch.7,[3] opposition-led legislative proposals are known as Private Members' Bills. The majority of these opposition-sponsored Bills do not survive the second stage of the Dáil/Seanad and never become law.[4] The first Private Member's Bill to be enacted was the Meath Hospital Act 1951, but perhaps the most famous of the Private Members' Bills to be enacted in Ireland is the Judicial Separation and Family Law Reform Act 1989, as this was the first Private Member's Bill to become legislation in 30 years, and it paved the way for the introduction of divorce.

15–04 Legislative drafting is a particular skill, and the members of the Government are supported in the production of legislation by a team of specialised lawyers known as parliamentary draftsmen located in the Office of the Parliamentary Counsel to the Government, which is a section of the Office of the Attorney General.[5] The legal English employed in the drafting of legislation is very technical and precise. Consequently, it can be off-putting to read legislation for the first time.[6] To a certain extent, this is because it is the function of legislation to specify or prescribe the law relating to a particular matter. The majority of legislation is focused on addressing the law in relation to one specific area; for example, the Non-Fatal Offences against the Person Act 1997

1 Chapter 2, para.2–26.
2 Chapter 7, para.7–01.
3 Chapter 7, Box 7.2.
4 Chapter 7, Box 7.2, text to fn.69.
5 For more on the functions of the Attorney General, see Ch.12, Section E.
6 See Ch.4, Sections C–H for detailed consideration of why issues of the best way to interpret legislation arise and the tools that can be used to help resolve these questions.

is concerned with crimes against people that do not result in the death of the victim. Therefore, legislation is very detailed, and is written in an exact and precise manner. In this way, it is different to the law as set out in the Constitution. While the Constitution is written in a general manner, legislation fills in the details and stipulates exactly how the law operates in particular circumstances.

15–05 All legislation follows a prescribed format and this can be enormously helpful for the reader in terms of navigating through various legislative provisions. We will now consider the various elements of legislation. Understanding what each part is can help with reading legislation. However, it is also important when reading legislation to be mindful of the tools for legislative interpretation employed by the courts. These were detailed in Ch.4.

1. The Short Title

15–06 This is the title by which the legislation is commonly known. It will usually be found either at the very beginning of the legislation on the very first page, or at the very end of the legislation in the final section. For example, s.1(1) of the Regulation of Lobbying Act 2015 states that "[t]his Act may be cited as the Regulation of Lobbying Act 2015." Contrastingly, it is the final section of the Betting (Amendment) Act 2015 (s.40) that contains the short title of that legislation.

2. The Official Citation of the Act

15–07 Each Act is given an official citation. Acts are numbered according to the chronology in which they are passed into law in a particular calendar year. Thus, for 2023 the chronology and consequent official citation for the first few Acts of the Oireachtas is as follows:

No 1/2023 – National Cultural Institutions (National Concert Hall) (Amendment) Act 2023;
No 2/2023 – Oil Emergency Contingency and Transfer of Renewable Transport Fuels Functions Act 2023;
No 3/2023 – Criminal Justice (Mutual Recognition of Custodial Sentences) Act 2023;
No 4/2023 – Communications Regulation and Digital Hub Development Agency (Amendment) Act 2023.

However, when we cite statutes in our writing, we exclude the chronological detail, and just provide the name of the statute which includes the year in which it was enacted.

3. The Long Title of the Act

15–08 The long title explains the purpose of the legislation and why it is being introduced. If we examine the Regulation of Lobbying Act 2015, we see that the long title informs us that it is:

> "[a]n Act to provide for establishing and maintaining a register of persons who carry on lobbying activities; to provide for a code of conduct relating to carrying on lobbying activities; to impose restrictions on involvement in lobbying by certain former designated public officials; to amend the Ethics in Public Office Act 1995; and to provide for related matters."

4. The Date of Promulgation

15–09 As we know from Ch.7, an Act is promulgated when the President officially signs it into law.[7] The date of promulgation is simply the date upon which the President performs that particular function in relation to that particular Act. This will usually be found at the right-hand margin of the legislation immediately under the long title of the Act. In relation to the Regulation of Lobbying Act 2015, the date of promulgation was 11 March 2015.

5. List of Acts Referred to

15–10 This is quite simply a list of all the Acts that the legislation you are reading refers to. The Wildlife (Amendment) Act 2023, for example, lists six other Acts that it mentions in setting out its scheme to enable the creation of natural heritage areas and the preservation of bog habitats. These Acts cover a broad range of areas: Companies Act 2014; Forestry Act 1988; Harbours Act 1996; Local Government Act 2001; Planning and Development Act 2000; and Wildlife (Amendment) Act 2000.

---

[7] See Ch.7, Section D.

15–11 By cross-referencing legislation in this explicit manner, legislation is designed to ensure that the law remains open, transparent and knowable. However, it is important to note that each Act lists those Acts that are mentioned, amended or repealed by this new piece of legislation. Thus, it is evident that legislation is liable to change with great regularity. The challenge, then, for the reader of legislation is to ascertain precisely whether, where and how the law contained in any individual piece of legislation might have been amended or changed. These changes can happen almost immediately following enactment. Take, for example, the Gender Recognition Act 2015 which, as enacted on 22 July 2015, included a requirement in s.9(2)(b) that applicants for gender recognition swear a statutory declaration that they are neither married nor a civil partner. That requirement—that applicants neither be married nor in a civil partnership in order to be granted a gender recognition certificate—was removed on 29 October 2015 with the passing of the Marriage Act 2015 which, in s.24, deleted s.9(2)(b) and all other sections of the Gender Recognition Act 2015 that required those applying for a gender recognition certificate to not be married or in a civil partnership. Yet, if you were to download the Gender Recognition Act 2015 from *www.irishstatutebook.ie*, or another official source, you would read a version of the Act as it appeared on the day it received the presidential signature—in other words, it will still contain the single applicant requirement that has now been repealed by the Marriage Act 2015.[8] Thus, when reading legislation, it is important to double check that the legislative provision you are reading is still valid law. You can check this by consulting the online Legislation Directory, which attempts to set down where primary Acts have been repealed or amended in whole or in part.[9] As discussed in Ch.14, the Law Reform Commission has an ongoing project producing Revised Acts—consolidated versions of legislation that contain all the amendments since the original enactment, in order to make reading the legislation more accessible and reflective of the actual current law.[10] Finally, some commercial publishers, such as Westlaw IE, produce consolidated versions of significant legislation.[11]

8 For more on the Gender Recognition Act 2015, see Ch.7, Section E.
9 For discussion on the Legislation Directory, see Ch.14, paras 14–15 to 14–16.
10 See further discussion on the Revised Acts section of the Law Reform Commission website in Ch.14, para.14–25.
11 See Ch.12, Section C.2.

6. Marginal Notes

15–12 As you read older legislation, you will notice that in the margins alongside the sections are brief descriptions of what the specific section addresses. These are known as marginal notes and they facilitate a quick or skim-read of legislation by identifying what each section is about, without the need to read through the legislation in detail. Section 3 of the Charities Act 2009 sets out a legislative definition of a charitable purpose. The section begins:

> "3.—(1) For the purposes of this Act each of the following shall, subject to subsection (2), be a charitable purpose: ..."

As can be seen, it dives straight into the subject matter of the section. The marginal note alongside the beginning of s.3 simply states "Charitable purpose", and so we know when skim-reading the legislation that this is what will be covered in s.3. Sometimes the marginal notes do not quite appear in the margins but rather seem to be headings at the start of each section. This is how the marginal notes are presented in the Regulation of Lobbying Act 2015. This manner of identifying the subject matter of sections is more recent and as some of the legislation recently or currently enacted may have been initially drafted prior to the introduction of this manner of marginal annotation, not all new Acts have abandoned the more traditional location for such information, i.e. in the margins of the Act, although all the Acts published in 2015 have adopted this new heading format.

7. Interpretation or Definition Section

15–13 Most legislation will begin with a section that is alternately labelled the interpretation or definition section. In essence, this is the dictionary for this particular legislation and defines all the key terms that will be used in the legislation. Thus, it informs the reader exactly how the defined words are to be understood and interpreted. This is a significant aid to interpreting each piece of legislation. The interpretation or definition section is usually located towards the beginning of the legislation. It is important to note that this is not always the first or second section. In the Regulation of Lobbying Act 2015, for example, the interpretation section is s.5. Furthermore, for lengthy statutes with many parts, there may be a definition or interpretation section towards the beginning of each part. A good example of this is the Work Life Balance and Miscellaneous Provisions Act 2023.

8. Commencement Section

15–14 The commencement section, which is usually found either in the first or the final section of an Act, identifies a designated person who commences, or activates, an Act or section of an Act.[12] Where legislation includes a commencement section, this means that the Act does not immediately become law once the President signs it. Rather it requires the identified person, usually the relevant government minister, to activate the section/Act. A good example of this is the Policing, Security and Community Safety Act 2024. The stated purpose of the Act is to implement the recommendations of the 2018 *Report of the Commission on the Future of Policing in Ireland*.[13] As of the time of writing, only s.302(b) has been commenced. Thus, the vast majority of the provisions contained in the legislation, and consequently the recommendations of the Commission, are technically on the books but remain inactive. By contrast, the Environmental Protection Agency (Emergency Electricity Generation) (Amendment) Act 2023 was signed into law on 10 March 2023. A commencement order was issued by the Minister for the Environment, Climate and Communications to bring the whole Act into operation on 30 March 2023.

9. Repeals

15–15 When a piece of legislation renders an older piece of legislation obsolete, it is said to repeal that legislation. Where an Act repeals one section of another legislative enactment, it will simply state that it does so. Section 37 of the Betting (Amendment) Act 2015 repeals s.32 of the Betting Act 1931 and it does this simply as follows: "Section 32 of the Principal Act is repealed."

[12] See the previous discussion of commencement sections in Ch.4, Box 4.1.

[13] For details of the background and purpose of the legislation, see Policing, Security and Community Safety Bill 2023 Explanatory Memorandum, p.1, available at: *https://data.oireachtas.ie/ie/oireachtas/bill/2023/3/eng/memo/b0323d-memo.pdf.* See further, Commission on the Future of Policing in Ireland, *Report of the Commission on the Future of Policing in Ireland* (2018) available at: *https://www.gov.ie/en/publication/3c5c3-the-commission-on-the-future-of-policing-in-ireland-cofpi/*. See also Ch.10, Box 10.3.

15–16 Occasionally, legislation will repeal so much other legislation and will be so far-reaching in its scope that it will include a specific section on repeals. This is the case with s.4 of the Civil Registration Act 2004 which states that "[t]he enactments specified in the Second Schedule are repealed to the extent specified in column 3 of that Schedule." In other words, the repeal section has identified that there are so many repeals contained in the legislation, including the repeal of entire Acts, that there needs to be a schedule (or an appendix) to the Act which has a table outlining exactly which section of which Acts are repealed.

10. Schedules

15–17 Sometimes an Act will include a schedule. A schedule is essentially an appendix to the main Act and contains details that are supplementary to the principal purpose of the Act. The Regulation of Lobbying Act 2015 includes one schedule. That schedule consists of a list of bodies that are not considered public service bodies for the purposes of the legislation.

C. Reading Cases

15–18 Judgments are at the heart of common law systems such as that operating in Ireland. As discussed in Ch.5, the law has evolved over centuries of consideration of individual cases by courts. In order to ensure that the law was common, or the same, in all parts of the country, the doctrine of precedent evolved. In essence, this means that courts are obliged to treat similar cases in a similar fashion. The merits of this approach are that it ensures that the courts act with certainty, stability and predictability in the manner in which they dispose of cases. In other words, parties to a dispute before the courts can be confident they will be treated fairly and impartially.

15–19 This confidence in the legal system derives from adherence to precedent. However, the precedent in each case is not necessarily presented in a perfectly formed package. Cases do not arrive before the courts because lawyers want to understand what a particular rule means. Rather they emerge from disputes, fights and arguments between people. Law is a messy business. Lawyers for each side will present the facts and the law in such a manner as will best reflect upon their client and increase their chance at winning. Thus, there may be many layers to the argument a lawyer makes for their client. They may raise many different legal points. Some will hit their target and persuade the court, while others will fall flat.

15–20 In Ireland, written judgments can be lengthy. Our judges like to take their time in explaining how they have reached the decision in a case. Where more than one judge hears a case, each is entitled to give their own judgment and explain what it was about the facts and the law that persuaded them to find in favour of one side over the other. Not all judges necessarily agree on the outcome of a case. Thus, there may be more than one judgment in a case.[14] Generally speaking, there are three types of judgment if multiple judgments are issued. The leading judgment is the main one written and gives the decision of the court as to which party has won the case and the reasons for that decision. Concurring judgments are those that agree with the outcome of the leading judgment but may disagree on the reasons for that decision or may expand on that reasoning. Dissenting judgments disagree with the outcome of the case, would find in favour of the other side, and again include the reasons for the dissent.

15–21 Reading judgments can be a daunting prospect. That said, there is a certain consistency to how judgments are written and once we become familiar with judgments, it is easier to navigate through them, and ascertain the aspects that are important to the decision in each case and to the development of precedent overall. As discussed in Ch.5,

[14] Previously, Article 34.4.5° of the Constitution required that when the Supreme Court was considering the constitutionality of a law, the court had to issue a single unanimous judgment. This was known as the "one judgment" rule and was in place to quell any question of dissent amongst the judges and to strengthen the weight of judicial pronouncements on the constitutionality of legislation. This rule was removed from the Constitution as a result of the referendum on the Thirty-third Amendment of the Constitution, which also established the Court of Appeal. As a consequence, judges may now issue dissenting judgments in cases where the constitutionality or otherwise of a law is at issue. The "one judgment" rule is also contained in Article 26.2.2° as regards a referral by the President of a Bill to the Supreme Court to test its constitutionality prior to signing by the President. The Thirty-third Amendment did not amend Article 26 in any way, and thus the "one judgment" rule persists in these rare cases. For further discussion on the abolition of the "one judgment" rule, see C.A. Casey, "Foreword: Charter or Higher Law? The Constitution under the New Supreme Court" (2024) 44(1) *Dublin University Law Journal* 1.

cases generally follow a set, four-part structure: facts that raise legal issues; the law that the opposing parties argue governs those issues; the application of the relevant law to the material facts of the case; and the decision as to which party will win.[15] Unfortunately, there is no "short cut" through this process, and deft reading of case law is, like driving a car, a skill that is learned through regular practice. The following quote by Scott Turow, who is a lawyer but is more famous for his legal thrillers such as *Burden of Proof* and *Presumed Innocent*, both of which were made into movies, is a good description of what it is like when you first start reading cases:

> "OK. It was nine o'clock when I started reading. The case is four pages long and at 10.35 I finally finished. It was something like stirring concrete with my eyelashes. I had no idea what the words meant. I must have opened *Black's Law Dictionary* twenty-five times and I still can't understand many of the definitions."[16]

One of the rewards of investing time in developing this skill is that when we regularly read cases, we become immersed in the language of the law. We can see how legal arguments are formed and deployed. We can identify successful arguments from those that failed. In other words, we learn to think like a lawyer and can begin to appreciate how the subtleties and nuances of language and of logical legal argument can determine the outcome of a case.

1. The Parties to a Case

15–22 All cases involve at least two parties: the person bringing the case to court is usually termed the "plaintiff" or the "applicant", while the person defending a case is usually termed the "defendant" or the "respondent". The name of a case will usually tell us the names of the parties involved. So, for example, *Molloy v Reid* [2014] IESC 4 gives us a wealth of vital information about the case. It tells us the names of the parties: Molloy was the plaintiff and Reid was the defendant. The full citation also lets us know the year in which the judgment was given

---

15 See Ch.5, para.5–33.

16 S. Turow, *One L: What They Really Teach You at Harvard Law School* (London: Spectre, 1988), p.28 (quoted in J. Holland and J. Webb, *Learning Legal Rules*, 7th edn (Oxford: Oxford University Press, 2010), p.182).

(2014) and this neutral citation[17] tells us that it took place in the Supreme Court of Ireland (IESC).

15–23 The parties to a case need not necessarily be human people. Companies have what is known as "legal personality"[18] and, consequently, are recognised as being people for the purposes of engaging in legal activities such as signing contracts. *James Elliott Construction Ltd v Irish Asphalt Ltd*[19] is an example of a case where two companies were involved in a suit to determine which of them should bear the cost of extensive remedial works carried out to the Ballymun Central Youth Facility following damage due to the inclusion of pyrite in the infill for the foundations.

15–24 The State can also be involved in court cases. According to Article 5 of the Constitution, "Ireland is a sovereign, independent, democratic state." Initially, the belief was that the State had inherited the Crown's common law immunity from liability for its employee's torts. In other words, it was believed that the Irish State could not be sued. In *Byrne v Ireland*,[20] the Supreme Court held that the State is not immune from suit. It is not only Ireland as a State that can be involved in court proceedings; officers of the State, such as various government ministers, can also be parties to court proceedings. In *Dowling v Minister for Finance*,[21] three shareholders in the Irish Life and Permanent Holding Group challenged the legality of the acquisition of the company by the State as part of the recapitalisation of the bank. The Minister for Finance, as the relevant government minister, was the defendant to the suit.

15–25 Office-holders who regularly appear as parties in cases include both the Attorney General and the Director of Public Prosecutions (DPP).[22] The Attorney General is the legal counsel to the Government and regularly appears as a party to proceedings in which there is a significant matter of public interest at issue. For example, the Attorney

---

17 A neutral citation enables us to identify a case without reference to any commercial law report, such as the *Irish Reports* or the *Irish Law Reports Monthly*.
18 See Ch.4, para.4–32, fn.56 for a brief discussion on how this is a "legal fiction".
19 [2014] IESC 74.
20 [1972] I.R. 241.
21 [2014] IEHC 418.
22 See also, Ch.12, Section E.

General was a defendant in *McGee v Attorney General*[23] where it was found that the constitutional right to marital privacy had been infringed by the State in confiscating contraceptives which the plaintiff had ordered from England on medical advice. The Attorney General can also initiate (or start) proceedings where they believe that it is in the public interest to do so. In *Attorney General v Dowse*,[24] the Attorney General successfully brought proceedings to protect the interests of Tristan Dowse, an Indonesian-born boy who became an Irish citizen on foot of his adoption by an Irish couple. The couple returned him to the orphanage in Indonesia and sought to have the record of his adoption deleted from the Register of Foreign Adoptions in Ireland. MacMenamin J., in the High Court, ruled that the adoptive parents had breached their constitutional duties as parents and had to support Tristan until he turned 18. The judge also directed that Tristan be removed from the Register of Foreign Adoptions. However, he held that the boy would retain his Irish citizenship and succession rights to his former adoptive parents' property. Many prosecutions in the State are run by the DPP's office on behalf of the people and, consequently, the DPP is always a party to such proceedings. For example, in *DPP v Monaghan*, the court ruled that "the community is the ultimate party wronged when a crime is committed", and so there does not need to be an identifiable complainant to enable the DPP to initiate proceedings.[25]

15–26 The names of the parties to a case can also give an indication of the type of issue that is involved in the case. As seen above, where the Attorney General is a party to a case, this indicates that there is a public interest element to it. Similarly, the presence of the DPP amongst the parties to a case lets us know that it concerns criminal matters. Where the case involves particularly sensitive matters, the parties may be anonymised. *Attorney General v X*[26] concerned the ability of a 14-year-old girl to travel to the UK to avail of an abortion to end a pregnancy that resulted from rape. The name of X was never publicised. Similarly, cases relating to family law matters are usually held in camera (in private) and reported substituting initials for the names of the parties, as in *N v HSE*[27]

[23] [1974] I.R. 284. The *McGee* case was considered in Ch.3, paras 3–29 to 3–30.
[24] [2006] IEHC 64.
[25] [2007] IEHC 92 at para.16.
[26] [1992] 1 I.R. 1.
[27] [2006] IEHC 278.

which concerned a dispute over custody of a child known as "Baby Ann" between her potential adoptive parents and her birth parents where the birth parents withdrew their consent to the adoption.

2. The Facts of a Case

15–27 This is the story of the case. What happened between the parties to bring them before the court? Usually, the facts of the case will be outlined towards the beginning of the leading judgment in a case. The facts of a case can be very complex. Each side will attempt to present the facts to strengthen the argument in their favour. Discussion of the facts may also arise in the context of complicated legal analysis in the case. Consequently, it can be challenging to sort through this information to identify those facts that were essential to making the decision. Ultimately each case turns on its own facts. While the development of the law in general is an important part of judgment reading, we must recall that the primary purpose in delivering a judgment is to resolve the dispute between the parties before the court. Consequently, judges will hone in on those facts that they regard as crucial or material to the dispute as a means of logically justifying finding in favour of either party. As Jackson J. of the US Supreme Court famously said, "it may sound paradoxical, but most contentions of law are won or lost on the facts".[28] Essentially, the facts of a case help us to understand which laws are applicable to bring about a resolution of the particular dispute.

15–28 Understood from this perspective, the importance of the ability to discern those facts that were material or vital to securing the judgment in favour of the winning side is evident. We must be sure to separate the facts that existed prior to the case beginning its journey through the legal process, and those twists and turns that might have emerged as part of that process and thus become part of the "story" of the case but that are not its material facts.

15–29 A final aspect of considering the facts of a case is the ability to distinguish the material facts from other facts present in a case. The material facts of a case are those that were essential to helping the court reach its decision in the case. As Professor Goodhart points out:

[28] R.H. Jackson, "Advocacy before the United States Supreme Court" (1951) 37 *Cornell Law Quarterly* 1.

> "The judge, therefore, reaches a conclusion upon the facts *as he sees them*. It is on these facts that he bases his judgment, and not on any others. It follows that our task in analysing a case is not to state the facts and the conclusion, but to state the material facts as seen by the judge and his conclusion based on them. *It is by his choice of the material facts that the judge creates law*."[29]

We will return again to this point when discussing the ratio decidendi of the case, but for present purposes it is sufficient that when reading a case, we keep a close eye out for those facts that are essential to assisting the court reach its decision.

Box 15.1: Case Focus
***Keogh v ESB* [2005] 3 I.R. 77**

In this case, Peart J. includes the following information amongst the facts of the case:

> "The plaintiff, who was aged 30 years at the time, was speaking on the telephone on Christmas Day, 1997 when she experienced an electric shock through the receiver which she was holding to her ear with her right hand. It was severe enough to render her unconscious and for her to sustain burns to her finger tips, her neck and her right hip. Her right hip had been in contact with a metal sink at the time. She has no recollection of the incident itself and says that she recalls going to make the phone call and then waking up in an ambulance.
>
> She was admitted to the Burns Unit in Loughlinstown hospital, County Dublin. She was kept in hospital for 48 hours and was then discharged to the care of her general practitioner for dressings to her injuries.
>
> In her statement of claim she pleads that this shock was caused as a result of electricity escaping from an electricity transformer which is on land adjoining her house at Ballybeg, Redcross, County Wicklow, and being transmitted to her telephone handset by an underground telephone cable.

[29] A.L. Goodhart, "Determining the *Ratio Decidendi* of a Case" in A.L. Goodhart (ed.), *Essays in Jurisprudence and the Common Law* (Cambridge: Cambridge University Press, 1931), p.10 (emphases in original).

A very relevant fact in this case is that on Christmas Eve, 1997 weather conditions in the area of the plaintiff's home at Redcross were severe, such that there was extensive damage caused to electricity cables and supply to homes, including the plaintiff's. This undoubtedly stretched the resources of the defendant to deal with all faults and cable damage. Evidence from Met Éireann is that a vigorous storm depression of 972 hPa. tracked East-Northeastwards over the northern half of the country on the afternoon/evening of the 24th December 1997, and that the strongest winds in the Redcross area occurred during that period with mean speeds reaching 60 to 85 km/h, possibly gusting over 150 km/h, and that these conditions would have led to structural damage. On Christmas Day itself, there were still very windy conditions, though not as severe as those on Christmas Eve.

The plaintiff's evidence is that because of the weather conditions she had no electricity at her home from about 7 p.m. on Christmas Eve, 1997 and that everywhere around her home was also cut off. When she got back home after her discharge from hospital on the 27th December, 1997, she recalls that the electricity transformer near her home was being repaired at the time, and power returned that day also.

The plaintiff's partner gave evidence of what happened when the plaintiff made the phone call on Christmas Day, 1997. He said that he was talking to the plaintiff in the kitchen. He then walked away and heard a bang. He turned around and saw the plaintiff sliding downwards to the floor. He saw that she could not speak, her eyes were rolling around and there was a brown substance coming out of her mouth. He said that she could not talk to him and looked to be in what he called 'a bad way'. An ambulance was called and she was taken to hospital.

He also gave evidence of what had happened on Christmas Eve as far as the weather and loss of electricity was concerned. He states that on Christmas Eve he telephoned the defendant because he had been outside the house and saw sparks coming out of the transformer and there was no power in the premises. He remembers telling this to the person he spoke to in the defendant [company]. He recalls that the wind was certainly very strong but that the pole was not down and there was no lightning. He remembers having seen an electrical cable knocking against the side of the transformer. It had apparently broken away from the transformer itself. He recalls also that on the Saturday after Christmas day (the 27th December, 1997) the defendant restored

> power, put up a new transformer on the pole and took away the old transformer. When he was cross-examined by counsel for the defendants, he agreed that the weather conditions were very bad and that there were many power blackouts in the county of Wicklow over those days. But he could not comment when it was put to him that the defendant's crews would have been very stretched to deal with all the necessary repairs. It was also put to him that in fact power was restored on the 26th December, 1997, but he was certain that it was the day on which the plaintiff was discharged from hospital which was Saturday, the 27th December, 1997."[30]

The material facts are summed up in the headnote to the case report as follows:

> "The plaintiff sustained an electric shock through the telephone receiver in her house which was caused by electricity escaping from an electricity transformer on land adjoining her house. The transformer had been damaged in very high winds and had been reported as damaged and sparking the day before the accident by the plaintiff's partner. The defendant pleaded that the incident was an 'inevitable accident' or act of God."[31]

It does not matter to the ultimate legal determination to whom the plaintiff was speaking on the phone at the time she experienced the electric shock. Nor is it legally relevant that this incident happened on Christmas Day. Yet the inclusion of this information does help to contextualise what happened in the case. Often judges will include these extra facts to give a more complete picture of events to the reader of the judgment. Having read the judgment, it becomes clear which facts recounted by the judge are material and which are not.

3. Procedural History

15–30 The procedural history is the story of the case through the legal system until it appeared before the court whose judgment you are reading. You should note whether this is the first time that this case has been heard by a court. In other words, is it a first instance case before the High Court? If so, you simply need to note that. This is important as

[30] [2005] 3 I.R. 77 at paras 1–7.
[31] [2005] 3 I.R. 77 at 77.

it will fasten in your mind the precedential value of the case, bearing in mind the hierarchy of the courts and that the decisions of courts further up the hierarchy bind courts below them. However, some cases may take a more circuitous route and be heard by many courts prior to the one that produced the judgment you are reading. In some instances, the case may have concluded at a lower court but what you are reading is a determination by the Supreme Court as to whether it will hear an additional appeal beyond that already heard by the Court of Appeal, or whether it will hear an appeal directly from the High Court without need for the case to first appear before the Court of Appeal. These kinds of decisions are known as Supreme Court determinations.[32] In this event, you should briefly outline where the case has been before it arrived at its present hearing.

15–31 It can be a simple matter to identify where the case currently is, as typically the judgment will state, at the very top, the court from which the judgment issued, i.e. High Court, Court of Appeal or Supreme Court. Neutral citations are especially useful in this regard as they immediately identify the court from which the judgment comes. Uncovering where the case has been previously can usually be resolved by reading the judgment or the leading judgment if there is more than one. When recounting the facts of the case, the judge will often detail how the case has come before their court.

Box 15.2: Case Focus
***Garvey v Minister for Justice, Equality and Law Reform* [2006] IESC 3**

The case of *Garvey* is a very good illustration of the complicated path a case can take. This case arose as a result of an incident in Mountjoy Prison on 18 September 1999 involving trouble and riotous misconduct by prisoners. One of the offending prisoners sustained substantial injury to his face resulting, it was alleged, from a kick to the face by the appellant who was a prison officer responding to the incident. An internal investigation of the incident was begun and the appellant was suspended on 24 September 1999, initially without pay, although this

[32] For more on Supreme Court determinations, see Ch.14, para.14–21.

was subsequently amended to a reduced pay of 75 per cent while the investigation was ongoing.

The appellant successfully applied to the High Court for permission to challenge the lawfulness of his suspension by way of judicial review on 1 November 1999, and McGuinness J. ordered that he be paid full pay while he was suspended and pending the outcome of the judicial review proceedings.[33]

While waiting for the judicial review hearing to take place, the DPP brought criminal charges against the appellant for assault causing harm and assault causing serious harm under ss.3 and 4 of the Non-Fatal Offences against the Person Act 1997.

While waiting for the criminal trial to take place, the hearing for the judicial review took place on 8 May 2001 and it was struck out without any order by the courts on terms agreed by the parties.

The criminal trial began on 18 February 2002 and lasted for five weeks in Dublin Circuit Criminal Court and the jury returned verdicts of not guilty on each count.

Following this, the appellant requested that his suspension be lifted. However, on 27 April 2002, he was presented with an envelope containing a series of disciplinary charges under the Prison (Disciplinary Code for Officers) Rules 1996. Although the letter acknowledged that he had been acquitted of criminal charges, it nonetheless maintained that he "may have committed a breach of prison discipline under the code" and that there was "a case to be answered" on his behalf.[34]

Internal prison disciplinary proceedings were also begun against the other prison officers involved in the incident in April 2002 but they were abandoned as a result of independent judicial review proceedings brought by those officers and the subsequent order of the High Court from November 2002. Thus, the only prisoner officer still facing disciplinary proceedings relating to this incident was the appellant.

The appellant then applied to the High Court again on judicial review challenging the legitimacy of the disciplinary proceedings. In a reserved judgment, Ó Caoimh J. in the High Court refused the application on all grounds put forward, including that the disciplinary proceedings were to relate to the exact same allegation on foot of which the appellant had been acquitted on the merits.[35]

The appellant then appealed the refusal to the Supreme Court.

[33] [2006] IESC 3 at para.6.
[34] [2006] IESC 3 at para.9.
[35] [2006] IESC 3 at para.13.

4. Issue Presented

15–32 This is the legal issue that the plaintiff raises before the court. Sometimes this is clearly stated in the judgment, but other times it can be more difficult to identify exactly what the legal issue is. In such circumstances, you have to read the judgment carefully in order to identify the legal issue. Ideally, this should be something that you can state very simply in a sentence or so. It can be helpful to phrase this as a question with a "yes" or "no" answer. In *Keogh v ESB*, discussed above,[36] the issues could be phrased as follows:

- Did the ESB owe a duty of care to Ms Keogh?
- If so, was the ESB in breach of that duty?
- If so, was there a causal link between the breach of the duty and the injury suffered by Ms Keogh?

5. Holding / Finding

15–33 This outlines what the court held or found in a particular case. In other words, it means how did the court answer the questions identified in the issues presented in the points above? Be aware of the fact that where you have multiple judgments, there may be a number of answers to various questions. In such circumstances, the party in favour of whom the majority of judges found is the successful litigant.

15–34 The holding is not always immediately evident at the beginning of a judgment and so you may have to read the judgment closely to determine how each point that is argued is resolved. A good tip is to read the final few paragraphs of a judgment to uncover the result of the case once you have identified the issue. This can help focus your reading as you read through the entire case in terms of understanding how the reasoning developed.

6. Legal Principle

15–35 Where relevant, what was the legal principle underpinning the decision of the judge? Remember, some cases will be resolved on the basis of their particular facts. In other words, the facts of the case identify which legal rule is to apply, which, when it is applied, determines the

[36] [2005] 3 I.R. 77, considered in Box 15.1.

outcome. In these instances, there is no need for the judge to engage in detailed interpretation of the law. For example, in *Harkin v Towpik*,[37] the plaintiff, having discovered information online from a UK source, travelled to Poland for a breast reduction in a cosmetic clinic located there. Although she paid a deposit through her Irish bank, the majority of the fee was paid in Poland and it was in Poland that she was first examined by the defendant doctor, signed the consent form and underwent the procedure. On the facts of the case, the court found that the contract was concluded in Poland; the company in no way sought consumers from the Irish market, and thus the court struck out the plaintiff's claim for damages for personal injury arising from the procedure.

15–36 Other cases are resolved by interpreting the legal rules. In *Donoghue v Stevenson*, Lord Atkin developed the neighbour principle.[38] This principle places a duty on people to ensure that they take reasonable care to avoid acts or omissions that they can reasonably foresee would be liable to injure their neighbour: "'[n]eighbour' in this context is understood to mean any person so closely and directly affected by my act that I ought to have them in reasonable contemplation as being so affected when I am directing my mind to the acts or omissions which are called in question."[39] This point of legal principle has been at the heart of the development of the law of negligence. An example where the courts had to consider whether a duty of care arose was in the case of *Dempsey v Waterford Corporation*.[40] The defendant was carrying out sewage works and, as a result, sewage seeped into the plaintiffs' house from a culvert laid in the seventeenth century, around the time the house was built. The existence of the culvert was not recorded on any map, nor was it known to the defendant. Peart J. held that there could be no duty of care in these circumstances, as fulfilling such a duty would require the defendant to dig up the street "on the off chance that a culvert would be discovered".[41] As there was no breach of duty, the court found it was not necessary to consider whether the damage was reasonably foreseeable.

37 [2014] 1 I.L.R.M. 51.

38 [1932] A.C. 562. See discussion of the development of this principle in Ch.5, Section C.1.

39 [1932] A.C. 562 at 580.

40 [2008] IEHC 55.

41 [2008] IEHC 55 at para.32.

7. Reasoning / Ratio Decidendi

15–37 This is the manner in which the court reached its decision. What were the logical steps that the court took to get to its finding? Why did the court reach this decision? Tracing through the reasoning of the court can be a complicated business. You have to carefully note all the issues that arise as you read through each judgment and see how each judge resolved that issue. What were the legal principles that were considered important? What were the material facts that helped the court decide the case and how did the relevant legal principles apply to these particular facts?

Box 15.3: Case Focus

***Pharmaceutical Society of Great Britain v Boots Cash Chemists (Southern) Ltd* [1953] 1 Q.B. 401**

The defendant ran a self-service pharmacy. Customers picked the items themselves from the shelves, which clearly displayed the price, put them in a basket, and brought the basket to the cash register at the exit. The pharmacist would be able to supervise any transactions from his station. In 1951, in one of the defendant's stores, two customers purchased medicines containing small amounts of poisonous substances whose sale was controlled by Part I of the Poisons List compiled under s.17(1) of the Pharmacy and Poisons Act 1933.

The plaintiff brought the case claiming that the defendant was in breach of s.18(1)(a)(iii) of the 1933 Act, which requires that the sale of poisons be effected by or under the supervision of a registered pharmacist. The plaintiff argued that the pharmacist must be present from the moment the sale is effected. It further contended that displaying goods for free selection was an offer and that customers accepted this offer by placing the goods in their basket. Consequently, it argued that as the selection of the product was not done under supervision, a breach of the relevant statute occurred.

Ratio Decidendi

All three judges of the Court of Appeal agreed with the decision of the High Court. They found that the goods on display in a store are an invitation to buy. The offer is made by the customer when placing goods in a basket. This offer can then be accepted or rejected under the supervision of the pharmacist at the cash register. Consequently, the proper supervision was in place at the moment of sale as required by the legislation.[42]

A customer, it was found, has not given any acceptance while browsing in a store. Were it to be held that a shopkeeper's display of goods amounted to an offer, then customers would be committed to purchase any and all items placed in a shopping basket and would not be able to change their mind afterwards. Self-service stores merely allow customers to view products they may then wish to purchase, by making an offer to the cashier.

8. Concurring / Dissenting Opinions

15–38 If there is more than one judgment, you should examine each judgment in turn to identify the reasoning in that particular judgment. Once you know why each judge reached the particular decision they did, then you are equipped to fully engage with the case and offer logical, reasoned critique thereof. It is also important to note the reasoning used in any dissenting arguments, as this reasoning (which is an obiter in the case) may be relied upon as a persuasive precedent in a future case.

Box 15.4: Time to Reflect

Exercise

In light of the various aspects of a case highlighted above, write a brief case note (short summary) on *R. v Flattery* (1876–77) L.R. 2 Q.B.D. 410.

D. Reading Academic Legal Commentary

15–39 Finally in this chapter, we turn to a short consideration of reading academic legal commentary. It is not the law itself but rather discussion about the law. Engaging with what others have to say about the law can help you to understand the law, both in terms of what the law actually is and also why it is this particular way. Reading legal commentary can also help us to develop our skills at critically analysing the law. We can see what others have to say about the law and can compare and contrast

[42] This is an English example of a word being given its legal rather than its literal meaning, as previously encountered in *Minister for Industry and Commerce v Pim Brothers Ltd* [1966] I.R. 154, as discussed in Ch.4, Section E.2.

what different writers have to say about an issue. We are exposed to legal analysis, including criticisms of the law. In this way we can uncover suggestions as to how law might be reformed.

15–40 When reading what others have to say, it is important to remember that what you read is only the opinion of that writer. You need to read their analysis critically. To do this, you first need to be able to identify what is the argument advanced by the writer. What is it that the writer has to say about the law? Do they think that the law is valid or do they think it is ripe for reform? Compare the writer's analysis with the original case or legislation. Does it actually say what the writer argues it says? If you think that the commentary you are reading has misinterpreted the decision of the court, this gives you something to tease out in your writing. How is the writer wrong in their argument? How do you interpret the case differently? Perhaps you will agree with the commentary you read on a particular point. If so, then you should discuss why you find it persuasive. What resonates with you in terms of that writer's analysis of the law? You should identify for yourself how the commentary you have read clarifies your position on the law. Ultimately it is important that your essays contain your own analysis of the law. Academic legal commentary is useful as it can help refine and perfect your own critique of the law.

E. Conclusion

15–41 In this chapter we have considered how to read the law. We have identified the various parts of legislation in order to note how these can assist us to navigate through the legislation. We have also explored how cases can be read and identified those common aspects of cases that will facilitate you to grow in confidence as an adept reader of cases. Finally, we considered how reading academic commentary can deepen your understanding of the law and engender in you an ability to think critically about law.

Chapter 16

Legal Writing and Advocacy

"George Orwell once wrote that '[g]ood prose is like a window pane.' What I take Orwell to have meant by that remark is that when people read good prose, it makes them feel as if they've 'seen' something (whatever the author was trying to convey) more clearly. Put another way, if a writer can induce his or her reader to feel that the reader would have come to the same conclusion that the author reached had the reader done his or her own investigation of the subject matter, the writer has achieved a kind of 'window pane' effect on the reader."

P. Samuelson, "Good Legal Writing: Of Orwell and Window Panes" (1984) 46 *University of Pittsburgh Law Review* 149 at 149.

In this chapter we:

- identify the style points of good prose;
- discuss how to build a persuasive legal argument;
- introduce one particular referencing citation guide.

A. Introduction

16–01 Legal writing is always persuasive. You always write for an audience. As lawyers, we write to convince the reader that our interpretation of the law is the correct one. It is the same when we engage in oral advocacy: we need to persuade our audience that we are correct and our logic is sound. When a client reads the legal advice we have written, they should be able to make a decision on whether or not it is worth pursuing the claim to court. When studying law, a lecturer will look at whether you have communicated ideas and concepts in an intelligible manner and in a way that shows significant depth of knowledge and understanding of a legal area. If you are asked to examine a piece of legislation, by the end of your analysis the reader should understand the core points covered by it.

16–02 Often before we begin to study the law, our understanding of lawyers is coloured by popular culture. We imagine that to be an effective lawyer we will need to master an entirely new way of speaking and writing. We think we will need to express ourselves in complicated sentences full of sub-clause upon sub-clause and big words and Latin phrases. Nothing could be further from the truth. Our job as lawyers is not to make the simple complicated; rather, it is to make the complicated simple. Verbosity is the enemy of clarity. Opaque obfuscation obscures comprehension. As Strong notes, "[i]f you confuse the reader in any way or make it difficult for the reader to follow your thoughts, either through the introduction of difficult concepts, illogical structure or awkward language, you cannot communicate, let alone persuade".[1] Keep it simple. This is a good starting point for prose. Simple English is easily understood.

16–03 A good image to keep in mind when writing is the hourglass. You conduct lots of research that gets distilled into a narrow point—your final document. This document is merely the tip of the iceberg that your readers can explore through excavation of your references, citations and bibliography to undertake their own research.

Figure 16.1: The Hourglass of Research

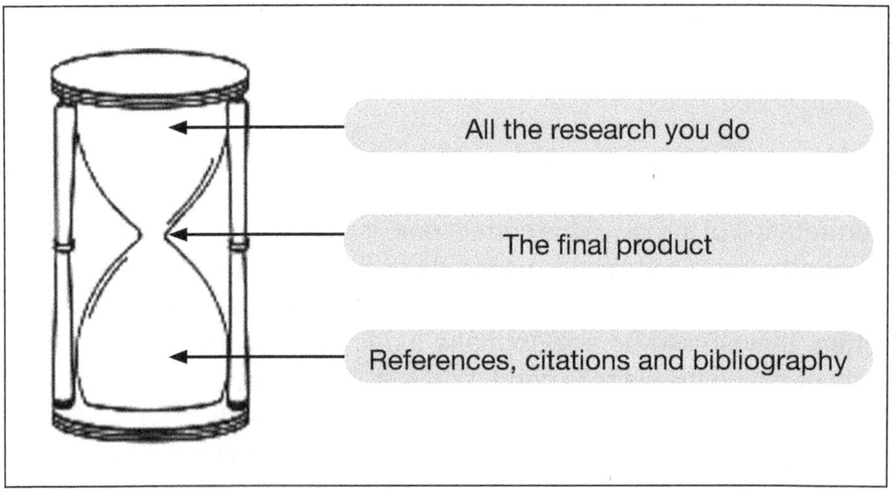

1 S.I. Strong, *How to Write Law Essays and Exams*, 4th edn (Oxford: Oxford University Press, 2014), p.134.

B. Style Points for Good Prose

1. The Basics of a Sentence

16–04 All sentences should consist of a verb, a subject and an object. The subject of the sentence is the thing the sentence is about. The verb is the action being carried out. The object is the thing having the action done to it. In the English language, sentences are constructed on a subject-verb-object structure. So:

Judge Smith	sits	on the bench.
(subject)	(verb)	(object)

The verb "sits" in the sentence above is a finite verb: it only applies to Judge Smith. An infinitive verb is one that could apply to any person, for example "to sit". Please note that it is inappropriate to place a word between the two parts of an infinitive verb, i.e. the "to" and the "sit". This is known as splitting an infinitive. It is a frequent grammatical error in legal writing, particularly where the author uses complex or long sentences. Therefore, Captain Kirk was making a basic error when he stated that the mission of the Starship Enterprise was "to boldly go ...". A final point regarding simple sentence structure is that there must be agreement between the subject and the verb of the sentence. In other words, if the subject is singular, then the verb must also be singular. If the subject is plural, then the verb must be plural. So both of the following sentences are correct:

> Judge Smith sits on the bench.
>
> The judges sit on the bench.

However, "the judges sits on the bench" is incorrect as the subject of the sentence, "the judges", is plural but the verb of the sentence, "sits", is singular.

16–05 Other important elements of a sentence are nouns. There are a few different types of nouns and we will now briefly discuss each. A noun is the name of a person, place, living creature or thing. In the example above, the words "Judge Smith" form a noun. A proper noun is the name of an actual place or person and is usually entitled to a capital letter regardless of where it comes in the sentence. Therefore, it is correct to write:

> The bench broke when Judge Smith sat on it.

Any noun that is not a proper noun is known as a common noun and does not usually have a capital letter. Finally, a pronoun is a word that replaces a noun. Singular pronouns are "I", "you", "he", "she" or "it", and plural pronouns are "we", "you" and "they", although "they" is now also frequently used as a gender-neutral singular pronoun where an unspecified person is being referred to or where a specified person is non-binary. We have used "they" instead of "s/he" when referring to unspecified persons throughout this book.

16–06 Adjectives, adverbs and conjunctions may also appear in sentences. Each of these things performs a particular function. An adjective is a word that describes a noun, e.g. "the dark night", "the quick runner". The words "dark" and "quick" tell us more about the night and the runner. Adverbs perform a similar function for verbs and add a layer of description to the sentence. Compare the following two sentences.

> "She smiled brightly."
>
> "She smiled tightly."

In both sentences she has smiled, but the inclusion of the adverbs enhances our appreciation of the kind of smile she gave. We can differentiate between the nature of the smiles due to the choice of adverb. Perhaps she is happy in the first sentence and less content in the second.

16–07 In formal prose, such as legal writing, adverbs are unnecessary. The inclusion of adverbs weakens an argument you wish to make. Stephen King observed that "the road to hell is paved with adverbs".[2] Adverbs suggest that the author is aware that his writing lacks clarity but is unsure how to address this. Consider the following sentence:

> "The facts of this case are overwhelmingly similar to those in *Murphy v O'Connor*."

[2] S. King, *On Writing: A Memoir of the Craft* (New York: Pocket Books, 2000), p.95.

Are they? The author is asserting that they are but does not demonstrate this. The sentence would be more persuasive if the author gave you the information necessary for you to reach the same conclusion. In a similar vein, consider this sentence:

> "Essentially, the court concluded that the plaintiff was correct."

In this sentence, the use of "essentially" introduces an element of doubt to the idea being conveyed. Did the court reach the conclusion that the plaintiff was correct or not? Employing a term such as "essentially" informs your reader that the court's conclusion was more complex than this, without explaining how it is more complicated, which can result in a confused reader. Thus, the clarity that ought to be central to good legal writing is lost. Adverbs introduce ambiguity and so are best avoided in formal legal writing where the primary aim is clear, concise communication.

16–08 A conjunction joins two parts of a sentence together: "Judge Smith sat on the bench and delivered his judgment." Examples of common conjunctions include "for", "and", "nor", "but", "or" and "yet". Note that, as a general rule, you should not start a sentence with a conjunction.

16–09 A clause is a group of words containing a subject and verb. An independent clause can stand on its own and may form a simple sentence, e.g. "Judge Smith sat on the bench." Where the sentence expands to include a second clause, as in "Judge Smith sat on the bench and delivered his judgment", a dependent clause is introduced. The dependent clause "and delivered his judgment" requires the independent clause, also known as the main clause, to make sense and cannot by itself form a complete sentence. Clauses always contain a finite verb; in other words, there must be a subject.

16–10 A phrase is a group of words without a subject-verb component. Therefore, it cannot convey a complete thought in the manner a clause can. Consider the following sentence:

> "Having considered the evidence, the judge found in favour of the appellant."

The first part of the above sentence cannot exist without the second part. It is a phrase and, by itself, it lacks completeness.

2. Paragraphs

16–11 A paragraph is a unit of text. It is made up of sentences that connect with each other to form a clear, discrete thought. This may be an entirely new thought or an expansion of the thought in the previous paragraph. Paragraphs are used to help your reader follow the logic of your argument. The end of a paragraph indicates to your reader that the writing is about to move in another direction. In this way, paragraphs can operate as signposts, helping your reader navigate through your writing in a logical manner.

3. Punctuation

16–12 Punctuation plays an important role in assisting the reader to understand the meaning of written text. It is a typographical strategy to clarify meaning in written text. It can also bring a text to life by introducing pitch, pace, pause, inflection, tone and body language to writing. It is the emoji of formal writing. Effective punctuation will enable the reader to gain a deeper appreciation of the information being communicated. Carefully selected punctuation can convey the attitudes of the author: we can perceive their passion, discover their distaste, and experience their empathy. In this way, punctuation can assist you to find your active voice and to produce energetic, dynamic prose.

16–13 To illustrate this point, consider the following passage:

> "Dear John I want a man who knows what love is all about you are generous kind thoughtful people who are not like you admit to being useless and inferior you have ruined me for other men I yearn for you I have no feelings whatsoever when we're apart I can be forever happy will you let me be yours Gloria"[3]

Unpunctuated as it is, the above passage does not engage the reader in any particular sense. In fact, it is somewhat confusing as the reader is not certain what message it is attempting to convey. Look at the

[3] *Games Magazine* (Chicago: Playboy, 1984).

following, punctuated version to read a definite statement, conveying a clear message.

> Dear John,
>
> I want a man who knows what love is all about. You are generous, kind, thoughtful. People who are not like you admit to being useless and inferior. You have ruined me for other men. I yearn for you; I have no feelings whatsoever when we're apart. I can be forever happy. Will you let me be yours?
>
> Gloria.

However, if you make small changes to the punctuation then the meaning of the sentence alters:

> Dear John,
>
> I want a man who knows what love is. All about you are generous, kind, thoughtful people, who are not like you. Admit to being useless and inferior. You have ruined me. For other men I yearn; for you I have no feelings whatsoever. When we're apart I can be forever happy. Will you let me be?
>
> Yours,
>
> Gloria.

16–14 We will now consider some punctuation marks and how they are used. This review should aid you to become sophisticated in your deployment of punctuation. Keep in mind that if a sentence is becoming very difficult to correctly punctuate, you might be better advised to rephrase your writing to ensure greater clarity. Typically, good punctuation passes unnoticed. Poor punctuation draws attention, may damage your credibility as a writer and thus undermine the argument you wish to advance.

(a) The full stop .

16–15 The full stop, also known as the period, is usually found at the end of a sentence expressing a statement. For example: "The court found in favour of the plaintiff."

(b) The question mark ?

16–16 The question mark is found at the end of a direct question. For example: "Who is the Chief Justice of Ireland?" Question marks do not appear following an indirect question: "Counsel for the plaintiff asked whether visibility had been poor at dusk."

(c) The exclamation mark !

16–17 This punctuation point is used to express surprise or very strong feeling. It is employed at the end of an emphatic declaration, interjection or command. For example: "Sit down now!" The exclamation mark can also be employed to close a question in a manner that conveys extreme emotion: "Where are you going? Stop!" Exclamation marks can emphasise a word in a sentence: "Despite being visible on CCTV footage, John was found not guilty(!) of theft." When noting mimetic sounds in writing, the exclamation point is employed: "The dog went *woof!* and the bear responded *grr!*" The final use of the exclamation mark is at the end of a fragment, word or phrase that is not a complete sentence in itself: "Should we advise Jack to bring his case? Absolutely!" In formal legal writing, the exclamation mark is very rarely used. So the simple rule for using exclamation marks in your formal writing is: don't! Ever!

(d) The comma ,

16–18 The comma vies with the full stop for the honour of being the most commonly used punctuation mark. Commas show readers how extra information has been added to a sentence. Commas set off introductory phrases in a sentence: "Having evaluated the evidence, the judge then turned to consider whether the burden of proof had been met." To highlight that something is an interrupting clause (i.e. additional information that is not strictly necessary for the thought in the sentence which enhances understanding of the point), the comma is employed thus: "The witness stated that he, not the defendant, was driving the car at the time of the accident." The comma is also used to separate items in a list: "The accused, her family and the members of the public all wept openly when the jury returned the guilty verdict." Finally, a comma can be used before a conjunction to separate two clauses in a sentence where the second clause introduces a new subject and verb: "The court found in favour of the plaintiff, and the defendant immediately sought leave to appeal the decision."

(e) The apostrophe '

16–19 The apostrophe is used for a few different reasons and we will examine each of them in turn. Apostrophes indicate possession or ownership: "The respondent's argument consisted of three points." Please note its position when you are indicating plural possession: "The judges' decision was unanimous." The apostrophe also indicates that there are letters missing from words, particularly in the context of informal contractions such as "wouldn't", "can't", "don't" or "shouldn't". By their very name, informal contractions are inappropriate in formal legal writing. Accordingly, you should not use contractions in your essays and assignments.

16–20 In this context, please note the special rules regarding "its" / "it's". "Its" is the possessive form of the pronoun "it". In other words, the thing belongs to it. "It's", by contrast, is the informal contraction for "it is". Simply put, "its" may have a place in legal writing, but "it's" should never appear in formal writing as it is an informal contraction.

16–21 Finally, the apostrophe does not indicate plurals. Consider the following two sentences:

> "The rules on this issue are long settled by the courts."
>
> "The court's finding was that a duty of care did exist."

The first sentence refers to more than one court while the second tells us that a particular court made a particular decision.

(f) The colon :

16–22 The colon is used to separate a general statement from following specifics.

> "The power of government is divided between three branches: the executive branch, the legislative branch and the judicial branch."

The information that comes after the colon tells us more about the statement that came before it. We now know that a contract has three parts and that these are the offer, acceptance and consideration. Put another way, what follows a colon explains the statement made immediately before the colon.

16–23 Inserting a colon in your writing creates a sense of anticipation. In this way the colon can highlight crucial information by adding emphasis to that which follows it. Consider the wording of Article 15.2.1° of the Constitution of Ireland:

> "The sole and exclusive power of making laws for the State is hereby vested in the Oireachtas: no other legislative authority has power to make laws for the State."

The colon following "Oireachtas" in the above Article strengthens the prohibition on law-making by anyone other than the Oireachtas.

16–24 Using colons adds vibrancy and life to your writing and makes it more engaging for the reader. This is a dramatic punctuation point. Beware of overuse of the colon lest it render your writing melodramatic. If every paragraph has its "dun, dun, dun" moment, then your reader will lose confidence in your writing.

(g) The semicolon ;

16–25 The semicolon links two sentences without the need for a conjunction such as "and", "but", "yet" and so on. In doing this, the semicolon transforms the sentences such that they become inexorably linked. For example, the semicolon in the following sentence links the two separate clauses such that they become interdependent: "The evidence was ruled inadmissible; the accused was found not guilty." Consequently, semicolons highlight connections between ideas that will help the reader gain a deeper understanding of your argument.

16–26 A second use of the semicolon is to separate lists where the components are longer than one word or where one component contains a comma: "The elements of defamation include a defamatory statement concerning another; publication to a third party; and fault amounting to at least negligence."

(h) The ellipsis …

16–27 This is a very useful punctuation mark when quoting material from another source. The ellipsis indicates that some words or phrases have been omitted from the quotation:

> "If the purpose is within one of the heads of charity forming the first three classes … the Court will easily conclude that it is a charitable purpose."[4]

The missing words from this quotation are "in the classification which Lord Macnaghten borrowed from Sir Samuel Romilly's argument in Morice v. Bishop of Durham,". By omitting these words, the point made by the above quotation is clearer than if they had been included.

16–28 Thus, the ellipsis helps to keep legal writing succinct and facilitate clearer understanding of the quoted material by enabling the omission of text that is not necessary for present purposes. You need to be cautious in employing the ellipsis to ensure that you do not manipulate the source to make it seem as if it says something it does not, lest you damage your credibility.

4. Avoid the Passive Voice

16–29 The active voice is more direct and vigorous than the passive voice. When the subject of the verb is the actor of the verb, i.e. the person doing the thing, then the active voice is at play. If the subject of the verb is the target of the action, then the passive voice is being used. Take the following two sentences as an example:

> "The cat ate the mouse."
>
> "The mouse was eaten by the cat."

The first sentence is in the active voice; the second is in the passive voice. The first sentence is more dynamic than the second. Often the

[4] *National Anti-Vivisection Society v Inland Revenue Commissioners* [1948] A.C. 31 at 65 per Lord Simonds.

use of the passive voice can sacrifice clarity. It is not always obvious who is performing the action of the sentence. Consider the following sentence:

> "As time passed, attempts were made to fit new fact scenarios under the umbrella of negligence so that compensation could be awarded for hurt caused."

It is not clear who is performing the action described in the above sentence. By contrast, the sentence below makes the same point but is more precise and focused:

> "As time passed, plaintiffs attempted to fit new fact scenarios under the umbrella of negligence so they could win compensation for hurt caused."

16–30 Sometimes reworking a clunky sentence such as the first one can be frustrating as you cannot seem to identify who performed the action. If this is the case, you have identified a problem: you do not know the information you are trying to convey. Attempting to rewrite a sentence in the active voice is a good example of how the writing process itself can help you to identify what you need to learn about a subject.

5. Be Clear

16–31 As the quote that began this chapter in referencing Orwell stated, "[g]ood prose is like a window pane".[5] In other words, it is clear. When reading good prose, it is possible to see straight through to the point that the author wanted to convey. Your perception may be influenced by the frame surrounding the window, yet your view into the room will be unobstructed. It is essential to remember that lawyers are professional communicators. If your reader cannot understand the point you are trying to make, you have failed to communicate your message.

16–32 What, then, makes writing clear? To begin with, clarity requires proper grammar and punctuation. As Dernbach has said:

---

[5] P. Samuelson, "Good Legal Writing: of Orwell and Window Panes" (1984) 46 *University of Pittsburgh Law Review* 149.

> "Errors in grammar, punctuation and spelling suggest that the writer is sloppy and careless – qualities that people do not want in a lawyer. Minor errors distract the reader from the message to be conveyed. Major errors may distort the message or make it unintelligible."[6]

16–33 There is, of course, more to clear writing than simple adherence to grammatical rules. Clear writing also uses ordinary words and simple sentence structures. You should avoid "legalese" and other sentence structures that complicate the message you are trying to communicate. Phrases such as "nevertheless" or "hereinafter" will not make your writing appear more learned; rather, use of such phrases will read as padding, as if you are unclear what it is you are trying to say, and thus detract from your work. In Ch.4 on legislation, we looked at the Plain English Movement and considered the virtue of writing the law in simple, ordinary language.[7] The same arguments hold true for writing about the law. The language of everyday will most often communicate the message you wish to convey in the quickest and easiest manner. However, the Plain English Movement is not without its critics.[8] The main critique levelled against the movement is that overreliance on ordinary words can cause writing to lose the precision that using technical legal language can give. Words such as "interlocutory injunction", "consideration" and "fee simple" are legal terms of art and they convey particular concepts that are not caught with the same degree of precision if translated into plain English. This potential tension was identified by the Law Reform Commission in its *Report on Statutory Drafting and Interpretation: Plain Language and the Law*.[9] It resolved this tension by recommending that in most situations plain English should be employed, while acknowledging that occasionally it might be necessary to use slightly more complex language in order to ensure legal certainty.[10]

---

6 J.C. Dernbach et al., *A Practical Guide to Legal Writing and Legal Method*, 4th edn (New York: Aspen Publishers, 2010), p.200.

7 Chapter 4, Box 4.3.

8 D. Crump, "Against Plain English: The Case for a Functional Approach to Legal Document Preparation" (2001–2002) 33 *Rutgers Law Journal* 713, and B. Hunt, "Plain Language in Legislative Drafting: Is It Really the Answer?" (2002) 23 *Statute Law Review* 24.

9 Law Reform Commission, *Report on Statutory Drafting and Interpretation: Plain Language and the Law* (LRC 61-2000).

10 Law Reform Commission, *Report on Statutory Drafting and Interpretation: Plain Language and the Law* (LRC 61-2000), para.6.22.

16–34 When writing about the law, it is best to think about the audience for each piece of writing that you produce. Is your reader a legal professional or a non-lawyer? How you describe the law will differ depending on the answer to this question. For the legal professional, the most efficient and clear way to communicate may be to use the legal term of art. For the non-lawyer, a better way to communicate may be to use the legal term, together with a lay explanation of what it means.

16–35 A sensible structure can also help bring clarity to your work. You should have a well-thought-out plan for your work. It should have a start, middle and end. A bit of careful planning at the beginning of the writing process can ensure that your reader follows your argument and can perceive the logical progression of your thoughts.

16–36 In this context, careful use of headings can be of great assistance. Headings are the window frames that support your pane of glass. They operate as signposts through your writing, guiding the reader through your work. Legal writing is not, after all, a suspense novel. Your reader is not waiting with bated breath for the shocking denouement. The best way to approach structuring your legal writing is to tell your reader what you are going to say, say it, and then remind the reader of what you have said. Repeating the main points in this way serves to highlight and reinforce the manner in which they support your overarching argument.

6. Be Concise

16–37 Good legal writing is always concise. Do not confuse concision with brevity. By concise, we mean that good legal writing is always efficient. There should not be words or sentences in your work that do not move your analysis forward. Concise writing is focused and precise, with the appropriate level of detail. It makes its point in an economical way. As Strunk and White explain, "[a] sentence should contain no unnecessary words, a paragraph no unnecessary sentences, for the same reason that a drawing should have no unnecessary lines, and a machine no unnecessary parts."[11]

[11] W. Strunk and E.B. White, *The Elements of Style*, 4th edn (New Jersey: Longman, 2000), p.23.

16–38 Concise writing is clearer than writing that is not concise. Consequently, it is easier for your reader to follow the argument you are advancing if it is not ponderous. Consider the following statement of facts from Denning L.J.'s judgment in *Hinz v Berry*:

> "It happened on April 19, 1964. It was bluebell time in Kent. Mr. and Mrs. Hinz had been married some 10 years, and they had four children, all aged nine and under. The youngest was one. Mrs. Hinz was a remarkable woman. In addition to her own four, she was foster-mother to four other children. To add to it, she was two months pregnant with her fifth child.
>
> On this day they drove out in a Bedford Dormobile van from Tonbridge to Canvey Island. They took all eight children with them. As they were coming back they turned into a lay-by at Thurnham to have a picnic tea. The husband, Mr. Hinz, was at the back of the Dormobile making the tea. Mrs. Hinz had taken Stephanie, her third child, aged three, across the road to pick bluebells on the opposite side. There came along a Jaguar car driven by Mr. Berry, out of control. A tyre had burst. The Jaguar rushed into this lay-by and crashed into Mr. Hinz and the children. Mr. Hinz was frightfully injured and died a little later. Nearly all the children were hurt. Blood was streaming from their heads. Mrs. Hinz, hearing the crash, turned round and saw this disaster. She ran across the road and did all she could. Her husband was beyond recall. But the children recovered.
>
> An action has been brought on her behalf and on behalf of the children for damages against Mr. Berry, the defendant. The injuries to the children have been settled by various sums being paid. The pecuniary loss to Mrs. Hinz by reason of the loss of her husband has been found by the judge to be some £15,000; but there remains the question of the damages payable to her for her nervous shock – the shock which she suffered by seeing her husband lying in the road dying, and the children strewn about."[12]

In just over 300 words, Denning L.J. outlines all the facts of the case. We are now in possession, not only of the bald information pertinent to the legal question at issue, but we also have a flavour of how Mrs Hinz must

[12] [1970] 2 Q.B. 40 at 42.

have been traumatised by what she witnessed. Denning L.J. does not overwork the recitation of facts. The story he tells is a simple one. We, the reader, see clearly through to its core.

16–39 The value of concise writing is that, as in the example above, it enables the reader to extract from the writing the information that is essential for the reader to possess. Practising legal professionals have little time to read briefing documentation. Concise writing is efficient as it makes its point quickly and with the appropriate level of detail such that the busy reader can maximise the limited time they have to devote to reading the document. Thus, concise legal writing ensures that the document is succinct yet contains all the pertinent information necessary to understand a complex subject with relative ease.

7. Be Engaging

16–40 Finally, good legal writing is engaging. It is important that your writing be engaging so that your reader does not lose interest in what you are saying before you get to say it. Denning L.J. explains why this is important:

> "No matter how sound your reasoning, if it is presented in a dull and turgid setting, your hearer – or your reader – will turn aside. They will not stop to listen. They will flick over the pages. But if it is presented in a lively and attractive setting, they will sit up and take notice. They will listen as if spellbound. They will read you with engrossment."[13]

16–41 How then can we make our writing engaging? Unsurprisingly, the same techniques that will make any prose engaging will elevate legal writing such that we are enthralled. Denning L.J.'s quote from *Hinz v Berry* above contains many elements that engage the reader. The opening is both precise (giving the exact date) and apparently whimsical (noting the bluebells). Denning L.J. engages us by telling us the story of the day: who was in the car, where they were going, the promise of the picnic, the trip across the road to pick bluebells. Thus, he depicts an idyllic springtime family outing. In this context, the out-of-control car

[13] A. Denning, *The Family Story* (Virginia: Lexis Law Publishing, 1981), p.216.

is a clear interloper. The contrast between the delightful opening and the conclusion of the second paragraph where Mr Hinz is dead and the children have blood "streaming from their heads" could not be more pronounced. The dissonance between the two images is shocking. In this way, Denning L.J. evokes in us, the reader, a small echo of how Mrs Hinz must have felt. We are now in her shoes. We empathise with her situation. We want to know how this situation is resolved and hope that it is in her favour.

16–42 There are a number of techniques that we, as writers, can employ to make our writing more engaging. Typical writing tools to engage readers are alliteration and assonance. Alliteration is the repetition of the same stressed sound in a number of words, which occur close together in a series. It creates a musical effect in the writing that enhances the pleasure of reading it. Thus, it makes reading and recitation of the writing attractive and appealing: it is easier to take in that which is alliterative. The repetition of the "r" in "reading and recitation" and the "a" in "attractive and appealing" in the previous sentence are examples of alliteration. Assonance occurs where two or more words close to one another repeat the same vowel sound but start with different consonant sounds. An example of assonance is the phrase "the r**ai**n in Sp**ai**n st**ay**s m**ai**nly on the pl**ai**n". The "ay" sound made by both the "ai" and "ay" letter combinations is repeated regularly here. Once again, assonance contributes to the musicality of a piece of writing.

(a) Variety

16–43 Introduce some variety into your writing. Contrast long sentences with short ones. This change in tempo will keep the interest of your reader. Similarly, contrasting a long paragraph with one that is short will achieve a similar impact. Consider the following extract from the decision of Henchy J. in *McGee v Attorney General*,[14] a case involving the illegal importation of contraceptives, where he discusses s.17 of the Criminal Law Amendment Act 1935, which outlawed the use of contraceptives in Ireland:

---

[14] [1974] I.R. 284. See the previous discussion of the *McGee* case in Ch.3, paras 3–29 to 3–32.

"The Act of 1935, as its long title shows, is not aimed at population control but at the suppression of vice and the amendment of the law relating to sexual offences. Section 17 follows immediately on a section directed against the practice of prostitution in public and immediately precedes a section making criminal certain acts which offend modesty or cause scandal or injure the morals of the community. The section creates a criminal prohibition in an area in which the legislature has thought fit to intervene in the interests of public morality. What it seeks to do, by means of the sanction of the criminal law, is to put an end, as far as it was possible to do so by legislation, to the use of contraceptives in the State. It does not in terms make the use of contraceptives a crime, but the totality of the prohibition aims at nothing less. Presumably because contraceptives are of differing kinds and vary in the ways, internal and external, they can be used, and because of the difficulty of proving their use in the intimacy of the sexual act, the section strikes at their availability. Sub-section 1 of s. 17 of the Act of 1935 makes it an offence to sell, or expose, offer, advertise, or keep for sale or to import or attempt to import for sale any contraceptives. In effect, this makes it legally impossible to sell or buy a contraceptive in the State. Had the prohibition stopped there, it would have left the loophole that contraceptives could be imported otherwise than for sale. That loophole, however, is sealed by sub-s. 3 of s. 17 which makes contraceptives prohibited articles under the customs code so that their importation for any purpose, if effected with the intention of evading the prohibition, is an offence: see s. 186 of the Customs Consolidation Act, 1876; *Frailey v. Charlton* [1920] 1 K.B. 147; *Attorney General v. Deignan* [1946] I.R. 542.

Because contraceptives are not manufactured in this State, the effect of s. 17 of the Act of 1935 as a whole is that, except for contraceptives that have been imported without the intention of evading the prohibition on importation, it is not legally possible to obtain a contraceptive in this State. It is doubtful if the legislature could have taken more effective steps by means of the criminal law to put an end to their use in the State."[15]

[15] [1974] I.R. 284 at 324.

In the second short paragraph, Henchy J. sums up the practical effect of the legislative analysis in the preceding paragraph. In this way, he guards against his analysis becoming turgid.

16–44 Varying the sentence and paragraph structures in this way maintains interest in the topic. You do not wish to risk your writing becoming like something written to teach people how to read English, which, although concise, is rarely engaging. Hence, it is important to ensure your writing is vibrant in its structure.

(b) Imagery

16–45 Imagery is the use of figurative language to represent objects, actions and ideas in such a way that it appeals to our physical senses. A well-chosen image can concisely convey exactly what the writer is thinking about in a way that an attempt to describe manages less clearly. A good example of this can be seen in the judgment of Black J. in *People (Attorney General) v Kennedy* where he uses the image of looking closely at a small section of a painting to explain the importance of the *ejusdem generis* and *noscitur a sociis* rules of statutory interpretation:[16]

> "A small section of a picture, if looked at close-up, may indicate something quite clearly; but when one stands back and examines the whole canvas, the close-up view of the small section is often found to have given a wholly wrong view of what it really represented. If one could pick out a single word or phrase and, finding it perfectly clear in itself, refuse to check its apparent meaning in the light thrown upon it by the context or by other provisions, the result would be to render the principle of *ejusdem generis* and *noscitur a sociis* utterly meaningless; for this principle requires frequently that a word or phrase or even a whole provision which, standing alone, has a clear meaning must be given quite a different meaning when viewed in the light of its context."[17]

16–46 The use of images is commonplace in the law. We often, for example, see courts discussing the need to balance competing legal

---

[16] For an explanation of both the *ejusdem generis* and *noscitur a sociis* aids to statutory interpretation, see Ch.4, Section F.1(b) and (c).

[17] [1946] I.R. 517 at 536.

rights—thus drawing on the image of the balance or the scales of justice. The need to "balance" the competing rights to life of the mother and her unborn child is evident throughout the decision in *Attorney General v X*.[18]

(c) Storytelling

16–47 Telling a story is a simple, yet very effective, way to engage a reader. Denning L.J. excelled at this in his judgments. Recall the compelling recitation of the facts in *Hinz v Berry* above.[19] Similarly, Denham J. in *O v Minister for Justice, Equality and Law Reform* stated:

> "Over thousands of years waves of people have come ashore on the island of Ireland. However, the island found by those early migrants was very different from the Ireland of today. The differences included those of the landscape, society and governance. Tales of early refugees to Ireland are told in myth and legend. In pseudohistory they may be discovered also. Lebor Gabála ... described the first invasion as by the relatives of Noah who had been refused entry to the ark before the flood. Today Ireland is not covered by great oak forests. Raths have been replaced by housing estates and apartment blocks. The Brehon law has been displaced by modern Irish law. The principles and law governing Irish society today come from the people and are to be found in the Constitution of Ireland, 1937, and the legislation of the Oireachtas. It is to that Constitution and law we must look to determine the issues of our times. The days when migrating people would sail long boats up an Irish river, pull the boat up the shingle, and set up home in Ireland, without recourse to a central government, are long gone. Today people who migrate to Ireland may arrive by many means but they must comply with the Constitution and the law.
>
> The essence of the issue in these cases is as follows. Where a non-national married couple arrive in Ireland and a child is born to them, is the entire family entitled to remain in Ireland (or at least until the child reaches his majority) as a consequence of the Irish citizenship of the child and the constitutional right of the child to

[18] [1991] 1 I.R. 1. For more on the *X* case, see Ch.8, Box 8.3.

[19] See para.16–38.

> the care and company of his parents, no matter how long or short a time the parents and child have been in Ireland?"[20]

Although this opening paragraph is long, it is easy to read. It comprises a series of short, uncomplicated sentences. It narrates the facts of the case but in a compelling and persuasive manner. Thus, Denham J engages the interest of the reader in this case, which involved a judicial review of a refusal of an asylum claim.

(d) Proper tone

16–48 It is difficult to define precisely what is meant by proper tone. At its simplest, where the subject matter of the writing and the writing techniques are in harmony, proper tone is achieved. Thus, in formal legal writing, when the writing techniques reflect and respect this formality, the proper tone is achieved. Where the subject matter is serious and the writing techniques are frivolous, this discord reflects the lack of proper tone adopted by the writer. One example of a wholly inappropriate tone, from the not-too-distant past, is to be found in the following description by Flood J. of a respondent, C.M.: "She has a very attractive face, a very slim and well-proportioned figure and is beautifully walked. I would think that in her early 20's [sic] she would have been a very physically attractive young woman with quite an aura of sexuality ... ."[21]

C. Building a Persuasive Legal Argument

16–49 Lawyers are professional communicators. Lawyers are also professional persuaders. We write to convince someone that our perspective on the law is correct. As students of law, you will write for two different audiences: your lecturers and your "clients"; in other words, the academic who is evaluating your work and someone with basic knowledge of the law but limited understanding of the area of law that

[20] [2003] 1 I.R. 1 at 43. For a critique of this and other decisions as regards the rights of residence of Irish children and their non-Irish national parents, see S. Mullally and L. Thornton, "The Rights of the Child, Immigration and Article 8 in the Irish Courts" in U. Kilkelly (ed.), *ECHR and Irish Law*, 2nd edn (Bristol: Jordans, 2009).

[21] *BJM v CM* [1996] 2 I.R. 574 at 577. Flood J. granted a decree of nullity to the petitioner, BJM, who was married to CM for 17 years and together had six children, on the basis that she had significant scarring.

you are writing about and are educating them on. Generally speaking, essays are produced as if writing from one academic to another; thus, your audience is an academic one. By contrast, in problem questions you are advising a client who may have little knowledge of the law. This will impact on how to approach your writing. If you have to write something as though you are educating someone, then you are less likely to skip steps in your logic, which leads to better analysis overall. The risk is if you focus only on the academic reader, you will assume that the reader knows things, but it is not the academic's knowledge that is being tested, it is yours. The following pointers may prove useful to remember.

1. Have a Point—Answering the Question Posed

16–50 As stated, when you write about the law, you are writing with a purpose. You need to communicate or persuade your audience, the reader, about your point. Consequently, as a basic starting point, you need to have a point to make. What is your argument? Do you agree or disagree with the statement? Should your client bring the case to court? Once you identify for yourself exactly why you are writing this piece of work, it will bring clarity to your writing. All too often, law students lack a point (that is, a thesis or argument) when they write about the law and no analysis of any aspect of law will work without it contributing to the bigger argument you wish to advance.

2. Make the Point

16–51 Once you have identified your thesis, you need to make your point at the outset. As stated above, you are not writing a mystery novel, but making an argument. It will help your reader to understand the flow of your argument if you briefly explain it at the beginning. The nuances of this argument will be developed in the body of your work, but begin by letting your client know if you think they should bring the case; let your academic colleague know if you think the law in this particular area needs reform.

3. Sensible Structure

16–52 When determining how to structure your writing, you need to think about how you wish to influence your reader. How can you outline your point so that your reader becomes convinced of the inevitability of the argument you are advancing? Remember the point made above about giving your reader signposts through your work. Use headings. Explain what you are about to say, say it, and explain what you have said. This simple structure will ensure that your reader remains engaged throughout your analysis.

4. Break Analysis Up into Parts and Develop Each Part in Full

16–53 A very simple structure often adopted by law students is ILAC. For each issue raised by the topic, employ this structure and you will ensure that you do not neglect to analyse any point and furthermore your reader will follow your thought process through the analysis.

I: Issue—what is the legal issue involved?
L: Law—what does the law have to say on this point?
A: Apply the law to the scenario under discussion (if you are answering a problem question); or
A: Analysis and context (if you are answering an essay question).
C: Conclude—come to a conclusion on each issue discussed.

16–54 This is a very logical and simple structure, which will ensure that your reader can easily discern the development of your analysis. By employing such a structure, you break your analysis up into component parts that enable each element to be explored and developed in a logical structure. In this way, your analysis will support your main thesis or argument and will ensure that your overall work retains clarity and concision.

16–55 Note that an average essay will require you to discuss more than one issue. Therefore, your basic essay structure may look something like this:

Figure 16.2: Basic Essay Structure

Introduction to essay

↓

Define issue 1 → Identify the law relevant to issue 1 → Apply/Analyse that law → Present your conclusion on issue 1

↓

Define issue 2 → Identify the law relevant to issue 2 → Apply/Analyse that law → Present your conclusion on issue 2

↓

Define issue 3 → Identify the law relevant to issue 3 → Apply/Analyse that law → Present your conclusion on issue 3

↓

Overall conclusion to essay, bringing together the various sub-conclusions above

D. Legal Citation

16–56 Citation is crucial to good legal writing. For a legal argument to be persuasive, it must draw on the existing law to indicate why, in this particular instance, the law should be resolved in this manner. In other words, persuasive legal writing consists of an argument based on an analysis of the law. Citation is the method by which writers about the law gain powers of persuasion. Citation demonstrates the legal authorities relied upon to advance the argument made and attributes or acknowledges those other commentators whose ideas you have adopted, referenced and engaged with as you develop your thesis. Citation shows you have done your research and credits those who helped you to develop your analysis. Every time you use ideas, theories, arguments, or any kind of information originating from another source, you *must* refer to (or cite) the original source.

16–57 There is no universal citation guide for law. Every publisher has their own individual or quirky way of citing references employed by their authors. This book, for example, is published by Round Hall and so adopted the Round Hall house style of citation. However, increasingly, law schools in Ireland employ the OSCOLA style of legal citation. Therefore, we will use the OSCOLA style to explain how best to reference in legal writing. Please note that the citation style discussed here will be different from the citation style evident in the footnotes, as we were obliged to comply with Round Hall's own citation style, which differs significantly from OSCOLA.

16–58 OSCOLA stands for Oxford Standard for Citation of Legal Authorities. It is a referencing system for legal materials developed by the Oxford University Law Faculty and is, as stated above, becoming widespread as a citation system employed in law schools across Ireland.

16–59 The OSCOLA style consists of two aspects:

(1) the use of in-text superscript note identifiers (expressed as running numbers) throughout the text that direct the reader to appropriate
(2) footnotes, where full bibliographic details of sources are provided in the first note, and brief follow-up notes provided for subsequent references to the same source.

Finally, each work should contain a full bibliography that outlines the bibliographic details of every source consulted throughout the research conducted.

16–60 The OSCOLA citation guide is available to download online from: *https://www.law.ox.ac.uk/oscola*. The variation for Irish legal resources is available from the following website: *http://legalcitation.ie/wp-content/uploads/2016/04/OSCOLA-Ireland-2016.pdf*.

1. Why Cite / Reference?

16–61 As stated above, referencing is a fundamental aspect of academic writing. You employ referencing for a number of different purposes: to acknowledge the ideas and intellectual property of others whose work you have consulted; to identify the range of research you have conducted; and to enable readers of your work to find the sources that you used in your research so that they can conduct their own study of the topic.

16–62 Acknowledging the ideas of others is important in formal legal writing. It is a form of professional respect and courtesy but it also fulfils the very important job of ensuring that you are protected from suspicion of plagiarism. Plagiarism is the taking of someone else's work or idea and presenting it as if it were your own. Within the academic community, plagiarism is taken very seriously and, if proven, can result in academic misconduct hearings, censure or even dismissal from a programme. Thus, it is essential that you learn to defend against a potential allegation of plagiarism by correctly and accurately referencing your research.

16–63 The second function of accurate referencing is to demonstrate the breadth and depth of the research you have conducted. Arguments and analysis based on detailed research are more credible than those that stand on flimsy research foundations. Demonstrating the extent of the research you have undertaken as part of your work enhances the quality of your work and lends support and gravitas to any reform proposals or conclusions that you draw.

16–64 Finally, referencing enables your reader, and yourself at a future date, to return to the research you have conducted and to explore aspects of it in more depth. In this way, it assists in the dissemination of ideas and intellectual argument and contributes to the growth of scholarship in a given area.

2. When to Reference

16–65 Any time you use, rely upon, or reference an idea that you did not invent, you need to include a citation. You should include a citation for all of the following categories of information (please note this is *not* an exhaustive list): cases, legislation, constitutional provisions, treaties, official reports, textbooks, monographs, journal articles, newspaper articles, radio programmes, television programmes, documentaries, videos, films, images, tables, graphs, statistics, diagrams sourced from any medium whether hard copy or soft copy, sound files, image files, recordings or personal communications whether found online or offline or in any other way. Whether you directly reference the source by quotation or indirect quotation, attribution, paraphrase, reference or oblique mention, you must include a citation.

16–66 Information that can be considered "common knowledge" does not require a citation. However, there is no consensus as to what constitutes "common knowledge". Generally speaking, it consists of those ideas, thoughts, facts, opinions and phrases that, while not distinctive to any particular source, are well known within the particular discipline. From a legal perspective, the fact that the Irish legal system is a common law system is common knowledge and would not require a citation. However, it is important to note that you should not make unsubstantiated claims in your work. Where a statement or idea is not referenced, it risks enabling bias and uninformed conjecture to be included in an essay. Therefore, it is important to seek an authoritative source for all the arguments and analysis you wish to advance. A good guide is: if in doubt, cite.

3. How to Reference

16–67 Referencing is a very simple part of the research and writing process. It becomes easier if you remember to gather the information you need for complete citations as you engage in the research process. The following four-point plan should enable you to stay on top of your referencing.

1. Keep accurate notes of all bibliographic information as you conduct your research. For every source you consult you should keep a note of the following information: the author's name, the title of the work, the publisher, place and year of publication. If you intend to quote from a text in your final work, note the page on which the quote appears.
2. Insert the footnotes as you write. Each time you mention something you did not invent yourself, insert a footnote that references the original source of that idea/thought. The first time you mention a particular source you should note the full bibliographic information.
3. Build your bibliography alongside your text. As you insert a citation in your footnotes, copy it into your bibliography. This will ensure that you do not neglect to include any source in your bibliography and will also save you time at the end trawling though your notes, footnotes, etc. to retrospectively build a bibliography.

4. When you mention a source for the second time, you can cross-reference back to the original citation you made, thus keeping your work streamlined and tightly referenced.

Box 16.1: Skills Insight

Tips for Using Referencing and Citation Tools in Microsoft Word

Every word-processing programme, including the various versions of Microsoft Word, is slightly different, but these general notes will aid you in your navigation of the programmes.

Inserting footnotes

To insert a footnote in a document using Microsoft Word you need to click on the references tab. This will give you a number of options. Focus on the section named "Footnotes".

You should now click on the "Insert Footnote" button (identified above with the arrow). This will immediately insert the superscript number next to the punctuation point.

husband has been found by the judge to be some £15,000; but there remains the question of the damages payable to her for her nervous shock - the shock which she suffered by seeing her husband lying in the road dying, and the children strewn about.[12]

Immediately the cursor will move you to the footnotes section at the bottom of the page and be prepared for you to write your footnote:

engrossment.[13]

[12]

[13] Lord A. Denning, *The Family Story*, (Virginia: Lexis Law Publishing, 1981), p216.

Now you simply need to type in all your citation information and you have successfully inserted a footnote.

[12] *Hinz v Berry* [1970] 2 QB 40 at 42.
[13] Lord A. Denning, *The Family Story*, (Virginia: Lexis Law Publishing, 1981), p216.

Cross-referencing footnotes

If you use the tools in Word to cross-reference your citations and footnotes, it will enable you to keep your work up to date without needing to manually update footnote cross-references as you draft and redraft your work.

When completing your citation information as you write your footnote, indicate that you are about to cross-refer by including the words "*supra* n" and then immediately use the cross-reference tool to insert the correct footnote number you are referring to.

[12] *Hinz v Berry* [1970] 2 QB 40 at 42.
[13] Lord A. Denning, *The Family Story*, (Virginia: Lexis Law Publishing, 1981), p216.

To cross-reference to a previous footnote, click on the references tab. In the "Captions" section you will see a symbol called "Cross-reference".

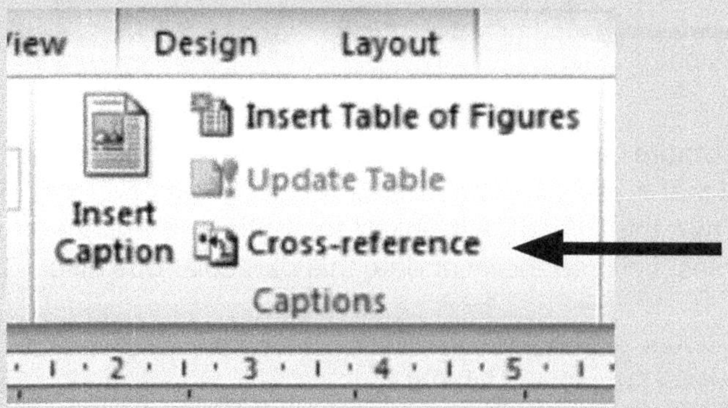

Click on the cross-reference icon and a new window will open. Click on the drop-down arrow under "Reference type".

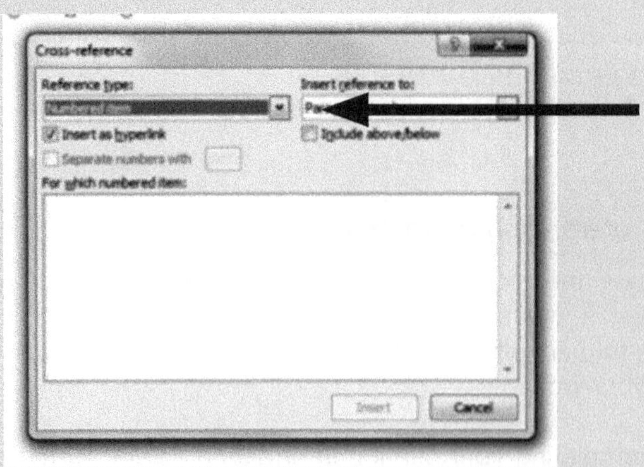

Select "Footnote". Using the list that appears, scroll down to choose the correct footnote number, in this case no. 12, and click "insert".

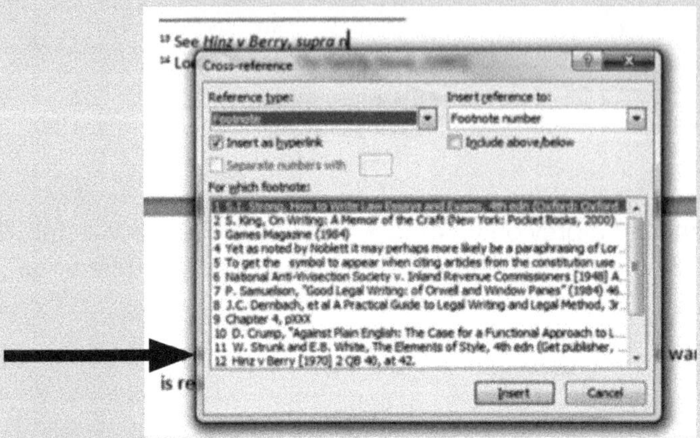

The footnote number will now automatically appear in your text. You will notice that if you click on that number, it will appear grey. This lets you know that this reference is linked to another so that if you update your footnotes, you can easily update this particular one also.

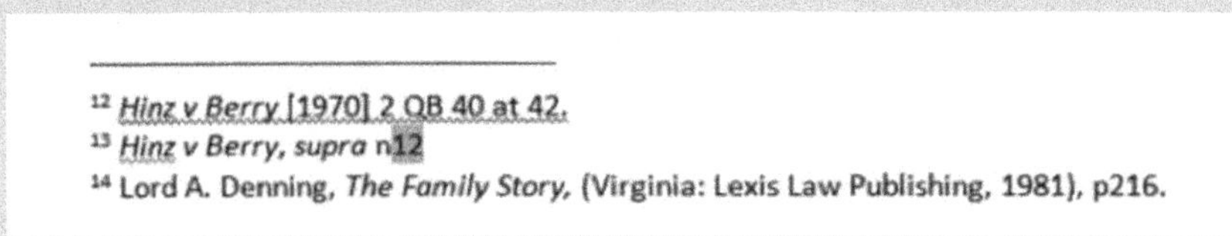
[12] *Hinz v Berry* [1970] 2 QB 40 at 42.
[13] *Hinz v Berry, supra* n12
[14] Lord A. Denning, *The Family Story,* (Virginia: Lexis Law Publishing, 1981), p216.

Updating footnotes

If when drafting and redrafting your work you include or delete footnotes, there is a simple mechanism by which to update all your footnotes simultaneously without needing to revisit and edit each individual footnote.

Let us assume from the example above that a series of new footnotes have been inserted so that our previous footnote 12 is now footnote 15.

[15] *Hinz v Berry* [1970] 2 QB 40 at 42.
[16] *Hinz v Berry, supra* n12
[17] Lord A. Denning, *The Family Story*, (Virginia: Lexis Law Publishing, 1981), p216.

This has the effect that our earlier cross-reference now appears to be incorrect. While it is linked to the new footnote 15, the number 12 will continue to appear in your text.

[15] *Hinz v Berry* [1970] 2 QB 40 at 42.
[16] *Hinz v Berry, supra* n12
[17] Lord A. Denning, *The Family Story*, (Virginia: Lexis Law Publishing, 1981), p216.

Updating this link so that the correct footnote number appears in the text is simple. Please note that this procedure updates ALL footnote cross-references.

Click in your footnote text. Then "select all" of the text. All the footnotes throughout the document will be highlighted and the cross-referenced number will appear grey at this point.

[15] *Hinz v Berry* [1970] 2 QB 40 at 42.
[16] *Hinz v Berry, supra* n12
[17] Lord A. Denning, *The Family Story*, (Virginia: Lexis Law Publishing, 1981), p216.

Simply press the F9 key on your keyboard. A warning window will ask do you wish to take this step as it cannot be undone.

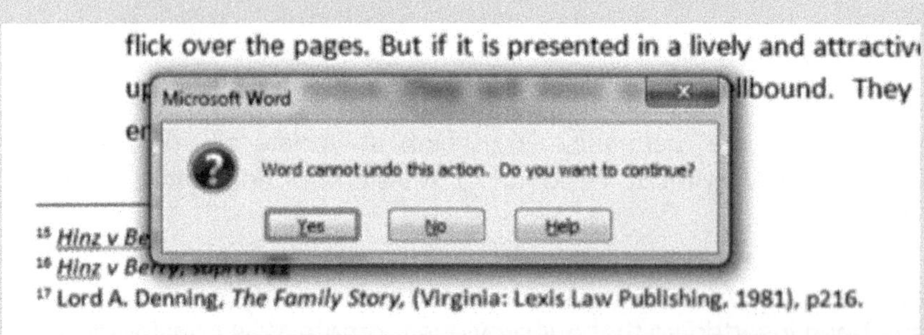

Click the "Yes" button and the numbers will automatically update throughout the document. You can see that the text of the footnotes remains highlighted but in the grey box where your cross-reference number is, it has updated from 12 to 15.

You have now successfully updated your cross-references throughout the document.

4. The OSCOLA Method of Citation

16–68 The OSCOLA method of citation is very detailed and includes instructions for how to cite every conceivable source you may draw upon when researching and writing your work. We will now examine how to cite the main types of legal sources you may refer to in your work. This is not intended to be an exhaustive list and you should look to the official OSCOLA guidelines for any source type omitted in this discussion.

(a) Citing primary sources of law

(i) The Constitution

16–69 Simply cite the Constitution as "The Irish Constitution (Bunreacht na hÉireann)". When referring to the Constitution in your work, use a capital letter. Similarly, when you reference a particular Article of the Constitution, a capital letter should be employed:

e.g. The Constitution provides in Article 34.4 that …

You do not capitalise the word "article" if you are referring to articles of the Constitution more generally.

e.g. Other articles in the Constitution concern ...

When you are referring to a subsection of a subsection of a particular constitutional Article you should employ the degree symbol °:

e.g. The unenumerated rights doctrine is located in Article 40.3.1° of the Constitution.

Box 16.2: Skills Insight

Tip to Make a Degree Symbol Appear in Word Using the Keyboard

To make the degree symbol appear without needing to draw upon the insert symbol box, simply press the "alt" key together with 0176 on the number keypad. For Mac users, press option shift 8.

(ii) Legislation

16–70 The format for citation of primary legislation, as in Acts of the Oireachtas, is as follows:

short title | year, | parts, | sections, etc.

e.g. Urban Regeneration and Housing Act 2015, s12(2)

16–71 For secondary legislation such as regulations and ministerial orders, note the following:

Short title | year, | Statutory Instrument number, | regulations, etc.

Regulation of Lobbying Act 2015 (Designated Public Officials) Regulations 2015, SI 2015/367, reg 4(a)

16–72 For legislation from the United Kingdom, the format is similar: the Modern Slavery Act 2015. Secondary legislation from the UK is noted as: Modern Slavery Act 2015 (Duty to Notify) Regulations 2015, SI 2015/1743, reg 3.

16–73 For treaties and protocols from the European Union, use the following format:

legislation title | [year] | OJ series | issue/first page

Treaty on the Functioning of the European Union (Consolidated version 2016) [2016] C 202/01

16–74 For EU secondary legislation such as regulations, directives, decisions, recommendations and opinions, use the following format:

legislation type | number | title | [year] | OJ L issue/first page

Council Decision (EU) 2015/1289 of 13 July 2015 imposing a fine on Spain for the manipulation of deficit data in the Autonomous Community of Valencia [2015] L 198/19

16–75 When citing legislation from other jurisdictions, simply use whatever citation method is employed in that jurisdiction. It may be necessary to include the jurisdiction in round brackets at the end of the citation.

Succession to the Crown Act 2015 (Australia)

Patient Protection and Affordable Care Act 2010 (United States)

(iii) Case law

16–76 When citing Irish cases, you need to give the parties' names, the neutral citation[22] and then any vendor citation such as the *Irish Reports* or the *Irish Law Reports Monthly*. The reports are referenced using shorthand. The website *http://www.legalabbrevs.cardiff.ac.uk* has a search function whereby you can search by either abbreviation or title to discover the identity of the source you are using or the shorthand notation for citation purposes.

16–77 Cases with neutral citations are cited as follows:

case name | [year] | court | number, | [year] OR (year) | volume | report abbreviation I first page

[22] A neutral citation enables us to identify a case without reference to any commercial law report such as the *Irish Reports* or the *Irish Law Reports Monthly*.

MacCarthaigh, Inspector of Taxes v Cablelink Ltd & Ors [2003] IESC 67, [2003] 4 IR 510

16–78 Reported cases without a neutral citation are cited as follows:

case name | [year] OR (year) | volume | report abbreviation | first page | (court)

D.P.P. v Cooney [1997] 3 IR 205 (SC)

16–79 Ordinarily, when citing reported judgments, the year of publication appears in square brackets. An exception to this rule is where the volumes in a series of reports are independently numbered; in other words, where the identification of the exact year is not essential to finding the case and the volumes in the series are sequentially numbered regardless of year of publication. In such circumstances, the year of reporting is recorded in round brackets.

In bonis Mitchell (1966) 100 ILTR 185

16–80 When citing an unreported decision, i.e. one that has not been reported in the published reports such as the *Irish Reports*, the *Irish Law Reports Monthly* or some other published reports, use the neutral citation. If there is no neutral citation available, then give the court and the date of judgment in brackets after the name of the case.

Wanze Properties (Ireland) Ltd v Five Star Supermarket (HC, 24 October 1997)

16–81 When citing cases from the UK, the method is the same as citing cases from the Irish courts.

16–82 For cases originating from the EU, employ the following method:[23]

Type of decision | full date, | *case name,* | case number in the register, | ECLI code, | paragraph cited

Judgment of 12 July 2005, *Schempp*, C-403/03, EU:C:2005:446, paragraph 19

[23] For further details see: *https://curia.europa.eu/jcms/jcms/P_126035/en/.*

Where the decision is not published in full in the reports, use the following method to cite it correctly:

> Type of decision | full date, | *case name*, | case number | not published, ECLI code
>
> Judgment of 6 June 2007, *Walderdorff v Commission*, T-442/04, not published, EU:T:2007:161

16–83 For judgments from the European Court of Human Rights, you can cite with reference to either the official reports, known as the *Reports of Judgments and Decisions* (ECHR) or the *European Human Rights Reports* (EHRR). Whichever you choose, be consistent throughout your work.

> *Goodwin v United Kingdom* [2002] ECHR 588
>
> *Jordan v United Kingdom* (2003) 37 EHRR 2

For unreported judgments of the European Court of Human Rights, cite as follows:

> *case name* | Application Number | (Court, date of judgment)
>
> *Winterstein v France* Application No 27013/07 (ECtHR, 17 October 2013)

16–84 Cite cases from other jurisdictions as they are cited in their own jurisdiction, but without full stops in abbreviations. If the law report series cited does not indicate the court, and if the identity of the court is not obvious from the context, you should identify the court in round brackets at the end of the citation.

> *Roe v Wade* 410 US 113 (1973)
>
> *Re the Marriage of C and D (falsely called C)* (1979) 35 FLR 340 (Family Court of Australia)

(b) Citing secondary legal sources

(i) Books

16–85 The OSCOLA format for citation of books is as follows:

> author, | *title* | (additional information, | edition, | publisher | year)
>
> Fiona de Londras, *Principles of Irish Property Law* (Clarus Press 2007)

When a second or subsequent edition of the book has been published, this constitutes additional information, hence cite as follows:

> Fiona de Londras, *Principles of Irish Property Law* (2nd edn, Clarus Press 2011)

16–86 Where a book has two to three authors, cite as follows:

> Genevieve Coonan, Kate O'Toole & Mary O'Toole, *Criminal Procedure in the District Court* (2nd edn, Round Hall, 2022)

16–87 Where a book has three or more authors:

> Liz Campbell and others, *Criminal Law in Ireland: Cases and Commentary* (2nd edn, Clarus Press 2021)

16–88 Where a book is an edited collection of chapters written by many different authors:

> James Gallen and Tanya Ní Mhuirthile (eds), *Law, Responsibility and Vulnerability: State Accountability and Responsiveness* (Routledge, 2022)

16–89 When you wish to cite just one chapter in such an edited collection:

> Tanya Ní Mhuirthile, 'Recent Reforms in Law on LGBT Rights in Ireland: Tightening the Tourniquet in the Rights of Vulnerable Intersex People' in James Gallen and Tanya Ní Mhuirthile (eds), *Law, Responsibility and Vulnerability: State Accountability and Responsiveness* (Routledge, 2022), 167.

16–90 When you cite a translation of a book from another language, the name of the translator is the additional information indicated above. Include the letters "tr" after the translator's name to identify that person as the translator of the work.

> Michel Foucault, *The Will to Knowledge: The History of Sexuality, Volume 1* (Robert Hurley tr, Penguin Books 1998)

16–91 Where you are citing a very old book, a newer copy of which you have consulted, do so as follows:

> John Stuart Mill, *On Liberty* (first published 1859, Penguin Classics 1985)

(ii) Journal articles

16–92 When citing journal articles, you have a choice to either write out the entire name of the journal or employ the accepted abbreviation. Once again, the website *http://www.legalabbrevs.cardiff.ac.uk* is an excellent resource for identifying these abbreviations whether you know either the journal name or the abbreviation.

16–93 The format for citing hard copy articles (or articles that are not available exclusively online) is as follows:

> Author, | 'title' | (year) | volume | (issue number) | journal name or abbreviation | first page of article
>
> Liam Thornton, '*C.A. and T.A.*: The Direct Provision Case' (2014) 17(4) Irish Journal of Family Law 116

This could also appear as follows if the accepted abbreviation for the journal name is used.

> Liam Thornton, '*C.A. and T.A.*: The Direct Provision Case' (2014) 17(4) IJFL 116

It does not matter whether you choose to cite by reference to the full journal name or by the abbreviation. What is important is that you are consistent throughout your document. Thus, you should decide at the outset whether you will use full journal names or abbreviations and then stick with that choice as you work through the document.

16–94 Increasingly there are legal journals emerging that only publish in an online format. When you are citing an article from such a journal you should do so as follows:

> Author, | 'title' | [year] / (year) | volume | journal name or abbreviation | article number | web address | date accessed
>
> Síofra O'Leary, 'Why the European Convention on Human Rights Still Matters' (2023) IJSJ 20 https://www.ijsj.ie/editions/2023-edition-2/#why-the-european-convention-on-human-rights-still-matters Accessed 13/11/2023

(iii) Parliamentary reports

16–95 Parliamentary reports record every word stated in the official chamber of parliament. In Ireland, there are three series of parliamentary reports: the reports of proceedings in the Dáil, reports of proceedings in the Seanad, and reports of debates in Oireachtas committees. The format for citing from the Oireachtas debates is as follows:

> Dáil Deb OR Seanad Deb | date, | volume, | column
>
> Dáil Deb 5 October 2005, vol 606, col 1690

16–96 Oireachtas Committees are cited as follows:

> Committee name | Deb | date, | page number
>
> Special Committee Wildlife Bill, 1975 Deb 1 July 1976, 4

(iv) Official publications

16–97 Official publications are those that are published by the State. They can consist of white or green papers published by government departments, government responses to Joint Oireachtas Committee reports, government responses to reports of committees of inquiry, and relevant treaties. Official reports are cited as follows:

author, | *title* | (document number, year)

Committee on Procedure and Privileges, *The Proceedings of the Sub-Committee on the Abbeylara Incident Established by the Joint Committee on Justice, Equality, Defence and Women's Rights* (Pn 10210, 2001)

(v) Law Reform Commission publications

16–98 The Law Reform Commission publishes consultation papers and subsequent reports on a broad variety of areas. Reports from the Law Reform Commission are cited as follows:

author, | *title* | (LRC | number-year)

Law Reform Commission, *Report on Prevention of Benefit from Homicide* (LRC 114-2015)

Consultation papers from the Law Reform Commission are cited as follows:

author, | *title* | (LRC CP | number-year)

Law Reform Commission, *Consultation Paper on Third Party Litigation Funding* (LRC CP 69-2023)

16–99 Issues papers from the Law Reform Commission are cited as follows:

author, | *title* | (LRC IP | number-year)

Law Reform Commission, *A Regulatory Framework for Adult Safeguarding* (LRC IP 19-2019)

16–100 Discussion papers from the Law Reform Commission mirror the numbering of reports and are cited as follows:

author, | *title* | (LRC | number-year)

Law Reform Commission, *Discussion Paper on Domestic Implementation of International Obligations* (LRC 124-2020)

Thus, it is clear that the difference between Law Reform Commission reports, consultation papers, issues papers and discussion papers from the perspective of citation is the inclusion of the letters "CP" in the Commission number from consultation papers and "IP" for issues papers.

(vi) Websites, blogs and podcasts

16–101 Websites are cited as follows:

> author, | 'title' | (Source or type of document (if relevant), | date) | web address | date of access
>
> Courts.ie, 'Remembering Our Past' https://www.courts.ie/remembering-our-past Accessed 13/11/2023

16–102 Blog posts and podcasts are cited in a similar fashion:

> Gillian O'Hanlon BL, 'High Court: Civil Servant Appointment Took Effect Without Positive Decision' (Irish Legal News, 13 November 2023) https://www.irishlegal.com/articles/high-court-civil-servant-appointment-took-effect-without-positive-decision Accessed 13/11/2023
>
> Vicky Conway, "Policing and Racism in Ireland" (Policed with Dr. Vicky Conway, 8 July 2021) https://tortoiseshack.ie/25-policing-and-racism-in-ireland/ Accessed 25/08/2023

(vii) Newspaper articles

16–103 Articles from newspapers are cited as follows:

> author, | 'title of article' | *title of newspaper* | (city of publication, | date)
>
> Tanya Ní Mhuirthile, 'Gender Recognition is "Transformative", but Bill Falls Short' *Irish Examiner* (Cork, 4 August 2015)

(viii) Personal communications

16–104 A personal communication is an email or a letter; these should be cited as follows:

Type of communication | from | name of author | to | name of recipient | date

Email from Amazon.com to Author 22 September 2015

(c) Secondary referencing

16–105 Occasionally, when researching you might come across a quotation in another source but are unable to locate the original source. Yet you may wish to use this quoted material. Secondary referencing, or second-hand referencing, is the term used to mean this kind of referencing. From the perspective of research, you should make every effort to locate the original source lest the secondary source is employing the quote in error or in an incorrect context. You should only cite works that you have consulted yourself. In this context, you should reference the second-hand source, as this is the source with which you have engaged. Cite second-hand references as follows:

Citation as per the kind of source consulted citing reference as included in secondary source

Raymond Byrne and J Paul McCutcheon, *The Irish Legal System* (5th edn, Butterworths 2009) 17 citing Robert P George (ed), *Natural Law Theory: Contemporary Essays* (Clarendon Press 1992).

(d) Subsequent referencing to a source already cited

16–106 When citing a source for the first time, you should include all the bibliographic information as appropriate for the type of source in the relevant manner discussed above. When you return to that source on a second or subsequent occasion you do not need to give all the bibliographic information again. In such situations you need only note the name of the author and cross-reference to the previous footnote where the full citation first appeared.

(e) Pinpointing

16–107 When you have quoted material directly from a source, or reference an idea that occurs on a particular page of a source, you should identify this to the reader. This process is called pinpointing. A pinpoint is simple to insert. At the end of the citation, replace the full stop with a comma and note the page number and end with a full stop.

> Catherine O'Sullivan, 'The Curious Case of the High Court's Rejection and Adoption of the UK Prosecutorial Policy in Respect of Assisted Suicide: An Analysis and Critique of *Fleming v Ireland*' (2014) 52 Irish Jurist 44, 56.

It is also possible to pinpoint to podcasts or YouTube videos. This information would go after the date on which the resource was posted:

> Vicky Conway, "Policing and Racism in Ireland" (Policed with Dr. Vicky Conway, 8 July 2021) 30:35–33:40, https://tortoiseshack.ie/25-policing-and-racism-in-ireland/ Accessed 25/08/2023.

(f) Quotations

16–108 When you include quoted material in your document, the quote should be faithful to the original. Where the quotation is fewer than three typed lines, it should be included directly in the body of your text within single quotation marks and immediately preceded by a colon. Quotations of longer than three typed lines should be indented from the left-hand margin, do not require quotation marks, and should be introduced by a colon. An example of the inclusion of a quote of fewer than three typed lines is evident below:

> They argued that the inability of science to agree on the exact aetiology of transsexuality was of secondary importance: '[r]espect for privacy rights should not, as the legislative and societal trends referred to above demonstrate, depend on exact science.'[24]

As can be seen in these circumstances, the quotation becomes part of the sentence you are writing. As that entire extract is longer than three typed lines, it has been indented here to illustrate how larger quotations are incorporated into your text.

---

[24] T. Ní Mhuirthile, "Article 8 and the Realisation of the Right to Legal Gender Recognition" in S. Egan, L. Thornton and J. Walsh (eds), *Ireland and the European Convention on Human Rights: 60 Years and Beyond* (Dublin: Bloomsbury, 2014), p.208, quoting *Sheffield v UK* (1999) 27 E.H.R.R. 163 at 201.

16–109 When a quotation begins in the middle of a sentence but you wish to use it as the start of a sentence, capitalise the initial letter but place it between square brackets to indicate that you have made this change. Similarly, if you wish to use a quotation that was the beginning of a sentence in the middle of one of yours, put the initial letter of the quote in lower case letters between square brackets. An example of this is evident in the quote above, where you can see the square brackets noting that the sentence quoted began with the word "Respect" but as it is now included part way through a sentence, this has been changed to a lower case "r".

16–110 Where you wish to exclude a word or words from the quotation, employ the ellipsis to indicate that a word or more has been omitted from the original quote. An example of this was outlined above when discussing the ellipsis as a punctuation mark: "[i]f the purpose is within one of the heads of charity forming the first three classes ... the Court will easily conclude that it is a charitable purpose."[25]

16–111 Punctuation follows after the close quotation marks unless it is part of the quotation itself. In the same way, any footnote superscript number will be located after the punctuation point after the close quotation marks, or immediately following the close quotation mark, should the punctuation point be located before the close quotation marks.

(g) Order of sources in footnotes

16–112 When you have more than one source in a particular footnote, you should list the most relevant ones first. Cite the remaining references in chronological order in a new sentence beginning with "See also". Do not include the word "and" prior to the final source in the list. Cite sources in hierarchical order within each footnote, save where a particular source is most relevant to the point in the main text, i.e. primary sources first in the order of their precedence (articles from the Constitution, legislation, case law), then secondary sources, again in hierarchical order (books, journal articles, official reports, etc.).

[25] *National Anti-Vivisection Society v Inland Revenue Commissioners* [1948] A.C. 31 at 65 per Lord Simonds.

(h) Bibliography

16–113 Your bibliography should also be organised based on source type and, within that, organised alphabetically by author's surname (if there is more than one author, list the source according to the surname of the first author's name that appears in the citation). One difference between the citation in a footnote and the citation in the bibliography is that bibliographies are organised by author's surname. Thus, you will need to note your author surname first and need only note the initials or first name(s). Below is a sample bibliography based on the examples used to describe the OSCOLA system above.

Box 16.3: Skills Insight
Example of a Bibliography

Bibliography

PRIMARY SOURCES

Constitutions

Constitution of Ireland (Bunreacht na hÉireann) 1937

Legislation

Australia

Succession to the Crown Act 2015

Ireland

Urban Regeneration and Housing Act 2015, s12(2)
Regulation of Lobbying Act 2015 (Designated Public Officials) Regulations 2015, SI 2015/367

European Union

Treaty on the Functioning of the European Union (Consolidated version 2016) [2016] C 202/01

Council Decision (EU) 2015/1289 of 13 July 2015 imposing a fine on Spain for the manipulation of deficit data in the Autonomous Community of Valencia [2015] L 198/19

United Kingdom

Modern Slavery Act 2015
Modern Slavery Act 2015 (Duty to Notify) Regulations 2015, SI 2015/1743

United States of America

Patient Protection and Affordable Care Act 2010

Case Law

Australia

Re the Marriage of C and D (falsely called C) (1979) 35 FLR 340 (Family Court of Australia)

European Court of Human Rights

Goodwin v United Kingdom [2002] ECHR 588
Jordan v United Kingdom (2003) 37 EHRR 2
Winterstein v France Application No 27013/07 (ECtHR, 17 October 2013)

European Union

Judgment of 12 July 2005, *Schempp*, C-403/03, EU:C:2005:446, paragraph 19
Judgment of 6 June 2007, *Walderdorff v Commission*, T-442/04, not published, EU:T:2007:161

Ireland

D.P.P. v Cooney [1997] 3 IR 205 (SC)
In bonis Mitchell (1966) 100 ILTR 185
MacCarthaigh, Inspector of Taxes v Cablelink Ltd & Ors [2003] IESC 67, [2003] 4 IR 510
Wanze Properties (Ireland) Ltd v Five Star Supermarket (HC, 24 October 1997)

United States of America

Roe v Wade 410 US 113 (1973)

SECONDARY SOURCES

Books

Campbell, L. and others, *Criminal Law in Ireland: Cases and Commentary* (2nd edn, Clarus Press 2021)

Coonan, G., O'Toole, K., and O'Toole, M., *Criminal Procedure in the District Court* (2nd edn, Round Hall 2022)

de Londras, F., *Principles of Irish Property Law* (2nd edn, Clarus Press 2011)

de Londras, F., *Principles of Irish Property Law* (Clarus Press 2007)

Foucault, M., *The Will to Knowledge: The History of Sexuality, Volume 1* (Robert Hurley tr, Penguin Books 1998)

Mill, J.S., *On Liberty* (first published 1859, Penguin Classics 1985)

Redmond, J. and others, *Sexual Politics in Modern Ireland* (Irish Academic Press 2015)

Edited collections

James Gallen and Tanya Ní Mhuirthile (eds), *Law, Responsibility and Vulnerability: State Accountability and Responsiveness* (Routledge 2022)

Chapters in books

Tanya Ní Mhuirthile, 'Recent Reforms in Law on LGBT Rights in Ireland: Tightening the Tourniquet in the Rights of Vulnerable Intersex People' in James Gallen and Tanya Ní Mhuirthile (eds), *Law, Responsibility and Vulnerability: State Accountability and Responsiveness* (Routledge 2022), 167.

Journal Articles

Síofra O'Leary, 'Why the European Convention on Human Rights Still Matters' (2023) IJSJ 20

Catherine O'Sullivan, 'The Curious Case of the High Court's Rejection and Adoption of the UK Prosecutorial Policy in Respect of Assisted Suicide: An Analysis and Critique of *Fleming v Ireland*' (2014) 52 Irish Jurist 44

Liam Thornton, '*C.A. and T.A.*: The Direct Provision Case' (2014) 17(4) Irish Journal of Family Law 116

Parliamentary Reports

Dáil Deb 5 October 2005, vol 606, col 1690
Special Committee Wildlife Bill, 1975 Deb 1 July 1976, 4

Official Publications

Committee on Procedure and Privileges, *The Proceedings of the Sub-Committee on the Abbeylara Incident Established by the Joint Committee on Justice, Equality, Defence and Women's Rights* (Pn 10210, 2001)

Law Reform Commission Publications

Law Reform Commission, *Report on Prevention of Benefit from Homicide* (LRC 114-2015)

Law Reform Commission, *Consultation Paper on Third Party Litigation Funding* (LRC CP 69-2023)

Law Reform Commission, *A Regulatory Framework for Adult Safeguarding* (LRC IP 19-2019)

Law Reform Commission, *Discussion Paper on Domestic Implementation of International Obligations* (LRC 124-2020)

Websites, Blogs and Podcasts

Courts.ie, 'Remembering Our Past' https://www.courts.ie/remembering-our-past Accessed 13/11/2023

Gillian O'Hanlon BL, 'High Court: Civil Servant Appointment Took Effect Without Positive Decision' (Irish Legal News, 13 November 2023) https://www.irishlegal.com/articles/high-court-civil-servant-appointment-took-effect-without-positive-decision Accessed 13/11/2023

Vicky Conway, "Policing and Racism in Ireland" (Policed with Dr. Vicky Conway, 8 July 2021) https://tortoiseshack.ie/25-policing-and-racism-in-ireland/ Accessed 25/08/2023.

Newspaper Articles

Ní Mhuirthile, T., 'Gender Recognition is "Transformative", but Bill Falls Short' *Irish Examiner* (Cork, 4 August 2015)

Personal Communications

Email from Amazon.com to Author 22 September 2015

5. Using Citation Management Software

16–114 There are several different companies offering digital support software to manage your references and citations such as Endnote, Zotero, Cite Them Right, etc. Each of these citation management systems aims to assist you to gather the most accurate bibliographic information about the research you undertake; organise it in a systemised manner; and include accurate citations within your text as you draft your work. Including correct citations and references to support your writing as you are writing is an excellent practice regardless of whether you decide to use software to help with this. It will ensure that you do not lose those references as you draft your work. These citation management systems are pre-programmed with all the requirements for many different citation styles, e.g. OSCOLA, Harvard, Chicago. Thus, you merely need to select the style your assignment requires you to use, and the citation management system will ensure that all your references are accurately noted in that style. Using these software packages can also streamline creating a bibliography for you. Where you have created your footnotes using such a system, it is usually only a matter of clicking a button and a bibliography will be generated for you. Many of these systems are free to use for simple projects. It may be that your institution has a subscription to a particular system, or prefers you to use a particular system, and has expert librarians who can offer training and support on that system. It is a good idea to adopt a system at the beginning of your studies, and you can bring it with you throughout your career. As these systems update regularly, and as they are all slightly different from an operational perspective, we have not detailed how to use any particular system in this book. You can very easily find up-to-date instruction videos online if you would like to find out more about them.

E. Conclusion

16–115 In this chapter we have considered how to produce legal writing that is of high quality and that is persuasive. We have examined the grammatical rules underpinning good prose. We have also considered how to approach legal writing in order to build an argument that persuades the reader that your point is correct. Finally, we have examined how to substantiate your work and explicitly demonstrate the breadth and depth of your research through referencing and accurate citation.

Index